THE OXFORD HANDBOOK OF

FREE WILL

THE OXFORD HANDBOOK OF

FREE WILL

Edited by

ROBERT KANE

OXFORD

UNIVERSITY PRESS

2002

OXFORD
UNIVERSITY PRESS

Oxford   New York
Athens Auckland Bangkok Bogotá Buenos Aires Cape Town
Chennai Dar es Salaam Delhi Florence Hong Kong Istanbul Karachi
Kolkata Kuala Lumpur Madrid Melbourne Mexico City Mumbai Nairobi
Paris São Paulo Shanghai Singapore Taipei Tokyo Toronto Warsaw

and associated companies in
Berlin   Ibadan

Published by Oxford University Press, Inc.
198 Madison Avenue, New York, New York 10016

Oxford is a registered trademark of Oxford University Press

Library of Congress Cataloging-in-Publication Data
The Oxford handbook of free will / edited by Robert Kane.
p.   cm.
Includes bibliographical references and index.
ISBN 0–19–513336–6
1. Free will and determinism.   2. Philosophy, Modern—20th century.
3. Ethics, Modern—20th century.   I. Kane, Robert, 1938–
BJ1461 .F74 2002
123'.5—dc21   00–052872

1 3 5 7 9 8 6 4 2

Printed in the United States of America
on acid-free paper

To Claudette

Acknowledgments

I owe a debt to Peter Ohlin of Oxford University Press, who conceived this project and was indispensable in carrying it out, also to several anonymous readers of the original proposal whose suggestions helped to improve the project, and finally to the contributors for their efforts and dedication, and for putting up with an often headstrong editor.

To Blackwell Publishers, London and Cambridge, MA, for permission to reprint "Free Will Remains a Mystery" by Peter van Inwagen from *Philosophical Perspectives* 14 Action and Freedom, edited by James E. Tomberlin. Oxford: Blackwell Publishers (2000): 1–19.

To Kluwer Academic Publishers, Dordrecht, The Netherlands, for permission to reprint selections from "Responsibility and Self-Expression" by John M. Fischer. *Journal of Ethics* 3 (1999): 277–97.

To The University of Chicago Press, Chicago IL, for permission to reprint selections from "Recent Work on Moral Responsibility" by John M. Fischer. *Ethics* 110 (1999): 109–25.

To Imprint Academic, for permission to reprint "Do We Have Free Will?" by Benjamin Libet. *Journal of Consciousness Studies* 6 (1999): 47–57.

To MIT Press, Cambridge, MA, for permission to reprint selections from *Neurophilosophy of Free Will* by Henrik Walter, 2001. (Forthcoming 2001.)

Contents

PART III. THE MODAL OR CONSEQUENCE ARGUMENT FOR INCOMPATIBILISM

PART IV. COMPATIBILIST PERSPECTIVES ON FREEDOM AND RESPONSIBILITY

PART V. MORAL RESPONSIBILITY, ALTERNATIVE POSSIBILITIES, AND FRANKFURT-STYLE EXAMPLES

PART VI. LIBERTARIAN PERSPECTIVES ON FREE AGENCY AND FREE WILL

PART VII. NONSTANDARD VIEWS: SUCCESSOR VIEWS TO HARD DETERMINISM AND OTHERS

PART VIII. NEUROSCIENCE AND FREE WILL

CONTRIBUTORS

....

Mark Bernstein is Professor of Philosophy at the University of Texas at San Antonio. His articles concerning free will and fatalism appear in *Philosophical Studies, Mind, The Monist,* and other journals. He edited *Free Will, Determinism and Moral Responsibility* (*Philosophical Studies,* 1994) and is the author of *Fatalism* (1992). Bernstein's other major philosophical interests include normative and applied ethics, especially animal ethics, which are subjects of his most recent work *On Moral Considerability: An Essay on Who Morally Matters* (1998). Department of Philosophy, University of Texas, San Antonio, TX 78249. E-mail: markb@io.com

Bernard Berofsky is Professor of Philosophy at Columbia University. He is the author of *Liberation from Self* (1995), *Freedom from Necessity* (1987), and *Determinism* (1971), as well as articles on the subjects of free will, moral responsibility, autonomy, determinism, and causality. His works have appeared in various journals, including *American Philosophical Quarterly, Mind, Journal of Philosophy, Nous,* and *Philosophy and Phenomenological Research.* He serves on the Editorial Board of the *Journal of Philosophy.* Department of Philosophy, 705 Philosophy Hall, Columbia University, 1150 Amsterdam Avenue, New York, NY 10027.

Robert C. Bishop holds a research position in philosophy of science and physics in the Abteilung für Theorie und Datenanalyse of the Institut für Grenzgebiete der Psychologie (Freiburg, Germany). His current areas of research are philosophy of science, conceptual foundations of physics, free will, philosophy of mind, and philosophy of social science. His writings on determinism, chaos, free will, and emergence include the co-authored "Is Chaos Indeterministic?" (*Selected Contributions to the Tenth International Congress of Logic, Methodology, and Philosophy of Science,* 1999). Institut fur Grenzgebiete der Psychologie, Wilhelmstrasse 3A, D-79098, Freiburg, Germany.

Randolph Clarke is Associate Professor of Philosophy at the University of Georgia. He has published a number of articles on action theory and free will, including "Toward a Credible Agent-Causal Account of Free Will" (1993), "Indeterminism and Control" (1995), and "Agent-Causation and Event-Causation in the Production of Free Action" (1996). Department of Philosophy, University of Georgia, Athens GA 30602. E-mail: rclarke@arches.uga.edu

Daniel Dennett is Distinguished Professor of Arts and Sciences and Director of the Center for Cognitive Studies at Tufts University. He is the author of numerous books and articles, including, on the topic of free will, *Elbow Room: The Varieties of Free Will Worth Wanting* (1984), "Mechanism and Responsibility" (1973), "On Giving Libertarians What They Say they Want" (1978), and "I Could Not Have Done Otherwise. So What?" (1984). Department of Philosophy and Center for Cognitive Studies, Tufts University, Medford MA 02155.

Richard Double is Associate Professor and Chair of the Department of Philosophy at Edinboro University of Pennsylvania. He is the author of three books, *The Nonreality of Free Will* (1991), *Metaphilosophy and Free Will* (1996), and *Beginning Philosophy* (1999). He has authored over sixty articles and reviews on the philosophy of mind, epistemology, and ethics and is nearing completion of a fourth book, *The Elusiveness of Morality*. Department of Philosophy, Edinboro, University, Edinboro, PA 16444. E-mail: rdouble@vax.edinboro.edu

Laura Waddell Ekstrom is Associate Professor of Philosophy at the College of William and Mary in Williamsburg, Virginia. She is author of *Free Will: A Philosophical Study* (2000) and the editor of *Agency and Responsibility: Essays on the Metaphysics of Freedom* (2001). Her articles on autonomy, causation, responsibility, and free will have appeared in *Synthèse, American Philosophical Quarterly, Australasian Journal of Philosophy*, and *Philosophy and Phenomenological Research*. Department of Philosophy, College of William and Mary, Williamsburg, VA 23187–8795. E-mail: lwekstr@facstaff.wm.edu

John Martin Fischer is Professor of Philosophy and Director of the University Honors Program at the University of California, Riverside. He received his Ph.D. in philosophy from Cornell University in 1982. He is author of numerous papers on free will, moral responsibility, death, and issues in ethics, is the editor or co-editor of five volumes, and is author of two books, *The Metaphysics of Free Will: An Essay on Control* (1994) and (with Mark Ravizza) *Responsibility and Control: A Theory of Moral Responsibility* (1998). Department of Philosophy, University of California-Riverside, Riverside, CA 92521.

Carl Ginet is Professor of Philosophy Emeritus at Cornell University. He is the author of two books, *Knowledge, Perception and Memory* (1975) and *On Action* (1990) and numerous articles. Philosophy Department, Goldwin Smith Hall, Cornell University, Ithaca, NY 14853. E-mail: cag2@cornell.edu

Ishtiyaque Haji is Associate Professor of Philosophy at the University of Minnesota, Morris. He is the author of articles in ethical theory, metaphysics, and action theory, and of the book *Moral Appraisability* (1998). Department of Philosophy, Division of Humanities, University of Minnesota-Morris, Morris, MN 56267. E-mail: hajiih@mrs.umn.edu

David Hodgson is Chief Justice in Equity and an Additional Judge of Appeal of the Supreme Court of New South Wales. Although his career has been in the law, he has had a long interest and involvement in philosophy. He has published two philosophical books with Oxford University Press, *Consequences of Utilitarianism* (1967) and *The Mind Matters* (1991), and in recent years he has published many articles on consciousness, plausible reasoning and free will. Supreme Court of New South Wales, Queen's Square, Sydney, NSW 2000, Australia. E-mail: raeda@ozemail.com.au

Ted Honderich is Grote Professor Emeritus of Philosophy at University College, London. He is author of *A Theory of Determinism* (2 volumes; 1988), *How Free Are You?* (1993) and editor of *Essays on Freedom and Action* (1973) among many other writings on free will, mind and body, and other philosophical topics. Department of Philosophy, University College-London, Gower Street, London WC1E 6BT, UK. E-mail: t.honderich@ucl.ac.uk

Robert Kane is University Distinguished Teaching Professor of Philosophy at the University of Texas at Austin. He is the author of *Free Will and Values* (1985), *Through the Moral Maze* (1994), *The Significance of Free Will* (1996), (which was awarded the 1996 Robert W. Hamilton Faculty Book Award) and other writings in the philosophy of mind and action, ethics, the theory of values and philosophy of religion. Department of Philosophy, Waggener Hall 316, The University of Texas, Austin, TX 78712. E-mail: rkane@uts.cc.utexas.edu

Tomis Kapitan is professor of philosophy at Northern Illinois University. He has taught at Birzeit University and East Carolina University and has recently been a visiting professor at the American University of Beirut. He is author of *Philosophical Perspectives on the Israeli-Palestinian Conflict* (1997) and co-editor of *The Phenomeno-Logic of the I: Essays on Self-Consciousness* (1999). He has published papers in metaphysics, logic, and the philosophy of language, including "Deliberation and the Presumption of Open Alternatives" (1986), "Doxastic Freedom: A Compatibilist Alternative" (1989), and "Autonomy and Manipulated Freedom" (2000) and is currently writing a book dealing with the free will problem. Department of Philosophy, Northern Illinois University, DeKalb, IL 60115. E-mail: kapitan@niu.edu

Benjamin Libet is Professor in the Department of Physiology at the University of California, San Francisco. He received a Ph.D. in neurophysiology, supervised by Ralph Gerard (founder and Honorary President of the Society for Neuroscience). Libet also worked with K.A.C. Elliott on brain metabolism and with Sir John Eccles on synaptic mechanisms. In 1958 he began a series of highly influential experimental studies in human subjects relating brain activities to the appearance or production of conscious experience. Department of Physiology, University of California, San Francisco, San Francisco, CA 94143–0444.

Alfred R. Mele is William H. and Lucyle T. Werkmeister Professor of Philosophy at Florida State University. He is the author of *Irrationality* (1987), *Springs of Action* (1992), *Autonomous Agents* (1995), and *Self-Deception Unmasked* (2000). He is also the editor of *The Philosophy of Action* (1997) and co-editor of *Mental Causation* (1993). Department of Philosophy-1500, Florida State University, Tallahassee, FL 32306. E-mail: almele@mailer.fsu.edu

Timothy O'Connor is Associate Professor of Philosophy at Indiana University. He has written extensively on the topic of free will, editing *Agents, Causes, and Events* (1995) and authoring *Persons and Causes: The Metaphysics of Free Will* (2000). He has also written on the concept of emergence as applied to the philosophy of mind and is currently writing a book on the metaphysics of modality and its application to the cosmological argument for theism. Department of Philosophy, Indiana University, Sycamore Hall 026, Bloomington, IN 47405. E-mail: toconnor@indiana.edu

Derk Pereboom is Professor and Chair in the Department of Philosophy at the University of Vermont. He received a BA from Calvin College and a Ph.D. from UCLA (1985) with a dissertation on Kant's Theory of Mental Representation. He is the author of *Living Without Free Will* (2001) and articles on Kant, philosophy of mind, philosophy of religion, and free will. Department of Philosophy, University of Vermont, Burlington, VT 05401. E-mail: Derk.Pereboom@uvm.edu

Paul Russell is Professor of Philosophy at the University of British Columbia. He is the author of *Freedom and Moral Sentiments: Hume's Way of Naturalizing Responsibility* (1995). He has held a Research Fellowship at Sidney Sussex College, Cambridge and also visiting positions at the University of Virginia, Stanford University, and the University of Pittsburgh. Department of Philosophy, University of British Columbia, 1866 Main Mall, Vancouver B.C., Canada V6T 1Z1. E-mail: prussell@interchange.ubc.ca

Saul Smilansky is Professor in the Department of Philosophy at the University of Haifa, Israel. He works primarily on ethics and on the free will problem. His book *Free Will and Illusion* was published by Oxford University Press in 2000. Department of Philosophy, University of Haifa, Haifa 31905, Israel. E-mail: smilsaul@research.haifa.ac.il

Galen Strawson is Professor of Philosophy at the University of Reading. He is the author of three books, *Freedom and Belief* (1986), *The Secret Connexion: Realism, Causation and David Hume* (1989) and *Mental Reality* (1995), and he is the keynote author in *Models of the Self*, ed. S. Gallagher and J. Shear (1999). Department of Philosophy, University of Reading, Reading RG6 2AA, UK.

Christopher Taylor is Assistant Professor of Piano Performance, University of Wisconsin at Madison. He has a summa cum laude BA in mathematics from

Harvard University (1992) and is completing a doctorate in Musical Arts at the New England Conservatory of Music. His piano recordings include a CD (Phillips) of works by Messiaen and Boulez which was released shortly after his third-place finish in the 1993 Van Cliburn competition. This is his first publication in philosophy. Center for Cognitive Studies, Tufts University, Medford, MA 02155.

Peter van Inwagen has been John Cardinal O'Hara Professor of Philosophy at the University of Notre Dame since 1995. He received his Ph.D. from the University of Rochester in 1969 and subsequently taught at Syracuse University for twenty-four years. He is author of *An Essay on Free Will, Material Beings, God, Knowledge and Mystery: Essays in Philosophical Theology, Metaphysics, Ontology, Identity and Modality*, and numerous essays. Department of Philosophy, University of Notre Dame, Notre Dame, IN 46556–5639. E-mail: pvaninwa@nd.edu

Henrik Walter, M.D., Ph.D., is a neurologist, psychiatrist, and philosopher and has also studied psychology. In philosophy his writings on the problems of free will and intentionality include *Neurophilosophie der Willensfreiheit* (1998), translated into English and published by MIT Press as *Neurophilosophy of Free Will* (2001). Since 1998 he has been at the newly founded Psychiatric University Clinic doing clinical psychiatry and research in cognitive neuroscience on working memory, emotions, semantic information processing, and other topics. He will welcome serious proposals and collaboration to test philosophical theories on mental phenomena by doing neuroimaging experiments. Department of Psychiatry, University Clinic Ulm, Leimgrubenweg 12, 89075 Ulm, Germany. E-mail: henrik.walter@medizin.uni-ulm.de

David Widerker is Associate Professor of Philosophy at Bar-Ilan University in Israel. He has published widely on the topics of free will and moral responsibility, including "On an Argument for Incompatibilism" (*Analysis*, 1987), "Troubles with Ockhamism" (*Journal of Philosophy*, 1990), "Libertarianism and Frankfurt's Attack on the Principle of Alternative Possibilities" (*Philosophical Review*, 1995), and "Frankfurt's Attack on the Principle of Alternative Possibilities: A Further Look" (*Philosophical Perspectives*, 2000). Department of Philosophy, Bar-Ilan University, Ramat-Gan 52900, Israel. E-mail: widerd@mail.biu.ac.il

Linda Trinkaus Zagzebski is Kingfisher College Chair of the Philosophy of Religion and Ethics, University of Oklahoma and formerly Professor of Philosophy, Loyola Marymount University, Los Angeles, CA. She is author of *The Dilemma of Freedom and Foreknowledge* (1991), *Virtues of the Mind* (1996), and many articles on philosophy of religion, epistemology, and ethics. Her current research is on theory of emotion and emotion-based virtue theory. Department of Philosophy, 455 West Lindsey, Room 605, University of Oklahoma, Norman, OK 73019. E-mail: lzagzebski@ou.edu

THE OXFORD HANDBOOK OF

FREE WILL

CHAPTER 1

INTRODUCTION: THE CONTOURS OF CONTEMPORARY FREE WILL DEBATES

ROBERT KANE

There is a disputation [that will continue] till mankind is raised from the dead, between the Necessitarians and the partisans of Free Will

Jalalu'ddin Rumi, twelfth-century Persian poet

THE problem of free will and necessity (or determinism) is "perhaps the most voluminously debated of all philosophical problems," according to a recent history of philosophy.[1] This situation has not changed at the end of the twentieth century and the beginning of a new millennium. Indeed, debates about free will have become more voluminous in the past century, especially in the latter half of it—so much so that it has become difficult to keep up with the latest developments. This handbook was compiled as a remedy in the form of a sourcebook or guide to current work on free will and related subjects for those who wish to keep up with the latest research.

The focus of the volume is on writings of the past thirty to forty years, an era of reborn interest in traditional issues regarding free will in the context of new developments in the sciences, philosophy, and humanistic studies. While references are frequent throughout this volume to major thinkers of the past who have discussed free will, the emphasis is on recent research.[2] Many of the writers of the following essays are long-time contributors to contemporary debates about free will; others are younger scholars who are beginning to make significant contributions. By surveying and evaluating recent writings, the hope is that their essays will serve as a guide to the latest work and a resource for future research.

What is often called "the free will issue" or "the problem of free will," when viewed in historical perspective, is related to a cluster of philosophical issues—all of them to be dealt with to some degree in this volume.[3] These include issues about (1) moral agency and responsibility, dignity, desert, accountability, and blameworthiness in ethics; (2) the nature and limits of human freedom, autonomy, coercion, and control in social and political theory; issues about (3) compulsion, addiction, self-control, self-deception, and weakness of will in philosophical psychology; (4) criminal liability, responsibility, and punishment in legal theory; (5) the relation of mind to body, consciousness, the nature of action,[4] and personhood in the philosophy of mind and the cognitive and neurosciences; (6) the nature of rationality and rational choice in philosophy and social theory; (7) questions about divine foreknowledge, predestination, evil, and human freedom in theology and philosophy of religion; and (8) general metaphysical issues about necessity and possibility, determinism, time and chance, quantum reality, laws of nature, causation, and explanation in philosophy and the sciences. Obviously, this volume does not discuss every aspect of these complex issues, but it does attempt to show how contemporary debates about free will are related to them.

In the remainder of this introduction, I describe the contours of contemporary free will debates, placing them—and the essays to follow—in historical and dialectical perspective.

1. FREE WILL AND CONFLICTING VIEWS
ABOUT PERSONS

The problem of free will arises when humans reach a certain higher stage of self-consciousness about how profoundly the world may influence their behavior in ways of which they were unaware (Kane 1996: 95–6). Various authors have described this stage of self-consciousness as the recognition of a conflict between two perspectives we may have on ourselves and our place in the universe

(P. F. Strawson 1962; Nagel 1986; Bok 1998; Blackburn 1999). From a *personal* or *practical* standpoint, we see ourselves as free agents capable of influencing the world in various ways. Open alternatives seem to lie before us. We reason or deliberate among them and choose. We feel it is "up to us" what we choose and how we act; and this means that we could have chosen or acted otherwise—for, as Aristotle succinctly put it, "[W]hen acting is up to us, so is not acting" (1915b: 1113b6). This "up to us-ness" also suggests that the origins or sources of our actions are in us and not in something else over which we have no control—whether that something else is fate or God, the laws of nature, birth or upbringing, or other humans.[5]

These two features of the personal or practical standpoint are pivotal to what has traditionally been called free will: we believe we have free will when (a) it is "up to us" what we choose from an array of alternative possibilities and (b) the origin or source of our choices and actions is in us and not in anyone or anything else over which we have no control. Because of these features free will is frequently associated with other valued notions such as moral responsibility, autonomy, genuine creativity, self-control, personal worth or dignity, and genuine desert for our deeds or accomplishments (Anglin 1990; Kane 1996: ch. 6). These two features of free will also lie behind various reactive attitudes that we naturally assume toward our behavior and that of others from a personal standpoint (P. F. Strawson 1962). Gratitude, resentment, admiration, indignation, and other such reactive attitudes seem to depend upon the assumption that the acts for which we feel grateful, resentful, or admiring originated in the persons to whom we direct these attitudes. We believe that it was up to them whether they performed those acts or not (cf. Nathan: 1992: 46).

But something happens to this familiar picture of ourselves and other persons when we view ourselves from various *impersonal, objective* or *theoretical* perspectives (Nagel 1986: 110). Perhaps we only seem to "move ourselves" in a primordial way when in fact our actions are caused by physical forces over which we have no control (Trusted 1984). Perhaps our choices from among alternative possibilities are determined by unconscious motives and other psychological springs of action of which we are unaware (Hospers 1958). These thoughts take many forms in human history, but in all their forms they threaten our self-image and cause a corresponding crisis in human thinking (Farrer 1967, Kenny 1978). Such is the case when we learn that much of our character and behavior is influenced by heredity or environment (Felt 1994), or that our thoughts and behavior can be covertly influenced by social conditioning (Waller 1990; Double 1991), or by subtle chemical imbalances of the neurotransmitters or hormones of our brains or bodies.

Free will becomes an issue when, by reflections such as these, humans realize how profoundly the world may influence them in ways previously unknown.

The advent of doctrines of *determinism* or *necessity* in the history of ideas is an indication that this higher stage of awareness has been reached—which accounts for the importance of such doctrines in the long history of debates about free will (Woody 1998).[6] Determinist or necessitarian threats to free will have taken many historical forms—fatalist, theological, physical or scientific, psychological, and logical—all of which are discussed in this volume. But a core notion runs through all these forms of determinism, which explains why these doctrines appear to threaten free will. Any event is determined, according to this core notion, just in case there are conditions (such as the decrees of fate, the foreordaining acts of God, antecedent physical causes plus laws of nature) whose joint occurrence is (logically) sufficient for the occurrence of the event: it *must* be the case that *if* these determining conditions jointly obtain, the determined event occurs. Determination is thus a kind of conditional necessity that can be described in various ways. In the language of modal logicians, the determined event occurs in every logically possible world in which the determining conditions (e.g., antecedent physical causes plus laws of nature) obtain. In more familiar terms, the occurrence of the determined event is *inevitable*, given these determining conditions.

Historical doctrines of determinism refer to different kinds of determining conditions, but they all imply that every event (including every human choice or action) is determined in this general sense.[7] One can understand as a consequence why such doctrines pose a threat to free will. If one or another form of determinism were true, it seems that it would not be (a) "up to us" what we chose from an array of alternative possibilities, since only one alternative would be possible; and it seems that (b) the origin or source of our choices and actions would not be "in us" but in conditions, such as the decrees of fate, the foreordaining acts of God, or antecedent causes and laws, over which we had no control. But these apparent conflicts can only be the first word on a subject as difficult as this one. Many philosophers, especially in modern times, have argued that, despite intuitions to the contrary, determinism (in all of its guises) poses no threat to free will, or at least to any free will "worth wanting," as Daniel Dennett (1984) has put it.[8]

As a consequence, debates about free will in the modern era (since the seventeenth century) have been dominated by two questions, not one—the "Determinist Question": "Is determinism true?" and the "Compatibility Question": "Is free will compatible (or incompatible) with determinism?" Answers to these questions give rise to two of the major divisions in contemporary free will debates, that between determinists and indeterminists, on the one hand, and that between compatibilists and incompatibilists, on the other. Let us look at the two questions in turn.

2. THE DETERMINIST QUESTION AND MODERN SCIENCE

One may legitimately wonder why worries about determinism persist at all in the twentieth-first century, when the physical sciences—once the stronghold of determinist thinking—seem to have turned away from determinism. Modern quantum physics, according to its usual interpretations, has introduced indeterminism into the physical world, giving us a more sophisticated version of the Epicurean chance "swerve of the atoms" than the ancient philosophers could ever have conceived. We have come a long way since the beginning of the nineteenth century, when Pierre Simon, marquis de Laplace, could claim that discoveries in mechanics and astronomy unified by Newton's theory of gravitation have made it possible

> to comprehend in the same analytical expressions the past and future states of the system of the world.... Given for an instant an intelligence which could comprehend all the forces by which nature is animated and the respective situation of the beings who compose it—an intelligence sufficiently vast to submit these data to analysis—it would embrace in the same formula the movements of the greatest bodies of the universe and those of the lightest atom; for it nothing would be uncertain and the future, as the past, would be present to its eyes. (1951: 3–4)

Twentieth-century physics threatened this Laplacean or Newtonian determinist vision in several related ways. Quantum theory, according to its usual interpretations, denies that elementary particles composing the "system of the world" have exact positions and momenta that could be simultaneously known by any such intelligence (the Heisenberg Uncertainty Principle); and it implies that much of the behavior of elementary particles, from quantum jumps in atoms to radioactive decay, is not precisely predictable and can be explained only by probabilistic, not deterministic, laws. Moreover, the uncertainty and indeterminacy of the quantum world, according to the orthodox view of it, is not merely due to our limitations as knowers but to the nature of the physical world itself.

In the light of these indeterministic developments of twentieth-century physics, one may wonder why physical or natural determinism continues to be regarded as a serious threat to free will, as evident in many essays of the volume.[9] Indeed, it is an important fact about the intellectual history of the twentieth century that, while universal determinism has been in retreat in the physical sciences, determinist (and compatibilist) views *of human behavior* have been thriving (while antideterminist and incompatibilist views of free will continue to be on the defensive).

What accounts for these apparently paradoxical trends? There are four reasons, I believe, why indeterministic developments in modern physics have not disposed of determinist threats to free will, all of them on display in this volume. First, there has been, and continues to be, considerable debate about the conceptual foundations of quantum physics and much disagreement about how it is to be interpreted. Orthodox interpretations of quantum phenomena are indeterministic, but they have not gone unchallenged. These issues about determinism and indeterminism in modern physics and related sciences, and their implications for the free will problem, are the subject of two essays of this volume, by David Hodgson and Robert Bishop.

Second, contemporary determinists about free will often concede that if modern physics is correct, the behavior of elementary particles is not always determined (see Honderich 1988; Weatherford 1991; Pereboom 1995). Yet they insist that this has little bearing on how we should think about human behavior, since quantum indeterminacy is comparatively negligible in macroscopic physical systems as large as the human brain and body. Since physical systems involving many particles and higher energies tend to be regular and predictable in their behavior for the most part, according to quantum physics itself, modern determinists argue that we can continue to regard human behavior as determined at the macroscopic level "for all practical purposes" (or "near-determined," as one of them has put it[10]) even if microphysics should turn out to be indeterministic; and this is all that determinists need to affirm in free will debates. (For this line of argument, see the essays in this volume by Ted Honderich and Derk Pereboom; and for discussion of conflicting views about the role indeterminism might play in macroscopic systems, see the essays of Hodgson and Bishop.)

Third, one often hears the argument in contemporary free will debates that if quantum jumps or other undetermined events did sometimes have non-negligible effects on the brain or behavior, this would be of no help to defenders of an incompatibilist free will. Such undetermined effects would be unpredictable and uncontrollable by the agents, like the unanticipated emergence of a thought or the uncontrolled jerking of an arm—just the opposite of the way we envision free and responsible actions (for example, Dennett 1984; G. Strawson 1986; Honderich 1988; Double 1991). This argument has been made in response to suggestions by prominent twentieth century scientists (such as Nobel laureates Louis De Broglie and A. H. Compton [1935] in physics and Sir John Eccles [1970] in neurophysiology) that room might be made for free will in nature if undetermined events in the brain were somehow amplified to have large-scale effects on human choice and action. Unfortunately, such a modernized version of the Epicurean chance swerve of the atoms seems to be vulnerable to the same criticisms as its ancient counterpart. It seems that such undetermined events in the brain or body would occur spontaneously and would be more of a nuisance—or perhaps a curse, like epilepsy—than an enhancement of an agent's freedom. (For this line of argument and others about the limitations of indeterminist free will, see the essays in this volume by Galen Strawson, Honderich, and Christopher Taylor and Daniel Dennett.)

The fourth and final reason why indeterministic developments of twentieth-century physics have not undermined determinist thinking about human behavior is perhaps the most important. While determinism has been in retreat in the physical sciences during the twentieth century, developments in sciences other than physics—in biology, neuroscience, psychology, psychiatry, social and behavior sciences—have been moving in the opposite direction. They have convinced many persons that more of our behavior is determined by causes unknown to us and beyond our control than previously believed. These scientific developments are many, but they clearly include a greatly enhanced knowledge of the influence of genetics and heredity upon human behavior (the recent mapping of the human genome is a symbolic as well as real indication of this influence, naturally arousing fears of future control of behavior by genetic manipulation); greater awareness of biochemical influences on the brain; the susceptibility of human moods and behavior to drugs; the advent of psychoanalysis and other theories of unconscious motivation; development of computers and intelligent machines that mimic aspects of human cognition in deterministic ways; comparative studies of animal and human behavior suggesting that much of our motivational and behavioral repertoire is a product of our evolutionary history; influences of psychological, social, and cultural conditioning upon upbringing and subsequent behavior, and so on. (The impact of such trends on contemporary free will debates is discussed in essays by Taylor and Dennett, Paul Russell, Richard Double, Benjamin Libet, and Henrik Walter.)

In sum, there continues to be considerable debate about determinism and indeterminism in the physical world, and about the relationship of both to human behavior, while contemporary sciences other than physics provide continuing support for deterministic thinking about human behavior. Worries about determinism in human affairs therefore persist with good reason in contemporary debates about free will.[11]

3. The Compatibility Question and Arguments for Incompatibilism

These worries about determinism make the second pivotal question of modern free will debates, the Compatibility Question, all the more important. Is free will compatible (or incompatible) with determinism? The free will problem arose historically because it was assumed that there was some kind of conflict between free will and determinism. If it turns out, to the contrary, that determinism is no threat to free will because the two can be reconciled, then worries about determinism would be misplaced. The traditional problem of free will would not only be solved, but in a manner "dissolved," for the supposed conflict with determinism that gave rise to it in the first place would have been shown to be illusory.

Such a "dissolutionist" strategy has been the reigning strategy of modern compatibilists about free will since Thomas Hobbes in the seventeenth century. The strategy led in the twentieth century to claims by logical positivists and others that the traditional problem of free will is a "pseudo-problem" or a "dead issue" and ought to be laid to rest. This has not happened, of course; debates about free will are more alive than ever today. But compatibilist views have had a powerful influence throughout the twentieth century. The idea that free will and determinism are compatible continues to be a majority view among philosophers and scientists because it seems to offer a simple resolution of the conflict between ordinary views of human behavior from a practical standpoint and theoretical images of human beings in the natural and social sciences. (Philosophers always believe they have made progress when they discover something we don't have to worry about—or when they discover something we *do* have to worry about.)

So while the debate over the Compatibility Question has not ended, the burden of proof has shifted back to those who believe in a traditional free will that is *incompatible* with determinism. One cannot simply assume that if determinism is true, we would lack freedom or free will in an important sense. Arguments must now be provided to show this; and one of the interesting developments of the past thirty years is that new arguments for incompatibilism have indeed been proposed to meet the challenge. These incompatibilist arguments have in turn provoked more sophisticated compatibilist responses, and new theories on both sides of the Compatibility Question, as we shall now see.

Two features of free will were mentioned earlier that seem to imply its incompatibility with determinism—(a) it is "up to us" what we choose from an array of alternative possibilities and (b) the origin or source of our choices and actions is in us and not in anyone or anything else over which we have no control. Most modern arguments for the incompatibility of free will and determinism have proceeded from feature (a)—the requirement that an agent acted freely, or of his or her own free will, only if the agent had *alternative possibilities*, or *could have done otherwise*.[12] Let us refer to this requirement as the AP condition (for "alternative possibilities") or simply AP. (It is also sometimes called the "could have done otherwise" condition or the "avoidability" condition.)

The case for incompatibility from this AP (or "could have done otherwise") condition has two premises:

1. The existence of alternative possibilities (or the agent's power to do otherwise) is a necessary condition for acting freely, or acting "of one's own free will."

2. Determinism is not compatible with alternative possibilities (it precludes the power to do otherwise).

Since it follows immediately from these premises that determinism is not compatible with acting freely, or acting of one's own free will, the case for incompatibilism (and the case against it) must focus on one or another of these premises. In fact, there have been heated and labyrinthine debates in recent philosophy about both premises. Premise 1 is just the AP condition itself (free will requires alternative possibilities or the power to do otherwise) and it has been subjected to searching criticisms. But I shall begin with premise 2, which is usually regarded as the most crucial (and vulnerable) premise since it asserts the incompatibility of determinism with the power to do otherwise.

The most widely discussed argument in support of premise 2 in recent philosophy has been the so-called "Modal" or "Consequence" Argument for incompatibilism. This argument was first formulated in varying ways by Carl Ginet (1966, 1980), David Wiggins (1973), Peter van Inwagen (1975, 1983), James Lamb (1977), and (in a theological form) by Nelson Pike (1965).[13] Alternative formulations have since been proposed and defended by many others.[14] Van Inwagen (1983), who offers three versions of the argument, regards these as versions of the same basic argument, which he calls the "Consequence Argument," and states informally as follows:

> If determinism is true, then our acts are the consequences of the laws of nature and events in the remote past. But it is not up to us what went on before we were born; and neither is it up to us what the laws of nature are. Therefore, the consequences of these things (including our present acts) are not up to us.
> (p. 16)

To see the connection between this argument and premise 2, recall that something's being "up to us" implies our having the power to bring it about or not to bring it about. Given this assumption, the claims in the quote that "it is not up to us what went on before we were born" or "what the laws of nature are" imply that there is nothing we *could have done* to alter the past before we were born or the laws of nature. But if determinism is true, the past before we were born and the laws jointly entail our present actions. So it seems that there is nothing we can do to alter our present actions. We do not have the power to do otherwise and hence lack alternative possibilities.

This Modal or Consequence Argument for incompatibilism is the topic of two essays in this volume, one by Tomis Kapitan, a compatibilist critic of the argument, the other by Peter van Inwagen, one of its best-known incompatibilist defenders. The first half of Kapitan's essay surveys various formulations of the Consequence Argument and criticisms made against it over the past three decades. Like many of the argument's critics, Kapitan believes its soundness depends upon how one interprets modal notions such as "power" or "ability" (to bring something about) and "could have done otherwise"; and the argument also depends on how one interprets related conditional statements about what *would* or *might* have happened if various abilities or powers had been exercised. Kapitan explores these topics in the latter part of his essay and, in the light of them, considers possible compatibilist strategies for answering the argument.

In the first half of his essay, van Inwagen restates and reaffirms a formal version of the Consequence Argument first presented in van Inwagen (1983) (which has become the most widely discussed version of the argument in the 1990s) and then defends this version against a recent objection by Thomas McKay and David Johnson (1996). In the second part of his essay, van Inwagen turns to a different topic that we will consider later—how one is to make sense of the incompatibilist or nondeterminist kind of freedom that the Consequence Argument seems to require. Van Inwagen believes that no one to date has been able to give an intelligible account of incompatibilist freedom; and he has doubts about the possibility of doing so. Yet because he also thinks the Consequence Argument is undeniably sound, he argues that we must continue to believe in an undetermined free will even if we do not know how to give an intelligible account of it.

4. Classical Compatibilism: Interpretations of "Can," "Power," and "Could Have Done Otherwise"

Most compatibilists believe that the Consequence Argument and all arguments for incompatibilism can be defeated by giving a proper analysis of what it means to say that agents *can* (or have the *power* or *ability* to) do something; and consequently there has been much debate in recent philosophy about the meaning of these notions. Traditionally, compatibilists themselves have defined *freedom* in terms of "can," "power," and "ability." To be free, most compatibilists have insisted, means in ordinary language (1) to have the *power* or *ability* to do what we will (desire or choose) to do, and this entails (2) an absence of *constraints* or *impediments* preventing us from doing what we will, desire, or choose. The constraints or impediments they have in mind include physical restraints, lack of opportunity, duress or coercion, physical or mental impairment, and the like. You lack the freedom to meet a friend in a cafe across town if you are tied to a chair, are in a jail cell, lack transportation, someone is holding a gun to your head, or you are paralyzed. Compatibilists have typically insisted that (1) and (2) capture what freedom means in everyday life—that is, an absence of such constraints and hence the power (= ability plus opportunity) to do whatever you will or want to do.

A view that defines freedom in this way has been called "classical compatibilism" by Gary Watson (1975); and this is a useful designation. Classical compatibilists include well-known philosophers of the modern era such as Thomas Hobbes, David Hume, John Stuart Mill, and numerous twentieth-century figures (such as A. J. Ayer 1954, Moritz Schlick 1966 and Donald Davidson 1973).[15] Despite differences in detail, we can say that what these classical compatibilists have in common is that they define the freedom to do something in terms of (1) and (2). What do they say about the freedom *to do otherwise*? It is also defined by classical compatibilists in terms of (1) and (2). You are free to do otherwise than meet your friend when you (1) have the power or ability to avoid meeting him, which entails in turn that (2) there are no constraints or impediments preventing you from avoiding the meeting (e.g., no one is forcing you at gunpoint to meet him). Of course, an absence of constraints and hence the freedom to do something does not mean you will actually do it. But for classical compatibilists it does mean that you *would* do it, *if* you wanted or desired to do it. Thus they hold that (1) and (2) entail a third feature of classical compatibilism, namely, that terms such as *can, power, ability*, and *freedom* should be given a *conditional* or *hypothetical* analysis: (3) that an agent can (has the power, is able, is free, to) do something means that the agent would do it, if the agent wanted (or desired or chose) to do it.

Such conditional or hypothetical analyses of *can, power*, and *freedom* were not invented by compatibilists to thwart the Consequence Argument. They were invented long before that argument in an effort to represent ordinary notions of freedom. But, if conditional analyses are correct, they *would* effectively thwart the Consequence Argument and other arguments for the incompatibility of freedom and determinism that appeal to alternative possibilities, or the power to do otherwise. For if the power to do otherwise means only that you would have done otherwise if you had wanted or desired, it would be consistent with determinism. It might be true that you would have done otherwise if you had wanted, though it is determined that you did not in fact want otherwise. Likewise, if the power to do otherwise has only such a conditional meaning, it would not require changing the past or violating laws of nature. To say "you could have done otherwise" would only amount to the counterfactual claim that you would have done otherwise, if (contrary to fact) the past (or the laws) had been different in some way, for example, if you had wanted or desired or chosen otherwise.[16]

"Character examples" of this kind have their source in David Hume's well-known observation that we cannot be held responsible (or be said to act from "our own" free wills) unless our actions are to a considerable degree determined by our characters or motives in regular ways. The obvious truth of this claim gives character examples, like Dennett's Luther example, an undeniable force. Yet there is reason to think such character examples do not provide conclusive evidence that free will does not require alternative possibilities and hence that free will is compatible with determinism. For the following response to such examples is available to incompatibilists and has been made by some of them in recent debates (see Kane 1985, 1996; van Inwagen, 1989; Shatz 1997; Ekstrom 2000).

It may be true that Luther's "Here I stand" might have been a morally responsible act done "of his own free will," even if he could not have done otherwise at the time he performed it and even if his act was determined by his then-existing character and motives. But this would be true only to the extent that one could assume other things about the background of Luther's action that made him responsible or accountable for it—namely, that he was responsible by virtue of earlier choices and actions for making himself into the kind of person he now was, with this character and these motives, and that he could have done otherwise with respect to at least some of those earlier acts. If this were not so, one might argue, there would have been nothing he could have *ever* done to make himself different than he was—a consequence that is difficult to reconcile with the claim that he is morally responsible for being what he is.[18] (The implications of this line of reasoning for issues about moral responsibility, desert, and freedom are discussed—from differing points of view—in several essays of this volume, including, those of Paul Russell, Galen Strawson, Laura Ekstrom, and Robert Kane.)

This argument, even if correct, would not show of course that character examples like that of Luther lack significance—far from it. Such examples seem to show that alternative possibilities need not be required for *every* morally responsible act done of our own free wills; and, if correct, this would be a significant implication. Yet the preceding argument also seems to show that, if we take a broader view of an agent's life history, rather than focusing on individual acts in isolation, it does not necessarily follow that free will and moral responsibility do not require alternative possibilities *at all*, that is, at any times, in the course of an agent's life.[19] A stronger argument would be needed to show this; character examples alone do not suffice.

This leads to examples of the second kind mentioned earlier—Frankfurt-style examples or Frankfurt-style cases—which, according to many philosophers, *do* provide the stronger argument needed to show that alternative possibilities are not required at all for free will or moral responsibility. Examples of this kind were originally introduced by Frankfurt (1969) with the intent of undermining what he called the "Principle of Alternative Possibilities" (PAP): "[A] person is morally responsible for what he has done only if he could have done otherwise" (p. 829). This is our AP condition applied to "morally responsible" acts rather than to acts done "of our own free will." (The AP variant would be "a person acts of his own free will only if he could have done otherwise.") The two principles (PAP and AP) would be equivalent, if the moral responsibility at issue (in PAP) were precisely the kind that free will (in AP) is suppose to confer; and this assumption has been commonly made in free will debates. But we shall see that this assumption (linking moral responsibility and free will) has also come into question in contemporary free will debates, specifically in connection with examples of the Frankfurt type.

Frankfurt-type examples typically involve a controller who can make an agent do whatever the controller wants (perhaps by direct control over the agent's brain). The controller will not intervene, however, if the agent is going to do on his own what the controller wants. Frankfurt argues that if the controller does not intervene because the agent performs the desired action entirely on his own, the agent can then be morally responsible (having acted on his own)—even though the agent literally could not have done otherwise (because the controller would not have let him). If this is so, the Principle of Alternative Possibilities, PAP, would be false: the agent would be morally responsible, though he could not in fact have done otherwise. If PAP and AP turn out to be equivalent, AP would be false as well. Neither moral responsibility nor free will (in the moral responsibility-entailing sense) would require alternative possibilities; and arguments for incompatibilism, such as the Consequence Argument, would be thwarted.

Frankfurt-style examples of this sort involving "pre-emptive" (or "counterfactual") control have proliferated since they were first introduced. The literature on them is now enormous and has had a significant impact on contemporary free will debates. Note that Frankfurt-style examples provide extra leverage against PAP and AP that character examples do not provide. For one might go on to imagine a "global" Frankfurt controller hovering over agents throughout their entire lifetimes, so that the agents never could have done otherwise; and yet the controller never in fact intervenes because the agents always do on their own what the controller wants. Such a global controller would be a mere observer of events, never actually intervening in the agents' affairs (a mere "counterfactual intervener," in John Fischer's words). It seems that the agents would act "on their own" throughout their entire lifetimes and would be responsible for many of their actions even though they never could have done otherwise and never had any alternative possibilities.[20]

Contemporary debates about the implications of Frankfurt-style examples are the subject of three essays of this volume, by John Martin Fischer, Laura Ekstrom, and David Widerker. Fischer, whose prior writings have contributed as much as any contemporary philosopher to our understanding of the implications of these examples, provides a comprehensive survey of arguments about Frankfurt-style examples over the past thirty years. He considers various strategies by which critics of these examples have tried to rescue the Principle of Alternative Possibilities, PAP (or variations of it) from arguments based on such examples; and various responses to these strategies. Fischer himself is a defender of Frankfurt-style examples, who believes that moral responsibility does not require alternative possibilities (that is, he denies PAP). But, surprisingly, he is also an advocate of his own version of the Consequence Argument (Fischer 1994) and believes that *freedom* does imply alternative possibilities (that is, he affirms AP). This view, which Fischer calls *semi-compatibilism*, is defended by him and also by Mark Ravizza in a number of recent writings (Fischer 1994; Ravizza 1994; Fischer and Ravizza 1998).[21] It amounts to the claim that moral responsibility is compatible with determinism (since it does not require the power to do otherwise), while freedom (which does require the power to do otherwise) is not compatible with determinism.[22]

Laura Ekstrom and David Widerker look at Frankfurt-style examples from an opposing incompatibilist or libertarian perspective. Ekstrom, along with other incompatibilist critics of these examples (for example, van Inwagen 1978, 1983; Kane 1985, 1996a; Lamb 1993; Widerker 1995a, and b, Ginet 1996; Copp 1997; Wyma 1997), has argued that Frankfurt-style examples do not refute every relevant form of PAP and do not show that moral responsibility is compatible with determinism (cf. Ekstrom 2000: ch. 6). In her essay for this volume, she defends a number of objections to Frankfurt-style examples, arguing that intuitions to the effect that agents are morally responsible in such examples beg the question against those who believe free will is incompatible with determinism. Ekstrom also discusses a new Frankfurt-style example put forward in an influential article by Alfred Mele and David Robb (1998), which was designed to answer objections to earlier Frankfurt-style cases by incompatibilist critics such as Widerker (1995a and b) and Kane (1985, 1996a).

Widerker is the author of several articles (notably, 1995a and b) that have had a significant impact on recent debates about Frankfurt-style examples. In his essay for this volume, he defends the main theses of these articles by responding to new Frankfurt-style examples put forward in the past decade to answer his and other incompatibilist objections. Since Widerker has discussed the Mele/Robb example elsewhere (2000a), and it is dealt with by Fischer and Ekstrom in this volume, he focuses on other recent Frankfurt-style examples designed to answer incompatibilist objections—examples suggested by Eleonore Stump (1996a, 1999b), David Hunt (1996a), and others. Widerker's essay also discusses some theological implications of Frankfurt-style cases. He concludes with a general argument (called the "W-defense") designed to show that it would be unreasonable to hold an agent morally *blameworthy* for an action if the agent could not have avoided performing the action. In the light of this defense, Widerker argues for a version of PAP for at least one kind of moral responsibility—moral blameworthiness—against supporters of Frankfurt, such as Fischer (1994).

6. BEYOND CLASSICAL COMPATIBILISM: NEW COMPATIBILIST APPROACHES TO FREEDOM AND RESPONSIBILITY

In addition to semi-compatibilism, a host of other new compatibilist views of both freedom and responsibility have been introduced in the past forty years in the attempt to answer objections to classical compatibilism. These new compatibilist theories are described and critically evaluated in two further essays of this volume, by Ishtiyaque Haji and Paul Russell.

Haji's essay deals with two broad categories of contemporary compatibilist views of freedom and responsibility, which he calls *reactive attitude theories* and *mesh theories*. Mesh theories are further divided into "hierarchical theories," "valuational theories," "reason theories," and others. Compatibilist theories of the first category—reactive attitude theories—have their roots in another seminal essay of modern free will debates, P. F. Strawson's "Freedom and Resentment" (1962). Strawson argues that free will issues focus pivotally on the conditions required to hold persons responsible for their actions; and he argues that responsibility is constituted by persons adopting certain reactive attitudes toward themselves and others—attitudes such as resentment, admiration, gratitude, indignation, guilt, and the like. To be responsible, according to Strawson, is to be a fit subject of such attitudes. It is to be enmeshed in a "form of life" (to use Ludwig Wittgenstein's apt expression for this view) in which such reactive attitudes play a constitutive role.

Moreover, this form of life of which the reactive attitudes are constitutive is such that, according to Strawson, we would not give it up even if we found that determinism was true, because we could not give up assessing ourselves and others in terms of the reactive attitudes if we continued to live a human form of life. So Strawson contends that the freedom and responsibility required to live a human life (whatever else they may involve) must be compatible with determinism. Freedom and responsibility do not require some mysterious indeterminist or "contracausal" free will, as incompatibilists claim. This Strawsonian reactive attitude view has inspired considerable debate since the 1960s, which is documented in Haji's essay. It has also gained new adherents in the 1990s, one of whom is R. Jay Wallace, whose book *Responsibility and the Moral Sentiments* (1994) is the most thoroughly developed Strawsonian view in the recent literature. Wallace's view is also critically evaluated in Haji's essay.

Mesh theories, which form another influential class of new compatibilist theories, insist that the freedom required for responsibility is a function of the appropriate "mesh" or connection between agents' choices or actions, on the one hand, and their reasons or motives for acting, on the other. The most widely discussed of mesh theories are the *hierarchical theories* of motivation of Gerald Dworkin (1970), Harry Frankfurt (1971), Wright Neely (1974), and others. In his seminal essay "Freedom of the Will and the Concept of a Person" (1971), Frankfurt argued that persons, unlike similar animals, "have the capacity for reflective self-evaluation that is manifested in the formation of second-order desires" (p. 7)—desires to have or not to have various first-order desires. Free will and responsibility require that we assess our first-order desires or motives and form "second-order volitions" about which of our first-order desires should move us to action. Our "wills"—the first-order desires that move us to action—are *free*, according to Frankfurt, when they conform with our second-order volitions, so that we have the *will* (first-order desires) we *want* (second-order desires) to have and in that sense we "identify" with our will.

Classical compatibilism is deficient, according to hierarchical theorists such as Frankfurt, because it gives us only a theory of freedom of *action* (being able to do what we will) without a theory of freedom of *will* in terms of the conformity of first-order motives to higher-order motives (being able, so to speak, to will what we will). Hierarchical theories remain compatibilist, however, since they define free will in terms of a conformity (or "mesh") between desires at different levels without requiring that desires at any level be undetermined. It does not matter, as Frankfurt puts it, how we came to have the wills we want to have, whether by a deterministic process or not. What matters is that we have the wills we want and the power to realize them in action. That is what makes us free.[23]

Hierarchical views are an improvement in many ways over classical compatibilism since they provide a compatibilist account of free will as well as of free action and a richer picture of the human person. But hierarchical views are not without problems; and they have also been subjected to searching criticisms, which Haji considers in his essay. Some of the criticisms of hierarchical views have given rise to other "mesh theories" that depart from the hierarchical model in various ways. Among further mesh theories discussed in Haji's essay are "valuational" theories, such as that of Gary Watson (1975), and Susan Wolf's "reason view" (1990). For Watson, the relevant mesh required for free agency is not necessarily between higher-and lower-order desires, but between an agent's "valuational system" (beliefs about what is good or ought to be done), which has its source in the agent's reason, and the "motivational system" (desires and other motives), which has its source in appetite. Watson thus revives the ancient Platonic opposition between reason and desire—arguing that freedom consists in a certain conformity of desire to reason.

Susan Wolf's "reason view" takes this approach in yet another direction that also has ancient roots. She argues that freedom consists in being able to do the right thing for the right reasons, which requires in turn the ability to appreciate "the True and the Good." Wolf's theory thus has a stronger normative component than many other mesh theories. According to her, you are free only when you are doing the *right* thing for the *right* reasons. Another recent theory that shares this particular kind of normative component and has affinities to Wolf's, though it is original, is put forward by Phillip Pettit and Michael Smith 1996. Normative theories of freedom of somewhat different kinds have also been defended by Michael Slote (1980) and Paul Benson (1987), among others.[24] Wolf's reason view has some unusual and controversial implications that Haji also evaluates in his essay. For example, her view contains an "asymmetry thesis" according to which we act freely when we do the right thing for the right reasons, but do not act freely when we act wrongly or otherwise fail to do the right thing for the right reasons. Finally, Haji's essay discusses yet another compatibilist mesh theory of recent vintage put forward by Hilary Bok (1998).

Paul Russell's essay considers a number of other contemporary compatibilist views, some of which fit into Haji's categories, but most of which are not easily classified. Russell organizes his essay around themes from Daniel Dennett's influential compatibilist work, *Elbow Room* (1984), and in the light of these themes considers other compatibilist views along with Dennett's, including those of Paul Benson (1987), Martha Klein (1990), John Fischer and Mark Ravizza (1998),[25] Robert Audi (1993), and Kevin Magill (1997). Through these authors and a number of other authors cited in his essay, Russell discusses a variety of topics that have been of concern to contemporary compatibilists, such as control, reflexivity, responsiveness to reasons, "moral luck," the place of character in moral evaluation, ultimacy, blameworthiness, and normative elements of freedom.

As noted, Russell's discussion of Dennett focuses on the latter's earlier *Elbow Room* (1984). Dennett's more recent views may be seen in the essay he himself has contributed to this volume in collaboration with Christopher Taylor. Taylor and Dennett argue in defense of compatibilism that objections to compatibilist accounts of free agency are based on a flawed understanding of the relation of such notions as *possibility* and *causation* to freedom and agency; and they undertake an analysis of the relevant notions of possibility and causation to show this. Taylor and Dennett also employ analogies to the functioning of sophisticated computers to argue that the flexibility, reflexivity, and creativity that free will requires are consistent with the hypothesis that the behavior of humans, like that of intelligent machines, is determined. As their essay illustrates, appeals to intelligent machines and computer simulations of human cognition and behavior have come to play an increasingly important role in modern debates about free will.

7. Libertarian or Incompatibilist Theories of Free Will: The Intelligibility Question

Let us now turn from compatibilist theories to contemporary incompatibilist views of free will. Those who believe that free will is incompatible with determinism and who also affirm that free will exists (thus denying the truth of determinism) are usually referred to as *libertarians* in twentieth-century writings on free will. Libertarianism in this sense is not to be confused with the political doctrine of the same name. In free will contexts, libertarians are those who believe in the existence of a traditional antideterminist (or incompatibilist) free will, which does not necessarily commit them to political beliefs about freedom associated with political libertarianism. To avoid confusion, it would be more accurate to speak in free will debates of "free will libertarians" or "libertarians about free will" or "defenders of an incompatibilist free will"—making clear that the designation *libertarian* and its cognates is an abbreviation for these longer expressions—as it is assumed to be throughout this volume.

Contemporary free will libertarians must not only answer the Determinist and Compatibility questions by denying determinism and denying the compatibility of free will and determinism. They face an even more daunting task of answering a third pivotal question that has been at the heart of modern debates about free will and may be called the Intelligibility Question. Can one make sense of a freedom or free will that is incompatible with determinism? Is such an incompatibilist freedom coherent or intelligible, or is it, as many critics contend, essentially mysterious and terminally obscure?

The threat to free will from the perspective of this Intelligibility Question does not come from determinism, but from its opposite, *indeterminism*. If free will is not compatible with determinism, it does not seem to be compatible with indeterminism either. (One might say that the Compatibility Question is about the first half of this ancient dilemma, while the Intelligibility Question is about the second half.) An event that is undetermined might occur or not occur, given the entire past. Thus, whether or not it actually occurs, given its past, would seem to be a matter of chance. But chance events are not under the control of anything, hence not under the control of the agent. How then could they be free and responsible actions? Reflections such as these have led to charges that undetermined choices or actions would be "arbitrary," "capricious," "random," "irrational," "uncontrolled," "inexplicable," or merely "matters of luck or chance," not really free and responsible actions at all. It appears that the indeterminism that libertarians demand for free will would not in fact enhance freedom but would undermine it.

One of the significant features of recent free will debates is that an increasing amount of attention has been given to this Intelligibility Question concerning libertarian free will. It is one thing for libertarians to put forth arguments for incompatibilism or to point out flaws in compatibilist accounts of free agency (as they have often done); it is quite another to give a positive account of the libertarian free agency that will show how such a free will can be reconciled with indeterminism and how it is to be related to modern views of human behavior in the natural and human sciences. Recent efforts to give positive accounts of incompatibilist or libertarian free agency are discussed in four essays of this volume, by Timothy O'Connor, Randolph Clarke, Carl Ginet, and Robert Kane.

It is instructive in reading these essays to sort recent libertarian theories into two broad categories—(1) *agent-causal* (or *AC*) theories and (2) *teleological intelligibility* (or *TI*) theories (see Kane 1989). Agent-causal or AC theories, in O'Connor's words (1995a: 7), posit "a *sui generis* form of causation by an agent that is irreducible (ontologically as well as conceptually) to event-causal processes within the agent." (I shall follow a common practice in recent writings on free will of hyphenating expressions such as "agent-cause" and "agent-causation" when talking about AC theories to indicate that a special kind of relation is intended.) AC theories have taken many historical forms. Indeed they have been the most common kind of libertarian theory until recent times. But, despite differences, they are usually motivated by a common line of reasoning. Since undetermined free acts might occur or not occur, given all the same prior events or states of affairs involving the agents, if we to avoid saying such acts merely happen by chance, we must posit some additional causal factor over and above (and not reducible to) prior events or state of affairs to account for their occurrence. This additional causal factor would be the agent itself, which cannot be caused in turn by prior events because it is not an event and therefore not of the right type to be the effect of any cause. The agent-cause, to use Roderick Chisholm's notable expression (1982b: 30), must be a kind of "prime mover unmoved."

Libertarian theories of the teleological intelligibility (or TI) variety, by contrast, attempt to make undetermined free actions intelligible in terms of reasons or motives and intentions or purposes (hence *teleologically* intelligible), without postulating *sui generis* kinds of agency or causation that cannot be spelled out in terms of events or states of affairs involving the agent. TI theories in turn fall into two categories, depending on how they interpret the relation of reasons and intentions to actions: (1) *simple indeterminist* (or *noncausalist*) TI theories maintain, again from O'Connor (1995: 7), "that free agency doesn't require there to be any sort of causal connection (even of an indeterministic variety) between the agent ['s reasons] and his free actions"; while (2) *causal indeterminist* (or *event-causal*) TI theories maintain that agents cause their "free actions via [their] reasons for doing so, but indeterministically" (ibid.).

As a consequence of these distinctions, recent positive libertarian theories have often been sorted into three categories: agent-causal, simple indeterminist, and causal indeterminist theories (see O'Connor 1993, 1995a; Clarke 1995, Ekstrom 1999), the latter two being TI theories. But it is interesting to note that current agent-causal or AC theories can also be divided into two categories, depending on whether they interpret the relation of reasons to actions noncausally or causally. Some AC theorists maintain that reasons for acting play an essential (probabilistic) *causal* role in agent-causation (for example, Clarke 1993, 1996a), while other agent-cause theorists question this (see, e.g., O'Connor 1995a, 2000). So there are really at least four types of libertarian theory in the contemporary literature: AC theories of noncausalist and causalist kinds and TI theories of noncausalist (simple indeterminist) and causalist (causal indeterminist) kinds. All four types are discussed in the four essays of this volume on current libertarian views. Indeed, the authors of the four essays represent each of the theories: O'Connor and Clarke are AC theorists of the noncausalist and causalist kinds, respectively; while Ginet and Kane are TI theorists of the noncausalist and causalist kinds, respectively.

O'Connor's essay provides an overview of recent agent-causal (or AC) theories, explaining what motivates them through a discussion of mechanism, teleology and agency. He considers different accounts of the agent-causal relation by, among others, libertarians such as C. A. Campbell (1967), Roderick Chisholm (1966, 1976a), Richard Taylor (1967), John Thorp (1980), Michael Zimmerman (1984), Richard Swinburne (1986),[26] Godfrey Vesey (in Flew and Vesey 1987), Alan Donagan (1987), William Rowe (1991),[27] Randolph Clarke, (1993, 1996a) and O'Connor himself (1995a, 2000). O'Connor also poses the question whether agent-causal theories require a substance dualism of mind and body—as many philosophers have suspected they must, since they posit a sui generis causal relation between an agent and action that is irreducible to ordinary modes of causation. O'Connor argues that AC theories do not necessarily require substance dualism but may require some sort of strong emergence of mind from matter. He also discusses some contemporary dualist accounts of free agency in the light of this question (for example, those of John Eccles and Karl Popper 1977 and Richard Swinburne 1986, among others [28]).

Clarke's essay critically examines TI theories of both the simple indeterminist and causal indeterminist kinds. (He prefers to call the former "noncausal" theories and the latter "event-causal" theories—two alternative designations that are also common in contemporary discussions.) With regard to *simple indeterminist* or *noncausal* TI theories, Clarke critically examines two representative views, those of Carl Ginet (1990) and Hugh McCann (1998) (while also citing other views of this sort, for example, of Storrs McCall 1994 and Stewart Goetz 1997). Clarke poses questions about how well these theories account for the relation of reasons to action and how well they are able to account for the causal role of agents in the control of free actions. His discussion of the second kind of TI theory, *causal indeterminist* or *event-causal* theories, is more complicated in that there are two distinct forms such theories have taken. The general possibility of causal indeterminist libertarian theories (as alternatives to both agent-causation and simple indeterminism) was first suggested, though not worked out, by David Wiggins (1973), Daniel Dennett (1978), Richard Sorabji (1980), and Robert Nozick (1981). Attempts to develop such theories in more detail have taken two forms in the 1980s and 1990s.

In one form, the causal indeterminism is placed earlier in the deliberative process, in the coming to mind of considerations for choice or in the formation of preferences. It is these processes that are said to be undetermined. Dennett (1978) and Kane (1985) first suggested views of this sort (which have been called "Valerian" libertarianisms[29]), but neither unqualifiedly endorsed them.[30] (Indeed, Dennett, a compatibilist, suggested such a view only to criticize it.) Clarke critically examines two more recent versions of this kind of causal indeterminist view, those of Alfred Mele (1995) and Laura Ekstrom (2000).[31] For causal indeterminist theories of the second kind, the indeterminism is not only placed earlier in the deliberative process, but also later, in choices themselves and in efforts of will preceding choice and action. Clarke also critically examines the most developed version of this second form of causal indeterminist theory, the view of Robert Kane (1985, 1996a). With regard to both versions of causal indeterminism, Clarke (as he did with simple indeterminist theories) considers questions about how well they are able to account for the rationality and control agents are supposed to exercise over their free actions. He concludes his essay with an assessment of the evidence for the indeterminism in nature which these and other libertarian theories would require.

Ginet's essay focuses on the issue that distinguishes causalist from noncausalist forms of both AC or TI theories—that is, the issue of how explanations of actions in terms of reasons or motives (beliefs, desires, intentions, and other motivating psychological attitudes) are related to causal explanations of behavior. This has been a central issue in the philosophy of action generally for the past forty years; and Ginet has been a major contributor to the debates about it. *Causalists* hold that reasons explanations are a form of causal explanation and require that there be a causal connection between the agent's reasons or motives and the actions they explain. *Noncausalists* deny that reasons explanation are a form of causal explanation and deny that such explanations require a causal connection between reasons and the actions they explain.

Ginet is a noncausalist and he defends a noncausalist account of reasons explanation in his essay, as he has in other writings (for example, Ginet 1990). He notes that the issue has an obvious bearing on the free will problem, for if reasons can explain actions noncausally, then actions could be explained without the supposition that they are either caused or determined. But noncausalist accounts of reasons explanations have been controversial and have been criticized by compatibilists and many incompatibilists as well, ever since the publication of Donald Davidson's seminal article on the subject, "Actions, Reasons and Causes," in 1963. Ginet surveys these debates since Davidson's essay and undertakes a defense of noncausalism against its critics. In the process, he also criticizes Clarke's (and O'Connor's) agent-causal views, which Ginet, as a TI theorist and simple indeterminist, also rejects.

Kane agrees with Ginet that a special kind of agent- or nonevent causation is not needed to account for libertarian free will. As a TI theorist, he too rejects sui generis forms of causation, such as AC theories postulate. But, as a causal indeterminist, Kane disagrees with Ginet on the causalist issue: he does not think libertarians should deny that reasons explanation are a kind of causal explanation; nor need they deny that there are causal relations between reasons and actions in order to give an adequate account of incompatibilist free will. What matters is that the relevant causal relations involving reasons not always be deterministic (they may sometimes be nondeterministic or probabilistic). In short, "undetermined" need not mean "uncaused; and reasons, like other causes, may "incline without necessitating." If "undetermined" did mean "uncaused," one could see why libertarians might be tempted to posit (as AC theorists do) some extra kind of causation or agency to account for how free actions can be caused or produced, given that they are undetermined by events. Libertarian freedom, Kane contends, must be indeterminist, but it need not be "contra-causal."[32]

But it is one thing to make such claims, and another to give an adequate account of libertarian free agency without appealing *either* to some special kind of agent-or nonevent causation *or* to the claim that reasons explanation are not causal. Kane undertakes this task in his essay and attempts to show how a TI account of free will of such a kind might be reconciled with modern conceptions of human beings in the natural and human sciences. His essay also addresses the Compatibility Question in addition to the Intelligibility Question, suggesting a novel route to incompatibilism that avoids direct appeals to alternative possibilities (AP) and the Consequence Argument, relying instead on a notion of "ultimate responsibility" (UR).

8. Hard Determinism, Successor Views, and Other Nonstandard Theories

Not all of those who believe that free will is incompatible with determinism affirm the existence of free will (as libertarians do). Some incompatibilists also believe that determinism is true and so are committed to denying the existence of free will. Those who take such a stand are commonly referred to as *hard determinists*. The designation originated with the American philosopher and psychologist William James (1907), who distinguished "soft" from "hard" determinists. Both groups believe that all human behavior is determined. But soft determinists are *compatibilists* who insist that determinism does not undermine any free will or responsibility worth having, while hard determinists are *incompatibilists* who take a harder line: since determinism is true, free will does not exist in a sense required for genuine responsibility, accountability, blameworthiness, or desert.

Few thinkers have been willing to embrace such a hard determinist position unqualifiedly, since it would require wholesale changes in the way we think about human relations and attitudes, how we treat criminals and criminal behavior, and so on. This has not prevented hard determinism from being unequivocally endorsed by some (for example, Baron d'Holbach in the eighteenth century and Clarence Darrow and Paul Edwards 1958 in the twentieth), but unequivocal endorsement has been rare. The principle at work seems to have been that of the Victorian lady who exclaimed when she first heard of Darwin's theory. "Descended from the apes," she said: "let's hope it isn't true. But if it is, let's hope it does not become generally known."

Nonetheless, a core or kernel of the traditional hard determinist position has persisted into the twentieth century and continues to play a significant role in contemporary free will debates. This kernel persists in what might be called Successor Views to classical hard determinism. These Successor Views cannot strictly speaking be called hard determinist in the classical sense; and those who hold them would disown that title. But these views do contain a kernel of the classical hard determinist position that—detached from its traditional moorings—presents a powerful challenge to both compatibilist and libertarian views of free will. This kernel is defended in one form or another by four contributors to this volume, Galen Strawson, Ted Honderich, Derk Pereboom, and Saul Smilansky. None of them would accept the label of hard determinist with its classical connotations[33]; and their views differ from each other. But each accepts an important kernel of traditional hard determinism; and each accordingly presents a challenging alternative to both contemporary compatibilist and libertarian views.

The kernel may be identified as follows. Classical hard determinism consists of three theses: (1) free will (in the strong sense required for ultimate responsibility and desert) is not compatible with determinism; (2) there is no free will in this strong sense because (3) all events are determined by natural causes (that is, determinism is true). What I am calling Successor Views to classical hard determinism accept (1) and (2), but remain noncommittal about (3)—whether universal determinism is true. Aware of developments in twentieth-century physics, advocates of Successor Views are less confident than classical hard determinists about the truth of universal determinism; and they prefer to leave that question to the scientists. They remain convinced, however, that (1) free will—in what Galen Strawson (1986) calls the "true-responsibility entailing" sense—is incompatible with determinism, and that (2) there is, no such incompatibilist or libertarian free will.

This is the kernel—theses (1) and (2). Though this kernel is clearly not hard "determinism" in the classical sense, because it does not unqualifiedly affirm universal determinism (3), it still represents a pretty "hard" view since it rejects free will in the "true-responsibility entailing" sense. According to it, persons cannot be responsible or deserving for what they do in the ultimate sense assumed by believers in traditional free will. But what is especially interesting about this kernel is that it puts advocates of Successor Views who hold it at odds with *both* contemporary libertarian *and* compatibilist views. For, anyone holding the kernel holds (against compatibilism) that free will in the true-responsibility entailing sense is *not* compatible with determinism—thesis (1)—and (against libertarianism) that incompatibilist or libertarian free will does not exist—thesis (2).

But why do advocates of Successor Views think libertarian free will does not exist, if they remain noncommittal about the truth of universal determinism? One answer lies in the dilemma of free will mentioned earlier: if free will is not compatible with determinism, it does not seem to be compatible with indeterminism either. In response to this dilemma, compatibilists try to refute the first horn (by arguing that free will can be reconciled with determinism) while libertarians try to refute the second horn (arguing that free will can be reconciled with indeterminism). Many Successor Views (Pereboom's is an exception) reject both reconciliation projects and accept both horns of the dilemma. Thus, for these Successor Views, another thesis tends to play the role played by the thesis of universal determinism (3) in classical hard determinism, namely (3'): free will is not compatible with determinism and it is not compatible with indeterminism either. The first part of (3') is just (1) and the second half implies (2); so the kernel is reached in a different way without assuming the truth of determinism.

But this is not quite the whole story about Successor Views either. While they remain noncommittal about whether determinism holds universally in nature, most advocates of Successor Views do in fact believe that *human behavior* is regular and determined for the most part and that if indeterminism did exist in the microphysical world, its macroscopic effects on human behavior would be negligible and of no significance for free will. If the effects of indeterminism on the human brain and behavior are insignificant, as most advocates of Successor Views believe, then the traditional problems posed by determinism for free will remain unchanged, whatever one's view about the microphysical world. More important, most advocates of Successor Views insist that if indeterminism at the micro-level did sometimes have macroscopic effects on human behavior, it would be of "no help" to believers in free will, since such indeterminism would not enhance, but would only diminish, freedom and responsibility.

As noted, theses (1) and (2) put advocates of Successor Views at odds with both libertarians and compatibilists. We should not be surprised, therefore, to find the four contributors to this volume who defend Successor Views—Strawson, Honderich, Pereboom, and Smilansky—arguing against both existing libertarian and compatibilist solutions to the free will problem. In his essay, for example, Galen Strawson defends his influential argument that libertarian free will is an impossibility, whether determinism is true or not (Strawson 1986, 1994a, 2000). Strawson argues that either libertarian free will requires an impossible infinite series of backtracking free choices by which we formed ourselves or it terminates in mere chance events over which we have no control. Strawson has also been a critic of positive accounts of libertarian free agency, like those considered in the previous section. And he has criticized compatibilist views as well (including the "reactive attitude" view of his father, P. F. Strawson) for failing to give us all that we want in the way of true responsibility-entailing freedom (1986: ch. 5).

In the process of revisiting arguments against incompatibilist or libertarian accounts of freedom in this volume, Strawson focuses attention on a different line of argument for incompatibilism from those we have so far considered. Recall the two features of traditional free will that seem to imply its incompatibility with determinism: (a) it must be "up to us" what we choose from an array of alternative possibilities and (b) the origin or source of our choices and actions must be "in us" and not in anyone or anything else over which we have no control. As noted, most arguments for incompatibilism (of which the Consequence Argument is the prime example) have proceeded from feature (a). But another noteworthy feature of recent free will debates, especially of the past two decades, is that more attention has been directed toward the comparatively neglected condition (b), the idea that agents must be the "ultimate sources" of their own wills and actions in a sense that entails that they, and they alone, are ultimately responsible for being the kinds of persons they are.[34] In his essay, Strawson subjects this so-called "ultimacy" or "ultimate responsibility" condition to searching examination. Compatibilists are criticized for failing to recognize the importance of ultimacy for free will, while libertarians are criticized for thinking it is a realizable condition. (It is instructive in this regard to read Strawson's essay in conjunction with the preceding essay in this volume by Kane. Both philosophers argue that notions of ultimate responsibility and desert are crucial for free will, but they differ about whether the freedom required for ultimate responsibility and desert is intelligible and can be realized in the actual world.[35])

Ted Honderich also argues for theses (1) and (2) of the kernel of classical hard determinism, as he has done in other influential writings (1988, 1993). Honderich thinks that the traditional notion of free will requires a power of ultimate "origination" of choices or actions that is incompatible with determinism (thesis [1]).[36] But he also argues that no such power of ultimate origination is possible or could exist in the real world (thesis [2]). Of all the Successor Views canvased in this volume, Honderich's comes closest to affirming the whole package of classical hard determinism, but even he does not quite affirm it all. The first clause of the title of his essay, "Determinism as true," suggests that he does, but it requires interpretation. The determinism Honderich affirms is a qualified "macro-determinism" of *human behavior* that, he says, is consistent with micro-indeterminism of the kind that standard quantum theories postulate. Honderich's sympathies do clearly lie on the side of universal determinism, since he also questions whether quantum physics should be interpreted indeterministically and whether it will turn out to be the last word about the physical world. But he does not take a final stand on these issues or on the truth of universal determinism, as classical hard determinists do. Honderich's main concern in the latter part of his essay (which he calls "the real problem" of free will) is how humans should react to the realization that their behavior is mostly determined and libertarian free will impossible. Some important "life-hopes" must be abandoned, he believes, if determinism is true, but many other life-hopes that matter to us can be retained.[37]

Derk Pereboom also defends both theses of the kernel of classical hard determinism—that (1) genuine free will is incompatible with determinism and (2) libertarian free will does not exist, offering his own arguments for each thesis. Pereboom calls the resulting position—which amounts to a rejection of both compatibilism and libertarianism—"hard incompatibilism" (see Pereboom 2001). He candidly admits that accepting such a position involves "relinquishing our ordinary view of ourselves as blameworthy for immoral actions and praiseworthy for actions that are morally exemplary."[38] The question that chiefly concerns Pereboom in his essay is whether affirming such a view would have the dire consequences many people fear for a host of everyday concerns that matter to us—for example, for moral reform and education, for crime prevention, interpersonal relations, our reactive attitudes of indignation, guilt, gratitude, love and repentance, the ways we treat others, including children, and generally, for our form of life. Pereboom discusses each of these topics, arguing that the consequences of hard incompatibilism would not be as destructive as many people believe and would be compensated by benefits in the form of more humane treatment of others.

Saul Smilansky is another philosopher who holds the kernel of hard determinism without being a hard determinist in the traditional sense. But Smilansky's view is unusual among contemporary views of free will, including the other Successor Views we have been discussing. His view is defined by two radical theses, both of which he defends in his essay for this volume and in a recent work (Smilansky 2000). The first thesis, Fundamental Dualism, states that we can and should be both incompatibilists and compatibilists about freedom and responsibility. There is no reason, Smilansky argues, why it should not be the case that certain forms of moral responsibility, desert, and blame require libertarian free will, while other forms can be sustained without it. Thus, if libertarian free will is impossible (as he believes), there is no reason why we have to choose between hard determinism or compatibilism. We can hold a mixed view that embraces what is true in both hard determinism and compatibilism, while denying that either has the whole truth.

Smilansky's second thesis, Illusionism, is even more radical. In contrast to both Honderich and Pereboom, Smilansky thinks the consequences for humanity of widespread belief that we lack libertarian free will *would* be dire and destructive. Illusion on free will is therefore morally necessary, he argues (this is the thesis of Illusionism). It is not that Smilansky thinks we need to induce illusory beliefs in people—in Brave New World fashion—but rather that such beliefs are already "in place" (for example, most people either don't question whether they have libertarian free will or, if they are compatibilists, assume they have all the freedom and responsibility they need); and these illusory beliefs play a largely positive social and moral role, he thinks. Recognizing that this thesis of Illusionism is likely to meet with considerable resistance (to put it mildly), Smilansky offers a series of arguments in the latter part of his essay to show the necessity of illusion by explaining the difficulties that would prevail without it. In this connection, he considers issues concerning guilt and innocence, value and worth, remorse and integrity, and related issues.

Richard Double defends yet another nonstandard view on free will which falls entirely outside the category of Successor Views we have been considering. Double calls his view *free will subjectivism*. The goal of his essay is to show how such a view and the free will problem in general are related to *metaethical* questions about the objectivity and subjectivity of value. In the process, he also considers how free will debates are influenced by differences in *metaphilosophy*—by differing views about the nature of philosophy (see Double, 1991, 1996a). Double thinks that people generally designate by "free will" the amount and kind of freedom that is required for moral responsibility. But ascriptions of moral responsibility, he also believes, do not attribute objective properties to persons; rather they express our subjective moral and evaluative attitudes toward people and their behavior. Consequently, ascribing free will to persons is also not a matter of ascribing some objective property they may or may not possess, but of expressing subjective attitudes toward them and signaling how they will be treated—for example, through reactive attitudes, verbal recrimination, praise and blame, retributive punishment or reward, and so on.

Double relates this free will subjectivism to metaethical views about value in the first part of his essay and argues that such a view best explains the persistent and seemingly irresolvable disagreements that have characterized debates about free will. In the second part of his essay, he compares and contrasts his view with those of other prominent contributors to contemporary free will debates, including several contributors to this volume: B. F. Skinner (1948, 1971), Daniel Dennett (1984), Bruce Waller (1990), Galen Strawson (1986), P. F. Strawson (1962), Thomas Nagel (1986), Ted Honderich (1993), and Peter Unger (1984).

Finally, Alfred Mele defends another nonstandard position on free will that does not fit into any of these categories. In his essay for this volume, Mele arrives at this position by a discussion of three topics that have been intertwined with contemporary debates about free will: *autonomy*, *self-control*, and *weakness of will*. Mele follows Aristotle in taking self-control (*enkrateia*) and weakness of will (*akrasia*) to be contraries—weakness of will being a deficiency of self-control. His essay begins with a survey of recent debates about the nature of self-control and weakness of will—debates to which Mele himself has been a significant contributor (Mele 1987, 1995).[39] This survey leads him to an account of what he takes to be an "ideally self-controlled agent."

Mele then poses the question whether an ideally self-controlled agent so conceived would necessarily also be *autonomous* (that is, self-governing or self-legislating) in a manner that many contemporary philosophers would associate with free will. He discusses this question in the context of the growing corpus of recent philosophical writing on the topic of autonomy (including works by Feinberg 1986; Dworkin 1988; Benn 1988; Lehrer 1997; Haworth 1986; Lindley 1986; Christman 1991; Berofsky 1995; among others). Mele argues that autonomy—and hence also free will—requires more than self-control, including ideal self-control, and he considers the additional conditions required, showing how contemporary discussions of autonomy are interwined with debates about free will (compare Mele 1995). Do these further conditions for genuine autonomy require that we choose between compatibilist and incompatibilist accounts of autonomy (and hence free will)? Mele thinks not, because one can give a "robust, satisfiable" set of adequate conditions for both compatibilist autonomy and incompatibilist autonomy. One can thus remain agnostic on the Compatibility Question regarding autonomy and free will without giving up the belief that there are autonomous human beings. He calls this view "agnostic autonomism."

9. NEUROSCIENCE AND FREE WILL

Contemporary debates about determinism in human behavior have by no means been confined to the implications of modern physics. As noted in section 2, while determinism was in retreat in the physical sciences during the twentieth century, developments in sciences other than physics—in biology, neuroscience, psychology, psychiatry, social and behavior sciences—have convinced many persons that more of their behavior is determined by causes unknown to them and beyond their control than previously believed. Of particular significance among these scientific developments is the growing knowledge of genetics and physiology, of biochemical influences on the brain, including the susceptibility of human moods and behavior to drugs and biochemical sources of psychiatric disorders. All this, coupled with advances in understanding human cognition and neural networks, has led to a growing interest during the past two decades in the implications of the cognitive sciences and neurosciences for traditional issues about free will. This interest is reflected in two essays of this volume, by Benjamin Libet and Henrik Walter.

Benjamin Libet, professor of psychology at the University of California, San Francisco, has been a pioneer in the neurophysiological study of *volition* and *willed action*. In 1958 he began a series of groundbreaking experimental studies in human subjects (in collaboration with neurosurgeon Bertram Feinstein) relating brain activities to the appearance or production of conscious experience and willed action that have been much discussed by philosophers as well as scientists. In his essay for this volume, Libet discusses the implications of these experiments for traditional debates about free will, with special reference to the role that *consciousness* plays in free voluntary action.

Libet and his collaborators found that voluntary acts are preceded by a specific electrical charge in the brain (the "readiness potential") which begins several hundred milliseconds before the human subjects become consciously aware of their intention to act. This suggests that the volitional process is initiated unconsciously. While some philosophers and scientists have been tempted to conclude from Libet's findings that willed actions are determined by unconscious forces and hence that our awareness of conscious control is illusory, Libet himself has a more nuanced view of the results, which he presents in this essay. He believes there is still a role for consciousness in controlling the outcome of willed actions, since consciousness can veto the act once underway. Thus, free will is not necessarily excluded, though novel neuroscientific findings place constraints on how free will could operate and how we are to make sense of it in terms of current research on the brain.

Henrik Walter is a neuropsychiatrist and philosopher who has also written perceptively about the implications for neuroscientific research for issues about free will. His contribution to this volume consists of excerpts from his *Neuro-philosophie des Willensfreiheit*, published in Germany in 1996 and in English as *Neurophilosophy of Free Will* in 2001. In the excerpts, Walter discusses the role of the frontal cortex (and particularly the prefrontal association cortex) of the brain in the planning of actions, the selection from various options, and the organizing of behavior over time. He discusses neurological evidence for and against the claim that this region of the brain is the seat of the "will" in human beings, which some scientists have suggested (for example, Crick 1994). Walter's view is that the functions of willing (deliberation, planning, and the like) are distributed throughout the brain, though the prefrontal areas play a pivotal role since they provide a link between the cortical regions involved in higher cognitive functioning and other parts of the brain that are the sources of emotions, feelings, and motor reactions.

Walter also discusses fascinating neurological evidence suggesting that interruption of circuits involving the frontal cortex and related parts of the brain due to lesions or other deficiencies gives rise to disturbances in the feeling of agency. These include, among other examples, "alien hand syndrome" (where the patient's hand seems to have a "will of its own"), obsessive-compulsive disorders, and the "self-disorder" of schizophrenics, where patients feel that certain experiences and mental actions no longer belong to themselves or are produced outside of themselves. In the book from which these excerpts are taken, Walter defends a compatibilist view of free will. He sides with those who believe that libertarian free will cannot be made intelligible. But he thinks that justice can be done to many libertarian intuitions, if we take a neurophilosophical approach to the notions of autonomy and free will.

For further references to research in the neurosciences relevant to current debates about free will, readers should consult the bibliographical references in the essays of Libet and Walter as well as two noteworthy recent anthologies, *The Volitional Brain: Towards a Neuroscience of Free Will* (1999), edited by Libet, Anthony Freeman, and Keith Sutherland, and *Neurobiology of Decision Making* (1956), edited by A. Damasio, H. Damasio, and Y. Cristen.

10. THEOLOGICAL DETERMINISM AND FATALISM

While determinist threats to free will from the natural and human sciences have taken center stage in modern free will debates, the scientific challenges have not been the only ones of importance to current debates. Other historically important determinist threats to free will of continuing interest are dealt with in two further essays of this volume—*theological* determinism (in Linda Zagzebski's "Recent Work on Divine Foreknowledge and Free Will") and *fatalism*, or *logical* determinism (in Mark Bernstein's "Fatalism").

The theological implications of the free will problem have been a central preoccupation of many religious traditions, Jewish, Christian, and Muslim, among others, as well as a central preoccupation of Western intellectual history in general, especially since St. Augustine's seminal work, *On the Free Choice of the Will*. In his classic poem *Paradise Lost*, John Milton describes the angels debating about predestination and free will—wondering how they could have freely chosen to serve or reject God, given that God had made them what they were and had complete foreknowledge of what they would do. Milton tells us that the angels debating this issue were in "Endless Mazes lost," not a comforting thought for us mortals.[40]

Many theologians through the centuries have believed that God's power, omniscience, and providence would be unacceptably compromised if one did not affirm that all events in the universe, including human choices and actions, were foreordained and foreknown by God. But many other theologians argued, with equal force, that if God did in fact foreordain or foreknow all human choices and actions, then no one could have chosen or acted differently, making it hard to see how humans could have ultimate control over their actions in a manner that would justify divine rewards or punishments. In such a case, the ultimate responsibility for good or bad deeds, and hence responsibility for evil, would devolve to God—an unacceptable consequence for traditional theists.

In the past thirty years, there has been renewed interest among philosophers and theologians in these issues of theological determinism or theological fatalism; and contemporary debates about them have surpassed even medieval discussions in labyrinthine complexity. Most of the recent literature on this topic has focused on the relation of divine foreknowledge and divine providence to human freedom and the implications of these topics to such things as divine omniscience and power, prophecy, petitionary prayer, the relation of time and eternity, and numerous other religious concerns. Linda Zagzebski's essay is a comprehensive and illuminating guide to the contemporary literature on theological determinism by a philosopher who has herself contributed significantly to current discussions of the religious implications of free will issues.

Mark Bernstein's essay deals with yet another historically important source of determinist thinking. The earliest of determinist or necessitarian doctrines that posed a threat to free will involved *fate*, conceived either as an impersonal cosmic force, or in the words of the ancient philosopher Empedocles, "an oracle of Necessity, an ancient decree of the gods, eternal, sealed fast with oaths."[41] Ancient concerns about fatalism were taken one step farther early in the development of Western philosophy when ancient Greek thinkers of the Megarian and (later) the

Stoic schools conceived the idea that laws of logic alone might imply that human wills are fated and not free. If every proposition must be true or false (as the logical law of bivalence requires), and if this is the case for propositions about the future as well, then it seems that every future event would be fated either to occur or not to occur. If the proposition "a sea fight will occur tomorrow" were true today (to use an example made famous by Aristotle), then a sea fight could not but occur tomorrow. If the proposition were false, then a sea fight could not occur. Either way, the outcome would be necessitated by the past, together with the requirement that every proposition be true or false. This esoteric doctrine of *logical fatalism* or *logical determinism* has exercised thinkers for centuries and continues to be discussed in contemporary philosophy. Recent discussions of it are the subject of Mark Bernstein's essay.

11. PLAN OF THE VOLUME

This is a sourcebook. Each essay can be read on its own and the references within each essay direct the reader to further writings in that topic area. While the essays can be read in any order, some naturally go together and are grouped into sections, guided by the three central questions discussed in this introduction.

The Determinist Question. The first four essays consider various determinist threats to free will and the contemporary debates they have generated, from theological and fatalist doctrines that posed the earliest threats (part I: essays of Zagzebski and Bernstein) to considerations of determinism and indeterminism in the modern physical sciences (part II: essays by Hodgson and Bishop).

The Compatibility Question. The Modal or Consequence Argument for incompatibilism, the most widely discussed recent argument for the incompatibility of free will and determinism, is discussed in part III (essays by Kapitan and van Inwagen). Part IV considers compatibilist responses to the Consequence Argument and surveys a variety of contemporary compatibilist perspectives on freedom and responsibility (essays by Berofsky, Haji, Russell and Taylor and Dennett). Part V considers issues about moral responsibility and alternative possibilities posed by so called "Frankfurt-style examples" and discusses doctrines of "semi-compatibilism" (essays by Fischer, Ekstrom, and Widerker).

The Intelligibility Question. The essays of Part VI consider various incompatibilist or libertarian perspectives on free will and agency and address the question of whether traditional doctrines of free will that require indeterminism can be made intelligible. They also consider issues about the nature and explanation of action, the relation of reasons to causes, control, rationality, and metaphysical issues about mind and body, agency and personhood (essays by O'Connor, Clarke, Ginet and Kane).

Part VII considers recent nonstandard views on free will, including Successor Views to hard determinism. The essays of this part also discuss a variety of further topics related to free will, including metaethical issues about the objectivity and subjectivity of value, morality and ultimate desert, criminal punishment, autonomy, self-control and weakness of will, illusion, and metaphilosophy (essays by Strawson, Honderich, Pereboom, Smilansky, Double, and Mele).

Finally, Part VIII takes a look at all three questions—determinism, compatibility, and intelligibility—from the perspective of the neurosciences, which have begun to influence debates about free will in the past decade and are likely to have further influence in the immediate future (essays by Libet and Walter).

NOTES

1. Matson 1987, vol. 1: 158.
2. I contemplated including essays on the history of free will debates in non-Western as well as in Western cultures but found this task excessive for one volume. Another volume with a historical or comparative focus would be a valuable project in its own right, but it also goes beyond the scope of this work. Some recent works on historical figures in the Western tradition do have relevance to contemporary debates about free will, and many are cited in various essays of this volume. Some prominent examples (by no means a complete list) include, on Aristotle, Hardie (1968), Kenny (1969b), Sorabji (1980), Irwin (1980), (1988), Fine (1981), Broadie (1991), Meyer (1993); on other ancient thinkers, Mi. White (1985); on Augustine, Babcock (1988), MacDonald (1999), Hunt (1996a, 1999); on Thomas Aquinas, Stump (1990), Kenny (1993), Loughran (1994), Gallagher (1994), Pink (1997), MacDonald (1998): on medieval thinkers in the period from Aquinas to Scotus, Kent, (1995); on Ockham, M. Adams (1987); on Molina and Molinism, Freddoso (1983, 1988): on Locke, Yaffe (forthcoming); on Leibniz, R. Adams (1982, 1994), Blumenfeld (1988a), Sleigh (1990, 1994), Paull (1992), Murray (1995); on Thomas Reid, Rowe (1991), O'Connor (1994); on Hume, Russell (1995); and on Kant, Wood (1984); Allison (1990).
3. Introductions to the problem of free will which appeared in the past twenty years include C. Williams (1980), Trusted (1984), Flew and Vesey (1987), Thornton (1990), Honderich (1993), Felt (1994), Dilman (1999), Ekstrom (2000). Anthologies of readings on free will in the same twenty-year period include Watson (1982), Fischer (1986), Fischer and Ravizza (1993), O'Connor (1995), Mongkin and Kellner (1998), Ekstrom (2001a), Kane (2001), and for theological issues about free will and divine foreknowledge, Fischer (1989).
4. There is an enormous literature on the "philosophy of action" (or "theory of action") in the period covered by this volume, much of it relevant to issues about free

will and frequently cited in this volume. Influential book-length treatments and anthologies include Goldman (1970), von Wright (1971), Castaneda (1975), Brand and Walton (1976), Tuomela (1977), Aune (1977), Thomson (1977), Thalberg (1977), Davis (1979), Peacocke (1979), Davidson (1980), Hornsby (1980), O'Shaughnessy (1980), Brand (1984), Bratman (1987), Donegan (1987), Frankfurt (1988), Dretske (1988), J. Bishop (1989), Velleman (1989), Wilson (1989), Ginet (1990), Lennon (1990), Schick (1991), Mele (1992), (1997b), Audi (1993), Bennett (1995), McCann (1998).

5. To be sure, this personal or practical standpoint involves other presuppositions as well, for example, that we as persons are enduring objects with a continuing identity in time. If one reduces persons to successions of causally related physical and mental events—denying they are enduring substances—as does Derek Parfit (1984) or much of the Buddhist tradition, then it may be argued that free agency and free will go by the board as well, in the normal way we understand them from a practical standpoint. (See Timothy O'Connor's essay in this volume for a discussion of some of these issues.) In an insightful article, Mark Siderits (1987) argues that the Buddhist reductionist conception of persons yields a novel compatibilist position on free will.

6. Woody (1998) provides an in-depth study of the historical and personal sources of free will issues.

7. For further discussion of definitions of determinism, see the essay by Robert C. Bishop in this volume. The sense of determinism I have in mind here that is relevant to free will is what Jordan Howard Sobel (1998) calls determinism by "ancient causes." Sobel identifies ninety varieties of determinism, but he indicates that the ones that pose problems for free will are those that imply that all events have ancient causes (i.e., they are events that, for any past time, have sufficient antecedent causes earlier than that time). Other influential works on determinism of the past thirty years include Berofsky (1971), Montague (1974), Earman (1986), and Honderich (1988).

8. Those persons, like Dennett, who believe that freedom in every sense worth having is compatible with determinism, usually note that notions of freedom in ordinary language, such as freedom from coercion, from addiction, physical restraint, or political oppression are all consistent with determinism. An interesting variation of this compatibilist strategy is exhaustively pursued by Christine Swanton (1992), who lists scores of ordinary statements in which we talk about agents' being free and tries to devise a "coherence theory" of freedom, as she calls it, satisfying all of them.

9. E.g., those of Hodgson, Bishop, Kapitan, Russell, Taylor and Dennett, Honderich, Pereboom, Strawson, Smilansky, Libet, and Walter.

10. Honderich (1988, 1993).

11. I have been speaking here of various kinds of scientific or *causal* forms of determinism (by antecedent causes and laws of nature), which have been the focus of most of the attention in modern debates about free will. There continue to be worries about other sources of determinism of theological and logical, rather than causal, varieties in contemporary philosophy. These are discussed in a later section of this introduction and in essays in this volume by Linda Zagzebski (on theological determinism) and Mark Bernstein (on logical fatalism), chs. 2 and 3, respectively.

12. While the vast majority of contemporary arguments for incompatibilism have taken this route, there are exceptions. A few contemporary philosophers have chosen to argue for incompatibilism by way of condition (b)—the requirement of ultimate origins or sources—rather than from condition (a) for alternative possibilities. For discussion of

this alternative approach to incompatibilism, see section 8 of this introduction and essays by Strawson, Kane, and Russell, chs. 19, 18, and 10, respectively. In addition, there has been a tradition of arguing that a notion of indeterminacy is logically built into the notion of a free choice (see Mackay 1967; Popper 1972), or that Godel's incompleteness theorem has implications concerning the compatibility of human reasoning and determinism (Lucas 1970; Penrose 1989). Finally, an unusual self-referential argument for incompatibilism is presented in Boyle, Grisez, and Tollefson (1976).

13. Pike's theological form of the argument is discussed in Linda Zagzebski's essay (ch. 2) in this volume which discusses the theological aspects of the free will problem. I return to Zagzebski's essay and the theological issues later in this introduction.

14. E.g., Widerker (1987), Talbott (1988), Hasker (1989), Ginet (1990), O'Connor (1993, 2000), Fischer (1994), Warfield (1996) and Finch and Warfield (1998). Differences of various formulations and their implications are discussed in Kapitan's essay, ch. 6.

15. For further discussion of classical compatibilism, see the essays of Russell and Berofsky.

16. The role and interpretation of such counterfactual conditionals have therefore been important topics of discussion in free will debates. See the essays in this volume by Kapitan, Berofsky and Taylor and Dennett, chs. 6, 8, and 11, respectively.

17. Shatz (1997) is an insightful discussion of character examples and one of the most thorough discussions of this topic in the recent literature. See also van Inwagen (1989) and Kane (1996: ch. 3).

18. Cf. Kane (1996: ch. 3) and Shatz (1997). Also see M. Zimmerman (1989, 1996) and Haji (1998) for this sort of argument applied to morally blameworthy actions.

19. Robert Audi is a compatibilist who, unlike most other recent compatibilists, has emphasized the importance of responsibility for *character* as well as for individual actions (see, e.g., Audi 1991b for a perceptive account of responsibility for character). Audi's view allows him to concede the points made in this paragraph about a need for the power to do otherwise, but he is also one of those compatibilists who offers a compatibilist account of the power to do otherwise (1974, 1993) rather than denying its importance for responsibility.

20. One can see why Frankfurt-style examples have also had an impact on debates about theological determinism. For discussion of their theological implications, see the essays in this volume of Zagzebski and Widerker, chs. 2 and 14, respectively.

21. Semi-compatibilists must of course show what moral responsibility does require if it does not require the power to do otherwise. Fischer (1994) and Fischer and Ravizza (1998) attempt to do this in terms of notions of (what they call) *guidance control* and *reasons-responsiveness*. There is a discussion of their use of these notions in the essay by Russell in this volume.

22. The possibility of separating moral responsibility and free will in this regard is a new wrinkle in free will debates. Once one conceives the possibility of disentangling them, one might consider going the other way—regarding moral responsibility as incompatible with determinism, while freedom is compatible with determinism. Such a view has in fact a modern defender in Bruce Waller (1990), whose view is discussed in Richard Double's essay for this volume ch. 23. The separation might also be considered in theological contexts. Some incompatibilists, such as Eleonore Stump (1990, 1996a) and Linda Zagzebski (1991, 2000), influenced by Frankfurt-style examples, have also en-

tertained the view that, while free will is incompatible with causal determinism, moral responsibility is not. See Zagzebski's essay in this volume, ch. 2.

23. Two forthcoming collections of essays involving critical discussion of Frankfurt's views are Buss and Overton, eds. (n.d.) and Betzler and Guckes, eds. (2000a, and b).

24. A number of other distinguished philosophers, such as Bernard Williams (1986) and Thomas Scanlon (1988), defend normative approaches to the free will problem of compatibilist kinds that differ in certain respects from those mentioned in these paragraphs. Williams is a compatibilist, but he does not think determinism can be reconciled with our "ethical conceptual scheme . . . as it stands" (1986: 12), which is strongly influenced by Judeao-Christian and Kantian ideas of moral duty and conscience. Incompatibilism does seem to fit this scheme, Williams thinks. But he also thinks that modern "morality" conceived in this Kantian or deontological manner is deficient and thinks we have to "recast our ethical conceptions" (p. 13) by returning to ancient Aristotelian models of the ethical life which he argues are compatible with determinism. One's views about free will therefore depend on how one conceives the ethical life. (See Richard Double's essay in this volume on this point, ch. 23). Likewise, Scanlon's compatibilist view (1988) is related to his influential contractualist ethical theory. What gives free choice and action their special value and moral significance, Scanlon holds, is the desire to regulate one's behavior by standards that other persons could not reasonably reject in an informed and unforced contractual agreement and the desire to justify one's behavior to others in accord with such standards. What the satisfaction of these desires requires by way of freedom and responsibility is the capacity for critically reflective, rational self-governance (which Scanlon spells out in a manner similar to hierachical theorists like Frankfurt). Yet another compatibilist who believes that the view one takes on the freedom/determinism issue depends upon one's conception of ethics and the good life is Richard Warner (1987).

25. Fischer and Ravizza are of course only (semi-)compatibilists about moral responsibility, not freedom. But their account of responsibility in terms of "reasons-responsiveness" employs strategies, examined by Russell, that throw light on compatibilist views in general.

26. O'Connor says that while Swinburne appears to be an AC theorist, some of his statements suggest otherwise.

27. Rowe (1987, 1991) develops his view as an interpretation and defense of the theory of Thomas Reid, the seventeenth-century philosopher who is regarded by many AC theorists as the modern originator and inspiration for their view.

28. Other noteworthy recent defenses of a dualist solution to the free will problem include Foster (1991) and Moreland and Rae (2000).

29. The expression "Valerian" refers to the French poet Paul Valery, who argued that freedom and creativity involved the "intelligent selection" from a number of undetermined alternatives. Dennett (1978) quotes Valery to this effect; and subsequently Mark Bernstein dubbed views of this sort "Valerian libertarianisms." See also Double (1988a) and Kane (1988).

30. Fischer (1995) contains another more recent suggestion for a view of this kind.

31. See the essays of Mele and Ekstrom in this volume, chs. 24 and 13, respectively, for defenses of their respective views against such charges.

32. Even where "causal" has the ordinary sense of "event-causal."

33. Honderich comes closest, but even the determinism he affirms is not the universal determinism of classical hard determinism, as I explain later.

34. Examples of philosophers who have focused more attention on this so-called "ultimacy" condition include Paul Gomberg (1975), Richard Sorabji (1980), Robert Nozick (1981), Robert Kane (1985, 1996a), Thomas Nagel (1986), Ted Honderich (1988), W. S. Anglin (1990), Martha Klein (1990), Derk Pereboom 2001, and Strawson himself (1986). Not all of these figures think this condition can be realized (indeed many of them argue against the possibility of its realization); but they all think it is a significant feature of free will in the traditional sense.

35. Paul Russell's essay (ch. 10) also considers issues of ultimacy, but from a compatibilist perspective.

36. The assertion in the title of his essay that "Compatibilism and Incompatibilism are False" might suggest that Honderich is denying thesis (1) of the kernel, but this is not so. What he is claiming is that compatibilists go wrong when they insist that compatibilist freedom is the *only* kind worth having and incompatibilists go wrong when they claim incompatibilist freedom is the *only* kind worth having. Both kinds support significant "life-hopes."

37. Another philosopher who has construed the free will issue in terms of conflicts between certain of our beliefs and our deeply held desires is Nicholas Nathan. In his work *Will and World* (1992), Nathan develops a general view about the nature of philosophical issues as involving conflicts between beliefs and desires, applying such a metaphilosophical theory not only to the question of free will, but to other philosophical problems as well.

38. This volume, p. 479.

39. There is a rich recent literature on the problem of weakness of will or *akrasia*, much of which Mele refers to in his chapter. Significant recent works include Audi (1979), Bigelow, Dodds, and Pargetter (1990), Charlton (1988), Dunn (1987), Davidson (1970), Gosling (1990), Hurley (1993), Jackson (1984), Kenny (1975), Mortimore (1971), Pears (1985), Pugmire (1994), K. Robinson (1991), A. Rorty (1980a), Walker (1989), and Watson (1977).

40. These theological questions about free will also played a pivotal role in the Arab retrieval of ancient philosophical texts, so important in the development of late medieval Western culture. When Muslim scholars (about a century after the death of Mohammed) asked the caliphs if they could look at the ancient scrolls of the Greek philosophers hidden away in the libraries of the Middle East, one of their primary motives was to see if the pagan philosophers would provide insight into the vexing question of predestination and free will, which the Koran did not resolve.

41. Wilbur (1979: 163).

PART I

THEOLOGY AND FATALISM

CHAPTER 2

RECENT WORK ON DIVINE FOREKNOWLEDGE AND FREE WILL

LINDA TRINKAUS ZAGZEBSKI

Two important doctrines of traditional monotheistic theology threaten to lead to fatalism. One is the doctrine of infallible divine foreknowledge; the other is the doctrine of divine providence. In the first doctrine the source of the fatalist danger is God's intellect; in the second it is God's will. Foreknowledge threatens fatalism because if God knows the entire future in a way that cannot be mistaken, then it looks as if nothing can happen differently than it does. If so, and if human freedom requires the ability to do otherwise, it appears that we are not free. Divine providence threatens fatalism because if everything occurs under the control of the divine will, then apparently everything happens the way God determines it and, again, it looks as if we lack the power to act differently and so we are not free.

Both fatalism due to foreknowledge and fatalism due to providence have precursors in Stoic philosophy; in fact, a central aspect of Stoic ethics was its teaching that human happiness resides in willing conformity to a preordained divine plan. More important for Christian philosophy, the doctrines of foreknowledge and providence have roots in Scripture, albeit in an ambiguous form, as is the case with most metaphysical doctrines (e.g., Psalm 33:13–15, Matthew 6:26–34). There may even be a hint of fatalism in the Bible—God determines the outcome of the casting of lots (Proverbs 16:33)—but for the most part the Bible is not fatalistic.

Contemporary philosophers of religion are virtually unanimous in treating fatalism as unacceptable, so if either foreknowledge or providence leads to fatalism, it must be rejected or at least modified.[1]

Often foreknowledge and providence have been linked. Some philosophers have thought that foreknowledge is useful, perhaps even required, for providential purposes. Recently this idea has come under attack, as we will see in section 6. A more common traditional link was the reverse: God knows the future through his knowledge of his own creative will (Aquinas, *Summa Theological* 1.14.8).[2] The priority of the divine will over the divine intellect was the source of the Calvinist doctrine of predestination: God eternally decrees eternal life for some, eternal damnation for others (*Institutes*, bk. 3, ch. 21, sec. 5). However, it is difficult to find a contemporary philosopher who defends this doctrine in its strong form, and predestination is not an issue that has been widely debated in the recent literature (see Flint 1997b: 576). In contrast, the debate over foreknowledge and free will is as strong as ever. But as we will see, there has been a change in the popularity of some of the solutions.

1. CONTEMPORARY FORM OF THE DILEMMA AND SUMMARY OF SOLUTIONS

During the last few decades, the statement of the foreknowledge dilemma has been refined and the key premises and definitions clarified. The problem is usually posed by defining infallible belief and then considering three sequential moments of time: (1) some random moment in the past; (2) the present; and (3) some arbitrary moment in the future in which you will perform an act that is a good candidate for a free act if anything is. For simplicity let us use yesterday, today, and tomorrow for these three moments of time,[3] and let us suppose that tomorrow you will get out of bed exactly seven minutes after you wake up. Call the proposition that you will perform this act on the day in question "B." Let us also define "infallible belief" as "belief that cannot be mistaken." Hence, if God believes B infallibly, then God cannot be mistaken in believing B. A typical contemporary way of stating the argument that if God knows B infallibly then you do not get out of bed freely is the following:

1. Yesterday God infallibly believed B. (Supposition of infallible foreknowledge)

2. It is now necessary that yesterday God believed B. (Principle of Necessity of the Past)

3. Necessarily, if yesterday God believed B, then B. (Definition of infallibility)

4. So it is now necessary that B. (2–3, Transfer of Necessity Principle)

5. If it is now necessary that B, then you cannot do otherwise than get out of bed tomorrow exactly seven minutes after you wake up. (Definition of *necessary*)

6. Therefore, you cannot do otherwise than get out of bed tomorrow exactly seven minutes after you wake up. (4–5, modus ponens)

7. If you cannot do otherwise when you do an act, you do not do it freely. (Principle of Alternate Possibilities)

8. Therefore, when you get out of bed tomorrow, you will not do it freely. (6–7, modus ponens)

By parity of reasoning you can argue that no act any human person performs is done freely.

There is a consensus that this argument or something close to it is a very strong threat to the compatibility of infallible foreknowledge and human free will. Attention has therefore focused on the key premises, (1), (2), and (7), and the only arguable inference, the one from (2) and (3) to (4). Let me begin, however, by commenting on the claim that God has beliefs infallibly (premises [1] and [3]). Notice that omniscience *simpliciter* is too weak to generate the dilemma, but essential omnscience is stronger than is required. Omniscience is usually defined as simply the property of knowing the truth value of all propositions. A being S is omniscient if and only if for every proposition *p*, S knows whether *p* is true or false. But this definition of omniscience commits us to nothing about whether it is *possible* for an omniscient being to be mistaken. An omniscient being *is* not mistaken in any of his beliefs, and he *has* a belief corresponding to every proposition, but omniscience is not the same as essential omniscience; a being could be omniscient even though he might have made a mistake. Such a being is omniscient, although he might not have been. Given that to be infallible is to believe in such a way that the believer cannot make a mistake, omniscience does not entail infallibility. Premises (1) and (3) could be false even though God is omniscient and believes B.

Suppose now that God is *essentially* omniscient. In that case God would not only be omniscient as things actually are, but he could not be anything but omniscient. In the common parlance of possible worlds, to say that God is essentially omniscient is to say that God is omniscient in every possible world. Not only is God not mistaken in any of his beliefs, he *cannot* be mistaken. Necessarily, God believes B if and only if B. Hence, if God is essentially omniscient and believes B, then God believes B infallibly and (1) and (3) are true. Essential omniscience entails infallibility.

Notice, however, that believing infallibly does not require essential omniscience. The latter is more than we need for the truth of (1) and (3), because essential omniscience not only involves the impossibility of making a mistake in a belief; it also includes having a belief corresponding to every proposition. But this argument generates a problem for any belief God has that is infallible, regardless of the scope of his other beliefs. This means that the fatalist argument does not rely on omniscience or essential omniscience, so those who wish to avoid the fatalist conclusion by limiting God's foreknowledge must not only deny divine omniscience on the above definition but must deny that God knows *any* proposition about future free human acts in an infallible way.

We are now ready to classify the traditional and contemporary responses to this argument. I will begin with two that are not in fashion. One is to deny that contingent propositions about the future have a truth value. This apparently was Aristotle's position in the famous Sea Battle Argument of *De Interpretatione* 9. In the recent literature, this view has been defended by J. R. Lucas (1989), Richard Purtill (1988), and Joseph Runzo (1981), but it has received little attention in the past decade. The reason for the lack of interest in this way out of the problem no doubt comes from logic rather than theology. The idea that propositions, or the bearers of truth value, are tenseless and have their truth value immutably has a strong hold on the contemporary philosophical mind. Giving up the view that future contingents have truth value would require a serious alteration in the general theory of propositions. But consider logical fatalism, the view that future truth makes the future necessary. It is usually thought to be easy to refute any argument for logical fatalism. But if any such argument is valid, we seem to be forced to give up the premise that there are true propositions about the contingent future. Lately the argument that theological fatalism is equivalent to logical fatalism has resurfaced (Warfield 1997; Finch and Warfield 1999). If someone is convinced of that equivalence, he or she could either conclude with Warfield that theological fatalism is as harmless as logical fatalism, or that logical fatalism is as threatening as theological fatalism. If the latter move attracts any adherents, there might be a resurgence of interest in the position that future contingents have no truth value. We will look at these recent essays on the connection between logical and theological fatalism in section 7.

A second response unpopular in the current literature is that human beings do not have libertarian free will; that is, that the sense in which humans are free is compatible with determinism. Virtually all discussants of the foreknowledge issue agree that the problem is not solved unless the solution preserves free will in a sense that is incompatible with determinism. I know of no prominent writer on the issue since Anthony Kenny (1967a), who resolves the problem by claiming that even though God's foreknowledge determines our future acts, we are still free in a good enough sense of *free*. But I suspect that the absence of this solution from the recent foreknowledge literature is misleading, because determinists probably refrain from participating in that discussion only because their solution is so simple—they can give it in one sentence. One would expect them to devote their attention to writing about determinism rather than foreknowledge. It is possible, then, perhaps even likely, that this position is more common then it appears from the discussions of foreknowledge.

Let us return to the key premises in the argument for theological fatalism in order to classify the other solutions to the problem. One way is to deny premise (1). That premise is straightforwardly denied by those who deny that God knows the future infallibly even though future contingents have a truth value. Such a position is currently popular and will be discussed in section 6. But premise (1) can be rejected for reasons that do not limit God's knowing power. If God either does not have beliefs or does not exist in time, then God did not literally believe anything yesterday. The former move appears in an essay by William Alston (1986) but has not been widely discussed. I suspect that the lack of literature on this solution is not due to a lack of intellectual worth as much as to the problem of figuring out where to go with it. I do consider reasonable the notion that God's way of knowing is sufficiently superior to our own that attributing beliefs to him is problematic. Nonetheless, we need to say something about God's mental states, including those that are analogous to our beliefs. The foreknowledge dilemma arises from a minimal assumption about those states—that they exist at moments of time. Those who question whether God has beliefs therefore tend to use this idea to bolster their doubts that God's past epistemic states have the necessity of the past (the Ockhamist solution). This is, in fact, what Alston does with this suggestion that God does not have beliefs. A related approach has been attempted by David Hunt (1995a, 1995b), who has worked out a dispositional account of God's knowledge to circumvent the problem.

The latter move, that premise (1) is false because God does not exist in time, has a long history stemming from Boethius and Aquinas and remains one of the most respected solutions to the dilemma of theological fatalism. This solution received a boost in recent philosophy of religion from Stump and Kretzmann (1981) and Brian Leftow (1991a and b), but the coherence of the doctrine of time-lessness and its desirability for Christian theology have been under sustained attack for some time. The popularity of this solution in published work has declined in recent years, although I see no reason to think it will not regain favor in the future. I will address the literature on this Boethian solution in section 2.

Another historically important way out of the problem is to deny premise (2); that is, to deny that God's past beliefs have the necessity of the past. The idea that the past has a kind of necessity or fixity that the future lacks is expressed in the aphorism, "There is no use crying over spilt milk." The idea is simple enough, but it is notoriously difficult to figure out how to identify past events that have this kind of necessity. The proposal that God's past beliefs are not really, or strictly, past comes from William of Ockham and was brought into the contemporary literature by Marilyn Adams (1967). This solution enjoyed considerable popularity and frequent debate throughout the seventies and eighties, but discussion about it has declined in the past decade. The literature on this solution will be discussed in section 3.

Another possibility is to deny the principle warranting the inference to (4), the principle that the necessity of the past is preserved under entailment: If the proposition that God believed B yesterday now has the necessity of the past and that proposition entails B, then B now has the necessity of the past. There have been recent attempts to deny this principle (e.g., Zagzebski 1991: 162–68); and Alfred Freddoso (1988: 57–58) says that Molina implies a rejection of the principle as well. Michael Tooley (2000) has argued against my use of this move. John Martin Fischer critically discusses the attempt to reject a different but related principle in "Scotism" (1985a). But we should consider any move of this kind only after rejecting virtually all others.

The last disputable premise is premise (7), the Principle of Alternate Possibilities (PAP): If when you do an act you cannot do otherwise, you do not do the act freely. Harry Frankfurt (1969) presented a famous set of counterexamples to this principle, generating a considerable literature in which determinists argue that Frankfurt-style cases succeed in falsifying PAP and libertarians argue that they fail. (On this literature, see the chapters of this volume by Fischer, Ekstrom, and Widerker [12, 13 and 14]). Recently, however, a few defenders of Frankfurt cases have been libertarians who argue that even though Frankfurt has succeeded in showing the falsity of PAP, determinism is false as well. Hence, the argument for theological fatalism falters at the last step (Zagzebski 1991; ch. 6; Hunt 1999). Hunt argues that a solution of this kind can be found in Augustine. This is the newest solution in the literature and, if Hunt is right, it also has important historical precedent. I will discuss the literature on this solution in section 5.

This brings us to the Molinist solution, an important way out of the problem, and one that has generated considerable debate in the past decade. Luis de Molina and others developed the theory of middle knowledge, according to which God knows what any possible free creature would freely choose in any possible circumstance. By knowing the circumstances in which future creatures will be placed, God knows what they will freely choose. Hence, God has foreknowledge because he has middle knowledge. Freddoso's translation of and introduction to Molina's *On Divine Foreknowledge* (Freddoso 1988) brought this solution into the contemporary debate. Curiously, it is not at all clear which step of the argument for theological fatalism the middle knowledge solution rejects. A discussion of this literature will be the topic of section 4.

I know of one more way out of the dilemma. This is the solution of Leibniz, discussed in articles by Robert Sleigh (1994) and Michael J. Murray (1995). According to Murray, Leibniz developed a unique position according to which a sufficient reason for a free act is found in dispositions of intellect and will. These dispositions neither metaphysically nor physically necessitate choice but necessitate them only "morally," a kind of necessitation compatible with free will. God can foreknow human choices by knowing these dispositions. This solution is another one that rejects premise (7).

2. The Boethian Solution

A timeless being lacks temporal location and has no temporal properties. Hence, a timeless being has no beliefs at moments of time. In the sixth century Boethius gave a classic definition of eternity as "the complete, simultaneous, and perfect possession of illimitable life" (*The Consolation of Philosophy*, book V, prose 6). It may not be immediately obvious that this definition has anything to do with time, but it is clear that Boethius intended his definition to have the consequence that an eternal being is timeless, indeed, more than timeless, and God is eternal. All things are present to God, not in the sense of being temporally simultaneous, but in the sense of being "before the mind." This includes everything that is future to us. Since the foreknowledge dilemma arises only for an infallible being within the flow of time, it does not apply to an eternal God. There is no problem in attributing comprehensive infallible knowledge to God, including knowledge of the precise moment you will pull yourself out of bed tomorrow.

Aquinas took up the Boethian solution, using some of the same metaphors, for example, the circle analogy. Both Boethius and Aquinas compared the way an eternal God is present to each and every moment of time to the way in which the center of a circle is present to each and every point on the circumference. The points on the circle are spatially ordered in such a way that no point coincides with any other, yet each point is equidistant from and directly opposite the center of the circle. Likewise, although the moments of time are ordered in such a way that they are truly distinct from one another, each is present to eternity.[4]

The metaphysics of eternity is certainly dramatic and while we are no doubt right to be skeptical of analogies, the fact that we have no experience of a timeless realm is not in itself any reason to think there is no such realm; and if the timeless realm exists, the need for metaphors is unsurprising. An important attempt to bring the Boethian concept of eternity into the contemporary idiom was Stump and Kretzmann's article, "Eternity" (1981). Stump and Kretzmann took themselves to be explicating Boethius but introduced the idea of atemporal duration as an aspect of God's eternity. This idea generated much controversy, but as far as I can see, it is not important for the use of the idea of God's timelessness as a way out of the foreknowledge dilemma. What is important for that dilemma is Stump and Kretzmann's idea of E-T simultaneity, which they use to explain the relation between God's timeless knowing state and contingent temporal events that are the objects of knowledge. E-T simultaneity is intended to be a species of simultaneity in which every moment of time is simultaneous with eternity but no moment of time is simultaneous with any other—the point of the circle analogy of Boethius and Aquinas. An important aspect of this kind of simultaneity is that it is defined relative to an observer, either in the temporal sphere or in eternity. Events that are simultaneous relative to a timeless observer are not simultaneous relative to a temporal observer. Criticisms of Stump and Kretzmann's view on eternity appear in several places, including Hasker (1989a), Wierenga (1989), Widerker (1991b), and Padgett (1992). Stump and Kretzmann argue that the eternity doctrine provides an adequate solution to the foreknowledge dilemma in (1991) and defend their view of eternity in (1992).

Objections to the timelessness solution to the foreknowledge dilemma usually focus on objections to the doctrine of timelessness itself, either in the form presented by Stump and Kretzmann or in some other. This literature is important for natural theology, but from the point of view of the problem of theological fatalism, the important issue is whether God's timelessness would get us out of the dilemma anyway. One reason has been proposed in recent years for thinking that it would not (Zagzebski 1991: ch. 2). It seems to me that a dilemma structurally parallel to the argument for theological fatalism can be posited for timeless knowledge as well as for foreknowledge. Such an argument would mirror the argument given at the beginning of section 1, but in place of premise (2), which is about the necessity of the past, we would have a premise about the necessity of eternity: (2') It is now necessary that God timelessly believes G. Surely the timeless realm is as ontologically determinate and fixed as the past. Perhaps it is inappropriate to say that timeless events are *now* necessary. Even so, we have no more reason to think that we can do anything about God's timeless knowledge than about God's past knowledge. If there is no use crying over spilt milk, there is no use crying over timelessly spilling milk either. If we cannot do anything about God's timeless knowing state, then it also looks as if we cannot do anything about what those states entail. There may, of course, be solutions to the timeless knowledge dilemma as well as to the foreknowledge dilemma. My point is that timelessness alone does not solve the problem. David Hunt (1999: 11) has recently made the same observation.

Another argument that timelessness does not escape the problem has been given by Robert Brown (1991), who argues that timeless omniscience is compatible with human free will only if God lacks immutability and aseity. Brown maintains that the real threat to human freedom comes from the latter attributes, not from God's knowing our future.

Another kind of objection to Boethianism has received attention in recent years. It is not actually an objection to the effectiveness of this approach as a way out of the foreknowledge dilemma but a point about the motive for attributing either foreknowledge or timeless knowledge to God at all. This is the argument of Basinger (1986) and Hasker (1989a) that neither simple foreknowledge (without middle knowledge) nor timeless knowledge is any help to God's providence. As mentioned at the beginning of this chapter, some people think the theological motive for attributing to God knowledge of what is for us the contingent future is just that God can then use this knowledge in arranging a providential outcome for human history. If timeless knowledge is useless for this purpose, then some philosophers claim that we lose the motive for attributing such knowledge to God. This issue will be addressed in section 6.

3. THE OCKHAMIST SOLUTION

Nelson Pike's important article "Divine Omniscience and Voluntary Action" (1965) set the agenda for much of the debate in the ensuing twenty-five years and is largely responsible for the popularity of Ockhamism during that period. Pike posed the problem as follows:

> If God existed at T1 and if God believed at T1 that Jones would do x at T2, then if it was within Jones' power at T2 to refrain from doing x, then (1) it was within Jones' power at T2 to do something that would have brought it about that God held a false belief at T1, or (2) it was within Jones' power at T2 to do something which would have brought it about that God did not hold the belief He held at T1, or (3) it was within Jones' power at T2 to do something that would have brought it about that any person who believed at T1 that Jones would do S at T2 (one of whom was, by hypothesis, God) held a false belief and thus was not God—that God (who by hypothesis existed at T1) did not exist at T1. (p. 34)

In this presentation of the dilemma, there are only three possible ways out. The first appears to be incompatible with God's infallibility. The second appears to be incompatible with the necessity of the past. The third appears to be impossible *simpliciter*. When the problem is posed in this way, the most promising (or least unpromising) way out is the second. But (2) is not worded correctly as it stands. What it should say instead is:

(2') It was within Jones' power at T2 to do something such that if he did it, God would not have held the belief he in fact held at T1.

Unlike (2), (2') does not commit us to backward causation. It does commit us to backward counterfactual dependency, which is less implausible than backward causation. Nonetheless, (2') is incompatible with one way of understanding the asymmetry between past and future. David Lewis (1979) claims that it is constitutive of temporal asymmetry that whereas we now have it in our power to act so that the future would be different from what it will be, we do not have it in our power to act so that the past would have been different from what it was. Therefore, (2') runs up against a deep intuition about time.

In a well-known response to Pike, Marilyn Adams (1967) argued that Pike's three alternatives are all unacceptable only if God's past beliefs are really or strictly in the past. But following Ockham, she argued that both God's existence and God's past beliefs are not strictly past. They are "soft" facts about the past. A strict, or "hard," fact about the past, she proposed, is one that is not at least in part about a time in the future. This idea can generate a solution to the foreknowledge dilemma provided that the fixity or necessity of the past applies only to the "hard" past and propositions stating God's past beliefs are not hard facts.

Adams's article led to a series of articles on the hard fact/soft fact distinction, some attempting to define "hard fact" and "accidental necessity" (the necessity of the past) in a way that preserves the Ockhamist solution, some arguing that the solution was doomed. Probably the best known Ockhamist proposal after Adams was Alvin Plantinga's article, "On Ockham's Way Out" (1986). Plantinga defined the accidentally necessary in terms of lack of counterfactual power, and argued that counterfactual power over God's past beliefs is coherent. God's past beliefs are not accidentally necessary. Ockhamism was also defended by Freddoso (1983), Hoffman and Rosenkrantz (1984), Jonathan Kvanvig (1986), Zemach and Widerker (1987), Reichenbach (1988), Wierenga (1989, 1991), Craig (1990), and Talbott (1993). Critical discussions of Ockhamism appeared for some time—for example, Fischer (1983b and 1985b), Hasker (1985, 1989a), Widerker (1990), and Pike (1993). Discussion on both sides of the issue has abated in the last several years, but Dale Brant (1997) has recently given an interesting argument against Plantinga. Brant argues that Plantinga's defense of Okhamism is logically defective because he implicitly makes the following assumptions: (1) Equivalent propositions are either both about a given time or neither is; (2) If a proposition is about a given time, so is its negation; (3) If two propositions are about a given time, so is their conjunction. Surprisingly, Brant argues, although these assumptions are plausible, they are inconsistent.

In my opinion a serious problem with Ockhamist solutions is that even if they can produce an account of temporal asymmetry that has the consequence that God's past beliefs do not have the necessity of the past, it is unlikely that this can be done in a way that is independently plausible. That is true because a divine past belief seems to be as good a candidate for something that is strictly past as anything we can think of—say, an explosion that occurred last week. (I argue this in Zagzebski 1991: ch. 3). Therefore, if the Ockhamist solution is to be convincing, it should be supplemented with some account of God's belief states that makes it intuitively plausible to think of a temporal deity as independent of the modalities of time aside from our interest in resolving the foreknowledge problem. Otherwise, the solution is in danger of being ad hoc. I attempted to import some aspects of the Thomistic view of how God knows into Ockhamism to bolster this solution (ibid.), to which Tooley (2000) has responded. In any case, the Ockhamist solution has been discussed less frequently in recent years.

A more straightforward way of interpreting Pike's second alternative is to claim that backward agent causation is possible and that our free acts bring about or cause God's past beliefs. Many people think backward causation makes no sense, but since the direction of causation from earlier to later is only one of the arrows of time, it is not obviously impossible (see Stephen Hawking 1988: ch 9). In the philosophical literature, Michael Dummett gave a famous defense of the possibility of backward agent causation (1964), and the possibility has been discussed by Freddoso (1982), Mavrodes (1984), Forrest (1985), Talbott (1986), and Reichenbach (1987), but I know of no defenses of it in the past decade. Alan Padgett (n.d.) has attempted to demonstrate its impossibility, and it seems likely that this is one of the solutions that awaits further work on the philosophy of time.

4. THE MOLINIST SOLUTION

The middle knowledge solution has received a lot of attention in the past decade. One of its advantages is that it is an account of *how* God knows the contingent future, not just an argument that infallible foreknowledge of free acts is not impossible. Another advantage is that a strong view of divine providence is included in the same theory as an account of foreknowledge. The theory is highly controversial, but it is undeniably ingenious and powerful. As mentioned earlier, the theory was brought into the contemporary literature by Freddoso's translation of Molina (1988), and it received a recent boost from its defense by Thomas Flint (1998). Much earlier, Alvin Plantinga had independently thought of the idea as a way out of the problem of evil (1973, 1977). Middle knowledge is said to be "middle" because it stands between God's knowledge of necessary truths and his knowledge of his own will. The objects of middle knowledge are counterfactuals of free-dom: *If person P were in circumstances C, P would freely do X*. Middle knowledge requires that there are true counterfactuals of this form corresponding to every pos-sible free creature and every circumstance possible for that creature. These propo-sitions are contingent, but they are prior to God's creative will. In fact, God uses them in deciding what to create. By combining his knowledge of what he wills to create with his middle knowledge, God knows the entire actual future.

Recently, William Hasker (1989a) and Robert Adams (1991) have argued against the possibility of middle knowledge. Hasker and Adams argue that it fol-lows from Molinism that we do not bring about the truth of any counterfactual of freedom about us. Hasker uses as a premise in his argument a controversial Power Entailment Principle (PEP):

> PEP: If it is in my power to bring it about that P, and "P" entails "Q" and "Q" is false, then it is in my power to bring it about that Q. (p. 49)

Let us apply PEP to the example used in our fatalist argument. Suppose that I get up tomorrow seven minutes after I wake up and I do it freely. That means that I have the power to get up at a different time, say, four minutes after I wake up. But a proposition to the effect that I get up four minutes after I wake up entails the following counterfactual of freedom: If the circumstances tomorrow morning when I wake up obtained, I would freely get up four minutes after I wake up. Call this counterfactual C. C is false and by PEP it is in my power to bring it about that C. But how can I have the power to bring it about that C when, by hypothesis, the falsehood of C is prior to God's creative will?

In Adams's version of the argument, Molinism is committed to the position that the truth of all counterfactuals of freedom is explanatorily prior to God's decision to create us. But, Adams argues, the truth of a counterfactual to the effect that I do A in C is strictly inconsistent with my refraining from A in C, and so my refraining from A in C is precluded by something prior in the order of explanation to my action in C. But that is inconsistent with my acting freely in C. The key premise in Adams' argument is the following:

> AP   If I freely do A in C, no truth that is strictly inconsistent with my refraining from A in C is explanatorily prior to my choosing and act-ing as I do in C.

Craig critiqued the Adams argument (1994), Hasker defended a version of it (1995) and responded to Craig (1997), Craig replied to Hasker (1998), and Hasker gave a rejoinder to Craig (2000). Flint also attempted to rebut Adams (1998: ch. 7). Arguments against PEP are given in my book (1991) and by Craig (1998). Hasker replies to my arguments (1993) and I give a rejoinder (1993). Flint tries to show that the notion of bringing about can be understood in so many different ways that arguments employing power entailment principles are often guilty of equivocation (1991, 1998, ch. 6). See also Gaskin (1993) for a discussion of other problems with the logic of middle knowledge. A good recent defense of middle knowledge is given by Eef Dekker (2000).

A different kind of objection to Molinism has been given by Jerry Walls (1990). In "Is Molinism as Bad as Calvinism?" Walls argues that since Molina maintained that God chooses to put people in situations in which he knows they will choose damnation, Molinism is as morally abhorrent as the Calvinist doctrine of predestination. According to Molina God does not give an equal opportunity to all to be saved. For example, particular persons would have been saved had they lived longer or died sooner. This is a form of the problem I have elsewhere called "religious luck" (1994). It seems to me, however, that it is compatible with middle knowledge that God does give an equal opportunity to all to be saved (regardless of what Molina thought himself). Perhaps none of the damned would have been saved had they died at a different time. In any case, this is a problem for more theories than Molinism.

Let us assume, however, that God has middle knowledge and knows the contingent future in the way described by Molina. How, exactly, does that solve the dilemma of section 1? Freddoso says in the introduction to his translation of Molina (1988:57–58) that Molina rejects the principle that accidental necessity is closed under entailment. But someone could reject that principle without adopting the theory of middle knowledge and someone could accept middle knowledge without rejecting the transfer principle. The Molinist solution, then, seems to include more than middle knowledge.

One of the interesting twists in the debate about middle knowledge is the claim by Basinger (1986), Hasker (1989a) and some others that simple foreknowledge is useless for providence and hence, either God has middle knowledge or there is no point in affirming foreknowledge. Since they think middle knowledge has been refuted, they argue that the most viable position is to give up the traditional view that God has infallible foreknowledge. This view will be addressed in section 7.

5. THE FRANKFURTIAN/AUGUSTINIAN SOLUTION

A large literature on the Principle of Alternate Possibilities (PAP) was sparked by Harry Frankfurt's famous counterexamples (1969)(see chapters 12, 13, and 14 of this volume). Frankfurt intended to drive a wedge between responsibility and alternate possibilities, and he thought he could thereby drive another wedge between responsibility and libertarian freedom. I have argued that PAP is false even if libertarianism is true and hence, premise (7) of the argument of section 1 is false (1991, ch. 6). Hunt has also defended this position (1999, 2000) and claims that it can be found in Augustine (1996b, 1999). Apart from the application to foreknowledge, support for the Frankfurtian rejection of PAP from an incompatibilist perspective can be found in Stump (1990, 1996a), Zagzebski (2000), and Pereboom (2000).

A typical Frankfurt-style case follows:

> Black, an evil neurosurgeon, wishes to see White dead but is unwilling to do the deed himself. Knowing that Mary Jones also despises White and will have a single good opportunity to kill him, Black inserts a mechanism into Jones's brain that enables Black to monitor and to control Jones's neurological activity. If the activity in Jones's brain suggests that she is on the verge of deciding not to kill White when the opportunity arises, Black's mechanism will intervene and cause Jones to decide to commit the murder. On the other hand, if Jones decides to murder White on her own, the mechanism will not intervene. It will merely monitor but will not affect her neurological function. Now suppose that when the occasion arises, Jones decides to kill White without any "help" from Black's mechanism. In the judgment of Frankfurt and most others, Jones is morally responsible for her act. Nonetheless, it appears that she is unable to do otherwise since if she had attempted to do so, she would have been thwarted by Black's device.[5]

Two sorts of objections to the use of Frankfurt cases to falsify PAP have been given in the recent literature. One is the argument that the description of cases like this presupposes determinism. The Frankfurt machine cannot operate unless it is possible to be a perfect predictor in a nondeterministic universe. But since that is impossible, a Frankfurt machine is impossible. Robert Kane (1985, 1996a) and David Widerker (1995a, and b) have independently given this objection. One kind of response to it has been given by Mele and Robb (1998), and another by Stump (1996a). Other replies appear in Hunt (1999), Pereboom (2000), and Zagzebski (2000). In brief, the point of the latter class of replies is to describe a case in which the Frankfurt-style manipulator intervenes whenever a causally necessary but insufficient condition for the act the machine does not want occurs. Such a scenario prevents the agent from doing otherwise without presupposing determinism. (See essays by Fischer, Ekstrom, and Widerker in this volume for further discussion of this literature [chapters 12, 13, and 14]).

A second type of objection to the use of Frankfurt cases to falsify PAP is the argument that even if F cases are successful against some forms of PAP, some other form of PAP survives. A number of writers have given arguments of this type, and I will only mention a few. An early version of this response to Frankfurt appears in Naylor (1984), and another in Wierenga (1989: 85). More recent versions appear in McKenna (1997) and Otsuka (1998). Fischer defends Frankfurt in several places, e.g., Fischer (1994). For very recent discussion of these debates see Pereboom (2000) Zagzebski (2000) and chapters 12, 13, and 14 herein.

I have argued that PAP might be false even if we have libertarian freedom, but there is an important disanalogy between the Frankfurt cases and infallible foreknowledge that arguably permits the defender of the compatibility of foreknowledge and free will to preserve PAP. The point of Frankfurt cases is to describe a situation in which the agent deliberates and chooses in the usual way, but his or her will is thwarted in close possible worlds—worlds in which the machine operates. But in the foreknowledge case, the agent's will is not thwarted by God in any world, at least not due to his foreknowledge. If God's knowledge is infallible, the closest Frankfurt analogy would be a case in which the machine is set to make the agent do whatever she decides to do anyway. In worlds in which she chooses C, the machine is set to make her choose C if she does not do so on her own, and in worlds in which she chooses not C, the machine is set to make her choose not C if she does not do so on her own. It is, of course, hard to see how such a case can be coherently described, but the point is that that is the way the case would have to be for it to be parallel to divine foreknowledge. And what is important about such a case is that it is most reasonably described as one in which the agent *can* do otherwise. He does otherwise in counterfactual circumstances in the same way he would in the absence of a God with foreknowledge. If the point of Frankfurt cases, as Frankfurt says himself, is that the machine makes no difference to what the agent does, surely the point is even stronger in the case of a foreknowing deity. Not only does foreknowledge make no difference to what the agent actually does, it does not even make any difference to what she might have done instead. (I argue this point in Zagzebski 1991: ch. 6, sec. 2.2). Nonetheless, like the Molinist solution, it is not clear what premise of the argument for fatalism should be rejected if we take this approach.

6. THE "OPEN GOD" VIEW

Recently a group of philosophers and theologians have been promoting what they call the "openness of God" theory, or alternatively, "free will theism." Their claim is that the classical Christian view of a God who knows the contingent future is problematic both philosophically and biblically. In *The Openness of God* (1994), Clark Pinnock, Richard Rice, John Sanders, William Hasker, and David Basinger reject divine timelessness, immutability, impassibility, and infallible foreknowledge, ideas that were anticipated in this century by the process theology of Whitehead and Hartshorne.[6] Although discussion of process thought has waned in recent decades, it had considerable influence throughout most of the twentieth century. The "open God" view, according to its advocates, is less radical than process theology, however, in that the "open God" theorists claim their position is not unorthodox but more faithful to Scripture than the classical notion. The philosophical motive for their position is the view that infallible foreknowledge is inconsistent with human free will, but they also maintain that a God who "takes risks," who enters into genuine give-and-take relationships with human persons, is better supported in Scripture than the God of classical Christian theology. God knows everything that logically can be known, they say, but God does not know the truth value of all propositions; for example, he does not know, at least not infallibly, whether you will get up tomorrow exactly seven minutes after you wake up.

From one point of view, this position does not count as a solution to the dilemma of this chapter, since it capitulates in the face of the fatalist argument and admits that it is forced to give up the doctrine of foreknowledge. But these theorists argue that one of the primary motives for the doctrine of foreknowledge is a misconception. Basinger (1986), Hasker (1989), and Sanders (1997) argue that foreknowledge without middle knowledge (what they call "simple foreknowledge") is useless for providential purposes. In contrast, middle knowledge would be providentially useful but is unsupportable. They conclude that the open God view is the position of choice. God has neither foreknowledge nor middle knowledge.

The argument that simple foreknowledge is useless for providential purposes goes roughly as follows: Suppose that God would be providentially motivated to intervene to prevent some future event from occurring, say, a plane crash. If God has foreknowledge of such an event, then that event is in the actual future. But if it is in the actual future, then ipso facto God will not prevent it. In fact, God's knowledge of the entire future includes both the knowledge that the plane crash will occur and the knowledge that he will not intervene to prevent it. How, then, can he use knowledge of the future to prevent the future from occurring? He can't prevent what will occur from occurring, but he can prevent what would have occurred without his prevention from occurring. To do that, he must know, not what *will* occur but what *would* occur in alternative futures; he would have to have middle knowledge. Comprehensive knowledge of the entire future is in itself of no use, whether such knowledge is foreknowledge or timeless knowledge.

One of these "free will" or "openness of God" theorists, John Sanders, discusses an alternative model of simple foreknowledge for providential purposes, the tape analogy (1997). According to this model God unrolls the tape of the future in his mind a little at a time. He stops it at any point at which he wants to intervene, writes his intervention onto the tape, then unrolls the tape further, deciding whether and how to intervene again, and so on. Sanders argues that God's ability to intervene on this model is no greater than it is on the open view, since on this model God's response is always later in time than the event to which he is responding. A God without foreknowledge can do as much.

David Hunt (1993a) defends the providential use of simple foreknowledge and responds to two critics (Kapitan 1993 and Basinger 1993) in the same journal issue. But while this debate will no doubt continue, it seems to me unlikely that the historical motive for affirming infallible foreknowledge was that it is necessary for divine providence, as the open view claims. Instead, it seems to me that infallible foreknowledge was affirmed because it was thought to be an aspect of cognitive perfection and hence a requirement for a perfect being. Nonetheless, the open God theorists are right to call attention to the connections between the doctrines of providence and foreknowledge since historically they have been connected, whether or not it is in the way they maintain.

7. Logical and Theological Fatalism

Arguments for the equivalence of logical and theological fatalism have surfaced from time to time. For example Plantinga (1986) argues that Jonathan Edwards's argument for theological fatalism reduces to logical fatalism. (For further discussion of logical fatalism, see Mark Bernstein's essay in this volume). Nonetheless, most writers on foreknowledge take the theological form of the argument to be more threatening because the principle of the necessity of the past is more persuasive when applied to God's past knowing states than when applied to the past truth of a proposition. Recently Warfield (1997) has argued for the equivalence of the two forms of fatalism if God is necessarily existent and essentially omniscient. Under that assumption, the following two propositions are logically equivalent:

1. It was true in 50 A.D. that Plantinga will climb Mount Rushmore in 2000 A.D.
2. God knew in 50 A.D. that Plantinga will climb Mount Rushmore in 2000 A.D. Since almost everyone rejects logical fatalism, they must agree that (1) is consistent with
3. Plantinga will freely climb Mount Rushmore in 2000 A.D.

But since (3) is logically consistent with (1), (3) is also logically consistent with anything logically equivalent to (1); in particular, (3) is also logically consistent with (2). Therefore, anyone rejecting the argument for logical fatalism must also reject the argument for theological fatalism.

Responses to Warfield have been given by William Hasker (1998) and Anthony Brueckner (2000). Brueckner argues that rejection of an argument does not force one to hold that there is a possible world in which the premises are true and the conclusion false. The conclusion might be true in all possible worlds for independent reasons. So one could be right to reject the argument for logical fatalism even though human beings lack free will in all possible worlds. In such a case, he says, it would be "incautious" to express the rejection of any argument for logical fatalism by saying that (1) and (3) are logically consistent since there is no possible world in which (1) and (3) are both true. We would say instead that the logical fatalist has not identified what makes us lack freedom. Something else does; perhaps it is divine foreknowledge. Brueckner concludes that the compatibility of foreknowledge and free will cannot be demonstrated by the strategy Warfield employs. Warfield responds both to Brueckner and to Hasker in Warfield (2000).

8. RELATED PROBLEMS AND ANOTHER DILEMMA

One issue related to foreknowledge is petitionary prayer about the past. Suppose that Smith receives a letter telling him whether he did or did not get tenure. Before he opens the letter, does it make sense for him to pray that the contents of the letter are favorable even though the outcome has already been decided? It seems as if prayer at that late date is either useless or superfluous, but if God has foreknowledge, he could take Smith's prayer into account in deciding whether to intervene on Smith's behalf. If that is possible, however, it seems as if Smith's prayer should also be efficacious after he reads the letter. Yet nobody would offer a petitionary prayer after they know the letter's contents. Michael Dummett (1964) raised this issue many years ago in a famous articles, and I believe it deserves more attention. See Flint (1997a) for the middle knowledge perspective on the problem.

The foreknowledge problem also raises the issue of how the various solutions to the problem (Boethian, Ockhamist, and so on.) deal with prophecy. Some authors (for example, Widerker 1991a, Freddoso 1988) claim that prophecy creates special problems for attempts at resolving free will and foreknowledge. It is a problem for the eternity solution because prophecy seems to bring some bit of eternal knowledge into time, thus transforming it into foreknowledge. It is a problem for the Ockhamist solution because it is hard to make a case that past prophetic knowledge infallibly communicated by God is not a strict fact about the past. A recent attempt to deal with the issue from the Boethian perspective is given by Stump and Kretzmann (1991), while Wierenga (1991) approaches it from the Ockhamist perspective.

Another problem related to theological fatalism is that of how an agent can freely perform an act while knowing what that act will be. For example, if Jesus tells Peter that he will deny him three times before the cock crows and Peter believes him and keeps his belief in mind, is Peter able to decide whether to deny Christ? We might call this the problem of self-foreknowledge. A recent discussion of this problem and its relation to the problem of this chapter appears in Hunt (1996a), which includes references to recent literature on the issue.

At the beginning of this chapter I remarked that in addition to foreknowledge the Christian doctrine of providence threatens to lead to fatalism. There are many forms of this doctrine (see Flint 1997b for a summary), and not all of them are so threatening, but the doctrine of predestination has always been problematic. It is hard to find any philosopher of religion these days who supports a strong form of predestination, but a recent article by Hugh McCann (1995b) argues that God's determining decisions are compatible with our possessing libertarian free will, to which there is a reply by William Rowe (1999).

Finally, I have proposed another dilemma that shows a direct conflict between the assumption of an essentially omniscient foreknower, the law of excluded middle, and the modal asymmetry between past and future. ("A New Foreknowledge Dilemma," 1990; also in 1991, appendix, and in 1997). If I am right that this argument is valid, only a strong form of Ockhamism would suffice to save the hypothesis of an essentially omniscient foreknower. The dilemma has nothing to do with free will.

NOTES

1. Most of the recent literature is by Christian philosophers, but the problem occurs in Jewish and Muslim philosophy as well. For a recent collection of essays from a Jewish perspective, see Mongkin and Kellner (1998). For a Muslim perspective, see M. A. Rauf (1970).

2. See Brian Shanley (1997) for a contemporary exposition of Aquinas on how an eternal God knows things other than himself by causing them. Shanley (1998) discusses the problem of how Thomas's view is consistent with human freedom.

3. Obviously, the referents of "yesterday," "today," and "tomorrow," change each day, so for precision you may fill in the dates of these three days in the argument below. I have chosen the indexical terms because it makes the language of the argument more natural.

4. For Boethius see *Consolation* book IV, prose 6, and *De Trinitate*, 354.78–366.82. For Aquinas see *Summa contra gentiles* I, ch. 66.

5. This adaptation of Frankfurt's example, which uses a neurological device, is similar to some of the cases described by John Martin Fischer. An early use of this type of example appears in "Responsibility and Control," *Journal of Philosophy* 89 (January 1982), pp. 24–40.

6. See A. N. Whitehead (1978), Charles Hartshorne (1941) and (1967), and Griffin and Cobb (1976).

CHAPTER 3

....

FATALISM

....

MARK BERNSTEIN

FATALISM is the thesis that whatever happens must happen; every event or state of affairs that occurs, must occur, while the nonoccurrence of every event and state of affairs is likewise necessitated. With respect to human affairs, fatalism claims that we lack the power (capability, ability) to perform any actions other than the ones that we do, in fact, perform. Our belief that there are alternative courses of action available to our decisions and choices is mistaken. As a result, there is no such thing as (libertarian) free will. If, as many believe, this sort of freedom is necessary for the justified ascription of moral responsibility, then there can be no legitimate attributions of moral responsibility. As a result, the common assessments of persons being praiseworthy and blameworthy are unwarranted. It would be difficult to imagine any thesis whose truth would prove so destructive to our self-concept.

Fatalism is frequently characterized as a conceptual or logical thesis.[1] This is somewhat misleading for two reasons. If this characterization is meant to suggest that fatalists see themselves arguing for a logical or conceptual truth, it is unfair to all but the most sophomoric fatalists. It is true that upon the discovery of some logical truth we may realize that some goal of ours is impossible to fulfill. Hobbes, for example, thought he could, and actually did, square the circle. We realize now, as some knew then, that Hobbes could not have squared the circle. It is mathematically impossible (and I take this to be a type of a conceptual or logical impossibility) that anyone could square the circle. Alternatively, it is logically impossible that anyone has the power to square the circle and that anyone who believes that they have such a power is (logically) necessarily mistaken. Nevertheless, although some fatalists do view themselves as arguing for the logical necessity of their thesis, most do not. Most fatalists attribute what may be called "meta-physical necessity" to their thesis; the nature of their 'must', although not of the force of logic, is still powerful enough, so they believe, to eradicate the possibility of any robust free will.[2]

The second way in which the description of fatalism as a logical thesis misleads is that in so classifying it we may foster the impression that the premises used in the argument refer only to laws of logic. Again, unless we restrict ourselves to the most implausible of arguments, the impression is illusory. Serious arguments for fatalism employ premises that refer to some (putative) fundamental facts about the nature of time and truth. As a result, the type of necessity that attaches to the fatalist's thesis, the necessity that I have categorized as 'metaphysical', is the ne-cessity that all past events acquire when they become past. That is, when the sophisticated fatalists claim that everything that occurs, must occur, or that we lack the power (ability, capability) to perform acts other than the ones that we actually do perform, what they are saying is that in the sense that we have no power to perform actions that would alter the constitution of the past, we are equally powerless to choose (or decide) among alternative courses of action in the future. The belief that we have the ability to pick among different courses of action—the belief that we have (libertarian) free will—is false.

One would hope that philosophers would feel some uneasiness about sum-marily dismissing a subject that, in the ancient world alone, occupied Aristotle, the Stoics, the Peripatetics, and other thinkers. This proud pedigree should at least suggest the thought that the issue has been unfairly caricatured. When we interpret fatalism charitably, as a sophisticated, substantive thesis, it provides entry into some thorny problems regarding the nature of truth and time. In fact, I will suggest that when properly understood, reports of the death of fatalism are at least somewhat exaggerated.

1. SOME COMMON MISUNDERSTANDINGS (OR WHY NOT TREAT FATALISM LOGICALLY)

Fatalism is not the view that what will be, will be. It is true, of course, that whatever will happen will happen, but this is a mere tautology. For similar rea-sons, fatalism is not the view that necessarily what will occur, will occur, where the *necessarily* is given wide scope. When the *necessarily* is seen governing the proposition "what will happen, will happen," we have merely a proposition that expresses the tautologous nature of the first mistaken understanding of fatalism.

It is sometimes suggested that fatalism implies that what happens, happens *no matter what*, that is, that the occurrence of whatever happens is, in some sense, inevitable or unavoidable. Such a view suggests that fatalism mocks the relationship of causality, at least where causes are viewed as necessary conditions of effects. If some states of affairs will occur no matter what else occurs, and more particularly will occur regardless of what events or states of affairs antedate the state of affairs in question, it may be that no particular event can be a causally necessary condition for any state of affairs. Some interpret fatalism as having this implication and thus conclude it is a sham (Ayer 1963: 238; Grunbaum 1953: 772; Morgenbesser and Walsh 1962: 1; van Rensselaer Wilson 1955: 70–71). Some who believe that fatalism does not have this implication believe that if it did, it would be a fraud, even a logically inconsistent one (Cahn 1967: 19). Their reasoning for this is straightforward. Suppose that Jones will meet his grandfather Wednesday and that this will happen no matter what. This is seen as absurd since if Jones gets killed Tuesday, then he cannot meet his grandfather tomorrow. Thus, if fatalism really is committed to an occurrence happening no matter what else occurs, the thesis should be quickly dismissed.

Fatalism does not have this implication. If it is true that Jones will meet his grandfather Wednesday, then no one has the power to prevent this meeting. If Jones's being killed Tuesday would prevent that meeting, then Jones is not capable (lacks the capacity) of being killed tonight. None of this suggests to the metaphysical fatalist that the true proposition "Jones meets his grandfather Wednesday" is a tautology or logically necessary truth. Jones, however, can relax. If it is true that he will meet his grandfather tomorrow, and being killed would prevent this meeting, then he (metaphysically) cannot be killed beforehand.

2. FATALISM AND DETERMINISM

Determinism, like *fatalism* is, in some measure, a term of art. The thesis of determinism, like that of fatalism, can also be stated as "whatever happens must happen." The theses also share the presumption that any acceptable elucidation of them would threaten the existence of free will. Yet important differences exist between the two theses; the *must* or necessity of fatalism is distinct from the *must* of determinism.

Grounding the thesis of determinism is the intuitive idea that the world works in ways that continually reflect regularities. Unimpeded dropped books fall to earth, glass tends to be shattered when met by massive, fast-moving objects, ingestion of bread and tofu disposes nourishment. Let us call these and other regularities, these workings of the world, "laws of nature." The term *law* is suggestive; violations are *naturally* impossible, a thought manifested in the work of many philosophers and theologians who characterize miracles as events that violate these laws and whose cause can only be a supernatural or divine being. We natural, mortal creatures lack the power to bring about any event that is in violation of a law of nature.

Consider now the existence of certain events governed by natural laws. It appears as if any such events must occur. Given a prior state of the world that is governed by laws of nature, a unique state of the world is forthcoming. It is helpful to think of the laws of nature operating as mathematical functions and the antecedent events as arguments for these functions. Once the function and the argument (input of the function) are settled, the output is necessitated. To implement the mathematical analogy, let $f(x) = 5x + 2$ and the input to the function be 3. The output of $f(3)$ is 17, a mathematically necessitated result relative to the function and argument. Just as any other result is mathematically impossible—a violation of the rules or laws of mathematics—any event other than the one that actually occurs, relative to the antecedent state of the world and the laws of nature, is naturally impossible. Only by supernatural interference could an outcome other than the actual one occur in a world with the identical prior state and laws. Determinism can then be defined as claiming that it is logically impossible that there are worlds with natural laws and pasts congruent with the actual world and yet with futures distinct from that of the actual world.

Deterministic necessity attaches to an event just in case the event appears in every logically possible world that shares the natural laws and antecedent state of affairs of the actual world. Consider a logically possible world congruent to that of the actual world up to and including a specific time but immediately afterward containing a different set of natural laws than that of the actual world. There is no reason to believe that this world's future will be anything like, let alone identical to, the future of the actual world. Books may well rise when dropped, glass may no longer shatter when struck by massive high velocity objects, and bread may no longer nourish. All bets are off concerning what events may occur once the laws of nature diverge. Next, reflect upon the scenario where logically possible worlds contain natural laws that are unflaggingly identical to those of the actual world, but whose antecedent states of affairs diverge from those of the actual world. Obviously, some of these worlds will differ greatly from the actual one. Since some of these worlds will simply not contain any books, there will be no future consisting of books plummeting to earth when they are released. The necessity of determinism therefore requires (depends upon, is contingent upon) the intelligibility of transworld identity of natural laws and prior events.

Subtleties aside, it is natural to understand deterministic necessity as a species of causal necessity—more particularly, a type of efficacious causality where the causal antecedents of a state of affairs make or bring about a subsequent state rather than exist as mere concomitant accoutrements. What, then, is the relationship between fatalism and determinism? Were fatalism merely a logical thesis, it would be consistent in both indeterministic and deterministic worlds. Logical truths are completely unaffected by the causal relationships that may hold between states of affairs. Conceptual fatalism, a view of the happenings of the world that makes their occurrence logically mandated, does eviscerate cause and effect of any efficacy. Tautologies are not, and cannot be, true by virtue of some set of antecedent events.

Given our understanding of both the metaphysical necessity of fatalism and the causal necessity of determinism, the natural task is to describe their relationship. If an event is metaphysically fated, we are as unable to influence it as we are incapable of modifying the past. I see no reason to think that this same event might not be causally necessitated. Of course, if it is causally necessitated, this relationship of causal necessitation is itself metaphysically necessitated if (metaphysical) fatalism is true. But there is no logical impediment to this. The two types of necessity are compatible.

3. Arguments for Fatalism

The simplest historical argument for fatalism does in fact appeal only to the laws of logic, thus fostering the view that fatalism is merely a logical thesis.

1. it is (logically) necessary that: each individual proposition is either true or false.
2. Therefore each individual proposition is either (logically) necessarily true or (logically) necessarily false.

The usual rejoinder is to accept the truth of premise (1), which is basically an expression of the principle of logical bivalence, but to deny the argument's validity. Logical necessity does not distribute over a disjunction. Consider the present weather conditions. It is (logically) necessary that it is either raining or not raining. Yet surely if it is raining, this event is not logically necessitated. The cumulus clouds (logically) could have passed by the neighborhood; they just did not. Likewise, if it is not raining, it (logically) could be; rain clouds could have dropped precipitation in the area; they just did not. Thus this argument for fatalism is invalid.

Fatalists can, of course, always claim that this argument is question-begging. To insist that logical necessity does not distribute over a disjunction is tantamount to denying the fatalist's thesis. But given a choice between the logical principle prohibiting distribution of necessity over a disjunction and the fatalist's thesis, most people find the former far more plausible.

Thankfully, most fatalistic arguments are versions of the one to be found in Aristotle's *De Interpretatione*, bk. 9, in which concerns about truth and time, in addition to the laws of logic, come into play. It is fair to claim that the following version (call it RF for 'representative fatalism') owes its inspiration to Aristotle and is representative of the great majority of subsequent arguments purporting to demonstrate the truth of fatalism.

1. There will be a sea battle on 1/1/2010 or there will not be a sea battle on 1/1/2010.
2. If there will be a sea battle on 1/1/2010, then it was always true that (it was always a fact that) there will be a sea battle on 1/1/2010; if there will not be a sea battle on 1/1/2010, then it was always true that (it was always a fact that) there will not be a sea battle on 1/1/2010.
3. If it was always true that (it was always a fact that) there will be a sea battle on 1/1/2010, then there was never a time at which anyone or anything could prevent the sea battle; if it was always true that (it was always a fact that) there will not be a sea battle on 1/1/2010, then there was never a time at which anyone or anything could bring about the sea battle.
4. Thus either no one (or nothing), at any time, could prevent the sea battle or no one (or nothing), at any time, could bring about the sea battle.
5. Thus, either the occurrence of the sea battle is necessary (that is, no one and no thing has the power, at any time, to prevent the sea battle) or the nonoccurrence of the sea battle is necessary (that is, no one and no thing has the power, at any time, to bring about the occurrence of the sea battle).
6. Thus, in general, fatalism is true.

Unsurprisingly, philosophers have questioned this argument in a host of ways. Some, most notably Aristotle, denied premise (1) when the disjuncts concerned future contingents (cf. Cahn 1967: chs. 7, 8). Although each disjunct in isolation had to be either true or false, a disjunction of future contingents is neither. This radical response is currently unpopular. It seems to most philosophers ad hoc. They are inclined to look for other responses to the argument before restricting the application of the logical Law of Excluded Middle and its close relative, the principle of bivalence. One would hope less draconian measures would be required to meet the fatalist's challenge. Some have questioned the legitimacy of the inference from "there will be a sea battle" to "it was always true that there will be a sea battle" involved in the step from (2) to (3). But while it is clear that the fatalist employs this inference, it is less clear what motivation we have to reject it other than the question-begging reason that it leads to a result with which we do not want to be saddled.

A more frequently voiced criticism takes aim at the very intelligibility of tensed facts and tensed propositions. It is claimed that to speak of an event or state of affairs as always (that is, at all times) being the case (or not) and to speak of a proposition always being true (or false) makes as little sense as the putative unintelligibility of imputing spatial attributes to facts or propositions. Just as it is (allegedly) senseless to speak of a state of affairs being the case in Connecticut or a proposition being true in New York, it is meaningless to speak of states of affairs obtaining at certain times or propositions having truth-values at particular times.

But there may be less to this objection than meets the eye. We can understand "proposition p is true in place q" as "had anyone uttered in q the sentence that expresses proposition p, he would have expressed a true proposition." Similarly, we can analyze "proposition p is true at time t" as "had anyone uttered at t the sentence that expresses proposition p, he would have expressed a true proposition." In effect, the translation assigns to the moment of utterance the dispositional property of containing a true proposition p had anyone uttered the sentence "p."[3]

If this Aristotelian argument (RF) were sound, we would be left with the task of explaining how we can be legitimately said to have libertarian free will regarding any of our actions in the face of its antecedently being true that we will perform one particular act. At least at first blush, it seems that if we had the ability to choose between alternative courses of action, then we would have the ability to change the past. We would have the ability to make a proposition that was true at some prior time false at that time or to make one false at a prior time true. Fatalists thus allege that the denial of their position commits one to the intolerable result that we have the power to alter the past and so commits us to denying the self-evident fact that the past is inviolable or fixed. Belief in the inviolability or fixity of the past amounts to the belief that if the sea battle has occurred at some particular time, then we now lack the power to make it the case that it did not occur at that time and if the sea battle has not occurred at some particular time, we now lack the power to make it the case that it did occur at that time.

While most philosophers would accept the fact that we lack the power to alter the past, many would claim that we do not need this power to falsify step (3) of RF. Many claim that the expression "it was always a fact that the sea-battle will occur" does not refer to a fact that concerns the past, or, at least, does not refer to a fact solely about the past. As such, the power that we normally believe we have regarding this fact is real, and the exercise of this power does not violate the legitimate stricture concerning the impossibility of altering the past. The distinction, difficult as its exact expression is, between facts that are truly about the past (often called "hard" facts) and so unamenable to any of our powers, and those facts "about the past" over whose existence we do have some say (called by contrast "soft" facts), finds its medieval ancestor in Ockham. Expression of soft facts may masquerade as hard facts, but we need not be taken in by the illusion. We can make it a fact (a fact that was "always the case," if you like), that the sea battle will not occur by simply making the captain realize that entering into such a battle would have an exorbitant human cost. In so doing, we are not violating the principle that the past cannot be changed. Rather, we are performing some act, an act that fatalism has given us no reason to think that we cannot perform, such that as a result, the constitution of the world is different than it would have been had we not exercised our power to perform this act. Using the fatalist's jargon, in speaking to the receptive captain, we are making it the case that it was always a fact that the sea battle will not occur. We sometimes have the power to perform acts that make it the case that some states of affairs have always been facts.

It may be helpful to consider a scenario where the Yankees win the pennant in 2010, the Indians win in 2011, and the sport of baseball is terminated prior to the 2012 season. To the fatalist, it was always true that (always a fact that) the Yankees won the penultimate American League pennant. Yet, the Ockamist claims that this fact is at least partially a product of something that occurred just prior to the 2012 season. If the season had been terminated just prior to the 2013 season, then it would not be a fact (and never would have been a fact) that the Yankees won the penultimate American League pennant. We should not be misled by the expression "always the case that" into thinking that the truth or fact has already been fixed in the past. While hard facts about the past are "fully accomplished" and "over and done with" (Fischer 1989: 5), some soft facts, like the *penultimacy* of the Yankee pennant, are determined, at least in part, by what occurs afterward. In 2011 or any time before the termination of the 2012 baseball season, it was a soft fact that the Yankees were the penultimate team to win the American League pennant, although it was a hard fact, in 2011, that the Yankees won the 2010 pennant. While all hard facts are fixed, not all soft facts are. If the 2012 baseball season had not been terminated (let us imagine that the commissioner ordered it to be played), it would not have been a fact that the Yankees won the penultimate American League pennant. When we speak of the fixity or inalterability of the past, we are expressing what we take to be the relationship between our powers and hard facts.

Do these Ockhamist considerations destroy the viability of (metaphysical) fatalism? I think not. The problem is not merely to make a hard fact/soft fact distinction[4] but to explain why such a distinction should carry so much weight. Ockhamists appear guilty of question-begging if they simply assume that hard facts about the past are fixed while some soft facts are not. Whether one can distinguish between facts that are essentially temporally related to subsequent times from those that are not, is not the crucial issue. What fatalists want to know is why this distinction makes (some) soft facts immune from their argument. Fatalists may grant that in 2010 the fact that the Yankees won the penultimate pennant in the American League may be different—in some ways—than the fact, in 2010, that Lincoln delivered the Emancipation Proclamation. They may also grant the merely verbal point that we will call facts of the former sort "soft" facts and call the latter "hard" facts. Still, they will insist on an explanation of how we can make it the case that the Yankees won the American League's penultimate pennant if it was always true that they would be the League champions. How, precisely, can something that has always been a fact depend upon events that are in our power to perform? To be told, in effect, that this is just the way some temporally relational facts work, is not to give an answer but to abruptly end the dialogue. The fatalist is not likely to be converted. At this point, the ever-recurring meta-issues regarding burden of proof and question-begging are likely to resurface.

Some believe that we can adopt a bolder position. Perhaps we should question the dogma that there are hard facts; that is, what if we challenge the common assumption shared by Ockhamists, fatalists, and ordinary persons, that we lack, indeed, necessarily lack, the power to bring about and prevent past events. What if we not only have the power to bring about past events that have already occurred and the power to prevent the occurrence of possible but nonactual past events, but even have the more remarkable power to bring about past events that did not occur and to prevent events that did occur? If, somehow, these powers are not, as they seem on the surface, impossible, then we may have the most direct, and stunning, defeat of fatalism that we can imagine. If our powers regarding the past are like our powers regarding the world's future, we may be relieved of the fear that we lack free will.

Some believe that such powers are possible (for example, Mavrodes 1983). But we must be very careful about how we conceive the nature of such power. It is not the power to bring it about that there was a past time at which it was true that some event occurred and a subsequent time at which it was not true that that very same event occurred. That is, advocates of even this remarkable power do not conceive it as a power to change the actual existence status of events relative to different times. Rather, the remarkable power is conceived as the power to make it the case that states of affairs that have been facts for some time are henceforth not facts anymore.

How can such a remarkable power exist? I think that we must conceive it as a 'meta-ability' (Bernstein 1992: 106ff.) or a 'generalized power' (Hasker 1989a:

ch. 7). We must view the power not as an ability to perform a particular act in particular circumstances (for, if we did, then, there could be no such power), but rather as an ability to gain the ability to perform acts of a certain kind. Neither my friend nor I can speak Russian; we both lack sufficient knowledge to do so and it would be the height of foolishness to take either of us as tour guides of Moscow. Still, my friend, unlike myself, is quite good at learning new languages. Put in the right settings, with proper instruction, she would learn competent Russian. I, on the other hand, am linguistically challenged; the greatest Russian teachers in the world would be forever stymied in their attempts to teach me the language. While neither my friend nor I can speak Russian, only she has the meta-ability to speak it.

The power, then, to prevent states of affairs that have been facts up to this point from ever being facts, requires (a) the possibility of there being an act such that if I presently performed it, the state of affairs that was a fact up to this point would never had existed, and (b) the meta-ability to perform such an act. Of course, such a possibility requires the possibility of backward (or retro-) causation, but this, relatively speaking, is a small price to pay. (After all, the relatively simple power requires this.) And we need to understand that, given our present situation, we lack the ability (and so, on the "lower level," we cannot) perform such an act. The fact that the Yankees won the 1927 pennant is safe from revision; we can no more do this than I can learn Russian despite the greatest tutelage the world has to offer.

What bearing does this have on free will? Have these considerations lived up to the aforementioned hope that we can demonstrate that free will exists despite the arguments of the (metaphysical) fatalist? In a word, no. The easiest way to see this is to concede that there is a sort of power that we may well have that is compatible with changing (affecting, causing, bringing about) the past. But libertarian free will, unlike a compatibilist version of free will, demands the ability, in the very circumstances that the individual finds herself, to choose among various alternative courses of action. Putting it another way, libertarian free will requires the ability, not merely the meta-ability, to do this; it requires the particular (or specific) ability and not generalized ability. Picturesquely, libertarianism demands that there are alternative paths available to us, *right then and there*, and not merely that under certain causally possible conditions, though not the ones present, we would have such available options. (In fact, this shows that this understanding of power really seems, at bottom, to be a compatibilist rendition). Only under these conditions do the libertarians see freedom having the robustness that we demand of free individuals. Thus, regardless of how successful one believes this account is for articulating a notion of power (ability) to accommodate our ability to affect the past, it fails to resolve the issue in favor of the antifatalist.

4. FATALISM AND LOGIC

It is worthwhile to note an interesting implication of (logical) fatalism to the way we usually characterize argumentation. Deductive arguments are distinguished from inductive ones by the fact that the evidential link between the premises and the conclusion is absolute; there is no (logical) possibility of all the premises being true and the conclusion false. Inductive arguments are those where there is at least one possible world where all the premises are true and the conclusion false. Deductiveness and inductiveness are not matters of the actual truth-values of any of the statements involved. Consider an argument that we normally would consider inductive in which all the premises and conclusion are true. If fatalism is true, then this argument is not truly inductive, for there is no possible world where the conclusion is false. This trivially follows from the idea that fatalism collapses the possible worlds into the actual one. Indeed, fatalism entails that the only inductive arguments are those in which all the premises are true and the conclusion is false. Assimilating, as is common, deductivity with logical validity and inductivity with logical invalidity, this highlights the point that the domain of the most significant logical notions is greatly altered under fatalism.

Does this signal the death-knell for fatalism? Not necessarily. The (logical) fatalist is free to suggest that some logical distinctions that we have made, canonized though they may be in our logic textbooks, need to be modified. What antifatalists view as a fundamental, perhaps decisive criticism, fatalists consider an illuminating insight.

5. THEOLOGICAL FATALISM

For centuries, the driving force behind most discussions of fatalism has come from religion. There is at least a powerful prima facie case that the existence of a Judeo-Christian God is incompatible with human freedom. More particularly, the divine attribute of eternal infallible omniscience is seen to clash with libertarian human freedom.

Consider the case of Sue, who forgoes eating dinner this coming Thursday evening. God, being omniscient, believes, from time immemorial, that Sue would not be eating dinner this Thursday. Being infallible, God cannot be mistaken in this belief. Employing the Ockhamist terminology, this belief of God seems to be a hard fact. God infallibly believed one thousand years ago, for example, that Sue will forgo eating this Thursday dinner. It would appear to be beyond our power to make it the case that God did not so believe. Thus, it appears as if Sue *cannot* eat dinner this coming Thursday, for if she could, then it would be in her power to make it the case that God did not believe that she would refrain from Thursday's dinner. Generalizing, we are to conclude that if God exists, humans never have the ability to act other than they do.

This argument for incompatibility is fairly characterized as fatalistic as opposed to deterministic. There is no reference to causation or natural laws. The argument would be unaffected if, as scientists currently popularly believe, the workings of the world are, at bottom, indeterministic. Still, it is important to notice how this type of fatalistic argument differs from arguments like RF that purport to establish fatalism. After all, while some contemporary philosophers accept the theological argument for the incompatibility of God's foreknowledge with human freedom, few, if any of them, accept the similar fatalist argument against human freedom. For these philosophers, therefore, that *God believes* a certain fact must have pivotal significance over and above the truth of the fact.

I have already alluded to one key difference between this argument and the general argument for fatalism that makes no reference to the beliefs of anyone, mortal or divine. We have seen that the currently fashionable response to the general fatalistic argument is to claim that the fatalist has given us no reason to think that we cannot alter some soft facts about the past. In so doing, we are not violating our commonsense precept that we cannot alter hard facts about the past. Assuming that it is true that Sue will not eat dinner this coming Thursday, it is arguably an alterable soft fact about the past that it was always true that Sue will forego dinner this Thursday. The key difference with the theological version is that by granting Sue the power to eat dinner this coming Thursday, we apparently grant her the power to change a belief that God has at some earlier time. But the having of a belief—by anyone, mortal or divine—at some earlier time seems clearly to be a hard fact, a fact that is fully accomplished and over and done with. To see the force of this, notice that even the destruction of the world 500 years ago would not alter the fact that God (or anyone else, for that matter) 1,000 years ago had the belief that Sue would not eat dinner this coming Thursday. The having of the belief, in other words, does not seem to be temporally relational in the manner of the sort of soft facts regarding the past over which we seem to have some control. Granting Sue the power to eat dinner this Thursday, so it seems, does violate the stricture that no one has the power to change the past.

Why is it important that an infallibly omniscient God have this belief rather than a mere mortal like you or me? An infallibly omniscient being has, and can have, all and only true beliefs. There is no truth that God does not believe and God can have no false beliefs. We, on the other hand, can have false beliefs. Suppose that both God and we believe, at some antecedent time, that Sue will not eat dinner at some later time. If Sue exercised her power to eat dinner (a possibility that the antifatalist insists upon), then she would have the power to bring about a change in the propositional content of God's belief; that is, Sue would have the power to bring about a change of belief in God. It appears that had Sue exercised her power then, since God is infallibly omniscient, God would have believed at the earlier time that Sue would have eaten her Thursday dinner. Thus, it appears that Sue has power over the content, an inherent or intrinsic property, of God's belief. Since having a belief at an earlier time does seem to be a hard fact (a fact that is over and done with), attributing the power to Sue of doing other than what she actually does, appears to violate of the principle that the past cannot be altered. On the other hand, if you or I had the belief, the implementation of Sue's power would not have changed a hard fact, but only the truth value of our belief. Not being infallibly omniscient, the content of our belief would not need to, and presumably would not change, since having the mortal belief at an earlier time is just as much a hard fact as a divine earlier belief. And this, so it has been alleged, is merely a change of an appropriate soft fact and does no violence to our belief in the fixity of the past.

An Ockhamist may respond by submitting that this Cartesian conception of belief is mistaken. What makes a belief the belief that it is, is not, as the Cartesian would suggest, merely a matter of what is going on "inside the head." It is not as though we could look inside the mind (or brain) of an individual and read off what a person believes. Appropriating Hilary Putnam's idea that meanings and beliefs "ain't in the head," the Ockhamist may claim that if Sue eats dinner this coming Thursday, then the state of God's mind that actually constituted God's belief would not have constituted this belief (Putnam 1975: 215–71).[5] To Putnam, the belief, for example, that water is wet would have been a different belief had XYZ and not water constituted the oceans, lakes, and streams. Although my state of mind—the formal reality of my idea, so to speak—would have been identical whether water or XYZ made up the oceans, lakes, and streams, my belief would have been different. Instead of believing that oceans were made of water, I would have believed that the oceans were made of XYZ. Transporting this idea to theological fatalism yields the Ockhamist conclusion that God's belief is partially a function of what Sue freely decides to do this coming Thursday evening. Of course, one would need to argue for the plausibility of an "externalist" conception of belief before this idea gains many apologists. The argument is further complicated by the worry that an externalist conception may militate against the Judeo-Christian conception of divine omniscience.

Ockhamism is not the only strategy available to compatibilists regarding human free will and divine foreknowledge. Assuming consensus on the facts that God does have beliefs at times and that some of these beliefs concern human acts at subsequent times, the Molinist offers an account of how we humans can have power over the past (Hasker 1989a: ch. 2; Zagzebski 1991: ch. 5). The theory holds that God knows, in advance, what every possible free creature would freely choose to do in every possible situation in which a free choice can be exercised. God knows not only what will happen from time immemorial but also what *would* happen even if in fact it will not. Humans make free choices, but God chooses to create them and place them in particular situations. Applying this view of so-called middle knowledge, we can imagine God realizing that a free choice that I would make in 2010 that would have great benefits for all of humanity would be possible only if God made it the case the Lincoln never existed. No doubt this is an unlikely scenario, but one in which we have an example of *counterfactual power* over the past. In this same sense we are said to have power over the earlier beliefs of God. We can freely perform an act such that if we performed it, God would not have the belief that he previously had.

Most of the contemporary criticism of middle knowledge comes from putative problems concerning the so-called counterfactuals of freedom. Middle knowledge requires that some relevant conditionals of the form "if conditions X occurred, P would freely do Y" be both capable of being true (and so meaningful) and knowable by God. Pre-philosophically, we tend to have no particular problem in assigning truth values to (some) counterfactuals of freedom. It surely seems true that had my university offered me a $20,000 raise, I would have accepted it. I would claim to know this with a very high degree of certainty. What, then, are the problems inherent in the counterfactuals of freedom that are necessary to the viability of Molinism?

Robert Adams (1977) and William Hasker (1989a) have worried that counterfactuals of freedom seem to have no grounding.[6] Hasker claims not to understand how a counterfactual of freedom can be true. This metaphysical concern, I think, can be managed straightforwardly. What makes a simple declarative proposition true is the fact that it references; "snow is white" is true in virtue of snow being white. Using the semantics of counterfactuals developed by Stalnaker (1968) and Lewis (1973), we assign truth to a counterfactual just in case some possible world in which the antecedent and consequent are true is more similar to the actual world than any world in which the antecedent is true and the consequent false. While there may be obscurities and difficulties with this semantic analysis of counterfactuals, there appears to be no special reason why this analysis cannot be used to provide the "grounding" for counterfactuals of freedom. It is true, of course, that we need to consult other possible worlds in order to assign truth-values, but this is normally taken as a mere heuristic device to deal with modalities in general.[7]

Adams's worry about grounding is different and aimed more specifically toward the personal liberty that is supposed in the counterfactuals of freedom. He claims to be unable to see how a counterfactual of freedom can be true. He suggests that the antecedent of such a conditional can neither logically nor causally necessitate the consequent and, as a result, speculates that no connection between antecedent and consequent of a true counterfactual of freedom would allow the consequent to be contingent in a sense that is required for libertarian freedom.

It seems, however, that whatever the merit of these rather technical problems, Molinism still fails to solve the foreknowledge/free will dilemma. Counterfactual power, based on the theory of middle knowledge, is a misnomer. It is not power worth the name and is certainly not robust enough to satisfy either the ordinary man or the libertarian, both of whom believe that we have free will. Molinism tells us that God's knowledge of a particular future human action is contingent. Assume, that as a matter of fact, God believes from time immemorial that Sue will not eat her Thursday dinner. We are also told that Sue is free to eat or not eat this Thursday's dinner. To the libertarian, this means that Sue, as she is at the very moment of choice, in her very psycho-physical state at the moment, has these two alternatives open to her. It would seem, then, that Sue has the power to change a belief of God, a possibility that Molinism expressly precludes. Molinists claim that if Sue (freely) chose to eat this Thursday's dinner then, God would never have believed that Sue would not eat this Thursday's dinner. In fact, God would have always believed that Sue would eat this Thursday's dinner. Sue, though, exerts no causal influence over God; no one can, let alone does, do that. It is just that God, being infallibly omniscient, would have always had the true belief about Sue and her upcoming dinner. Sue's power to eat and not eat dinner, her freedom of will at this particular moment, entails the possibility of there being a realizable world in which she eats dinner. But this is not enough for libertarian freedom. If God knows from time immemorial that Sue will not eat dinner this Thursday, then Sue, on Thursday, does not have alternative courses of action from which to choose. If she really did have this libertarian freedom, then she would have the power to bring about a change in God's beliefs, and this, the Molinist concurs, is impossible.

Boethius, Anselm, and Aquinas are the sources of the eternalist tradition that God is an atemporal being and as such it makes no sense to attribute temporal qualities to him.[8] In particular, it is unintelligible to claim that God knows some proposition at a certain time or that God believes something before or after an event occurs. God is timeless and God's beliefs and knowledge are timeless as well. The incompatibility problem putatively evaporates (rather than being resolved), for the premise that is necessary to generate the problem, namely, that God knows or believes what will happen *before* it happens, is taken to be necessarily inapplicable to a timeless God.

Problems for this view can be usefully divided into two groups. Some objections submit that the timeless view of God is inconsistent with the scriptural accounts of a Judeo-Christian God; others derive from the worry that, even if coherent, atemporal knowledge only serves to re-establish the dilemma in a slightly altered form. The Judeo-Christian God is a personal God, one who thinks and acts. These seem like activities or processes and as such require that the agent have a temporal dimension. On the other hand, one wonders whether the timeless knowledge of what we will do really mitigates the problem of reconciliation with free will. Although timeless knowledge would not be burdened with necessity of the past (metaphysical necessity), it arguably attracts a similar onus. As Marilyn Adams has put it (1987: 1135), "[I]f the necessity of the past stems from its ontological determinateness it would seem that timeless determinateness is just as problematic as past determinateness." I take the point to be that determinateness, manifested in either its past or timeless guises, precludes us from having any effect upon the future. As far as the question of our powers is concerned, the necessities of pastness and timelessness accomplish the same purpose (compare Zagzebski 1991).

We should always be wary of reports that proclaim that a philosophical problem has been solved, dissolved, or shown to be without merit. Fatalism provides us with further confirmation of this platitude.[9]

NOTES

My thanks to Robert Kane and Michael Almeida for very helpful comments.

1. Cahn (1967:8) tell us that fatalism "is the thesis that the *laws of logic alone* suffice to prove that no man has free will, suffice to prove that the only actions which a man can perform are the actions which he does, in fact, perform, and suffice to prove that a man can bring about only those events which do, in fact, occur and can prevent only those events which do not, in fact, occur" (my emphasis). J. M. Fischer (1989: 8) tells us that fatalism "is the doctrine that it is a logical or conceptual truth that no person is ever free to do otherwise." Van Inwagen (1983: 23) says that he will understand by fatalism "the thesis that it is a logical or conceptual truth that no one is able to act otherwise than he in fact does; that the very idea of an agent to whom alternative courses of action are open is self-contradictory." For some recondite formulations of fatalism, see Sobel (1998).

2. This terminology is used and justified in Bernstein (1992). The terminology is closely related to the medieval notion of accidental necessity, although I am hesitant in identifying the two for fairly arcane reasons. For a helpful introduction to the genesis of accidental necessity, see Zagzebski (1991: ch.1).

3. See van Inwagen (1983), especially the interesting note 16 (pp. 228–29), and Wirderker (1989: 97–105).

4. The discussion of the hard fact/soft fact distinction has grown to a cottage industry. Many of the best articles can be found in Fischer (1989). In addition to his very helpful introduction concerning this issue, I would especially recommend the contributions of Pike (1995), Wirderker (1989), and Hasker (1989a).

5. Fischer (1983b) exploits this idea in "Freedom and Foreknowledge," reprinted in idem (1989).

6. These and other objections are discussed in Zagzebski, (1991: 141–52).

7. This may be unfairly dismissive. Since libertarian freedom allows, indeed insists, on the possibility of two worlds being identical up to the moment of distinct choices or overt personal actions, it would appear arbitrary to think of one of these two worlds as being "closer" to the actual world. If this is what Hasker has in mind, the problem is more of *assessment* of counterfactuals of freedom than their grounding, although I would not want to place too much weight on a point that may be merely a verbal quibble. Adams, discussed later in the text, may be bothered by this problem as well. See Flint (1998) for a very recent and detailed account of Molinism.

8. For an extensive discussion of the eternalist tradition, see Hasker (1989a: chs. 8–10), Robinson (1995), and Zagzebski (1991: ch.2). It may be worth consulting Bernstein (1989), where it is argued that the 'block conception' or eternalist conception of time has no fatalistic consequences.

PART II

PHYSICS, DETERMINISM, AND INDETERMINISM

CHAPTER 4

QUANTUM PHYSICS, CONSCIOUSNESS, AND FREE WILL

DAVID HODGSON

By about 1920, classical relativistic physics—the physics of Newton and Maxwell and Einstein—provided an account of the workings of matter and energy in space and time that was apparently accurate and comprehensive. Two outstanding features of this account were (1) that it was deterministic and (2) that it required locality of causation.

Looking first at *determinism*, classical physics postulated that the material universe develops or changes over time wholly in accordance with definite and unequivocal physical laws, so that for any inertial frame of reference (any frame of reference not itself subject to any acceleration) the state of the universe at any time is wholly and unequivocally determined by the state of the universe at prior times and the physical laws of nature. Or, to put essentially, the same idea in the language of relativity theory, independently of frames of reference: any event at any location in space-time is wholly determined by events within its past light cone and the physical laws of nature.[1]

The last statement links with the second important feature of classical physics, *locality of causation*. In classical physics, anything that happens at any location in space-time is entirely unaffected by events with spacelike separation from it—that is, events occurring at locations in space-time other than within its past or future light cones. In fact, classical physics restricts locality of causation even more strictly than this: what happens at any location in space-time is considered as determined either by matter coming to that location by passing through adjacent regions of its past light cone, or else by force or energy fields the state of which at any location in space-time depends on its state in adjacent regions of its past light cone.

These features of classical physics would leave little room for free will, in any strong sense. If one accepts classical physics, free will must apparently be explained as being *compatible* with determinism. The only alternative to compatibilism, if sense is to be made of free will, would be to postulate that the laws of physics do not have universal application and that human free will can cause things to happen contrary to those laws. It might be suggested that Kant found a third alternative, but if so it is one I am unable to understand. Furthermore, any strong sense of free will requires that mental events, such as those involved in decisions and voluntary actions, have efficacy in the physical world. Mental events appear to be associated with patterns of physical events spread over substantial regions of the brain; so that if the mental events, as such, are to have an impact on the world, this would seem to suggest some non-locality in causal histories.

Then in the 1920s came quantum mechanics (QM). And QM seemed to indicate that the world was not deterministic; that the past plus laws of nature did not determine outcomes unequivocally but rather left open a spectrum of alternative outcomes, with varying probabilities. Further, QM seemed to indicate that causation was not entirely local, but rather that what happens in one location can be interdependent with and thus affect and/or be affected by what happens at another location with spacelike separation from it.

Not surprisingly, some people saw the indeterminism of QM as making possible an account of a strong sense of free will, as being incompatible with determinism, and as selecting from the outcomes left open by the past and (quantum) physical laws of nature. Notably, this approach was put forward by Arthur Eddington in *The Nature of the Physical World* (1929), and a similar suggestion appeared in Compton (1935). However, this view did not appeal to neuroscientists or philosophers: they pointed out that the indeterminism suggested by QM is mere randomness, which is hardly conducive to rational choice; and that in any event in systems as hot, wet, and massive as neurons of the brain, quantum mechanical indeterminacies quickly cancel out, so that for all practical purposes determinism rules in the brain. Eddington was strongly attacked, for example, by Susan Stebbing in *Philosophy and the Physicists* (1937); and it was not until quite recently that the possibility that quantum physics was relevant to free will was again taken up in any substantial way.

However, another feature of QM, namely its treatment of measurement and observation, was seen by some as suggesting an intimate link between QM and consciousness. I will be looking later at von Neumann's treatment of measurement, which has been taken to indicate that QM presupposes and depends upon the existence of conscious observers (see London and Bauer 1983; Wigner 1983).

By the early 1980s, physicist Henry Margenau was publishing views to the effect that QM was relevant to free will (see Margenau 1984; LeShan et al. 1982), and later in the 1980s the idea that QM may be relevant to consciousness in general and free will in particular began to receive significant attention. The most prominent recent exponent of the view that QM is relevant to consciousness is mathematician Roger Penrose, whose book *The Emperor's New Mind* was published in 1989 and has caused considerable debate. In the same year, philosopher Michael Lockwood published *Mind, Brain and the Quantum*; and since then there have been a number of books relating QM with consciousness, including my own *The Mind Matters* (1991), *Mind, Matter and Quantum Mechanics* by physicist Henry Stapp (1993), *How the Self Controls Its Brain* by neuroscientist John Eccles (1994), and *Shadows of the Mind* by Roger Penrose (1994).[2] Some of these books (notably Lockwood's) do not directly support a strong sense of free will, but all are of relevance to the debate.

In addition to QM, one other area of twentieth century physics is seen by some as relevant to free will, namely chaos and complexity theory. One finding of this area of physics is that in complex systems the minutest differences in initial conditions can produce great differences in outcomes. Most scientists and philosophers do not see this as supporting indeterminism, much less free will: rather, they see it as explaining why there can be unpredictability in complex systems, even when they are strictly deterministic. However, a respectable minority think that the impossibility of 100 percent accuracy in measuring initial conditions and consequent large uncertainties in outcomes could signal actual indeterminism that is not dependent on quantum theory (see Prigogine and Stengers 1984; Polkinghorne 1996). I will not consider this view in any detail in this essay, although it will come up in passing. (There is discussion concerning this approach in Robert Bishop's essay [chapter 5] in this volume.)

In this essay I will focus on the relevance of QM to the free will debate. First, I will outline how QM involves three features potentially of relevance to free will, namely indeterminism, nonlocality, and what may be called observer-participation. Second, I will look at interpretations of QM that might be seen as restoring determinism to physics, namely the many-worlds interpretation and the Bohm interpretation. Third, I will outline some objections that have been raised to the notion that QM is relevant to free will. Fourth, I will briefly discuss the approaches of some of the authors mentioned above. And last, I will outline some of my own thoughts on the matter.

1. Indeterminism, Nonlocality, and Observer-Participation

I will begin by briefly saying something about the way in which QM represents physical systems and then suggest how this gives rise to the three features I have mentioned.

1.1. QM Representations

In classical physics, the quantities of observable properties (or 'observables') of physical systems, such as position or momentum or energy, are represented directly by mathematical objects—so that for example one may expect to find the energy of a system represented by a symbol such as E, and one may take that to mean that the system really does have the quantity of energy that E indicates. However, in QM the mathematical objects used do not generally represent directly the quantities of the observables but rather indicate the *probabilities* of various observables being disclosed on measurement, *if* an appropriate measurement should be made.

A typical representation in QM of the *state* of a physical system is by the mathematical object $|\psi>$, which carries the information that, if a measurement of an observable, such as the energy of the system is made, the possible results are energy levels $E_1, E_2, \ldots, E_n$, etc., with respective probabilities $P_1, P_2, \ldots, P_n$, etc. Each quantity E_n is associated with a different possible state (called an 'energy *eigenstate*') of the system, represented by mathematical objects $|\psi_n>$—so that $|\psi_1>$ is associated with E_1, $|\psi_2>$ is associated with E_2, and so on. The probability P_n that the system will be measured as a particular E_n is $|c_n|^2$, the absolute square of a number c_n, generally complex, which is given by a relationship between $|\psi>$ and $|\psi_n>$, called an *inner product* and written $<\psi_n|\psi>$. The inner product $<\psi_n|\psi_n>$ is 1; and in the special case where the system before measurement happens to be in an eigenstate $|\psi_n>$, an energy measurement will disclose the particular E_n with certainty (probability 1): otherwise, as noted earlier, $|\psi>$ will give only a range of possible results and their respective probabilities.

Consistently with the preceding discussion, once the energy of the system has been measured and found to be a particular E_n, then, according to QM, the state of the system has been *reduced* from the general state $|\psi>$ to the eigenstate $|\psi_n>$; and a further measurement of energy, made immediately, before the system has time to change, will give E_n with certainty.

The orthodox view of QM is that the failure of $|\psi>$ generally to indicate a particular energy does not mean that there is some incompleteness in what $|\psi>$

tells us about the energy of the system. Rather, unless and until a measurement is made, the system is not considered to have any particular energy, but rather to be in a *superposition* of all the possible energy eigenstates $|\psi_n>$, weighted by the numbers c_n—one reason for this being that the behavior of such systems is most readily understood in terms of the existence of such superpositions and the interaction of their elements. Such a superposition can be written $\Sigma c_n|\psi_n>$, where $c_n = <\psi_n|\psi>$, and $\Sigma|c_n|^2 = 1$. It is different from what is called a *statistical mixture* in classical physics, in that, although a statistical mixture indicates probabilities for a range of states that a system may be in, such a mixture is considered to indicate that the system actually *is* in one of those states but only the probabilities are *known*.

Another feature of QM is that representations of systems involve a minimum indeterminacy of certain *combinations* of observables, such as position and momentum. Broadly, for any $|\psi>$, the product of indeterminacies of position and momentum must always be at least of the order of Planck's constant h, a very small quantity of a variable called action; and this means that if either position or momentum is measured precisely, the other becomes wholly indeterminate. This is Heisenberg's uncertainty principle.

1.2. Indeterminism

Just as classical physics has equations that specify how a physical system will change over time, so also does QM. And these equations are just as deterministic as those of classical physics: according to QM, a QM state $|\psi>$ will change deterministically over time, so long as no measurement of the system is made. However, orthodox QM is nevertheless fundamentally indeterministic, for two reasons.

First, what changes deterministically is a QM state $|\psi>$ which, as we saw, itself involves minimum indeterminacies of certain combinations of observables. The product of indeterminacies of position and momentum of any system must, according to QM, always be at least of the order of h; and application of deterministic laws to initial conditions with such indeterminacies can produce great indeterminacies in outcomes, particularly in complex systems like the human brain.

Second, even in relation to observables made certain by an initial quantum state $|\psi>$, deterministic time-development of $|\psi>$ results in indeterminacy and thus indeterminism in outcomes. Deterministic change of $|\psi>$ will generally change the probabilities $|c_n|^2$ for the various observables that could be found on measurement. For example, if energy has been measured and found to be a particular E_n, and if the system is *not* remeasured immediately but allowed to change, then there will be a deterministic development of the system that will change it away from the particular state $|\psi_n>$ corresponding to the particular energy E_n; and this will mean in turn that, if the energy of the system is subsequently measured, the outcome could be any of a spectrum of E_ns, with the probabilities given by the new values of the $|c_n|^2$s produced by the deterministic development of the system. That is, indeterminism is involved in the reduction of the quantum state that is considered as happening upon measurement.

1.3. Nonlocality

When two QM systems (say $|\psi>$ and $|\phi>$) interact, they become correlated or entangled; and until this entanglement is destroyed, for example by a measurement, the systems cannot accurately be represented separately as superpositions of the possible states of the respective systems, because this would leave out the way in which possible states of $|\psi>$ and $|\phi>$ are correlated with each other. In some cases, measurement of a particular state of $|\psi>$ will mean that $|\phi>$ would certainly be measured to be in a particular state, even though the systems $|\psi>$ and $|\phi>$ are some distance apart.

This can be demonstrated in the case of polarization of photons.

When photons have passed through a polarizer, they are plane-polarized in the direction of the axis of the polarizer (let us say, vertical); and they will then all pass with certainty through another polarizer of the same orientation. However, if instead they encounter a polarizer orientated at an angle θ to the vertical, then only about $\cos^2\theta$ of the photons will pass, and about $\sin^2\theta$ of them will be absorbed. According to QM, the vertically polarized photons are indistinguishable from each other as to their polarization, and it is not determined in advance which will pass the θ-orientated polarizer and which will be absorbed. QM treats each photon as being in a superposition of θ-oriented polarization states $c_1|\theta>$ $+ c_2|\theta + \pi/2>$, where $c_1 = \cos\theta$ and $c_2 = \sin\theta$ and asserts that, if its polarization in the θ direction is measured by means of the θ-orientated polarizer, the probability that it will be measured as $|\theta>$ by passing the polarizer is $\cos^2\theta$, and the probability that it will be measured as $|\theta + \pi/2>$ by not passing is $\sin^2\theta$ (cf. Dirac 1958: 4–7).

When two photons have interacted in a particular way, their polarization states become correlated in such a way that, after the photons separate, they will be measured in a way consistent with their having the same plane polarization. Accordingly, if one photon in such a pair passes through a vertically orientated polarizer, there is certainty that the other would pass through such a polarizer, whether or not this is actually put to the test; and there is $\cos^2\theta$ probability that the other would pass through a θ-orientated polarizer. Experiments conducted by

Alain Aspect in the 1980s, combined with a theorem devised by the late John Bell, showed that it cannot be the case that, prior to measurement, a photon pair will have properties that determine with certainty that its component photons will or will not pass through the polarizers orientated in each of *three* distinct directions (such as vertical, 30° from the vertical, and 60° from the vertical). Since *any* direction can be measured, this means that, even though the photons when measured have spacelike separation, the polarization of one photon, when it is measured, is then instantaneously correlated with, and thus affects or is affected by, the polarization of the other photon (see Aspect et al. 1982b; Bell 1987; Davies and Brown 1986; Mermin 1985). This is an example of the *nonlocality* implicit in QM.

1.4. Measurement and Observers

For most practical applications, the inability of QM to do more than give probabilities of measurements does not matter much, since the indeterminacies and indeterminism of QM are generally at atomic scales, and in fact QM both gives virtual certainties for the behavior of systems comprising large numbers of particles of matter or radiation, and also confirms the substantial accuracy of classical physics for macroscopic systems.

Thus, if one has a collection of radioactive atoms, with a half-life of (say) one year, then the probability that any particular atom will decay within one year is 0.5; and it is generally accepted that all of such atoms are relevantly identical, that there is nothing to distinguish those that will decay within a year (or indeed, within a second) from those that will not. Yet, there is near-certainty as to the relative frequencies of decay and non-decay of large numbers of such atoms over a period of time; namely, that very close to one half of (say) one billion atoms will decay within one year, and one half will not. One may compare this with the tossing of coins. In 10 tosses of an unbiased coin, the probability that there will be between 4 and 6 heads (5 heads ± 20%) is about 0.66; while in 50 tosses, the probability that there will be between 20 and 30 heads (25 heads ± 20%) is about 0.93. In a billion tosses, the probability that there will be a half a billion heads ± 20% (or even ± 1%) is very close indeed to 1.

According to QM, the regularity of the behavior of macroscopic objects depends on the high probabilities of relative frequencies in the behavior of vast numbers of particles. For most nonconscious macroscopic systems in most circumstances, the probabilities amount to virtual certainties, so that for ordinary purposes we can safely proceed on the assumption that the middle-sized objects that we deal with in our everyday lives do exist, independently of being observed, in definite positions and with definite motion and do behave in accordance with the laws of classical physics.

However, on a theoretical approach, there is a considerable mystery. The fact remains that these ordinary middle-sized objects are composed of atoms that generally do not have determinate position or motion or energy, and in respect of which the most fundamental laws of physics assert a determinate position or motion or energy only in terms of a probability of observation.

QM suggests that, prior to measurement, a system will generally have no definite energy but be in a superposition of energy eigenstates; that measurement of energy will disclose a particular energy associated with a particular energy eigenstate; and that, immediately after measurement, the system will be in this particular energy eigenstate. How, then, is it that measurement brings about this reduction of a superposition of eigenstates to one particular eigenstate? This is the measurement problem of QM. It is a problem because the mathematics of QM, in dealing with the way systems change over time, deals only with deterministic development in the absence of measurement and does not indicate how measurement can select out one element of a superposition.

Schrodinger's cat is a cliché, but it is a graphic illustration of the measurement problem. Readers will be familiar with the thought experiment that Erwin Schrodinger (1983: 157) described in the following words:

> A cat is penned up in a steel chamber, along with the following diabolical device (which must be secured against direct interference by the cat); in a Geiger counter there is a tiny bit of radioactive substance, so small that perhaps in the course of one hour one of the atoms decays, but also, with equal probability, perhaps none; if it happens, the counter tube discharges and through a relay releases a hammer which shatters a small flask of hydrocyanic acid.

We suppose that the device switches off after one hour, and some time later the experimenter opens the chamber. We suppose that the relevant region of the world is divided into three parts: (1) the system actually observed (the radioactive substance); (2) the measuring instrument (the Geiger counter, hammer, and acid; the cat; and the steel chamber); (3) the actual observer.

According to QM, after one hour, the radioactive substance (unmeasured) would be in a superposition of states

$$c_1|\text{not decayed}> + c_2|\text{decayed}>,$$

where $|c_1|^2 = |c_2|^2 = 0.5$. If one treats (1) alone as developing according to the rules of QM, and the whole of (2) and (3) as measuring (1), then (1) would in fact be measured as having decayed if and when the Geiger counter discharged, and otherwise as not having decayed. However, if one treats (1) and part of (2) (say, the Geiger counter, hammer, and acid) as developing according to the rules of QM, then the state of this system (unmeasured) after one hour would be

$$c_1|\text{not decayed, flask unbroken}> + c_2|\text{decayed, flask broken}>,$$

and this system would be measured by the state of the cat, alive and dead. And if one treats (1) and the whole of (2) as developing according to the rules of QM (as one can), then the state of this system after one hour would be the superposition

$$c_1|\text{not decayed, cat alive}> + c_2|\text{decayed, cat dead}>,$$

and it would remain in this state (apart from possible phase changes, which need not concern us) until the observer opened the chamber and observed either a live or dead cat. One can go even farther, treating the observer as part of the measured system, which is developing in accordance with the rules of QM, and introduce, say, a supervisor as the measuring part of the world. On that approach, when the observer opens the box, the system would go into the superposition

$$c_1|\text{not decayed, cat alive, live cat observed}>$$
$$+ c_2|\text{decayed, cat dead, dead cat observed}>,$$

and measurement would take place only when the supervisor became aware of what the observer discovered when he opened the chamber.

Von Neumann dealt with this problem in his 1932 treatise on the mathematics of QM (1955: 417–45) with his "projection postulate," which suggests that, in measurement, two things happen: (1) the QM superposition $\Sigma c_n|\psi>$ becomes a classical mixture, so that only one of the $|\psi_n>$s actually obtains, with probability $|c_n|^2$; and (2) this particular $|\psi_n>$ becomes known to the observer. He called this process 1, so as to distinguish it from the deterministic development of systems, in the absence of measurement, which he called process 2. He gave no explanation, in QM terms, of how or why process 1 occurred in measurement: rather, he argued that no such explanation was necessary, because it did not matter how much of (1), (2) and (3) one treated as the measured system—the ultimate observer would always detect a particular $|\psi_n>$ in system (1), with probability $|c_n|^2$, whether this be considered as brought about by an immediate measuring instrument (such as a Geiger counter), or by a higher level measuring device (such as live or dead cat), or by an intermediate observer (such as a person who opens the steel chamber and reports what he sees to a supervisor).

Now, if one accepts that physical theories such as QM are no more than mathematical models that enable accurate predictions of observations and measurements, then one may well be satisfied with this. That line is taken, for example, by Stephen Hawking in *A Brief History of Time* (1988: 9, 139); and he thereby evades the tricky questions concerning his central concept of imaginary time, as well as any necessity of even mentioning the measurement problem of QM. However, I think most of us expect more of science than mere prediction: we want to know about what things exist and how they actually work. And it is difficult to sustain a consistent "models" approach. Hawking does not do so: contrary to his statements about models, most of his book in fact consists of assertions about what things exist and how they work (see, for example, ibid.: 10, 13, 168–69, 174–75).

Furthermore, since the laws of QM enable more accurate predictions of observations than do the laws of classical physics, as well as accounting for all the predictions that follow from the laws of classical physics, it is reasonable to believe that we should get a *better* indication of what things exist and how they work from the laws of QM than from the laws of classical physics; so that it is reasonable to look for an explanation of what is really going on when measurement of a quantum system occurs.

1.5. Solving the Measurement Problem?

There are various proposals for interpreting or modifying QM so as to dispense with reference to observation, without surrendering to Hawking's "models" approach. Three broad alternatives can be identified.

First, some proposals acknowledge that QM is substantially accurate in its account of process 2 (deterministic development) and seek to account for process 1 (reduction to a single eigenstate) as a purely objective physical process (see, for example, Ghirardi et al. 1986; Penrose 1989: 367–71). However, no single one of these has wide support, and it appears that any such account would alter the statistical predictions of QM, which are well confirmed (see generally d'Espagnat 1989). Further discussion is beyond the scope of this essay.

Second, there is the suggestion that, although QM's account of process 2 is accurate, there is in fact *no* process 1. This "many worlds" interpretation of QM asserts that process 2 development correlates the system being measured and the measuring part of the world (including any conscious observers) into a superposition that associates each possible state of the measured system with a relative state of the measuring part of the world, and that there is in fact no selection from this superposition of observers, measuring devices, and possible states of the measured system: all elements of this superposition are taken as not merely possibilities but actualities, and all of them are taken to continue in existence after measurement. Nonlocality is affirmed, but indeterminism and observer-participation are denied. This version of QM has been supported by distinguished cosmologists (such as Barrow and Tipler 1988), science writers (such as Gribbin 1985), and philosophers (such as Lockwood 1989). Despite many criticisms, it is still advocated in Deutsch and Lockwood (1994) and Deutsch (1998) and seemingly approved in Weinberg (1993: 65, 186, 224) and Gell-Mann (1994: 137–65). Since this approach could be seen as a way of undermining the support free will may have from the observer-dependence and indeterminism of QM, I will take a little time in the next section to show why I believe that this version of QM is untenable.

Third, there are suggestions that QM is inaccurate or incomplete in its account of *both* process 2 *and* process 1, and that there are "hidden variables" underlying the probabilities of QM. The most developed candidate for "completing" QM in this way, and thus removing the need to postulate measurement or observation, is the theory of the late David Bohm, which, like the many-worlds interpretation, affirms nonlocality; but it could be seen as denying indeterminism and observer-participation, so I will say a little about it also in section 2.

I have not in this review mentioned an interpretation of QM that is said to be gaining acceptance in recent years, the so-called "consistent histories" interpretation (see Whitaker 1996: 292–97; Omnès 1994). I find it less than clear; and I believe that, if it is not an objective reduction theory like that of Ghiradi and his collaborators, then it is really (as suggested in Gell-Mann 1994: 138–53) a variation of the many-worlds version, so that it can escape the objections to that version only by retreating to the "models" approach.

Thus, none of the proposals has general acceptance; and it remains a reasonable possibility that, while QM enables superbly accurate predictions of the *outcomes* of observation and gives a better indication than classical physics of what things exist and how they work, it does not and cannot give a precise account of what happens in the *process* of observation or indeed in the *absence* of observation. This leaves as a possibility that no theory invoking mathematical laws can do so, which suggests in turn that reference to observations may always remain a fundamental feature of basic physical theory, and thus that matter is to some degree dependent on mind. As we will see, this approach is advocated by Henry Stapp (and see also d'Espagnat 1989).[3]

2. Many-Worlds and Bohm

2.1. Many-Worlds

According to the many-worlds or relative state version of QM, when the observer opens the steel chamber containing Schrodinger's cat, the superposition

c_1|not decayed, cat alive, live cat observed>
+ c_2|decayed, cat dead, dead cat observed>

does actually obtain: so that there are thereafter two instances of the observer, one that sees the live cat and one that sees the dead cat, each unaware of the other. No element of the superposition is eliminated. This (it is said) is what the mathematics of QM indicates, unless one introduces the unexplained process 1; and it cannot be disproved, because there is no possibility of either version of the observer being able to detect the existence or nonexistence of the other.

In order to show what I believe to be the absurdity of this view, I will first suggest a modification of the Schrodinger's cat thought experiment. By reducing the amount of radioactive material, and having the device switch itself off after (say) two minutes, the probability of an atom decaying and of the cat being killed is reduced from 0.5 to 0.01. The experiment is performed 100 times. According to the many-worlds version, each time the steel chamber is opened, there occur two instances of the observer, of which one observes a live cat, and the other observes a dead cat. After the experiment has been performed twice, there will be 4 observer histories: observer sees live cat, then live cat; observer sees live cat, then dead cat; observer sees dead cat, then live cat; observer sees dead cat, then dead cat. After 100 performances, there will be 2^{100} observer histories. And just as, after 2 performances, two of the four histories showed an equal number of observations of live and dead cats, so also, after 100 performances, the 2^{100} histories will be grouped, in a bell-shaped curve, around results showing equal numbers of observations of live and dead cats. QM would predict that the histories should be grouped around results showing 99 observations of live cats for every one observation of a dead cat.

We can see what has happened. In standard QM, the probabilities 0.99 and 0.01, respectively, for each observation of a live or dead cat are reflected (1) in the high degree of confidence (approaching certainty) that one can have, in making each observation, that it will be of a live cat and not of a dead one; and (2) in the distribution of results over many observations. Both (1) and (2) depend upon one of the possible results occurring on each occasion, and the other *not* occurring: so that by postulating that both possible results always actually occur, the many-worlds interpretation excludes these reflections of probability.

This line of argument has been noted by advocates of many worlds (see, for example, Graham 1973; Lockwood 1989: chapters 12 and 13); although surprisingly it is entirely ignored in Deutsch (1998), a prominent book that advocates a worldview based on the many-worlds approach. Three main responses have been suggested: (A) that probabilities of individual occurrences are reflected in probabilities of relative frequencies, and worlds split only in respect of relative frequencies; (B) that probabilities are reflected in the number of worlds or histories produced when splitting occurs; and (C) that (in some sense or other) some of the worlds or histories that actually occur are more or less probable and so should (in some way or other) count more or less than others. None of these is acceptable.

Response (A), suggested by Graham (1973), notes that the regularities in our world are due to the relative frequencies of huge numbers of quantum events; so that, except in those rare cases where individual quantum events are observed, there is no need to suggest that worlds or histories split for individual quantum events. Accordingly, it is said, for all practical purposes, the many-worlds approach can take account of probability.

However, even though QM does indicate very high probabilities for relative frequencies consistent with the regular behavior of matter, it also gives finite, albeit very low, probabilities for other relative frequencies that are inconsistent with such behavior—just as ordinary probability theory gives very high probabilities for about 50 percent of heads in a billion tosses of an unbiased coin, and finite, albeit very low, probabilities for results widely diverging from this (including for 2, 1, or even 0 heads in a billion tosses). On Graham's view, there must be an actual world or history for each possibility, including those with as little probability as 0 heads in a billion tosses (see Squires 1994: 203).

Turning to response (B), we could suggest that, in my modified Schrodinger's cat thought experiment, each time the steel chamber is opened, there occur 100 instances of the observer, one of which sees a dead cat and 99 of which see a live cat. Then, after 100 performances, the 100^{100} histories will be grouped around results showing 99 observations of live cats for every one observation of a dead cat, appropriately reflecting the statistical predictions of QM.

However, it is crazy to suggest that the *number* of worlds or histories created in measurement should depend on what happen to be the numerical probabilities of the possible outcomes of the particular measurement that is made—particularly when some observables can take values anywhere within a continuous range, with no limit in principle to the precision of measurement, and thus no limit to the number of worlds or histories created (on this approach) by measurement. In fact, as pointed out by Squires (1991: 285), there will be deviations from the predictions of quantum theory to a degree that increases with time *unless* the number of worlds or histories is *infinite*; and this is just what is proposed by Lockwood (1989) and discussed by Albert (1992). According to the approach discussed by Albert, associated with each observer are an infinite number of minds, and QM probabilities of the result of any measurement are reflected in the proportion of minds for each possible result.

This overcomes the problem of determining the number of possible worlds or histories—but has absurdities of its own. Suppose one takes a piece of radioactive substance with a billion particles, having a half-life of one year, and sets up a Geiger counter so that it will signal any decays and display the number of decays on a dial. After one year, assuming no malfunctions, the probability that the dial will show no decays is one in $2^{1000000000}$: yet on the approach under consideration there will be an infinity of minds associated with an observer who then reads the dial, which observe that the dial shows no decays. (Infinity divided by $2^{1000000000}$ is still infinity!)

So what this means is that QM, devised to explain the regular behavior of objects in our world, on the basis of the virtual certainty of the statistics of the behavior of vast numbers of particles, leads, in this many-worlds version, to the postulation of the *actual existence* of myriad infinities of worlds or histories or minds, for which there is no such regular behavior, because the statistical predictions of QM do not hold good; indeed, in Albert's version, an infinity of minds for every possible outcome of every quantum process, however wildly improbable (one in $2^{1000000000}$, or one in $2^{1000000000}$ raised to the power of $2^{1000000000}$, and so on). The statistics of QM, and the regularity of the behavior of matter with which we are familiar, are then supposedly explained by the ratios between all these infinities. This is not merely metaphysical baggage, as is sometimes said of the many-worlds view, it is an utter absurdity.

Response (C) is that the probabilities indicated by QM are reflected in the probabilities of the different worlds or histories; so that, in relation to my modified Schrodinger's cat thought experiment, the great majority of the 2^{100} observer histories, reflecting probabilities for dead as against live cats much in excess of one in one hundred, are themselves highly improbable and can be discounted accordingly (see DeWitt and Graham 1973: 163).

By suggesting that one world or mind for each possible outcome is enough, this response avoids the absurdity of postulating an infinity of worlds or minds for each possible outcome; but this deprives the central concept of probability of any meaning. Since every possible outcome *actually does occur* in *just one* world or for *just one* mind, no meaning can be given to what are said to be the different probabilities of the different outcomes.

Thus, none of the three responses answers the probability argument. Standard QM asserts that in measurement on each occasion only one result actually occurs, and the other possible results do not occur, with these actual occurrences and nonoccurrences over many measurements reflecting the statistical predictions of QM. The many-worlds version asserts that, on every occasion, every possibility actually occurs—so that the probabilities of QM cannot be expressed in the statistics of actual occurrences and nonoccurrences *because there are never any nonoccurrences*. This makes nonsense of QM. So I contend that, of all the main interpretations of QM, the many-worlds version can most confidently be dismissed.

2.2. The Bohm Version

Although I introduced Bohm's version of QM as identifying "hidden variables," Bohm himself, in his last comprehensive statement of his interpretation, preferred to call it an *ontological* interpretation (Bohm and Hiley 1993: 2), because his theory was concerned with what actually exists and happens, in contrast with orthodox QM, which as we have seen relates to measurements or observations and thus can be considered as directed primarily toward *epistemology*.

One central feature of Bohm's interpretation is that particles of matter such as electrons are considered as always having a well-defined position, independently of any observation or measurement: in this respect Bohm's version is like classical physics. However, the motion of the particles is affected, not merely by forces recognized by classical physics, but also by a force due to what Bohm calls a quantum field. This field is unlike classical fields, particularly in that its effect is considered to be independent of the strength of the field but totally dependent on its form, with the result that this effect does not decrease with distance.

The quantum field proposed by Bohm is such that the position of individual particles cannot be controlled or predicted, and that in ordinary circumstances the statistical results of orthodox QM will be produced. In certain circumstances, the Bohm system could give rise to statistics different from those of orthodox QM, but it has not yet been possible to investigate those circumstances (see Bohm and Hiley 1993: 345–48).

The Bohm interpretation is like orthodox QM in embracing nonlocality: in situations like those dealt with by the Aspect experiments, the quantum field is seen as able to instantaneously correlate the polarization of distant particle pairs. As noted above, it is unlike orthodox QM in making no reference to observation or measurement.

As regards indeterminism, the interpretation could be considered deterministic *if* it were accepted as final and comprehensive. However, Bohm took the view that "nature in its total reality is unlimited, not merely quantitatively, but also qualitatively, in its depth and subtlety of its laws and processes" (Bohm and Hiley 1993: 321; compare Bohm 1984). For this reason, Bohm claimed that reality is neither absolutely deterministic nor absolutely indeterministic, but "somewhere between and beyond [these views], as indeed it is beyond what can be captured in thought, which is always limited to some abstraction from the totality" (Bohm and Hiley 1993: 324). So Bohm himself does not rule out the possibility of indeterministic free will, supported by postclassical physics.[4]

3. MARGINALIZING QM

As noted earlier, the possible relevance of QM to consciousness in general and free will in particular has been taken up again over the last couple of decades. In general and overall, it seems that philosophers and neuroscientists have tended to dismiss this approach, and that its principal advocates have been a few physicists and just one neuroscientist. I will look briefly at the grounds on which QM is dismissed, and also at what two prominent philosophers have said about the relevance of QM to free will; and then, in section 4, at the views of some scientists who argue that QM is relevant at least to consciousness, if not also free will.

3.1. Standard Arguments

As I have said, (1) the orthodox interpretation of QM involves a measure of irreducible indeterminism in the development over time of systems in the world. Also, (2) QM contradicts the causal locality and reductionism of classical physics which is still generally assumed in the broader scientific orthodoxy, thus opening up the possibility that an agent's conscious mental activity could act holistically in exercising a causal influence not fully explicable from a physical viewpoint. And (3) the mathematics of QM links not objective events but *observations* of events; so that the participation of conscious subjects is presupposed, and the total dependence of consciousness upon matter, which is assumed in the scientific orthodoxy, is thus put into question.

These considerations have so far had little effect on the orthodox scientific worldview.

The first is dealt with by acknowledging that there may be some indeterminism in the world, but suggesting that this is of little moment and in particular does not allow for any exercise of free will independent of physical causation. Any indeterminism (it is said) occurs at levels of scale in size and time which cannot be relevant to any supposed exercise of free will; and in any case, the indeterminism involves only randomness, which (as shown by Hume) would not be conducive to efficacious human choice.

The second consideration, combining nonlocality with holism, is generally ignored, or at best dismissed as again occurring at scales and in circumstances irrelevant to free will. Although nonlocality sits uneasily in various ways with the theory of relativity, it is in fact generally accepted that quantum nonlocality does not permit the transmission of a detectable signal at faster than the speed of light—so that for practical purposes it might seem that locality of causation is maintained. The scientific orthodoxy, it is said, is thus not threatened by this exotic implication of QM which is so remote from anything significant for the operations of the brain.

The third consideration, the presupposition of observers, is assumed to be a temporary feature of QM, which will be supplanted when QM is better understood. As we have seen, there are various theories about QM in which the observer is not presupposed; and although none of these has general acceptance, it is reasonable (it is said) to believe that the wholly implausible idea that matter is to some extent dependent on mind will be rooted out of QM.

Philosopher David Chalmers has jokingly called the project of relating QM to consciousness a strategy for the minimization of mysteries (McCrone 1994): QM is a mystery, consciousness is a mystery, so by saying they are the same mystery, you have reduced the number of mysteries by one.

3.2. Dennett

In his major work on free will, *Elbow Room* (1984), Daniel Dennett dismisses QM as irrelevant to free will. He points out (77n) that QM indeterminism would not involve macroscopic indeterminism of human action unless there happened to be something of the nature of natural Geiger counters in our brains, so as to amplify QM indeterminism to the requisite macroscopic scale; but he adds that in any event it is difficult to discern the point of such mechanisms. His reason is that any possible advantage of random processes, for example in throwing up alternatives for acceptance or rejection, could equally well be served by pseudo-random processes such as those used by present-day computers (see ibid.: 120, 151).

He also makes the point (ibid.: 136) that, if free will and responsibility depended upon our actions being "the magnified effect of quantum-level indeterminacies occurring in our brains," then it is extremely unlikely, given the complexity of our brains even at the molecular level, that we could ever know whether any particular act was or was not one for which the person was responsible—and this, he says, is absurd.

3.3. Honderich

Ted Honderich is another philosopher who has considered QM in relation to the free will question, and concluded it is irrelevant.

He makes the point (Honderich 1993: 37) that, if someone is to be responsible for his or her mental state following what is supposed to be a free choice, then that mental state must follow reliably from the mental processes involved in the choice; yet for indeterministic free will, the mental processes involved in the choice itself must not follow reliably from their precursors. Even then, he says, QM only postulates random or chance events, and we cannot be responsible for chance events.

He also advances an argument (ibid.: 61–66) to the effect that QM does not really provide a sound basis for believing in indeterminism, which could be relevant to human choices. He argues that the success of the formalism of QM does not guarantee the truth of particular interpretations of QM, that in any event much that QM suggests not to be deterministic effects are not the sort of thing that determinists claim to be deterministic effects, and that the lack of evidence for chance events in the ordinary macroscopic world makes it reasonable to doubt that QM really could produce such events.

4. QM and Consciousness

4.1. Penrose

As mentioned earlier, the most prominent advocate in recent years of the relevance of QM to consciousness is mathematician Roger Penrose.

A central plank of Penrose's argument is the nature of human rationality, and the capacity of humans to solve problems one cannot solve by applying rule-based procedures or algorithms. This capacity, he argues, requires *understanding*, which in turn requires consciousness. He supports this by reference to Godel's theorem, developing an argument previously advanced by philosopher John Lucas (1970). Penrose (1994) contains a very extensive discussion and elaboration of this argument.

Penrose then asks what kind of physical process could possibly support non-algorithmic rationality. He points out that both classical physics and von Neumann's process 2 in QM are algorithmic: in each case, time-development proceeds strictly in accordance with definite rules in a way that is, in principle at least, computable. However, von Neumann's process 1 in QM is different. According to standard QM, it is purely random within probability parameters established by the process 2 development; but Penrose suggests both that standard QM is inadequate in its account of process 1, and that an adequate account of process 1 may involve nonalgorithmic development of the type required for consciousness and human rationality.

Penrose argues that QM needs a new account of process 1, the reduction of the quantum state, as an objective process—what he calls OR, or objective reduction. He suggests that both nonalgorithmic rationality and consciousness are associated with nonlocal co-ordinated objective reductions occurring over extended regions of the brain.

Now it would seem that such nonlocal quantum events, if they are to be associated with conscious experiences, would require QM entanglement or *coherence* extending over substantial areas of the brain for periods of time of the order of at least (say) one-tenth of a second; so Penrose considers whether there are any features of the brain that could support the spread and duration of entanglement to that extent. And he adopts a suggestion, first made by anesthetist Stuart Hameroff, that structures within the neurons of the brain called *microtubules* could isolate quantum states in such a way as to do just that.

On the question of free will, Penrose believes that the nonalgorithmic processes of his theory could make free will possible, but that such processes could also be compatible with determinism. He gives a simple example (Penrose 1997) of a "toy universe" in which each step of time-development depends on whether a plane can be tiled by a shape determined by the previous time-step: such a universe would be deterministic, but its development would not be computable by application of algorithms.

4.2. Stapp

Another prominent advocate of the relevance of QM to consciousness and free will is the physicist Henry Stapp, a collaborator of QM pioneer Wolfgang Pauli. Unlike Penrose, Stapp does not suggest that QM is in need of significant modification but rather embraces QM's reference to observation as the basis for a theory of the relationship and interaction of mind and matter.

Stapp adopts the general approach of von Neumann and Wigner, suggesting that the mathematical representations of QM do not refer to mind-independent observable properties that exist independently of observers: rather, they refer to objectively existing *informational structures*, carrying the maximum information that *can be had* about the world. The process 1 of von Neumann can then be understood as *changing* in that maximum information, through measurement and observation. This is not the same as saying that the observer's consciousness of the result of measurement has the physical effect of changing the otherwise mind-independent physical state of the observed system, as is sometimes said about this type of approach: it is the more subtle view that the representations never do precisely specify mind-independent physical states at all but rather specify the maximum information that can be had about them. Nor is it the same as saying that there are no mind-independent physical states: the informational structures, and indeed physical states underlying them, are treated as objectively existing, and not dependent on being actually known by any particular mind or consciousness.

Stapp believes that classical physics provides us generally with very close approximations to the observable properties and functioning of mind-independent macroscopic physical entities in the world, including human brains; and that if one is to show that QM plays a significant role in the functioning of the brain, an explanation is required as to how this can be, given what we know about the conditions obtaining in the brain. In Stapp (1993: ch. 6), he postulates that a function of brain activity is to process information about the world coming in from sensors, in order to produce a "template for action" that can give rise to appropriate action. One feature of the complex dynamic systems studied in chaos theory is that, while minute differences in initial conditions can give rise to huge differences in outcomes, calculation of outcomes often shows high probabilities for outcomes approximating closely to a small number of states, called *attractors*. Stapp suggests (1998: 243) that this may be so for the brain, with the various attractors representing the various possible templates for action. He goes on to analyze the effect of Heisenberg uncertainties in the position and momentum of presynaptic calcium ions and concludes that this involves uncertainties as to discharge of neurotransmitters, which in turn breeds myriad different possibilities, each of which could be expected to evolve into something very close to one of a small number of different attractors. The selection between the attractors could then occur by a "reduction of the wave packet," that is, by a process 1 reduction of the quantum state. Stapp concludes (ibid.: 244):

> It should be emphasized that this effect is generated simply by the Heisenberg uncertainty principle, and hence cannot be simply dismissed or ignored within a rational scientific approach. The effect is in no way dependent upon macroscopic quantum coherence, and is neither wiped out nor diminished by thermal noise. The shower of different macroscopic possibilities created by this effect can be reduced to the single actual macroscopic reality that we observe only by a reduction of the wave packet.

Thus, Stapp argues, whereas classical physics has no room for consciousness and offers no possibility of any explanation of or role for consciousness, the picture of the world provided by QM incorporates consciousness in a natural and parsimonious way.

On the relevance of all this to free will, Stapp does not question that the outcomes of process 1 reductions are random within the probability parameters given by relevant quantum states; but he points out that outcomes depend very much upon *what measurements* are made and *with what frequency*. For example, according to QM, there are cases where the probability for a particular outcome increases over time, in the absence of measurement, in such a way that the probability of that outcome can be made to approach zero by sufficiently frequent observations: this is called the quantum Zeno effect (or "a watched pot never boils": see Sudbery 1986: 192–93). Although of course we do not deliberately select what "measurements" to make of the quantum states of our brains, our intentional actions could make measurements that constrain outcomes in this sort of way.

4.3. Eccles

The last advocate of the relevance of QM to consciousness that I will consider is the late John Eccles, a prominent neuroscientist and Nobel laureate. He has advanced (Eccles 1994) a hypothesis that focuses on the triggering of the discharge of neurotransmitters, giving rather more anatomical detail than Stapp.

It is well known that the neocortex of the human brain contains thousands of millions of nerve cells called neurons. Each neuron consists of a body or soma, fibers called dendrites through which signals are received from other neurons, and a fiber called an axon through which it sends signals to other neurons. The axon itself ends in many branches, and these branches terminate in synaptic knobs or boutons, each of which closely abuts the surface of a spine from a dendrite, or of the soma of the receiving neuron: each such area of functional contact is called a synapse. When a neuron signal reaches a bouton, discharge of neurotransmitters (or *exocytosis*) may occur, the probability of such occurrence being of the order of 0.25. If exocytosis occurs, neurotransmitters cross the synaptic space or cleft to the receiving neuron and there make an excitatory or inhibitory contribution to the firing of that neuron. Whether or not a neuron fires will depend upon the total of such contributions, through all the synapses of its dendrites and soma, which may number several thousand for a single neuron.

Something like one-half of the neurons of the neocortex have pyramid-shaped bodies and dendrites ascending from their apexes towards the surface of the brains. As they ascend, these dendrites become closely grouped in bundles or clusters, which comprise dendrites from about 70 to 100 neurons. The dendrites from each neuron have about 2,000 spine synapses, some as many as 5,000, so that each cluster has over 100,000 spine synapses. Eccles contends that these clusters of dendrites, which he calls dendrons, are basic anatomical units of the cortex.

Eccles gives close consideration to the structure and contents of the presynaptic boutons. Each bouton generally contains something like 2,000 vesicles, quantal packages of neurotransmitter molecules, with each vesicle containing about 5,000 to 10,000 molecules. At any time, about 30 to 50 of these vesicles are located in a grid that adjoins the synapse, and thus are ready for exocytosis. When a neuron signal reaches the bouton, one (but no more than one) of these vesicles may discharge the whole of its contents into the synaptic cleft; and this happens only with a probability of the order of 0.25, or one in four. It is Eccles's contention that this probability is an indeterministic quantum mechanical effect, and not merely an expression of our ignorance of hidden variables. His hypothesis is that the self affects brain processes by momentarily increasing the probabilities of exocytosis in all of the 100,000 or so boutons of a "dendron." Chapter 9 of Eccles (1994) contains calculations that suggest that the quantities of energy, distance, and time involved in the process are sufficiently small for quantum mechanical effects to be significant; and also that conservation laws would not be violated. On the other hand, simultaneously increasing the probabilities of exocytosis in as many as 100,000 boutons could macroscopically affect brain processes and thereby contribute to the realization of subjective intentions.

Now Eccles advocated a dualist theory, according to which there is a conscious spiritual self distinct from the brain; and he proposed the hypothesis I have outlined in order to account for interaction between the spiritual self and the physical brain. As noted later, I believe there are very powerful objections to that kind of dualism. However, the central thesis of Eccles's book, the proposed mechanism for interaction between the self and the brain, could equally explain how the mental aspect of the brain-and-mind can contribute to physical processes without violation of any physical law; and it does stand as a plausible hypothesis as to how quantum mechanical indeterminism could give rise to alternatives for choice.

5. CONCLUSION

I will conclude with a brief statement of some views of my own.

First, I agree with Stapp that classical physics has no place and no role for consciousness. If the development over time of the physical world proceeds according to physical laws that admit of no alternatives and engage with physical quantities of mass, electric charge, distance, momentum, and so on, then consciousness would seem to be an accidental superfluity, having no causal role other than just going along with the developments required by physical laws that engage with physical states and events upon which consciousness, on this approach, supervenes.

Take pain, for example. Pain has useful functions that explain why evolution has selected in its favor: namely, it draws our attention to possible damage to ourselves and gives us a strong motive to take steps to remedy it and to avoid damage in the future. Yet if our actions were based upon computation-like procedures governed by classical physics, then the pain would be a superfluity. A computer does not need pain, or any other consciously felt incentive, to make it run in accordance with its program, as required by physical laws of nature; so why would we?

Second, I agree with Penrose that our rationality is not merely algorithmic. Of course, it can plausibly be argued that, although our rationality cannot be fully explained in terms of known algorithmic rules, such as those of logic, mathematics, and probability, nevertheless it is entirely algorithmic or computational, in the sense that it uses computational procedures unknown to us but selected for their efficacy over millions of years of evolution. But our rationality seems to have much more general application than this argument would suggest; and it also seems to depend on consciousness, in a way for which this argument has no explanation (see Hodgson 1991: ch. 5; 1995; 1999).

Certainly, our brains perform staggering computations, outside consciousness, such as the preconscious calculations necessary to achieve three-dimensional vision and apparent stability of a viewed scene despite voluntary movements of head and eyes, and those necessary for walking on uneven ground and for catching balls. Compared with these nonconscious feats, our conscious efforts may in fact seem paltry: conscious performance of such tasks as simple mental arithmetic is clumsy and prone to error, conscious reasoning generally is riddled with fallacies and biases, and conscious awareness of a crisis can bring on irrational panic. One might therefore have expected that evolution, which has given us both our prodigious nonconscious computing capabilities *and* our fallible conscious processes, would have made sure that, for really important decisions, and especially in a crisis, our consciousness would be shut off, in order that our nonconscious processes could work away without interference to find the solution and give effect to it. Yet, as we know, the reverse is true. When faced with an important decision, and particularly in a crisis, our conscious attention is automatically brought to bear, so that we cannot help addressing the problem with full consciousness. This strongly suggests that something about our conscious processes gives them an advantage over wholly nonconscious computations, which cannot be explained in terms of algorithms that could be carried out unconsciously.

Third, I believe that the locality of causation entailed by classical physics is a further reason why classical physics must be inadequate to account for consciousness. Whatever else consciousness involves, it involves a bringing together or chunking, into broadly unified experiences, of multitudes of events in extended regions of the brain; and the occurrence of these experiences, and any causal roles they may have, possess a nonlocal character beyond anything that can be explained in terms of classical physics or indeed any science that assumes the correctness of classical physics. Current attempts to solve this "binding problem" of consciousness in terms of co-ordinated 40-Hertz oscillations seem to me to be hopelessly inadequate, so long as these oscillations are considered as arising and having effects attributable to the local causation of classical physics (see Hodgson 1996).

Fourth, for all these reasons it is very strange to me that so many scientists and philosophers are dogmatic in their dismissal of the relevance of QM to consciousness, and in their insistence that consciousness can be explained in terms of classical physics.

Their strongest argument is that, in systems as massive, hot, and wet as neurons of the brain, any quantum entanglement and indeterminacies would be eliminated within times far shorter than those necessary for conscious experiences; and that this is well and good, because any significant quantum indeterminism would only prejudice rationality. Recent calculations by Max Tegmark have suggested that any macroscopic quantum entanglement in the brain would be destroyed in times of the order of 10^{-13} to 10^{-20} seconds (see Seife 2000).

However, Tegmark's arguments have been criticized by Hameroff and Hagan (2000), while Stapp (2000) claims they do not affect his position. In any event, even if arguments such as Tegmark's were to show that orthodox QM cannot assist in explaining consciousness, they would not overcome what I say is the clear inadequacy of classical physics to do so. And arguments to the effect that indeterminism must prejudice rationality miss the points that our rationality seems to be nonalgorithmic, that the operation of QM in the brain may permit nonalgorithmic rational processes in ways such as those suggested by Penrose and Stapp, and that, if there were any ways in which quantum processes could be used to advantage in the brain, it is likely that evolution would have found them.

Fifth, plausible accounts can be given of how nonalgorithmic rationality could give rise to free will.

I do not believe this can be achieved by a dualistic theory such as that of Eccles, which raises the question, exactly what is the self's contribution to actions and decisions? Eccles is content to postulate that the self's willing of intentional action can, by the mechanism he describes, be effected by the physical brain. What he does not consider is whether, and if so to what extent, the physical brain is involved in forming the intentions in the first place. If Eccles were to say that intentions are formed by the self, without assistance from related brain activity, then further questions arise. How can it do so? What is the self's (presumably nonphysical) structure that enables it to form intentions, and why does it need to have such a complicated brain to do no more than put intentions into effect? On the other hand, if Eccles were to say that physical brain processes are involved in forming intentions, then he would have to identify the respective roles in this of the brain and the self: if the self cannot form intentions on its own, exactly what can it do, what is its distinctive contribution? And as before, one may also ask how the self makes this contribution: what structure does it have to enable it to do so?

For such reasons I do not accept outright dualism but say rather that the brain-and-mind (or brain-and-self) is a physical-and-mental whole, whose causal properties are not fully captured by the physical aspect.

The approaches of Penrose and Stapp, on the other hand, could support an account of rational indeterministic free will. Stapp, for example, treats process 1 reduction as involving two elements not included in process 2 deterministic evolution: the selection and application of a particular "measurement" and the partially random result. The first of these elements may as a practical matter determine the outcome; and that element may occur as "willed" by the whole prechoice conscious state associated with the prechoice physical state of the brain. This in turn would provide a way in which the totality of conscious experiences may contribute nonrandomly to outcomes not predetermined by physical laws of nature.

For a fuller statement of my views, I refer readers to Hodgson (1991; 1996; 1999): in the last of these, I argue at length that the supposed dichotomy between determinism and randomness, relied on by Dennett and Honderich among many others, is a fallacy. And for a careful presentation of a view similar to mine, I refer readers to Kane (1996a). In chapters 8 to 10, Kane endorses four of the key contentions that I have advocated in my writings:

1. The contention that, prior to a choice being made, an agent's reasons are characteristically inconclusive, inter alia because they are incommensurable; and that it is the agent's choice or decision that resolves the issue (1991: 133–35; 1999). Kane (1996a) endorses the idea of incommensurability at p. 167; and at p. 133, he postulates that, in situations where an agent has to choose between alternative courses of action and has reasons or motives supporting each alternative, the agent *makes* one set of reasons or motives prevail over the others by *deciding*.

2. The contention that what the physical perspective can only treat as a chance occurrence may correctly be seen from the mental or experiential perspective as an agent's choice (1991: 389–93, 444–47; 1999). Kane says (1996a, 147), that from the physical perspective, *free will looks like chance*, since from a physical perspective, there is just an indeterministic chaotic process with a probabilistic outcome, whereas experientially considered, the process is the agent's effort of will and the single outcome is the agent's choice.

3. The contention that the problem of free will is closely interlinked with the problems of consciousness and of the indeterminism disclosed by QM (1991 *passim* and esp. 393–94; 1999). Kane asks (1996a, 148) "How can a physical process of the brain be at the same time a consciously experienced effort of will?" and suggests that this is just part of the mystery of "how neural firings in the brain could be conscious mental events." On pp. 150–51, he suggests it is also implicated with the general problem of indeterminacy-in-nature introduced by quantum physics.

4. The contention that the objective probabilities for various outcomes are to some extent reflected in the subjectively felt strength of reasons; and that rational decisions may nevertheless favor actions with lower antecedent probabilities (1991: 392–93; 1999). Kane (1996a: 177) points out that antecedent probabilities of available alternatives do not necessarily indicate which of them are more or less rational for the agent to choose.

Kane's position might seem at variance with mine in that, whereas he apparently eschews special forms of agency or causation, I distinguish between what I call physical causation (apparently proceeding in accordance with laws of nature and randomness) and what I call volitional causation[5] (manifested in the decisions and actions of conscious agents, and selecting between alternatives left open by physical causation). But I believe that a closer consideration shows that his rejection of special forms of agency or causation is qualified in a way that makes it less than decisive, and that the latter part of his book, where he comes close to my position, does involve an implicit introduction of a special form of agency or causation.[6]

One other possible difference between Kane's position and mine is that he appears to distinguish sharply between theoretical reasoning, or deciding what to believe, and practical reasoning, or deciding what to do (pp. 22–23), and he considers free will only in relation to the practical reasoning, whereas, consistently with my agreement with Penrose, I closely link free will with consciousness and plausible reasoning generally and suggest that volitional causation can be exercised in deciding what to believe, as well as what to do. This brings out what I see as the important link between volitional causation and rationality; and it makes possible an account of volitional causation and free will as a natural and vital part of human activity, and understandable as a product of evolution.

NOTES

1. The past light cone of an event is all that region of the totality of space-time *from which* the location of the event could be reached by traveling at light speed or less; while its future light cone is all that region of space-time that *could be reached from* its location by traveling at light speed or less.

2. Others include Wolf (1984), Zohar (1990), Squires (1990), Herbert (1993), and Jibu and Yasue (1995).

3. For further approaches to the interpretation of QM by two philosophers, see Maxwell 1988 and Price 1994.

4. Indeed, physicist Jack Sarfatti has devised a theory of consciousness and free will based upon Bohm's version of QM, or post-QM. Sarfatti's unorthodox work does not yet appear in any book or published article, but it can be found on the internet at http://stardrive.org/title.shtml

5. I have previously used the term "agent causation"; but because of certain connotations of that term, I now think it best to use a different term.

6. See Hodgson (1999: 214).

CHAPTER 5

CHAOS, INDETERMINISM, AND FREE WILL

ROBERT C. BISHOP

1. PHYSICAL DETERMINISM

UNDERSTANDING the nature of determinism is notoriously difficult. At an abstract level of analysis, there are at least ninety varieties of determinism (Sobel 1998: 77–166). Furthermore, there are several ways to construe determinism (for example, physical, psychological, theological, logical, metaphysical). Since the question of how physical laws are related to the exercise of free will appears explicitly in free will discussions (see, for example, the essays in this volume on the Consequence Argument by Kapitan (ch. 6) and van Inwagen (ch. 7); Kane 1996a), my primary focus will be on physical determinism, the thesis that everything is determined to occur according to physical laws. This choice removes only part of the complication, however, because there are several conceptions of physical determinism as well. It could be viewed as a metaphysical thesis where all of physical reality is ontologically determined. Or it could be viewed as an observed phenomenon of our experience. Alternatively, physical determinism might be a concept relevant to the mathematical models of physics and other sciences, while its relevance to the world of everyday choice and action is questionable.

There have been numerous attempts to clarify and explain physical determinism (for example, Earman 1986; Kellert 1993; Laplace 1951; Montague 1974; Popper 1982; Russell 1953; Stone 1989; van Fraassen 1988 and 1991). Syntactic approaches favored by the logical positivists have largely been abandoned, having proven inadequate for describing scientific practices (Bishop and Kronz 1999: 129–30). Even innovative approaches trying to combine formal systems and semantics such as Richard Montague's (1974: especially 303–60) do not break free of serious limitations. The types of second-order formal languages Montague studies can only represent a finite number of physical magnitudes and so are inadequate for cases where an uncountable number of distinct physical magnitudes interact to produce determinism. The laws and models of physics are more appropriately described by mathematical equations. The important questions for physical determinism in such laws and models are the existence and uniqueness properties of the solutions, not necessarily questions of quantification or logical entailment.

1.1. The Laplacean Vision

Our modern notion of physical determinism is largely drawn from classical physics and extended to other sciences. The mathematical models of physics and their implications have given rise to the Laplacean vision for determinism (Bishop n.d.(a) Stone 1989: 124–25; Kellert 1993: 49–62):

> (DD) *Differential dynamics.* There exists a nonprobabilistic algorithm relating a state of a model at any given time to a state at any other time.
> (UE) *Unique evolution.* A model is such that a given state is always followed by the same history of state transitions.
> (VD) *Value determinateness.* Any state of a model can be described with arbitrarily small (nonzero) error.
> (AP) *Absolute prediction.* Any state of a model can be generated from the algorithm with arbitrarily small (nonzero) error from any other state of the model.

The equations of physical theories along with their initial and boundary conditions provide the motivation for DD expressing the Laplacean belief that there are no indeterministic events in classical physics. UE is closely associated with DD and captures the Laplacean belief that models of classical physics will repeat their behaviors exactly if the same initial and boundary conditions are specified. The third element of this vision, VD, is motivated by the Laplacean belief that there is nothing in principle in classical physics that prevents mathematical descriptions of arbitrary accuracy. The final element, AP, is a prima facie reasonable expectation that given DD, UE, and VD, it should be possible in principle to predict the exact state a model would take on at any time. This implication, however, does not follow (Bishop n.d.).

1.2. Unique Evolution

I take UE to be the crucial element of the Laplacean vision in the relationship between physical determinism and free will. Imagine a typical physical model as a film. UE means that if we start the film over and over at the same frame (returning the model to the same initial state), it would repeat every detail of its total history over and over again and identical copies of the film would produce the same sequence of pictures. So no matter whether we start *Jurassic Park* at the beginning frame, the middle frame or any other frame, it plays the same from that frame forward or backward. No new frames are added to the movie nor is the sequence of frames changed simply by starting it at an arbitrary frame. In other words, any model isomorphic to our original model, each having the same initial and boundary conditions, would follow the same sequence of state transitions.

By contrast, suppose it was the case that returning the model to the same initial state produced a different sequence of state transitions on some of the runs. Consider a computer that generates a different sequence of pictures on some occasions when starting from the same initial picture. Suppose further that the computer has the property that simply by choosing to start with any picture normally appearing in the sequence, it is sometimes the case that the chosen picture is not followed by the usual sequence of pictures or that some pictures often do not appear in the sequence or new ones are added from time to time. Then there is no guarantee that identical copies of a model with this behavior starting from identical initial states would follow the same sequence of state transitions. Such a model violates UE and is incompatible with the Laplacean vision.

More formally UE may be stated as follows: Let M stand for the collection of all models sharing the same set L of physical laws and suppose that P is the set of relevant physical properties for specifying the time evolution of a model recognized by L. Then

> A model m ε M exhibits UE if and only if every model m' ε M isomorphic to m with respect to P undergoes the same evolution as m (Bishop and Kronz 1999: 131).[1]

UE can be given two readings when abstracted from the rest of the elements of the Laplacean vision. It can be construed as a statement of *causal determinism* where "every event has a cause that is an event that takes place at some antecedent time or times" (Sobel 1998: 84). It may also be read as a statement of *block-universe determinism* characterized by William James as "[t]he whole is in each and every part, and welds it with the rest into an absolute unity, an iron block, in which there can be no equivocation or shadow of turning" (1956: 150). As Jordan Sobel points out, these two forms of determinism can be distinguished (1998: 102–5). The former derives from the causal principle that every event has an antecedent cause, a flow from cause to effect, if you will, that may be continuous or have gaps. The latter reflects the intuition that a difference anywhere in the universe requires a difference everywhere. For example, in this context Sobel distinguishes "fast-starting" series of causally linked states (1998: 89). These are series where every state has a temporally antecedent determining cause, but the series itself has no antecedent deterministic cause (its beginning is undetermined by prior events and may have a probabilistic cause) and no state in the series occurs before a specified time. The causal principle that every event has an antecedent cause would fail for a fast-starting series as a whole though it would apply *within* such a series. This would be an example where causal determinism failed, but where block-universe determinism would still hold.[2] On the other hand, if one explicates the causal principle in terms of the laws L and properties P, then the idea that a difference anywhere in a model m' isomorphic to m requires a difference everywhere in m' with respect to m can be explicated in terms of differences in either L or P.

1.3. Fixed Laws and the Past

I will make no attempt here to explicate the notion of physical laws L other than to gesture at the fact that in classical physics laws are often taken to be expressed by the equations fulfilling DD, UE, and VD. There is currently no consensus among philosophers of science on a problem-free conception of natural laws (for example, Bunge 1998; Cartwright 1983 and 1989; Giere 1999; Suppe 1989; van Fraassen 1988 and 1991)[3] and, fortunately, this minimal construal of physical laws is sufficient for many free will discussions such as the various versions of the Consequence Argument. By restricting the notion of laws of nature occurring in the Consequence Argument to the set L (P should also be included, strictly speaking), one can discuss the fixedness of the past in terms of the principles or models in the practice of physics. One can construe the current understanding of the evolution of the universe as evidence for change of L or P over time or the emergence of new laws or properties in the history of this evolution. In the practice of physics, however, this evolution is seen as the unfolding of the consequences of L and P, and the history of the discovery of new laws or properties is simply the temporal discovery of fixed elements of the sets L and P that have always existed.

There are cases such as the standard models of the evolution of the universe, where particular epochs are characterized by a smaller set of laws and properties while others exhibit the emergence of new laws and properties (Kolb et al. 1986; Kolb and Turner 1990). In such cases these "new" laws and properties are viewed as consequences of the "old" laws and properties and often the former can be mathematically derived from the latter, given appropriate conditions (though this derivation is not a logical entailment; see Primas 1998). In this sense the set of laws L and properties P are still considered as fixed. One can object to construing L and P as fixed for these cases, but over the time span relevant to human history, we have no evidence suggesting that L and P are anything but fixed, so the history of human choices and actions takes place within a domain over which L and P are fixed.[4]

Fixed L and P, combined with DD, UE, and VD, leads to a strong sense in which past events are fixed such that given the same L and P for two identical models m and m', the past histories of both m and m' as well as their future histories will be identical. If this conception is applied to the history of all events in the world, then the world's past and future history of events—including all human motives, reasons, decisions, actions, and so on—are fixed and the consequence argument, under the Laplacean vision, bites very deeply.

2. INDETERMINISM

The past (as well as the future) history of events may not be fixed even though L and P are fixed, however, if indeterminism is present.[5] Indeterminism can enter into the models of physics given fixed L and P by making various modifications to the Laplacean vision. There are two ways of getting indeterminism. The first is to modify DD by making the equations of the model irreducibly indeterministic or by introducing irreducibly indeterministic initial or boundary conditions. The second way to get indeterminism is to drop UE (for example, Lucretius's atom where indeterminism emerges from the lack of unique evolution: the famous Epicurean "swerve" of the atom).[6] Clearly the first strategy implies the second as irreducibly indeterministic equations, and initial or boundary conditions guarantee that it is a contingent matter whether identical models will follow the same history of state transitions. The second strategy does not imply the first, since the loss of UE alone does not imply that the evolution equations be explicitly probabilistic (van Fraassen 1991:51). In order for our models obeying L and P to have any *intelligible* content other than their being indeterministic, however, an explicitly probabilistic prescription is required.[7]

2.1. Quantum Mechanics, Probabilistic Causation, and the Nature of Indeterminism

This lack of explanation (or sufficient reason) can lead one to think that inde-terministic models are noncausal even if probabilities are brought explicitly into the mathematical models.[8] This forms the basis for one of the most common objections to incompatibilist theories of free will which draw on indeterminism in some crucial fashion: namely, if indeterminism is important in determining the outcome of an agent's decision to do A, then there would be no sufficient reason for the agent having chosen to do A rather than otherwise. Everything was a matter of chance and as such, fails to explain the agent's decision nor explain the agent's power to decide (see Kane 1996a: 105–23 for a discussion of and response to this type of argument).

Quantum mechanics is the paradigm indeterministic theory in physics. Its explicit probability assignments have been verified in a wide range of laboratory experiments and made possible a number of now common devices found in every-day life (for example, transistors, lasers, NMR scanners). Let me illustrate the difference between the quantum mechanical world and our everyday world in the following way. In our everyday world, stoplights operate with a predictable pattern of green, then yellow, then red. To comprehend how different the quantum realm is, suppose quantum stoplights have two possible patterns: either green, yellow, red or green, red, yellow.

The key feature of quantum stoplights is that they have a 50 percent prob-ability for exhibiting the green-yellow-red pattern and 50 percent for exhibiting the green-red-yellow pattern. Let me emphasize that the probability refers to the green-yellow-red pattern or the green-red-yellow pattern, not to the appearance of any individual color.[9] If you were approaching a quantum stoplight that was currently yellow, you would not know if the light was going to turn red or green next, because you would not know what pattern the light was exhibiting based on the color you were seeing. You could observe the quantum stoplight over a long period of time to determine probabilities for the two patterns. But, according to conventional interpretations of quantum mechanics, you have no way of knowing *in advance* which pattern the light will exhibit as you come to the intersection because the patterns at the level of observation are indetermin-istic.

If the quantum stoplights are observed to be in a particular pattern, an ex-planatory account can be given for why that pattern was exhibited in terms of the equations and probabilities governing the model. Take radioactive decay as a concrete example. Our models for radioactive decay do not allow us to predict the precise time a radioactive atom will decay, but only the probabilities for a decay event in a specified time range. We can then take measurements to test the predictions. Based on the physics of radioactive atoms, we can explain why the atom decayed in the time range it did with the predicted probability.

Radioactive decay, tunneling of particles through energy barriers, and the absorption and emission of light are typical quantum phenomena that fit this kind of probabilistic form of explanation. Philosophers of science have developed a rich literature on the notion of indeterministic or probabilistic causation (for example, Baker 1999; Collins 2000; DeVito 1996; Eells 1991; Good 1961 and 1962; Hall 2000; Harper and Skyrms 1988; Hitchcock 1993: 335–64; Humphreys 1980: 25–37 and 1989; Koons 2000; Lewis 1986a: vol. 2, 175–85 and 2000; Mellor 1986: 166–86 and 1999; Menzies 1996; Noordhof 1998 and 1999; Paul 2000; Pearl 1997 and 2000; Reichenbach 1956; Salmon 1984, 1993: 137–53 and 1998; Shaffer 2000; Skyrms 1999; Skyrms and Harper 1988; Suppes 1970). The general idea of probabilistic causation is this: for an event (or set of events) C to be a cause of an event E, C's occurring must raise the probability of E's occurring and this probability is conditional on an appropriately chosen set of background factors B. The probability must be conditionalized on background factors so that the increase in probability picks out a genuine case of causation rather than a spurious case of accidental correlation. There are two particularly difficult problems for theories of probabilistic causation: (1) The causal relevance of (some of the events) C may appear or disappear as the partition of the factors B is refined (e.g., in terms of the level of detail). Related to this problem is another: (2) the fact that C's occurring raises the probability of E's occurring on B should be robust with respect to B in the sense that additions to B (e.g., new experience) do not introduce such changes to the probabilities that these facts no longer hold. Although these problems are difficult to address in a general theory (indeed, they seem to tell against the prospects for such a general theory), focusing on a specific context like quantum mechanics makes the difficulties more tractable (though not necessarily less messy!). We can then reference the appropriate laws in L and properties in P as well as the particular experimental setup for the background B and explicate causal relevance and robustness in terms of B.

While it is possible to give a philosophical account of probabilistic causation in quantum mechanics, the nature of the probability involved remains an open question. Let us return to our quantum stoplights for a moment. There is a 50 percent probability for each pattern to be exhibited by such lights. The key question is whether to understand the nature of this probability as epistemic or ontic. Along epistemic lines, one possibility is that there is some additional factor (a hidden mechanism) such that once we discover and understand this factor, we would be able to predict the observed behavior of the quantum stoplight with certainty (physicists call this approach a "hidden variable theory"; for example, Bell 1987: 1–13, 29–39; Bohm 1952a and b; Bohm and Hiley 1993; Bub 1997: 40–114; Holland 1993; see Hodgson in this volume ch. 4). Or perhaps there is an interaction with the broader environment such as the neighboring buildings, trees, and so on that we have not taken into account in our observations, to explain how these probabilities arise (physicists call this approach decoherence or consistent histories; see, for example, Giulini et al. 1996; Omnès 1994; Zurek 1981, 1982, and 1991). We would then interpret the indeterminism we observed in the behavior of the stoplights as an expression of our ignorance about the actual workings. Under an ignorance interpretation, indeterminism would not be a fundamental feature of quantum stoplights, but merely epistemic due to our lack of knowledge about the system. Quantum stoplights would turn out to be deterministic after all.

The alternative possibility is that the indeterminism we observe is ontic in the sense that there are no factors to fully determine what pattern the stoplights are going to exhibit at any given moment as in the so-called von Neumann projection postulate (see, for example, Rae 1986; von Neumann 1955) or quantum stochastics (for example Diósi 1988 and 1989; Diósi, Gisin, and Strunz 1998; Ghirardi, Rimini, and Weber 1986; Gisin 1984 and 1989; Gisin and Percival 1992; Plenio and Knight 1998). Under an ontic interpretation, indeterminism would be a fundamental feature of quantum stoplights.

3. FREE WILL AND PHYSICS

By now it is perhaps clear how physics in the form of the laws L and properties P under the Laplacean vision of determinism is relevant to free will discussions. The fundamental principles of physics certainly play a role in the brain (a bio-*physical* organ), which in turn is involved in consciousness and free will (although not necessarily in a reductive sense). If classical physics in this Laplacean picture is the whole story of the matter, then whatever free will amounts to, it must be influenced (if not completely determined) by L and P.

Since quantum mechanics is more fundamental than classical mechanics and quantum mechanics is one of the most empirically successful of our physical theories, many authors have looked to it to support theoretical accounts of human freedom (for example, Beck and Eccles 1992; Compton 1935; Eccles 1970; Kane 1996a; Penrose 1989, 1994, and 1997; Stapp 1993; Hodgson [ch. 4, this volume] discusses the views of a number of these authors). Still it has been less clear to many that quantum mechanics is relevant to free will. For example, an early objection to quantum effects influencing human volitions was offered by philosopher J.J.C. Smart (1963: 123–24). Smart accepted the truth of indeterminism at the quantum level but argued that the brain remains deterministic in its operations because microscopic events are insignificant by comparison. After all, a single neuron is known to be excited by on the order of a thousand molecules, each molecule consisting of ten to twenty atoms. Quantum effects, though substantial when focusing on single atoms are presumed negligible when focusing on systems involving large numbers of atoms. So it seems that quantum effects would be too insignificant in comparison to the effects of thousands of molecules to play any possible role in deliberation.

3.1. Routes for Amplification:
Chaos and Quantum Mechanics

Arguments such as Smart's do not consider the possibility for amplifying quantum effects through the interplay between chaos (Baker and Gollub 1990; Hilborn 1994) at the level of the classical world (for example, chairs, trees, brains) on the one hand and quantum effects (for example, tunneling through energy barriers, radioactive decay) on the other. Philosophers Jesse Hobbs (1991) and Stephen Kellert (1993; 69–75) have argued that chaos in classical systems can amplify quantum fluctuations due to sensitivity to the smallest changes in initial conditions. Briefly, the reasoning runs as follows. Given two chaotic models m and m' of classical mechanics in nearly identical initial states (for example, specification of the initial positions and velocities of the model), they will evolve in radically different ways in a relatively short time period as the slight differences in initial conditions are amplified. Because no known lower limit to this sensitivity exists, there is the possibility of chaotic macroscopic systems being extremely sensitive to quantum fluctuations because quantum mechanics sets a lower bound on how precisely the initial conditions can be specified. Hence UE must fail for chaotic models in classical mechanics.

Along these lines, suppose the patterns of neural firings in the brain correspond to decision states. Chaos could amplify quantum events, causing a single neuron to fire that would not have fired otherwise. If the brain (a macroscopic object) is also in a chaotic dynamical state, which makes it sensitive to small perturbations, this additional neural firing, small as it is, would then be further amplified to the point where the brain states would evolve differently than if the neuron had not fired. In turn these altered neural firings and brain states would carry forward such quantum effects that affect the outcomes of human choices.[10]

There are several objections to this line of argument. First, the presence of chaos in the brain and its operations is an empirical matter currently hotly debated and inconclusive (Diesmann, Gewaltig and Aertsen 1999; Kaneko, Tsuda and Ikegami 1994 103–89; Lehnertz et al., Forthcoming; Vandervert 1997; see also Walter [ch. 26 in this volume]). Second, these kinds of sensitivity arguments depend crucially on how quantum mechanics itself and measurements are interpreted (Bishop and Kronz 1999: 134–38). As discussed in §2.1, some versions of quantum mechanics are ontically deterministic and others are ontically indeterministic, so the nature of the small quantum effects amplified by chaos is open to interpretation.[11] Third, although the abstract sensitivity arguments do correctly lead to the conclusion that the smallest of effects can be amplified, applying such arguments to concrete physical systems shows that the amplification process may be severely constrained. For example, investigating the role of quantum effects in the process of friction in sliding surfaces indicates quantum effects can be amplified by chaos to produce a difference in macroscopic behavior, provided that the effects are large enough to break molecular bonds and are amplified quickly enough (Bishop 1999: 82–86). In the case of the brain, we currently do not know what constraints on amplification exist.[12]

3.2. Routes for Amplification: Nonequilibrium Statistical Mechanics

An alternative possibility avoiding many of the difficulties exhibited in the chaos + quantum mechanics approach of §3.1 is suggested by the research on far-from-equilibrium systems by Ilya Prigogine and his Brussels-Austin Group. Their work offers reasons to search for a different type of indeterminism at both the micro and macrophysical levels (Antoniou and Prigogine 1993; Petrosky and Prigogine 1996 and 1997; Prigogine 1997).[13]

If a system of particles is distributed uniformly in position and momentum in a region of space, the system is said to be in thermodynamic equilibrium (like cream uniformly distributed throughout a cup of coffee). In contrast, a system is far-from-equilibrium (nonequilibrium) if the particles are arranged so that highly ordered structures appear (for example, a cube of ice floating in tea). The following properties characterize nonequilibrium statistical systems:

- Large number of particles
- High degree of structure and order
- Collective behavior
- Irreversibility
- Emergent properties[14]

The brain possesses all these properties, so that the work of the Brussels-Austin Group can be applied to analyzing the brain as a nonequilibrium system.

Let me quickly sketch a simplified version of the approach in order to point out why the developments of the Brussels-Austin Group offer an alternative for investigating the connections between physics and free will. Conventional physics describes physical systems using particle trajectories as a fundamental explanatory element of its models (this is clear from the way the Laplacean vision is articulated in §1). This means that the behavior of a model is derivable from the trajectories of the particles composing the model. The equations governing the motion of these particles are reversible with respect to time (they can be run backward and forward like a film). When there are too many particles involved to make these types of calculations feasible (as in gases or liquids), coarse-grained averaging procedures are used to develop a statistical picture of how the system behaves rather than focusing on the behavior of individual particles.

In contrast, the Brussels-Austin approach views these systems in terms of models whose fundamental explanatory elements are distributions; that is to say, the arrangements of the particles are the fundamental explanatory elements and not the individual particles and trajectories.[15] The equations governing the behavior of these distributions are generally *irreversible* with respect to time. In addition, focusing exclusively on distribution functions opens the possibility that macroscopic nonequilibrium models are irreducibly indeterministic, an indeterminism that has nothing to do with ignorance about the system. If true, this would mean that probabilities are as much an ontologically fundamental element of the macroscopic world as they are of the microscopic and are free of the interpretive difficulties found in conventional quantum mechanics.

One important insight of the Brussels-Austin Group's shift away from trajectories to distributions as fundamental elements is that explanation also shifts from a local context (set of particle trajectories) to a global context (distribution of the entire set of particles). This implies that a system acting as a whole may produce collective effects that are not reducible to a summation of the trajectories and subelements composing the system (Petrosky and Prigogine 1997). The brain exhibits this type of collective behavior in many circumstances (Engel et al. 1997), and the work of Prigogine and his colleagues gives us another tool for trying to understand that behavior. Though it is still speculative and contains some open technical questions (Bishop nd.(b) and (c)), this approach offers both an alternative for exploring the relationship between physics and free will and a new possible source for exploring indeterminism in free will theories.[16]

4. Final Thoughts

One way to characterize free will debates is as an attempt to find a home for free will in a physical world picture that seems hostile to such freedom. There would seem to be no viable sense of free will without some form of determination or ordered realm of causes and influences in which to act and make a difference. On the other hand, that freedom has to be real and meaningful and cannot just amount to the effect of causes that play upon the human agent. It is possible to argue that the full reality of free will and constraints upon it can only be fully explicated in terms of an emergent realm of human social and rational influences and counter-influences that depends upon the physical world for its existence but is not reducible to physical processes (Martin and Sugarman 1999). The contemporary developments in determinism and physics surveyed in this chapter indicate that the existence of pockets of determinism in physics do not imply that determinism holds sway over all domains of physics, so that the existence of creases or joints in the causal fabric of our world for genuine human action becomes more plausible (Richardson and Bishop n.d.).

NOTES

1. Both Hobbs and Kellert use John Earman's construal of "Laplacian Determinism" (Earman 1986: 13) to spell out UE. However there are technical reasons for preferring the definition given in the text (Bishop and Kronz 1999: 130–31).

2. Sobel suggests that such fast-starting series could be seen as free actions because they "leave open that they should be produced by 'out-of-the-world' agency" but is dubious that such agency makes sense (1998: 97). Perhaps this supposed need for "out-of-the-world" agency might be alleviated in shifting to a "dialogical" conception of agency. Here within-the-world processes of mutual influence and shaping among persons (e.g., conversations) could provide a genuine source of influence for free actions provided that dialogical influence is treated at least on par with efficient causation (Gadamer 1989; Bishop 1999; 156–93; Richardson and Bishop n.d.).

3. Among the more extreme positions on physical laws is that of Nancy Cartwright, who argues that our conception of nature as a seamless web of causal law-like connections is mistaken. Although short on details, John Dupré (1996), drawing on Cartwright's work, argues against the idea that every event is governed by some quantitatively precise law, so that the causal order turns out to be partial and incomplete. He conceives of human agents as sources of causal power and order acting in this partially complete causal web and bringing order to this web. Though Dupré does not propose a positive account of agency, he suggests that clarifying human agents as causal sources of freedom and action requires viewing agents as embedded in the languages and practices of society (1996: 400; cf. Bishop 1999; 156–93 and 211–32 and Richardson and Bishop n.d.).

4. An additional complication arises from considering the possibility that new properties arise in physical systems that are not implied by L and P but are due solely to the organization of the components of the systems in question (Beckermann, Flohr, and Kim 1992). A strong emergentist might argue that among these emergent properties

are causal powers that, while not fully constrained by L, P, and the constituents of the physical system, nevertheless are able to influence or manipulate the physical system in question. Jaegwon Kim has argued forcefully against this strong emergentist possibility (for example, 1993: 265–84, 309–35, 1999); however there are counterexamples to his arguments in physics and chemistry in the phenomena of temperature, chemical potential, chirality, and others (Primas 1998). What these counterexamples mean regarding the fixedness of L and P is an open question.

5. Earman has discussed several cases in the context of Newtonian mechanics where determinism in the form of UE appears to fail. Particularly noteworthy are his discussions of so-called space invaders cases (1986: 33–35 and 45–47) and systems of colliding billiard balls (ibid.: 39–40). These cases have been critically discussed in (Bishop 1999: 34–39; Bishop and Kronz 1999: 132–33).

6. Some have thought that relaxing VD would introduce indeterminism into the models of physics (Glymour 1971: 744–45); however, determinism can be revised to allow for set- and interval-valued properties evolving along uniquely determined paths (Earman 1986: 217–18; Fine 1971; Teller 1979).

7. I have stated this requirement for intelligibility only in the context of physical models and theories. This is not meant to suggest that human rationality is limited to algorithmic processing (either deterministic or probabilistic). See Hodgson (this volume, ch. 4).

8. This is true mainly because the principle of sufficient reason (PSR) does not hold for such models. An insightful treatment of PSR and its related principles and axioms may be found in Kane 1986.

9. The patterns of my quantum stoplights are analogous to a two-state system. The green-yellow-red pattern would be an up state and the green-red-yellow pattern would be a down state. Approaching the intersection would be analogous to a measurement on the system.

10. Eccles (1970) and Kane (1996a) make explicit use of such amplifications in their accounts of free will (see also Hodgson's [ch. 4] discussion of Eccles in this volume).

11. Ted Honderich relies on these interpretive difficulties as his main line of argument against the relevance of quantum effects for questions about free will and determinism (1988: vol 1, 269–304).

12. There are two other lines of argument worth mentioning, regarding the relevance of quantum mechanics to free will, one by Roger Penrose (1989, 1994, and 1997) and the other by Henry Stapp (1993). Penrose argues that the conscious acts of thinking and choosing are tied directly to the processes of resolving quantum superpositions of potentialities to one actuality requiring the presence of a kind of large-scale quantum coherence in the brain. Stapp's approach focuses on the nonlocal correlations exhibited in the Einstein-Podolsky-Rosen experiments (Einstein Podolsky, and Rosen 1935; Aspect, et al. 1982a and b; Bell 1987; 14–21; Stapp 1993: 5–9). Roughly, these experiments seem to question a commonsense assumption about locality: if a pair of simultaneous measurements is made in two far-apart regions of an extended system, the two measurements should be independent of each other. Stapp argues that nonlocal holism exhibited by these so-called EPR experiments implies that quantum effects play an important role in consciousness and decision making, where quantum mechanics provides the basis for a Heisenberg-Whiteheadean ontology for reality that is neither dualist nor physicalist, but instead involves a kind of mind/body duality (1993: especially ch. 6). Stapp's view is ulti-

mately deterministic in that he construes quantum indeterminism as existing due to our ignorance (ibid: 91–92).

13. For a critical historical review, see Bishop (n.d. (b) and (c).

14. Whether these properties are strongly emergent in the sense of note 4 this chapter, or in some weaker sense is usually left open.

15. Many, including me, have at times concluded that Prigogine and collaborators were arguing that trajectories did not exist. The matter is somewhat technical and the Brussels-Austin Group has been notoriously unclear in writing about this point (see Bishop n.d. (b) and and (c).

16. Although I am unaware of anyone actively exploring this direction in the literature, related to and indeed influenced by the Brussels-Austin work is a proposal by John Polkinghorne that the randomness in macroscopic chaotic models and systems be interpreted as representing a genuine indeterminism rather than merely a measure of our ignorance (1991: 34–48). He shares a deep skepticism that the interpretive difficulties of quantum mechanics raised in §3.1 will be overcome soon, casting doubt, in his mind, on whether this is the right source for the openness or indeterminism he thinks important to the free will and action we experience (ibid: 40–41). Polkinghorne argues that the physical world must possess openness (causal creases or joints if you will) for human free will to operate in the sense we experience (as well as for God to be active in the world; see idem: 1988 and 1989). In essence the sensitivity to small changes exhibited by the systems and models studied in chaotic dynamics, complexity theory, and nonequilibrium statistical mechanics is taken to represent an opening at the ontic level in the physical order for human choice to cause physical changes (for example, bodily changes such as beginning to walk). However, the sensitivity upon which Polkinghorne relies would also be open to quantum influences whether deterministic or indeterministic.

PART III

THE MODAL OR CONSEQUENCE ARGUMENT FOR INCOMPATIBILISM

CHAPTER 6

A MASTER ARGUMENT FOR INCOMPATIBILISM?

TOMIS KAPITAN

THE past twenty-five years have witnessed a vigorous discussion of an argument directed against the compatibilist approach to free will and responsibility. This reasoning, variously called the "Consequence Argument," the "Incompatibility Argument," and the "Unavoidability Argument," may be expressed informally as follows: If determinism is true, then whatever happens is a consequence of past events and laws over which we have no control and which we are unable to prevent. But whatever is a consequence of what is beyond our control is not itself under our control. Therefore, if determinism is true, then nothing that happens is under our control, including our own actions and thoughts. Instead, everything we do and think, everything that happens to us and within us, is akin to the vibration of a piano string when struck, with the past as pianist, and could not be otherwise than it is.

While a number of philosophers interpret this reasoning as vitiating the prospects of compatibilism, others challenge its assumption that unavoidability "transfers" from sufficient condition to necessary condition or from cause to effect. The ensuing debate has occasionally been vitriolic—Hume once remarked that the free will issue is "the most contentious question of metaphysics, the most contentious science"—yet undeniably fruitful in generating more detailed examinations of ability and practical freedom. Whether we incline toward compatibilism or incompatibilism, this latter development is likely to be of lasting value.

As a compatibilist, I believe that the Consequence Argument fails to prove incompatibilism, and here I will develop criticisms of it that, for the most part, are already in the existing literature. Although a short chapter cannot provide the theoretical account of practical freedom needed to underpin and justify this compatibilist critique, it will clarify the tasks that lie ahead.

1. DEVELOPMENT OF THE ARGUMENT

The Consequence Argument was independently developed in the 1970s by David Wiggins (1973), Peter van Inwagen (1975), James Lamb (1977), and Carl Ginet (1980). Since then, versions have been advanced in van Inwagen (1983), Widerker (1987), Ginet (1990), O'Connor (1993a and 2000), and Fischer (1994) among others. The core reasoning is similar to the "Master Argument" of Diodoros Cronos, who argued that since the past is fixed and inevitable, and the impossible cannot follow from the possible, then nothing is possible except the things that do happen or will happen. Given an apparent assumption of the argument, namely, that the past determines the present and future, then nothing other than what does happen or will happen can happen and, consequently, no one can do other than one does or will do (Mates 1961: 36–40; White 1985: 69–91; Knuuttila 1993: 14–16).

The emergence of formal representations for modal reasoning has led to a renewed examination of the modal elements in descriptions of action and capabilities. Abbreviating an agent S's ability at time t to bring about a situation p as "$A_{s,t}p$" then "$\sim A_{s,t}p$" expresses S's inability at t to bring about p, "$\sim A_{s,t}\sim p$" is S's inability at t to prevent p, and "$N_{s,t}p$" the claim that p is unavoidable for S at t, that is, "p & $\sim A_{s,t}\sim p$." So represented, proposals about the governing principles of these *practical modalities* can be more readily discerned and debated.

In several publications Peter van Inwagen has forcefully presented a clear formulation of the Consequence Argument (see 1975, 1983, and ch. 7 here). It utilizes an operator "N" where "Np" expresses the universal unavoidability of p or, in van Inwagen's preferred locution, "p and no one has or ever had any choice about whether p," and the following inference rules:

α $\Box$p ∴ Np
β   Np, N(p ⊃ q) ∴ Nq.

Then, where "$\Box$" expresses logical necessity, "P_0" the state of the world at some time in the remote past, "L" the conjunction of the laws of nature, and "P" an arbitrary true proposition, the following is a consequence of determinism:

1. $\Box((P_0 \ \& \ L) \supset P)$.

It is easy to derive NP as follows:

2. $\Box(P_0 \supset (L \supset P))$ 1, propositional logic
3. $N(P_0 \supset (L \supset P))$ 2, rule α
4. NP_0 premise
5. $N(L \supset P)$ 3, 4, rule β
6. NL premise
7. NP 5, 6, rule β

Accordingly, determinism renders every truth unavoidable. Van Inwagen takes the premises of this argument as "obviously true," rule α as "obviously valid," and rule β as something that "appeals immediately to the reflective intellect" (1983: 124). While he notes that β is the most difficult element of the argument to defend (ibid.: 96) and the "most doubtful thesis the incompatibilist must accept" (ibid.: 222), he stresses that "one could have no reason for being an incompatibilist" without accepting this rule (1989: 405).

While it is often true that the consequences of what is unavoidable are themselves unavoidable (van Inwagen 1983: 98), the argument makes itself felt when it rules out certain abilities simply because events are determined, abilities we would normally assume agents to have. For example, suppose that in a large office at 11:59:30 AM EST on March 12, 2005, Margo notices a copy of *Lady Chatterley's Lover* on Suzanne's desk. She picks it up, reads a few sentences, and decides that she would like to read a bit more in the evening. Since Suzanne is on her coffee break and no one else is in the immediate vicinity, Margo discretely slips the book into her briefcase at 11:59:50. She briefly considers returning it but then moves on, leaving the book in her briefcase the rest of the day. Let P represent the state of affairs of the book being in Margo's briefcase at exactly noon. If determinism is true, then some remotely past state of the universe, P_0, together with laws of nature, L, necessitate that P obtains and that no one has any choice about that. According to the argument, since no one is able to prevent P_0 and L from obtaining, then no one is able to prevent P from obtaining, including Margo who at 11:59.52 is alert, cognizant that it is Suzanne's book and that she ought not steal it, and possessed of the physiological and psychological capacities needed to stop, remove the book from her briefcase, and return it to the desk within the next eight seconds. If responsibility for returning the book implies an ability to do so— and van Inwagen understands his "having a choice" locution to be relevant to moral responsibility (1983: 104–5, 184–88)—then Margo is not responsible for her theft if determinism is true; indeed, no one is responsible for anything.[1]

Rule β, or similar closure rules and principles that "transfer" unavoidability from antecedents to consequents, is common to all versions of this elegant argument for incompatibilism.[2] Rule β is also featured in Ginet's rendition (1980, 1983), while others (for example, Fischer 1994: ch. 1) appeal to an indexed counterpart:

β' $N_{s,t}p$, $N_{s,t}(p \supset q)$ ∴ $N_{s,t}q$, for any agent S and time t.

Wiggins uses a variant of the Diodoran principle that the impossible cannot follow from the possible, namely, that if at time t it is inevitable that not-p, then p cannot follow from what *could* be the case at a later time t' (1973: 43–44). So if I could bring about q but do not, and my not doing so is caused by not-p, then my bringing about q would entail p. Since not-p is inevitable then, by the principle, I could not bring about q. The argument offered by Lamb assumes that if an event E is a logical consequence of a set F of true propositions, and S can prevent E, then S can do something such that some member of F would be false (1977: 23, 29). When combined with the premises that the past and laws cannot be altered, this principle of "can-entailment" justifies an inference to the conclusion that no agent can refrain from doing what is determined.

The arguments by Wiggins and Lamb differ from the van Inwagen/Ginet version in that the past and laws are connected to the unavoidable action or its result through entailment rather than the relation expressed by "N(p ⊃ q)." What is common to the two approaches is the assumption of the "transfer" or "closure" of unavoidability under a consequence relation, that is,

R1.   Whatever is a consequence of what is unavoidable is itself unavoidable.

Assuming that unavoidability is a type of necessity, this principle gains credibility from the widely accepted modal law,

M1.   Whatever is a consequence of a necessity is itself necessary.

The point is that there are versions of R1 besides β which are capable of generating the consequence argument, including those that are immune to counterexamples suggesting that β would fail in an indeterministic universe (Widerker 1987; Vihvelin 1988).[3] Some writers favor this version of R1:

R2.   Np, $\Box(p \supset q)$ ∴ Nq,

with "N" read in Ginet's fashion (Widerker 1987: 41). Alicia Finch and Ted Warfield (1998) also favor R2, describing it as "less vulnerable to criticism" than van

Inwagen's β (ibid.: 522) and as "clearly valid" (ibid.: 525). With it, a simpler version of the Consequence Argument is available:

1. $\square((P_0 \& L) \supset P)$ premise
2. $N(P_0 \& L)$ premise
3. NP 1, 2, R2.

An indexed counterpart of R1 appears in Talbott 1988: 247, and this counterpart of R2,

    R3. $N_{s,t}p$, $\square(p \supset q)$ ∴ $N_{s,t}q$, for any agent S and time t,

is deemed by Timothy O'Connor to be "clearly even *more* intuitive" than rule β' (O'Connor 2000: 9). It is easy to derive both R2 and R3 from rules α and β, though neither β nor β' follow from R2 or R3 without additional assumptions. Finally, O'Connor (1993b: 209) has also proposed,

    R4. $N_{s,t}p$, $N_{s,t}(p \supset q)$ ∴ $N_{s,t}q$, for any p, q such that q is made true later than p,

in order to avoid counterexamples to β' found in Widerker 1987 and Zagzebski 1991: 165–68.

    Another problem for rule β is presented in McKay and Johnson 1996, which shows that if the ability to bring about p is an ability to *ensure* that p obtains, then rules α and β support the inference from Np and Nq to N(p & q)—the so-called rule of agglomeration. That is, since $\square(p \supset (q \supset (p \& q)))$ is logically true, then N(p $\supset$ (q $\supset$ (p & q))) follows by rule α. By successive applications of rule β, we get N(p & q). However, just as ability to ensure does not distribute over a disjunction, unavoidability is not closed under conjunction. Suppose a man is able to flip a coin but does not. Then, both "the coin does not land heads" and "the coin does not land tails" are true, and there is nothing he can do to prevent them from being true since it is not within his power to ensure that the coin lands head nor within his power to ensure it lands tails. Thus, both "N(the coin does not land heads)" and "N(the coin does not land tails)" are true. However, the conjunction "The coin does not land heads and the coin does not land tails," while true, is within his power to prevent because he is able to flip the coin. Thus, "N(the coin does not land heads and the coin does not land tails)" is not true.

    This difficulty is not insurmountable. That unavoidability is not agglomerative does not show that the particular propositions NP$_0$ and NL could be true and N(P$_0$ & L) false (Finch and Warfield 1998: 523), and we need not go through agglomeration to justify the premise $N(P_0 \& L)$ since it is true in its own right (ibid.: 523–24). Even if we abandon rule β, the McKay-Johnson argument does not affect R2 or R3; agglomeration cannot be derived in the above manner by means of these rules since $\Box(q \supset (p \& q))$ is not true (though Blum 2000 provides a different derivation). McKay and Johnson suggest reading "Np" as "p and no one can or could (choose to) do anything that *might* lead to p's being false." This yields a strong unavoidability that rules out even a weak ability to prevent p, that is, an ability to do something such that p might be true (an ability that is disjunctive-distributive), but preserves the premises of van Inwagen's argument. The coin toss counterexample to agglomeration for this strengthened operator fails, so the barrier is removed to accepting a rule structurally identical to β, with "N" so understood and retaining van Inwagen's original argument. In this volume van Inwagen (chapter 7) also construes the unavoidability operator along these lines, providing a model that validates both β and agglomeration. (I will say something about his revision in section 4.)

Regardless of what version of the Consequence Argument is adopted, its appeal would be considerably diminished were it insisted at the outset that a necessary condition of one's being able to prevent a situation q is that it not be already determined that q will occur, or, in what comes to the same thing, that not-q be consistent with the past and laws. For suppose that Np holds and that the entailment of q by p is a consequence of determinism; then it is already determined that q holds and that no one will bring about q. If so, then according to the proposed condition, no agent is able to prevent q and Nq follows immediately. Naturally, those who have not yet ruled out compatibilism will hardly be persuaded by an argument that begins by placing an indeterministic condition on ability. What makes the Consequence Argument so attractive is that it is plausible *prior* to any analysis of ability (Foley 1979: 73–74; van Inwagen 1980b: 100; Slote 1982: 22).

2. COMPATIBILIST RESPONSES

Compatibilists have attacked the Consequence Argument from the outset (for example, Stoic critics of the Diodoran version (White 1985: ch. 4)). Some deny its relevance to moral responsibility by rejecting the assumption that moral responsibility requires an ability to do otherwise (Frankfurt 1969; Dennett 1984; Fischer 1994). There is considerable debate whether a principle of alternative possibilities can be so easily abandoned, but, in any case, the parallel direct argument against the compatibility of determinism and responsibility remains to be contended with (see note 1 this chapter). Another compatibilist response is that rule β fails on the conditional analysis of ability that compatibilists have traditionally favored (Gallois 1977; Foley 1979). However, the conditional analysis suffers from defects of its own (Lehrer 1964; Berofsky 1987; Kane 1996a), and van Inwagen emphatically rejects it (1977a and b, 1980, 1983, 1990a).

Despite the failure of the conditional analysis, the strategy of attacking the Consequence Argument through an account of the relevant practical modalities is ultimately the route a compatibilist must pursue. This point is emphasized by Michael Slote (1982), who argues that rule β rests on the questionable assumptions that the unavoidability operator is both agglomerative and closed under entailment (ibid.: 10). He contends that not all modal operators are agglomerative, closed under entailment, or governed by β-like rules, for example, certain epistemic and deontic operators, as well as the alethic modality of "nonaccidentality." Such modalities are *selective* inasmuch as they hold only relative to certain circumstances, say, as an obligation holds relative to a particular promise but not to another. Perhaps unavoidability is similarly selective. For example, a particular event in the past may be unavoidable relative to our present desires, beliefs, skills, and dispositions insofar as they are incapable of changing that event, yet relative to these same factors we might be able to do other than what we are caused to do (ibid.: 19–20). If so, rules like β and R2 fail.

These are rich suggestions if the ability needed for practical thinking and responsibility is "selective" as Slote suggests, especially if it includes epistemic elements (Dennett 1984: 148–49; Slote 1985: 328, Kapitan 1986b). Unfortunately, Slote's largely promisory remarks have left his essay open to criticism. Some deny that he has adequately motivated the denial of the closure principles for any type of necessity (O'Connor 1993b: 212–14), and even if a β-like principle fails for some types of necessity, he has not shown it to fail for van Inwagen's notion of unavoidability (Fischer 1986a; van Inwagen 1990a). Moreover, even if a prospective action is not unavoidable given the agent's present doxastic and motivational states, it may be *relevantly* unavoidable with respect to yet other conditions that have nothing to do with such states (Fischer 1994: 40–44).

A more detailed compatibilist response to the Consequence Argument begins by challenging the premises that the past cannot be altered or that the laws of nature cannot be violated (Narveson 1977; Gallois 1977; Lewis 1981; Horgan 1985). On the face of it, this approach seems utterly absurd; how are we mortals *able* to alter what has already happened or change the laws that govern the course of nature? Are not the following principles absolutely ironclad?

Fixity of the Laws: No one is able to bring about that a law of nature is violated.

Fixity of the Past: No one is able to bring about that the past is altered.

(Here, the extension of *the past* is fixed by the time at which the ability is possessed.) In fact, the response in question is subtler than a brute denial of these apparent truths. The critical move is that there is more than one concept of an *ability to bring about* a situation, thus, more than one concept of unavoidability, and while on some construals the Fixity Principles are beyond challenge, there is another in which they are jeopardized. Moreover, the concept of unavoidability for which the Fixity Principles are correct is *not* closed under a relation of consequence, whereas when closure does hold then one or both of the Fixity Principles is endangered. This type of argument—hereafter, the "main compatibilist response"—requires a careful look at the relevant practical modalities.

In general terms, an agent is able to bring about a situation p just in case he or she is able to perform an action of which p would be a consequence. However, different sorts of consequence relation permit distinctions among types of ability. One type is captured by the following:

> *Broad Ability*: S is broadly able at t to bring about p iff there is a course of action K such that at t (1) S is able to do K, and (2) were S to do K then p.[4]

This formula leaves open what consequence relation underlies the conditional in (2). The entailment of p by the action is one candidate, but since what we are able to do typically depends upon the cooperation of the environment, for example, bringing it about that a door is open, we can also interpret the conditional as asserting that p would be a "consequence" of S's K-ing if p would obtain were S to do K *in* the prevailing circumstances. Counterfactual dependency is one variety of such conditional dependency.

So defined, one is broadly able to bring about logical and mathematical necessities, an odd-sounding result given that the locution *brings about* suggests causation, as when I bring about the vibration of a tuning fork upon striking it against a hard surface or when my team wins by scoring a winning goal. So understood, what is "brought about" comes to obtain as a result of one's action, that is, its causal effects, and therefore it cannot be a situation that obtains of necessity or prior to undertaking that action. More liberally, let us say that one brings about whatever *becomes* true or *begins* to obtain by virtue of one's action, so that those who killed John Kennedy brought it about that Mrs. Kennedy became a widow, that a certain trigger was pulled, that John Kennedy perished while Churchill was still living, and that the conditional "the Eifel Tower is in Paris ⊃ John Kennedy is dead" is true. Expressing it by the phrase "make it the case that," we may characterize this liberal notion of causal ability as follows:

> *Causal Ability*: S is causally able at t to bring about p iff there is a course of action K such that at t (1) S is able to do K, and (2) S's doing K would make it the case that p.[5]

Causal ability is obviously more restrictive than broad ability, though the latter remains a necessary condition so that broad *in*ability implies an analogous causal inability. Both notions capture the sense in which ability involves *opportunity* to achieve a certain result, namely, that in the prevailing circumstances one would achieve that result were one to undertake a certain action.

Return to the main compatibilist response. Granting that Margo is able to return the book to Suzanne's desk, then she is both broadly and causally able to bring it about that the book is on the desk at noon. Since it is entailed by the past (P_0) and the laws (L) that the book is in Margo's briefcase at noon (P), then, were she to return the book to Suzanne's desk at noon, P would not obtain. However, if P were to not obtain then P_0 & L would not obtain, in which case,

a. Margo is able to do something such that if she did it then P_0 & L would not obtain. Consequently, by definition, Margo is *broadly* able to bring about $\sim(P_0 \& L)$, and if this is so, then one of the following would be true:

b. Margo is able to do something such that if she did it then P_0 would not obtain.

c. Margo is able to do something such that if she did it then L would not obtain.

Compatibilists differ about which is preferable; while the "local miracle" approach opts for (c), the so-called backtracking approach favors (b).[6] In either case, Margo is broadly able to bring about either that L does not obtain or that P_0 does not obtain. So, if the unavoidability operator is defined in terms of broad ability, then one of the premises of both van Inwagen's and the simpler version of the consequence argument is false.[7]

To continue the main compatibilist response, if ability to bring about is interpreted in the causal sense, then the premises of the Consequence Argument are true; Margo cannot *change* the past or laws, that is, she cannot "make it the case that" either P_0 or L does not obtain through anything she does. However, since Margo *is* able to return the book to Suzanne's desk and by so doing would make it the case that $\sim$P, then she is causally able to bring about $\sim$P. We thereby have a counterexample to rule β, and to any of the other mentioned candidates for a transfer rule with unavoidability interpreted in the causal sense. In sum, the main compatibilist response is this: while the Consequence Argument is valid on the broad sense of ability, its premises are false, and though the premises hold on the causal sense, it is invalid since the appropriate closure rule fails. As David Lewis (1981: 120–21) concluded, there is no one consistent reading of the critical modality that would render the argument sound.

3. STRICT ABILITY

The main compatibilist response faces two immediate problems. First, as it stands, it operates with an undefined notion of an "ability to do," one that allows that agents are able to do other than what they are caused to do. Those who wonder about the viability of compatibilism are correct to demand a fuller account. Second, neither broad nor causal ability is rich enough to account for all ascriptions of responsibility, since neither can explain certain cases where one lacks responsibility *because* one is unable to bring about a desired result. Here I will develop this second problem and argue that the main compatibilist response can withstand the necessary qualifications, and I will reserve the first problem until the next section.

Like broad ability, causal ability is also extraordinarily liberal given the manner in which we ordinarily ascribe ability. While it is clear enough that one is causally unable to bring about necessary truths, the definition allows that one is causally able to bring about what one produces accidentally or unintentionally, or without the faintest conception of what is being accomplished. For example, my daughter bowled a strike the very first time she rolled a bowling ball down the lane. Five-year-old novice that she was, she was unable to duplicate that feat in the next five-hundred or so tries. Was she *able* to throw a strike on her maiden attempt? It might be thought that one is able to do whatever one does. Yet her throwing a strike was a matter of pure luck; we wouldn't hesitate to explain her subsequent failures to throw a strike by saying that she lacked the general ability or *skill* to throw a bowling ball in such a way to knock down all the pins. In short, there is a further sense of ability whereby she was *unable* to bring it about that all the pins are knocked down on a single roll even though on a particular occasion she was able to do so in both the broad and causal senses.

How does skill differ from luck? One difference is that a skilled bowler can roll a strike regularly, that is, on all or a relatively high percentage of attempts (Brown 1988, 1990). It might be thought that skill is simply a causal ability to regularly bring about a certain sort of result by performing a particular kind of action, what we might call *regular* causal ability. Yet, even this is not enough, whether or not regularity is construed as a guarantee or a comparatively high degree of probability. I am able to hit a certain sequence of keys on my computer keyboard even though I never have before. Suppose that any time I were to hit that sequence I would invariably log onto a particular Pentagon computer; then I have a regular causal ability to bring about my being logged onto that computer, since being logged on would be a regular result of hitting just that sequence. Do I have the *skill* to bring it about that I am logged on to that computer? It would seem not. Do I have this skill if I actually hit a sequence of keys that logs me on? Again, it seems not, or at least this is what I hope the FBI would conclude after a proper investigation. After all, I am an amateur, not a seasoned hacker, and I blindly stumbled into the Pentagon computer system. I lacked proper know-how, not in hitting the particular sequence of keys I did—I may have done that very deliberately—but in logging onto the particular Pentagon computer as a result. If I can remember how I got there, then I may very well *acquire* the skill as a result of my experiment, but only because I have picked up a valuable piece of information.[8]

The point is that skill involves some measure of know-how in addition to a regular connection between action and result. If we add opportunity to know-how and regularity, we may speak of an agent as having the *strict* ability at a time to bring about a certain result. To characterize this notion more precisely, we first define a notion of consequence:

> *Reliable Consequence*: p is a reliable consequence of S's doing action K at time t just in case (1) S's intentionally K-ing at t made it the case that p, (2) at t, S acted on a plan according to which his K-ing then would make it the case that p, (3) there is a regular connection between S's doing K-type actions and p-type results as envisioned in S's plan at t.

This relation can obtain even when p is not brought about intentionally and S only tacitly envisions the appropriate plan, for it is sufficient if p is embedded in the plan as a foreseen or foreseeable result of a K-type action.[9] Accordingly, p *would be* a reliable consequence of S's K-ing at t just in case p would result from S's undertaking by way of a plan then envisioned by S. In this sense, strict ability requires know-how. So we have,

> *Strict Ability*: S is strictly able at t to bring about p iff there is a course of action K such that at t (1) S is able to do K, and (2) p would be a reliable consequence of S's doing K.

Strict ability entails broad and causal ability, but it differs in requiring that "bringing about" involves both a regular connection between an undertaking and a result *as well as* the agent's conceptions of the undertaking, the result, and a strategy for producing the latter from the former.[10]

The notion of strict ability is critical to our discussion; its absence can block both prospective and retrospective ascriptions of responsibility despite presence of a corresponding regular causal ability. Think of what is accomplished through the use of computers, from writing an e-mail message to landing an airplane safely to selling stocks online, situations that result from simple basic actions that people perform with the slightest movements. Suppose a machine operator, Bradley, can freeze the operation of his machine, should he receive notice of a safety threat, by pressing the keys F1, K, A, N, O, N, in that order, followed by "Enter" on his computer keyboard. One day he is instructing a trainee, Mike, and is about to tell him the six-membered code when he receives an emergency signal. The alarm causes Bradley to suffer a heart attack from which he immediately perishes before he can give the code to Mike. The latter, who has heard only that the code is a six-membered sequence, frantically tries various combinations that spring to mind, but to no avail; the machine fails to shut down and several workers are injured. Was Mike responsible for the injuries suffered? Presumably not, and the reason is that he was *unable* at that point to bring the machinery to a halt. On a keyboard with seventy-five keys, there are nearly two hundred billion possible six-membered sequences, not counting those with double-keyed members, and Mike can hardly be blamed for not hitting the right sequence in the short interval he had. Yet the action of hitting keys F_1, K, A, N, O, N, in that order, followed by "Enter" is easily something he was then able to do, and had he done it then, he would have stopped the machine and prevented the injuries. In short, Mike had the regular causal ability to stop the machine but lacked the strict ability to do so.

The point is that there are cases when an agent lacks responsibility for a situation *because* of a strict inability to prevent it despite the presence of both broad and causal abilities to prevent it. This is evidence that both prospective and retrospective ascriptions of responsibility are governed by the principle that S is morally responsible at t_1 for bringing about p at t_2 only if S is strictly able at t_1 to bring about p at t_2. If so, then the Consequence Argument poses a threat to compatibilism only if it can be shown that determinism precludes strict ability to do otherwise, and interpreting "N" in this strict fashion makes the argument no less plausible.

Yet, on the face of it, the main compatibilist response easily withstands the shift to strict ability. Obviously Margo lacks the strict ability to prevent P_0 & L, but if she does have the causal ability to bring about the book's being on the desk at noon, it is but a small step from there to claim that she also has the strict ability to do so; all we need to add is that ~P would be a *reliable* consequence of the action that she is able to perform. The case has been described in a way that makes this addition reasonable.

4. REPLIES AND REJOINDERS

The second problem facing the main compatibilist response is more challenging. The assumption that agents are *able* to do other than what they are caused to do has been thought to beg the question against the incompatibilist, since it appears to "presuppose" that an ability to do otherwise is compatible with determinism (an objection noted in Kane 1996a: 51–52). Van Inwagen writes that it would be "nice" to see a counterexample to rule β that did not presuppose compatibilism (1983: 102), and some would make this a condition on any acceptable counter-example (Ekstrom 2000: 40–41; Crisp and Warfield 2000: 175). Three things should be pointed out here. First, the compatibilist need not argue *from* compatibilism to the claim that Margo, say, has the ability to do otherwise, and thus, he or she is not "presupposing" the compatibility thesis *qua* premise. Second, the ability claim is offered as an unproblematic assessment of Margo's current skills, oppor-tunities, and knowledge. As long as this ascription is not prima facie outlandish, then the ball is thrown back into the incompatibilist's court; why isn't Margo able to return the book to Suzanne's desk? In what way is she incapacitated? Incom-patibilists have made similar undefended ability claims in their discussions of the transfer principles (for example, that an agent is able to refrain from tossing a coin; McKay and Johnson 1996). Third, the response that Margo is unable to place the book back on Suzanne's desk *because* she is caused to do otherwise is tanta-mount to begging the question on behalf of the incompatibilist. Defending the consequence argument by stipulating that a counterexample to β must not be consistent with or "presuppose" an assumption that an agent is able to do other than what is determined, is unlikely to impress anyone not already committed to incompatibilism.

Nevertheless, if the compatibilist's claim that Margo is able to do otherwise cannot be separately explicated and defended, then the consequence argument has not been *shown* to be unsound on either the broad, causal, or strict readings of ability. To be sure, an account of the ability-to-do or of the "openness" of a course of action is essential to *secure* the counterexample to the argument, but why suppose that such an account is not available? While the familiar conditional analyses of old-fashioned compatibilism might be deficient, these are not the only candidates to be found in the literature.[11] It will not do to scoff and complain that the alternative accounts obviously misuse the term *able* prior to any exami-nation of their merits; rejecting any one of these compatibilist analyses must be based on an argument that it is inadequate for the purposes of ascribing respon-sibility.

Still, by acknowledging that Margo is able to do something that would imply a difference in the past or in the laws, the compatibilist must agree that if deter-minism is true then agents have abilities whose exercise would *require* either prior miracles or an altered past. This conditional may appear "incredible," as O'Connor insists:

> When I wonder what is now in my power to do, I am wondering what is open to me given the way things are and have been and the laws that constrain how things might be. . . . I want to know which of those abilities I am able to exer-

cise *in the present circumstances.* . . . An 'ability' to act here and now, the actual
exercise of which strictly requires a prior condition that is lacking and which I
cannot in any way contribute to bringing about, is, in the sense at issue, no
ability at all. (This is essentially what closure under logical entailment for unavoidability implies.)[12]

Several points can be made in response. First, the locutions "given the way things
are and . . . might be" and "the present circumstances" must fall within the scope
of "wondering" and "know," respectively, if O'Connor's description of what happens in deliberation is accurate. Given our limited grasp of the actual facts, what
we wonder about and want to know is what we can do given what we *take* to be
the relevant past, present, and future circumstances. However, the conviction that
what we take to be relevant allows for different open alternatives is entirely consistent with adopting a deterministic stance (Kapitan 1986a). Second, that one is
strictly able to do something that would require a change in the past or laws if
we did it may seem incredible, but why any more so than the incompatibilist's
affirming that Margo would be *unable* at 11:59:52 A.M. to return the book to
Suzanne's desk by noon if determinism were true, especially when we grant that
Margo would retain the requisite skill, knowledge, and opportunity to take the
book out of her briefcase and place it on Suzanne's desk during the said interval?
Third, in his last sentence, O'Connor assumes the closure of ability under entailment—or, under the relation denoted by "requires"—noting that it is implied by
closure for unavoidability. But any compatibilist who disputes the latter will
equally reject closure for ability, as argued in sections 5 and 6.

In this volume (ch. 7), van Inwagen speaks of an agent's ability to bring about
p in terms of "access" to a region (world) in which p is true. To avoid the McKay-
Johnson counterexample to rule β, he introduces the notion of *exact access* to a
region, defined as access to a region but to none of its proper subregions, and
proposes the following construal of "N":

Np iff p and every region to which anyone has exact access is a subregion
of p.

This, he claims, gives us the notion of the *sheer inescapability* from p, that is, from
the region or world determined by p, that is, the idea that nothing one can do
even *might* lead to the falsity of p. Now, if Np and N(p ⊃ q) are true, then every
region to which anyone has exact access is a subregion of both p and p ⊃ q, so
that no one has exact access to any region outside q. Hence, Nq is true and rule
β is valid. Similarly, agglomeration is retained, for if both Np and Nq hold, then
the only regions to which anyone has exact access are subregions of both p and
q, that is, to subregions of p & q.

Van Inwagen is well aware that compatibilists will not accept his account of
ability and, instead, would favor an analysis—no doubt "some version of the

conditional analysis"—that will sanction the conditional that an agent like Margo can perform an act such that if she did it then P_0 & L would be false.[13] But this move, he writes, "... is contrived and ad hoc; ... it seems that our freedom can only be the freedom to add to the actual past; it seems that our freedom can only be the freedom to act in accordance with the laws of nature" (p. 167). Contrived? Ad hoc? No more so than van Inwagen's own rendition of "N" in terms of exact access to regions of logical space. Nor does it beg the question any more than insisting that one is able to do only what is consistent with the past and laws. According to van Inwagen's account, if Np holds, then not only is p unavoidable for everyone, but so is anything that p implies, for if one had exact access to q where q implies $\sim$p, then one would have exact access to $\sim$p. Similarly, if N(p ⊃ q) holds, then anything anyone is able to do must preserve the truth of p ⊃ q, in which case no one has exact access to $\sim$(p ⊃ q). It immediately follows that the truth of q must be preserved by anything anyone is *able* to do. But A $\sim$ p can be true only if someone has exact access to a region in which $\sim$p is true, that is, only if some region to which someone has exact access is not a subregion of p. No one has such access if Np and N(p ⊃ q) hold. Of course rule β can be validated in this manner, but only through a construal of ability that *explicitly* excludes anyone from being able to prevent what is already determined. Predictably, the compatibilist will reject this analysis.

I noted earlier that the neutral observer should be unimpressed by a presentation of the Consequence Argument that *begins* with an analysis of ability explicitly requiring that what one is able to bring about must be consistent with the past and laws. Similarly, he or she should not be swayed by a defense of the argument that *relies* upon such an analysis.

5. The Diodoran Strategy

At this stage, it might seem that the debate has reached an impasse (Fischer 1994: 83–85; Kane 1996a: 51–52), and some readers might harbor a suspicion that the compatibilist-incompatibilist divide over free will is unresolvable.[14] I think this would be premature; since the study of the practical modalities has a healthy future in front of it, there is little ground for supposing that the powerful reasoning underlying incompatibilism can be so easily quieted. Other possibilities of developing the Consequence Argument turn on new interpretations of, or on interrelations among, the notions of ability and unavoidability. I examine a few in the the three sections that follow.

Recall that the conclusion of the Consequence Argument is relevant to moral responsibility only if it is interpreted as asserting a *strict* unavoidability of whatever is determined. Abbreviating broad, causal, and strict ability by "A^b," "A^c," and "A^s" respectively, letting '$\rightarrow$' represent entailment, and taking uniform indices and operands to be implicit, these operators are related as follows:

$$A^s \rightarrow A^c \rightarrow A^b.$$

Contraposing, there is this pattern of entailment for types of inability:

$$\sim A^b \rightarrow \sim A^c \rightarrow \sim A^s.$$

and, similarly, for unavoidability:

$$N^b \rightarrow N^c \rightarrow N^s.$$

This shows that insofar as something is unavoidable in *any* of the three senses of unavoidability, then it is also strictly unavoidable. If so, establishing the Consequence Argument is a matter of justifying the inference that P is unavoidable in *some* sense—for then it will also be strictly unavoidable—whenever P_0 & L is unavoidable in some sense (see Ginet 1990: 97). Satisfying this *minimal inference pattern* is necessary if the Consequence Argument is sound.

The next thing to note is that the interdefinability of the practical modalities suggests that a suitable closure rule for unavoidability might be derivable from a simpler and more appealing closure rule concerning ability. This method for defending the Consequence Argument begins by noting the similarity of the pattern,

P1.   *Ap*, q is a consequence of p ∴ *Aq*

where *A* is an ability operator, to the Diodoran principle,

M2.   Whatever is a consequence of a possibility is itself possible.

Accordingly, if rules like β, R1, and their variants acquire plausibility through similarity to the modal law,

M1.   Whatever is a consequence of a necessity is itself necessary,

then P1 gains credibility from M2. Moreover, just as M1 and M2 are equivalent, perhaps an instance of P1 could be used to derive a suitable instance of,

P2.   *Np*, q is a consequence of p ∴ *Nq*

where N is an unavoidability operator correlated to A. Consider, for example, the following refinement of P1:

P3. Ap, p entails q $\therefore$ Aq.

Since entailment contraposes, we can easily derive,

P4. $A{\sim}q$, p entails q $\therefore$ $A{\sim}p$,

which van Inwagen has described as "clearly analytic" (1977b: 94) and a "trivial truth" (1983:72). From P4 we obtain,

P5. ${\sim}A{\sim}p$, p entails q $\therefore$ ${\sim}A{\sim}q$,

Proof. Suppose that ${\sim}A{\sim}p$ and that p entails q. If ${\sim}A{\sim}q$ were false, then we would have $A{\sim}q$ and, by P4, $A{\sim}p$. But this contradicts the supposition. With P5, it is but a short step to

P6. Np, p entails q, $\therefore$ Nq.

Similar reasoning allows us to derive other forms of closure for unavoidability.[15] Can this "Diodoran" strategy of arguing for incompatibilism from a P1-like rule provide a means for satisfying the minimal inference pattern of the Consequence Argument?[16]

At issue is whether the Diodoran strategy applies to appropriate *instances* of these general patterns set forth in terms of the three types of ability and unavoidability so far uncovered. Consider, first, the following rule for broad ability:

C1. $A^b p$, p entails q $\therefore$ $A^b q$.

Proof. Suppose that $A^b p$ and p entails q. Then, by the definition of "broad ability," there is a course of action that S is broadly able to do such that p would obtain. Since p entails q, then q would also obtain. Then S is broadly able to do something that would result in q, that is, $A^b q$. By the reasoning that took us from P3 to P6, we derive the following instance of P6:

C2. $N^b p$, p entails q $\therefore$ $N^b q$.

Similarly, with

C3 $A^b p$, $N^b(p \supset q)$ $\therefore$ $A^b q$

(see note 15) we obtain

C4. $N^b p$, $N^b(p \supset q)$ ∴ $N^b q$.

Proof. Suppose both $N^b p$ and $N^b(p \supset q)$. Being broadly unable to prevent p, there is no course of action that S is broadly able to do whose performance would result in ~p, and similarly for $p \supset q$. So there is no course of action S is able to perform that would result in ~q; if there were, then by C3 S would be broadly able to do an action which would ensure ~p, contrary to the supposition. Hence, $\sim A^b \sim q$. Since q follows from the supposition, we have $N^b q$, and in this way we derive both C2 and C3. Of course, with $N^b q$ we can immediately prove $N^s q$, in which case the following rule is also valid:

C5. $N^b p$, p entails q ∴ $N^s q$,

which would deliver the incompatibilist's goal in one step.

Do we have the means for satisfying the minimal inference pattern by virtue of these lines of reasoning? Not at all. Return to the case of Margo and recall that her ability to return the book to Suzanne's desk by noon yields her strict ability to bring about ~P, that is,

(a) $A^s \sim P$,

which is the cornerstone of the main compatibilist response. Accepting this ability claim under the assumption that P is already determined, the compatibilist must deny both that

(b) $N^s P$ (P is strictly unavoidable),

and, by the previous entailments, that

(c) $N^b P$ (P is broadly unavoidable),

Given that $(P_0 \& L)$ entails P, then the valid rules C2 or C3 require the compatibilist to deny

(d) $N^b(P_0 \& L)$.

The appeal to the Fixity Principles is of no avail in defense of (d). As long as we are speaking of broad ability, then C1–C5 must be accepted, and given that Margo is broadly able to bring about ~P and that $P_0 \& L$ entails P, then she is able to do something such that $P_0 \& L$ would be falsified. Hence, Margo is broadly able to bring about $\sim(P_0$ & L), contrary to (d), and the main compatibilist response is safe despite the derivation of C2, C4, and C5.

Does the situation change if we shift to causal ability? Here the Fixity Principles are unquestionably true and we can readily accept

(e) $N^c(P_0$ & L) (the past and the laws are causally unavoidable),

and consequently,

(f) $N^s(P_0$ & L).

The question now is whether a plausible closure rule can carry us from either (e) or (f) to the strict unavoidability of P and thereby secure a sound instance of the minimal inference pattern. Is the Diodoran strategy of any help here?

Let us consider. If we had

C6. $N^c p$, p entails q $\therefore$ $N^c q$,

then from (e) we could derive

(g) $N^c P$ (P is causally unavoidable)

and we could prove what is desired, namely,

(b) $N^s P$ (P is strictly unavoidable),

contrary to the compatibilist's (a). Similarly, if we had

C7. $N^c p$, $N^c(p \supset q)$ $\therefore$ $N^c q$,

we could derive (g) and our work would be finished. Now, can either C6 or C7 be justified? We could derive C6 by the reasoning that allowed the derivation of P6 from P3 if we had the relevant instance of P3 for causal ability, namely,

C8. $A^c p$, p entails q $\therefore$ $A^c q$.

But since what is entailed by what someone brings about need not itself be something that is *brought about*, for example, necessary truths, then C8 fails. However, a related principle holds:

C9. $A^c p$, p's obtaining would make it the case that q obtains $\therefore$ $A^c q$, if we assume that the "makes it the case" relation is transitive. Now if we had

C10. $\sim A^c \sim p$, p's obtaining would make it the case that q obtains.$\therefore A^c \sim q$,

we could derive

C11. $N^c p$, p's obtaining would make it the case that q obtains $\therefore N^c q$

and use it to obtain (g) from (e). But we cannot establish C10 from C9 in the manner in which we derived P5 from P3 because the "makes it the case" relation does not contrapose. This is a good thing, for C10 is invalid in any case. Consider that my having been born with a certain deformity in my hands (p) would have made it the case that I cannot play Beethoven's *Moonlight* Sonata on the piano within the next hour (q). I am not now causally able to bring it about that I was not born with that deformity, so $\sim A^c \sim p$ holds. However, since I am able to play that sonata on the piano within the next hour, then I am able to prevent my *not* playing it on the piano within the next hour, in which case $A^c \sim q$ holds and $\sim A^c \sim q$ does not. Consequently, C10 fails.

An alternative Diodoran route to C6 and C11 goes through

C12. $A^c p$, p entails q, q is false $\therefore A^c q$,

that is, if an agent can do something that makes it the case that p then, since p entails q and q is false, the agent's making it the case that p would also make it the case that q. With this principle—deemed "unassailable" by William Hasker (1989a: 112–114)—we avoid the problem that doomed C8. Moreover, C12 is particularly relevant to the compatibilist claim that a person is able to bring about a situation which is already determined not to obtain. If C12 is true, we can establish C6 as follows. Suppose that we have both $N^c p$ and p entails q, but that $N^c q$ is false, that is, $\sim N^c q$. Then $\sim(q \,\&\, \sim A^c \sim q)$, that is, either $\sim q$ or $A^c \sim q$. Since p entails q and $N^c p$ implies p, then q is true. Accordingly, $A^c \sim q$ is true. Since $\sim q$ entails $\sim p$ and $\sim p$ is false, then, by C12, $A^c \sim p$. But $A^c \sim p$ contradicts $N^c p$, which is given. Consequently, with C12 we establish C6 and, by similar reasoning, C11. With either C6 or C11, we have the means for deriving (g) and, hence (b) from the premise (e). The conclusion of the Consequence Argument would then be secured by way of acceptable premises.

Does this clinch it? Once again, the compatibilist who thinks that Margo is able to return the book to Suzanne's desk accepts

(h) $A^c \sim P$

and consequently rejects

(g) N^cP

and thereby concludes that C6, C7, and C11 are all invalid. Since C6 and C11 are derivable from C12, then the compatibilist is forced to deny the validity of C12. Is this feasible? Yes, and the route to so doing is to recognize that the following instance of C12 is invalid:

(i) $A^c\sim P$, P entails $\sim(P_0 \& L)$, it is false that $\sim(P_0 \& L)$ $\therefore$ $A^c(P_0 \& L)$.

Accepting (h), each of the premises of (i) can be granted, but since Margo is unable to make it the case that $\sim(P_0 \& L)$ obtains, then the conclusion is obviously false. So C12 is invalid and the proof of C6 and C11 collapses.

It is important to distinguish C12 from the valid C9 and, thus, from this equally valid refinement of C9:

C13. A^cp, p's obtaining would make it the case that q obtains, q is false $\therefore$
A^cq,

While this rule cannot be used to derive C11, it might be thought to show that the compatibilist is committed to denying one or both of the fixity principles. Consider this instance of C13:

(j) $A^c\sim P$, $\sim P$'s obtaining would make it the case that $\sim(P_0 \& L)$ obtains, it is false that $\sim(P_0 \& L)$ $\therefore$ $A^c\sim(P_0 \& L)$.

Since (h) holds, and it is false that $\sim(P_0 \& L)$, one might be tempted to use (j) in deriving,

(k) $A^c\sim(P_0 \& L)$

which would violate the Fixity Principles. One way to avoid this is to deny (h), but if we do this, then we are committed to affirming (g) and, thus, the desired (b). To block this inference, the compatibilist need only notice that while (j) is valid, the premise

(l) $\sim P$'s obtaining would make it the case that $\sim(P_0 \& L)$ obtains

is clearly false, since the counterfactual dependency of $\sim P$ upon $\sim(P_0 \& L)$ is simply not of the "make it the case" variety. Hence, C13 does not threaten the compatibilist with an embarrassing denial of the fixity principles.

Despite its initial appeal, the Diodoran strategy affords no effective reply to the compatibilist critique as long as discussion is confined to broad and causal ability. The valid rules C2, C4, and C5 for broad ability cannot be coupled with true premises to satisfy the minimal inference pattern, and the considerations raised against C6, C7, and C11 suggest that there is little hope for finding a valid closure rule for causal unavoidability.

6. STRICT ABILITY AND THE CLOSURE PRINCIPLES

Perhaps the minimal inference pattern can be satisfied by considerations of strict ability alone. Since

(f) $N^s(P_0 \,\&\, L)$

is undoubtedly true, perhaps we can infer

(b) N^sP

directly by means of a closure principle for strict unavoidability, namely,

C14. N^sp, p entails q ∴ N^sq

or

C15. N^sp, $N^s(p \supset q)$ ∴ N^sq.

Are these rules valid? No. Once again, the example of Margo is as effective against C14 and C15 as it is against C6 and C7. Furthermore, even if C14 and C15 follow from a Diodoran rule for strict ability such as

C16. A^sp, p entails q ∴ A^sq

or

C17. A^sp, if p were the case then q would be the case ∴ A^sq, the cognitive requirements on strict ability block the closure of strict ability over the involved consequence relations. The computer examples of section 3 show that an agent might be strictly able to bring about that a certain sequence of keys is struck within a ten-second interval, but not strictly able to bring about each of the causal consequences of that event or the abstruse necessary truths it entails since these would not be reliable consequences. Again, by virtue of certain biological laws, my inhaling cigar smoke may entail that my nervous system is in chemical state NIC. Ignorant as I am of physiology, I have utterly no conception of this state much less than that it is brought about by my smoking a cigar. It was induced by something I did intentionally, but, lacking the requisite concepts, I did not bring it about reliably. These examples render the likes of C16 and C17 futile.[17]

Do *any* closure principles hold for strict ability and unavoidability? How do we deal with the powerful suggestion that if unavoidability is a type of necessity and ability is a type of possibility then both practical modalities should be governed by closure principles akin to the modal laws M1 and M2? In fact, the classifications are only partly correct. A critical difference between these practical modalities and the alethic modalities is that strict ability and strict unavoidability harbor epistemic elements that the ordinary alethic modalities lack. While allusions to "blind necessity" (and "blind possibility") are entirely apt, the sort of ability worth caring about is blessed with vision, fortunately.

Still, is it not correct to maintain that you can do what is *required* by what you can do (O'Connor 2000: 17)? For example, Jenine might be obligated to see to it that her son is enrolled in the college of his choice, and in most institutions of higher learning this would involve her undertaking a substantial course of action composed of many subsidiary steps, for instance, paying the application fee. Assuming that she is able to act as she ought, must she not also be able to perform all the subsidiary actions required to complete the larger course of action? Well, of course, but this answer must be properly formulated in terms of the appropriate consequence relation suggested by *required*. For example, the following principle is plausible:

C18. $A^s p$, q would be a reliable consequence of S's bringing about p $\therefore$ $A^s q$

where the temporal parameter on the consequence relation is the same as that on the ability operator. That is, if at t agent S correctly envisions both that p would result from a considered action and that q would result from p, then at t S accurately anticipates that q would be a result of his action. It is in this way that S's ability to bring about p implies an ability to bring about whatever is reliably "required" by bringing about p. So if Jenine is strictly able to enroll her son in the chosen college, then she is strictly able to perform any act reliably required by so doing. As a refinement of C18 we have

C19. $A^s\sim p$, $\sim q$ would be a reliable consequence of S's bringing about $\sim p$ ∴ $A^s\sim q$

and so,

C20 $\sim A^s\sim q$, $\sim q$ would be a reliable consequence of S's bringing about $\sim p$ ∴ $\sim A^s p$.

Hence,

C21. $N^s q$, $\sim q$ would be a reliable consequence of S's bringing about $\sim p$ ∴ $N^s p$.

While each of C20–C213 holds, the following rule,

C22. $N^s p$, q would be a reliable consequence of S's bringing about p ∴ $N^s q$.

is invalidated any time S possesses more than one way of reliably bringing about q. Inability to prevent a situation from obtaining does transfer to any action that would reliably prevent it, but there is no automatic transfer from sufficient conditions to actions.[18]

Compatibilists need have no quarrel with any of C18–C21, since these rules cannot be used to support the Consequence Argument. To illustrate, suppose, as before, that P_0 & L entails P and we accept the counterfactual

(m)   If Margo were to bring about $\sim P$, then $\sim(P_0$ & L) would obtain,

as well as what the compatibilist insists upon, namely,

(n)   Margo is strictly able to bring about $\sim P$.

If we had C17, then we could infer the implausible

(o)   Margo is strictly able to bring about $\sim(P_0$ & L)

and thereby reveal the implausibility of the compatibilist's position. However, C17 is invalid. Alternatively, one might try to infer the implausible (o) from (n) by means of the valid C18 if the following held:

(p) $\sim(P_0$ & L) would be a reliable consequence of Margo's bringing about $\sim$P.

Yet it is pretty certain that (p) fails. Even if a theory of causation allowed that $\sim(P_0$ & L) would be a *causal* consequence of Margo's bringing about $\sim$P, it would be a *reliable* consequence only when Margo correctly envisions a route from her returning the book to Suzanne's desk to $\sim(P_0$ & L). But this sort of envisionment is clearly impossible for any finite agent like ourselves, since $\sim(P_0$ & L) is beyond our cognitive grasp.[19] So (p) is implausible as well. Alternatively, from C14 and the obviously true

(q) P_0 & L and Margo is strictly unable to prevent P_0 & L,

we could infer the negation of the compatibilist's (n). However, we have noted that C14 and other rules of the P2 sort for strict ability are invalid. On the other hand, the valid C20 could be used to infer the negation of (n) from the negation of (o) if (p) were true, contrary to what the compatibilist wants. However, (p), as we have seen, is false.

The upshot? The Diodoran strategy is of no more use in deriving a suitable closure rule for strict unavoidability than it was for causal unavoidability, and the closure rule that is valid, namely (C21), is something the compatibilist can live with. To the extent that we have so far articulated the practical modalities, the Consequence Argument has not succeeded.

7. STRENGTHENING THE UNAVOIDABILITY OPERATOR

While I have distinguished three senses in which an agent S is able to bring about p, they are alike in that the action S is able to do that would bring about p is such that its exercise would *ensure* p. But now we must deal with a weaker notion whereby S is able to bring about p if S is able to act so that it *might* be the case that p (O'Connor 2000: 13), an adjustment that yields weakened senses of broad, causal, and strict ability. From the standpoint of responsibility ascriptions, we should not restrict attention to actions that ensure a result since there are relevant senses of ability that do not require any such guarantee. Prospectively, we can ascribe responsibility for probable outcomes of acts (see Kane 1996a: 55). Retrospectively, uncharitable fans might blame a basketball player for missing a layup in a closely contested game even though any of the actions open to him would only make it highly probable that the ball would go through the basket. Again, a teacher might blame a student for failing to submit a paper on time even though, when the paper was assigned, there was no plan of action at the student's command that would guarantee that the paper would be completed and submitted on time. Sometimes the probabilities of success are slight; if I deliberately feed you a kind of mushroom I know to be 5 percent fatal, I am blamable for bringing about your death should you perish upon eating it.

A weakened sense of the ability to bring about corresponds to a strengthened unavoidability operator so that $N_{s,t}p$ holds just in case "p is true and the agent s cannot act (at or subsequent to t) in such a way so much as *might* be the case that not-p" (O'Connor 2000: 13; McKay and Johnson 1996: 119, and van Inwagen Ch. 7, this volume). Whether this operator is to be interpreted as broad, causal, or strict unavoidability, or is better defined in terms of regular causal ability, is uncertain, so let us simply give it a new label, "N^w," assume that it entails strengthened *strict* unavoidability, and see if we can justify the appropriate reasoning in accord with the minimal inference pattern. As before, there is no barrier to accepting

(r) $N^w(P_0 \& L)$

with the operator indexed to Margo at 11:59:52. The proposed transfer principle is either

C23. N^wp, p entails q ∴ N^wq

for O'Connor, or

C24. N^wp, $N^w(p \supset q)$ ∴ N^wq

for McKay and Johnson and van Inwagen. Have we here a means of justifying the main inference pattern? Not at all, for anyone who accepts (r) and resists the conclusion

(s) N^wP

will take the case of Margo and the book to be as much a counterexample to C23 and C24 as it is to C6, C7, C11, C14, and C15. If we grant that Margo is strictly able to ensure that ~P, that is,

(a) $A^s{\sim}P$

then it follows that she is able to do something that *might* bring about ~P, that is,

(t) $A^w{\sim}P$

holds when interpreted in the strict sense. If so, then by the definition of unavoidability,

(u) N^wP

is false read in the strict sense. But since we can readily concede (r) whenever P is entailed by P_0 & L, then C23 and C24 are invalidated when N^w is taken in the strict sense. Since, by hypothesis, the strict reading of N^w is entailed by the broad and causal readings of N^w, it follows that C23 and C24 are also invalid in the broad and causal senses. Therefore, the revised argument of O'Connor, McKay and Johnson, and van Inwagen fares no better than its predecessors do. The main compatibilist response emerges unscathed, as before.

8. CONCLUSION:
THE COMPATIBILIST'S TASK

At this stage I have explored the Diodoran strategy and concluded that it fails to generate a valid closure rule of unavoidability that can justify the reasoning of the minimal inference pattern. Of the closure rules that are valid, either they cannot be mated to corresponding true premises, as is the case with C1–C5, C9, and C13, or they are unable to generate the desired conclusion from its premises, as with C18–C21.

Nothing precludes the definition of still further senses of *able* and *unavoidable*, or the proposal of further closure principles in terms of which the incompatibilist's argument might be cast. One route is to understand that since an undefined notion of *consequence* was used in the characterization of broad, causal, and strict ability, then there are as many species of ability under each of these three headings as there are consequence relations. So, with n distinct consequence relations, we have $3n$ concepts of ability to bring about and $3n$ unavoidability operators. Every such operator would be correlated with n different candidates for transfer rules, each asserting the closure of that operator under a specific consequence relation, generating $3n \times n$ distinct rules for unavoidability in all. Perhaps among this multitude there are some capable of providing the right sort of inferential mechanism that the Consequence Argument needs. Until they are unearthed, however, I conclude that there is good reason to be suspicious of the claim that any variant of the Consequence Argument can achieve a wholesale refutation of compatibilism.[20]

This assessment provides compatibilists with momentary breathing room at best. As indicated in section 4, those who accept that responsibility for a situation implies ability to bring it about and, perhaps, an ability to prevent it, must explain how agents are *able to do* other than what they are caused to do. Without it, they can give no defense of their counterexamples. With it, they can be confident that the Consequence Argument, by itself, is no refutation of their position. Incompatibilists might shake their heads in exasperation, even scorn, about the prospects for success in this endeavor and insist that the compatibilist misuses the term "able." But as long as the compatibilist provides *an* account of the ability-to-do that will underwrite the main compatibilist response to the Consequence Argument, then the incompatibilist has no choice but to confront the proposed account squarely. The battle can only be decided on the terrain that drives concern about free will, specifically, the nature and presuppositions of moral responsibility. While the standard conditional analysis of ability is flawed, we are not automatically pushed to accept an indeterminist analysis if the other compatibilist accounts of practical freedom already in the market place do the job (see n. 11). If they are ultimately shown to be deficient, it should be remembered that the field of modality is rich with possibilities, theoretical as well as practical, and with a sharpened set of metaphysical tools the compatibilist may yet produce what is needed.

NOTES

I am indebted to Robert Kane and Saul Smilansky for their helpful comments on an earlier version of this essay.

1. If responsibility does not imply "having a choice," a parallel argument can be given by construing "Np as "no one is, or ever has been, even partly responsible for the fact that p," an argument whose rules and premises van Inwagen takes to be equally plausible (1983, 104–5, 183–88). This "direct" argument for the incompatibility of determinism and responsibility is criticized in Kapitan (1986b), Ravizza (1994), and Fischer and Ravizza (1998: ch. 6). It is defended in Warfield (1996) against Ravizza (1994), and a refined version is given in an unpublished manuscript by Michael McKenna, who criticizes the treatment of the argument in Fischer and Ravizza (1998).

2. John Fischer (1994: 62–66) presents what he calls the "conditional version" of the "Argument for Incompatibilism" and contends that it does not utilize a "transfer principle" of the sort used in van Inwagen's argument. Van Inwagen (1994: 99) alleges that

this argument is invalid, though Fischer is careful to point out that while the argument is not formally valid it is nonetheless reasonable to accept its conclusion given the content of its premises (Fischer 1994: 228 n.43, and see Fischer and Ravizza 1996: 220–22). Contrary to Fischer's contention, I have argued that his conditional version tacitly relies on a type of transfer principle (Kapitan 1996: 432–33).

3. The proposed counterexamples to rule β by David Widerker (1987) and Kadri Vihvelin (1988) depend upon an assumption of indeterminism. For this reason they do not achieve what a compatibilist might hope, namely, a demonstration that β fails in a deterministic universe, a point emphasized by McKay and Johnson (1996: 118). The indeterministic examples are also discussed in O'Connor (1993a and 2000: 9–14) and Crisp and Warfield (2000).

4. See, for instance, John Fischer, who writes: "The strategy I have been presenting construes certain statements of the form, 'S can bring about such-and-such,' as implicitly involving conjunctions. The two conjuncts are a 'can-claim' such as 'S can do X' and a conditional, such as 'If S were to do X, then Y would occur' " (Fischer 1994: 75). Gallois (1977: 102) also suggested this analysis, and arguably, van Inwagen's definition of "can render false" fits the pattern as well (1983: 68). The apparent circularity of the definition can be mitigated by treating the definiendum as "ability to bring about" and offering a separate account of the "ability to do" of the definiens (as I do in Kapitan 1996).

5. Carl Ginet provides a similar formula: "It was open to S at t to make it the case that p if and only if it was open to S at t to act in such a way that had S so acted, S would thereby have made it the case that p" (Ginet 1990: 102). I merely economize in calling this sort of ability "causal," acknowledging a difference between 'causing' and 'making it the case that' (see Kim 1974 and Hasker 1989a: 105). The distinction between broad and causal ability is noted in Gallois (1977: 102–4), Lewis (1981: 120); and Horgan (1985: 347). Vihvelin (1991, 1995a and b) argues that counterfactual power over the past or laws is not itself a causal ability, even given Lewis's counterfactual analysis of causation. Ekstrom (1995, 1998a) contests Vihvelin's claim, suggesting that the proponent of the Consequence Argument can profit by adopting a Lewisonian analysis of causation. However, a problem with this analysis is that it ignores the apparent temporal directionality of causation.

6. David Lewis's local miracle approach does not require that the action Margo is able to do is itself a law-breaking event; rather, the law may be broken by some "divergent miracle" occurring shortly before her action (Lewis 1981; Horgan 1985; and Kapitan 1991b: 337–38nn. 4 and 5). That the compatibilist might opt for a backtracking approach is noted in Greenspan (1976) and articulated in several places, including Narveson (1977), Foley (1979), Fischer (1983a), Horgan (1985), and Peacocke (1999: ch. 7, sec. 4). Choice of either alternative depends partly upon one's approach to counterfactuals. While the backtracking theory requires the entire past to be substantially altered in order to retain the laws, the local miracle approach alters the laws and requires only a slight adjustment of the past.

7. If unavoidability is not agglomerative, then the correlated notion of ability is not disjunctive-distributive. Thus, even if Margo is able to bring about ($\sim P_0$ or $\sim L$), it would not follow that she is able to bring about $\sim P_0$ or able to bring about $\sim L$. But then one must either defend the claim that the truth of (a) does not require the truth of one of (b) or (c), or avoid interpreting the premises in terms of broad ability.

8. Mark Brown (1988) accounts for skill in terms of what he calls a "reliable" connection between action and result: I am able to reliably bring about p if p is true at every world within a relevant cluster of worlds, where a cluster is *relevant* if it "corresponds to choices of actions of which I am actually *capable*" (p. 5). For example, a skilled archer reliably brings about the arrow's hitting the bull's-eye since in every world—or in most worlds—in which he intentionally performs certain actions the arrow hits the bull's-eye. While an ordinary archer might not hit the bull's-eye at will, he may very well be able to reliably bring about the arrow's hitting the target. By omitting cognitive elements, Brown's notion of reliability does not capture what I am here calling "strict ability" or "skill." The principal shortcoming of his account—and hence, of his semantics for the language of ability—is that its concept of ability is not rich enough for responsibility ascriptions, as I argue in the next three paragraphs of the main text. Both O'Connor (1993a, 2000) and Ginet (1990) acknowledge that there is *a* notion of ability that includes a cognitive requirement, though it plays little role in their development and defense of the consequence argument. Others who acknowledge cognitive conditions on ability include Dennett (1984: 116–18), Vihvelin (1988), Kapitan (1989, 1991a, 1996), and Glannon (1995).

9. There are several accounts of intentional action where the intentional status of projected actions is understood in terms of plans or envisioned routes. See, for example, Goldman (1970: ch. 3), Castañeda (1975: ch. 12), Brand (1984: chs. 1, 8, and 9), Bratman (1987, chs. 3 and 8); and Moser and Mele (1994).

10. The problem with the definitions of broad and causal ability is that by allowing someone to be able to bring about whatever results from his or her undertakings they squeeze ability out of blind luck. That the sort of ability relevant to responsibility requires skill has been emphasized by several philosophers, notably Kenny (1975), Gert and Duggan (1979), Shatz (1988: 185), and Brown (1988, 1990). On the importance of general ability (skill) for responsibility, see Wallace (1994: 182–92). See also John Fischer's discussion of Kenny's example in (1994: 25–29).

11. See, for example, the accounts offered in Dennett (1984); Berofsky (1987); Mele (1996), and Bok (1998). In previous writings I have a defined a notion of doxastic openness as follows: a course of action A is *doxastically open* at time t to agent Sam, say, just in case relative to what Sam then takes himself to believe, (1) if he undertook to A then he would A, and if he undertook to refrain from A-ing then he would refrain, and (2) his undertaking A is as yet contingent (Kapitan 1996: 437). Only actions that an agent conceives can be doxastically open for him or her. I then argue that by adding the efficacy conditionals, namely, that Sam actually would do A (or refrain from doing it) depending on whether he undertook to do so (or not), we produce a notion of the ability-to-do (or, of a course of action being an "open alternative") that is rich enough to justify ascriptions of responsibility (see Kapitan 1986b, 1989, 1996, 2000).

12. O'Connor (2000: 17). See also Greenspan (1976: 244), which makes a similar point.

13. Here's an example of a compatibilist analysis in terms of access to regions of logical space. For any time t and course of action K, an agent S at t has access to both (1) some region in which S performs K whenever K is an open alternative for him at t and (2) to some region corresponding to p whenever p would be a reliable consequence of S's K-ing. Then $N_{s,t}p$ holds whenever p is true and there is no course of action S is able to do that would reliably result in $\sim p$. On this analysis, rule β fails. Naturally, the

notion of an agent's being *able* to perform an action, must itself be characterized in compatibilist terms (see n. 11).

14. Strawson (1986) and Double (1991) express skepticism that the debate between compatibilists and incompatibilists can ever be satisfactorily resolved or that either position can be adequately defended, but I have argued that their critiques are unconvincing (Kapitan 1990, 1994). A more promising, less skeptical, "hybrid" view that combines elements of both compatibilism and incompatibilism is developed in Smilansky (2000).

15. For example, if we have "Ap, $N(p \supset q)$ $\therefore$ Aq," a refinement of P1, we can obtain "Np, $N(p \supset q)$ $\therefore$ Nq," assuming that $N(p \supset q)$ contraposes to yield "$A\sim q$, $N(p \supset q)$ $\therefore$ $A\sim p$." Likewise, "Np, If p were the case then q would be the case $\therefore$ Nq" is derivable from "Ap, if p were the case then q would be the case $\therefore$ Aq" given the transitivity of conditional dependency, a defensible claim when the relevant contexts or circumstances in which the dependency holds are held constant, as argued by Lycan (1984: 449); Honderich (1988: 33), and Lowe (1990: 84–85). Note that a pattern F is a *refinement* of pattern G just in case any structure that exhibits F also exhibits G (compare Castañeda 1975: 69).

16. The Diodoran strategy is explicit in Talbott (1986a: 458–60) and Hasker (1989a: 111–15), but employed whenever the Consequence Argument is defended by appeal to a closure principle for ability (for example, in van Inwagen 1983: 72 and O'Connor 2000: 17).

17. If we acknowledge cognitive requirements on the ability-to-do (n. 11), then a similar argument can be used against the principle: "If S can do X and doing X would be truly describable as doing Y, then S can do Y." On the other hand, if the description of S's action as being one of doing "Y" is external to "can" because it falls outside the constitutive cognitive operator, however, as J. M. Fischer suggests (1994: 28), then while the principle is true enough, it cannot be used to refute compatibilism since "can" would have no more force than "broadly able," thereby inviting the main compatibilist response once again.

18. J. M. Fischer makes a similar point in arguing against the principle that if S cannot do X and doing X would be doing Y then S cannot do Y (Fischer 1994: 29). It should be noted that C22 cannot be derived from C18 in the manner in which P6 was obtained from P3, since the relation of reliable consequence does not contrapose to produce the required lemmas.

19. This provides another means of countering Laura Ekstrom's attempt to rescue the Consequence Argument by means of David Lewis's theory of causation (see n. 5).

20. Two other versions of the Consequence Argument are presented in Ginet (1990: 101–6) and Fischer (1994: 62–66). I have criticized the former in Kapitan (1991a: 238–39 and 1996: 433–35), and the latter in (1996: 432–33).

CHAPTER 7

....

FREE WILL REMAINS
A MYSTERY

....

PETER VAN INWAGEN

THIS chapter has two parts. In the first part, I concede an error in an argument I have given for the incompatibility of free will and determinism. I then show how to modify my argument to avoid this error, and conclude that the thesis that free will and determinism are compatible continues to be—to say the least—implausible. But if free will is incompatible with determinism, we are faced with a mystery, for free will undeniably exists, and it also seems to be incompatible with *in*determinism. That is to say; we are faced with a mystery if free will *is* incompatible with indeterminism. Perhaps it is not. The arguments for the incompatibility of free will and indeterminism are plausible and suggestive, but not watertight. And many philosophers are convinced that the theory of "agent causation" (or some specific development of it) shows that acts that are undetermined by past states of affairs can be free acts. But the philosophical enemies of the idea of agent causation are numerous and articulate. Opposition to the idea of agent causation has been based on one or the other of two convictions: that the concept of agent causation is incoherent, or that the reality of agent causation would be inconsistent with "naturalism" or "a scientific worldview." In the second part of this paper, I will defend the conclusion that the concept of agent causation is useless to the philosopher who wants to maintain that free will and indeterminism are compatible. But I will not try to show that the concept of agent causation is incoherent or that the real existence of agent causation should be rejected for scientific reasons. I will assume—for the sake of argument—that agent causation is possible and that it in fact exists. I will, however, present an argument for the conclusion that free will and indeterminism are incompatible even if our acts or their causal antecedents are products of agent causation. I see no way to respond to this argument. I conclude that free will remains a mystery—that is, that free will undeniably exists and that there is a strong and unanswered prima facie case for its impossibility.

1. THE ARGUMENT FOR INCOMPATIBILISM

I have offered the following argument for the incompatibility of free will and determinism. [1] Let us read "Np" as "p and no one has or ever had any choice about whether p." I employ the following two inference rules:

α $\Box p \vdash Np$
β $Np, N(p \supset q) \vdash Nq$.

(The box, of course, represents necessity or truth in all possible worlds.) Let "L" represent the conjunction of the laws of nature into a single proposition. Let "P_0" represent the proposition that describes the state of the world at some time in the remote past. Let "P" represent any true proposition. The following statement, proposition (1), is a consequence of determinism:

(1) $\Box((P_0 \ \& \ L) \supset P)$.

I now argue,

(2) $\Box \ (P_0 \supset [L \supset P])$ 1, standard logic
(3) $N(P_0 \supset [L \supset P])$ 2, α
(4) NP_0 Premise
(5) $N(L \supset P)$ 3, 4, β
(6) NL Premise
(7) NP 5, 6, β.

Since the two premises are obviously true—no one has any choice about the past; no one has any choice about the laws of nature—(7) follows from (1) if the two rules of inference are valid.[2] And from this it follows that if determinism is true, no one has any choice about anything.

Are the two rules of inference valid? Rule α obviously is, whatever Descartes would have us believe about God. The question of the soundness of the argument comes down to the question whether β is valid. And although β does not, perhaps, share the "luminous evidence" of α, it nevertheless seems plausible. One way to appreciate its plausibility is to think in terms of regions of logical space, by which I mean a space whose points are possible worlds. (Distances between points correspond to the "distances" that figure in a Lewis-Stalnaker semantics for counterfactual conditionals; areas or volumes represent probabilities.[3]) Consider figure 7.1.

Suppose Alice is inside p and has no choice about that; suppose she is also inside the region that corresponds to the material conditional whose antecedent is p and whose consequent is q (the heavily shaded region)—and has no choice about *that*. Alice will, of course, be inside the intersection of p and q, and hence inside q.[4] Has she any choice about that? It would seem not. As an aid to our intuitions, let us think of the regions displayed in the diagram as physical regions. Examination of the diagram shows that any way out of q—any escape route from q, so to speak—will either take Alice out of p or out of the shaded region. Therefore, *because* Alice has no way out of p and no way out of the shaded region ($p \supset q$), she has no way out of q. To be inside a region and to have no way out of it is to be inside that region and to have no choice about whether one is inside it. Rule β, therefore, would seem to be valid. This intuitive, diagrammatic argument is very plausible, and at one time I found it, or something very like it, cogent. Unfortunately, as any student of geometry knows, figures can be misleading, since a figure may have unintended special features that correspond to unwarranted assumptions. And this must be so in the present case, owing to the fact that McKay and Johnson have discovered what is undeniably a counterexample to β.[5]

McKay and Johnson begin by noting that α and β together imply the rule of inference that Michael Slote has called Agglomeration:

Np, $Nq \vdash N(p \ \& \ q)$.

(To show this, assume Np and Nq. The next line of the proof is "$\Box(p \supset ([q \supset (p \ \& \ q)]))$." The proof proceeds by obvious applications of α and β.) Rule α is obviously correct. To show β invalid, therefore, it suffices to produce a counterexample to Agglomeration. McKay and Johnson's counterexample to Agglomeration follows:

> Suppose I have a coin that was not tossed yesterday. Suppose, however, that I was able to toss it yesterday and that no one else was. Suppose that if I had tossed it, it might have landed "heads" and it might have landed "tails" and it would have landed in one way or the other (it is false that it might have landed on edge, it is false that a bird might have plucked it out of the air . . .), but I should have had no choice about which face it would have displayed. It seems that

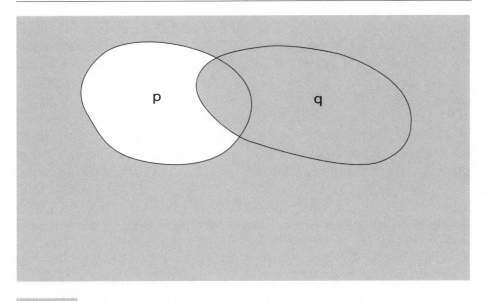

$p \supset q$

Fig. 7.1

N   The coin did not land "heads" yesterday

N   The coin did not land "tails" yesterday

are both true—for if I had tossed the coin, I should have had no choice about whether the tossed coin satisfied the description "did not land 'heads,' " and I should have had no choice about whether the tossed coin satisfied the description "did not land 'tails.' " But

N   (The coin did not land "heads" yesterday & the coin did not land "tails" yesterday)

is false—for I did have a choice about the truth value of the (in fact true) conjunctive proposition *The coin did not land "heads" yesterday and the coin did not land "tails" yesterday*, since I was able to toss the coin and, if I had exercised this ability, this conjunctive proposition would have been false.

The case imagined is, as I said, undeniably a counterexample to Agglomeration. Agglomeration is therefore invalid, and the invalidity of β follows from the invalidity of Agglomeration. Our diagrammatic argument for the validity of β therefore misled us. But what is wrong with it?

We may note that a similar intuitive, diagrammatic argument could have been adduced in support of Agglomeration. Imagine two intersecting regions, p and q. Their region of overlap is, of course, their conjunction. Suppose one is inside p and has no way out of p; and imagine that one is inside q and has no way out of q. One will then be inside p & q; but does it follow that one has no way out of p & q? Inspection of the simple diagram that represents this situation shows that any way out of p & q must either be a way out of p or a way out of q. What is wrong with *this* argument?

To answer this question, we must examine the concept of "having a way out of a region of logical space." Suppose we know what is meant by "having access to" a region of logical space. (A region of logical space corresponds to a proposition, or to a set containing a proposition and all and only those propositions necessarily equivalent to it. To have access to a region of logical space is to be able to ensure the truth of the proposition that corresponds to that region, or to be able to ensure that that region contains the actual world. If one is inside a region, one ipso facto has access to that region. If one has access to p, one ipso facto has access to the regions of which p is a subset—to the "superregions" of p.) To have a way out of a region p of logical space that one is inside is then defined as follows: to have access to some region that does not overlap p—or to have the ability to ensure that the proposition that corresponds to p is false. Now consider figure 7.2.

Suppose I am "inside" the region p & q. Suppose I have access to and only to the following regions: (a) p & q and the other regions I am inside, and (b) r and the superregions of r. ("But what about the subregions of r?" From the fact that one has access to a certain region of logical space, it does not follow that one has access to any of its proper subregions. I may, for example, be able to ensure that the dart hit the board, but unable to ensure with respect to any proper part of the board that it hit that proper part.) It follows from these suppositions that I am inside p and have no way out of p—for every region to which I have access overlaps p. (And, of course, the same holds for q: every region to which I have access overlaps q.) But I do have a way out of p & q, for I have access to a region—r—that does not overlap p & q. (It is not essential to the example that r be a nonconnected region. It might have been "horseshoe-shaped" or a "ring." What is essential is that r overlap p and overlap q and not overlap p & q.)

If one thinks about the issues raised by McKay and Johnson's counterexample in terms of diagrams of logical space, it is easy enough to construct a counterexample to β itself (at least in the sense in which figure 7.2 represents a counterexample to Agglomeration).[6] Here is a simple counterexample to β. Consider three regions of logical space, related to one another as in the following diagram:

Suppose I am inside p and inside $p \supset q$. (Or, what is the same thing, suppose I am inside p & q.) Suppose I have access to and only to the following regions: (a) the regions I am inside, and (b) r and its superregions. Then I have no way out of p (every region to which I have access overlaps p) and no way out of $p \supset q$ (every region to which I have access overlaps $p \supset q$), but I have a way out of q, for I have access to a region—r—that does not overlap q.

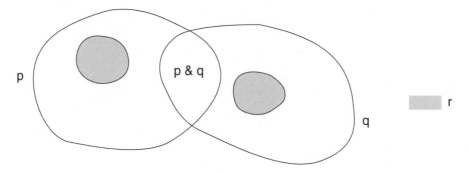

Fig. 7.2

How did figure 7.1 and the intuitive argument based on it mislead us? The answer is simple. The informal argument invited us to think of "having a way out of a region" as something like having available a path or line leading from a particular point inside that region *to a particular point* outside that region. (Recall my use of the term "escape route.") That, after all, is what it is normally like to have a way out of a region of physical space, and our intuitive grasp of any sort of space is mainly by way of analogy with physical space. But if we exercise our imaginations, we can think of ways in which one might have an ability to change one's position in physical space that is entirely different from the ability to follow a path that leads to a given point. We might for example suppose that one can bring it about that one changes one's position in space without moving—by magic, perhaps—and that when one changes one's position by this means, one might arrive at *any* of the points that make up some extended region.

Now consider once more Alice and figure 7.1 (but add to figure 7.1 a region *r* that is related to *p* and *q* just as *r* is related to *p* and *q* in figure 7.3). Our intuitive argument for the conclusion that a way out of *q* must either be a way out of *p* or a way out of $p \supset q$ (the shaded region) was this:

> As an aid to our intuitions, let us think of the regions displayed in the diagram as physical regions. Any way out of *q*—any escape route from *q*, so to speak— will either take Alice out of *p* or out of the shaded region.

As long as Alice moves by following a continuous path through space (an "escape route"), this is correct: any continuous path that leaves both *p* and the shaded region must leave *q*. But suppose that although Alice has no way of crossing any of the boundaries shown in the diagram by following a continuous path through space, she has a single magical resource: a magical lamp such that if she rubs it, the Slave of the Lamp will instantaneously translate her to a randomly chosen point inside the region *r*. Has Alice a way out of *p*? Has she a way out of $p \supset q$? The answers to these questions, perhaps, depend on how one defines "a way out."

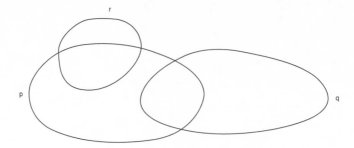

Fig. 7.3

But if we define "a way out" in a way parallel to our definition of "a way out of a region of logical space," that is.

> If one is inside a region of space *r*, one has a way out of *r* just in the case that one is able to ensure that one is inside a region that does not over-lap *r*,

the answer to both questions is no: she has no "way out" of either of these regions. But Alice *does* have a way out of *q*: rubbing the lamp constitutes a way out of *q*, for rubbing the lamp will ensure that she is not in *q*. Our intuitions about physical space therefore misled us. As the world is, the only way to leave a region of physical space is to follow a continuous path out of that region, and our intuitions reflect this fact. Our diagrams of logical space are, of course, drawn in physical space and the diagrams therefore invite us to think of one's having access to a region *r* of logical space (a false proposition, a region not containing the actual world) in terms of one's ability to move along a line drawn from the point in the diagram that represents the actual world to some point inside the section of the diagram that represents *r*. Our "diagrammatic" argument misled us into thinking that there could be no counterexample to β (or to Agglomeration) because noth-ing in the concept of "access to a region of logical space" corresponds to the "continuous path" requirement that the real world imposes on our intuitions about "access to a region of physical space." A continuous path through physical space terminates in a single point, not in an extended region. To "have access" to an extended region of physical space is therefore (normally) to have access to one or more of the points that make up that region. To have access to a region of logical space, however, is in no possible case to have access to a point in logical space (a single possible world): Since one's power to direct the course of events is limited, from the fact that one is able to ensure that *some* possible world in which, say, the coin is tossed is actual, it does not follow that one is able to ensure with respect to any given world in which the coin is tossed that one will be able to ensure that *that* world is actual. And of course, one never is able to ensure this; if one were, one would not only be able to ensure that a tossed coin lands on one particular face, but one would be able to determine the truth value of every contingent proposition.

My definition of "N*p*" was "*p* and no one has or ever had any choice about whether *p*." The definiens is equivalent to

> *p* and every region of logical space to which anyone has, or ever had, access overlaps *p*.

Why? Well, suppose that *p*, and that I did not do but was able to do X (and was able to do nothing else that was relevant to the truth value of *p*), and that if I had done X, *p* might have been true and might have been false. It seems wrong in that case to say that I had a choice about the truth value of *p*. If, for example, the coin was untossed and I was able to toss it, and if I had tossed it, it might have fallen "heads" and might not have fallen "heads," it is wrong to say that I had a choice about the truth value of the (true) proposition that the coin did not land "heads." (This point is the essence of the McKay-Johnson counterexample to Agglomeration.) Now if it were important that the coin have landed "heads" (if someone's life depended on its landing "heads," say), there would be something wrong with my defending my failure to toss the coin by saying, "Look, the coin *didn't* land heads, and I didn't have any choice about that." And it is perhaps intuitively plausible to suppose that if *p* and if I had no choice about whether *p*, then I cannot properly be held morally responsible for *p*. But I do not think that this consideration has any tendency to show that I had a choice about how the coin fell. If I did offer the imagined lame excuse, the proper response would not be, "You did too have a choice about whether the coin landed 'heads' "; it would rather be, "You had a choice about whether the coin was tossed, and if you had tossed it, it might have landed 'heads.' What you are to blame for is not doing your best to bring it about that the coin landed 'heads.' " In sum, if *p* is a true proposition, having a choice about the truth-value of *p* implies being able to *ensure* that *p* is false.[7] And, as we have seen, the following is possible: *p* is true and no one is able to ensure that *p* is false; the conditional whose antecedent is *p* and whose consequent is *q* is true, and no one is able to ensure that that conditional is false; someone is able to ensure that *q* is false.

McKay and Johnson are therefore right. Rule β is invalid, and my argument for the incompatibility of free will and determinism is invalid.

This, of course, does not imply that free will and determinism are compatible, or that there is no plausible argument for the incompatibility of free will and determinism. I think, in fact, that my original argument for the incompatibility of free will and determinism can be turned into a valid argument by a minor modification of rule β.[8] Suppose that, instead of defining "N*p*" as "*p* and no one has, or ever had, any choice about p"—that is, as "p and every region to which anyone has, or ever had, access overlaps p"—, we were to define "Np" as follows:

> p and every region to which anyone has, or ever had, *exact* access *is a subregion of p*.

One has *exact* access to a region if one has access to it *and to none of its proper subregions*. Intuitively, one has exact access to p if one can ensure the truth of p but of nothing "more definite." The properties of the "exact access" relation differ from those of the "access" relation in several important ways. If I am inside a region, I do not in general have exact access to that region. (This is an understatement: the only region I am inside and have exact access to is the actual world.[9]) If I have exact access to a region, then, by definition, I have exact access to none of its (proper) superregions.[10] If I have exact access to the region of logical space in which Hillary Clinton proves Goldbach's Conjecture, it follows that I do *not* have exact access to the region in which *someone* proves Goldbach's Conjecture—although it follows that I *do* have *access* to that region. It is, unfortunately, impossible to give a plausible example of a nonactual region to which I have exact access. Suppose that, although I do not throw the dart, it is within my power to ensure that it hit the board—*and* that, for no proper part of the board is it within my power to ensure that the dart hit that part. Do I have exact access to a region in which the dart hits the board? Presumably not, for presumably I have access to a region in which the dart hits the board *and* I exclaim, "Ah!" For one to have exact access to the nonactual region p, it must be the case that one can ensure the actuality of p but not the joint actuality of p and any logically independent region. If one could ensure the actuality of some nonactual *world*, one would have exact access to that world, of course, but obviously no one can do that—or no one but God. Still, it seems evident that there must be regions of logical space to which any given human being has exact access, simply because a human being's ability to ensure the truth of things, to "fine-tune" his or her actions and their consequences, must come to an end somewhere.

Consider now our operator "N," redefined as I have suggested. I think that this is what I was trying to capture when I defined "Np" as "p and no one has, or ever had, any choice about p." What McKay and Johnson's counterexample shows is that the concept "not having a choice about" has the wrong logical properties to capture the idea I wanted to capture—the idea of the *sheer inescapability* of a state of affairs. But if "N" is redefined in the way I have proposed, the redefined "N" does capture this idea. If every region to which I have access overlaps p, it may nevertheless be true that there is some action I can perform such that, if I did, then p *might* be false. But if every region to which I have *exact* access *is a subregion of p*, every action I can perform is such that, if I did perform it, p would be true: it is not the case that p might be false.

Now if "N" is redefined as I have suggested, rule β is valid—for the simple reason that every set that is a subset of both p and $p \supset q$ (that is, of p & q) is a subset of q. Thus, if every region of logical space to which anyone has exact access is within both p and $p \supset q$, every region of logical space to which anyone has exact access is within q. (And, of course, rule α is valid: every region of logical space to which anyone has exact access is a region of logical space.)

What about the two premises of the argument for the incompatibility of free will and determinism? These both seem true—or at least the reasons for thinking them true are no worse than they were on the "no choice" understanding of "N." Every region of logical space to which anyone has exact access will be a subregion of P_0; every region of logical space to which anyone has exact access will be a subregion of L. (The compatibilist will disagree. The compatibilist will define "is able" in some way—will no doubt employ some version of the "conditional analysis of ability"—that will have the consequence that each of us is *able* to perform various acts, such that, if he or she did perform them, then the conjunction of P_0 and L would be false. Thus, the compatibilist will argue, we do have exact access to regions that are not subregions of both P_0 and L. But this is an old dispute, and I have nothing new to say about it. I will say only this—and this is nothing new—the compatibilist's "move" is contrived and ad hoc; it is "engineered" to achieve the compatibility of free will and determinism; it *seems* that our freedom can only be the freedom to add to the actual past[11;] it *seems* that our freedom can only be the freedom to act in accordance with the laws of nature.)

It seems, therefore, that I now have what I thought I had when I thought rule β was valid on the "no choice" understanding of "N": a valid argument for the incompatibility of free will and determinism whose premises seem to be true. And this, *mutatis mutandis*, is all that can be asked of any philosophical argument. At any rate, no more can be said for any known philosophical argument than this: it is valid and its premises seem to be true.

2. AGENT CAUSATION AND THE *MIND* ARGUMENT

Free will, then, seems to be incompatible with determinism. But, as many philosophers have noted, it also seems to be incompatible with *in*determinism. The standard argument for this conclusion (which I have called the *Mind* Argument because it has appeared so frequently in the pages of the journal, *Mind*) goes something like this:

If indeterminism is to be relevant to the question whether a given agent has free will, it must occur because the acts of that agent cannot be free unless they (or perhaps their immediate causal antecedents) are undetermined. But if an agent's acts are undetermined, then *how* the agent acts on a given occasion is a matter of chance. And if how an agent acts is a matter of chance, the agent can hardly be said to have free will. If, on some occasion, I had to decide whether to lie or to tell the truth, and if, after much painful deliberation, I lied, my lie could hardly have been an act of free will if whether I lied or told the truth was a matter of chance. To choose to lie rather than tell the truth is a *free* choice only if, immediately before the choice was made, it was up to the agent whether he lied or told the truth. That is to say, before the choice was made, the agent must have been able to lie and able to tell the truth. And if an agent is faced with a choice between lying and telling the truth, and if which of these things the agent does is a *mere matter of chance*, then it cannot be up to the agent which of them he does.

(At any rate, this is one way to formulate the *Mind* Argument. Other statements of the argument are available, including some that do not appeal to the concept of chance. I will presently return to this point.) In *An Essay on Free Will*, I tried to show that the *Mind* Argument depended on the "unrevised" version of rule β. If this is correct, then, since "unrevised β" is invalid, the *Mind* Argument is invalid. But perhaps I was wrong to think that the *Mind* Argument depended on "unrevised β," at least in any essential way. Perhaps the *Mind* Argument depends only on the employment of some rule of inference *of the same general sort* as "unrevised β." Perhaps, indeed, the Mind Argument could be rewritten to depend only on "revised β." I will not consider these possibilities. I will not try to answer the question whether the *Mind* Argument is in fact valid. I have a different project. I wish to consider the *Mind* Argument in a very informal, intuitive form, to contend that in this intuitive form the argument has a great deal of plausibility, and to use this contention as the basis of an argument that the concept of *agent causation* is entirely irrelevant to the problem of free will. This is no trivial conclusion. Most philosophers who have thought carefully about the problem of free will maintain that the concept of agent causation is incoherent—and perhaps also maintain that if, *per impossibile*, this concept were coherent, it would be contrary to naturalism or to some other important philosophical commitment to suppose that it applied to anything in the real world. A sizable and respectable minority of the philosophers who have thought carefully about the problem of free will maintain that the concept of agent causation is coherent and, moreover, that agent causation is real and figures in an essential way in the acts of free agents. But almost everyone seems to think that if there really *were* such a thing as agent causation, its reality would constitute a solution to the problem of free will. I will try to show that even if agent causation exists, even if it is an element in the acts of free agents, the problem of free will is just as puzzling as it would have been if no one had ever thought of the idea of agent causation. I am going to try to show that even if agent causation is a coherent concept and a real phenomenon, and we know this, this piece of knowledge will be of no help to the philosopher who is trying to decide what to say about free will.

I begin my argument by characterizing the problem of free will and the concept of agent causation.

The problem of free will in its broadest outlines is this. Free will seems to be incompatible with both determinism and indeterminism. Free will seems, therefore, to be impossible. But free will also seems to exist. The impossible therefore seems to exist. A solution to the problem of free will would be a way to resolve this apparent contradiction. There would seem to be three forms a solution could take, three ways in which one might try to resolve the apparent contradiction. One might try to show, as the compatibilists do, that, despite appearances, free will is compatible with determinism. Or one might try to show, as many incompatibilists do, that, despite appearances, free will is compatible with indeterminism. Or one might try to show, as many "hard determinists" do, that the apparent reality of free will is mere appearance. (To be reasonably plausible, a solution of the third type would probably have to incorporate some sort of argument that moral responsibility does not, as it appears to, require free will— or else an argument that a belief in the reality of moral responsibility is not, as it appears to be, an indispensable component of our moral and legal and political thought.) This is the problem to which, in my view, agent causation is irrelevant. (Perhaps there is some *other* problem that could reasonably be called "the problem of free will" and to which agent causation *is* relevant. I can only say that if such a problem exists, I don't know what it is.)

Agent causation is, or is supposed to be, a relation that agents—thinking or rational *substances*—bear to events. Agent causation is opposed to *event* causation, a relation that events bear to events. The friends of agent causation hold that the causes of some events are not (or are only partially) earlier events. They are rather substances—not *changes* in substances, which are of course events, but "the substances themselves." Thus, they say, Thomas Reid caused the movements of his fingers when he wrote the sentence, "There is no greater impediment to the advancement of knowledge than the ambiguity of words." These movements, they insist, were caused simply by *Reid*, and not by any change in Reid. Or, speaking more carefully, since they are aware on empirical grounds that these movements were in fact caused by changes in Reid's hand and arm and spinal cord and brain, they will say that there were *some* events, events that occurred no more than a few seconds before these movements and were among their causal antecedents, events that presumably occurred within the motor centers of Reid's brain, that were caused by Reid and not by any prior events. Speaking even more carefully, they may say that at any rate there were causal antecedents of the movements of

Reid's fingers to whose occurrence Reid, Reid himself, the thinking substance, *contributed causally*—thus allowing the possibility that earlier events in Reid's brain *also* contributed causally to the occurrence of these events.

Let this suffice for a characterization of the problem of free will and the concept of agent causation. Now how is the concept supposed to figure in a solution of the problem? I believe that the reality of agent causation is supposed to entail that free will and indeterminism are compatible. The idea is something like this. A certain event happens in Reid's brain, an event that, through various intermediate causes, eventually produces a bodily movement that constitutes some voluntary action of Reid's—say, his writing the sentence "There is no greater impediment to the advancement of knowledge than the ambiguity of words." (Perhaps we need not attempt to explain the notion of a bodily movement's "constituting" a voluntary action. The idea is illustrated by this example: certain movements of Reid's arm and hand and fingers constitute his writing the sentence "There is no greater impediment, and so on.") And Reid is, let us suppose, the agent-cause of the aforementioned brain-event that was a causal antecedent of his writing this sentence—or at any rate he contributes agent-causally to its occurrence. (From this point on, I will neglect the distinction between agent-causing an event and contributing agent-causally to its occurrence.) The action, or the event that is Reid's performing it, is not determined by the state of the universe at any time before the antecedent brain-event occurred. (And why not? Well, because the event that was his agent-causing the antecedent brain-event was not determined to occur by any prior state of the universe. And if that event—his agent-causing the antecedent brain-event—had not occurred, his hand and fingers would not have moved and he would not have written the sentence.) And yet it is as obviously true as anything could be that he is responsible for this event, for he was its cause: it occurred because *he* caused it to occur. It was therefore an act of free will, and free will is therefore consistent with indeterminism.

In the sequel, I will take it for granted that the relevance of the concept of agent causation to the problem of free will is to be found in the supposed fact that the reality of agent causation entails that free will is compatible with indeterminism. And I will take it for granted that the argument of the preceding paragraph is a fair representation of the argument that is supposed to establish this compatibility. If there is some other reason agent causation is supposed to be relevant to the problem of free will, or if the argument of the preceding paragraph is a poor or incomplete representation of the reasons for supposing that the concept of agent causation can be used to establish the compatibility of free will and indeterminism, then the argument of the remainder of this chapter will be at best incomplete and at worst entirely beside the point.

In my view, this argument does not successfully in show that the reality of agent causation entails the compatibility of free will and indeterminism. Its weak point, I believe, is the reasoning contained in its last two sentences: "And yet it is as obviously true as anything could be that [Reid] is responsible for [the antecedent brain-event], for he was its cause: it occurred because *he* caused it to occur. It was therefore an act of free will, and free will is therefore consistent with indeterminism." It is not my plan to make anything of the fact that Reid knew even less than I about what goes on in the motor centers of human brains—or of the fact that other agents, agents who act freely if anyone does, do not even know that they *have* brains. Any doubts about the argument that might be based on these facts have to my mind been adequately answered by Chisholm, and I shall not bother about them.[12] Nor shall I raise questions about the cause of the event "its coming to pass that Reid is the agent-cause of the antecedent brain-event."[13] Again, I think Chisholm has seen what the friends of agent causation should say about the cause of this event, to wit, that Reid was its agent-cause—and was, moreover, the agent-cause of the event "its coming to pass that Reid is the agent-cause of the event 'its coming to pass that Reid is the agent-cause of the antecedent brain-event,' " and so *ad infinitum*.[14] Some may object to the thesis that, as an indispensable component of his writing a certain sentence, Reid, without being aware of it, became the agent-cause of an infinite number of events; I do not.

In order to see what I *do* object to in the argument, let us return to the question why some have thought that free will was incompatible with indeterminism. Let us, that is, return to the "mere matter of chance" argument. I will try to state this argument more carefully. (In *An Essay on Free Will*, I had a very short way with any attempt to state the *Mind* argument in terms of an undetermined act's being a random or chance occurrence.[15] I argued there that the words 'random' and 'chance' most naturally applied to *patterns* or *sequences* of events, and that it was therefore not clear what these words could mean if they were applied to single events. It will be evident from what follows that I no longer regard this argument as having any merit.) Let us suppose undetermined free acts occur. Suppose, for example, that in some difficult situation Alice was faced with a choice between lying and telling the truth and that she freely chose to tell the truth—or, what is the same thing, she seriously considered telling the truth, seriously considering lying, told the truth, and was able to tell the lie she had been contemplating. And let us assume that free will is incompatible with determinism, and that Alice's telling the truth, being a free act, was therefore undetermined. Now suppose that immediately after Alice told the truth, God caused the universe to revert to precisely its state one minute before Alice told the truth (let us call the first moment the universe was in this state "t_1" and the second moment the universe was in this state 't_2,' and then let things "go forward again." What would have happened the second time? What would have happened after t_2? Would she have lied or would she have told the truth? Since Alice's "original" decision, her decision to tell the truth, was undetermined—since it was undetermined whether she would lie or tell the truth—her "second" decision would also be undetermined, and this question can therefore have no answer; or it can have no answer but, "Well, although she would either have told the truth or lied, it's not the case that she would have told the truth and it's not the case that she would have lied; lying is not what she would have done, and telling the truth is not what she would have done. One can say only that she *might* have lied and she *might* have told the truth."

Now let us suppose that God *a thousand times* caused the universe the revert to exactly the state it was in at t_1 (and let us suppose that we are somehow suitably placed, metaphysically speaking, to observe the whole sequence of "replays"). What would have happened? What should we expect to observe? Well, again, we can't say what would have happened, but we can say what would *probably* have happened: sometimes Alice would have lied and sometimes she would have told the truth. As the number of "replays" increases, we observers shall—almost certainly—observe the ratio of the outcome "truth" to the outcome "lie" settling down to, converging on, some value.[16] We may, for example, observe that, after a fairly large number of replays, Alice lies in 30 percent of the replays and tells the truth in 70 percent of them—and that the figures 30 percent and 70 percent become more and more accurate as the number of replays increases. But let us imagine the simplest case: we observe that Alice tells the truth in about half the replays and lies in about half the replays. If, after 100 replays, Alice has told the truth 53 times and has lied 48 times,[17] we'd begin strongly to suspect that the figures after a 1,000 replays would look something like this: Alice has told the truth 493 times and has lied 508 times. Let us suppose that these are indeed the figures after 1,000 replays. Is it not true that as we watch the number of replays increase, we shall become convinced that what will happen on the *next* replay is a matter of chance? (The compulsive gamblers among us might find themselves offering bets about what Alice would do on the next replay.) If we have watched 726 replays, we shall be faced with the inescapable impression that what happens on the 727th replay will be due simply to chance. Is there any reason we should resist this impression? Well, we certainly know that nothing we could learn about the situation could undermine the impression, for we already know everything that is relevant to evaluating it: we know that the outcome of the 727th replay will not be determined by its initial state (the common initial state of all the replays) and the laws of nature. Each time God places the universe in this state, both "truth" and "lie" are consistent with the universe's being in this state and the laws of nature. A sheaf of possible futures (possible in the sense of being consistent with the laws) leads "away" from this state, and if the sheaf is assigned a measure of 1, surely we must assign a measure of 0.5 to the largest subsheaf in all of whose members Alice tells the truth and the same measure to the largest subsheaf in all of whose members she lies.

We must make this assignment because it is the only reasonable explanation of the observed approximate equality of the "truth" and "lie" outcomes in the series of replays. And if we accept this general conclusion, what other conclusion can we accept about the 727th replay (which is about to commence) than this: each of the two possible outcomes of this replay has an objective, "ground-floor" probability of 0.5—and there's nothing more to be said? And this, surely, means that, in the strictest sense imaginable, the outcome of the replay will be a matter of chance.

Now, obviously, what holds for the 727th replay holds for all of them, including the one that was not strictly a *replay*, the initial sequence of events. But this result concerning the "initial replay," the "play," so to speak, should hold whether or not God bothers to produce any replays. And if He does not—well, that is just the actual situation. Therefore, an undetermined action is simply a matter of chance: if it was undetermined in the one, actual case whether Alice lied or told the truth, it was a mere matter of chance whether she lied or told the truth. If we knew beforehand that the objective, "ground-floor" probabilities of Alice's telling the truth and Alice's lying were both 0.5, then (supposing our welfare depended on her telling the truth) we could only regard ourselves as *fortunate* when, in the event, she told the truth. But then how can we say that Alice's telling the truth was a free act? If she was faced with telling the truth and lying, and it was a mere matter of chance which of these things she did, how can we say that— and this is essential to the act's being free—she was *able* to tell the truth and *able* to lie? How could anyone be able to determine the outcome of a process when it is a matter of objective, ground-floor chance?

This is the plausible, intuitive version of the *Mind* Argument that I have promised to discuss. I must now show that the concept of agent causation cannot undermine the intuitive plausibility of this argument.

Let us suppose that when Alice told the truth, she agent-caused certain brain-events that, in due course, resulted in those movements of her lips and tongue that constituted her telling the truth. And let us again suppose that God has caused the universe to revert to precisely its state at t_1, and that this time Alice has lied. I do not see how to avoid supposing that in this "first replay" Alice *freely* lied— for if one has to choose between telling the truth and lying, and if one freely chooses to tell the truth, then it must be the case that if one had chosen instead to lie, the choice to lie would have been a free act. (One cannot say that an agent faces exactly two continuations of the present, in one of which he tells the truth but was able to lie and in the other of which he lies and was *un*able to tell the truth.) Now if Alice's lie in the first replay was a free act, she must—according to the friends of agent causation—have been the agent-cause of some among the causal antecedents of the bodily movements that constituted her lying. And so, of course, it will be, *mutatis mutandis*, in each successive replay. If God produces 1,000 replays, and if (as I have tacitly been assuming) the state of the universe at t_1—the common initial state of all the replays—determines that Alice will *either* tell the truth or lie, then, in each replay, Alice will *either* agent-cause cerebral events that, a second or so later, will result in bodily movements that constitute her telling the truth or agent-cause cerebral events that, a second or so later, will result in bodily movements that constitute her lying. She will, perhaps, agent-cause events of the "truth antecedent" sort 508 times and events of the "lie antecedent" sort 493 times.

Let us suppose once more that we are somehow in a position to observe the sequence of replays. We may again ask the question, "Is it not true that as we watch the number of replays increase, we shall become convinced that what will happen in the *next* replay is a matter of chance?" I do not see why we should not become convinced of this. And what might we learn, what is *there* for us to learn, that should undermine this conviction? What should lead us to say that the outcome of the next replay, the 727th, will not be a matter of chance? What should lead us to say that it is anything other than a matter of chance whether Alice will agent-cause truth-antecedent cerebral events or lie-antecedent cerebral events in the about-to-occur 727th replay? Well, one might say this: If it turns out that Alice agent-causes truth-antecedent cerebral events, this will not be a matter of chance because it will be she, *Alice*, who is the cause of the event "its coming to pass that Alice agent-causes truth-antecedent cerebral events." But have we not got every reason to regard the occurrence of *this* event—that is, the occurrence of "its coming to pass that Alice agent-causes the event 'its coming to pass that Alice agent-causes truth-antecedent cerebral events' "—as a matter of chance? If the three events "the truth-antecedent cerebral events"/ "its coming to pass that Alice agent-causes the truth-antecedent cerebral events"/ "its coming to pass that Alice agent-causes the event 'its coming to pass that Alice agent-causes truth-antecedent cerebral events' " are the first three terms of an infinite series of agent-caused events, is not the simultaneous occurrence of all the events in this sequence (as opposed to the simultaneous occurrence of all the events in an infinite sequence of agent-caused events whose first member is "lie-antecedent cerebral events") a mere matter of chance?

Nothing we could possibly learn, nothing God knows, it would seem, should lead us to distrust our initial inclination to say that the outcome of the next replay will be a matter of chance. If this much is granted, the argument proceeds as before, in serene indifference to the fact that we are now supposing Alice to be the agent-cause of various sets of cerebral events that are antecedents of the bodily movements that constitute her acts. And the argument proceeds to this conclusion: if it is undetermined whether Alice will tell the truth or lie, then—*whether or not* Alice's acts are the results of agent-causation—it is a mere matter of chance whether she will tell the truth or lie. And if it is a mere matter of chance whether she will tell the truth or lie, where is Alice's free will with respect to telling the truth and lying? If one confronts a choice between A and B and it is a matter of chance whether one will choose A or B, how can it be that one is *able* to choose A?

I close with an example designed to convince you of this.

You are a candidate for public office, and I, your best friend, know some discreditable fact about your past that, if made public, would—and should—cost you the election. I am pulled two ways, one way by the claims of citizenship and the other by the claims of friendship. You know about my situation and beg me not to "tell." I know (perhaps God has told me this) that there exist exactly two possible continuations of the present—the actual present, which includes your begging me not to tell and the emotional effect of your appeal on me—in one of which I tell all to the press and in the other of which I keep silent; and I know that the objective, "ground-floor" probability of my "telling" is 0.43 and that the objective, "ground-floor" probability of my keeping silent is 0.57. Am I in a position to promise you that I will keep silent, knowing, as I do, that if there were a million perfect duplicates of me, each placed in a perfect duplicate of my present situation, 43 percent of them would tell all and 57 percent of them would hold their tongues? I do not see how, in good conscience, I could make this promise. I do not see how I could be in a position to make it. But if I believe that I am able to keep silent, I should, it would seem, regard myself as being in a position to make this promise. What more do I need to regard myself as being in a position to promise to do X than a belief that I am *able* to do X? Therefore, in this situation, I should not regard myself as being able to keep silent. (And I cannot see on what grounds third-person observers of my situation could dispute this first-person judgment.)

Now suppose God vouchsafes me a further revelation: "Whichever thing you do, whether you go to the press or keep silent, you will be the agent-cause of events in your brain that will result in the bodily movements that constitute your act." Why should this revelation lead me to conclude that I am in a position to promise to keep silent—and therefore that I am able to keep silent? Its content simply does not seem relevant to the above argument for the conclusion that it is false that I am able to keep silent. I confess I believe there *is* something wrong with this argument. (I expect I believe this because I fervently *hope* that there is something wrong with it.) But it seems clear to me that if there is, as I hope and believe, something wrong with the argument, its flaw is not that it overlooks the possibility that my actions have their root in agent-causation.

NOTES

I am grateful to Ted A. Warfield (*il miglior fabbro*) for reading part 1 of this essay and for offering valuable criticisms. I hope I have made good use of them.

    1. See van Inwagen (1983: 93–104).

2. Or this will do as a first approximation to the truth. But the statement in the text is not literally true, since at least one of the two premises is a contingent truth. ("P_0" is a contingent truth, and "NP_0", which has "P_0" as a conjunct, is therefore a contingent truth. "L" is *probably* a contingent truth, and "NL" is therefore probably a contingent truth.) Here is a more careful statement. If the two rules of inference are valid, then an argument identical in appearance with the argument in the text can be constructed in any possible world and premises (4) and (6) of any of these arguments will be true in the possible world in which it is constructed if "P_0" expresses a proposition that describes the state of the world (= "universe") in that possible world before there were any human beings, and "L" expresses the proposition that is the conjunction of all propositions that are laws of nature in that possible world. Thus it can be shown (if the two rules of inference are valid) with respect to each possible world that if determinism is true in that world, then none of its inhabitants has any choice about anything. And if this can be shown with respect to each possible world, then free will is incompatible with determinism.

3. That is, if a region of logical space occupies 23.37 percent of the whole of logical space, the probability of its being actual (containing the actual world) is 0.2337: the "intrinsic probability" of a proposition that is true in just that region of logical space is 0.2337. See van Inwagen (1997: 69–87).

4. In this chapter, the symbols "p" and "q" and so on will sometimes be schematic letters representing sentences and sometimes variables ranging over propositions or regions of logical space. Although I normally deprecate this sort of logical sloppiness, it does have its stylistic advantages, and it is easily eliminable at the cost of a little verbal clutter. Similar remarks apply to "&" and "⊃."

5. McKay and Johnson (1996: 113–22).

6. The McKay/Johnson counterexample to Agglomeration is not a counterexample to β—although, since the validity of β entails the validity of Agglomeration, the existence of a counterexample to Agglomeration entails the existence of counterexamples to β.

7. It implies more than this. It implies something about knowledge, generally knowledge of cause and effect. If p is true, and if p would be false if I did X (which I was able to do), for me to have a choice about the truth value of p, I must have known (or at least be such that I *should* have known) that doing X would result in the falsity of p.

8. Other ways to repair the argument have been suggested. One of these ways—similar to my own proposal—has been suggested by McKay and Johnson themselves (1996: 118–21). For a different suggestion, see Finch and Warfield, (1998).

9. This statement assumes that no nonactual world is as close to the actual world as the actual world is to itself. Without this assumption, we should have to say: the only region I am inside and have exact access to is the set of worlds that are as close to the actual world as it is to itself.

10. Suppose I have exact access to r. Then I have access to r. Let R be any (proper) superregion of r. If I have exact access to R, I have exact access to a region and to one of its proper subregions (r)—which is contrary to the definition of exact access.

11. Compare. Ginet (1990: 102–3).

12. Chisholm (1966: 20–21).

13. The event "its coming to pass that Reid is the agent-cause of the antecedent brain-event" is the same event as "Reid's acquiring the property *being the agent-cause of the antecedent brain event*." Presumably, there is a moment of time before which Reid has not agent-caused the antecedent brain-event and after which he has, and that is the moment when this event occurs.

14. At any rate, I *believe* that Chisholm has considered this problem and has defended the "and so *ad infinitum*" solution. But I have been unable to find this solution in his writings.

15. Van Inwagen 1983: 128–29.

16. "Almost certainly" because it is *possible* that the ratio not converge. Possible but most unlikely: as the number of replays increases, the probability of "no convergence" tends to zero.

17. After 100 replays, Alice has told the truth or lied 101 times.

PART IV

COMPATIBILIST PERSPECTIVES ON FREEDOM AND RESPONSIBILITY

CHAPTER 8

....

IFS, CANS, AND
FREE WILL: THE ISSUES

....

BERNARD BEROFSKY

THE first prominent philosopher of the twentieth century to advance a compatibilist solution to the free will problem based on a conditional or hypothetical analysis was G. E. Moore (1912). We exercised free will in doing A rather than B, according to Moore, in virtue of the conditional fact that we would have done B had we chosen to do so. Moreover, free will is compatible with determinism insofar as this fact does not preclude the possibility that action A was determined by the actual choice (along with other factors). All the hypothetical proposition says is that a different outcome—action B—would have ensued had the causal chain leading to action A been different.

The eighteenth-century Scottish philosopher David Hume, to whom many twentieth-century compatibilists rightly pay homage, had propounded a conditional analysis of freedom in *An Inquiry Concerning Human Understanding*:

> By liberty, then, we can only mean a power of acting or not acting according to the determinations of the will; that is, if we choose to remain at rest, we may; if we choose to move, we also may. Now this hypothetical liberty is universally allowed to belong to everyone who is not a prisoner and in chains (Hume 1955: 104)

Similar sentiments had earlier been expressed by Thomas Hobbes:

> For he is free to do a thing, that may do it if he have the will to do it, and may forbear, if he have the will to forbear (Hobbes 1962: 240)

During the first half of the twentieth century, variants of the analysis appeared. Some replaced *choose* with *try* or *want*. Others permitted a looser, probabilistic conditional. (He probably would, if he tries.) The basic line of thought was generally received favorably among Moore's successors, the Anglo-American analytic philosophers. Further support came from their cousins, the logical positivists, including, Moritz Schlick (1966) and A. J. Ayer (1954), who saw in this approach a strategy for reaching a speedy resolution of yet another traditional philosophical problem that had resisted solution during the many centuries that had been deprived of the positivist vision.

The use of the hypothetical analysis was typically supplemented with the other standard elements of the compatibilist repertoire. Basically, the compatibilists charged the opposition with two confusions. Causation, which is not freedom-undermining even in its deterministic forms, is confused with compulsion or coercion, which, of course, is freedom-undermining. A physical barrier or even an internal compulsion or addiction can be an impediment to action; but when one acts simply because one wants to, one is not being impeded from acting otherwise. Hence, one is expressing one's freedom by doing what one wants. Second, although determinism entails that all human behavior is subsumable under universal law, freedom is not thereby threatened, for the sorts of laws involved are merely descriptive (natural, scientific), not prescriptive, like the laws of a legislative body. They just describe the way in which people behave; they do not force or constrain adherence. Finally, the compatibilists argued that indeterminism would not be more desirable since, under indeterminism, behavior is random and not under the control of the agent, a situation actually antithetical to freedom.

Compatibilism and its defense via the hypothetical analysis held sway in the Anglo-American philosophical world at midcentury, around which time chinks began to form in its armor. An internal and an external development helped to undermine complacency. C. Campbell (1951), the Scottish libertarian, challenged several underlying assumptions of the analysts with a lucidity equal to the best of their own practitioners. With respect to the hypothetical analysis, he observed that its truth is at best a necessary condition of the sort of freedom that is essential to moral responsibility. Campbell thereby reminded the analysts of the danger of divorcing the practice of philosophical analysis from the contexts that generate a concern in the issues. It is surely true that in everyday ascriptions of freedom, we often mean nothing more than that the agent would have acted differently had she chosen. But if she has no control over her choices, we would not hold her morally responsible. Thus, for moral responsibility, it must be the case that one could have chosen otherwise.

In saying this, Campbell was actually reiterating what Moore, the compatibilist, had earlier conceded. Recognizing the legitimacy of the demand addressed to the simple hypothetical account of free will that it has also to be the case that one could have chosen differently, Moore contended that we often are just insisting that the agent would have chosen differently had he made a different, prior choice (Moore 1912: 93). For example, an alcoholic could have chosen to refrain from alcohol yesterday because she would have if only she had not earlier chosen to resume drinking with the knowledge that she would likely become addicted. The hypothetical analysis is thereby preserved.

Campbell insisted, however, that the re-application of the hypothetical analysis at the level of choice or will is problematic. For should the antecedent of the conditional whose consequent is "she would have chosen differently" refer to remote causal origins of choice, the analysis lacks plausibility. It may be true that I would have chosen differently had I been educated in a different way or had I been exposed to people with different personalities; but these facts do not imply that I, a person educated in a certain way and exposed to the people I was actually exposed to, now could have chosen differently.

Since we sometimes blame people for choices they make by virtue of prior choices, we might, in accordance with Moore's suggestion, salvage a limited version of the analysis by restricting freedom of choice to such cases.

The latter strategy, however, falls prey to an infinite regress argument. C. D. Broad (1952) defended incompatibilism by pointing out that it is possible to raise the question "But could the person have chosen differently?" at any level. If we demand that the person could have chosen differently, and we suppose that this power is constituted at least by the fact that she would have done so had she made a different prior choice, we must also demand that the person have been able to execute a different prior choice. It is then clear that the strategy of the hypothetical analysis fails, for no matter how often it is re-applied, it will never suffice to capture all relevant choices. There will always be a dangling choice over which, for all we know, the agent never had control.

1. Internal Challenges

The internal challenge to the hypothetical analysis came from the heart of analytic philosophy. One of its most brilliant practitioners, J. L. Austin, concluded, after a detailed and careful review in which the views of Moore and P. H. Nowell-Smith (1954), another leading advocate of compatibilism, were scrupulously examined, that "determinism, whatever it may be, may yet be the case, but at least it appears not consistent with what we ordinarily say and presumably think" (1961: 179).

As insightful as many of Austin's observations were, he offered no conclusive grounds to reject hypothetical analyses of "could have done otherwise." He saw that many "if-then" sentences, including both "He would have done otherwise if——" and "He could have done otherwise if———" are not genuinely conditional propositions, no less causal conditionals. Thus, "I could have done otherwise if I had wanted to (or if I had chosen to)" is clearly not a conditional proposition for, as normally intended, it alone entails "I could have done otherwise" and does not, therefore, assert a dependence of ability upon desire. The conditional form of "I would have done otherwise if I had chosen" is often misleading insofar as this sentence is typically used to make a categorical assertion roughly equivalent to "It was up to me." The latter point is important, for the compatibilist case rests on the idea that the antecedent ("if" clause) picks out a hypothetical antecedent condition whose presence would have led to a different action. That assumption establishes the consistency of determinism with freedom in the form of this genuinely conditional fact. The compatibilist case would survive Austin's criticisms so long as some plausible "if-then" proposition were found that fulfilled this compatibilist requirement. Although it has frequently been noted that, when we successfully do something we try to do, choose to do, or want to do, it is sometimes difficult to isolate as elements distinct from the action, the effort, the choice, or the desire, the compatibilist need only observe that often these elements are really bona fide antecedent conditions of action. We really do want to do something well before we do it and are led to do it in virtue of the felt urge. Or we actually announce to ourselves a decision to proceed and thence take steps to carry out our decision. Or we undertake efforts well in advance of the goal toward which these efforts are expended. So even if the statement "He could have done otherwise" is a categorical assertion of (1)ability, (2)opportunity, or (3)ability plus opportunity,[1] it does not follow that the analysis of any of these three does not take a conditional form.

Additional grounds against both the treatment of many sorts of "if, then" statements as bona fide conditionals and the interpretation of "can" statements as conditionals were adduced by many philosophers. M. R. Ayers (1968), for example, pointed out that, since Jones does A entails that Jones can do A, but entails no proposition of the form "If X, then Jones does A," "Jones can do A" cannot be interpreted as a conditional.

In addition, compatibilists face the infinite regress problem, restated by the libertarian Roderick Chisholm (1964) in his review of Austin's essay "Ifs and Cans." In a famous footnote, Austin had criticized the specific version of the hypothetical analysis in terms of trying on the ground that a golfer might well insist that he could have holed a putt even when he tried and failed to do so. Chisholm identified other problems for the analysis in terms of trying, including ones that bear directly on the infinite regress problem. He noted that there are things people can do only when they do not try to do them (the very effort interferes with successful execution) and there are very simple things people can do but cannot be said to try to do (open one's eyes). Chisholm proposed a revised analysis designed to evade these and other problems, but one that would still be subject to the infinite regress problem. It is: A can do X if and only if there is something such that if A tries to do it, he will do X.

The revision does address some of the problems of the original. For example, I can open my eyes even though I cannot normally be said to try to do so because I can try to look like someone waking up. But consider the case of a golfer who drives the ball to a very precise spot p_1 and thus can be said to be able to land the ball at p_1. We know that the simple analysis will fail for he will almost certainly fail if he tries to land the ball at p_1, and he may not have been trying to do that on the one occasion he succeeded. Chisholm's proposal for the action he must try to do which will yield success at landing the ball at p_1 is: what he tried to do when he was successful at landing the ball at p_1. But in all likelihood, the only occasion on which that strategy will work is the one occasion he did happen to succeed. That is, not only is he likely to fail to land the ball at p_1 if he tries; it is also highly probable that there is nothing he can again try to do that will yield this result. Thus, Chisholm's revision cannot be read as a generalized conditional. It must be read in a token sense as:

A can do X in concrete situation S: There is something Y such that had A tried to do Y in S, he would have done X in S.

The proposition is true just because A did X in S (no matter what he was trying to do).

In spite of the superiority of the revised version, the infinite regress problem remains for, since there are things I cannot even try to do, it may be that I cannot try to do any of the things that are required for me to do X.

In response, Donald Davidson (1973) proposed a simple solution. If the question compatibilists wish to bar is "But could he have X-ed?" where "X" is the hypothetical action picked out by the antecedent of the conditional whose performance would have led the agent to perform a different overt action, then all we need do is to adopt a version of the hypothetical analysis whose antecedent picks out states rather than actions. For example, if we analyze "She could have done otherwise" as "She would have done otherwise if she had wanted to," we cannot raise the worry that she might not have been able to want, for wanting is not something anyone *does*. Wanting is not an action.

Thus, Davidson proposes a conditional analysis of freedom for actions described as intentional, that is, for actions described in terms of the intention of the agent performing the action. An agent is free to (can do) A if and only if he would do A intentionally if he had desires and beliefs that would be reasons to do A. Since the analysis tells us that an agent would inevitably act in a certain way under certain psychological conditions, freedom demands universal laws linking mental states with actions and, since Davidson does not believe that such laws exist, he regards the quest for a causal (conditional) analysis of freedom as a failure.

Davidson has presented general arguments challenging the existence of psycho-physical laws; but another difficulty confronting the effort to formulate laws that would specify the causal path from attitudes to intentional action more completely concerns the way to avoid deviant causal chains. For we do not know how to rule out causation of actions by desires and beliefs when those actions are unintentional. (A man wants to inherit his uncle's money and believes that he would do so by running him over. This state unnerves him and causes him to take a drive during which he accidentally kills his uncle. The act of killing his uncle was caused by his desire to kill his uncle plus his belief that running him over would achieve this end; but he did not run his uncle over with the intention of killing him.[2]) Although the quest for a conditional analysis of freedom fails, Davidson retains the compatibilist view that freedom is a causal power of agents insofar as the free actions of agents are those which are caused by certain of their mental states, in particular, beliefs and desires.

Davidson's solution to the infinite regress problem is too simple. If I suffer from arachnaphobia, I am unable to remove the spider from the wall even though I would do so if I wanted to. My phobic condition prevents me from being in the state of wanting to remove the spider. There is no significant difference between inability to act and inability to enter a state. If my blameworthiness requires that I have been able to choose otherwise, then why would it not equally require that I have been able to enter the state of wanting otherwise?

Although the simple substitution of states for actions does not solve the infinite regress problem, an even simpler solution may be in the offing. The assumption that the agent must have power over the antecedent presupposes that the agent would not have the ability to do the action unless he performed the action through realizing the antecedent. But this is clearly not so for many hypotheticals. If God wills that I raise my arm, I would raise my arm. I have no power over God and cannot, therefore, bring about the antecedent condition. But I can raise my arm, for I don't need to bring God into the picture in order to do so. In other words, the hypothetical analysis posits a sufficient condition of the action I failed to, but was free to, do, and the objection, in demanding power over this sufficient condition, presupposes that it is also a necessary condition of the hypothetical action. The simple response, then, is that sufficient conditions need not also be necessary conditions.

For example, it is not implausible to read *desire* or *want* in a way that allows for intentional actions performed in spite of the absence of desire, for example, "Although I did not really want to do it, I did it because I thought I ought to." In such a case, if I actually fail to do my duty because my sense of duty is not strong enough, it may be true that I would have done the action if I had wanted to although the desire is not essential to the performance. Now, suppose one analyzes "I could have done otherwise" as "I would have done otherwise if I had wanted to." Not only is it then true that I could have done otherwise; one also blocks the infinite regress by rejecting the demand that I have been able to want to. For I could have done it even if I had not wanted to, so long as my feelings of obligation had been stronger.

If Davidson's solution is too simple, so is this response. For it generates the following question. One can evade the infinite-regress-generating query by choosing a sufficient condition that is not also a necessary condition. But surely there need to be constraints on the selection. "I can raise my hand" cannot mean "I would raise my hand if the Holy Grail were above me and I had been seeking it all my life" even if the latter is true. If our preference for "I would raise my hand if I tried" is grounded in the fact that I can readily make the antecedent (and, therefore, the consequent) true, then we have succumbed to the infinite regress. For if it must be the case that I can try and if "I can try" is to receive a hypothetical analysis, then the regress has begun.

Some compatibilists select the antecedent condition of the hypothetical not because the person has control over its occurrence, but rather because the condition is supposed to reflect origination in the self. If a free agent is one who determines her own actions, and this is interpreted to mean that she does what she does because she wants to, then a case exists for analyzing the freedom to have done otherwise as "She would have done otherwise if she had wanted to." To be self-determined is to be determined by one's own desires.

This view was challenged as simplistic by friends and enemies alike. Libertarians complained that, under determinism, the origins of desire can be traced back to factors beyond the self, heredity, and early environment. It is, therefore, simplistic simply to identify the agent with her desires. Moreover, in situations of conflict, agents sense that their deeper selves may indeed repudiate the desires that guide actions. Some compatibilists, for example, the hierarchical theorists, agreed, pointing out that even under determinism a person can, upon reflection, conclude that he would prefer not to be acting from the desire that is unfortunately overwhelming him. If he is addicted, he is doing what he most wants to do but would prefer not to be moved in this way.

These objections do not decisively refute more sophisticated hypothetical analyses. Although libertarians would complain about any version just because it is compatible with determinism, a compatibilist might replace "acting from desire" with a superior candidate for self-determination, perhaps acting from "deepest desire" or "desire arising from careful, rational, and independent reflection." The defender of the hypothetical analysis would then rest her case against the infinite regress argument on the primacy of self-determination (understood in her terms) over power. But if the power to be able to want (even deeply) otherwise is not important, why bother to insist upon a hypothetical analysis of freedom of action? Why say that a free agent is one who could have done otherwise, that is, one who would have done otherwise if he had wanted (deeply) to, if one regards self-determination, even in the absence of the power to do otherwise, as sufficient for freedom on the level of desire? Is not the position inherently unstable?

2. FREEDOM AND POWER TO DO OTHERWISE

The response of some compatibilists is indeed to say that power at either level is unnecessary. Those compatibilists abandon the conditional analysis, not on the grounds that it is an inadequate analysis of "could have done otherwise," but rather that freedom in the relevant sense is not constituted by the power to do otherwise. It is important to be able to do otherwise only if we want to do otherwise. If we do not want to do otherwise, then the power to do so, since it will not be exercised, is insignificant. How do we reach this position?

Suppose you force me to surrender my money by threatening to shoot me. So I give you my money, but not of my own free will. It is also true that, in giving you my money, I am displaying the power to do so. Thus, I have the power to do that which I do not do of my own free will, that for which I would not be held morally blameworthy. The fact that, in giving you my money, I am obviously displaying the power to give you my money does not vitiate the more important fact that I am giving you my money against my will, that is, unwillingly. Advocates of the hypothetical analysis have supposed an intimate connection between freedom and the power to do otherwise and have therefore ignored other senses of the term *free* that some believe are more important in the context of the classic free will problem.

Harry Frankfurt (1969), for example, has argued that the power to do otherwise (alternate possibility) is irrelevant in certain contexts. If the above example indicates the possibility of power without freedom, Frankfurt emphasizes the possibility of freedom without alternate possibility essentially on the grounds that the absence of the power to do otherwise may be present in a case in which a person acts willingly and would not do otherwise even if he had the power to do so. We must, then, view the hypothetical analysis as at best an analysis of one sense of *free*, in particular, the freedom to have acted otherwise, a sense that may not be as significant as the sense of freedom as full compliance or unqualified satisfaction.

If Frankfurt is right, it matters little to the issue of freedom and responsibility what the precise analysis of "could have done otherwise" is. Reflection on the robbery example reveals another basis for challenging the significance of this issue. We may say of a person who is confronted with a serious threat to his life and who chooses to sacrifice some money in order to annul the threat that he could not have done otherwise. What we mean in this case and most others is that it is unreasonable to expect a person in these circumstances to have done otherwise. The proposition is really normative and not purely "metaphysical." Thus, imagining that different norms prevail results in different interpretations of *can*. A person confronting a similar penalty for noncompliance may well be judged differently if he is also faced with an additional threat to the lives of thousands of other people he had agreed, with full knowledge of the dangers, to protect. Should he succumb to the threat, we may say that he could have done otherwise because we believe that he should have resisted the threat under these circumstances.

Thus, debates in real life about human capacities are inherently normative, depending on issues regarding rights, responsibilities, and the reasonableness of our expectations. Whether or not a person could have done otherwise depends on matters extremely remote from the deterministic or indeterministic nature of his decision. Patricia Greenspan (1978) observes that judgments of the unfreedom of action depend on the reasonableness of our expectations relative to the standards in force. So a person can be unfree or compelled even if he could have done otherwise.

Similarly, the definition of free will offered by Bernard Gert and Timothy J. Duggan (1979) rests on normative presuppositions. They define free will as the ability to will, an ability that is constituted essentially by the ability to have and to act upon a variety of beliefs concerning the existence of coercive and non-coercive incentives for action and inaction. For example, a person who is able to will to do A believes that there are coercive incentives for doing A and will almost always will to do A when any of these coercive incentives are present. A coercive incentive is then defined by Gert and Duggan as one it would be unreasonable to expect any rational agent not to act on. It is difficult enough to suppose that one can characterize in normatively neutral terms the principles adherence to which makes an agent rational. In addition, normativity enters in when we judge the reasonableness of a particular sort of action by a rational agent.

In spite of the fact that this objection rests on a plausible reading of the ordinary meaning of "could have done otherwise," I believe that the incompatibilist position that *can* can receive a purely metaphysical reading, is defensible. For the incompatibilist believes that we are literally incapacitated under determinism. (I know of no incompatibilist who believes that the sort of freedom that is of concern to him is one that can be present "in small doses" under certain deterministic scenarios.) Although most cases in which we allow "she could not have done otherwise" are cases in which she is not literally incapacitated, the incompatibilist believes that determinism does result in literal incapacitation. This view must be confronted and the observation that most uses of *can* are normative is only a way of evading an engagement with the incompatibilist metaphysics.

There is, however, yet another basis to relegate the issue of the analysis of "he could have done otherwise" to a subordinate status. Susan Wolf (1990) and Daniel Dennett (1984) draw our attention to individuals who are so good that in certain spheres they just cannot do the wrong thing. Dennett says of himself that he cannot be induced to torture someone for a thousand dollars. What makes these cases interesting is that we do not withdraw our praise from the actions of such individuals. In fact, we may well regard their inability to act wrongly as especially praiseworthy. And if freedom is a necessary condition of praiseworthiness, we must then regard such individuals as free.

Of course, we should withdraw our praise of Dennett if he is under the spell of a hypnotist or is the victim of intensive behavioral conditioning in which thoughts of succumbing to temptation are associated with bouts of nausea. Dennett and Wolf argue that not all cases of "moral compulsion" need be assimilated to such robotlike or addictive behavior. One can deliberately and intentionally do the right thing even when one could not have done otherwise. In these cases, since one's inability derives from one's own nature, not the machinations of some external force, the individual is free and responsible.

Wolf and Dennett part ways, however, on the status of people who do the wrong thing. For Wolf, under determinism, such individuals are unable to do otherwise and are therefore unfree. (Hence, Wolf talks about asymmetrical freedom; the implications of determinism differ depending on the moral nature of one's actions.) Dennett, a more robust compatibilist, sees determinism per se as having no such implications.

There is finally the effort to deflate the issue concerning the analysis of *can* by seeing it as a surrogate for a deeper issue. Robert Kane (1996a: 58–78) argues that these disagreements for the most part rest on a deeper disagreement that the parties do not usually recognize. Only the incompatibilist is committed to ultimate responsibility, the yearning to be original sources of value and creators in part of our own natures. We want to be responsible, not just for our actions, but also for our wills, that is, for the very reasons that motivate our decisions. We can have this Ultimate Responsibility (UR) only if we are responsible for any sufficient reason for our wills.

There is no doubt that this yearning is indeed an element of what is sought by seekers after free will. But the assumption that progress on the controversy can be obtained by shifting attention to UR (and away from the possibility of having done otherwise) assumes that the same issues will not arise at the level of UR. It is not clear to me, however, that the desire for UR is not the desire for power in disguise. For the worry about the presence of a sufficient reason is just that the agent cannot thereby resist acting on the motive.[3]

In reflecting on the connection of reasons to will, the incompatibilist worries that the agent under determinism plays no real role. For, as the incompatibilist sees it, in the presence of enabling conditions the sufficient reasons determine the choice, in which case the source of the choice lies outside the agent. What we really want is the "free" conversion by the agent of a reason into the reason for the choice. But is this not just the issue of whether or not my reasons "made me do it" that is the issue of power all over again? An incompatibilist wants the agent to be in charge. A compatibilist believes that, if the agent is in charge under indetermination, then, barring some special freedom-undermining consideration— gunpoint, addiction, and so on—he is also in charge under determination. Causes are not agents that take over in a way that undermines the putative agency of a normal person.

3. CONDITIONAL ANALYSIS OF POWER REJECTED

If defenders of a hypothetical analysis survive these onslaughts on the significance of the very issue they address, they must then confront a simple and apparently devastating argument against all conditional analyses of power, whether it be the power of human beings or inanimate objects. Keith Lehrer (1966b) has argued that, no matter what C is, "If C, then S X's" cannot mean "S can X," for the former is compatible with "S cannot X." It would be the case that S cannot X if both (a) C were not present and (b) the absence of C rendered S incapable of doing X. In other words, the following is a consistent triad:

If C, then S X's

Not-C

If not-C, then S cannot X

If the first proposition were equivalent to "S can X," then "S can X" may be substituted for "If C, then S X's." But the result would be a contradiction, since the second two propositions alone entail that S cannot X.

If we think of "C" as "S wants to X," then the third proposition asserts what we normally suppose to be highly implausible, for example, that, although we would raise our arms if we want to, thereby establishing that we can do so, we would be unable to do so were we not to want to. This point is irrelevant, however, for Lehrer's logical point hinges only on the compatibility of these three propositions, not the plausibility of any of them.

Bruce Aune (1967) objected to Lehrer's proof on the grounds that consistency of the three propositions had been assumed, not demonstrated. After all, deeper analyses of the notions might uncover an inconsistency. *Can*, for example, is ambiguous and the context should determine the way we disambiguate. For example, in one sense, I cannot lift my right arm because a heavy weight is resting on it. In another sense, I can lift my right arm because I can easily remove the weight. Clearly, I am free to lift my right arm and, if there were a morally pressing reason to do so, I would be morally blameworthy for failing to do so. We should, therefore, choose the interpretation according to which I can lift my right arm. Hence, the burden falls upon Lehrer to demonstrate that the appropriate sense of *can* yields a consistent triad.

Lehrer (1968) defended his case by repeating the point that it is logically possible that the failure to want, choose, or try to X causes the agent to be unable to X. He might also have said that Aune is free to interpret *can* in a morally relevant sense and plug that sense into the triad. We still come out with the same result: it is logically possible that the failure to choose to X causes the agent to be unable in any morally relevant sense that Aune chooses to X. Thus, Lehrer's point stands. Not only does he establish that *can* does not admit of a conditional analysis; he indirectly establishes the stronger claim that no conditional proposition alone implies a *can*.

A generalization of this result yields the view that the alethic modalities are irreducible. The concepts of necessity and possibility are interdefinable; but neither can be defined outside of this narrow circle of modal concepts. Lehrer's argument and the infinite regress argument lead to this conclusion since the best prima facie candidates for the reduction of modal propositions are conditional propositions. As has been said, the point is a general one, not depending on anything distinctive about human power and possibility. The statement that sugar can dissolve in water (sugar is soluble in water, it is possible to dissolve sugar in water) cannot for analogous reasons be read as; If sugar were placed in water, it would dissolve.

In the case of human power, we noted the importance of choosing an appropriate sufficient condition of action if one is advancing a conditional analysis. Comatose Harry, who loves to play poker, cannot now do so even though he would now be playing were he not comatose. Since it is also true that he would be playing poker now if he were to try to or if he wanted to, these candidates are equally unacceptable. Since Harry cannot now try and cannot now possess such a desire, he cannot now play poker.

We may try to blunt the sweeping charge of irreducibility by seeking distinctive features of human power. Central to M. R. Ayers's refutation of determinism, for example, is the significance of the distinction between "the powers of people and the powers of things" (1968: 102–18). Unique presuppositions accompany ascriptions of power and ability to people. We suppose that the targets of these ascriptions are conscious creatures, capable of forming and acting on intentions.

Perhaps we also suppose that they are language users and are possessed of at least minimal intelligence and maturity.

If we succeed at salvaging the analysis of "Harry can play poker now" as "Harry would play poker now if he were to try to do so" by insisting that the falsity of the former rests on the absence of a presupposition of the antecedent of the latter—that Harry is now conscious—we will have won the battle only to lose the war. First of all, the claim that a conditional proposition alone suffices to analyze can-statements will have been abandoned—we need explicitly to append additional presuppositions. Now, since the point of the hypothetical analysis is to defend compatibilism, defenders can live with this major modification so long as the new analysis is compatible with determinism. The more serious problem, then, is that the presuppositions themselves are formulated as powers or potentialities—the capacity to form intentions now (and perhaps to use language). We do not then have a clear demonstration of compatibility. If comatose Harry cannot play poker now because he cannot now form intentions, and if the latter incapacity is constituted by the falsity of some conditional, then the latter would have to refer in its antecedent to some "extrinsic" conditions. For although it is not false to say that Harry would form intentions now if his brain were altered in some coma-eliminating way, it is false to say that he would form intentions now if he were prodded in ways that normally produce intention-forming actions on his part.

Unfortunately, this strategy does not evade Lehrer's point. For the conditional analysis now being proposed—I can form intentions if and only if I would if prodded in appropriate ways—can be attacked in familiar ways. If I am not being prodded in the ways that would normally produce intentions on my part, then perhaps this failure renders me incapable of forming any intentions.

In uncovering unanalyzed modal concepts, we appear to reaffirm the irreducibility of the modal or, as Austin put it, "In philosophy, it is 'can' in particular that we seem so often to uncover, just when we had thought some problem settled, grinning residually up at us like the frog at the bottom of the beer mug" (1961: 179).

4. CONDITIONAL ANALYSES AND THE CONSEQUENCE ARGUMENT

If the defense of compatibilism via some conditional analysis had succeeded, then, of course, no argument for incompatibilism would be sound. The argument for incompatibilism that has most attracted the attention of philosophers in recent decades is called the Consequence Argument or the Transfer Argument. Its principal advocate, Peter van Inwagen (1975, 1983), presents a version of the argument according to which no one has the power to do other than what she actually does under determinism. Roughly, the claim is that, since no one has the power to alter the past or to alter the laws of nature, and since, under determinism, a proposition describing any person's actual action, say P_1, follows logically from a proposition that is a conjunction of the laws of nature and all the truths about the past, then no one has the power to alter the truth of P_1, even if P_1 describes a future action. The argument rests on the assumption that an inability to alter the truth of a proposition P entails an inability to alter the truth of any proposition that is a logical consequence of P. After all, if I am unable to visit Alaska, does it not follow that I am unable to falsify the proposition that either I do not visit Alaska or I do not visit Hawaii? For whether or not I can visit Hawaii, the falsification of the disjunctive proposition depends on my ability to falsify both disjuncts and, for that ability, I must be able to visit Alaska and I cannot do that.

We know that this argument must fail on a conditional analysis of power. Suppose that I can visit Alaska only if I choose to and that the Hawaii Office of Tourism is run by a powerful demon who is trying to divert tourists from Alaska to Hawaii. Whenever I contemplate the prospect of visiting Alaska, the demon intervenes to prevent me from deciding to do so. Although it is determined that I do not choose to visit Alaska, it is also true that I would visit Alaska if I were to choose to. Let us concede the plausible premise that I cannot alter the past or the laws of nature. Were I to try to do so, I would fail. Now, if determinism is true, it follows from a proposition that is a conjunction of the laws of nature and all the truths about the past—call it L—that I never visit Alaska—call it N. But the essential assumption that the inability to alter L transfers to the inability to alter N breaks down on the conditional analysis. For it is true that, were I to choose to falsify L, I would fail, but it is false that I would fail to falsify N if I were to choose to. I would visit Alaska if I chose to; I just cannot choose to.

Since the difficulties of the conditional analysis permit the advocates of the Consequence Argument to remain unfazed by this demonstration, compatibilists are obliged to find stronger responses. To indicate the difficulty compatibilists confront, let me explain why I believe one familiar response fails. Michael Slote (1982) has ingeniously argued that the transfer of power assumption cannot be made because the powerlessness over the past (or the laws of nature) rests on a sort of selectivity that is inapplicable to the future. More specifically, I cannot alter the past because alteration is impossible via my current desires and abilities— the features that are selected in the case of unalterability. No matter what my current desires and abilities happen to be, they are ineffective in bringing about changes in the past or the laws. But my current desires and abilities are clearly causally relevant to future actions. Thus, I might be able to alter some future action in the sense that that action depends on what I now want and can do.

The incompatibilist cannot deny the causal efficacy of desires and abilities for, even if she is also a determinist, she is not a fatalist. She believes that desires might be causally relevant (to future actions, of course) even if she also believes that the determination of those desires renders the agent unfree in acting on them.

Slote then concludes that the preceding undermines the incompatibilist's assumption of transfer of power, for one cannot now assume that powerlessness over the past and the laws entails powerlessness over future actions even if the proposition describing the future action follows logically from the laws conjoined with all the truths about the past.

The Consequence Argument survives this assault because the operator it invokes is unalterability. I am unable to alter the future because I am unable to alter the past plus the laws. In noting that my current desires are causally efficacious only in a forward direction, Slote cannot also suppose that I can alter the future in the relevant sense, that is, that I can falsify a proposition about a future action that follows logically from the laws plus the truths about the past. It would beg the question against incompatibilism to suppose that I could falsify such a proposition just because I can make it true (by acting on my desire). That the action depends causally on the desire does not in itself imply that I can bring it about that I do not perform the action. The incompatibilist can argue that I can make a proposition true that I cannot make false. Thus, Slote is talking about the operator "causing to be true" and the incompatibilist is talking about "causing to be false" (see Berofsky 1987).

The conclusion of the Consequence Argument can, of course, be blunted by those who do not see the power to do otherwise as per se important. Thus, John Martin Fischer (1994: 131–59) observes that, even if one is powerless to alter some proposition describing a future outcome, one may well be responsible for the outcome. For example, Sam knowingly and voluntarily brings about an outcome that would have resulted from powerful forces put in play only if Sam had freely decided not to produce the outcome himself. (See Fischer's essay in this volume, ch. 12, about these sorts of [so-called "Frankfurt-style"] examples.)

5. ABILITY, OPPORTUNITY, AND MOTIVATION

One common proposal for the analysis of the proposition that an agent can do something is that all the necessary conditions of her doing it are at hand. The earlier conclusion that no reductive analysis of *can* is available should make us suspicious of this proposal as well. And closer examination indeed reveals that it is problematic in several ways. If a necessary condition of her doing it is a condition whose absence would make it impossible for her to do it, that is, would make it such that she could not do it, then the analysis is circular and, therefore, unilluminating.

In order to see what else is wrong with this proposal, let us first explore important distinctions within the class of necessary conditions. In the free will context, for example, it is crucial to distinguish type ability from token ability or power. An individual with an ability may be unable to exercise it in a particular case because a temporary obstacle is present. Pete Sampras can play tennis; but he cannot play tennis now because he has no racket or he is asleep. Thus, he has a type ability, but not the token ability or power in this context. If our interest in freedom derives from an interest in moral responsibility, then we would concentrate on token rather than type ability. For a racket-deprived Sampras is not free to play tennis in the sense in which we might regard him as culpable for failing to play (unless, of course, he had the further token ability to obtain a racket now). He lacks the token ability and is, therefore, absolved of responsibility for failing to play (even though he can—in the type sense—play tennis).

Among the many conditions of power, we can distinguish roughly between ability-and opportunity-conditions. The lack of a racket (or court, or partner) deprives Sampras of an opportunity to exercise his ability. An individual who lacks the ability may be given the opportunity, but he will be unable to take advantage of it. Ability itself comprises various conditions and we may zero in on one or another, depending on context. A musical ignoramus cannot play middle C on the piano because he is deprived of knowledge. A paraplegic cannot play middle C for physical reasons. And a person who is perfectly fit physically may lack the ability to defeat Sampras because he lacks the requisite skills. Even one with opportunity, knowledge, and skills may lack the type ability or power for emotional reasons. (He "chokes" whenever he plays in a major tournament.)

A person who has the power to act may fail to do so for reasons having to do with her motivation or her will. She does not want to do so, she feels herself morally obliged not to do so, she has chosen not to do so or not to try to do so. Let us loosely collect these conditions under the label "conative." We normally distinguish between these and the other conditions (ability, opportunity), regarding only the latter's absence as depriving one of the power to act. Compatibilists, of course, cite this consideration when they say that someone could have done otherwise because he would have done otherwise if only he had wanted or tried to do otherwise. For compatibilists, it is crucial then to distinguish necessary conditions of power (ability, opportunity) from necessary conditions of its exercise (conative conditions). Hence, the analysis of "can do A" in terms of the presence of all necessary conditions of the doing of A fails. As we saw above, it is circular if a necessary condition is a condition whose absence annuls the power to do A;

and if a necessary condition is a condition in whose absence an agent will not do A, then there is no good reason to believe that an agent cannot do A just because he will not do A.

Incompatibilists do not usually just reject this fundamental distinction as unfounded—they do not just say that all the necessary conditions of an action are necessary conditions of the token ability to do the action. For them, the fact that it is determined that he not do A makes it the case that he cannot do A. No simple rebuttal of this position based on a hypothetical analysis of *can* is available. Let us explore one other strategy.

An individual possessed of a power can take advantage of an opportunity by virtue of some intrinsic characteristic. Objects that are soluble in water have a certain structure that confers this capacity on them. Sampras's neuromuscular system is significantly different from the systems of people lacking his tennis skills. This highly complex set of intrinsic traits is what makes it true that Sampras can play tennis well. Let us label this set "Sampras's tennis set" (obviously the sets of different athletes will vary somewhat), or TS.

Suppose that determinism is true and that Sampras chooses not to play a particular match. The opportunity is provided and Sampras is in no way disabled. Perhaps he just does not feel like playing now. Given determinism, there is a sufficient condition of his failure to play. Compatibilists will concede that Sampras could not have done otherwise if this sufficient condition fails in some way to include a conative condition—his desire not to play or his decision not to play. Call this conative condition (possibly a disjunctive one—he wants to play or he feels obliged to play or he decides to play or . . .) CS. So under the circumstances, TS is present and CS is absent.

The compatibilist position is that, since TS does and CS does not confer the power to play on Sampras, then the fact that not-CS is determined does not affect Sampras's power. If CS is not necessary for power, it does not matter how it came to be absent.

If the incompatibilist charges the compatibilist with begging the question at this point by just assuming that CS should not be a part of TS, that is, by assuming that the conative condition is not required for power, but only its exercise, the compatibilist can justly demand that a good reason must be advanced for collapsing the possible into the actual. For, again, that is what the incompatibilist is doing by insisting that all necessary conditions of the exercise of power are necessary conditions of the possession of power. And here again the incompatibilist is obliged to bring determinism into the story and he will do so willingly. For his fundamental contention is that determinism requires us to interpret sufficient conditions so that the presence of any sufficient condition under determinism necessitates the outcome, that is, renders it necessary in a way that annuls the agent's power to do otherwise. Under determinism, then, CS must be a part of TS just because Sampras's failure to play is determined.

How does determinism do this? Determinism tells us that Sampras's decision (or desire or subsequent nonaction) is subsumable under law. Thus, the incompatibilist must be able to argue from this assumption to the conclusion that Sampras lacks the power to do otherwise. It is obviously essential to this argument that laws be interpreted as necessary truths in some sense of the term that would license this result. The sort of necessity that laws possess must then be such that the subsumption under law of "Sampras does not play tennis here and now" renders this proposition "power necessary" for Sampras, that is, such that it is not in Sampras's power to make the proposition false.

The incompatibilist position is, then, that the determination of an action renders an agent powerless to perform any alternative action because the actual action is made necessary by its sufficient condition. Under determinism, only what is can be. The rebuttal of this position based on a hypothetical analysis of power is a failure. If the compatibilist is to succeed, then, she must find an alternative strategy. I mentioned earlier the radical option of divorcing free will from the power to do otherwise, a tack that would permit a believer in free will to look upon determinism as a benign possibility. (For this and other possible compatibilist strategies in the light of the failure of conditional analyses of power, see the essays in this volume by Kapitan, Haji, Russell, and Taylor and Dennett; chs. 6, 9, 10, and 11, respectively.)

6. A Superior Compatibilist Strategy

I close by mentioning an alternative compatibilist strategy that I believe is worth pursuing (see Berofsky 1979). As we have just seen, the incompatibilist case rests on the assumption that natural laws are necessary in a fairly strong sense of the term. This assumption has been challenged by philosophers inspired by another doctrine found in Hume's writings on causation, "the regularity theory," which contends that the difference between generalizations that just happen to be true and generalizations accorded the status of scientific laws is not based upon the necessity of the latter (in spite of the use of modal language in characterizing scientific laws—for example, our saying that sugar *must* dissolve when placed in water). In addition to establishing the difference between laws and other generalizations without positing the necessity of laws, the regularity theorist must then in effect define freedom. That is, if it is not the case that simple subsumption under law annuls my freedom, then what particular circumstances do annul my freedom? If the surrender of my money to the robber is not necessary in virtue of its being determined, then in what sense am I not acting "of my own free will"? I am being coerced, of course. But then a definition of coercion or compulsion must be provided and that is not a simple matter.

Of course, this has to be done anyway as these notions are central to our understanding of free will and there is no reason to believe that the compatibilist is at a disadvantage in providing these accounts. For the issues that arise about coercion and compulsion do not hinge on the simple question, Are laws of nature necessary truths?

For example, as we saw earlier, many people believe that a person is coerced in a way that absolves her of moral responsibility when the forces acting on her make it unreasonable for her to do otherwise. In handing the robber her money, she was coerced and hence neither free nor blameworthy, for we would not reasonably expect someone in those circumstances to jeopardize her life in order to save some money or to apprehend a criminal. The presence of freedom or responsibility does not hinge on the presence of some sort of metaphysical connection found in all cases of a nomic relation, for example, the relation between conditions and action posited by some scientific law, but rather turns on the presence of circumstances that demand a certain sort of moral evaluation.

Thus, though we are owed an account of freedom from coercion and compulsion and the like, every party to the dispute is saddled with this obligation. Of course, many incompatibilists will regard this exercise as insignificant since, if determinism is true, then freedom is a grand illusion and any further distinctions made in everyday life will be shallow and misleading.[4]

I believe that arguments for incompatibilism, and in particular, the powerful Consequence Argument, rest on a necessitarian interpretation of laws. For why do we believe that laws of nature are unalterable? No one can alter them because, once the antecedent condition is in place, the consequent is necessitated. If I could alter the outcome, then the generalization would lose its status as necessary.

To be sure, there are true non-laws that are unalterable, for example, "There are exactly 41 metals," and "All rocks situated 10 meters due south from the North Pole of the only planet of the star Rigel weigh exactly 1000 kilograms." But the unalterability of these generalizations depends upon the limitations of human beings and these limitations are surely based upon laws of physics, physiology, and so on. And these laws tell us that efforts at falsification are bound to fail since the generalizations in question are necessarily true.

Do we not suppose that, if laws are necessary truths, they will be so in a world devoid of people? And are we not then supposing that certain states of that world necessitate other states? If we wish to deny that the unalterability of certain facts rests upon these necessary connections, we shall have to say that the special character of those generalizations we designate as laws is bound up with the fact that, if there were people in such worlds, they would be unable to alter them. But is it not more plausible to believe that the truth of this counterfactual is itself grounded in necessity, that the reason that, if there were humans in this world, they would be unable to prevent sugar from dissolving in water, is that sugar must dissolve when placed in water?

If the regularity theory is correct, and unalterability can only be grounded in a necessity that turns out to be a fiction, it appears to follow that human beings would then be able to alter laws, that is, they would be able to produce outcomes rendered impermissible by some law of nature. While this result may be looked upon as a reductio ad absurdum of the regularity theory, some philosophers (Lewis 1981) have produced interpretations of alterability that allegedly render this possible. The claim is that although no one can break a law, perhaps a person can sometimes perform an action whose occurrence implies that some actual laws of nature are violated.

Suppose that the past and the laws entail that Jones does A. If we suppose that Jones had refrained from doing A, we must suppose that either the past had been different or that the laws had been violated. David Lewis's theory of counterfactuals suggests the latter. If so, then the argument that Jones cannot refrain from doing A on the grounds that he would have to violate a law falters if all that follows from "Jones can do A" is "Jones can do something such that, were he to do it, then some law would have been violated." (The latter is evidently not as helpful to incompatibilists since it is not clearly false.)

On the other hand, since Lewis's theory of counterfactuals is mute on the subject of can-statements, it does not tell us the conditions under which Jones can do A and does not, therefore, directly challenge van Inwagen's conclusion that (under determinism) Jones cannot do A. Yet the existence of an alternative interpretation of one of the premises of the Consequence Argument that permits it sometimes to be false provides a wedge for the compatibilist. Suppose, for example, that P is the state of the world at some time prior to my birth and that "If P, then I put on a red tie on April 6, 2000" is a law of nature (or, more plausibly, the consequence of the conjunction of all the laws). As I am getting dressed at 7 A.M. on April 6, 2000, the following instance of a consequence argument is advanced:

$N_{\text{7:01 A.M., April 6, 2000}}$ (P)

$N_{\text{7:01 A.M., April 6, 2000}}$ (If P, then R)

Therefore, $N_{\text{7:01 A.M., April 6, 2000}}$ (R)

How do we read "$N_{\text{7:01 A.M., April 6, 2000}}$ (If P, then R)"? If we read it as "No one can do something X at 7:01 A.M, April 6, 2000, such that if she were to do X, then 'If P, then R' is false," the premise is not self-evidently true. Thus, the acceptability of this premise cannot be grounded on the simple impossibility of performing a law-breaking act. On the other hand, the compatibilist cannot simply appeal to the Lewis theory of counterfactuals, for that in itself does not entail the falsity of the premise.

Van Inwagen might try to end this stalemate simply by insisting on the more plausible interpretation of N. If we read N (P) as saying that no one can perform an act that causes P to be false, then the argument regains its prima facie plausibility. For the premises in effect say that no one can affect the past or cause laws to be violated.

Further compatibilist responses to the Consequence Argument may be found in Tomis Kapitan's essay in this volume (ch. 7). At this point, the Consequence Argument is perhaps the most formidable weapon in the incompatibilist's armor. Even if the compatibilist constructs a successful response, she must concede that, in some way, laws limit our abilities. If she invokes the regularity theory, the specific relation between laws and abilities will be characterized in more complex ways than those suggested by the sweeping assumption of those who appeal to the necessity of laws. At this point in the debate, the compatibilist has yet to develop a credible defense of this idea.

NOTES

1. Austin (1961) called this sense of "can" the all-in sense.
2. The example is from Chisholm (1966).
3. Kane (1996a: ch. 5) agrees that the power to do otherwise is essential to self-forming actions, the heart of Ultimate Responsibility.
4. For an incompatibilist, the judgment that the victim of a robbery was unfree is true but misleading, for under determinism she would be unfree even if she handed over the money just because she felt generous or wanted to help someone in need. Certain incompatibilists—ones I would view as more reasonable—would allow that, even under determinism, we have real freedom of a limited sort (as opposed to the same sort of freedom, but less of it than is found under certain indeterministic scenarios). Even if it falls short of our ideals, the world we in fact find is better than one in which we are all puppets or slaves.

CHAPTER 9

··

COMPATIBILIST VIEWS OF FREEDOM AND RESPONSIBILITY

··

ISHTIYAQUE HAJI

DETERMINISM, the doctrine that the nonrelational facts of the past and the laws of nature entail one unique future, has been thought by many to be incompatible with freedom and moral responsibility for reasons that include the following. Traditionally, the most influential view about the sort of freedom required for responsibility postulates the availability, at various points in our lives, of genuinely accessible alternative possibilities. But there are powerful arguments for the conclusion that determinism expunges such possibilities and thus undermines the right sort of freedom for responsibility.[1] A second concern clusters around the idea that there is no room for "authentic agency" in the world if determinism is true. There are different ways to crystallize this somewhat amorphous idea. According to one prominent view, an agent is morally responsible for her behavior only if the antecedent actional elements, like her values, desires, or beliefs that cause that behavior, are "truly her own"; they are not, for example, the product of direct, surreptitious implantation. But it has been claimed that if determinism is true, this "authenticity" condition can never be met because our springs of action are ultimately the product of events long before our births and hence products of external sources over which we have no control. (See, for example, G. Strawson 1986; Kane 1995, 1996a and b; Pereboom 1995, 2001)

Compatibilist theories all share the common presumption that determinism does not undermine freedom and responsibility. The success of a compatibilist account depends partly but pivotally on how well it responds to the two afore-mentioned putative threats that determinism poses to responsibility. In this chap-ter, we will survey two broadly different kinds of compatibilist theories. Advocates of the first kind propose that responsibility is constituted by the "reactive atti-tudes" such as indignation, forgiveness, resentment, guilt, gratitude, and love that we display toward one another in response to behavior and traits of character. As there are no independent grounds external to the range of these attitudes that are relevant to responsibility ascriptions, the thought is that such an account of re-sponsibility is immune to threats of determinism. Proponents of the second kind of compatibilist theory develop the view that a person is responsible for his be-havior if there is an appropriate "fit" between that behavior and various psycho-logical elements of his or various features of the world. As this fit can obtain even if the world is determined, determinism, it has been claimed, is no threat to responsibility.[2]

1. P. F. STRAWSON'S ACCOUNT

One of the most influential advocates of the first kind of compatibilist theory is P. F. Strawson, who develops his account with the objective of reconciling tradi-tional disputants whom he calls "optimists" and "pessimists" in the free will debate (1962: 59–60). Optimists, who are compatibilists, defend a consequentialist con-ception of responsibility, holding that responsibility ascriptions like blaming and praising judgments are to be understood and justified by appeal to the useful consequences that follow from them. On their view, responsibility ascriptions provide a means of regulating social behavior, and such regulation, they claim, can be efficacious even if determinism is true. Pessimists, who are incompatibilists, insist that the sort of freedom required for responsibility is "contra-causal." Against the optimists, they argue that being responsible requires that the agent be *deserving* of, for example, blame, but this requirement of desert cannot be cap-tured by the social regulation view. The view, hence, leaves a glaring gap in our conception of responsibility, a gap, pessimists say, that is to bridged by the thesis of contracausal freedom.

Strawson rejects both optimist and pessimist accounts, but he hopes to draw concessions from either in an effort to better conceptualize responsibility. From the optimist, Strawson wants the admission that the social regulation view does overlook something vital to responsibility. From the pessimist, he desires acknow-ledgment that the vital element overlooked is not contracausal freedom, but the proper role that the reactive attitudes and feelings play in our interpersonal lives, which furnish the arena in which responsibility ascriptions are made (ibid.: 78–80).

In Strawson's view, the question about the conditions under which an agent is morally responsible is identified with the question of the conditions under which it is appropriate to hold an agent morally responsible. These conditions, in turn, are explained in terms of susceptibility to reactive attitudes. Strawson proposes that holding an agent morally responsible is an expression of certain basic needs and aversions: "It matters to us whether the actions of other people . . . reflect attitudes toward us of good will, affection, or esteem on the one hand or contempt, indifference, or malevolence on the other." The reactive attitudes are "natural human reactions to the good or ill will or indifference of others towards us as displayed in *their* attitudes and actions" (ibid.: 67); and they express "the demand for the manifestation of a reasonable degree of good will or regard, on the part of others, not simply towards oneself, but towards all those on whose behalf moral indignation may be felt" (ibid.: 71). Responsibility, then, is nothing more than—it is constituted by—our adopting these attitudes toward one another. On Strawson's view, holding responsible is as Gary Watson comments, "as natural and primitive in human life as friendship and animosity, sympathy and antipathy. It rests on needs and concerns that are not so much to be justified as acknowledged" (Watson 1987b: 259).

Strawson's account has generated a great deal of insightful, critical discussion. A worry developed by John Fischer and Mark Ravizza (1993: 18) builds on the strong connection that Strawson makes between being responsible and holding responsible. The worry is that one can hold a person responsible for something when intuitively he is not (and conversely, one can intuitively be responsible for something without being held responsible). As an illustration, Fischer and Ravizza ask us to imagine a society in which some class of people are systematically treated only as objects to be used in the interest of social utility, and others have no reactive attitudes toward members of the group. This fact alone, they claim, would not suffice to warrant that these persons are not morally responsible.

A cluster of criticisms has been directed against Strawson's response to the following twin claims of the pessimist. First, if determinism is true, we have reason to abandon the reactive attitudes and practices associated with moral responsibility, for determinism implies that excusing considerations apply to all human action and thus hold universally. Second, if we do have reason to abandon these attitudes and practices, we are psychologically and practically capable of doing so.

In response to the first, Strawson deploys the "rationalistic strategy,"[3] whose crux is that it would not follow from the truth of determinism that the typical excusing conditions for responsibility—such as acting in ignorance, or accidentally, or without forethought, or when psychologically abnormal, or morally undeveloped—exempt all causally determined agents from responsibility. For determinism does not entail that all our actions are done out of ignorance, accident, and so forth. In Strawson's summation, "it cannot be a consequence of any thesis which is not itself self-contradictory that abnormality is the universal condition" (1962: 68). So determinism would not provide us with any reason to modify, eschew, or suspend our reactive attitudes.

A concern against this strand of the rationalistic strategy is that reflection on one's developmental history can and does affect our reactive responses. For example, Watson (1987b: 267–80) has argued, drawing on Robert Harris's case, that appreciation of the causal influences of an abusive childhood on one's subsequent actions often *does* have the effect of mitigating degrees of blame. But if this is so, why can't reflection on the causal effects of determinism on our actions also serve to affect our reactive responses?

A second concern is that Strawson incorrectly construes pessimists as claiming that if determinism is true, then everyone would be *abnormal*, and that the abnormal cannot be held responsible. The pessimists' worry is really that determinism would *incapacitate* everyone in some way that undermines responsibility. Pessimists, for instance, might charge that no one can exercise contracausal freedom if all events are determined, but this sort of freedom is required for responsibility. (This criticism is raised in Russell 1992).

A second strand of the rationalistic strategy suggested by Strawson and developed by Jonathan Bennett (1980) is that, if we assume the truth of determinism, even if we did have choice over whether to abandon the reactive attitudes, it would be rational to retain them and our other practices of holding people responsible, in that the cost of abandoning these things would be too high. Given the connection between responsibility and the reactive attitudes, and given that these attitudes are inextricably associated with our interpersonal relations, to stop holding people responsible by forsaking the reactive attitudes would be to sacrifice all interpersonal relationships. This would greatly impoverish human life.[4]

Contesting this strand, Derk Pereboom (1995; 2001: ch. 4) has argued that although determinism would undermine judgments of responsibility like those of praiseworthiness and blameworthiness, abandoning responsibility in the face of determinism would not threaten good interpersonal relationships. In Strawson's view, some of the attitudes most important for interpersonal relationships are anger, resentment, forgiveness, gratitude, and mature love. Pereboom proposes that a number of these attitudes would have "analogues" that would survive determinism and would, hence, underpin or foster the interpersonal relationships that so concern Strawson.

Galen Strawson (1986) has raised a different sort of objection to this second strand of the rationalistic strategy. Against the elder Strawson's view that we would have overriding reasons to retain the reactive attitudes no matter what theoretical reasons like those advocated by incompatibilists were advanced against them, Galen Strawson argues that we have a commitment to truth, a propensity to live in accordance with the facts. But then if determinism is indeed incompatible with responsibility, it is not obvious that it would be rational to abandon our commitment to truth in favor of our commitment to sustaining a way of life in which our reactive attitudes figure prominently.

To turn briefly to the naturalistic strategy underlying P. F. Strawson's position, its point is that our human commitment to the reactive attitudes is so "thoroughgoing and deeply rooted" in our nature, that, *pace* the pessimists, it would be psychologically impossible to give them up or entirely abandon them even if we had theoretical grounds for doing so. It is thus "useless" and "idle" to ask whether or not it would be rational to suspend or abandon our reactive attitudes if determinism were true.

Criticizing this position, Paul Russell (1992) suggests that Strawson fails to distinguish between "type-naturalism" and "token-naturalism." The type naturalist plausibly holds that we have a general disposition to adopt the reactive attitudes which is partly constitutive of human nature, and consequently that this disposition is insulated from theoretical discoveries. In contrast, the token-naturalist says that we are prone to adopt particular tokens of, say, gratitude or resentment, under particular circumstances, and that we are so naturally constituted that we cannot abandon or suspend such tokens of specific attitudes under the relevant circumstances. Russell proposes that whereas type-naturalism is plausible, it cannot be used to discredit the pessimists' view that, confronted by adequate theoretical reasons, we would be able to abandon our reactive attitudes. For the pessimists' view is most charitably construed as the thesis that, in light of theoretical considerations, we are able to abandon *tokens* of, say, resentment, under certain (responsibility-undermining) circumstances; and that if determinism is true, we are all in such circumstances.[5]

Finally, Strawson's theory can be assessed according to whether it responds adequately to the putative threats of determinism to control and agency outlined previously. We have seen that Strawson holds that being morally responsible is nothing more than being a recipient of the reactive attitudes and a participant in the associated practices. The notion of responsibility is to be understood as largely the expression of our concerns and demands about our treatment of one another. Further, Strawson insists that responsibility is not a function of holding propositions "external" to the practice to be true, such as the proposition that responsibility requires contracausal freedom. So, similarly, one might think that Strawson's response to the putative first threat of determinism would be to say that the proposition that responsibility requires freedom to do otherwise is "external" to the germane practice and hence is not relevant to our understanding of responsibility. Similarly, in response to the putative second threat, he might say that the proposition that decisions that issue from sources over which we have no control are ones for which we cannot be responsible is, once again, "external" to our practices. These responses, though, to the two threats are suspect and we can appreciate this if we further explore the relevant practice.

If *practice* is construed narrowly to denote simply reactive responses to, or treatment of, others, then Strawson's account is objectionable. For then it would not be possible to explain why some of our reactive responses, like expressional blame, would be misplaced. I might believe that Jack is an appropriate candidate for blame with respect to a particular deed, and react accordingly; but unaware of certain pertinent facts, I might be mistaken. Presumably, though, Strawson would handle this sort of worry by construing *practice* broadly to include excusing and exempting conditions. But our practice of responsibility ascriptions includes clarifying the excuses and exemptions themselves, partly, by trying to discern the common features (if any) that they share so that we can frame, for example, legal policy. But a careful look at our practice reveals that several of our excuses tend to cluster around epistemic or control considerations. With respect to the latter, incompatibilists of a certain bent (for example, Edwards 1958) might insist that it is not improbable to assume that such considerations share lack of freedom to do otherwise. Further, incompatibilists of a different bent might argue that a number of the exemptions, such as psychological abnormality or systematic behavior control, share the feature that the agent is not in ultimate control of her decisions or actions; they are, in a transparent sense, the product of sources external to the agent (see, for example, Kane 1996a: ch. 5). But then, again, it is not far-fetched, these incompatibilists might say, to regard determinism as threatening responsibility in an analogous way: if it is true, then no one is in ultimate control of his or her decisions or actions.

2. R. Jay Wallace's Account

R. Jay Wallace (1994), who also develops a Strawsonian account, meets the objection regarding alternative possibilities head-on. Like Strawson, Wallace takes the question about the conditions under which persons are morally responsible to be tantamount to the question of the conditions under which it is appropriate to hold persons responsible; and holding persons responsible involves susceptibility to the reactive attitudes in relation to them. Unlike Strawson, Wallace restricts the reactive attitudes pertinent to responsibility to resentment, indignation, and guilt. These attitudes, he says, "hang together as a class," in that they are linked by related propositional objects: each is "explained exclusively by beliefs about the violation of moral obligations (construed as strict prohibitions or requirements), whereas other moral sentiments are explained by beliefs about the various modalities of moral value" (ibid.: 12).

On Wallace's view, a person is morally responsible for some action if and only if it would be appropriate to hold her responsible for that action (ibid.: 91). Because moral norms of fairness, Wallace contends, set the standards of appropriateness for responsibility ascriptions, this view is to be construed as the normative one that a person is morally responsible for an action if and only if it is *fair* to hold her responsible for that action.

Consonant with this interpretation, Wallace regards incompatibilists as claiming that "it would be unfair (and hence wrong) to hold people responsible if determinism is true" (ibid.: 110). Elaborating, Wallace attributes to incompatibilists the "generalization strategy" according to which what unifies the standard excusing and exempting conditions is that they are all different ways of showing that the agent could not have done otherwise.[6] Because determinism effaces alternative possibilities, it would, consequently, never be fair to hold people responsible. To meet the incompatibilists' charge, Wallace advances principles of fairness that include, as excusing and exempting conditions of responsibility, the very ones that we acknowledge, but that do not entail that what unifies these conditions is the generalization that agents are unable to do otherwise.

When excuses (such as coercion, physical constraint, duress, mistake, accident, and inadvertence) apply, Wallace proposes that what we find is that the agent has *not* violated a moral obligation. He explains that something is a moral obligation for an agent only if it is susceptible to direct influence by reasons (ibid.: 131). Mere bodily movements cannot be so influenced but only intentions or decisions, or, as Wallace prefers to say, "choices" of the agent (ibid.: 132). When, for example, a person harms another out of ignorance, the harm is not intentional, and so in most cases does not result from a choice to cause the harm; as such, the harm fails to issue from violation of a moral obligation. Wallace then advances the "no blameworthiness without fault" principle that it is unfair (because undeserved) to blame someone unless he has violated a moral obligation. Surely, Wallace, adds, it is "doubtful in the extreme that . . . determinism would entail that people never act on choices that violate moral obligations we accept" (ibid.: 135).

With the exemptions—psychopathy, behavior control, stress, insanity, addiction, childhood, hypnotism, deprivation, or torture—Wallace theorizes that the agent has been deprived of the ability to grasp and apply moral reasons, and the ability to control his behavior by such reasons (ibid.: 155–66). But if holding an agent responsible involves judging it appropriate to sanction her morally, and to sanction her as a result of the violation of moral obligations for which there are moral reasons, then it will be unreasonable to do this if she lacks the ability to apply the moral reasons that sustain the obligations violated. Another plausible principle of fairness is that it is unfair (because unreasonable) to blame someone for violating a moral obligation if she lacks the power to recognize and act on the moral reasons supporting that obligation. Again, Wallace indicates that determinism does not entail that people never have the power to recognize and act on moral reasons that underpin obligations. He concludes that the incompatibilists' generalization strategy fails, and the Strawsonian view developed vindicates the compatibilists' stance that determinism is no threat to responsibility.

I confine critical discussion of Wallace's rich account to the "no blameworthiness without fault" principle. The principle implies the following:

No Fault   A person is blameworthy for something (a choice or action, for example) only if that thing is morally wrong.

Wallace, it seems, accepts the Kantian *ought* implies *can* principle (ibid.: 221–25), which says:

K   S has a moral obligation to perform [not to perform] A only if S can perform [not perform] A.

A noncontroversial deontic principle that links obligation and wrongness is

OW   Agent S ought to do [not to do] A if and only if it is morally wrong for S not to do [to do] A.

K and OW enjoy both intuitive support and theory-based support—the latter as both are theorems within some of our best theories of the concept of moral obligation (for example, those of M. Zimmerman 1996 and Fred Feldman 1986). These deontic principles, in turn, entail that there is a requirement of alternative possibilities for overall wrong actions:

WAP   It is morally wrong for S to do [not to do] A only if S can refrain from doing [do] A.

Now if determinism eradicates genuine alternatives, and wrong actions require such alternatives, then the truth of determinism implies that no actions (where *action* is broadly construed to include choices) are wrong. But this result, in conjunction with No Fault, would saddle Wallace with the result, anathema to a compatibilist like him, that no one is blameworthy for anything in a determined world. In summary, if No Fault is true, then an incompatibilist might well exploit this principle, in conjunction with the fact that determinism subverts deontic wrongness, to argue for the view that no one can ever deserve blame for anything in a determined world. Such an argument need not hinge on any considerations of fairness. Rather, it would emphasize that alternative possibilities are required for deontic wrongness and that determinism undermines such wrongness.

Suppose, though, that No Fault is false, as many have argued (for example, Brandt 1958; M. Zimmerman 1988; Haji 1998). Then Wallace's account of why excusing conditions subvert responsibility straightforwardly fails because it invokes the "No fault without blameworthiness" principle, and No Fault is a false implication of that principle.

3. HIERARCHICAL ACCOUNTS: FRANKFURT AND DWORKIN

We now turn to an altogether different strategy for showing that freedom and responsibility are compatible with determinism. This strategy develops the idea that the sort of freedom required for responsibility is essentially a function of an appropriate "mesh" or connection between an agent's choices or actions and her other actional constituents like desires and preferences. We will start with hierarchical theories and then consider other types of "mesh theory" (a useful term introduced by Fischer and Ravizza 1998: 185).

The hierarchical theories of Gerald Dworkin and Harry Frankfurt are *internalist*. According to such theories, a person is responsible solely by virtue of facts internal to his psychology. *Externalists* hold that responsibility also requires that a person's motivations that give rise to choice or action be caused, in an appropriate way, by factors in the external world. Unlike internalists, externalists stress that the causal history of our springs of action are crucial to responsibility ascriptions.[7] Internalism appears to enjoy at least one theoretical advantage over externalism: if responsibility does not depend upon history, then compatibilism would be easier to defend.

In a seminal article, Frankfurt (1971) asserts that one essential difference between persons and other creatures is to be found in the structure of persons' wills. *Persons*, unlike simpler animals and young children, are able to form *second-order* desires and "have the capacity for reflective self-evaluation that is manifested in the formation of second-order desires" (ibid.: 7). Similarly, Dworkin's theory (1988) of personal autonomy, which attempts to capture the core idea of autonomy as self-government, appeals to the distinction between second-order and first-order desires. Unlike a first-order desire, whose object is an action or a state of affairs, a second-order desire's object is another actual or possible desire of the agent whose desire it is.

Dworkin proposes that a person is autonomous "if he identifies with his desires, goals, and values, and such identification is not influenced in ways which make the process of identification in some way alien to the agent" (1988: 61). Roughly, Dworkin conceives of identification as an agent's reflecting critically on a first-order desire and giving "higher order" approval of that desire. In early renditions of his theory that advance necessary conditions of responsibility, Frankfurt invokes both the idea of conformity between one's will (the first-order desire that moves one to action) and a second-order volition (a second-order desire that some first-order desire be one's will), and identification with one's will. Again, the key idea is that responsibility requires that we assess our first-order desires and form second-order preferences as to which first-order desire should move us to action.

Frankfurt has offered different accounts of the notion of identification.[8] So, for example, in one work (1987), he proposes that one identifies with a first-order desire when one has an unopposed second-order volition to act in accordance with it, and one judges that any further deliberation involving other higher order desires about the matter would result in the same decision. In recent essays, Frankfurt appeals to a distinction between passivity and activity with regard to one's desires in order to explain identification. He says that the desires with which a person has identified are "wholly internal to a person's will rather than alien to him; that is, he is not passive with respect to them" (1992b: 8). Further, "insofar as a person's will is affected by considerations that are external to it, the person is being acted upon. To that extent, he is passive. The person is active, on the other hand, insofar as his will determines itself" (1994b: 437).

To facilitate discussion, the basic structure of hierarchical theories can be summarized in this way: The hierarchical component is captured by the condition that an agent, S, identifies with a first-order desire, D, to perform some action, A, only if S has a second-order volition, V (relative to D), that D be S's motivating desire. Depending upon how the notion of identification is filled out, the condition will expand to a necessary and sufficient one for identification. We can then add that agent, S, exercises hierarchical control over action, A, if and only if S does A, and A is caused (in a nondeviant, appropriate way) by a desire with which S identifies. Finally, the proponent of an hierarchical theory can be taken to be committed to this principle:

HT   A person is morally responsible for performing an action only if she exercises hierarchical control over that action.

This sort of theory encounters problems that have invited illuminating and continuing discussion. Some of the more prominent of these include the following. First, the theory generates some counterintuitive results. For example, an addict (who, let us assume, has become addicted to a drug through no fault of his own) can identify with an irresistible desire for taking some drug. Assuming other conditions of responsibility (like epistemic ones) are satisfied, HT yields the result that the addict is morally responsible for taking the drug, even though, it seems, he is a slave to his relevant desire. Another example concerns akratic action that is free, intentional action contrary to one's best judgment. Assume that Mickey judges it best that he ought not to eat the pie, and he identifies with the desire to refrain from eating the pie. But suppose, succumbing to weakness, he akratically eats the pie. Developing the case in a certain fashion, critics have charged that though Mickey is blameworthy for eating the pie, HT yields the result that he is not, in that he does not identify with the desire to eat the pie. (Compare Mele 1992a for an illuminating discussion of akratic action and HT-type theories.)

A second sort of worry concerns a possible infinite regress of volitions. For an agent to be morally responsible by virtue of the conformity between his will and a second-order volition, V_1, V_1 must be freely willed. But for V_1 to be freely willed, there must be conformity between V_1 and some higher order volition, V_2, which must in turn be freely willed and so requires a yet higher order volition, and so forth (Watson 1975; Shatz 1985; Friedman 1986, Christman 1991; Zimmerman 1981; and Cuypers forthcoming). Indeed, the different notions of identification developed by Frankfurt reflect, in part, his efforts to meet this regress objection.

Third, some critics have claimed that HT rests on the unwarranted assumption that the agent's "real self" is to be identified with the cluster of her higher order volitions and those lower order elements selected by them (Thalberg 1989; Berofsky 1995).

Finally, there is the concern that identification can be "engineered" in such a fashion that the agent, contrary to the implications of HT, is not morally responsible. After all, the very components essential to reasoning, including one's values, desires, and beliefs, which are also central to identification, can be acquired via means (like unsolicited, direct electronic stimulation of the brain) that undermine responsibility (Slote 1980; Watson 1987a).[9] The underlying worry here is that hierarchical theories are too internalist; they are insufficiently sensitive to how one acquires one's springs of action.

How might theorists like Frankfurt respond to this last objection? On their behalf, I would urge distinguishing between concerns of responsibility-grounding control and those of ultimacy—roughly, those factors by virtue of which an agent's springs of action are truly an agent's own. The theorists could then be viewed as offering accounts of control and not ultimacy. To elaborate briefly, it has been customary to treat cases involving various sorts of manipulation as test cases for control. But they can also be used to cast doubt on accounts according to which the satisfaction of control (and epistemic conditions) is *sufficient* for responsibility. That these conditions are insufficient, I believe, is one of the deep morals to be drawn from appropriate cases of manipulation. This recommendation, if heeded, will help to refocus various debates concerning responsibility and control. For example, barring other difficulties with it, one would be misguided to charge that Frankfurt's theory is inadequate by virtue of its *control* dimension falling prey to suitable manipulation cases, on the assumption that the hierarchical machinery invoked by Frankfurt specifies the control and not ultimacy (or "ownership") requirement of responsibility.

To sum up, how well do HT-like theories cope with the two threats of determinism with which we began? First, to meet the charge that responsibility requires alternative possibilities, Frankfurt (1969) argues directly against the principle of alternate possibilities ("an agent is morally responsible for something only if he could have done otherwise") by invoking the now famous " 'Frankfurt-type' example" (adumbrated in the discussion that follows). I think this intriguing kind of example is by and large convincing. He then, of course, offers a hierarchical theory that does not imply that the sort of freedom required for responsibility entails the existence of genuinely open alternatives. Theories like HT, however, do not respond well to the second threat of determinism concerning agency. Indeed, I believe that such theories need to be supplemented by an account, roughly, of "authentic agency," or an account of what makes one's springs of action "truly one's own."[10]

Let us now examine further varieties of "mesh" theories, which require some suitable connection between the agent's action and other elements in the external world like values or reasons.

4. FURTHER MESH ACCOUNTS: WATSON AND WOLF

Gary Watson's account (1975), unlike Frankfurt's, is nonhierarchical but it is still a mesh account because it assumes that responsibility requires a suitable connection between the agent's behavior and her *values*. Reviving certain Platonic themes, Watson claims that our desires or preferences have different sources. Our "valuational" preferences originate in reason and express what reason recommends. Mere "motivational preferences," by contrast, have their source in "appetite." Mickey, for example, may most want to eat the pie in the sense of "most want" that amounts to having the causally strongest desire for something; yet, given his medical condition, reason does not sanction that desire but the opposed one to refrain. Watson suggests that we should identify free action not with an agent's causally strongest desire, but with her value judgment about what she ought to do. His view can be summarized in this way:

> Watson1   Agent, S, does A freely at time, t, if S most values doing A at t, S does A at t, and S's doing A at t issues in a nondeviant fashion from what S most values then.

Watson says that free agents have the capacity to translate their values into action; their actions flow from their "evaluational system." This (and other claims) suggest that Watson also endorses the following.

> Watson2   If an agent acts against what she most values at a time, then she acts unfreely at that time.

One problem with Watson's views lies with Watson2. There appear to be cases in which though a person acts against what she most values at a time, she then acts freely. Mickey's akratically eating the pie seems to be a case in point. Kadri Vihvelin (1994) gives another example: Person X lies to Customs officials. When questioned later, X agrees that breaking the law is wrong but candidly explains that he did it because he did not want to spend hundreds of dollars on import duties. X acted contrary to his judgment about what he ought to do; so he acted against what he most valued. But there is little reason to suppose that he acted unfreely.

Another worry concerns Watson1. One's values (or at least components of them), according to Watson, appear to be a subset of one's beliefs; they seem to be beliefs about what is right or wrong, or what one ought to do, or what is good and evil. If desires can be implanted in one against one's will or unbeknownst to one, so can beliefs, and hence so can values on Watson's conception of values. If an agent's behavior results from values surreptitiously implanted in her, then it is not clear, contrary to Watson1, that she is responsible for that behavior. Whether Watson's theory has the resources to cope with this objection, I suspect, will turn largely on refinement of the pertinent view of values.[11]

Susan Wolf's theory (1990) is another mesh theory that implies that responsibility is a function of an appropriate fit between an agent's behavior and values. A striking feature of her view (which she calls the Reason View) is that responsibility requires that agents have the normative ability to appreciate the "True and the Good" and to do the right thing for the right reasons:

> According to the Reason View, . . . responsibility depends on the ability to act in accordance with the True and the Good. If one is psychologically deter-mined to do the right thing for the right reasons, this is compatible with

having the requisite ability. . . . But if one is psychologically determined to do the wrong thing, for whatever reason, this seems to constitute a denial of that ability. For if one *has* to do the wrong thing, then one *cannot* do the right thing, and so one lacks the ability to act in accordance with the True and the Good. (ibid.:79)

As Wolf herself indicates, her Reason View is committed to the curious asymmetry thesis that whereas one can be responsible for a right (or good) action that one could not have avoided performing, one *cannot* be morally responsible for a wrong (or bad) action that one could not have avoided performing.

Wolf motivates her asymmetry thesis largely by contrasting examples of seemingly right and wrong (or good and bad) actions that are unavoidable. With respect to one part of her thesis, in one of the examples, a woman on an uncrowded beach sees a young boy struggling in the water in obvious need of aid. Thinking that the boy requires her help, she immediately swims to his rescue. Wolf assumes that it is literally impossible for the woman to refrain from saving the child "because her understanding of the situation is so good and her moral commitment so strong" (ibid.: 82). For a woman with her moral character, leaving the child to drown is either "unthinkable" or simply not a thought that can be taken seriously (ibid.: 59). Wolf concludes that even though the woman is not free to do otherwise, she is praiseworthy for saving the child. Wolf finds support for the other part of her asymmetry thesis in a class of cases involving kleptomania, drug addiction, hypnosis, and deprived childhoods, in which agents are apparently not blameworthy for performing seemingly wrong (or bad) actions even though they could not have done otherwise. Wolf claims that the judgment that they are not blameworthy stems from the fact that the agents could not do the right thing for the right reasons.[12] Such examples lead Wolf to conclude that the freedom requirement for moral responsibility is asymmetrical.

One shortcoming of the Reason View turns on Wolf's insistence that "it is only the ability to do the right thing for the right reasons . . . that is required for responsibility" (ibid.: 81). It appears that a person could deliberately harden his heart to the supplications of morality and so not be able to act in accord with the True and the Good and *still* be fully responsible for his actions. As an illustration, suppose Glaucon, who is well aware of moral restrictions, has decided to develop his character in such a way that his true guiding principle is one of self-interest. Imagine, now, that having "freely" and willfully developed his character in this direction, Glaucon is literally unable to refrain from pocketing a gold coin that he spies on the otherwise deserted stretch of road. When he pockets the coin, Glaucon acts in conformity with his character. His options are constrained by his earlier deliberate efforts to thwart requirements of the True and the Good in favor of maximizing self-interest. But although Glaucon cannot now act in accord with the True and the Good, it is clearly possible that he is blameworthy for pocketing the coin. His manner of conduct is relevantly analogous to what it would be were he to consent to being hypnotized for the purpose of ensuring that he pockets the coin. In the latter case, there would be little doubt about his culpability, even though he could not thwart the (let us suppose) powerful posthypnotic suggestion.

Wolf might respond to this case by saying that Glaucon is indirectly responsible for pocketing the coin because he was indirectly capable of acting according to reason. She might say, Glaucon freely decided, when he *did* have the capacity to act in accordance with the True and the Good, to shape his character in a certain way; consequently, he must be responsible for at least some actions that "issue from" his acquired character.

This reply, however, is not fully satisfactory. Wolf's view does support the reasonable verdict that Glaucon is responsible for acquiring his "self-interested character." But it fails to support the further plausible verdict that he is also responsible for pocketing the coin, a deed of his that issues from this character, *if* "it is *only* the ability to do the right thing for the right reasons ... that is required for moral responsibility."

A second problem with Wolf's view is that it, too, just like HT theories, seems to succumb to the problem of responsibility-undermining manipulation, on the reasonable supposition that an agent's ability (or inability) to do the right thing for the right reasons could be, for instance, electronically induced.

A third difficulty lies with Wolf's asymmetry thesis. Apparently Wolf runs together two different sets of concepts, one having to do with deontic rightness and wrongness and the other with deontic value. We can say that an act is *overall bad* if and only if, were it performed, it would produce more intrinsic evil than intrinsic goodness. Similarly, an act is *overall good* just in case its performance would produce more intrinsic goodness than intrinsic evil. It seems perfectly possible for an agent to be in a situation in which all her options are overall bad. Still, if we allow for even modest consequentialist considerations, it is not unreasonable to assume that of these options, the one that is least overall evil is the one the agent ought morally to do. Hence, what is overall bad need not be wrong and what is overall good need not be right or obligatory. So even if—and this is contentious—there is an asymmetry in alternative possibility requirements for moral responsibility for overall *good* and overall *bad* actions, it does not follow from *this* asymmetry that there is an analogous asymmetry for *right* and *wrong* actions.

Still, Wolf might reasonably claim that in the *range* of cases that interest her— the case of the upright mother, the agent with a depraved childhood, and so on—it *does* seem plausible to suppose that the overall good or bad actions performed are also, respectively, right or wrong. But even then, as John Fischer and Mark Ravizza (1992a) have argued, a deep worry plagues her asymmetry thesis. Fischer and Ravizza generate a Frankfurt-type case ("Villain") in which a vile character, Joe, is blameworthy for performing a bad action although he could not have done otherwise. Joe decides (for his own perverse reasons) to push a child off a pier for the purpose of causing her to drown in the violent surf. Had Joe shown any sign of not acting on his decision to kill the child, a device in his brain would have caused him to acquire the decision and to act on it. But Joe acts on his own, independently of any interference from the device. In this sort of case, it sensible to suppose that Joe is deserving of blame, and hence is morally blameworthy, for performing an overall bad action even though Joe could not have done otherwise. Fischer and Ravizza conclude that Wolf's asymmetry thesis is false; good and bad actions are symmetric with regard to the lack of a requirement of alternative possibilities for moral responsibility. In turn, if one (mistakenly) thinks that over-all bad actions are wrong and overall good actions right, Villain should impel Wolf to reconsider her asymmetry thesis.[13]

Let us next, examine one of the most recent incarnations of a mesh theory.

5. Bok's Account

Toward developing her version of a mesh account of free will, Hilary Bok distinguishes two standpoints, theoretical and practical, from which human actions can be regarded. The theoretical standpoint involves scientific (including psychological and historical) description and explanation of the phenomena in the universe. This standpoint, which is the determinist's, pictures the world as a place in which everything, human behavior included, is governed by natural laws. Now an agent has ultimate control over, say, his making some decision, when, roughly, there are no conditions "external" to him that are minimally causally sufficient for his making that decision. From the theoretical perspective, it appears that the libertarian's desideratum of ultimate control cannot be satisfied. The practical standpoint is the one we use to reason about what we should do and how we should live (1998: 62–63). Aligning herself with Kant, Bok contends that our ascriptions of freedom and responsibility are based on the requirements of the practical standpoint and that when we occupy that standpoint, we have every reason to regard ourselves as free and to hold ourselves morally responsible for our actions (ibid.: 52).

Next, Bok argues that the claims of theoretical and practical reasoning do not conflict (ibid.:ch.2), and that the freedom and moral responsibility presupposed by the practical standpoint is ultimately reconcilable with all our behavior's being completely determined by the natural laws. Central to establishing the consistency of freedom of the will and determinism is Bok's distinction between theoretical possibility (or possibility *tout court*) and practical (or narrow) possibility. Her view is that when we reason practically, all we assume is that our various alternatives are possible in the sense that we would perform them if we chose; we assume, in other words, a conditional or hypothetical conception of freedom to do otherwise. Given certain facts about deliberation (ibid.: 108), we do not assume in the practical standpoint that available alternatives are possible *tout court*, that is, we do not assume that, given the natural laws and the past, a person could have done other than what he or she in fact did.

Not surprisingly, on Bok's view the notion of practical possibility is relevant to free will. She writes:

> From the practical point of view . . . our use of this general [conditional] conception of possibility, as opposed to the narrower possibility *tout court*, is both unavoidable and rational. It is unavoidable because while we deliberate we cannot possibly employ a conception of the alternatives that are available to us that is narrower than the set of actions that we would perform were we to choose to do so. It is rational because, for the purposes of deliberation, we must regard the question what we will choose to do as open and because, if we regard that question as open, we should not regard the various actions that we would perform if we chose as differing with respect to their possibility, since any of them would be possible *tout court* if we chose to perform it. Moreover, to determine whether or not a particular action is one which we would perform if we chose is to determine whether or not we can regard it as a possible object of choice: an action about which question whether or not we have reason to perform it can legitimately be raised. (ibid.: 117–18)

Armed with the conception of practical possibility, Bok introduces her conception of freedom—the sort that is required for normative appraisals:

> a person is free if she is capable of determining her actions through practical reasoning; such an agent is free to choose among all those acts that she would perform if she chose to perform them, and she is free to perform a given action if she would perform it if she chose to do so. (ibid.: 120)

Bok remarks that freedom of the will has traditionally been claimed to involve two conditions: first, our wills are free only if we can choose among genuine alternatives (ibid.: 118); and second, freedom of the will involves stepping back and asking ourselves whether or not we should act on our various alternatives and desires (ibid.: 119). Both these conditions, she says, are met by her view of freedom: the first because when we engage in practical reasoning, constraints on knowledge dictate that we should regard all those actions that we would perform as genuine alternatives; and the second because determining our conduct through practical reasoning requires that we evaluate our motivations and decide which we have most reason to activate. In that her account satisfies this second feature, Bok claims, it is a "hierarchical" or, more aptly, a mesh account. She indicates that her account differs from those of, for example, Watson or Frankfurt in interpreting freedom as consisting in our ability to determine our conduct through practical reasoning, and not in our ability to act on our values or second-order volitions (ibid.: 119).

Bok then relates her conditional account of freedom to moral responsibility by advancing a particular conception of responsibility. Her view is that we are responsible for those actions that reveal the quality of our character and our will (ibid.: 139, 140, 152, 180). When my conduct reflects my will, I can appropriately hold myself accountable for it; it can legitimately be attributed to my charge (ibid.: 152). I can ask what such conduct reveals about me and my character and about ways in which it might be improved. As for blameworthiness, when, through exercise of my will—that is, through determining my actions by engaging in practical reasoning—I freely and knowingly violate my standards by performing some action, I am blameworthy for that action (ibid.: 167, 168, 192).

Let us begin evaluation of Bok's theory by focusing on ultimate control. Addressing the libertarian's worry that an action or choice that is ultimately caused by events outside an agent's control cannot be one for which the agent can be responsible, Bok writes:

> [O]ur main interest is in evaluating our contributions to the process whereby we came to act as we did. We want to discover whether we did anything that we think wrong: whether we were attentive to all those considerations we think we should have taken into account, whether we thought hard enough and seriously enough about what we were about to do, whether we made the right choices, and, if we did not, what explains our failure. It may be that it was determined that not only our act but the process whereby we came to perform it would fail to conform to our standards; but that fact is not relevant to the question whether or not it did fail to conform to them. And it is that question that we must answer if we wish to decide whether or not the fact that we did something that we regret indicates the existence of some fault in our wills that we can and should try to correct. (ibid.: 156)

Now it is true that the contributions that we make to the process whereby we come to act as we do are relevant to responsibility. But surely so are contributions of the past. In the case of Robert Harris discussed by Watson, when we learn, for example, about the parental abuse he suffered, and the neglect and the sordid conditions under which he spent his formative years, it is difficult to hold him fully responsible for his later vicious criminal behavior. If such past conditions mitigate responsibility—Harris would not be responsible to the same degree as he would be if his past were not so depraved—then contributions of the past, in addition to one's contributions to the process, which fuel one's actions, *do* bear on responsibility. But if we admit that certain conditions of the past over which one had no control can duly influence responsibility, then the compatibilist must squarely face the challenge of explaining why other conditions of the past over which one could not have had control—for example conditions that existed long before one was born—are not relevant to responsibility. And I believe this libertarian challenge has not been adequately addressed by Bok.

It might, in connection with this problem of past influences on responsibility, be noted that Wallace's normative conception of responsibility has a definite advantage over Bok's. Wallace, as we have seen, proposes that an agent is responsible for something insofar as it is fair to hold him responsible for that thing. In a case like Harris's, presumably, the normative approach would explain mitigation of responsibility by invoking considerations of fairness: given Harris's past, it is not fair to hold him responsible to the degree to which he would be held were it not for his unfortunate past.

Other compatibilist approaches relevant to past influences involve developing a conception of "authentic" springs of action, roughly, springs of action that are "truly one's one" (Fischer and Ravizza 1998: ch. 8; Haji 1998, chs. 6, 7). The strategy here is that with some such conception in hand, we could infer that, in a case like Harris's, some of Harris's springs of action, perhaps the values that he applies to evaluative best judgments that, in turn, give rise to decisions, are not truly, or are not fully truly, his own. Yet other approaches involve careful attention to the actual causal pathways that culminate in action with an eye toward isolating responsibility-undermining factors that might be present in some but not all of the pathways.

Another concern with Bok's mesh account is that it is susceptible to the problem of clandestine manipulation that also plagues other mesh accounts like Wolf's. If responsibility is a function of an appropriate fit between the choices an agent makes and her practical reasoning, and the very "inputs" of such reasoning can be surreptitiously controlled by an external manipulator, it appears that Bok's mesh condition can be satisfied even though the agent is not intuitively responsible.

Finally, there are concerns with Bok's views that are associated with "deontic morality."[14] Moral responsibility requires freedom or control. Similarly, other moral appraisals, like deontic ones of rightness, wrongness, and obligatoriness, presuppose freedom. This is perhaps most evident in the case of moral obligation. The verdict that the paraplegic ought to have walked across the lawn (or that he did wrong by failing to walk across the lawn), when *ought* denotes moral obligation or requirement, appears to be conceptually inconsistent. There is a control principle with intuitive and theoretical appeal associated with moral obligation, to wit, principle K, which is, recall, the *ought* implies *can* principle.

I want to evaluate Bok's suggestion that, from the standpoint of practical reasoning (ibid.: 62–65), the relevant conception of freedom presupposed by various moral appraisals (like those of moral responsibility or deontic ones) states that we are free only when we choose among courses of action that are truly open to us: in short, if we freely performed some action, we had genuine alternative possibilities. For Bok, the pertinent notion of possibility is the practical notion:

when we engage in practical reasoning, we assume that various alternative acts are possible in the sense that we would perform them if we chose (ibid.: 104–9). For purposes of deciding what one should do, then, it seems that Bok favors a conditional analysis of *can*:

CC   S can do A =df. S would do A if S chose to.

There are, however, problems with such an analysis.[15] J. L. Austin (1961) described cases in which, though it is true that some person could do something, it is false that she would do that thing if she chose to. In one of his best known examples, Austin imagined himself a golfer standing over a three-foot putt. Suppose he had made such putts in several but not in all relevantly similar situations in the past. Then it seems perfectly consistent to say, Austin proposed, that he could make the putt on this occasion, although he might miss (on this occasion). So his ability to make the putt does not entail that he would make the putt whenever he chose to do so. Keith Lehrer (1968) offers a different sort of counterexample against CC. There can be cases, Lehrer claims, in which although a person cannot do something, it is true that she would do it if she chose to. Suppose, for instance, that as a result of the traumatic experience of having been bitten by a snake in her youth, Leila has developed an extreme psychological aversion to snakes. Her aversion renders her unable to choose to pick up the harmless snake in her biology class. And (partly) because she cannot choose to pick up the snake, she cannot pick up the snake. Yet, Lehrer argues, it might be true that if she were to choose to pick up the snake, she would do so. So whereas Leila cannot pick up the snake because of her aversion, the conditional analysis yields the result that she can so act.

Deontic appraisals pose another challenge to Bok's conditional notion of freedom. To explain this challenge, we start by noting that there is a requirement of alternative possibilities for deontic acts. An outline of the argument for this requirement follows: We have seen that K (*ought* implies *can*) and principle OW (OW says that an agent S ought to do [not to do] A if and only if it is morally wrong for S not to do [to do] A) entail that overall wrong actions require alternative possibilities. Setting aside one complication,[16] it is straightforward to show that under conditions in which an agent lacks alternative possibilities, the agent's actions, besides not being overall wrong, are neither overall obligatory nor overall right. For if some action, A, is obligatory for some person, then failing to do A— an omission—is wrong for that person. But it is false that any action (or omission) in a world in which a person lacks alternative possibilities is wrong for any person, given WAP (it is morally wrong for S to do [not to do] A only if S can refrain from doing [do] A). So it is false that failing to do A is wrong for that person. Hence, in such a world, no action would be morally wrong or obligatory for that person.

There is no analogous way to show that rightness also requires alternative possibilities, for there is no analogous principle like OW that will allow us to infer that *right* implies "can refrain." But it is highly plausible to maintain that *right* does imply "can refrain." Otherwise, insofar as obligatoriness and wrongness do require alternative possibilities, we would have to contend with the unpalatable view that it is morally right for one to do whatever heinous acts one cannot avoid doing.

An alternative route to the conclusion that the primary deontic properties of rightness, wrongness, and obligatoriness require alternative possibilities assumes, very reasonably, that, just like *ought, right* and *wrong* also imply *can*. Then OW and the assumption that *wrong* implies *can* entail that there is a requirement of alternative possibilities for obligatory acts; OW and K entail that there is such a requirement for wrong acts; and we add to this the result that *right*, too, requires alternative possibilities.[17]

Now consider a standard "Frankfurt-type" case in which though an agent intentionally performed some action on "his own," he could not have refrained from performing it given the particular circumstances in which he found himself. In such cases, a counterfactual intervener or controller keeps vigil over the agent, ensuring that if the agent, say, Jones, shows any sign whatsoever of not performing the relevant act (for example, killing White), the controller will intervene and cause Jones to choose to act in the desired fashion. In his situation (assuming that he is not incapacitated to choose to kill White when he so chooses), Jones is unable to refrain from killing White. We have established that no one is able to perform an action that is right, wrong, or obligatory unless one is able to refrain from performing it. This fact and the pertinent ones of Jones's case entail that Jones's killing White lacks any of these moral statuses.

Bok's conditional notion of freedom yields the right results in this case. If one is able to do something, then it must be true that one has the opportunity to do that thing. In standard Frankfurt-type cases, although Jones has the ability to refrain from killing White, the counterfactual controller ensures that he lacks the opportunity to refrain from killing White. As it is false that Jones would have refrained from killing White had he so chosen, Bok's conditional notion of freedom correctly implies that Jones could not have refrained from killing White.

Suppose, now, that determinism is true. Then there is exactly one pathway for each person into the future. Just as the counterfactual intervener in standard Frankfurt-type cases ensures that Jones could not have refrained from doing what he in fact did, so, if determinism is true, the natural laws and the past ensure that each agent cannot do other than what she in fact does.

It is important here to understand the pertinent parallel between Frankfurt-type cases and a deterministic world. An agent is able to do something only if she has both the ability and the opportunity to do that thing. There are relatively weaker and stronger senses of *ability*. A relatively weak sense of *ability* entails merely that the agent has the germane capacity, whereas a relatively strong sense of *ability* entails, in addition, that the agent have pertinent skills and perhaps know-how. So, for instance, even if Fritz, who is unfamiliar with computers, succeeded in turning one on, his turning it on would be something of a fluke. As he did turn it on, he did have the weak ability—the capacity—to turn it on, but we would not want to say that he had the pertinent skills or know-how; he lacked the strong ability to turn it on.

As for opportunity, by and large advocates of the principle that *ought* implies *can* recommend that *opportunity* is to be understood broadly to include all circumstantial factors that would enable someone to exercise a pertinent ability. On this view, someone lacks the opportunity to perform an action just in case there is something (a bolted door or a state of unconsciousness, for example) that would prevent a successful exercise of the relevant ability or abilities.

In a standard Frankfurt-type case, the counterfactual intervener does not detrimentally affect Jones's *ability* to refrain from killing White; rather, the intervener ensures that Jones lacks *the opportunity* to refrain from doing other than what he does. Similarly, I agree with Kadri Vihvelin's (n.d.) insight that, once we realize that to have an ability is just to have a certain kind of capacity or skill, it should be uncontroversial that the possession of abilities, including unexercised ones, is compatible with deterministic as well as indeterministic laws. For any ability we might think relevant to the question of freedom and moral responsibility—such as mental abilities like reasoning and deliberating concerning possible actions, making evaluative judgments, forming intentions, and so forth—there is no reason to think that deterministic causal laws (or the past) would deprive us of this *ability*. Rather, determinism deprives agents of the *opportunity* to do anything other than what they in fact do. But if this is so, then, as advocates of K insist, because an agent can do something only if she has the opportunity to do that thing, determinism ensures that an agent cannot do other than what she in fact does.

One might worry that unlike Frankfurt-type cases, determinism has *actual* prior effects on the agent's capacities, abilities, character, and motives, whereas a merely counterfactual (but nonactual) intervener in Frankfurt-type cases does not have any actual effects on these things. So determinism, one might claim, does affect both one's capacities or abilities and one's opportunities.

In response, deep concerns still remain about how deterministic causal laws can undermine relevant abilities. Think of the matter in this way. When giving a positive account of free will, sophisticated indeterminists can adopt many of the pertinent views of compatibilists, including for example, views about the causal connections among one's values, best judgments, and intentions or decisions. Indeterminists of one brand (for example, Kane 1996a) typically postulate indeterminacy at some point or points in the pathway of intentional action. They theorize that some of the laws pertinent to the causal explanation of our choices or action will be nondeterministic or probabilistic ones. But surely nondeterministic causal laws do not detrimentally affect our having abilities, including unexercised ones, required for free action. If they do not, it is a puzzle why it should be thought that *deterministic* causal laws would detrimentally affect the appropriate abilities.

In any event, granting that determinism negatively affects both one's abilities and opportunities to do otherwise simply strengthens the case for the view that determinism expunges alternative possibilities.

One moral we can now draw is that if Jones's act of killing White is not wrong (or right, or obligatory) in a Frankfurt-type situation, and it is not wrong because he lacks the opportunity to do other than kill White, then Jones's act of killing White should also not be wrong (or right, or obligatory) in a deterministic world, as in such a world he would, again, lack the opportunity to refrain from killing White. Indeed, for any act performed (or intentionally not performed) by any agent in such a world, the agent would lack the opportunity to refrain from performing (or performing, in the case of an intentional omission) that action. So in such a world, no act could instantiate a primary deontic property.

Bok might object that one feature of Frankfurt-type examples that is absent from deterministic worlds and bears significantly on whether acts in such worlds can instantiate primary deontic properties: in Frankfurt-type examples, it is not the case that the agent like Jones would have done otherwise had he so chosen. But in a deterministic world this is not so; rather for example, Jones would have refrained from killing White had he so chosen. So the conditional notion of freedom, Bok might argue, yields this result: whereas in Frankfurt-type examples, Jones could not have refrained from killing White, Jones could have so refrained in a deterministic world. And, further, she might propose, merely the conditional notion of freedom to do otherwise is presupposed by deontic acts. Hence, she might rejoin, agents in deterministic worlds *can* perform acts that instantiate primary deontic properties.

But I believe that this objection is suspect. First, as we have seen, there are serious problems with the conditional analysis of *can*. (See, also, Berofsky's essay in this volume, ch. 8) More important, Bok's verdict that acts can be right or wrong or obligatory in deterministic worlds is predicated on her conditional notion of freedom. If this verdict is correct, then the view that an agent can perform an act only if she has the opportunity to perform it must be rejected by Bok, if *opportunity* is to be understood in the broad sense explained previously. We saw that in this broad sense of *opportunity*, an agent lacks the opportunity to perform an action if something prevents or would prevent a successful exercise of the relevant ability or abilities.

In a deterministic world, the natural laws and the past prevent or would prevent a successful exercise of each person's ability to do other than what he or she in fact does. An agent can lack the opportunity to do other than what he in fact does even if it is true that he would have done other than what he in fact did, had he chosen to do so. So, for instance, if S does A in situation U, S can lack the opportunity to do other than A in U even if it is true that S would have done other than A in U if S had chosen to.

Suppose Jones is in a deterministic world and he kills White. Then determinism ensures that he lacks the opportunity to refrain from killing White. But if he lacks this opportunity, he cannot, in his situation, refrain from killing White. As it must be true both that Jones can kill White and that he can refrain from killing White if his killing of White is to have a primary deontic property, his killing of White cannot have such a property if determinism is true. But if Bok believes otherwise, if she believes that Jones's killing White can have such a property in a deterministic world and she accepts WAP, then it seems that she must reject the view that one can perform an act only if one has the opportunity to do so. However, this view ought not to be rejected; it is not false. Hence, it follows that Bok's verdict is incorrect. Indeed, it follows that Bok's conditional concept of freedom is not the concept that is presupposed by deontic acts.

I believe that the discussion of Bok's conditional notion of freedom and deontic acts yet again casts doubt on her proposal that the practical and the theoretical standpoints can be isolated from one another when we think about freedom and normative appraisals.[18] As we have seen, Bok argues that when we engage in practical reasoning, we must use the conditional concept of freedom; and that when we act freely in this sense, we choose among genuine alternatives, and we should hold ourselves responsible for the acts we freely perform (Bok 1998: 205). As we can act freely in the conditional sense of *free* even if determinism is true, determinism, she believes, is no threat to responsibility. But this sort of "insulation argument" won't go through with deontic acts. Even granting that practical reasoning requires that we use the conditional notion of freedom, it seems that this notion of freedom is not presupposed by deontic acts as reflection on Frankfurt-type examples suggest. So even if we can act freely in the conditional sense of *free* in a deterministic world, acting freely in this sense will not sustain the conclusion that agents in such a world can perform acts that instantiate one or more of the primary deontic properties.

NOTES

Many thanks to Robert Kane for his comments and suggestions.

1. Arguments for the incompatibility of determinism and freedom to do otherwise have been advanced, for example, by Fischer (1983a, 1994), Ginet (1983, 1990), van Inwagen (1983, 1989), Warfield (1996), and Wiggins (1973). Critical discussion of these sorts of arguments can be found in Lewis (1981), Slote (1982), and Vihvelin (1990, 1991). See the

essays in this volume by van Inwagen (ch. 7) and Kapitan (ch. 6) for further discussion of these arguments.

2. Saul Smilansky (2000) defends the following interesting dualistic position in the free will debate. Smilansky claims that what he dubs the "Core Conception" captures the "basic intuition" (ibid.: 2) underlying the free will problem. This is the intuition that, with respect to things like moral responsibility, desert, justice, and punishment, the question of control or lack of it is morally crucial (ibid.: 2). This deep intuition, in turn, Smilansky proposes, has its roots in the obligation to respect persons (ibid.: 14–22). Smilansky argues that compatibilist forms of control are inadequate; if we have only such forms of control, "we are in serious difficulty in ethical and personal terms" (ibid.: 3). Similarly, he reasons that libertarian free will that demands "ultimate control" cannot be sustained. However, Smilansky's dualistic position, while not denying the hard determinist's lessons (the hard determinist rejects the possibility of responsibility in a determined world), especially the lesson that no one is "ultimately responsible" for one's choices and actions if determinism is true, also maintains that in order to be, for example, just, we have to be partial compatibilists. Compatibilism must be "taken into account" (ibid.: 92), he claims, "not only because of the pragmatic need for certain social arrangements [in which, for instance, considerations of desert are central], but also in a fundamental non-consequentialist moral sense, which stems from the Core Conception" (ibid.).

3. Paul Russell (1992) introduces the labels "rationalistic strategy" and "naturalistic strategy" to characterize Strawson's responses to the pessimist. Russell presents an insightful discussion of Strawson's views in Russell (1995: ch. 5).

4. Susan Wolf (1981) has also advanced this sort of Strawsonian thesis. Benson (1987) critically discusses both Wolf's and Bennett's development of this thesis.

5. Smilansky (2000: ch. 9) distinguishes two versions of Strawsonian (or "reactive") naturalism. Revisionist naturalism "seeks to change the perception that there is a theoretical need to justify common attitudes and practices, holding that there is no need for general grounding and that the reactions themselves provide all the (self-) grounding required" (ibid.: 222). Weaker nonrevisionist naturalism holds that "*in practice* common attitudes and behaviours remain constant, whatever the theoretical case may be" (ibid.: 224). On this view, our reactive attitudes, for example, cannot be threatened by the realization that (if Smilansky is right) there is no libertarian free will. Smilansky argues against both these versions of naturalism.

6. Watson (1987b: 259–60) usefully distinguishes between excusing and exempting conditions. Excusing conditions (like coercion or ignorance) inhibit responsibility locally; they don't imply that the agent is not a fit subject of responsibility. Exemptions (like insanity), in contrast, block responsibility globally; they do imply that the agent is not an appropriate candidate for responsibility ascriptions.

7. This sort of distinction between internalist and externalist theories is drawn by Fischer and Ravizza (1998: 252).

8. Relevant works include Frankfurt (1994a, 1993, 1992a, and b, 1988, and 1987).

9. Eleonore Stump attempts to meet this objection in Stump (1996b and 1993, 1990b). Critical discussion of Stump's views is to be found in Haji (1998).

David Zimmerman (2000) has recently developed a different sort of criticism of Frankfurt's hierarchical view. The criticism builds on the idea that a person who, for example, has fallen victim to manipulation at the hand of another party, can "take responsibility" for externally induced desires simply by bringing herself to identify with them wholeheartedly and decisively, despite their causal origins. Zimmerman argues that this view of taking responsibility commits Frankfurt to the morally repellent Stoic thought that "resignation to necessity is a path to liberation" (ibid.: 38). In addition to developing this objection, Zimmerman also proposes modifications to Frankfurt's hierarchical view that (Zimmerman believes) meet this objection.

10. Building on Frankfurt's 1987 essay, "Identification and Wholeheartedness," Michael Bratman (1996) provides, an account of identification that, among other things, tries to capture the sense in which one's motivations are fully one's own. Briefly, Bratman's approach develops Frankfurt's relatively early idea that the concept of decision is central to identification. The primary components of Bratman's suggestive account include the following. One treats one's desire as reason-giving when one treats it as setting an end that can, to some extent, justify performance of relevant means and/or relevant preliminary steps (ibid.: 9). For example, you treat your desire to pursue money as reason-giving if you treat that desire as setting, say, the end of amassing economic power, and this end justifies performance of relevant steps like careful investment. One is satisfied with a decision to treat some desire as reason-giving when that decision does not conflict with other standing decisions and policies about which desires to treat as reason-giving (ibid.: 11). An unwilling or grudging addict might treat her desire for the drug (to which she is addicted) as reason-giving, but this desire might conflict with a general policy of hers against treating her desire for the drug as reason-giving. In this case, the grudging addict is not satisfied with her decision to treat her desire for the drug as reason-giving. To identify with a desire, (1) one decides to treat that desire as reason-giving in some of one's practical reasoning and planning (ibid.: 8–9); (2) one is satisfied with that decision (ibid.: 10–11); and (3) one either treats that desire as reason-giving or is fully prepared to treat it as reason-giving were a relevant occasion to arise (ibid.: 11–2).

11. Watson could be interpreted as offering the following account of identification. Roughly, an agent, S, identifies with his desire to A, and so, if that desire moves S to A, with S's A-ing, if the desire to A is part of S's evaluational system and this desire causes S to A. But Watson renounces this view in "Free Action and Free Will" (1987a). He thinks that there can be cases in which one's act is fully one's own but the act is not caused by components of one's evaluational system. For example, it seems possible to identify with an action one does not think to be best or care most about. Watson says:

> I might fully "embrace" a course of action I do not judge best; it may not be
> thought best, but is fun, or thrilling; one loves doing it. . . . Call such cases, if
> you like, perverse cases. . . . There is no estrangement here. One's will is fully
> behind what one does. Of course, a person's evaluational system might be de-
> fined just in terms of what that person does, without regret, when it comes
> right down to it, but that would be to give up on the explanation of identifica-
> tion by evaluation. (1987c: 150)

12. The cases involving drug addiction and hypnosis are discussed by Wolf in Wolf 1980.

13. Philip Pettit and Michael Smith (1996) have advanced a different sort of mesh theory that, in some respects, resembles Wolf's theory. Having exposed certain assumptions that people make about each other and themselves when they engage in intellectual conversation, Pettit and Smith argue that authorizing a subject as a conversational inter-

locutor makes sense only if people treat themselves as having belief-forming and desire-forming capacities that satisfy three conditions: there are norms governing what they should believe and desire; they are capable of recognizing the demands of these norms; and by and large they have the capacity to respond appropriately to the demands they recognize (ibid.: 433–40). Pettit and Smith then propose that to regard an interlocutor as capable both of recognizing and of responding to these norms is to regard her as a subject who can be held responsible for what she believes and what she desires and does (ibid.: 441–44). They theorize, and here the salient resemblance to Wolf's view surfaces, that the sort of freedom required for believing freely and desiring freely is the ability of the agent, in the event of getting things (beliefs or desires) wrong, to get them right (ibid.: 444–47); that is, an agent's "beliefs and desires are free to the extent that they are the product of an ability, in the event of his being wrong, to get them right" (ibid.: 448n.21). On their view, the ability to believe or desire otherwise is "inherently attractive . . . only so far as it is the person's ability for anything that is not rightly believed or desired always to have believed or desired otherwise" (ibid.: 444). Responsibility in belief and desire, then, is a function of a suitable fit between an agent's beliefs and desires and certain yardsticks or demands (as dictated by the relevant norms) of right belief and right desire. Finally, Pettit and Smith propose that the natural position for them to take with respect to free choice is that "a subject's choices are free to the extent that they are the product—product, no doubt, 'in the right way'—of beliefs and desires that are themselves free" (ibid.: 448n.21). It would seem that this interesting approach regarding freedom in belief and desire (and choice) would succumb to one prominent sort of criticism that Fischer and Ravizza advance against Wolf's Reason View: Frankfurt-type examples, it appears, could be constructed in which though an agent "freely" believes or desires wrongly on his own, he could not have believed or desired otherwise because of the counterfactual intervener.

14. Some terminology will be helpful. Use the label "primary deontic properties" to refer to the moral properties of rightness, wrongness, and obligatoriness, and call any act that instantiates one or more of these properties a "deontic" act. The set of deontic acts comprises "deontic morality."

15. For further discussion of these problems, see the essay in this volume by Berofsky (ch. 8).

16. Briefly, the complication is this: one requires principles additional to OW and K to show that intentional omissions cannot be wrong when one lacks alternative possibilities. I discuss this issue in Haji (1999a).

17. If there is a requirement of alternative possibilities for deontic acts, then we have further reason to believe that Wolf is mistaken in claiming that right and wrong actions are asymmetric with respect to the requirement of alternative possibilities.

18. Kane (1999d: 30) also questions whether Bok can effectively shield the theoretical standpoint from practical questions about responsibility and guilt.

CHAPTER 10

PESSIMISTS, POLLYANNAS, AND THE NEW COMPATIBILISM

PAUL RUSSELL

> If a man is a pessimist, he is born a pessimist, and emotionally you cannot make him an optimist. And if he is an optimist, you can tell him nothing to make him a pessimist.
>
> Clarence Darrow

THE aim of this chapter is to examine recent contributions to compatibilist literature on freedom and responsibility that are not discussed in the prior chapters of part IV. Although the views of several authors will be considered, discussion will be organized primarily around Daniel Dennett's *Elbow Room*, an important work in the evolution of the "new compatibilism."

1. CHEERFUL COMPATIBILISM AND THE BOGEYMEN OF PESSIMISM

Dennett's discussion of the free will problem begins with the observation that this is a subject that people care about—it is not simply an intellectual puzzle looking for a solution. One group believes that if determinism is true, and "every deed and decision is the inexorable outcome . . . of the sum of physical forces acting at the moment," then the human condition would be a "terrible" and "frightening" existence (Dennett 1984: 1–5). Freedom would be an illusion, and we would be reduced to "awful" circumstances similar to those of individuals who find themselves imprisoned or paralyzed, or subject to (hidden) control and manipulation by others.

Incompatibilist views of this kind generate, and reflect, strong emotional responses that can be labeled as "pessimistic." Dennett's fundamental objective in *Elbow Room* is to discredit incompatibilist pessimism and to vindicate a more "optimistic" position (ibid.: 19, 169). According to Dennett, the thesis of determinism has none of these bleak implications for the human condition, and we do not require the metaphysical system building of libertarianism to "ward off non-existent evils" (ibid.: 4; and compare Strawson 1962).[1]

The opening chapter of *Elbow Room* provides a vivid and lively account of how incompatibilist pessimism acquires its psychological grip over us. Our worries and anxieties about determinism, says Dennett, are the product of "fearmongery" by philosophers. It is philosophers who have "conjured up a host of truly frightening bugbears and then subliminally suggested, quite illicitly, that the question of free will is whether any of these bugbears actually exist" (Dennett 1984: 4). The arguments of these pessimistic "gloomleaders," says Dennett, rely on thought experiments that serve as "intuition pumps" designed to produce the same relevant negative emotional response (ibid.: 12, 18). According to Dennett, however, these thought experiments do not so much illuminate the problem as artificially create it by means of misleading analogies and metaphors.

In Dennett's view, the analogies and metaphors concerned "do not in the slightest deserve the respect and influence they typically enjoy" (ibid.: 7). His method in *Elbow Room* is to examine carefully these incompatibilist intuition pumps and to show how they are systematically misleading. In this way, Dennett plays the part of a philosophical therapist, trying to release us from the set of worries and anxieties produced by these misleading analogies.[2] If the therapy succeeds, then the free will problem, as traditionally conceived, "dissolves".[3]

A particularly important subset of the bugbears that Dennett wants to discredit are various "bogeymen," viewed as agents who are really in control of us. The class of bogeymen can itself be subdivided into distinct groups. The first are those analogies that imply that our will somehow fails to govern our conduct, effectively disconnecting us from any (causal) influence on the world. These cases include, for example, imagining ourselves as living in a prison run by an invisible jailer, or being in the clutches of a puppeteer who controls our every movement no matter how we may struggle against him. These versions of the bogeymen control us not by controlling our will, but by moving our bodies directly and rendering our efforts and preferences inert.

Closely related to these bogeymen are more general worries about fate, the view that all our efforts and deliberations are futile. The concern here is that if determinism is true, and everything that we think and do is governed by causal laws, then we are subject to conditions of universal fate. This bugbear, says Dennett, "looms large" in the free will debate, and the intuition pumps described above do much to support and promote it.

Another subset of bogeymen operate on us in a different way. In these cases the worry is not that our wills fail to guide our conduct, but rather that the way we deliberate and will is controlled by another agent. In these cases, although actions are produced by our will, our will is not truly our own. Examples of this anxiety include cases of hypnosis, or manipulation by an evil neurosurgeon using electronic implants to control us. In such cases we may not even be aware that we are being controlled by another agent. We have the illusion of freedom.

A further worry—in some ways the opposite of the bogeymen anxieties—is that if determinism is true then there is no agent in control at all, since we are really nothing more than mere machines or automata responding in predictable ways to stimuli in our environment. On this view of things, human beings are not much different from simple insects, which can be easily manipulated by more sophisticated beings who control their environment. A wasp, for example, may look as if it makes choices and decisions, but it is really just biological machinery operating according to established causal laws—no real agent is at work. If determinism is true, says the incompatibilist pessimist, then human beings are not much better off than an insect operating in this fashion.

Dennett's objective is to show that all these intuition pumps are, in various ways, misleading. For the purpose of understanding his project, I will focus on his examples of bogeymen and the two different ways that they threaten human freedom. In order to distinguish among the various categories of pessimistic concern, I will introduce a spatial metaphor of distance. Close-range pessimism concerns those cases where the worry is that our will fails to guide our conduct. Middle-distance pessimism is the set of worries we have in circumstances where we believe that we are unable to properly regulate our own will, either because we cannot respond to available reasons or we are subject to manipulation of some kind. I also consider worries that our will is ultimately determined by causal antecedents that we cannot control. I refer to this concern as "pessimism at the horizon." (See the diagram at the end of this chapter)

2. CLASSICAL COMPATIBILISM AND CLOSE-RANGE PESSIMISM

A number of Dennett's basic arguments to discredit the bugbears of incompatibilism are taken straight from the shelf of classical compatibilism—as developed by empiricist thinkers from Hobbes and Hume to Schlick and Ayer. (Classical compatibilism still has distinguished defenders. See, for example, Davidson 1973.)[4] The classical arguments deal primarily with close-range pessimism. The position taken is that the traditional free will debate is a "pseudo-problem," the product of a series of conceptual or terminological confusions. The distinction that is fundamental to this position is that between caused and compelled action. According to this view, free actions are caused by our desires or willings. In contrast to this, unfree actions are brought about by "external" causes, independent of the agent's desires or will. Under these circumstances, the agent is forced or compelled and therefore not responsible for the action. In this way, the classical compatibilist position maintains that free action is to be distinguished from unfree action not by the absence of causes, but rather by the type of causes at work.

Another aspect of the classical position is a diagnosis of the source of incompatibilist confusion on this subject. The "metaphysical" interpretation of the causal relation is supposed to imply that a cause somehow forces or compels its effect to occur. Since freedom is, properly understood, opposed to compulsion, this would imply that an action that is caused must also be compelled, and so unfree. However, when the causal relation is properly understood in terms of a regular succession or constant conjunction of like objects, then all suggestion of causes forcing or compelling effects is removed. To say an action is caused by some antecedent willing by the agent is to say only that events of the first kind regularly follow events of the second kind—nothing more is involved.[5]

The classical compatibilist position also employs the distinctions introduced above to dismiss incompatibilist worries about fatalism. Incompatibilists argue that if determinism is true then all human beings are subject to fate, and any effort to alter or change the future is futile. According to classical compatibilism, this simply confuses two distinct issues.[6] Determinism is the thesis that everything that occurs, including our deliberations and decisions, are causally necessitated by antecedent conditions. Fatalism, by contrast, is the thesis that our deliberations and decisions are causally ineffective and make no difference to the course of events. Although there may be particular circumstances when we find that our efforts are futile ("local fatalism"), nothing about the thesis of determinism implies that this is the universal condition. On the contrary, as Dennett puts it, "deliberation is (in general) effective in a deterministic but nonfatalistic world" (Dennett 1984: 106).

Moral freedom, as the classical compatibilist understands it, involves being able to act according to the determination of our own will—that is, doing as we want to do or as we please (Hobbes 1962: 1, 66–8; Hume 1955: 95). On this account, therefore, freedom is a matter of freedom of action, the absence of any external impediments or obstacles. Accompanying this positive doctrine is the negative thesis that incompatibilist attempts to provide some account of free will, as distinct from free action, are radically mistaken and confused. More specifically, the notion of free will, it is claimed, is simply meaningless and absurd (Hobbes 1962: 1, 61–62). The only freedom that we need or want, according to this view, is to be able to guide our conduct by means of our own desires and willings. Any effort to go beyond this and explain moral freedom in terms of control over our own will inevitably leads to either metaphysical obscurity or the absurdity of an infinite regress.

3. REASON, SELF-CONTROL, AND MIDDLE-DISTANCE PESSIMISM

On the face of it, the classical compatibilist arguments deal effectively with close-range pessimist worries about being unable to regulate conduct through our own will. A determined world should not be assimilated to conditions of an invisible jail or being a puppet, since we can still distinguish circumstances where we act according to our will from those in which we do not.

These observations and reflections, however, fall far short of dealing with middle-distance pessimism. The most obvious difficulty facing any conception of moral freedom identified with the ability to act according to the determination of an agent's desires or willings is that such freedom is something that an animal, a child, or a mentally ill person might enjoy—all paradigmatic cases of individuals who lack moral freedom. Related to this point, some individuals, such as the kleptomaniac, appear to act according to compulsive desires. In cases of this kind, the agent's desires constitute *internal* obstacles to doing what the agent (reflectively) truly wants to do. Clearly, then, classical accounts of freedom understood simply as free action cannot draw the sorts of distinctions that we need to make in this sphere.[7]

These familiar incompatibilist objections to classical compatibilist accounts of freedom seem closely related to some of the worries raised by Dennett's "bogey-men." In the case of middle-distance pessimism, the concern is not that our will does not guide our behavior, but rather that we are unable to regulate our will according to reason or our own true values. Two of Dennett's examples speak directly to this problem—hypnotism and manipulation through neurological implants. The specific way that we interpret these cases, and the worries associated with them, will shape the way we judge the prospects of the "new compatibilism."

Dennett's interpretation of these cases, and the fears that they generate, center on two closely related issues. The first concerns the worry that we are not able to regulate our will in light of reasons that are available to us. The second is that our will is in some way being manipulated by another agent, and so our conduct is being indirectly controlled through control of our will. Under these circumstances our conduct reflects, not our own reasons and interests, but rather those of our manipulator. If Dennett can show that determinism has none of these unpleasant and disturbing implications then, he believes, he has discredited middle-distance pessimism.

The first step in his approach is to explain the nature of the relationship between our capacity for reason and the kind of freedom that is worth wanting. What we want, says Dennett, is to be the sort of creatures that are able to be "moved by reasons" (Dennett 1984: 25). Our reasons for acting are interpreted in terms of our fundamental interest in "self-preservation" and "self-replication." As finite beings, of course, our ability to represent all such reasons to ourselves is limited, but this does not mean that our sensitivity to relevant changes and variations in our environment is not significantly greater than that of other creatures. What is especially important to us, Dennett argues, is our ability to consider not only the direct objects of our desires, but also to reflect on our beliefs and desires themselves. This kind of reflective capacity enables us to question the evidential credentials of our beliefs, as well as the soundness and coherence of our desires. This constitutes, Dennett suggests, "a major advance in the cognitive arms race" (ibid.: 37). (This account of our reflective capacity is, of course, closely related to other "hierarchical" or "real self" theories of freedom, as advanced by, for instance, Frankfurt 1971 and Watson 1975.)

According to Dennett, the particular importance of this "power of reflexive monitoring" is that it helps us to deal with worries about manipulation by others. An agent who is able to examine and monitor his own beliefs and desires will detect "abnormalities" in their causation (ibid.: 1984: 30). With this ability, an agent can unmask "sneaky manipulators" or "evil tricksters"—which makes it difficult to trap him in disturbing situations of the kind suggested by middle-distance bogeymen. These abilities to self-monitor and escape the clutches of (evil) manipulators evolve and develop naturally and gradually—both in the individual and in the species. Nothing about the thesis of determinism suggests that we do not possess and exercise such abilities. What is crucial, however, is that we do not allow ourselves to be deceived by "intuition pumps" that conceal the complexity of our rational and reflexive powers. For the purposes of understanding human freedom, Dennett argues, *complexity matters* (ibid.: 12, 34, 37–38).

Central to clarifying the nature of freedom—and escaping our worries about bugbears—is recognizing that what we want or value is control. "We want to be *in control*," says Dennett, "and to control both ourselves and our destinies" (ibid.: 51, Dennett's emphasis). Any individual who is a "controller" must have states that include desires about the states of the "controllee," which must in turn have a variety of states that it can be in (ibid.: 52). Dennett uses the example of controlling an airplane to illustrate this point. By means of anticipating or predicting future states of the airplane, we can keep control of it. There are limits to the range of things that we can do with the plane (that is, degrees of freedom with respect to it). Nevertheless, if we judge things correctly, we can retain control over it. When it comes to self-control, this is what distinguishes us from "mere puppets." We are not helpless in using our foreknowledge and powers of deliberation to "take steps to prevent, avoid, preempt, avert, harness or exploit" wanted or unwanted circumstances. This power of control and self-control is what we want and value. Like the pilot of a airplane, we want to leave ourselves a "margin for error"—lots of "elbow room"—so we can keep control of the situation and do the things that we want to do (ibid.: 62–63).[8] Self-knowledge is essential to maintain and expand this freedom. While not "absolute" or unconditional, human beings enjoy a considerable amount of this kind of control. One implication of this understanding of control is that there are "degrees of freedom" (ibid.: 53; and compare Bernard Williams 1986: 5).

This account of freedom, as explained by Dennett, clearly goes well beyond the simple definitions suggested by classical compatibilism. On this account, it is not meaningless or absurd to say how free agents are able to control and regulate their own desires and wills. Our powers of reflection enable us to monitor our beliefs and desires, and, when necessary, to detect and "disconnect" unwelcome manipulators. Accompanying this positive doctrine, there are important negative theses about the nature of human freedom. First, a freedom that implies an ability to make arbitrary or causeless decisions or choices is not worth wanting, and not what we actually care about (Dennett 1984: 2). Second, and relatedly, the kind of freedom that Dennett has described does not presuppose that agents "could have done otherwise." This claim is particularly controversial, although it is consistent with Harry Frankfurt's well-known critique of the doctrine of "alternative possibilities" (Frankfurt 1969).

Dennett endorses Frankfurt's strategy but also argues that it is "insufficiently ambitious" (Dennett 1984: 132). In the first place, Dennett argues, a person may truly state that he could not do otherwise, but not in order to disown responsibility (ibid.: 133–35). Beyond this, if such a condition had to be satisfied to establish responsibility—that is, the agent could have done otherwise under the exact same circumstances—we could never know whether the agent was really responsible, given the epistemological difficulties involved. Finally, not only is the "traditional metaphysical question unanswerable"; even if we knew the answer, it would be useless. We want to know whether the agent is likely to repeat similar kinds of (undesirable) conduct again—and to know this we do not need to know if she actually had "alternative possibilities" available to her under the specific circumstances of her action. The question that matters to us is whether or not a flawed character trait needs to be corrected (ibid.: 137–38).

There is, according to Dennett, another insidious (middle-distance) bugbear that needs to be exorcised from the overactive incompatibilist imagination—one with, he believes, an especially powerful hold over us: the worry that if determinism is true then we are (somehow) "controlled by nature" or "controlled by the past" (ibid.: 50, 61, 72). This way of presenting the pessimist's anxieties does not rely on any fictional or hypothetical case of (evil) hypnotists or neurosurgeons at work. On the contrary, the source of the anxiety seems much closer to traditional theological worries about God's omnipotence and omniscience undermining the possibility of human freedom. Clearly God is not conceived of as evil, but vis-à-vis our aspiration to be true self-controllers, God may be viewed as a kind of cosmic bogeyman. In the secularized/naturalized version, however, the role of God is played by "Nature" or the "Past," but the same general worry persists: while we appear to be self-controllers, control nevertheless slips away through the causal chains to an external and alien source. Self-control, therefore, is really an illusion.

Dennett's reply is that such worries rest on simple confusion about the nature of control. To be a *controller*, as we have noted, involves being an agent with desires that can drive the controllee into some preferred state or another. The controller must also receive "feedback signals" from the object if it is effectively to control it (ibid.: 72). All talk of being controlled by Nature or by the Past plainly involves *personification* (ibid.: 57, 72). Without this, these bugbears disappear—neither Nature nor the Past can properly be said to be "controllers" of any kind, whether determinism is true or not. On Dennett's account this (basic) confusion about the nature of control motivates much of the incompatibilist's pessimism and accompanying resistance to the thesis of determinism.[9]

This analysis of incompatibilist worries covers three issues that we should carefully separate: (1) Do human purposes and choices have determining causes that ultimately originate externally (2) Is the ultimate source of our purposes and choices another intentional agent, who is in control of us? and (3) If there is such an agent in control of us, is the quality of its moral character good or evil? Pessimist anxieties, according to Dennett, depend largely on the last two issues. It is especially horrible to imagine ourselves under the control of another demonic or evil agent (for example, "hideous hypnotist" and the like). Nevertheless, even a benevolent controller, looking out for our interests, leaves us with a sense of chill, since there remains the fear that some other agent is "really in control of us."[10] When we consider the first issue by itself, Dennett maintains, we have no reasonable basis for being troubled or disturbed by the thought that the ultimate origins of our deliberations and choices lie outside of us.

Dennett associates worries about the ultimate origin of our deliberations and choices with the aspiration to "absolute agenthood"—to be a perfect, Godlike self-creator (ibid.: 83–85). It is his position that this aspiration is both impossible and unnecessary, since it is not needed for the kind of freedom that we care about (that is, "self-control" as he interprets it). The incompatibilist view is that, contrary to Dennett, worries about ultimacy or "absolutism" are essential to our conception of ourselves as true self-controllers, and libertarians maintain that this kind of freedom (which rules out determinism) is something that human beings are actually capable of. The distinct set of worries associated with ultimacy are the basis of "pessimism at the horizon." The critical question that faces us is whether Dennett is justified in dismissing these concerns at the horizon as both incoherent and unnecessary.

4. MIDDLE-DISTANCE REFINEMENTS AND DIFFICULTIES

It is clear that Dennett's version of the new compatibilism involves a number of controversial claims. At this stage, however, I want to consider some interesting amendments and modifications that have been suggested in two essays by Paul Benson. In "Freedom and Value" Benson argues that free agency requires another "equally significant ability" apart from control, the ability "to appreciate values." More specifically, to attribute free agency correctly in a given context depends, according to Benson, "partly on the content of the agent's normative understanding, not just on the agent's having some valuational point of view or other" (Benson 1987: 472). Benson maintains "that obstacles to competent appreciation of the norms that apply to our actions are as much impediments to full freedom as are certain obstacles to the expression of our evaluative judgments in our will or certain obstacles to the realization of our will in our conduct" (ibid.).

Benson points out that the omission that he is concerned with in compatibilist accounts of moral capacity (that is, normative competence) is addressed in Susan Wolf's essay "Asymmetrical Freedom" (Wolf 1980; and see also idem 1990), but he argues that what is missing from her account "is any discussion of why specifically *freedom* involves the competent appreciation of value" (Benson 1987: 474). To answer this question, we need to reflect on why the power of control is so important to us. We care about control, Benson suggests, because we care about the values by which our actions are assessed. This, in turn, reflects our "deep-seated desire to be able to justify our conduct" (Benson 1987: 475; and compare

Scanlon 1988: 170–72). Since the norms governing our actions are important to us, so too must be the ability to regulate our conduct by means of our evaluative judgments. Benson continues:

> [I]f we care deeply about the value of our actions, then we want more than the power to translate our own value judgments into effectual willing. We also want to be able to appreciate the relevant values and arrive at competent appraisals of the alternative courses of action we face. Our concern for those values would be practically impotent if we could not bring them competently to bear in our deliberations about what to do. (Benson 1987: 475)

Benson uses these observations about the importance of normative competence to shed light on another feature of fully free action that is intimately connected with it: the "enduring belief that a completely free act is fully our own" (ibid.).

Free acts are fully our own, Benson argues, "only insofar as they potentially afford appropriate bases for normative assessments of us in face of which we have no excuse" (ibid.: 482). When we lack any control over what we do (for example, cases of compulsion), the action provides no basis for "moral disclosure" and thus cannot be fully our own. Similarly, when agents lack normative competence, Benson argues, their conduct cannot reveal their moral values and so cannot disclose what they are like as persons in the relevant respect. The incapacity involved may be severe enough to render the individual wholly ignorant of normative standards and when and how they apply (as in the case of infants or severe mental illness). In other cases, the agent may adequately *appreciate* the pertinent values but cannot use their normative insights to *regulate* or guide their conduct (for example, older children, the severely deprived, and so on). (For a different compatibilist perspective on the issue of deprivation and blameworthiness, see Klein 1990: esp. ch.4, sec. 3. For another view closer to Benson's, see Wallace 1994: 231–35.) The general point, in all such cases, is that actions coming from agents who lack normative competence cannot reveal their moral values and, as such, cannot be said to be "fully their own."[11]

In a more recent essay, "Free Agency and Self-Worth," Benson modifies his position. He argues, in this context, that the "normative-competence condition" is too strong, insofar as it is "content specific." That is, Benson now accepts the view that "any desires, plans, values, beliefs, etc., can be involved in the motivation of free action"—free agents must be able to "commit themselves to whatever motives they please" (Benson 1994: 653, 663). On the new account, Benson refuses "to restrict substantively persons' desires, values, life plans or normative capacities in the name of freedom" (ibid.: 665; compare Christman 1991b: 356–59).[12] However, this more "permissive" position is not wholly "neutral" about content. The weaker condition that Benson now advances is a "self-worth condition." Free agents must "have a certain sense of their worthiness to act, or of their status as [competent] agents, which is not guaranteed by their abilities to act freely" (Benson 1994: 650).

The condition of self-worth, Benson argues, helps us to understand a variety of cases where agents do not face any of the "standard impediments" to free agency but are nevertheless not fully free. Among the cases that he cites are the effects of severe shaming and slavery, conditions that undermine a person's confidence in their own competence as an agent and, as such, constitute an assault on their sense of "moral dignity as persons." One particularly important aspect of this condition is that it draws our attention to the "social dimension of free agency" (ibid.: 661). Related to this point, this condition of free agency also clarifies that the value of free agency lies in part with "our sense of being in a position to answer for [our] conduct," which is itself "partly constitutive of [our] sociality" (ibid.: 668). "A blow to our freedom," Benson argues, "can obstruct our ability to express through our conduct who we are, but it can also be a blow to our sense of who we are as social creatures" (ibid.: 668).[13]

Another important set of issues that arise from Dennett's discussion concern the question of how freedom relates, in more precise terms, to our capacity to be guided by reason. Recent work by John M. Fischer and Mark Ravizza (1998) provides an influential and illuminating discussion of this problem. Fischer and Ravizza make clear that the relationship between "reason-responsiveness," on one side, and freedom and responsibility on the other, is open to very different interpretations. On the account that they provide, our capacity to respond to reasons depends on our (natural) "human deliberative mechanisms" (ibid.: esp. 34–41). A free agent, on a "strong" interpretation, operates with a mechanism that is *always* receptive and responsive to available reasons. Under these circumstances, the agent's reasons, choices, and actions reliably "track value" or "the reasons there are" in every case (Fischer and Ravizza 1998: 42; compare Nozick 1981: 317–62). Clearly, however, this condition is too demanding, since we would then be unable to hold an agent responsible when "tracking" reason *fails*. So what is required is a weaker theory that can accommodate cases where the (actual) mechanism fails, as well as cases where it succeeds.

Fischer and Ravizza employ considerable ingenuity trying to develop a "weaker" or "moderate" account that can deal with worries of this kind. A plausible account, which can serve the purposes of compatibilism, must describe "mechanisms" that can fail under some conditions, without being *systematically* unreliable (that is, too "weak"). We need, therefore, some principled way of distinguishing and identifying mechanisms that are sufficiently reliable in responding appropriately to reasons. When it comes to recognizing what reasons there are (that is, receptivity), there must be, Fischer and Ravizza argue, some appropriate *pattern* of reason-receptivity. That is to say, "the actual mechanism that issues in [the agent's] action must be at least 'regularly' receptive to reasons" (Fischer and Ravizza 1998: 70–1). This avoids the worry that the mechanism in question could be reason-receptive in an isolated case but otherwise fails systematically. When it comes to choosing in accordance with the available reasons (that is, reactivity), however, Fischer and Ravizza argue that the (stronger) demand for regular-reactivity or a pattern is not required. All that needs to be satisfied, they maintain, is the weak condition that in a given case the mechanism has been shown to be reactive to available reasons (Fischer and Ravizza 1998: 73–76).[14]

This account of "moderate reason-responsiveness" introduces an "asymmetry" between the receptivity and reactivity requirements. Fischer and Ravizza describe this as follows:

> In the case of receptivity to reasons, the agent . . . must exhibit an understandable pattern of reasons-recognition, in order to render it plausible that his mechanism has the "cognitive power" to recognize the actual incentive to do otherwise. In the case of reactivity to reasons, the agent . . . must simply display *some* reactivity, in order to render it plausible that his mechanism has the "executive power" to react to the actual incentive to do otherwise. In both cases the pertinent power is a general capacity of the agent's mechanism, rather than a particular ability of the agent (i.e., the agent's possession of alternative possibilities—the freedom to choose and do otherwise). (Fischer and Ravizza 1998: 75, emphasis in original)

Two (related) difficulties arise from these claims. The first problem is that it is unclear what justifies the "asymmetry." If a "pattern" or "regularity" is needed for receptivity, why is this not the case with reactivity? Clearly, Fischer and Ravizza hold that strengthening the reactivity requirement, in line with the receptivity requirement, would be too demanding, since we do not want to excuse agents whose mechanism is regularly receptive and has shown that it can react to reason. The controversial assumption that this position rests upon is that "reactivity is all of a piece in the sense that the mechanism can react to all incentives, if it can react to one" (Fischer and Ravizza 1998: 73–74). It may be argued, however, that this same reasoning can be applied to the receptivity requirement, which would result in a return to a "weak reason-responsive" view. On the face of it, therefore, the asymmetry that Fischer and Ravizza introduce, in order to arrive at a "moderate" position, seems to depend on ad hoc adjustments rather than principle-driven considerations.

There is, I believe, an even more fundamental difficulty for a reason-responsive view of the kind that Fischer and Ravizza seek to defend. The objection may be raised that it is unclear how the mere possession of such reason-responsive mechanisms or capacities can render agents sufficiently in control, unless they also have control over how the capacity is actually *exercised* within the particular conditions of action. On this view of things, the responsible agent needs more than simply the general capacity for reason-responsiveness (under some interpretation). What is also needed is a capacity of *exercise control*, which means that the agent is able to direct the specific way that her capacity for rational self-control moves her.

Any attempt to satisfy this demand is, of course, liable to lead us back into the conundrums associated with "ultimacy" and "absolute agency" (as discussed later in this chapter). While it may well be that exercise control is a demand that can never be satisfied, it will not suffice for the compatibilist to argue this point—since the "moral skeptic" or "hard determinist" may agree about this. The point that the compatibilist needs to establish is that exercise control is *unnecessary* for responsibility, and that the mere possession of powers of rational self-control will suffice. (For an interesting, although I think unsuccessful, attempt to make this case, see Wallace 1994: 180–93; and 161–62, 201–14.)

The difficulties that we have been considering relate primarily to the possibility that reason-responsive mechanisms may sometimes fail to respond appropriately to available reasons, without excusing the agent. There are, nevertheless, also difficulties associated with "strong" mechanisms that cannot fail (that is, always "track value"). In cases of this kind, since the agent is guided flawlessly by reason and enjoys perfect practical reason, she may be viewed as perfectly free. This view, however, does not entirely square with all our intuitions on this subject. More specifically, it may be argued that an agent who is *naturally* governed by (moral) reason, and so does what is required of her *effortlessly*, does not *deserve* moral praise. Moral praise should be reserved for those who must "struggle" to be good and do the right thing. Certainly, this claim captures the spirit of important strands of neo-Kantian incompatibilism (Campbell 1951: 130–33). However, some compatibilists, such as Martha Klein, embrace this view and have made it an essential element of a compatibilist approach to moral responsibility (Klein 1990: 167–71; compare Wolf 1990: 138–42).[15]

The general point that these observations bring to light is that reflection on both the success and failure of reason-responsive mechanisms present compatibilism with difficulties, and the relationship between rationality and freedom is by no means straightforward. Dennett's tendency to present incompatibilist concerns as based on confusion and exaggerated worries of various kinds leads him to underestimate the (genuine) difficulties and obscurities involved in articulating a plausible compatibilism as it relates to middle-distance issues.[16]

Nevertheless, while significant "gaps" in Dennett's compatibilist position are apparent, it is evident that he succeeds in outlining how compatibilists can deal with middle-distance worries about self-control, as they relate to questions of rationality and manipulation. Moreover, as Dennett's analysis of the "problem cases" suggests, these two categories are intimately connected, since cases of manipulation can be understood as "problematic" precisely because they involve a break-down in the agent's sensitivity to reasons. (See also Wallace 1994: 175–77, for a related account of how such "problem cases" can be interpreted in terms of a breakdown of rational self-control.) Dennett's strategy is to argue that our (natural) *complexity*, not indeterminism, provides us with the ability to be sensitive to available reasons and to guide our conduct on this basis. The same general ability gives us powers of "self-monitoring" that enable us to detect and escape from (threatening) manipulators. These incompatibilist bogeymen, therefore, need not frighten us anymore.

5. Ultimacy and Pessimism at the Horizon

Middle-distance pessimism, as we have seen, is generated by worries associated with intuition pumps and bogeymen that imply that we are somehow unable to regulate our will according to reason and what we reflectively care about. This is why we find (hypothetical) cases of manipulation disturbing: we want our will to respond to reason and we do not want another agent to control our will (in service of alien interests or reasons). Dennett maintains that in order to avoid these worries we do not need to be "absolute agents" capable of self-creation ex nihilo. More specifically, it is a false dilemma to suggest that either we are "a completely self-made self, one hundred per cent responsible for its own character" or we are "mere dominoes" in the causal chain (Dennett 1984: 100, 156–57). All that we want, says Dennett, is "to be as immune as possible from manipulation and dirty tricks and as sensitive as possible to harbingers of future vicissitudes that might cause us to alter course in the right ways—so that we can face the world with as much elbow room (as large a margin for error and as little relevant uncertainty) as we can get" (ibid.: 72–73).

Dennett refers to a number of philosophers who have presented objections that are supposed to show that our worries about determinism extend to issues on the horizon (ibid.: 33, 75, 83–84). He cites, for example, A. J. Ayer's description of "implanted" desires and beliefs (Ayer 1954: 9); Paul Edwards's observation that if determinism is true then even our efforts at self-creation must be "the result of factors that are not of [our] making" (Edwards 1961: 121); and Thomas Nagel's worries about "luck" as it concerns even "the stripped-down acts of the will itself" (Nagel 1979: 183). Each of these critics raises variations on the problem of ultimacy. For the purpose of this essay, however, I turn to Martha Klein's particular account of this problem.

Although Klein defends a ("partial") compatibilist position, she maintains, nevertheless, that our ordinary moral intuitions support certain incompatibilist claims (Klein 1990: 3 and ch. 4).[17] More specifically, according to Klein we generally accept "that one of the things which disqualifies an agent from blameworthiness is his not having been responsible for the causes of his decisions or choices" (ibid.: 51). This conviction commits us, she says, to a "U-condition" for agent accountability: the condition that "agents should be ultimately responsible for their morally relevant decisions or choices—'ultimately' in the sense that nothing for which they are not responsible should be the source of their decisions or choices" (ibid.: 51).[18] Klein's interpretation of the basic rationale behind the U-condition is that if agents acts are caused by factors for which they are not responsible, it is not obvious how they can be responsible for acting as a result of those factors (ibid.: 50). (This way of interpreting the U-condition and its significance is open to revision. See, in particular, Kane 1996a: esp. chs. 3 and 5; and also the essays by Kane and Galen Strawson in this volume, chs. 18 and 19.)

In support of the U-condition, Klein cites a number of "problem cases" that closely resemble Dennett's "bogeymen" examples (Klein 1990: 70–75, 89–90). These include victims of brain tumors, implantations, brainwashing, and hypnosis. The feature these cases share, Klein maintains, is that in each the agent's decisions can be traced to causes for which he is not responsible, and so he ought not to be blamed (ibid.:70). The example of the brain tumor is especially important to Klein's case for the U-condition, because it highlights the point that the real source of concern is not the "implantation" of desires and beliefs by others, but rather that the agent is not the true source or origin of his own motivations, since "he did not choose (to have) these states of mind" (ibid.: 73).[19]

Klein extends this reasoning and applies it "to the relatively pedestrian and non-threatening-sounding causes of genetic endowment and environment." The U-condition theorist reasons, says Klein, that since the agent "is no more responsible for his genetic endowment and upbringing than he is for the designs of a malevolent demon or brainwasher," it follows that he "is no more responsible for a personality which (perhaps) depends on his brain in a normal state, than he is for the personality change attributable to the brain tumour" (ibid.: 75). From the perspective of the U-condition advocate, unless this condition is met, it will simply be a "matter of luck" whether or not an agent's will is governed by "good" or "bad" desires (ibid.: 165–66). Under these circumstances it would be *unfair* to impose unpleasant treatment such as blame and punishment on an agent who is the (undeserving) "victim" of bad desires.

Dennett's initial line of reply to these worries is that his observations on middle-distance pessimism, and the bogeymen that it conjures up, discredit Klein's concerns about "ultimacy" or "absolute agency." Take, for example, worries that we may have about "implantation" of desires and beliefs. According to Dennett, so long as the agent possesses the relevant degree of "complexity" to be capable of self-monitoring, then she will be able (eventually) to unmask "the process of conditioning" (Dennett 1984: 33–34). Of course, if this capacity is destroyed or damaged by the conditioning process, then the agent is not a self-controller in the full sense of the term—but determinism itself does not imply this. What is worrying about brain tumors is not fears of manipulation by others, nor that our thoughts and actions are caused, but rather that we may become insensitive to reasons and consequently act in irrational and unpredictable ways (compare ibid.: 64–65). While *this* is frightening, there is no basis for supposing that determinism implies it. In sum, we do not need "absolute agency," says Dennett, to avoid the sorts of worries that Klein's "problem cases" present to us.

According to the U-condition theorist, this general line of reply entirely misses the point. It is not denied that agents may possess some relevant capacity to be "reason-responsive" and to revise and alter their character on the basis of re-flection. We might well be able to distinguish agents of this kind from individuals who lack these capacities (as new compatibilism suggests). Nevertheless, all this only postpones the fundamental difficulty. While our beliefs and desires may be subject to self-monitoring activities of various kinds, it remains true that these activities are themselves conditioned by factors that are not of the agent's own making.[20] Reflection on this process, therefore, strips away our confidence that we are truly "self-creators" *even in the normal case*. For this belief to be sustained, we must presuppose some power to undertake "self-forming actions" that enable us to be the (ultimate) origin of our character and conduct.[21] The sorts of capacities that Dennett and other new compatibilists in his mould describe fall short of this, and so their strategy fails to relieve pessimistic worries at the horizon.

Other lines of reply, however, are still available to Dennett. The first is to argue that many of these worries are motivated by confusion about "luck." It is simply a mistake, he claims, to suggest that individuals who are self-controllers of the kind that he has described are subject to "luck" because they fail the test of "absolute agenthood." These individuals are not "just lucky," he argues; they are "skilled" and "gifted" members of "the community of reason-givers and considerers" (ibid.: 92–100). When we identify individuals with these abilities we do not—and should not—treat them as simply "lucky" or "unlucky." On the contrary, we provide them with reasons and treat them accordingly.

This response, I believe, fails to confront the real worries that the U-condition presents. Without ultimacy, two crucial modes of control are absent: (1) The actual "reason-responsive mechanisms" that we possess are *acquired* in ways over which we have no final control (in both the normal and abnormal case). The character of these mechanisms, however, plainly determines the kind of choices and decisions that we will actually make.[22] (2) Apart from worries about how we acquire our (given) reason-responsive capacities, we may also worry about our ability to control the way that these capacities are *exercised* in specific circumstances (as discussed earlier). If determinism prevails, then the way capacities for self-creation and self-monitoring are exercised in a given situation will ultimately be determined by factors the agent cannot control.[23] Dennett is clearly right to assert that this does not reduce us to the condition of a "domino" or "zombie" and so on, but it is still true that without ultimate or absolute agency of some kind we lack these vital modes of (self-) control. It may be argued, therefore, that Dennett is too complacent in face of these problems, and consequently his "considerable optimism" (ibid.: 48) has the same pollyannish appearance that plagues classical compatibilism.

Dennett has, nevertheless, more cards to play. Up to this point his methodology has been faithful to the aims of "descriptive metaphysics."[24] That is to say, his position has been that our everyday attitudes and practices associated with moral freedom and responsibility are not threatened by any (confused) pessimist worries at the horizon. This is consistent with Dennett's "ordinary language" effort to expose the "bugbears" and "bogeymen" for what they really are—artificial creations of professional philosophers in the Western tradition. However, when it comes to dealing directly with worries at the horizon as they relate to issues of responsibility, Dennett takes a sharp turn in the direction of "revisionary metaphysics".[25] The argument here is that worries about ultimacy may be motivated by a conception of *responsibility* that, although deeply rooted in the Western philosophical and theological tradition, is nevertheless hopelessly incoherent and implausible—and so ought to be jettisoned. What really sustains "absolutism," on this view, is an understanding of responsibility that is committed to a conception of "total, before-the-eyes-of-God Guilt" (ibid.: 165–66; on related themes see also Bernard Williams 1986). An absolutist conception of *desert* of this kind takes issues of responsibility out of the relevant (human) practical contexts that should concern us and tries to place them on metaphysical foundations that are disconnected with these legitimate and intelligible concerns.

In opposition to the absolutist view, Dennett prefers a conception of responsibility that is thoroughly utilitarian and forward-looking, and he leans heavily on "engineering" metaphors when describing how this system operates (Dennett 1984: chs. 6, 7). Responsibility, he argues, should be understood in terms of "the rationale of punishment," and its rationale is to support the criminal laws of society. That is to say, we punish individuals when we think they are "mentally competent" enough to be deterred or reformed by the threat or imposition of sanctions. All this is not only a highly "revisionary" approach; it also takes a (large) step back in the direction of classical compatibilism.

Although the utilitarian features of Dennett's position are very familiar, a more unusual and interesting aspect of his discussion draws attention to the question of how responsibility and character are related—a subject that is generally treated lightly in free will literature. The view that Dennett defends is that in the realm of responsibility, what really interests us is what an action reveals about the character of the agent. More specifically, what we want to know is what we can *expect* from the agent in the *future* (ibid.: 137–38; compare Smart 1961: 300–305).

Isolated actions may be "regrettable," but they are only of moral interest to us insofar as they suggest ways that we can "redesign" agents so they will avoid future "errors" (Dennett 1984: 139–44). The importance of action, on this view, is that it allows us to identify character flaws that can be corrected by means of some relevant sanctions. Actions that do not serve this purpose can be dismissed as "don't cares"—that is, as cases that it is "rational to ignore" (ibid.: 141).

This view is plainly at odds with our ordinary moral assumption that agents are no less responsible for out-of-character action than for action that is in character. This certainly suggests that Dennett's "revisionism" is more radical than he acknowledges. Beyond this, the critic may also argue that, given that out-of-character action is still produced by the agent's own will, it is entirely reasonable to attribute such conduct to this agent, even if he is unlikely to repeat it in the future (compare Foot 1957: 105–6). Action that is produced through the agent's own will should not be treated the same way as action produced by another agent, or no (moral) agent at all.

The compatibilist can, of course, agree with Dennett that we ought to take the issue of responsibility for character more seriously, without endorsing his forward-looking, utilitarian perspective. Robert Audi has argued, for example, that agents can be held responsible for their character traits, but that this depends on the fact that their character is in some way generated or retained by more basic acts. According to Audi, "all (normative) responsibility traces to acts and ultimately to basic acts," (Audi 1991b: 307) because a person cannot be responsible "for something over which one has no control" (ibid.: 312). We can be responsible for our traits of character, therefore, only because we have control over our actions, which in turn affects our acquisition or retention of traits (ibid.: 312–3). A view of this kind, Audi maintains, can account for responsibility for character, consistent with compatibilist commitments, but without utilitarian commitments of the kind that Dennett embraces (ibid.: 319).[26]

Although Dennett gives considerable attention to the question of control and "self-creation," he is not committed to Audi's view, that responsibility for character requires the agent to have control (either generative or retentive) over it. On the contrary, an agent's character could be "implanted" or "conditioned" in ways she could not control, and yet it may still be true that sanctions or moral engineering will be effective in altering or changing her future conduct in desirable ways. Clearly, then, Dennett's pragmatic, utilitarian approach severs any (assumed) link between control and responsibility for character.[27]

My analysis reveals a deep tension in Dennett's entire project in *Elbow Room*. On his account, the relevant authorities or powers in society can (and should) use the conditioning influence of rewards and sanctions to control the character of others. In this way, even though the individuals concerned may possess rational and reflective capacities, in a (deeper) sense they may be truly described as "selves-made-by-others." The irony in all this is that Dennett's pragmatic, engineering approach to responsibility allows real worries about manipulation and "conditioning" to resurface. (There is, indeed, something of the spirit of B. F. Skinner's *Walden Two* to be found in his views on this subject.) To this extent, the first part of Dennett's project, which aims to relieve us of pessimistic anxieties about manipulative "bogeymen," is undermined by the second, which defends a conception of responsibility that places heavy emphasis on the benefits of "social engineering." (A good discussion of why we should be troubled by circumstances of this kind is presented in Kane 1996a: 65–70, 201–4).

In a review of *Elbow Room*, Gary Watson suggests that Dennett's "treatment of responsibility is the least instructive part of the book," and that the weaknesses of his general position are well illustrated by P. F. Strawson in his important essay "Freedom and Resentment" (Watson 1986: 522; and compare Dworkin 1986: 424). A central theme of Strawson's essay is that compatibilists or "optimists" who emphasize only forward-looking, utilitarian considerations in their account of moral responsibility leave an important "gap" in their position. More specifically, according to Strawson, conditions of responsibility must be understood in terms of our natural disposition toward "reactive attitudes and feelings" or "moral sentiments." Such responses to the good or ill will that we detect in the conduct of our fellow human beings are an "essential part of moral life as we know it" (P. F. Strawson 1962: 23). To a limited extent, we can suppress these reactions in particular cases or circumstances: there is no possibility however, that we can *systematically* abandon or suspend our commitment to the whole "complicated web of attitudes and feelings."

These observations, Strawson argues, are highly significant for the free will debate because they reveal what is wrong with both (classical) compatibilist optimism, as well as incompatibilist pessimism. Pessimists are right in saying that a purely utilitarian approach to responsibility leaves out "something vital in our conception of these practices" (ibid. 23). It is a mistake, however, to conclude on this basis that what is required to fill this "lacuna" in the optimist account is some form of libertarian metaphysics that involves denying determinism (ibid.: 23–25). Contrary to the pessimist, Strawson argues, no theoretical belief in the truth of determinism could lead us to abandon our commitment to the moral sentiments (ibid. 18: compare 10, 12). To suppose otherwise is "to over-intellectualize the facts" (ibid.: 23). When the role of moral sentiment is allowed its proper place in moral life, we can avoid both a crude utilitarian account of responsibility that is divorced from psychological reality, while at the same time avoiding the "panicky metaphysics" of libertarianism. Our sense of *desert* is founded, not on (incoherent) beliefs about undetermined conduct, but rather on the natural, emotional responses that are essential to human life as we know it.

A number of Strawson's followers have picked up on his "naturalistic" arguments and developed his twofold critique of utilitarian optimism, on one side, and of pessimistic worries at the horizon on the other side. (See Ishtiyaque Haji's essay, ch. 9 of this volume, for further discussion of Strawsonian strategies.) Among these contributions to Strawsonian themes is the work of Kevin Magill, who advances arguments that are relevant to Dennett's "revisionary" views about responsibility. Magill maintains, in line with Strawson, that we must resist the temptation to provide a general "justification for punishment, desert and moral responsibility." The "impulse" to do this, he claims, is based on the (misguided) assumption that a utilitarian principle can be applied to a sphere where a distinct and independent retributive principle operates (that is, that the guilty should suffer). According to Magill, both the utilitarian and retributive principles are "foundational to our moral thought and practices," and so any attempt to justify one in terms of the other involves us in "a kind of category mistake" (Magill 2000: 193–94; compare item 1997: ch. 2 and Mackie 1985).[28]

Dennett, as we have already noted, dismisses worries about ultimacy on the ground that they depend on a traditional absolutist conception of responsibility (that is, "guilty-before-the-eyes-of-God") that is simply unintelligible and should be (moderately?) "revised" in favor of a pragmatic conception based on "moral engineering" by means of sanctions. Against this, Strawson and his followers (for instance, Magill) argue that if compatibilists paid more attention to the role of moral sentiments in this sphere they could provide a richer, nonutilitarian understanding of responsibility. To the extent that this approach remains closer to the original spirit of Dennett's descriptive project, it is more satisfying than the revisionary, pragmatic account of responsibility that Dennett defends. What is not so evident, however, is that the Strawsonian view succeeds in providing us with a sure and easy way of setting aside pessimist worries at the horizon.[29]

It may be argued by the incompatibilist, for example, that our moral sentiments must be targeted only on individuals who possess some relevant set of moral capacities, and that this includes a capacity for ultimate control. Agents who have no control over the specific reason-responsive mechanisms that they have acquired, nor over how these mechanisms are actually exercised in particular circumstances, lack the kind of (ultimate) self-control that is required to sustain and support our moral sentiments. Human beings may possess reason-responsive mechanisms, and be (complex) self-controllers of the kind that Dennett and others have described, and yet still exercise these capacities in ways that stem ultimately from factors that they cannot control. In some sense, therefore, they have no final say about the moral quality of their own character and conduct.[30] It is not obvious, says the pessimist, that moral sentiments can be sustained when such considerations are pressed upon us.[31]

6. Pessimism and the Unbearable Limits of Finitude

In my view, the important and significant issues facing the new compatibilism of the kind advanced by Dennett lie primarily with problems of ultimacy at the horizon. The spatial metaphor of distance is helpful in this connection because it indicates that these horizon problems do not immediately present themselves to us in everyday moral life. Close-range and middle-distance issues differ in this respect. In our everyday moral dealings, we ask ourselves whether the conduct we are presented with is a product of the agent's own will, and if so, if the agent is a rationally competent (normal) adult, free from manipulation or coercive pressure. Concerns of this kind are part and parcel of ordinary moral life. Nothing about them is "artificial" or a peculiar product of the Western philosophical tradition.

The situation is not so straightforward at the horizon. Regarding worries about ultimacy, Dennett's general diagnosis of the free will problem seems more plausible. When action is produced by the agent's will, and the agent is clearly capable of rational self-control (that is, reason-responsive), further worries about the ultimate origin or source of the agent's will—in the absence of any worries about manipulation—seem remote from our usual concerns and interests. Worries of this kind seem likely to leave a typical moral audience unmoved. One reason why horizon concerns about ultimacy appear disconnected from ordinary moral life is that, unlike close and middle-distance issues, there is no obvious or decisive way to settle them. That is to say, when we raise questions about *ultimacy*, as distinct from issues of rationality and manipulation, there seems no way to *prove* that an agent was their ultimate source. The skeptic can always challenge such claims by arguing that any appearance of ultimate agency simply reflects our ignorance of the relevant causes at work. We become trapped, consequently, in issues and claims that can never be resolved. Beyond this, the skeptic is also likely to argue that it is not even clear what ultimacy *demands*—so how can we ever *verify* that it is satisfied in a given case? Clearly, general considerations of this kind lend credence to Dennett's claim that horizon problems are the artificial product of (overintellectualized) Western philosophy and theology.

There are, nevertheless, a number of reasons for rejecting this complacent attitude to horizon problems. First, worries of this kind—reaching beyond middle-distance problems of rationality and manipulation—emerge in legal contexts, where the problems are by no means the product of artificial philosophical reflection. On the contrary, lawyers and judges are plainly interested in evidence showing that a person accused of a crime had no control over factors that led to it.[32] Second, and relatedly, our understanding of the influence of genetic endow-

ment and the environment on human conduct and character is constantly advancing, and this presses horizon issues on us with increasing force—to refuse to
consider them seems mere evasion (compare. Klein 1990: 75 and Greenspan 1993).
Most important, it will not do to argue, as Dennett and others have done, that
because we are unable to provide a coherent account of how ultimate agency is
possible, that we can therefore dismiss worries that agents have no *final* control
over their character and conduct. On the contrary, it should be obvious that a
convinced skeptic on the subject of "libertarian metaphysics" may draw thoroughly pessimistic conclusions from this (as in the views of the "moral skeptic"
or the "hard determinist"). Arguing from the impossibility of ultimate agency to
the conclusion that there is no basis for pessimism in the realms of freedom and
responsibility is an egregious example of Pollyannaism.

There are interesting structural similarities between pessimism as it relates to
the free will problem and the question of human mortality. Consider, for example,
Pascal's profoundly pessimistic description of the human condition in the following passage:

> Imagine a number of men in chains, all under sentence of death, some of
> whom are each day butchered in the sight of the others; those remaining see
> their own condition in that of their fellows, and looking at each other with
> grief and despair await their turn. This is the image of the human condition.
> (Pascal 1966: 165/#434)

The conclusion that Pascal draws from this analogy is that "the only good thing
in this life is the hope of another life" (ibid: 157/#427). For our purposes, the
interesting thing about this passage is that Pascal uses an "intuition pump" to
justify *extreme* pessimism about the human condition. If there is no immortal
soul and future state, he suggests, then human life is nothing better than a painful
period during which we wait to be executed, along with everyone else.

The obvious reply to all this is that it grossly exaggerates and distorts the
limits and miseries of human life. Pascal is guilty of the same sort of abuse of intuition pumps that Dennett objects to in the free will problem. However, while
we may grant that Pascal's pessimism is *exaggerated*, it does not follow that all
worries about human morality and finitude are without foundation. We may, for
example, discredit Pascal's pessimism by pointing out (close and middle-distance)
pleasures and sources of happiness that can be found within the span of human
life. These show that, typically, our experience of human life does not resemble
being chained up and waiting to be executed. At some point, however, those of
us who are skeptical about the possibility of immortality must confront the reality of the limits of human existence—the duration of a human life is finite. Such
reflections do not impose themselves on us in our everyday concerns, so we are
not usually depressed or troubled by them. Nevertheless, to the extent that we

have the occasion, opportunity, and temperament to think about such matters, most people will find them sobering or rather melancholy to contemplate.[33] The important point is that we may not share Pascal's extreme pessimism on this subject and yet still appreciate why these reflections on human mortality occasion pessimism of some kind. The reasonable position on this subject, therefore, seems to lie somewhere between Pascalian pessimism and Pollyannaish optimism.

These observations on Pascal's pessimism shed light on both what is right and wrong in Dennett's attempt to discredit incompatibilist pessimism. The incompatibilist pessimism that Dennett has challenged is essentially Pascalian. It involves analogies and metaphors that are more misleading than illuminating. However, it does not follow from this that reflection on the limits of human agency is not disconcerting or unsettling. On the contrary, when we look beyond the close and middle-distance issues that are the focus of Dennett's attention, we must still confront horizon worries about ultimacy. Even if the worries here are not Pascalian, they provide no basis for Pollyannaish optimism.[34]

What these observations show is that, regarding the free will problem, we must carefully identify the source and quality of our pessimism and note the way they are related. More specifically, it is obvious that the *quality* of our pessimism will vary with the (perceived) *source* of worry. For example, Dennett is surely right to say that if close-range worries were justified (for example, we are in chains), then this would be a "terrible" condition. Much the same is true of middle-distance worries, which would also be "awful." It is not evident, however, that worries at the horizon have this quality or license an extreme negative emotional response. In the first place, concerns of this kind will vary depending on how lucky/unlucky individuals are with respect to their character and conduct.[35] A person of admirable character may occasion no feeling that her condition is "terrible" or "frightening"—unless, of course, we confuse horizon issues with close and middle-distance pessimism. Even a person whose character and conduct is deplorable cannot be assimilated to the condition of a person who is manipulated or incapable of rational self-control. The sort of pessimism occasioned by a lack of ultimacy must be qualitatively different (that is, reflecting a difference in the source of our concern). An awareness of finitude and contingency, as it relates to the (assumed) impossibility of ultimate agency, licenses a more modest sense of being *disconcerted*, rather than any form of Pascalian despair.[36] In general, it is a mistake to assume that incompatibilist pessimism must take the form of an all-or-nothing, homogeneous, and extreme sense of despair at the thought of the implications of determinism. The alternatives available to both the pessimist and the optimist are surely more subtle and nuanced than this.[37]

Free will and pessimism by degrees

Range	*	Scope of Concern
Close	3	*Freedom of Action*
	3	
	3	Is the agent's conduct regulated by his will?
	3	Are the agent's deliberations and choices futile?
	3	
	3	
Middle	3	*Rational Self-Control*
	3	
	3	Is the agent's will responsive to the available reasons and his true values?
	3	
	3	Is the agent subject to control or manipulation by others?
	3	
	3	

[**** The unstable boundary of ordinary moral life . . . *****]

	3	
Horizon	3	*Ultimate Agency*
	3	
	3	Is the agent's character and will ultimately determined by factors that he
	3	does not control?
	3	
	3	Does the agent have a final say about the nature of his character and
	3	conduct?
	3	
	3	
Cosmic	3	*Self-Creation*
	3	
	3	Is the agent an absolute, unconditioned (Godlike) self-creator?
	3	

NOTES

I am grateful to Robert Bunn, Ish Haji, Saul Smilansky, and Robert Kane for their helpful comments and suggestions.

1. Dennett's way of associating incompatibilism with "pessimism" is also a prominent feature of Strawson's influential essay "Freedom and Resentment" (Strawson 1962). Although this perspective on the free will debate reflects dominant tendencies in incompatibilist literature, there are some important complications to be noted. For example, the incompatibilist pessimist may well be an "optimist" about the existence of (libertarian) free will. Moreover, some incompatibilists would argue that our everyday beliefs and attitudes concerning freedom and responsibility are not *worth* salvaging, and so they find nothing "frightening" or "awful" about doing without them. As we will see, at times this attitude surfaces in Dennett. For the purposes of this chapter, however, I will work within the pessimist/optimist framework that Dennett (and Strawson) have constructed.

2. Dennett's methodology is self-consciously modeled after the ordinary language techniques of predecessors such as Ryle and Wittgenstein (Dennett 1984: 6, 18). (*Elbow Room* is dedicated to the memory of Ryle.)

3. Dennett argues that worries about free will are "an almost exclusively Western preoccupation" and that for most people "metaphysical freedom has just not been worth worrying about" (Dennett 1984: 4). Clearly, then, Dennett sees his audience as composed primarily of philosophers, who are victims of their own "induced illusions."

4. "Hobbes, Locke, Hume, Moore, Schlick, Ayer, Stevenson, and a host of others have done what can be done, or ought ever to have been needed, to remove the confusions that can make determinism seem to frustrate freedom" (Davidson 1972).

5. There are, in my view, significant problems with the efforts of (empiricist) compatibilists to defend their position on the foundations of a regularity theory of causation. For more on this, see Russell (1988).

6. "Fatalism says that my morrow is determined no matter how I struggle. This is of course a superstition. Determinism says that my morrow is determined through my struggle . . ." (Hobart 1934: 82). For criticism of this doctrine, see Russell (2000).

7. The usual point of criticism of classical compatibilism is that freedom of action does not imply freedom of will. Rogers Albritton, drawing on the same distinction, argues that an agent who is unable to *act* according to his own will (that is, faces "obstacles" of some kind) may nevertheless enjoy "perfect and unconditional" freedom of *will* (Albritton 1985). Indeed, Albritton is skeptical about the very possibility of *un*free will. Even the addict or compulsive, he claims, lacks only strength of will, which is a different matter. However, Albritton does not discuss "bogeymen" cases of the kind that Dennett describes, and these, in my view, show that his unqualified skepticism concerning the possibility of unfree will is misplaced.

8. According to Dennett, our deliberations about our "options" requires only "epistemic openness" (Dennett 1984: 122–23).

9. Kane comments on this aspect of Dennett's strategy as follows: "[Dennett] plays the old compatibilist tune in a new key. Just as classical compatibilists distinguish *constraint* from *mere causation*, he says we must distinguish *control* from *mere determination*" (Kane 1996a: 70).

10. Kane points out, for example, that children, as they reach maturity, "want an autonomy and dignity that they associate with the power to run their own lives," even though they "know that their parents are well-intentioned toward them" (Kane 1996a: 69).

11. It may be objected that no action that we condemn can be judged as fully the agent's own—since it manifests a failure of normative competence. Benson denies this implication on the ground that "we can sometimes freely do what we believe we should not" (Benson 1987: 480).

12. Christman argues that to hold "that freedom is a value only in relation to correct moral norms is to ignore the obvious noninstrumental value of self-mastery itself" (Christman 1991: 358).

13. Benson's interesting observations on the social dimension of responsibility, and how it relates to issues of normative competence, lead to further questions about the relevance of *emotional* competence to moral agency. I discuss these matters in more detail in Russell n.d.

14. There are, as Fischer and Ravizza point out, difficulties associated with "judgments about mechanism individuation" (Fischer and Ravizza 1998: 40n, 51–2n, 113, 216n; 251n). They offer, however, no "general way of specifying when two kinds of mechanism are the same" and rely, instead, on our "intuitive judgments" about such matters.

15. It may be argued that our interest in "moral effort" is closely connected with the question of how an agent actually exercises her rational capacities (that is, how she uses "exercise control"). The exact nature of this relationship is, however, open to a number of different interpretations.

16. Dennett claims that in the process of moral development "everyone comes out more or less in the same league"—unless they are "singled out as defective" (Dennett 1984: 96). According to this view, normal adults are all "gifted with powers of deliberation" and "self-control" and at this threshold can be treated as (fully) free and responsible agents (ibid.: 98). However, as indicated, this view leaves large problems unaddressed.

17. See esp. Klein (1990: ch.7), for the details of her effort to (partially) reconcile compatibilist and incompatibilist principles.

18. One of Klein's particular concerns is to argue that the U-condition is distinct from incompatibilist worries about "could have done otherwise" (Klein 1990: ch. 2). I will not discuss this aspect of her position.

19. Classical compatibilists, of course, insist that worries about the *source* of our moral qualities are misplaced, as this does not change the *value* of the qualities themselves. See, for example, Hobart (1934: 84): "It is the stuff certain people are made of that commands our admiration and affection. Where it came from is another question . . . Its origin cannot take away its value, and it is its value we are recognizing when we praise."

20. This is, of course, a familiar objection to "hierarchical" models of free will, such as Frankfurt (1971). For further discussion of this and related points, see Fischer and Ravizza (1993: 25–33).

21. The terminology of "self-forming actions" is from Kane (1996a: esp. ch. 6). Klein is a skeptic about the (empirical) possibility of ultimate agency. Kane (1996a) is a sustained and sophisticated attempt to work out the details of a libertarian metaphysics of this kind.

22. For an interesting and important effort to deal with this general problem, see Fischer and Ravizza (1998: 230–36).

23. It is arguable that our basic concerns about the way we acquire our reason-responsive mechanisms can be reduced to worries about whether we control the actual exercise of these capacities in particular circumstances. Note, for example, that if we had (ultimate) control over how our reason-responsive mechanism is actually exercised in the context of specific conditions, there seems to be no reason to worry about how the general capacity was acquired (for example, even if it was implanted in some deviant manner).

24. The distinction between "descriptive" and "revisionary" metaphysics is introduced and explained in Strawson (1959).

25. "My conclusions are neither revolutionary nor pessimistic. They are only moderately revisionary: the common wisdom about our place in the universe is roughly right" (Dennett 1984: 19).

26. It is evident that worries about ultimacy return on the account of responsibility for character suggested by Audi. Given that we must be able to "trace" character traits to actions that the agent could *control*, it may be argued that these ("self-forming") actions must satisfy the U-condition. For a libertarian argument along these lines, see Kane (1996a: 38–40).

27. Dennett's views on this subject may be compared and contrasted with Hume's. Hume also holds that a person may be (morally) evaluated for character traits over which he has little or no control. Indeed, he takes the more radical view that this includes "natural abilities" (intelligence, imagination, and so on), understood as pleasurable or painful qualities of mind. For a discussion of Hume's views, see Russell (1995: ch. 9).

28. Magill does not claim, on this basis, that "there are no grounds for being troubled by the suffering caused by punishment and blame" (Magill 1997: 47). On the contrary, his point is that the "true problem" that we face is "a practical one about opposing strains within our moral framework and conflicting (nonmetaphysical) moral sentiments within ourselves" (ibid.: 49). Regarding this problem, he claims, "there can be no general resolution of the tension between the principle of well-being and the principle of desert" (ibid.: 52). Nevertheless, "if we keep in mind that it is what we care about, informed by our personal, moral and political feelings and sentiments, that generally informs whether we take the objective or the reactive attitudes, we will not be faced with a helpless dilemma every time we confront decisions about whether to blame or to understand" (ibid.: 52). On the subject of moral sentiment and retributivism see also Russell (1995: ch. 10).

29. For the details of this, see Russell (1992).

30. There are a number of important complexities here that I cannot pursue. Suffice to note in passing, however, that this way of interpreting what is needed to satisfy ultimacy (that is, the forms of control missing from new compatibilist accounts) may set a standard that some suggested libertarian accounts of ultimacy still fail to meet.

31. An illuminating discussion of this problem is presented in Watson (1987b); but compare McKenna (1998b).

32. See, for example, Clarence Darrow's classic "hard determinist" defence of Leopold and Loeb (Darrow 1924). It is significant that Darrow did not argue that his clients did not understand what they were doing or lacked general powers of rational self-

control. On the contrary, his defense is based largely on the (assumed) existence of causes of their character and conduct that were ultimately beyond their control. It is also significant, however, that he refers to several different "bogeymen," which tends to obscure the exact nature of his case.

33. "Neither the sun nor death can be looked at steadily" (LaRochfoucauld 1678: #26). Although we generally assume that people have some shared *sensibility* about such matters, variations of response can always be found. This need not imply, however, any kind of intellectual confusion about the relevant considerations or issues involved.

34. It may be argued, of course, that the only way to escape from pessimistic worries of this kind, is to embrace libertarian metaphysics, much as some maintain that the only way to escape pessimism about the finitude of human life is to embrace the doctrine of the immortality of the soul.

35. Compare, for example, our sense of luck regarding the distribution of other qualities such as beauty or intelligence. It is not obvious that the beautiful or intelligent person will feel any sense of "despair" or "fear" when she contemplates her situation—although the (unfortunate) ugly or stupid person may view things differently.

36. Although I believe that reflection on horizon issues of ultimacy generate a sense of disconcertment, my reason is not that it threatens, systematically, to discredit our moral sentiments. On the contrary, when we reflect on considerations about the finitude of human agency, the thought that presses upon us is that who we are, and what we are responsible for to other human beings, depends ultimately on factors that we cannot control. This sobering thought makes us aware of the (uncomfortable) gap between our aspiration to be self-made selves and the evidence that this is an illusion. Such problems concern the relationship between fate (understood in terms of the issue of origination) and responsibility. A plausible compatibilism, I maintain, must acknowledge the legitimacy of concerns about origination and accommodate them by allowing for the possibility that agents who are subject to fate may nevertheless be justifiably held responsible. On this see Russell (2000).

37. There is, of course, a considerable amount of room to be found between Pascalian pessimism and Pollyannaish optimism in respect of the issues of determinism and origination. Other (divergent) positions of this general kind in the contemporary literature can be found in, for example Honderich (1993), Pereboom (1995), and Smilansky (2000), as well as Russell (2000). Smilansky's position, which involves the claim that illusion about libertarian free will is desirable and "morally necessary," is described in his essay in this volume (ch. 22).

....

CHAPTER 11

WHO'S AFRAID OF DETERMINISM? RETHINKING CAUSES AND POSSIBILITIES

....

CHRISTOPHER TAYLOR

DANIEL DENNETT

INCOMPATIBILISM, the view that free will and determinism are incompatible, subsists on two widely accepted but deeply confused theses concerning possibility and causation: (1) In a deterministic universe, one can never truthfully utter the sentence "I could have done otherwise," and (2) In such universes, one can never really take credit for having caused an event, since in fact all events have been predetermined by conditions during the universe's birth. Throughout the free will literature, one finds variations on these two themes, often intermixed in various ways. When Robert Nozick[1] describes our longing for "originative value," he apparently has thesis (2) in mind, and thesis (1) may underlie his assertion that "we want it to be true that in that very same situation we could have done (significantly) otherwise." John Austin, in a famous footnote, flirts with thesis (1):

> Consider the case where I miss a very short putt and kick myself because I could have holed it. It is not that I should have holed it if I had tried: I did try, and missed. It is not that I should have holed it if conditions had been different: that might of course be so, but I am talking about conditions as they

> precisely were, and asserting that I could have holed it. There is the rub. Nor
> does "I can hole it this time" mean that I shall hole it this time if I try or if
> anything else; for I may try and miss, and yet not be convinced that I could
> not have done it; indeed, further experiments may confirm my belief that I
> could have done it that time, although I did not.[2]

(In later sections we discuss at length the ways in which this particular quote can lead readers astray.) Meanwhile, Robert Kane, in *The Significance of Free Will*, eloquently proclaims the importance of our presumed ability truly to cause events, the ability that thesis (2) addresses:

> Why do we want free will? We want it because we want ultimate responsibility.
> And why do we want that? For the reason that children and adults take delight
> in their accomplishment from the earliest moments of their awakening as per-
> sons, whether these accomplishments are making a fist or walking upright or
> composing a symphony.[3]

Elsewhere in the free will debate, one often finds authors advancing definitions that confirm the relevance of possibilities and causes. Kane describes free will itself, for instance, as "the power of agents to be the ultimate creators ... and sustainers of their own ends and purposes."[4] The key words here are *power* and *creator*. Intuition suggests that the term *power* is intertwined with *possibility* roughly as follows: agent A has the power to do X if and only if it is possible that A does (will do) X. And certainly, to be a *creator*, one has to be the *cause* of changes in the world; one has to "make a difference" in how the world runs. Kane provides some other significant concepts:

> Alternative Possibilities (AP): The agent has *alternative possibilities* ... with re-
> spect to A at t [iff] at t the agent can (has the *power* or *ability* to) do A and
> can do otherwise.[5]

> Ultimate Responsibility (UR): An agent is *ultimately responsible* for some (event
> or state) E's occurring only if (R) ... something the agent voluntarily ... did or
> omitted and for which the agent could have voluntarily done otherwise ...
> causally contributed to E ..., and (U) for every X and Y ... [I]f the agent is
> personally responsible for X, and if Y is an *arche* (or sufficient ground or cause
> or explanation) for X, then the agent must also be personally responsible for
> Y.[6]

Carl Ginet in a similar vein proposes:

> Two or more alternatives are *open to me* at a given moment if which of them I
> do next is entirely up to my choice at that moment: Nothing that exists up to
> that moment stands in the way of my doing next any one of the alternatives.[7]

Whether or not these definitions are entirely dependable, they are emblematic of the central role of the concepts of causation and possibility in our understanding of free will.

In short, the acceptance of theses (1) and (2) lies at the heart of incompatibilism. Incompatibilists dread determinism because they suspect that a deterministic universe would lack the sorts of open possibilities that we cherish and deprive us of the ability to cause changes to the world in a meaningful way. Accordingly, they find heartening the discovery of indeterminacy in modern quantum mechanics, and they hope to discover indeterministic quantum events at the root of each free agent's decision-making ability. Kane ingeniously attempts a naturalistic, scientifically respectable account of indeterministic free will, and yet the arcane processes he describes are strangely dissatisfying as a new foundation for human freedom and dignity. Not only do they seem oddly "outside of our control," but they are so subtle that, very likely, scientists will be unable to confirm their relevance to our mental life for the foreseeable future.

To avoid the sort of impasse that Kane and other incompatibilists have apparently reached, we propose to reexamine the foundations of possibilities and causes, to understand why theses (1) and (2) look so compelling. We will discover that the desires incompatibilists describe, to have powers and to effect changes, can be satisfied without any recondite appeals to quantum indeterminacy. The suspicions to the contrary lose their force once we begin to untangle, with the aid of a little formalism, the complexities of the underlying concepts.

1. POSSIBLE WORLDS

While a complete account of possible worlds would require many extra pages, the following paragraphs outline an approach, compatible with modern scientific methods, that avoids various modal pitfalls identified by Quine (such as talk of *propositions, analyticity, essences,* and so forth).[8] Ideally, science strives for a description of the universe that is as thorough and comprehensive as possible, composed in an orderly mathematical idiom. A simple example of such ideal state-descriptions are the "Democritean" universes introduced by Quine.[9] A Democritean universe is completely specified using a function f that assigns to each quadruple (x,y,z,t) a value of either 0 or 1. If $f(x,y,z,t) = 1$, then at time t matter occupies location (x,y,z); otherwise point (x,y,z) is devoid of matter at t. Needless to say, modern physics has long since supplanted the tidy Democritean conception of reality, but even today the basic project of describing the world with (monstrously complex) functions remains intact. So despite its scientific shortcomings, the following definition provides a useful starting point as we struggle to discipline unruly pretheoretical intuitions:

A *possible world* is simply any function of the form described above (in mathematical notation, any function of the form $f: \mathbb{R}^4 \to \{0,1\}$).[10]

The set of all possible worlds we will denote by Ω a particularly noteworthy subset of Ω is Φ, which contains just the *physically* or *nomologically possible* worlds, in which no physical laws are violated.[11]

Given a possible world f, we of course have many ways to describe and make assertions about it. Often it will be natural to postulate *entities* within f: connected hypersolids in $\mathbb{R}^4$ that yield coherent life-histories for objects like stars, planets, living creatures, and everyday paraphernalia. One will also want to set up a system of *informal predicates* that apply to these entities, such as "has a length of 1 meter," "is red," "is human."[12] We may then form sentences like

$\exists x \; (x \text{ is human})$

and determine whether they apply in various different possible worlds (while recognizing that often enough one will encounter borderline worlds where incontestible verdicts prove elusive).

Worthy of special note are *identification predicates* of the form "is Socrates." "Is Socrates," we shall suppose, applies to any entity in any possible world that shares so many features with the well-known denizen of the actual world that we are willing to consider it "the same person." In the actual world, of course, "is Socrates" applies to exactly one entity; in others, there may reside no such being, or one, or conceivably several to whom the predicate applies equally well. Like other informal predicates, identification predicates suffer from vagueness and subjectivity, but they do not cause unusual problems.

With this machinery in place we can now explicate such sentences as:

Necessarily, Socrates is mortal.   (1)

We would propose the translation:

In every (physically?) possible world f, the sentence "$\forall x \; (x \text{ is Socrates} \Rightarrow x$ is mortal)" obtains.   (2)

Here "is Socrates" and "is mortal" are informal predicates of the sort just introduced. Paraphrase (2) strikes us as both plausible and free of the logical confusions Quine decries. Of course, deciding whether (2) is true does present considerable challenges, stemming largely from the unavoidable blurriness of the predicates. Moreover, we are not specifying the set of possible worlds over which one should allow f to range; perhaps some readers will advocate set Ω (all worlds), others Φ (the physically possible worlds), and yet others a still more restricted set X. Logic alone cannot resolve this issue, but logical language does help us to pinpoint such questions and recognize the sorts of vagueness we face. However we choose, we can employ the notation

$$\Box_x \phi$$

to indicate that sentence φ obtains for every world in set X.

As the dual of necessity, possibility yields to a similar analysis. Hence

Possibly, Socrates might have had red hair. (3)

means

There exists (within some set X) a possible world f in which the sentence "$\exists x$ (x is Socrates $\wedge$ x has red hair)" obtains. (4)

Analogous to the notation "$\Box_x \varphi$" we introduce

$$\Diamond_x \varphi,$$

meaning that φ holds for some world within X. The familiar sentence:

Austin could have holed the putt (5)

now becomes

$$\Diamond_x \exists x \ (x \text{ is Austin} \wedge x \text{ holes the putt}). \tag{6}$$

Notice that in this case we need to restrict X to a narrow range of worlds, all quite similar to actuality, if we are to do justice to Austin's meaning. For suppose that Austin is an utterly incompetent golfer, and that impartial observers are inclined to deny (5). If we let X range too widely, we may include worlds in which Austin, thanks to years of expensive lessons, winds up a championship player who holes the putt easily, thus validating (6) but distorting the presumed sense of (5). At the same time, as we shall see, there is no good reason to make X so small that only worlds *identical* to reality in the moments before the putt are included.

2. COUNTERFACTUALS

Using possible worlds, one can also profitably interpret sentences of the form

If you had tripped Arthur, he would have fallen,   (7)

as David Lewis has shown.[13] Roughly, (7) obtains if and only if in every world approximately similar to our own where the antecedent holds, so does the consequent. In other words,

$$\Box_x\ \varphi \Rightarrow \psi, \tag{8}$$

where φ stands for "you tripped Arthur," ψ stands for "Arthur fell," and X is a set of worlds similar to our own. As an alternative notation, let us also write,

$$\varphi \ \Box\!\!\rightarrow_x \psi. \tag{9}$$

Choosing an optimal value for X in (8) and (9) is not always easy, but we suggest the following loose guidelines:

In sentences like (8) and (9), X ought to

- contain worlds in which φ holds, $\sim\varphi$ holds, ψ holds, and $\sim\psi$ holds
- contain worlds otherwise very similar to the actual world (insofar as the preceding clause permits). (G)

So when analyzing (7), choose X to contain worlds in which you trip Arthur, worlds where you refrain from tripping him, worlds where he falls, and worlds where he remains upright. In the case of (10):

If the sun hadn't risen this morning, I would have overslept,   (10)

X will look quite different, since it includes strange worlds in which the sun fails to rise.

In *Counterfactuals*, Lewis cleverly devises a single connective $\Box\!\!\rightarrow$ appropriate for all φ and ψ, but in this chapter we settle for a family of connectives of type $\Box\!\!\rightarrow_x$. Doing so, we believe, forestalls various technical complications and accords equally well with intuition. Notice that for Lewis transitivity fails and, worse, so does the equivalence

$$\varphi \ \Box\!\!\rightarrow \psi \equiv \sim\psi \ \Box\!\!\rightarrow \sim\varphi.$$

With each operator $\Box\!\!\!\rightarrow_X$, on the other hand, transitivity and contraposition succeed, provided we hold X fixed. Of course, X can vary, as observed in the previous paragraph, so that the two sentences:

| If Bill had tripped him, he would have fallen | (11) |
| If he had fallen, he would have broken his glasses | (12) |

need not imply

| If Bill had tripped him, he would have broken his glasses. | (13) |

However, we can confidently assume that

| If Bill had tripped him, he would have fallen | (14) |

implies

| If he had not fallen, Bill would not have tripped him, | (15) |

since guidelines (G) yield the same set in each case.

3. CAUSATION

Fundamental as it appears, the language of causation has stirred up interminable debate and has (perhaps for that reason) been avoided by scientists. Many philosophers apparently hope some day to unearth the one "true" account of causation, but given the informal, vague, often self-contradictory nature of the term, we think a more realistic goal is simply to develop a formal analogue (or analogues) that helps us think more clearly about the world. Our preexisting hunches about causation will provide some guidance, but we should mistrust any informal arguments that masquerade as "proofs" validating or debunking particular causal doctrines.[14]

When we make an assertion like

| Bill's tripping Arthur caused him to fall, | (16) |

a number of factors appear to be supporting the claim. In an approximate order of importance, we list the following:

- Causal necessity. At least since Hume, philosophers have suspected that counterfactuals play some role in our causal thinking, and this factor and the next fall within the same tradition. Our assent to sentence (16) depends on our conviction that in any world roughly similar to our own in which Arthur falls, Bill must have tripped him up. Using the notation of the previous section, we have $\psi \; \Box\!\!\rightarrow_x \varphi$, where φ stands for "Bill tripped Arthur," ψ represents "Arthur fell," and X is the set of worlds similar to our own in which (1) Bill trips Arthur, (2) Bill doesn't trip him, (3) Arthur falls, or (4) he doesn't fall. As observed above, the sentence $\sim\!\varphi \; \Box\!\!\rightarrow_x \sim\!\psi$ has the same logical force; in other words, had Bill not tripped Arthur, he would not have fallen.

- Causal sufficiency. It may well be that whenever we affirm (16), we do so partly because we believe that (using the same notation as before) $\varphi \; \Box\!\!\rightarrow_x \psi$. In other words, we believe that Arthur's fall was an *inevitable outcome* of Bill's tripping: in any world where Bill places the obstruction in his path, Arthur goes toppling. (Or equivalently, if Arthur had *not* fallen, then Bill must in that case have refrained.) This second condition is logically entirely distinct from the first, and yet the two seem to get badly muddled in everyday thinking. Indeed, as we shall see, incompatibilist confusion often originates precisely here. Below we will discuss at greater length the relations between these two conditions.

- Truth of φ and ψ in the actual world. Although a relatively trivial requirement, it should be mentioned if only for completeness.

- Independence. We expect the two sentences φ and ψ to be logically independent: there must exist worlds, however remote from reality, in which φ obtains but not ψ, and vice versa. Hence "Mary's singing and dancing caused her to dance and sing" has a decidedly odd ring. This condition also helps rule out "1 + 1 = 2 causes 2 + 2 = 4."

- Temporal priority. A reliable way to distinguish causes from effects is to note that causes occur earlier.[15]

- Miscellaneous further criteria. Although less critical than the preceding points, a number of other conditions may increase our confidence when we make causal judgements. For instance, in textbook examples of causation, φ often describes the actions of an agent, and ψ represents a change in the state of a passive object (as in "Mary causes the house to burn down"). Further, we often expect the two participants to come into physical contact during their transaction.[16]

In order to understand these conditions better, let us try them out on a few test cases (some of which derive from Lewis).[17] First consider the sharpshooter aiming at a distant victim. Scrutiny of the sharpshooter's past record shows that the probability of a successful hit in this case is 0.1; if it makes any difference, we might imagine that irreducibly random quantum events in the sharpshooter's brain help determine the outcome. Let us suppose that in the current case the bullet actually hits and kills the victim. We unhesitatingly agree then that the sharpshooter's actions caused the victim's death, *despite their causal insufficiency*. Accordingly, it appears that in such cases, people rank necessity above sufficiency when making judgments about causes.

Still, sufficiency does retain some relevance. Suppose that the king and the mayor both have an interest in the fate of some young dissident; as it happens, both issue orders to exile him, so exiled he is. This is a classic case of *overdetermination*. Let φ_1 stand for "the king issues an exile order," φ_2 stand for "the mayor issues an exile order," and ψ, "the dissident goes into exile." In the current scenario, neither φ_1 nor φ_2 alone is necessary for ψ: for instance, had the king failed to issue any order, the dissident would still have been exiled thanks to the mayor, and vice versa. In fact $\varphi_1 \wedge \varphi_2$ satisfies the necessity requirement, but we are (perhaps unreasonably) reluctant to posit a disjunction as a cause.[18] Instead, sufficiency comes to the rescue and permits a choice between the two. After all, φ_2 fails this test: it is easy to imagine a universe where the mayor issues his decree yet the dissident gets off (just change the king's order into a pardon). The king's order, on the other hand, is truly *effective*; whatever small changes we make to the universe (including changes in the mayor's orders), the dissident's exile follows from the king's command. Accordingly we may dub φ_1 the "real cause" (if we feel the need to satisfy that yearning).[19]

Consider next the tale of Billy and Susie. Both children are throwing rocks at a glass bottle, and as it happens Susie's rock, traveling slightly faster, reaches the bottle first and shatters it. Billy's rock arrives a moment later at exactly the spot where the bottle used to stand, but of course encounters nothing but flying shards. When choosing between φ_1 ("Susie throws rock S") and φ_2 ("Billy throws rock B"), we vote for φ_1 as the cause of ψ ("The bottle shatters"), despite the fact that neither sentence is necessary (had Susie not thrown her rock, the bottle would still have shattered thanks to Billy, and vice versa) and both are sufficient (Billy's throw suffices to produce a broken bottle, whatever his playmate does, and likewise with Susie's). Why? The general notion of temporal priority (introduced above in connection with distinguishing cause from effect) strikes us as one critical consideration. As with priority disputes in science, art, and sports, we seem to put a premium on being the *first* with an innovation, and since rock S arrived in the vicinity of the bottle earlier than did rock B, we give credit to Susie. Further, it is clear that, although the bottle would still have shattered without Susie's throw, the shattering event would have been significantly different, occurring at a later time with a different rock sending fragments off in different directions. We can choose set X to reflect this fact (in keeping with guidelines (G)):

let it contain worlds in which either (1) the bottle doesn't shatter at all, or (2) it shatters in a way very similar to the way it shatters in reality. Then for every world in X,

$$\psi \Rightarrow \varphi_1$$

obtains; wherever in X the bottle shatters, we find Susie throwing her rock first. On the other hand,

$$\psi \Rightarrow \varphi_2$$

may well fail in X; X can certainly contain worlds where the bottle shatters but Billy refrains. In short, φ_1 is "more necessary" than φ_2, provided that we choose X right. The vagueness of X, though sometimes irksome, can also break deadlocks.

Not that deadlocks must always be breakable. We ought to look with equanimity on the prospect that sometimes circumstances will fail to pinpoint a single "real cause" of an event, no matter how hard we seek. A case in point is the classic law school riddle:

> Everybody in the French Foreign Legion outpost hates Fred, and wants him dead. During the night before Fred's trek across the desert, Tom poisons the water in his canteen. Then, Dick, not knowing of Tom's intervention, pours out the (poisoned) water and replaces it with sand. Finally, Harry comes along and pokes holes in the canteen, so that the "water" will slowly run out. Later, Fred awakens and sets out on his trek, provisioned with his canteen. Too late he finds his canteen is nearly empty, but besides, what remains is sand, not water, not even poisoned water. Fred dies of thirst. Who caused his death?[20]

4. DETERMINISM AND POSSIBILITY (THESIS 1)

Now that we have some formal machinery in place, we can reconsider the spuriously "obvious" fear that determinism reduces our possibilities. We can see why the claim *seems* to have merit: let φ be the sentence "Austin holes the putt," let X be the set of physically possible worlds that are *identical* to the actual world at some time t_0 prior to the putt, and assume both that Austin misses and that determinism holds. Then in fact φ does not hold for any world in X ($\sim \Diamond_X \varphi$), because X contains only one world: the actual one. Of course, this method of choosing X (call it the *narrow method*) is only one among many. We should note that the moment we admit into X worlds that differ in a few imperceptibly microscopic ways from actuality at t_0, we may well find that $\Diamond_X \varphi$, even when determinism obtains. (This is, after all, what recent work on chaos has shown: many phenomena of interest to us can change radically if one minutely alters the initial conditions.) So the question is: when people contend that events are possible, are they really thinking in terms of the narrow method?

Notice that Austin evidently endorses the narrow method of choosing X when he states that he is "talking about conditions as they precisely were" whenever he asserts he could have holed the putt. Yet in the next sentence he seemingly rescinds this endorsement, observing that "further experiments may confirm my belief that I could have done it that time, although I did not." What "further experiments" might indeed confirm Austin's belief that he could have done it? Experiments on the putting green? Would his belief be shored up by his setting up and sinking near-duplicates of that short putt ten times in a row? If so, then he is not as interested as he claims he is in conditions as they precisely were. He is content to consider "Austin holes the putt" possible if, in situations very similar to the actual occasion in question, he holes the putt.[21]

We contend, then, that Austin equivocates when he discusses possibilities, and that in truth the narrow method of choosing X does not have the significance he imagines. From this it follows that the truth or falsity of determinism should not affect our belief that certain unrealized events were nevertheless "possible," in an important everyday sense of the word. We can bolster this last claim by paying a visit to a narrow domain in which we know with certainty that determinism reigns: the realm of chess-playing computer programs.

Computers are marvels of determinism. Even their so-called random number generators only execute pseudo-random functions, which produce *exactly* the same sequence of "random" digits each time the computer reboots. That means that computer programs that avail themselves of randomness at various "choice" points will nevertheless spin out exactly the same sequence of states if run over and over again from a cold start.[22] Suppose, for instance, you install two different chess-playing programs on your computer and yoke them together with a little supervisory program that pits them against each other, game after game, in a potentially endless series. Will they play the same game, over and over, until you turn off the computer? Perhaps; but if either chess program consults the random number generator during its calculations (if, for instance, it periodically "flips a coin" to escape from Buridan's ass difficulties in the course of its heuristic search), then in the following game the state of the random number generator will have changed. Accordingly, different alternatives will be "chosen" and a variant game will blossom, resulting in a series in which the games, like snowflakes, are no two alike.[23] Nevertheless, if you turned off the computer and then restarted it, running the same program, exactly the same variegated series of games would spin out.

This gives us a toy model of a deterministic Democritean universe, in which zillions of bits are flipped in sequence, governed by a fixed physics. Rewinding and replaying the tape of life is really possible in such a toy world. Suppose we create such a chess universe involving two programs, A and B, and study the results of a lengthy run. We will find lots of highly reliable patterns. Suppose we find that A (almost) always beats B. That is a pattern that we will want to explain, and saying, "Since the program is deterministic, A was *caused* always to beat B" would fail to address that curiosity. We will want to know what about the structure, methods, and dispositions of A accounts for its superiority at chess. A has a competence or power that B lacks, and we need to isolate this interesting factor.[24] When we set about exploring the issue, availing ourselves of the high-level perspective from which the visible "macroscopic" objects include representations of chess pieces and board positions, evaluations of possible moves, decisions about courses to pursue, and so forth, we will uncover a host of further patterns: some of them endemic to chess wherever it is played (for example, the near certainty of B's loss in any game where B falls a rook behind) and some of them peculiar to A and B as particular chess players (for example, B's penchant for getting its queen out early).[25] We will find the standard patterns of chess strategy, such as the fact that when B's time is running out, B searches less deeply through the game tree than it does when in the same position it has more time remaining. In short, we will find a cornucopia of *explanatory* regularities, some exceptionless (in our voluminous run) and others statistical.

These macroscopic patterns are salient moments in the unfolding of a deterministic pageant that, looked at from the perspective of microcausation, is to a large extent all the same. What from one vantage point appear to us to be two chess programs in suspenseful combat, can be seen through the "microscope" (as we watch instructions and data streaming through the CPU) to be a single deterministic automaton unfolding in the only way it can, its jumps already predictable by examining the precise state of the pseudo-random number generator. There are no "real" forks or branches in its future; all the "choices" made by A and B are already determined. Nothing, it seems, is really *possible* in this world other than what actually happens. Suppose, for instance, that an ominous mating-net looms over B at time *t* but collapses when A runs out of time and terminates its search for the key move one pulse too soon; that mating net *was never going to happen*.[26] (This is something we could prove, if we doubted it, by running the same tournament another day. At exactly the same moment in the series, A would run out of time again and terminate its search at exactly the same point.)

So what are we to say? Is our toy world really a world without prevention, without offense and defense, without lost opportunities, without the thrust and parry of genuine agency, without genuine possibilities? Admittedly, our chess programs, like insects or fish, are much too simple agents to be plausible candidates for morally significant free will, but we contend that the determinism of their world does not rob them of their different powers, their different abilities to avail themselves of the opportunities presented. If we want to understand what is happening in that world, we may, indeed must, talk about how their choices cause their circumstances to change, and about what they *can* and *cannot* do.

Suppose we find two games in the series in which the first twelve moves are the same, but with A playing White in the first game and Black in the second. At move 13 in the first game, B "blunders" and its pattern goes downhill from there. At move 13 in the second game, A, in contrast, finds the saving move, castling, and goes on to win. "B *could have castled* at that point in the first game," says an onlooker, echoing Austin. True or false? The move, castling, was just as legal the first time, so in *that* sense, it was among the "options" available to B. Suppose we find, moreover, that castling was not only one of the represented candidate moves for B, but that B in fact undertook a perfunctory exploration of the consequences of castling, abandoned, alas, before its virtues were revealed. Could B have castled? What are we trying to find out? Looking at *precisely* the same case, again and again, is utterly uninformative, but looking at *similar* cases is in fact diagnostic. If we find that in many similar circumstances in other games, B *does* pursue the evaluation slightly farther, discovering the virtues of such moves and making them—if we find, in the minimal case, that flipping a single bit in the random number generator would result in B's castling—then we support ("with further experiments") the observer's conviction that B could have castled then. We would say, in fact, that B's failure to castle was a fluke, bad luck with the random number generator. If, on the contrary, we find that discovering the reasons for castling requires far too much analysis for B to execute in the time available (although A, being a stronger player, is up to the task), then we will have grounds for concluding that no, B, unlike A, could not have castled. To imagine B castling would require too many alterations of reality; we would be committing an error alluded to earlier, making X too large.

In sum, using the narrow method to choose X is useless if we want to explain the patterns that are manifest in the unfolding data. It is only if we "wiggle the events" (as David Lewis has said), looking *not* at "conditions as they precisely were" but at nearby neighboring worlds, that we achieve any understanding at all.[27] Once we expand X a little, we discover that B has additional options, in a sense both informative and morally relevant (when we address worlds beyond the chessboard). The burden rests with incompatibilists to explain why "real" possibility demands a narrow choice of X—or why we should be interested in such a concept of possibility, regardless of its "reality."

As we have seen, possibilities of the broader, more interesting variety can exist quite comfortably in deterministic worlds. Indeed, introducing indeterminism adds nothing in the way of worthwhile possibilities, opportunities, or competences to a universe. If in our sample deterministic world program A always beats program B, then replacing the pseudo-random number generator with a genuinely indeterministic device will not help B at all: A will *still* win every time. Though pseudo-random generators may not produce genuinely random output, they come so close that no ordinary mortal can tell the difference. A superior algorithm like A's will hardly stumble when faced with so inconsequential a change. And analogous conclusions could well apply in meatier universes like ours. To put it graphically, the universe could be deterministic on even days of the month and indeterministic on odd days, and we would never notice a difference in human opportunities or powers; there would be just as many triumphs, and just as many lamentable lapses, on October 4 as on October 3 or October 5. (If your horoscope advised you to postpone any morally serious decision to an odd-numbered day, you would have no more reason to follow this advice than advice to wait for a waning moon.)

5. SOME RELATED FEARS

In passing we mention a number of other misguided worries about determinism, clustered about the basic fear of lost possibilities. Some thinkers have suggested that the truth of determinism might imply one or more of the following disheartening claims: all trends are permanent, character is by and large immutable, and it is unlikely that one will change one's ways, one's fortunes, or one's basic nature in the future. Ted Honderich,[28] for example, has maintained that determinism would somehow squelch what he calls our life hopes:

> If things have gone well for a person, there is more to hope for in what follows
> on the assumption that the entire run of his or her life is fixed. . . . If things
> have not gone well, or not so well as was hoped, it is at least not unreasonable
> to have greater hopes on the assumption that the whole of one's life is not
> fixed, but is connected with the activity of the self. . . . Given the sanguine
> premiss of our reasonableness, there is reason to think that we do *not* tend to
> the idea of a fixed personal future. (Honderich 1988; p. 388–89)

Clearly such anxieties originate in a vague sense that true possibilities (for an improved lot, say) disappear under determinism.

One readily sees the baselessness of such fears by referring again to the field of computer science. Programmers have already demonstrated how deterministic computer algorithms can adapt themselves to changes in the environment and learn from their mistakes.[29] Chess programs A and B from the previous section could well incorporate such talents. If initially mediocre B possesses these abilities and A does not, then we may ultimately find B emerging victorious. And if B has this sort of structure in a deterministic world, its enviable capacity will not improve with the introduction of a genuinely indeterministic random-number generator. Nor will adding indeterminism to the universe help it if it lacks this ability.

In general, there is no paradox in the observation that certain phenomena are *determined* to be changeable, chaotic, and unpredictable, an obvious and important fact that philosophers have curiously ignored. Honderich finds disturbing the notion that we might have a "fixed personal *future*," but the implications of this notion are entirely distinct from the implications of having a "fixed personal *nature*." The latter is cause for dismay, perhaps, but not the former, for it could very well be one's fixed personal future to be blessed with a protean nature, highly responsive to the "activity of the self." The total set of personal futures, "fixed" or not, contains all sorts of agreeable scenarios, including victories over adversity, subjugations of weakness, reformations of character, even changes of luck. It could be just as determined a fact that you *can* teach an old dog new tricks as that you can't. The question to ask is, Are old dogs the kinds of things that can be taught new tricks? We rightly care about being the sorts of entities whose future trajectories are not certain to repeat the patterns found in the past. The general thesis of determinism has no implications about such issues—for answers to these questions, we must turn to specific fields like biology and social science (which themselves might be either deterministic or indeterministic domains).[30] And as the next section will show, creativity, the ability to author something of "originative value," is similarly independent of determinism.

6. Determinism and Causation (Thesis 2)

The hunch that determinism would eliminate some worthwhile type of causation from the universe has even less merit than the claim that it eliminates possibilities. We suspect this fear stems from the conflation of causal necessity with causal sufficiency—as we have seen, our language makes this confusion all too easy. Determinism is essentially a doctrine concerned with sufficiency: if σ_0 is a (mind-bogglingly complex) sentence that specifies in complete detail the state of the universe at t_0 and σ_1 similarly specifies the universe at a later time t_1, then determinism dictates that σ_0 is sufficient for σ_1 in all physically possible worlds. But determinism tells us nothing about what earlier conditions are *necessary* to produce σ_1, or any other sentence ψ for that matter. Hence, since causation generally presupposes necessity, the truth of determinism would have little bearing on the validity of our causal judgments.[31]

For example: according to determinism, the precise condition of the universe one second after the big bang (call the corresponding sentence σ_0) causally sufficed to produce the assassination of John F. Kennedy in 1963 (sentence ψ). Yet there is no reason at all to claim that σ_0 caused ψ. Though sufficient, σ_0 is hardly necessary. For all we know, Kennedy might well have been assassinated anyway, even if some different conditions had obtained back during the universe's birth.[32] More plausible causes of the event would include "A bullet followed a course directed at Kennedy's body"; "Lee Harvey Oswald pulled the trigger on his gun"; perhaps "Kennedy was born"; conceivably "Oswald was born."[33] But conspicuously absent from this list are microscopically detailed descriptions of the universe billions of years prior to the incident. Incompatibilists who assert that under determinism σ_0 "causes" or "explains" ψ miss the main point of causal inquiry.

In fact, determinism is perfectly compatible with the notion that some events have no cause at all. Consider the sentence "The devaluation of the rupiah caused the Dow Jones average to fall." We rightly treat such a declaration with suspicion; are we really so sure that among nearby universes the Dow Jones fell *only* in those where the rupiah fell first? Do we even imagine that every universe where the rupiah fell experienced a stock market sell-off? Might there not have been a confluence of dozens of factors that jointly sufficed to send the market tumbling but none of which by itself was essential? On some days, perhaps, Wall Street's behavior has a ready explanation; yet at least as often we suspect that no particular cause is at work. And surely our opinions about the market's activities would remain the same, whether we happened to adopt Newton's physics or Schrödinger's.

Of course, one might wonder why it is that causal necessity matters to us as much as it does. Let us return for a moment to chess programs A and B. Suppose our attention is drawn to a rare game in which B wins, and we want to know "the cause" of this striking victory. The trivial claim that B's win was "caused" by the initial state of the computer is totally uninformative. Of course the total state of the toy universe at prior moments was *sufficient* for the occurrence of the win; we want to know which features were *necessary,* and thereby understand what such rare events have in common. We want to discover those features, the absence of which would most directly be followed by B's loss, the default outcome. Perhaps we will find a heretofore unsuspected flaw in A's control structure, a bug that has only just now surfaced. Or perhaps the victory is a huge coincidence of conditions that require no repair, since the probability of their recurrence is effectively zero. Or we might find an idiosyncratic island of brilliance in B's competence, which once diagnosed would enable us to say just what circumstances in the future might permit another such victory for B.

Rationality *requires* that we evaluate necessary conditions at least as carefully as sufficient conditions. Consider a man falling down an elevator shaft. Although he doesn't know exactly which possible world he in fact occupies, he does know one thing: he is in a set of worlds *all* of which have him landing shortly at the bottom of the shaft. Gravity will see to that. Landing is, then, *inevitable* (un-avoid-able) because it happens in every world consistently with what he knows. But perhaps *dying* is not inevitable. Perhaps in some of the worlds in which he lands, he survives. Those worlds do not include any in which he lands headfirst or spreadeagled, say, but there may be worlds in which he lands in a toes-first crouch and lives. There is some elbow room. He can rationally plan action on the assumption that living is possible, and even if he cannot discover sufficient conditions to guarantee survival, he may at least improve the odds by taking whatever actions are necessary.[34]

In closing, let us return to the human desire pinpointed by Kane that motivates so much of this debate: the desire to be able to take full credit as the creators and causes of change in the world. Consider for instance the wish that we (Taylor and Dennett) have to be acknowledged as the authors of this essay. Suppose that determinism turns out to be true. Would that in any way undercut our claim that our activity nevertheless played an essential role in this essay's creation? Not in the least, even after we factor in the earlier deeds of our parents and teachers. Without our efforts, it is safe to say that no essay exactly like this (or even closely similar) would have been produced.[35] Hence we are entitled to claim some "originative value" for our unique accomplishment. The thirst for originality and causal relevance is not to be quenched by abstruse quantum events: all that we require is the knowledge that without our presence, the universe would have turned out significantly different.

Appendix: Van Inwagen's Consequence Argument

Peter van Inwagen (1975) hopes to bolster the incompatibilist sense of lost causal powers with the following basic argument:

1. Let φ be some event that actually occurs in agent A's life (missing a putt, say). Also let σ_0 be a comprehensive description of the universe's state at some time in the remote past, and let λ be a statement of the laws of nature.

2. Then, assuming determinism, $\lambda \wedge \sigma_0 \Rightarrow \varphi$ applies in every possible world. Equivalently, $\sim\varphi \Rightarrow \sim(\lambda \wedge \sigma_0)$.

3. If A has the power to cause α and $\alpha \Rightarrow \beta$ obtains in every possible world, then A has the power to cause β.

4. So if A has the power to cause $\sim\varphi$, then A has the power to cause the falsity of either λ or σ_0, which is absurd.

5. Therefore A lacks the power to cause $\sim\varphi$.

This argument illustrates nicely the confusion that causal necessity and sufficiency engender. As we have argued, counterfactual necessity is the single most crucial condition for causation, and accordingly we would recommend that van Inwagen's "power to cause α" be rendered as follows:

A has the *power to cause* α iff for some sentence γ describing an action of A and a world f close to actuality, $\gamma \wedge \alpha$ holds in f and $\alpha \Rightarrow \gamma$ in every world similar to f.

In other words, within some cluster of nearby worlds, there is a possible action of A (called γ) that is a necessary condition for α to occur. But under this definition, line 3 has no warrant whatever. Line 3 hypothesizes that $\alpha \Rightarrow \gamma$ in a cluster of nearby worlds, and that $\alpha \Rightarrow \beta$ in every world; if we could deduce that $\beta \Rightarrow \gamma$ in this cluster, we would be home free. But of course in Logic 101 we learn that $\alpha \Rightarrow \gamma$ and $\alpha \Rightarrow \beta$ do not entail $\beta \Rightarrow \gamma$, and so line 3 fails, and van Inwagen's argument with it.

NOTES

1. Nozick (1981: 313), "We want it to be true that in that very same situation we could have done (significantly) otherwise, so that our actions will have originative value."

2. Austin (1961: 166).

3. Kane (1996. 100).

4. Ibid. (p. 4).

5. Ibid. (p. 33).

6. Ibid. (p. 35).

7. Ginet (1990: 9).

8. See Quine (1980) for a discussion of these pitfalls.

9. Idem (1969: 147–55).

10. The average educated person's casual working assumptions about the cosmos still resemble the Democritean account, and philosophers traditionally rely on nothing more sophisticated when exploring the implications of determinism and indeterminism, causation and possibility.

Our suggestion that possible worlds simply *are* functions of the appropriate form may seem disturbingly reductive, particularly when one contemplates the particular function(s) that correspond to the actual world; accordingly David Lewis takes pains to distinguish possible worlds from their mathematical "handles." However one wishes to address these ontological scruples, nothing in the following discussion hinges on them.

11. Since we are restricting ourselves to the scientifically old-fashioned Democritean worlds, we would have trouble specifying the contents of Φ precisely—and besides, of course, we do not yet *know* all the laws of nature—but we can pretend that we know, and hence we can pretend that in most cases one can judge whether or not a particular world f accords with natural law.

John Horton Conway's Game of Life can be viewed as a particularly simple pseudo-Democritean universe, eliminating one spatial dimension and quantizing time. (See Dennett 1991: 27–51 or Idem 1995, for an introduction to Life.) The set of all possible sequences of bitmaps is then Ω, and the single (deterministic) rule of Life "physics" applied to every "initial" state gives us the subset Φ of Ω. Every variation on Conway's "physics" generates a different subset Φ.

12. Of course, these predicates unleash a horde of problems concerning vagueness, subjectivity, and (in such cases as "believes that snow is white") intentionality, but difficulties along these lines do not imperil the basic approach.

13. Lewis (1973a), *passim*.

14. See, for example, (Tooley 1987).

15. A vast amount of ink his been spilled arguing that the direction of causation is either independent of or logically prior to the direction of time, and to address the matter here would require too lengthy a digression. So we merely note the issue and tentatively take the direction of time as a given (originating ultimately in the Second Law of Thermodynamics) from which the direction of causation derives.

Gasking (1955) raises a number of interesting cases in which cause and effect appear to be simultaneous: for instance, if a piece of iron attains a temperature of (say) 1000°C and thereupon starts to glow, we still distinguish the former as cause and the latter as effect. But this apparent exception to the rule has a ready explanation that Gasking himself hints at: when a speaker refers to the iron "reaching 1000°," she is envisioning this event as the endpoint in a lengthy heating process. The heating process *does* precede the glowing, and so the latter is considered an effect.

Another category of "exceptions" includes diseases and their symptoms (say, a cold and sneezing), which might sometimes arise simultaneously. Yet often enough diseases *do* precede their symptoms, while symptoms (by definition) never appear before their diseases. Accordingly we grant diseases the status of "cause."

16. Notice that we do not in the previous clauses make any provision to ensure the transitivity of causation. Lewis (2000: 191–95), among others, feels it important to guarantee transitivity by making "causation" the ancestral of "causal dependence." But Lewis himself provides many examples of transitivity's counterintuitive consequences. For instance, suppose that agent A wants to travel to New York. Agent B, hoping to thwart A, lets the air out of the tires on A's car. In consequence, A takes the train instead and reaches New York only slightly behind schedule. If causation is transitive, than B has "caused" A's successful arrival, despite the fact that the two sentences "B lets the air out of A's tires" and "A arrives in New York" satisfy none of our more crucial conditions. Lewis finds the awkward implications of transitivity acceptable; we remain unpersuaded.

Hall (2000) goes to even greater lengths to defend transitivity. His account seems to imply that a pebble on the train tracks south of Paris that minutely alters the course of the Orient Express is a "cause" of the train's arrival in Istanbul several days later. Paul's "Aspect Causation" (2000) suggests a possible diagnosis for Hall's willingness to countenance such bizarre conclusions, as stemming from an overeager acceptance of the premise that causation is a relation between "events" (however this problematic term may be defined). At any rate, notice that on our account one can consistently consider false the sentence "Pebble p's lying on the tracks south of Paris caused the train's arrival in Istanbul," while accepting "Pebble p's lying on the tracks south of Paris caused the train's arrival in Istanbul via a minutely altered course in France."

17. Lewis (2000).

18. Obviously, a sentence like "Drugs or aliens caused Elvis's premature demise" abbreviates the cumbersome "Drugs caused Elvis's premature demise or aliens caused Elvis's premature demise"—a disjunction of two separate causes, not a single disjunctive cause.

19. Invoking causal sufficiency in this way solves, to our satisfaction, all of the analogous problem cases raised by Shaffer (2000). Note that Shaffer rather misleadingly suggests that "counterfactual accounts of causation" must always be formulated solely in terms of necessity (ibid.: 176). We, on the contrary, consider our account essentially "counterfactual" even though it allows for sufficiency along with necessity.

Lewis's formulation (Lewis 2000) of "Causation as Influence" can be viewed as an indirect way of introducing sufficiency into an originally necessity centered account. For present purposes we consider our approach more illuminating, but both strategies point in the same general direction.

20. A doubly elaborated version of the example due originally to McLaughlin (1925), first elaborated in Hart and Honoré (1959). The Hart and Honoré version has one less twist: "Suppose A is entering a desert. B secretly puts a fatal dose of poison in A's water keg. A takes the keg into the desert where C steals it; both A and C think it contains water. A dies of thirst. Who kills him?"

21. When Austin speaks of further experiments, could he be referring to experiments in the high-tech labs of physicists and microbiologists, experiments that would convince him that his brain amplifies indeterministic quantum events? Given the extreme impracticality of such experiments, and Austin's overall skepticism about the relevance of science in these contexts ("[A modern belief in science] is not in line with the traditional beliefs enshrined in the word can," Austin 1961: 166), this interpretation seems unlikely. But this is precisely the direction in which Kane and some other incompatibilists have headed. See also Dennett (1984: 133–37).

22. We are restricting our attention to programs that do not require or accept input from the external world, which could, of course, be random in any of several senses. The easiest way to ensure that there is variation in subsequent runs of a program is to have it call for inputs of these sorts: the time taken from the computer's clock, the presence or absence of a pulse from a Geiger counter, the last digit in the latest Dow Jones Industrial Average as taken off the Internet, and so on.

23. All this is independent of whether or not either chess program can "learn from its experience," which is another way their internal state could change over time to guarantee that no two games were the same.

24. Another case in which we could know all the deterministic microdetails but be baffled about how to explain the causal regularities is Dennett's example of the two black boxes (1995: 412–22).

25. Dennett (1978: 107).

26. Compare the comet plunging toward earth that is intercepted at the last minute by the other comet, unnoticed till then, that had been on its collision trajectory since its birth millions of years ago (Dennett 1984: 124).

27. If we exclude such variation, then trivially, castling in the second game was not "open to B," to use Ginet's terminology. Recall that Ginet requires that "nothing that exists up to that moment stands in the way of my doing next any one of the alternatives." The narrow method has the effect of treating the precise state of B's contemplation of the option of castling as something *external*, as something that can itself "stand in the way" at the moment of choosing, guaranteeing that *nothing about B* could *explain* B's choice, whatever it is. As Dennett notes, "If you make yourself really small, you can externalize virtually everything" (1984: 143).

28. Honderich (1988).

29. They have also demonstrated, all too often, the possibility of programs losing competence over time by accumulating deleterious effects from bugs. At any rate, just how significant are the many examples of "machine learning" that have been produced to date? The answer is contested, and it is true that the best chess programs today do *not* include substantial "unsupervised" learning capacities. Still, the feasibility of genuine learning in computer programs has not been in doubt since the self-improving checkers program created by Arthur Samuel in the 1950s. (See Dennett 1995: 207–12 for details.) John McCarthy has posed the question of what the minimal life-world configuration is, in which occupants learn the physics of their own world (ibid.: 175). One might also ask, Which variations on Conway's physics generate possible worlds in which occupants can know or learn anything at all?

30. This paragraph is drawn, with revisions, from Dennett 1988.

31. See the appendix to this chapter for an additional example of the conflation of necessity and sufficiency (in van Inwagen's Consequence Argument).

32. Imagine that we take a snapshot of the universe at the moment of Kennedy's assassination, then alter the picture in some trivial way (by moving Kennedy 1 mm to the left, say). Then, following the (deterministic) laws of physics in reverse, we can generate a movie running all the way back to the Big Bang, obtaining a world in which σ_0 subtly fails.

33. Of course, the last two options fail the sufficiency test so badly that we prefer not to countenance them as causes. As explained earlier, sufficiency does have *some* relevance in assigning causes, but not the overwhelming importance that incompatibilists imply.

34. The dependence of this concept of possibility on *epistemic* considerations has been suggested before (see Dennett 1984: 147ff.) but mischaracterized. It is true that if determinism held, and if the man knew *exactly* which world he inhabited, he would already know his fate.

35. Similarly, Deep Blue, in spite of its being a deterministic automaton, authored the games of chess that vanquished Kasparov. No one *else* was their author; Murray Campbell and the IBM team that created Deep Blue cannot claim credit for those games; *they* did not see the moves. The vast exploratory activity of Deep Blue itself was the originating cause of those magnificent games.

PART V

MORAL RESPONSIBILITY, ALTERNATIVE POSSIBILITIES, AND FRANKFURT-STYLE EXAMPLES

CHAPTER 12

FRANKFURT-TYPE EXAMPLES AND SEMI-COMPATIBILISM

JOHN MARTIN FISCHER

IT is a basic and pervasive assumption that in order to be morally responsible for one's behavior, one must have had (at some relevant point along the path to the behavior) alternative possibilities of a certain sort. This basic idea is encapsulated in the "Principle of Alternative Possibilities," the various versions of which require that moral responsibility be associated with the presence of alternative possibilities.[1] Now there are powerful reasons to think that causal determinism would rule out alternative possibilities.[2] So it has appeared to many philosophers that causal determinism is incompatible with moral responsibility.

There are, however, various ways of challenging the Principle of Alternative Possibilities. One way employs a thought-experiment with a distinctive structure; such thought-experiments are frequently called "Frankfurt-type examples," because of Harry Frankfurt's seminal presentation of them (1969) The examples contain a fail-safe mechanism that does not actually play any role in the relevant agent's deliberations, choices, and behavior, but whose presence ensures that the agent deliberates, chooses, and behaves just as he actually does.

1. FRANKFURT-TYPE EXAMPLES

The first "Frankfurt-type case" was given by John Locke in *An Essay Concerning Human Understanding*. Locke's example is a case in which "a man be carried whilst fast asleep into a room where is a person he longs to see and speak with, and be there locked fast in, beyond his power to get out; he awakes and is glad to find himself in so desirable company, which he stays willingly in . . ."[3] In Locke's example, the man stays in the room voluntarily and it seems that he does so "freely" (although Locke himself would use the term *voluntarily* rather than *freely*) and can be morally responsible for doing so, although unbeknownst to him he could not have left the room. Of course, the man *does* have various alternative possibilities (apart from special assumptions): he can choose to leave the room and try to leave the room, and so forth.

Frankfurt can be seen to be entering the debate at this point. Frankfurt seeks to construct examples in which even *these* sorts of alternative possibilities have been eliminated. To do this, Frankfurt employs the apparatus of a "counterfactual intervener"[4] who can monitor the brain and intervene in it, should the agent be about to choose to do otherwise. In order to flesh out these examples—although Frankfurt did not explicitly do this—it is useful to posit a "prior sign" that can be read by the counterfactual intervener and guide him in his activity. (This was David Blumenfeld's innovation: Blumenfeld, 1971.) If the sign indicates that the agent is about to choose to do what the counterfactual intervener wants him to choose, the intervener does not intervene. If, contrary to fact, the agent were about to choose differently, the prior sign would inform the counterfactual intervener (and he would intervene).

Here is a particular version of a "Frankfurt-type case." Suppose Jones is in a voting booth deliberating about whether to vote for Gore or Bush. After reflection, he chooses to vote for Gore and does vote for Gore by marking his ballot in the normal way. Unbeknownst to him, Black, a liberal neurosurgeon working with the Democratic Party, has implanted a device in Jones's brain which monitors Jones's brain activities. If he is about to choose to vote Democratic, the device simply continues monitoring and does not intervene in the process in any way. If, however, Jones is about to choose to vote, say, Republican, the device triggers an intervention that involves electronic stimulation of the brain sufficient to produce a choice to vote for the Democrat (and a subsequent Democratic vote).

How can the device tell whether Jones is about to choose to vote Republican or Democratic? This is where the "prior sign" comes in. If Jones is about to choose at T_2 to vote for Gore at T_3, he shows some involuntary sign—say a neurological pattern in his brain—at T_1. Detecting this, Black's device does not intervene. But if Jones is about to choose at T_2 to vote for Bush at T_3, he shows an involuntary sign—a different neurological pattern in his brain—at T_1. This brain pattern would trigger Black's device to intervene and cause Jones to choose at T2 to vote for Gore, and to vote for Gore at T3.

In that the device plays no role in Jones's deliberations and act of voting, it seems to me that Jones acts freely and is morally responsible for voting for Gore. And given the presence of Black's device, it is plausible to think that Jones does not have alternative possibilities with regard to his choice and action. Thus, the Frankfurt-type examples seem to be counterexamples to the Principle of Alternative Possibilities.

2. THE "DIVIDE AND CONQUER" STRATEGY OF RESPONSE TO THE FRANKFURT-TYPE EXAMPLES

Peter van Inwagen (1978; 1983) has developed what might be called the "divide and conquer" strategy of response to the Frankfurt-type examples. His basic point is that the proponent of the Frankfurt-type cases (as counterexamples to the Principle of Alternative Possibilities) is not sufficiently precise in specifying what the relevant agent is morally responsible for. We typically hold individuals morally responsible for various items, including actions, omissions, and consequences (envisaged either as "particulars" or more coarsely individuated "universals"). Van Inwagen's contention is that (in the Frankfurt-type cases and elsewhere) there is no one item of which it is true both that there is no alternative to it and that the agent is morally responsible for it. There are some items for which the agent may well be responsible, but these are items to which there are genuinely available alternative possibilities. And there are some items to which there are no such alternative possibilities; for these items the agent is not morally responsible, according to van Inwagen. Van Inwagen's diagnosis of the confusion of the proponent of the Frankfurt-type cases is that he is (perhaps implicitly) thinking of one sort of item when he is focusing on moral responsibility, and another when he is focusing on alternative possibilities.

Van Inwagen essentially distinguishes four principles. The "Principle of Alternate Possibilities" (strictly speaking) deals with actions which have been performed:

(PAP)   A person is morally responsible for what he has done only if he could have done otherwise.

The "Principle of Possible Action" pertains to actions which have not been performed (failures to act or omissions):

> (PPA)   A person is morally responsible for failing to perform a given act only if he could have performed that act.

Two additional principles deal with our moral responsibility for consequences of what we do (or omit). The first "Principle of Possible Prevention" applies to consequences considered as event-particulars:

> (PPP1)   A person is morally responsible for a certain event-particular only if he could have prevented it.

The second such principle applies to consequences considered as event-universals, which are individuated more broadly than event-particulars:

> (PPP2)   A person is morally responsible for a certain state of affairs only if (that state of affairs obtains and) he could have prevented it from obtaining.

Van Inwagen contends that (PPA), (PPP1), and (PPP2) cannot be refuted by Frankfurt-type cases. Further, he claims that if no one is morally responsible for having failed to perform any act, and no one is morally responsible for any event-particular or event-universal, then no one is morally responsible for *anything* (including actions) (1983: 181).

It will be useful to consider the arguments for and against each principle. Let us begin with the principle pertaining to omissions, (PPA). Van Inwagen's defense of the principle can be understood as follows. Suppose you are in your apartment looking out the window, and you see someone being mugged. You consider calling the police, but you just do not want any involvement, so you refrain from calling the police. Unbeknownst to you, the telephone wire has been cut by the criminal, and so even if you had tried to reach the police, you would have been unsuccessful. Van Inwagen's intuition is that you are not morally responsible for failing to call the police (in the sense of failing to successfully make contact with the police). You may be morally responsible for failing to *try* to reach the police, for failing to dial, and so forth; but you are not morally responsible for failing successfully to reach the police. Further, it is van Inwagen's crucial contention that this intuition is explained by the fact that you *could not have reached the police*, and thus that in general moral responsibility for failing to do X requires the ability to do X. Van Inwagen's strategy involves pointing to a number of cases of omissions in which the agent could not have done the act in question and in which it appears that we would base our exculpation of the agent on this inability.

At one point I accepted this sort of defense of (PPA), but because I reject (PAP), I defended an asymmetry between actions and omissions with respect to the requirement of alternative possibilities for moral responsibility. That is, I defended the thesis that whereas moral responsibility for performing act X does not require the ability to refrain from X-ing, moral responsibility for failing to perform X does require the ability to do X (Fischer 1985/86). But a number of insightful critiques convinced me that in fact (PPA) is just as problematic as (PAP) (Haji 1992; Clarke 1994; Zimmerman 1994; Frankfurt 1994; and Glannon 1995). The basic insight behind the critique of (PPA) is that there are omissions cases that are structurally similar to the Frankfurt-type action cases. Thus, van Inwagen's intuitions may well be valid for the cases (such as the case of the mugging and cut telephone wire described above) to which he points, but this is only a proper subset of the relevant cases.

So, for example, consider an "omissions version" of the Frankfurt-type case with which we began (in which Jones votes for Gore). Suppose everything is the same except that Jones actually refrains from voting at all. (He is disgusted by all the available candidates.) But suppose that Black is ready to directly stimulate Jones's brain, should Jones show a prior sign indicating that he is about to choose to vote (and to vote). It seems to me that Jones can in this case be morally responsible for refraining from voting, although he could not have voted. I do not see any relevant difference between this sort of case and the "action-version" of the example (see Fischer and Ravizza 1998).

Van Inwagen appears to concede that Frankfurt has in fact provided counterexamples to (PAP). Discussing an action version of the Frankfurt-type examples, van Inwagen writes, "It seems we must conclude that we have a genuine case in which an agent is morally responsible for having shot a certain man even though he could not have done otherwise than shoot that man. This case shows that the Principle of Alternate Possibilities is probably false" (1983: 164), I think that van Inwagen is correct here. But I have always been puzzled as to how he can say this, given that he has apparently argued that (PPA), (PPP1), and (PPP2), which he accepts, entail that moral responsibility for *anything* requires alternative possibilities.

Let us now turn to the principle as it applies to consequences. It will perhaps be illuminating to begin with the principle pertaining to consequence-universals, (PPP2):

(PPP2)   A person is morally responsible for a certain state of affairs only if (that state of affairs obtains and) he could have prevented it from obtaining.

Again, van Inwagen (ibid.: 164) develops a case in which the agent could not have prevented the state of affairs from obtaining and it appears that precisely this fact entails that he is not morally responsible for it. So suppose that Ryder has been kidnapped and involuntarily placed on a horse, Dobbin. Ryder comes to a fork in the road at which he can guide Dobbin to the right or left, but he cannot (at any point) cause Dobbin to stop before he gets to the end of the road. Further, unbeknownst to Ryder, both forks end up in Rome. Van Inwagen's intuition is that Ryder may well be morally responsible for causing Dobbin to take the left rather than the right fork, but he cannot fairly be held morally responsible for the state of affairs that Dobbin ends up in Rome (one way or another). And van Inwagen suggests that precisely the fact that Ryder could not have prevented this state of affairs from obtaining that makes it the case that he is not morally responsible for it.

But, again, as with omissions, it seems to me that Van Inwagen is focusing on a proper subset of cases. I believe that there are other cases in which it is plausible to say that the relevant agent is morally responsible for the obtaining of a state of affairs which he cannot prevent from obtaining. Consider, for example, "Assassin." Sam tells his friend, Jack, of his plan to murder the mayor. Jack also wants the mayor dead, so he has secretly implanted a device in Sam's brain which allows him to monitor all of Sam's brain activity and to intervene in it, if he desires. The device can be employed by Jack to ensure (via direct electronic stimulation of the brain) that Sam decides to kill the mayor and that he acts on this decision. Suppose, further, that Sam methodically and freely carries out his plan to kill the mayor. Jack thus plays absolutely no role in Sam's decision and action; Sam acts exactly as he would have acted had no device been implanted in his brain. It seems to me that in this case Sam is morally responsible not only for his act of shooting the mayor, but for the state of affairs universal, *that the mayor is shot*. And yet (given Jack's set-up) Sam cannot prevent the obtaining of this state of affairs (See Fischer and Ravizza 1998: 59.)

Consider, also, "Missile." Here an evil woman, Elizabeth, has obtained a missile and missile launcher, and she has decided (for her own rather perverse reasons) to launch the missile toward Washington, D.C. Suppose that Elizabeth's situation is like that of Sam; she has not been manipulated, brainwashed, and so forth. Further, imagine that she has had exactly the same sort of device implanted in her brain as had been put into Sam's and that there is a "counterfactual intervener" associated with her who would ensure that Elizabeth would launch the missile, if Elizabeth were to show any sign of wavering. Suppose also that, once the missile is launched toward the city, Elizabeth cannot prevent it from hitting Washington, D.C. When Elizabeth freely launches the missile toward Washington, D.C., it seems to me that she is morally responsible for the occurrence of the consequence-universal, *that Washington, D.C. is bombed;* and yet she could not prevent this state of affairs from obtaining (one way or another).

My contention, then, is that there are indeed cases in which an agent can legitimately be held morally responsible for bringing about a consequence-universal, even though she could not have prevented this universal from obtaining (one way or another). Van Inwagen's intuition to the contrary here, as in the context of omissions, is based on attending to a proper subset of the relevant cases and inappropriately generalizing from this subset. Further, I (and my co-author) have developed (elsewhere) a principled way of distinguishing among the cases.[5]

Now let us turn to the Principle of Alternative Possibilities as it applies to consequence-particulars:

(PPP1)   A person is morally responsible for a certain event-particular only if he could have prevented it.

Van Inwagen's argument in defense of (PPP1) proceeds as follows (1983: 167–70). He begins by accepting a criterion of event-individuation according to which the actual causal antecedents of a particular event are *essential* to it. Now Van Inwagen points out that in the alternative sequence in a Frankfurt-type case a different causal sequence (involving a different prior sign) from the actual sequence occurs; thus, according to van Inwagen, there is a different event-particular in the alternative sequence from the event-particular in the actual sequence. Thus, he contends that Frankfurt has not impugned (PPP1) by providing cases in which the agent is morally responsible and yet the same event occurs in the actual and alternative sequences.

Perhaps van Inwagen's strategy can be understood as follows. The proponent of (PPP1) essentially believes that moral responsibility requires that the agent have access to an alternative possible world in which a different event-particular results from his behavior. One way to show the falsity of this belief would be to display cases in which the agent is morally responsible and yet the relevant event-particulars are the same in the actual and alternative scenarios. But—given the fine-grained approach to event-individuation—Frankfurt has not succeeded in displaying such a case.

Some philosophers have questioned van Inwagen's "essentialist" principle of event-individuation, and they have thus contended that Frankfurt has in fact succeeded in presenting cases of the requisite sort (for example, Carter 1979). I do not know how exactly to resolve the dispute about event-individuation, but I also do not think that one's views about the Frankfurt-type cases should depend on this sort of issue. Against van Inwagen I would argue that Frankfurt's strategy for impugning (PAP) need not rest on the project of presenting cases in which the event-particulars are the same in the actual and alternative scenarios, because I believe that the proponent of (PPP1) should hold that moral responsibility requires that the agent have access to an alternative possible world in which a different event-particular results from his *voluntary* behavior. That is, if one believes that one's moral responsibility is grounded in the sort of control that involves genuine alternative possibilities, it seems to me that those alternative possiblities must contain voluntary behavior; how can adding a scenario in which the agent does not voluntarily bring about a different event-particular make it the case that the agent is morally responsible in the actual sequence? (Fischer 1994: 131–59; see also, Kane 1985: 60 and 1996a: 107–15.) To suppose that this is possible would be to believe in alchemy! Surely, in the Frankfurt-type cases, an agent is, intuitively speaking, morally responsible for bringing about an event-particular, and yet he does not have access to an alternative scenario in which he *voluntarily* brings about a different event-particular. So the Frankfurt-type cases are not best construed as cases of access to a different world with the same event-particular, but of *lack of access* to the *relevant* sort of alternative world. If the Frankfurt-type cases are construed in this way—as showing lack of access to the relevant alternative possibilities—then the issue about individuation of event-particulars becomes irrelevant.

To drive the point home, consider a variant on the Frankfurt-type case of Jones and Black. Here everything is as in the original Frankfurt-type example, except that if Black detects that Jones is about to choose to vote for Bush, Black will use his machine to destroy Jones's brain and thus kill him instantly. Here, again, Jones freely chooses to vote for Gore and does vote for Gore (in the normal way). He behaves just as he would have behaved, had there been no device implanted in his brain. And yet he could not have brought about a different event-particular. In this case it is clear that Jones's lack of ability to bring about a different event-particular does not come from his (sole) access to another possible world in which there is the same event-particular as in the actual world; rather, it comes from his *lack of access* to another possible world of *any* sort (and thus of the *relevant* sort). If I may immodestly dub this sort of case a "Fischer-variant" on the Frankfurt-type cases, I would claim that the Fischer-variants refute (PPP1) just as effectively as the original Frankfurt-type cases. The distinctive potency of the Frankfurt-type cases consists in showing that there can be moral responsibility even in cases in which the agent *lacks* access to the appropriate alternative scenarios, and thus van Inwagen's ingenious reliance on a fine-grained method of act-individuation to defend (PPP1) is in the end misguided and irrelevant.

I conclude, then, that none of van Inwagen's arguments in defense of (PPA), (PPP1), or (PPP2) is compelling. Indeed, I believe that Frankfurt-type cases provide powerful reasons to reject theses principles, along with (PAP).

When considering (PAP), someone might object in a manner similar to the way in which Van Inwagen objected to Frankfurt's critique of (PPP1). The original case of Jones is supposed to be one in which Jones is morally responsible for his choice and his act of voting for Gore, although he lacks alternative possibilities. At this point it may be objected that, despite the initial appearance, Jones *does* have at least *some* alternative possibility. Although Jones cannot choose or vote

differently, he can still exhibit a different neurological pattern in his brain N*
(from the one he actually exhibits, N). I have called such an alternative possibility
a "flicker of freedom" (Fischer 1994). The flicker theorist contends that our moral
responsibility always can be traced back to some suitably placed flicker of freedom;
our responsibility is grounded in and derives from such alternative possibilities.

It seems that one can always find a flicker of freedom in the Frankfurt-type
cases insofar as they are developed as "prior-sign" cases. That is, the agent will
always at least have the power to exhibit an alternative sign. But I contend that
the mere involuntary display of some sign—such as a neurological pattern in the
brain, a blush, or a furrowed brow—is too thin a reed on which to rest moral
responsibility. The power involuntarily to exhibit a different sign seems to me to
be insufficiently robust to ground our attributions of moral responsibility.

Note that in the alternative sequence (in which Jones shows neurological pattern N*, which is indicative of an impending decision to vote for Bush), the sign
is entirely involuntary and the subsequent decision and vote are produced electronically. Thus, in the alternative sequence, Jones cannot be said to be choosing
and acting freely and similarly cannot be thought to be morally responsible for
his choice and action. If my point in connection with van Inwagen's "act-
individuation" defense of (PPP1) is correct, then this sort of alternative possibility
cannot ground ascriptions of moral responsibility. It is insufficiently robust: it
lacks "voluntary oomph."

To help to see this, imagine, just for a moment, that there are absolutely no
alternative possibilities, even the flimsy and exiguous flickers of freedom we have
recently been entertaining. An alternative-possibilities control theorist would say
that under such circumstances the relevant agent cannot be morally responsible
for his choice and action. Now add the flickers of freedom we have been considering—the power to exhibit a different neurological pattern, N*. I find it very
hard to see how adding this power can transform a situation in which there is no
moral responsibility into one in which there is moral responsibility. How can
adding a pathway along which Jones does *not* freely vote for Gore and is *not*
morally responsible for voting for Gore make it the case that Jones actually *is*
morally responsible for voting for Gore? This, again, is the "problem of alchemy."
(Fischer 1994: 141)

I believe that this problem of lack of robustness—lack of voluntary oomph—
plagues various versions of the flicker of freedom strategy or response to the
Frankfurt-type examples. For example, suppose one follows Margery Bedford Naylor (1984) in arguing that what one is "really" morally responsible for is (say)
acting "on one's own" (and not as a result of coercion, manipulation, and so
forth). Now if this is so one could say that the agent does indeed have an alternative possibility—the option of not acting on one's own in this sense. But I
would contend that this sort of alternative possibility is a mere flicker of freedom
and insufficiently robust to ground attributions of moral responsibility.

My reason is that in the alternative sequence of a Frankfurt-type case the agent would not be voluntarily choosing not to perform the action on her own. That is, it is true that (in the alternative sequence of a Frankfurt-type case) the agent would not be choosing and acting on her own, but these features of the sequence would not be voluntarily adopted by him—they would be entirely fortuitous, from the point of view of his deliberations. It would then seem to me that the sort of alternative possibility identified by Naylor lacks voluntary oomph.

3. A DILEMMA FOR THE PROPONENT OF FRANKFURT-TYPE EXAMPLES

An important challenge to the position I have sketched (against the flicker theorist) has been presented by such philosophers as David Widerker (1995 a and b), Robert Kane (1985: 51; 1996a: 142–45)[6], Carl Ginet (1996), and Keith Wyma (1997). I will boil down the various versions of the argument into the following. It begins with a dilemma: either the proponent of the Frankfurt-type examples is presupposing the truth of causal determinism or indeterminism.

Let us start with the presupposition that causal determinism obtains. Now it appears as though the relevant agent, Jones, in the previous example, cannot choose or do otherwise (cannot choose at T2 to vote for Bush or vote for Bush at T3) because the "counterfactual intervener," the liberal neurosurgeon Black, can know, given the prior sign exhibited by Jones at T1, that Jones will indeed choose to vote for Gore at T2. If Jones were to choose at T2 to vote for Bush, the prior sign would have had to be different; thus, Jones cannot at T2 choose to vote for Bush at T3. But the problem is that the contention that Jones is morally responsible for choosing to vote for Gore and actually voting for Gore is put in doubt, given the assumption of causal determinism. That is, if causal determinism is explicitly presupposed, it does not seem that someone could say that Jones is obviously morally responsible for his actual choice and action, in a context in which the relationship between causal determinism and moral responsibility are at issue. To do so would appear to beg the question against the incompatibilist.

Now suppose that indeterminism (of a certain relevant sort) obtains. Under this supposition it would not be dialectically inappropriate to claim that Jones is morally responsible for his actual choice at T2 to vote for Gore and his vote for Gore at T3. But now the contention that Jones cannot choose at T2 to vote for Bush at T3 is called into question, because there is no deterministic relationship between the prior sign exhibited by Jones at T1 and Jones's subsequent choice at

T2. So, if we consider the time just prior to T2, everything about the past can be just as it is consistently with Jones's choosing at *T2* to vote for Bush at *T3*. Someone might think that if it takes some time for Jones to make the choice, Black can intervene to prevent the completion of the choice; but then Jones will still have the possibility of "beginning to make the choice," which is surely more robust than a mere flicker of freedom (say an involuntary twitch, blush, or neurological pattern). After all, beginning to make a choice is a voluntary undertaking (even if it is truncated through no fault of one's own)—it presumably has sufficient voluntary oomph to ground ascriptions of moral responsibility.

The proponents of the Frankfurt-type examples contend that they are non-question-begging cases in which an agent is morally responsible for her choice and action and yet the agent has no sufficiently robust alternative possibilities. But the counter-argument of Widerker, Kane, Ginet, and Wyma appears to show that the examples in question are neither uncontroversial cases in which the agent is morally responsible for his choice and subsequent behavior nor cases in which the agent lacks the alternative possibilities. This clearly important argument has been influential. Indeed, in a recent article Ted A. Warfield (1996: 221) claims that the rejection of the Frankfurt-type examples (as cases in which an agent is morally responsible yet lacks alternative possibilities) is "increasingly common."

4. A Reply on Behalf of the Proponent of the Frankfurt-type Examples

Despite this rising chorus I still remain convinced that the Frankfurt-type cases help to establish that moral responsibility does not require alternative possibilities.

4.1. The Assumption of Causal Determinism

Begin with the first horn of the dilemma: the assumption that causal determinism obtains. I agree that one cannot now simply and precipitously conclude, from consideration of the examples, that the agent is morally responsible for his choice and behavior. But in any case this is not the way I would have proceeded; I never have envisaged a simple "one-step" argument to the conclusion that (say) Jones is morally responsible for his choice and action. Rather, I employ the Frankfurt-type examples as the first (but obviously important) step of a slightly more complex argument to the conclusion that Jones is morally responsible for his choice and action (despite lacking alternative possibilities).

The argument goes as follows. First, one carefully considers the Frankfurt-type cases. Upon reflection, I believe that one should conclude that in these cases the lack of alternative possibilities does not in itself ground a claim that the agent is not morally responsible for his choice and action. In other words, I think that the examples make highly plausible the preliminary conclusion that *if* Jones is not morally responsible for his choice and action, this is *not* simply because he lacks alternative possibilities. After all, everything that has any causal (or any other kind of) influence on Jones would be exactly the same, if we "subtracted" Black entirely from the scene. And Jones's moral responsibility would seem to be supervenient on what has an influence or impact on him in some way.

So the relevant (preliminary) conclusion is, if Jones is not morally responsible for his choice and action, the reason is not simply that he lacks alternative possibilities. And it does *not* appear to beg the question to come to this conclusion, even if causal determinism obtains. The first step is to argue, based on the Frankfurt-type examples, that intuitively it is plausible that alternative possibilities are irrelevant to ascriptions of moral responsibility. One is supposed to see the irrelevance of alternative possibilities simply by reflecting on the examples. I do not know how to *prove* the irrelevance thesis, but I find it extremely plausible intuitively. When Louis Armstrong was asked for the definition of jazz, he allegedly said, "If you have to ask, you ain't never gonna know." I am inclined to say the same thing here: if you have to ask *how* the Frankfurt-type cases show the irrelevance of alternative possibilities to moral responsibility, "you ain't never gonna know."

The *second* step in the argument consists in asking whether causal determinism *in itself and apart from ruling out alternative possibilities* threatens moral responsibility. I have considered various possible reasons why someone might think that causal determinism does threaten moral responsibility in itself and apart from ruling out alternative possibilities, and I have come to the conclusion that it is not plausible to accept any of these reasons.[7] It seems to me that this two-stage argument is highly plausible and does *not* beg the question against the incompatibilist, even on the assumption of causal determinism. Thus I believe that the use of the "prior-sign" cases can be defended against the charge of begging the question.

4.2. The Assumption of Indeterminism

Let us now move to the second horn of the dilemma: the assumption of indeterminism. Here I admit that the prior-sign cases will not describe an agent who lacks alternative possibilities. But I want to sketch three strategies for modifying the Frankfurt-type case to address this difficulty.[8]

4.2.1. *Hunt's Approach*

A Frankfurt-type case which works as the ones sketched previously in this essay is a "prior-sign" case. But recall that the original "Frankfurt-type" case was presented by John Locke in *An Essay Concerning Human Understanding*. It is important to see that there can be *another* sort of Frankfurt-type case, which takes its cue more closely from Locke's example; I shall refer to such a case, developed by David Hunt (2000), as a "blockage case." Note that in Locke's example the door to the room is actually locked *no matter whether the man is inclined to choose to stay in the room or not*. Imagine, then, that although the actual neural processes in one's brain (one is here supposing that the mind supervenes on the brain) take place indeterministically, *all other neural pathways are blocked.*[9] This is a way of bringing the locked door, the blockage, into the brain. Just as in the case of the locked door, the pathways are actually blocked; in contrast to the structure of the prior-sign cases, the pathways' being blocked does not depend on prior features of Jones. This, then, is a different way of solving precisely the problem Frankfurt sought to solve—one that more simply and naturally takes its cue from Locke. And, importantly, it does *not* appear to introduce alternative possibilities.

4.2.2. *Mele and Robb's Approach*

Here is a second way of modifying the Frankfurt-type cases so that they (allegedly) "work" in a causally indeterministic context. Hunt's strategy involves "blockage" that is insensitive to prior signs. The second strategy, developed by Alfred Mele and David Robb, involves two simultaneously operating sequences, one of which is indeterministic, the other of which is causally deterministic; the indeterministic sequence actually leads to the result in question, but the deterministic sequence (the operation of which is insensitive to prior signs) would have issued in the same sort of result, if the indeterministic sequence had not. Mele and Robb (1998) develop their ingenious example as follows (changing our cast of characters slightly):

> At $T1$, Black initiates a certain deterministic process P in Bob's brain with the intention of thereby causing Bob to decide at $T2$ (an hour later, say) to steal Ann's car. The process, which is screened off from Bob's consciousness, will deterministically culminate in Bob's deciding at $T2$ to steal Ann's car unless he decides on his own at $T2$ to steal it or is incapable at $T2$ of making a decision (because, *e.g.*, he is dead by $T2$.) (Black is unaware that it is open to Bob to decide on his own at $T2$ to steal the car; he is confident that P will cause Bob to decide as he wants Bob to decide.) The process is in no way sensitive to any "sign" of what Bob will decide. As it happens, at $T2$ Bob decides on his own to

steal the car, on the basis of his own indeterministic deliberation about whether to steal it, and his decision has no deterministic cause. But if he had not just then decided on his own to steal it, P would have deterministically issued, at $T2$, in his deciding to steal it. Rest assured that P in no way influences the indeterminstic decision-making process that actually issues in Bob's decision. (ibid.: 101–2)

The actual sequence in the Mele/Robb example is indeterministic, and yet the agent could not have done otherwise due to the unfolding of a deterministic causal sequence that preemptively overdetermines the actual decision. And the relevant agent seems to be morally responsible for his decision and behavior.

4.2.3. *Stump's Approach*

The third strategy for modifying the Frankfurt-type cases to accommodate inde-terministic contexts is developed by Eleonore Stump (1990, 1995, 1996a, 1999a, which is a response to Goetz 1999). Stump assumes that there is some sort of one-many correlation between a mental act or state and the firings of neurons in the brain:

> When I suddenly recognize my daughter's face across a crowded room, that one mental act of recognition, which feels sudden, even instantaneous, to me, is correlated with many neural firings as information from the retina is sent through the optic nerve, relayed through the lateral geniculate nucleus of the thalamus, processed in various parts of the occipital cortex, which take account of figure, motion, orientation in space, and color, and then processed further in cortical association areas. Only when the whole sequence of neural firings is completed, do I have the mental act of recognizing my daughter. Whatever neural firings are correlated with an act of will or intellect, I take it that in this case, as in all others, the correlation between the mental act and the firing of the relevant neurons is a one-many relation. (Stump 1999a: 417)

On Stump's approach, it is crucial that if the firing of the whole neural se-quence correlated with a mental act is not completed, the result is not some truncated or incomplete mental act (say, the beginning of a choice or decision). It is no mental act at all:

> If the neural sequence correlated with my recognizing my daughter's face across a crowded room is interrupted at the level of the thalamus, say, then I will have no mental act having to do with seeing her. I won't for example, think to myself, "For a moment there, I thought I saw my daughter, but now I'm not sure." I won't have a sensation of almost but not quite seeing her. I won't have a premonition that I was about to see her, and then I mysteriously just don't see her. I will simply have no mental act regarding recognition of her at all. (ibid.: 417–18)

Let us suppose now that a mental event is identical to a series of neural firings.[10] A particular mental event, say, a choice, can be assumed to result from an indeterministic process. Further, a counterfactual intervener can be associated with the agent who could notice (in an alternative scenario) that a different neural sequence was beginning, and could then interrupt it before it can be completed. If Black, the counterfactually intervening liberal neurosurgeon, did interrupt a neural sequence that was beginning (and which is such that, if it were completed, it would constitute, or correlate with, a decision to vote for Bush), Jones would *not* (according to Stump) have engaged in the mental act of *beginning to make a decision*. Jones would have *no* mental act, just as Stump would not have begun to recognize her daughter, if the sequence of neural firings beginning in her retina had been terminated in the thalamus (ibid.: 418).

Thus, in Stump's version of the Frankfurt-type cases, the agent's choice is not causally determined, and it is also true that the agent cannot have chosen (or behaved) differently from how she actually chooses (and behaves). And yet it seems entirely plausible that the agent is morally responsible for her choice and behavior in these cases.

Despite the force and influence of the argument (presented by Widerker, Kane, Ginet, and Wyma) against the contention that in the Frankfurt-type cases the agent is morally responsible although he has no alternative possibilities, there is an attractive strategy of response. Even if causal determinism is true, it does not appear to be question-begging to use the cases as part of a two-stage argument (rather than an argument that simply assumes that the relevant agents are morally responsible in the cases). And if causal determinism is false (in certain ways), it still seems (at least at first blush) to be possible to construct versions of the Frankfurt-type cases in which it is plausible to say that the agent is morally responsible and yet lacks alternative possibilities.

5. ANALYSIS OF THE INDETERMINISTIC CASES

It is contentious, however, whether the indeterministic cases presented by such philosophers as Hunt, Mele and Robb, and Stump really work. Let us start by focusing on Hunt's approach. Recall that Hunt envisages a case in which the neural events resulting in the relevant choice are indeterministic, and yet all *other* neural pathways in the brain are "blocked" (as in Locke's "locked-door" example). The question could now be expressed as follows: Does the agent have access to a scenario in which his neural path makes contact with or "bumps up against" the blockage? If so, it would seem that the alternative possibility in question does after all exist, because if the neural path "bumps up against" the blockage, then presumably the agent is no longer the author of the subsequent act (and is not morally responsible for it).

But how exactly can the agent (or his neural events) bump up against the blockage? It would seem that access to the blockage would require an intermediate set of neural events, different from the actual neural events, that is—as it were, a "bridge" between the actual neural process and the blockage. (In Locke's example, the agent would have to walk over to the door and try to open it.) But even these intermediate events are presumed to be blocked in Hunt's example. So it may seem that Hunt has indeed provided an example of the required sort, that is, one in which the agent is morally responsible and yet does not have *any* alternative possibilities.

But the example is difficult to imagine (and thus properly to evaluate). If casual indeterminism obtains in the actual neural pathway, how exactly can it be the case that the agent does not have access to events consisting in bumping up against any of the barriers (intermediate or terminal)? And if the agent really does not have access to any such "bumping" events, how can it be the case that causal determinism does not actually obtain?

Consider the following somewhat rough analogy. Suppose one is driving on a freeway, with some space (as is safe!) between one's car and other vehicles. But imagine also that all of the off-ramps to the freeway are entirely bottled up with traffic, right from the beginnings of the off-ramps. The spaces between the cars represents that one's actual driving on the freeway corresponds to causal indeterminism, and the off-ramps' being blocked points to the lack of alternative possibilities.

But now someone will ask why, if there is indeed space between the vehicles, the driver cannot at least begin to guide his car toward an off-ramp. And if such possibilities of changing direction exist, then these would seem to be alternatives of the relevant sort, that is, characterized by sufficient voluntary oomph. So the example needs to be changed so that one is driving along on the freeway absolutely "up against" the bumpers of the cars in front and back, but not being pushed or pulled in any way by those cars. Of course, if one were being pushed or pulled along, then this would correspond to actual-sequence causal determination. The idea is that it at least seems possible to be driving in such a manner that one is not being pushed or pulled by the contiguous cars and yet (because of the positions of the cars) one does not have the power to change the direction of the car at all. But here again there seems to be the alternative possibility that involves pressure exerted on the contiguous cars. That is, the "bumping events" seem to be ineradicable features of the analogy, and thus it is hard to see how completely to eradicate the "bumping events" from the brain. (For another sort of reply to the blockage strategy, see Robert Kane 2000a.)

David Hunt has also suggested that the context of God's foreknowledge of future events is relevantly similar to Frankfurt-type examples.[11] Let us suppose that God exists within the same time framework as humans do, is essentially omniscient, and can know future contingent truths. Let us further assume that causal indeterminism obtains. (Of course, each of these assumptions is contentious, as is their combination.) I believe that it follows from the conjunction of these assumptions (suitably interpreted) that human agents cannot choose or do otherwise; and yet (given certain assumptions about God) God's knowledge plays absolutely no role in human choices and actions. Just as with the "counterfactual intervener" in a Frankfurt-type case, one could "subtract" God from the situation and everything that has a causal impact on the agent's choices and behavior would be exactly the same. If all the preceding is correct, then the context of God's foreknowledge would seem to be one in which an agent could be held morally responsible for her choice and behavior and yet have no alternative possibilities. Here the problem of the apparent ineradicability of the "bumping" events is eliminated, but of course the package of assumptions necessary to do the trick is controversial.

To recapitulate, it seems to me that both the approaches of Hunt and Mele and Robb are promising, but that they posit something contentious: that the actual sequence can be indeterministic and nevertheless absolutely no alternative possibilities exist (even including bumping events). This problem comes out in Mele and Robb at the point at which they contend that the deterministic process P "in no way influences" the indeterministic process X that actually issues in the decision, and yet that the agent has absolutely no alternative possibility. How exactly is it possible for P to "neutralize" all nonactual neural pathways without issuing in causal determination in the actual pathway? I do not think it is obvious that the critiques are decisive, but on the other hand it is unclear whether we have here plausible Frankfurt-type examples that work in indeterministic contexts. God's foreknowledge (envisaged in a certain way) *may* do the trick. Also, if Stump is correct, then "bumping" events may well be insufficiently robust to ground moral responsibility attributions, because the neural bumping events would be insufficient for a mental event with voluntary oomph.[12]

Recently Derk Pereboom has presented an intriguing version of the Frankfurt-type examples which is promising insofar as it appears to work in an indeterministic context. That is, this sort of indeterministic example involves alternative possibilities that *clearly* lack sufficient robustness to justify attributions of moral responsibility. Here is Pereboom's case:

> Joe is considering whether to claim a tax deduction for the substantial local registration fee that he paid when he bought a house. He knows that claiming the deduction is illegal, that he probably won't be caught, and that if he is, he can convincingly plead ignorance. Suppose he has a very powerful but not al-

ways overriding desire to advance his self-interest no matter what the cost to others, and no matter whether advancing his self-interest involves illegal activity. Furthermore, he is a libertarian free agent. But his psychology is such that the only way that in this situation he could choose not to engage in the tax evasion is for moral reasons. His psychology is not, for example, such that he could decide not to evade taxes for no reason or simply on a whim. In fact, it is causally necessary for his deciding not to evade taxes in this situation that a moral reason occur to him with a certain force. A moral reason can occur to him with that force either involuntarily or as a result of his voluntary activity (e.g. by his willing to consider it, or by his seeking out a vivid presentation of such a reason). But a moral reason occurring to him with such force is not causally sufficient for his deciding not to evade taxes. If a moral reason were to occur to him with that force, Joe could, with his libertarian free will, either choose to act on it or act against it (without the intervener's device in place). But to ensure that he decide to evade taxes, a neuroscientist now implants a device which, were it to sense a moral reason occurring with the specified force, would electronically stimulate his brain so that he would decide to evade taxes. In actual fact, no moral reason occurs to him with such force, and he chooses to evade taxes while the device remains idle.[13]

In Pereboom's version of the Frankfurt-type examples, the actual sequence is indeterministic, and the alternative possibility in question—the occurrence to the agent of a moral reason with a sufficient force—does not appear to be sufficiently robust to ground ascriptions of moral responsibility. This is in part because the occurrence of such a reason is not sufficient in itself for Joe to begin to *act* in accordance with it. The possibility of the mere occurrence of a reason (of a certain force) to an individual does not yet ground a claim of the possession of alternative possibilities sufficiently robust to ground moral responsibility. Thus Pereboom's example is promising as a way of both securing actual-sequence indeterminism and alternative possibilities without oomph.

6. A REPLY ON BEHALF OF THE FLICKER THEORIST: ESCAPABILITY OF AUTHORSHIP/RESPONSIBILITY

The critic of the Frankfurt-type examples has (at least) one more card to play. Consider, for example, the following remarks of Michael McKenna (1997):

> [W]hat intuitively drives [the proponent of the alternative-possibilities requirement] is the kind of control needed in order for us to avoid being the author

of a *particular* act and thus avoid being responsible for the production of *that* particular action . . . It is a matter of holding people accountable for what they do only if they can avoid any blame or punishment that might fall upon them for performing those very particular actions which they do perform. . . . (ibid.: 73–74)

McKenna elaborates as follows:

The issue . . . here is whether the will . . . places *my* stamp upon the world, and whether *it is up to me . . . to have that particular stamp or some other as my mark upon the world.* In the Frankfurt-type cases the alternatives are, either doing what one does of one's own intention, or being coerced into performing the same kind of action against one's will. These alternatives do seem to be quite impoverished; however, they mean all the difference between one's doing something of one's own will, and one's not doing that kind of thing of one's own will . . . What more fundamental kind of control can there be here other than the control for one to either have a particular will or not have it? (ibid.: 74–75)

McKenna is claiming that even in the Frankfurt-type cases, the relevant agent has a significant and robust power: the power either to be the author of his action or not, and thus the power to be morally responsible for his action or not. A similar point is made in recent article by Keith Wyma (1997). Wyma begins with an example which suggests that many of us experienced something like a Frankfurt-type example as we were growing up:

When I was four years old and learning to ride a bicycle, I reached a point where my father decided I no longer needed training wheels. But he still worried that I might fall. So on my first attempt "without a net," he ran alongside as I pedaled. His arms encircled without touching me, his hands resting lightly upon me, but not holding me upright. I rode straight ahead. My father did not push or guide me, but if I had faltered or veered suddenly to the side, he would have tightened his grip, keeping me vertical and on track. After finally braking to a stop, I was jubilant but somewhat hesitant over whether I should be. I wondered, had I really ridden my bike on my own? . . . Was the triumph of riding straight down the street mine or not? (ibid.: 57)

Wyma goes on to argue for an intuition very similar to McKenna's. On Wyma's view, moral responsibility requires a certain kind of "leeway." And this leeway is specified by what Wyma calls the "Principle of Possibly Passing the Buck" (PPPB):

A person is morally responsible for something she has done, *A*, only if she has failed to do something she could have done, *B*, such that doing *B* would have rendered her morally non-responsible for *A*. (ibid.: 59)

Of course, in a Frankfurt-type case the relevant agent would not be morally responsible in the alternative sequence; Jones would not be morally responsible for voting for Gore, in the circumstance in which Black's device were triggered. Thus Wyma has apparently identified a significant sort of "leeway," even in the Frankfurt-type examples. At the end of his article, Wyma returns to the analogy with which he started:

> I believe the bike riding triumph *was* mine, because even though I could not have fallen or crashed while my father hovered protectively over me, I could still have faltered enough that he would have had to steady me; and because I had leeway to falter but did not do so, the success of riding was truly mine. *PPPB* vindicates a similar kind of leeway as being necessary for ascriptions of moral responsibility. (ibid.: 68)

Additionally, Michael Otsuka has recently defended a principle similar to Wyma's Principle of Possibly Passing the Buck. Otsuka calls his principle the "Principle of Avoidable Blame":

> One is blameworthy for performing an act of a given type only if one could instead have behaved in a manner for which one would have been entirely blameless. (Otsuka 1998: 688)[14]

Thus, all three defenders of the alternative possibilities control requirement seem to be pointing to the same sort of alternative possibility, they claim is present quite generally, and hence in the Frankfurt-type examples. This is the freedom to "pass the buck" or "escape" or "avoid" moral responsibility. And it seems that this freedom is present in all of the modifications of the Frankfurt-type examples presented here. One might say that these theorists are seeking, perhaps with some success, to fan the flickers of freedom.[15]

7. A FURTHER REPLY ON BEHALF OF THE PROPONENT OF THE FRANKFURT-TYPE EXAMPLES

But I believe that problems similar to those of the earlier defenses of the alternative-possibilities control requirement also plague the new approaches. Recall that the problem with saying that the possibility of exhibiting a different prior sign or indicator of future decision (and action) grounds moral responsibility is that the envisaged possibility is too exiguous and flimsy. The displaying of such a sign would not even be voluntary behavior. How could moral responsibility rest on such a delicate foundation?

Now it might be thought that the possibility of avoiding authorship or the possibility of avoiding moral responsibility would be a more substantial basis for moral responsibility. But I believe there are similar problems here. Note that in the alternative sequence in a Frankfurt-type case the agent would indeed be avoiding, say, moral responsibility, but she would be doing so "accidentally." The agent would *not* be *voluntarily* avoiding responsibility. The suggestion that avoiding responsibility is a sufficiently robust basis for moral responsibility may derive some of its plausibility from the fact that in a typical context in which we would say that someone has avoided, say, blameworthiness, he would have performed some voluntary action. Typically, the relevant facts about the various paths available to the agent would be accessible to him, and he would voluntarily choose a right action (rather than a morally objectionable one). Here we would say that the agent avoided blameworthiness; but this is a very different sort of context from the Frankfurt-type cases. In the Frankfurt-type cases, the agent does not choose to be morally responsible rather than not—these issues play no role in his deliberations. And in the alternative scenario in a Frankfurt-type case, the agent does not choose to escape responsibility or voluntarily choose anything that implies her escaping responsibility.

To isolate this point out more clearly, note that in the alternative scenario in a Frankfurt-type case the agent does not deliberate about whether or not to embrace moral responsibility. So issues about whether or not to be morally responsible play no explicit role in his deliberations. Further, they play no "implicit" role either. They might play an implicit role in the sort of context discussed above, in which an agent has internalized certain norms on the basis of which he chooses to do what he takes to be the right action. If he successfully avoids blameworthiness here, it is partly attributable to his having internalized norms the relevant community shares. Given these norms, the agent can reasonably expect to escape blame, if he chooses as he does. But in the alternative scenarios in the Frankfurt-type cases issues about moral responsibility obviously do not play an implicit role of this sort.

To the extent that issues pertaining to moral responsibility play neither an explicit nor an implicit role, I shall say that moral responsibility is not "internally related" to the agent's behavior in the alternative sequence of a Frankfurt-type case. And my point is that it is very plausible that moral responsibility must be so related to the agent's behavior, in order for the alternative possibility in question to be sufficiently robust to ground ascriptions of moral responsibility.

Of course, I do not accept the alternative-possibilities control model of moral responsibility. But my contention is that, *if* you do buy into this traditional picture, then you should *also* acknowledge that the alternative possibilities must be *of a certain sort*—they must be sufficiently robust. (I developed this point in my discussion of van Inwagen's defense of PPP1 earlier.) This same point has been highlighted by a philosopher with a very different orientation from mine: Robert Kane (1985: 60, 1996a: 107–15), a libertarian who believes that alternative possibilities are required for moral responsibility. Kane emphasizes what he calls the "dual" or "plural" voluntariness (and responsibility) conditions on moral responsibility: the relevant alternative possibilities—that is, alternative possibilities sufficiently robust to ground moral responsibility—must themselves involve voluntary behavior (for which the agent is morally responsible). On Kane's picture, it is not enough that an agent have *just any sort of alternative possibility;* it must be an alternative in which the agent acts voluntarily and is morally responsible. Similarly, I would contend that the relevant alternative possibilities must contain voluntary, responsible behavior in which moral responsibility is internally related to the agent's behavior. My suggestion, then, is that the new defenses of the alternative-possibilities control requirement (presented by McKenna, Otsuka, and Wyma) fall prey to the same sort of problem that afflicted earlier such defenses: the alternatives they postulate are not sufficiently robust.

In my early essay, "Responsibility and Control" (1982), I argued that the critic of the Frankfurt-type case mixes up "possibility" and "ability" in a certain way. That is, I pointed out that even if another event (or set of events) occurs in the alternative sequence of a Frankfurt-type case, it does not follow that the agent has the *ability* (in the relevant sense) to bring about this alternative event (or set of events). I believe that the recent defenses of alternative-possibilities control simply reinscribe the same general problem. The lack of "internal relatedness" of moral responsibility to the events in the alternative sequence points to the fact that the agent lacks the relevant sort of ability, even if there exists the possibility of something different happening. So, even if there exists the possibility that the agent not be the author of his action (or avoid moral responsibility), it does not follow that the agent has the ability (in the relevant sense) to avoid authorship (or responsibility). It is a simple point that has played a crucial role in discussions of indeterministic conceptions of control and moral responsibility: the mere possibility of a different event's occurring does *not* entail that the agent has the *ability* to do otherwise. The point applies equally in the context of the Frankfurt-type examples.

Return to Wyma's striking claim about his early bike-riding experience, "I believe the bike riding triumph *was* mine, because even though I could not have fallen or crashed while my father hovered protectively over me, I could still have faltered enough that he would have had to steady me; and because I had leeway to falter but did not do so, the success of riding was truly mine" (Wyma 1997: 68). Whereas we could quibble endlessly about details of these sorts of examples, the *intuitive point* seems clear: it is *not* the possibility of faltering slightly that makes the young Wyma's bike-riding triumph truly his. This has to do *not* with whether he could have faltered slightly, but with how he rode the bike—how he moved the pedals, balanced, and so forth, and by what sort of causal process this all took place.

8. The "Nonstandard Response" to the Frankfurt-type Cases

What might be called the "standard" critique of the Frankfurt-type cases concedes that the relevant agent does not have available the sort of alternative possibility typically associated with responsibility, but claims that nevertheless one can find a suitable alternative possibility, even in the Frankfurt-type examples. The "nonstandard" response to the examples claims that even in the Frankfurt-type cases the agent has available a robust alternative possibility of precisely the sort normally associated with moral responsibility. So, for example, in the Frankfurt-type example with which we began (in which Jones chooses to vote for Gore and votes for Gore on his own but Black is poised to intervene should Jones show any sign of choosing to vote for Bush), the nonstandard response claims that Jones *does* have the ability (in the relevant sense) to vote for Bush (Lamb 1993; Campbell 1997; for replies, see Fischer and Hoffman 1994 and Mc-Kenna 1998a).

The basic claim of the nonstandard response is that insofar as Black's device does not play any *actual* role in Jones's deliberations or actions, it should be "subtracted" when one is considering whether Jones has a genuine ability to choose and do otherwise (to choose to vote for Bush and to vote for Bush). Put in terms of possible-worlds semantics, the compatibilist in general insists that the alternative possible worlds that establish that the agent has a certain power or ability can *differ* in various ways from the actual world. So, if a given agent does X rather than Y in the actual world, but it is intuitively true that the agent could have done Y instead, one looks for a possible world that can *differ* in certain ways from the actual world prior to the time in question in which the agent does indeed do Y. Given that Black's device does not actually play any role, the nonstandard theorist will say that it can be absent from a possible world that is nevertheless relevant to whether Jones actually has the power to choose to vote for Gore and the power to vote for Gore.

I have difficulty sympathizing with this response. First, note that it would seem to imply that the man who is, unbeknownst to him, locked in the room in Locke's example *can* leave the room. Or, similarly, if one has secretly been chained to one's desk (perhaps while asleep), it follows that one *can* leave one's office, despite the chains, as long as one is unaware of the chains. Also, if one has been struck by paralysis but is not yet aware of the paralysis, the nonstandard approach would seem to imply that the paralysis is no obstacle. But these results just seem very implausible.

I would offer the following diagnosis of the confusion of the nonstandard response. I believe that the nonstandard theorist is conflating general abilities with the sort of ability that corresponds to J. L. Austin's "all-in sense of 'can'," or "can in the particular circumstances." One may have a general ability without having the latter sort of ability, insofar as one does not have the opportunity to exerecise the general ability. Whereas I would certainly concede that the agent in a Frankfurt-type case has the relevant general ability, I would deny that he can under the particular circumstances choose and do otherwise. So, whereas Jones certainly has the general ability to choose to vote Republican and to do so, he cannot under the particular circumstances choose to vote Republican and vote Republican. It is the particularized notion of ability, and not the general one, that is typically associated with moral responsibility; certainly, the particularized notion plays a role in the Principle of Alternative Possiblities.

9. Some Putative Implications of the Frankfurt-type Cases

There has (obviously) been considerable ink spilled over the Frankfurt-type examples. Recently some philosophers have explored some previously unnoticed (or insufficiently noticed) aspects of the examples. The Frankfurt-type examples purport to be contexts in which an agent can be morally responsible, even though she lacks alternative possibilities. But consider the following argument, which has been presented and discussed recently by David Widerker (1991a), David Copp (1997), and Ishtiyaque Haji (1993).[16] Suppose someone does something that is intuitively "bad," such as lying just to bolster his reputation. If this act is blameworthy, then it must be wrong. And if it is wrong, it must be the case that the agent should have done something else instead (where this could include simply refraining from doing anything). But "ought implies can," so if the agent should have done something else instead, then he must have been able to do something else. Thus, if the agent had no alternative possibilities (and thus could *not* have done anything else), then his act of lying cannot be considered blameworthy.

This sort of argument threatens the idea that an agent can be genuinely blameworthy in a context in which he has no alternative possibilities. Insofar as an account of moral responsibility will certainly need to accommodate agents' blameworthiness on some occasions, the argument casts into doubt whether an adequate "actual-sequence" account of moral responsibility can be given.[17]

The argument is disturbing, and worthy of more careful attention than I can give it here. Instead, I briefly suggest various ways of responding to the argument. One might deny the maxim that "ought implies can." Various philosophers have rejected it on grounds independent of considerations pertinent to the Frankfurt-type cases. Typically these philosophers have been motivated to give it up in light of reflection on the logic of moral dilemmas.[18] Another approach is suggested by Haji, who rejects the contention that if an act is blameworthy then it is "objectively wrong." That is, the argument presupposes that blameworthiness is connected to objective wrongness, whereas Haji believes that blameworthiness is linked only with subjective wrongness. So, on Haji's view, if an agent is blameworthy for performing an action, it need not be the case that the action was wrong, only (roughly) that the agent believed it to be wrong (and nevertheless did it).[19]

My own inclination here is to reject the "ought implies can" maxim, according to which, if an agent ought to do X, then he can do X. But why exactly should one accept this maxim? That is, what justification could be offered for it? It is most natural, I think, to say that it is valid because if it were not, then there could be cases in which an agent ought to do X but in fact cannot do X (and never could do X). Thus, given the connection between its being the case that an agent ought to do X and the agent's being blameworthy for not doing X, there could be cases in which an agent is blameworthy for not X-ing and yet he cannot X. And this seems unfair.

But I argued earlier that some Frankfurt-type omissions cases are relevantly similar to Frankfurt-type cases with respect to actions. That is, there are cases in which an agent is morally responsible for not X-ing although he cannot in fact X. Some of these are cases in which an agent is blameworthy for not X-ing and yet he cannot X. In fact, I believe that anyone who accepts the Frankfurt-type action cases must accept that there are such omissions examples. Thus, precisely the basic intuitions elicited by the Frankfurt-type cases show that the most natural justification of the "ought implies can" maxim is faulty. It is therefore not ad hoc for anyone who accepts the standard interpretation of the Frankfurt-type cases to reject the "ought-implies can" maxim.[20]

10. AN ACTUAL-SEQUENCE APPROACH TO MORAL RESPONSIBILITY

In my view, the Frankfurt-type cases provide very strong reasons to think that moral responsibility does not require alternative possibilities. Of course, they fall short of providing *decisive* reason to abandon the Principle of Alternative Possiblities. But they should make a reasonable person abandon an endless attempt seeking to identify some sort of alternative possibility and instead set about identifying what about the actual sequence of events leading to an action (or omission or consequence) grounds ascriptions of moral responsibility.

The lesson of the Frankfurt-type cases is that in assessing moral responsibility we should focus on the properties of the actual sequence of events leading to the behavior in question. Of course it does not follow straightforwardly that causal determinism is indeed compatible with moral responsibility. It is still possible to argue for "actual-sequence incompatibilism"—the view that causal determinism rules out moral responsibility quite apart from ruling out alternative possibilities.[21]

My position here is that the argument for the incompatibility of causal determinism and alternative possibilities is *considerably stronger* than the argument that causal determinism rules out moral responsibility *directly* (that is, apart from considerations pertaining to alternative possibilities). I believe that reasonable people, not already committed to a particular position on the the free will debate, would find it highly plausible that causal determinism rules out alternative possibilities. As pointed out previously, the argument here proceeds from such plausible principles of common sense as the Principle of the Fixity of the Past and the Principle of the Fixity of the Natural Laws. In contrast, I do not see that any considerations would move a reasonable and fair-minded person not already committed to a particular position on the free will debate, to believe that it is highly plausible that causal determinism rules out alternative possibilities *directly*.[22]

Now I do not wish to contend that considerations cannot be invoked which claim that causal determination in the actual sequence rules out moral responsibility directly (and thus not by ruling out alternative possibilities). But I believe that these considerations do not have the broad appeal of those that seem to show that causal determinism rules out alternative possibilities. Further, given that there are strong motivations toward compatibilism between causal determinism and moral responsibility—especially the desire to protect our status as morally responsible agents from esoteric scientific discoveries about the form of the equations that describe the universe—I am inclined to adopt "semi-compatibilism," the doctrine that causal determinism is compatible with moral responsibility, even if causal determinism were to rule out alternative possibilities.

Of course, there are various ways of specifying and developing an "actual-sequence" approach to moral responsibility (see Fischer 1999a). My approach contends that when one "decodes" the information embedded in the actual sequence in which there is moral responsibility, one will find a certain sort of "control." Whereas typically it is thought that control must involve alternative possibilities, I believe there are two species of control. "Regulative control" does indeed involve alternative possibilities, but "guidance control" does not; guidance control is of the sort displayed by agents in the actual sequences of Frankfurt-type examples, and, in general, by agents who are morally responsible for their behavior.

My project has been to analyze of guidance control and to show that this sort of control is compatible with moral responsibility. (See Fischer 1994 and Fischer and Ravizza 1998.) In my view, guidance control of one's behavior has two components: the behavior must issue from one's own mechanism, and this mechanism must be appropriately responsive to reasons. I have sought to provide accounts of both components, mechanism ownership and reasons-responsiveness, and I have defended the idea that guidance control, so analyzed, is compatible with causal determinism.

NOTES

This chapter builds on—and relies considerably on—previously published work. In particular, I am grateful for permission from the University of Chicago Press to reprint parts of Fischer (1999a), and from Kluwer Academic Publishers to reprint parts of (1999b).

1. Some philosophers prefer "alternate possibilities," whereas others prefer "alternative possibilities." Harry Frankfurt offers a (somewhat curmudgeonly) defense of his use of the term "alternate possibilities" in Frankfurt (1999: 372).

2. See, for example, Ginet (1966 87–104) and Ginet (1990); Wiggins (1973: 31–62), van Inwagen (1983), and Fischer (1994).

3. Bk. II, ch. 11, sec. 10.

4. This term was introduced in Fischer (1982).

5. See Fischer and Ravizza (1998: 92–122). For helpful discussions of moral responsibility for consequence-universals, see Heinaman (1986) and Rowe (1989).

6. As far as I know, Kane was the first to articulate this strategy in reply to the Frankfurt examples: Kane (1985: 51).

7. Fischer (1994: 147–54). For further discussion of this issue, see Kane (1996a: 40–43) and Mele (1996: 123–41).

8. For yet another approach, see Fischer (1995), Widerker and Katzoff (1996), Hunt (1996a), and Speak (1999).

9. I borrow this example from Hunt (2000). He develops this—and related—examples further in, "Freedom, Forekenowledge, and Frankfurt" (n.d.).

10. This supposition is just for simplicity's sake; Stump's view is compatible with other stories as to the precise relationship between mental states and brain events.

11. Hunt, working paper.

12. It should be noted that the original proponents of the "indeterminist" strategy of reply to the Frankfurt examples, such as Kane and Widerker, have attempted to respond to the challenges of Fischer, Hunt, Mele and Robb, and Stump. Kane attempts to respond to Hunt and Fischer on blockage cases in Kane (2000a). He attempts to respond to Mele and Robb in "Responsibility, Incompatibilism and Frankfurt-Style Examples," unpublished manuscript to be published in a collection edited by McKenna and Widerker, and to Stump in (Kane 2000b). Widerker attempts to respond to all three strategies in Widerker (2000a).

13. Pereboom, (2001). (Chapter 2 of the book also contains a critical discussion of the Hunt, Mele/Robb, and Stump strategies.)

14. Otsuka qualifies the principle to apply to cases in which it is not the case that everything one is capable of doing at a given point in time is blameworthy because of some previous choice for which one is to blame.

15. Thanks to Dan Speak for this phrase.

16. There is an instructive, extended discussion of these issues in Haji (1998: 42–64 and 151–67).

17. Haji has employed a similar argument to call into question whether morality itself could exist in a world without alternative possibilities: Haji (1998: 42–54).

18. For a thorough discussion, see Sinnott-Armstrong (1998), who believes that the "ought-implies-can" maxim is not an entailment but rather functions as a conversational implicature.

19. There is a critical discussion of this view in Copp (1997).

20. I thank Mark Ravizza for helping me to see this point. Note that the Widerker/Copp argument is a challenge for *any* account of moral responsibility according to which responsibility does not require alternative possibilities, not just to those accounts motivated by Frankfurt-type examples. As I pointed out in the text, consideration of the Frankfurt-type cases provides a powerful way of rejecting the Widerker/Copp argument; it is not clear that one who wishes to eschew such examples has a similarly potent response.

21. Fischer (1982) and Kane (1996a). (Despite his status as an incompatibilist, Kane agrees with me that such a strategy ultimately will not work.)

22. Fischer forthcoming.

CHAPTER 13

LIBERTARIANISM AND FRANKFURT-STYLE CASES

LAURA WADDELL EKSTROM

AMONG the sources of interest in free will—its relevance to human dignity, independence, and creativity, for instance—the most pervasive is concern over the moral responsibility of ourselves and others. How should we respond to intentionally performed wrong actions, ranging from heinous crimes to minor personal slights? Are the persons who perform such acts worthy of our condescension, blame, and punishment? Do we ourselves deserve credit for our moral and practical successes?

The answer to these questions is widely viewed as dependent upon the extent to which we can control our actions or, in other words, upon the issue of whether or not we have free will. As traditionally conceived, free will requires the ability at some time to do otherwise than one does. The incompatibilist holds that free will cannot exist in a purely deterministic world. The position of "semi-compatibilism" endorses this incompatibilist claim and so is a type of incompatibilism. However, the semi-compatibilist maintains that free will is not required for moral responsibility.

Semi-compatibilism is an intriguing position. Its primary defender, John Martin Fischer, interprets it as an advantage of the view that our status as morally responsible agents—and so our ordinary practices of praise and blame, punishment and reward—are not "held hostage" to the pronouncements of scientists regarding the fundamental nature of the universe (Fischer forthcoming). Should determinism turn out to be true, we can still be morally responsible persons.

In arguing for semi-compatibilism, Fischer speaks quite a bit about what a "reasonable and fair-minded person, not already committed to a particular position on the free will debate" would conclude (ch. 12 here, pp. 292, 306). Most of us, of course, would like to count ourselves as fair-minded and reasonable people. We come to the table, nearly all of us, as pretheoretic incompatibilists; and after we consider the relevant arguments (Fischer and I agree), that is what we should remain. The arguments for incompatibilism concerning free will and causal determinism are overwhelmingly powerful. The question, then, is whether free will *is*, as traditionally believed, or *is not*, as semi-compatibilism maintains, required for moral responsibility.

I am perfectly willing to be convinced that it is not required. But I have seen no argument, particularly in the literature on Frankfurt-type scenarios, to convince me to overturn the traditional judgment. In this chapter, I explain and defend this traditionalism.

1. ALTERNATIVE POSSIBILITIES TO WHAT?

One issue concerning free will and moral responsibility (call it Issue 1) is whether moral responsibility for an action requires ability at the time of the performance of the action to do otherwise than that action. The answer to this question is negative. In order to see this, we need not employ elaborate scenarios involving an agent who could but does not intervene in our decision process (to make us choose to perform and to perform a certain action). Simpler cases suffice. For instance, Justin deliberately jumps into a large pit out of which he cannot climb, in order to avoid helping his brother haul fallen trees from the yard, as he had earlier promised to do. Once he is in the pit and as his brother begins the work, Justin cannot do otherwise than fail to help. Yet he is a plausible candidate for blame for not doing the work as promised. Hence a narrowly construed version of the principle of alternative possibilities—(PAP$_1$): a person is morally responsible for doing X at t only if at t he could have done otherwise than X—is false.

It is unclear whether Frankfurt-style examples are designed to overturn PAP$_1$. Frankfurt himself states "the principle of alternate possibilities" in the following somewhat ambiguous form:

> (PAP)   a person is morally responsible for what he has done only if he could have done otherwise.

Frankfurt's counterexamples to PAP are supposed to elicit the judgment that the agent is morally responsible for what he does since he does it "on his own," even though his action was inevitable due to the presence of a counterfactual intervener. Unlike Peter van Inwagen, however, I am agnostic about the responsibility of the agent in the typical Frankfurt-style scenario, since such scenarios leave unstated the reigning metaphysical conditions. Van Inwagen accepts the conclusion that Frankfurt's cases overturn PAP. Yet he defends other principles linking responsibility and alternative possibilities, thus defending his responsibility-determinism incompatibilism (van Inwagen 1983).

But I think this course is misguided. Instead, like David Widerker and Robert Kane, I believe that the right response to proponents of Frankfurt-style cases as counterexamples to PAP is to take a closer look at their assumptions (Widerker 1995a and b; Kane 1985, 1996a; Ekstrom 1998b). The matter need not have anything to do with prior signs. But the question to ask is whether proponents of Frankfurt-type cases are assuming that causal determinism is true in the scenarios. If so, then the counterfactual intervener is entirely *superfluous*, for agents in deterministic scenarios cannot do otherwise than act just as they do and could not ever have acted or decided otherwise. It is a mistake, then, for the libertarian to grant that the agent in a Frankfurt-type scenario is responsible; one ought to remain agnostic until the metaphysical presuppositions of the example are made explicit. And for the compatibilist to assume that the agent is morally responsible under the assumption of determinism is question-begging in a context in which the relation between moral responsibility and alternative possibilities is at issue.

One may attempt to rebut the charge of question-begging against a deterministically specified Frankfurt-type scenario by claiming that what is shown by such a scenario is the following: "*if* Jones is not morally responsible for his choice and action, this is *not* simply because he lacks alternative possibilities"[1] (See Fischer's essay in this volume, ch. 12). But it is entirely unclear how the scenario by itself is supposed to demonstrate this conclusion. Nothing about the case presents a diagnosis of the agent's hypothetical nonresponsibility. In order to test a principle stating a necessary condition for moral responsibility, the example, in fact, is supposed to elicit the judgment that the agent *is* morally responsible. But it is illicit to hold on to this judgment once the (suppressed) context of causal determinism is illuminated. Fischer answers:

> One is supposed to see the irrelevance of alternative possibilities simply by reflecting on the examples. I do not know how to *prove* the irrelevance thesis, but I find it extremely plausible intuitively. When Louis Armstrong was asked for the definition of jazz, he allegedly said, "If you have to ask, you ain't never gonna know." I am inclined to say the same thing here: if you have to ask *how* the Frankfurt-type cases show the irrelevance of alternative possibilities to moral responsibility, "you ain't never gonna know." (ch. 12, p. 292)

But it is evident that the examples do not demonstrate the moral responsibility of the agent; they only assume it, inviting the reader to play along with a natural tendency to project available alternative possibilities onto others' situations. In a causally deterministic scenario, there *are* no alternative possibilities open to the agent at any point, and the mere presence of a counterfactual intervener cannot *show* us their irrelevance to moral responsibility. Thus, perhaps unlike jazz but at least regarding this case, the reason we "ain't never gonna know" is that there is nothing there to be known.

Proponents of Frankfurt-type counterexamples, alternatively, might assume causal determinism to be false in the examples. Then at some moment(s) in each scenario there is more than one physically possible future, and this fact may leave room for the agent's having, at some point, an ability to act or to decide otherwise than as he does. But if so, then it is open to the libertarian to maintain that the agent in the Frankfurt-style case is morally responsible partially in virtue of the availability of the unchosen alternative.

Suppose one constructs the Frankfurt-style scenario such that the agent can only *begin* to decide otherwise or such that a pathway consisting of certain neural events can begin but would be stopped before an alternative mental event could be completed. Then one may respond to this horn of the dilemma for Frankfurt-style cases—the one supposing the falsity of causal determinism—by arguing that such "flickers" are too flimsy a base on which to ground moral responsibility. I agree. But one cannot legitimately claim to have thereby upheld the argument from Frankfurt-style cases against PAP. For where there is only an insubstantial flicker, the agent is not clearly morally responsible, and so the case cannot serve as a counterexample to a principle proposing a necessary condition of moral responsibility.

Suppose we specify an indeterministic Frankfurt-type case so that the agent *does* have a significant, robust ability to do otherwise *prior to* the inevitable act. Consider, for instance, a certain way of specifying an example recently presented by Mele and Robb:

> At t_1, Black initiates a certain deterministic process P in Bob's brain with the intention of thereby causing Bob to decide at t_2 (an hour later, say) to steal Ann's car. The process, which is screened off from Bob's consciousness, will deterministically culminate in Bob's deciding at t_2 to steal Ann's car unless he decides on his own at t_2 to steal it or is incapable at t_2 of making a decision ... As it happens, at t_2 Bob decides on his own to steal the car, on the basis of his own indeterministic deliberation about whether to steal it, and his decision has no deterministic cause. But if he had not just then decided on his own to steal it, P would have deterministically issued, at t_2, in his deciding to steal it. Rest assured that P in no way influences the indeterministic decision-making process that actually issues in Bob's decision. (Mele and Robb 1998: 101–2)

Bob's indeterministic deliberative process is called "process x." An "indeterministic process" is a sequence of events, some of which are connected by indeterministic causal relations. If there is an indeterministic causal relation between event e_a and event e_c, then given e_a, e_c might not occur, even in the absence of anything to frustrate e_a (Anscombe 1981). A "deterministic process" is a sequence of events connected entirely by deterministic causal relations.

Here is one way of representing the Bob case.[2] Let a solid-lined arrow represent a deterministic causal relation. Let a dashed-lined arrow represent an indeterministic causal relation. Suppose that e_k is Bob's action of stealing Ann's car. Let e_i be Bob's forming the intention to steal Ann's car. The double solid line represents the screening off of the deterministic process P by causal preemption. Parentheses enclose a causal relation that might have obtained, but happened not to obtain.

Suppose we take e_g to be Bob's forming the preference to steal Ann's car and we stipulate that Bob could have formed a different preference instead, given the prior occurrence of a particular consideration or set of considerations (e_e), as is depicted in figure 13.1. Then in my view it is reasonable to conclude that Bob acts freely in stealing Ann's car and that he is morally responsible for stealing it (provided that he meets any other conditions for moral responsibility). I have proposed and defended an account of free action as action on authorized preference. A preference counts as "authorized" if it is the uncoerced causally indeterministic outcome of considerations that occurred to the agent during his deliberative process (Ekstrom 2000, 2001b). The case of Bob, filled in as I have described, is one in which a person is a legitimate candidate for being held morally responsible for forming a particular intention even though at the time he could not have done otherwise.

Is libertarianism thus shown false?[3] To the contrary, this case ought to be completely untroubling to a libertarian. Since the scenario explicitly involves robust alternative possibilities, it certainly does not show that responsibility is consistent with a complete lack of alternative possibilities. Hence the scenario does not demonstrate or even help to demonstrate that semi-compatibilism is true.

The upshot of recent work on Frankfurt-style cases is that deterministically specified Frankfurt-type scenarios should be dismissed and that certain indeterministically specified Frankfurt-type scenarios do show the falsity of a narrowly construed PAP (that is, PAP_1). But we already knew PAP_1 to be false. So the literature on Frankfurt-type cases has not been useful concerning Issue 1. The scenarios are not *needed* to demonstrate the truth of the correct answer, and many of them do not *succeed* in demonstrating it, either.

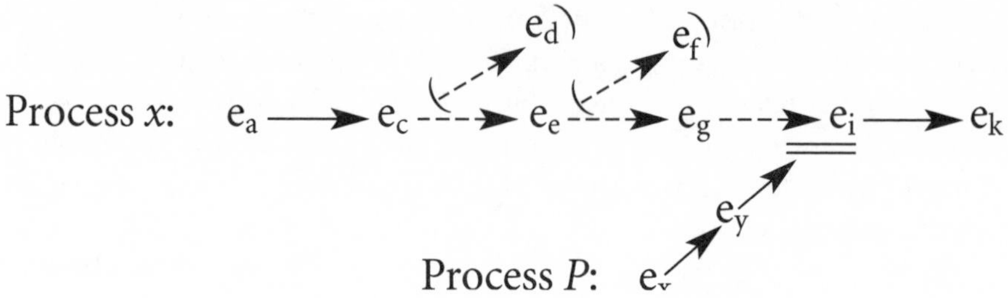

Process x: $e_a \longrightarrow e_c \dashrightarrow e_e \dashrightarrow e_g \dashrightarrow e_i \longrightarrow e_k$

e_d) e_f)

e_y

Process P: e_v

Fig. 13.1

2. ALTERNATIVES TO PAP$_1$

If PAP$_1$ is false, then what is the correct principle concerning the relation between alternative possibilities and moral responsibility? Many incompatibilist writers have sought to articulate such a principle.

Consider, for instance, the following:[4]

> *PAPh:* S is morally responsible for what he did at *t* only if (1) he could have done otherwise at *t* or (2) even though he could not have done otherwise at *t*, the psychological character on the basis of which he acted at *t* is itself partially a product of an earlier action (or actions) of his performed at a time when he could have done otherwise. (Mele and Robb 1998: 109)

PAPh takes as central the notion of the psychological character on which a person acts at the time in question, which has merit given the traditional libertarian emphasis on the importance of self-formation. David Hunt has recently discussed the following related principle:

> *PAP+:* S is morally responsible for A-ing at *t* only if (there is something) he could have done otherwise (and it is at least in part in virtue of what he could have done otherwise that he is morally responsible for A-ing at *t*) (Hunt 2000: 200)

Otsuka and Wyma consider as central, instead, the ability to avoid blame. Otsuka proposes the following:

> *Principle of Avoidable Blame:* One is blameworthy for performing an act of a given type only if one could instead have behaved in a manner for which one would have been entirely blameless (Otsuka 1998: 688)

Otsuka's principle is similar to the one defended by Wyma:

Principle of Possibly Passing the Buck (PPPB): A person is morally responsible for something she has done, *A*, only if she has failed to do something she could have done, *B*, such that doing *B* would have rendered her morally non-responsible for *A*. (Wyma 1997: 59)

Consider, alternatively, this principle:

Disjunctive Principle Concerning Alternative Possibilities: A person *S* is morally responsible for doing *X* at *t* only if either *S* could have at *t* done otherwise than *X* or *S* could have at some time done something other than what s/he did, something that would be reasonably expected to have the result that *S* would do otherwise than *X* at *t* (Ekstrom 2000: 211)

To illustrate: Catherine is morally responsible for missing the wedding she had promised to attend only if either she could have done otherwise at the time (that is, she could have attended the wedding) or she could have earlier done something that would have been reasonably expected to have the result that she would have attended the wedding as promised. Since Catherine deliberately flashed a police officer one hour prior to the wedding, thereby getting herself arrested and detained, she could not, at the time of the start of the wedding, have attended the wedding. Nonetheless, she may be morally responsible for missing the wedding if she could have refrained from flashing the police officer. Refraining from flashing the police officer one hour prior to the wedding would be reasonably expected to have the result that Catherine would attend the wedding on time, as promised.

Further libertarian work should address the relative merits and defects of such principles. Nonetheless, *all* of the previous principles would be false if moral responsibility were consistent with causal determinism, as semi-compatibilism maintains. Thus the second fundamental issue concerning free will and moral responsibility (call it Issue 2) asks whether being morally responsible for an action requires the falsity of the doctrine of causal determinism. Since determinism rules out available alternatives to every choice and action, one way it could be shown that moral responsibility requires the falsity of determinism would be to show that one's being morally responsible for an action is inconsistent with a complete lack of available alternatives to choice and action at every point in one's life. And so the question arises as to whether or not Frankfurt-style scenarios help to settle this issue.

The standard scenarios clearly do not resolve Issue 2. In the typical Frankfurt-type scenario the counterfactual intervener is involved in only one action or decision of the agent, leaving room for alternative possibilities earlier in the causal history of that act or decision. A more complex and interesting matter is whether or not more recently formulated "global Frankfurt-style cases" settle Issue 2.

Consider, for instance, Mele and Robb's extension of the Bob case. They write, "If our case falsifies PAP, an expanded version of the case falsifies PAPh."[5] In the *global Bob case*, we are to imagine that in any instance in which Bob makes a decision to A, a deterministic process like P was under way that *would have* resulted in Bob's deciding to A *if* Bob had not decided on his own, by way of an indeterministic process, to A. Further, we are to imagine that the same is true of all of Bob's actions that are not decisions. Mele and Robb comment:

> This global fact about Bob is quite remarkable, but it is a coincidence nonetheless. Given this fact, Bob could never have done otherwise than he did. But since he did everything on his own, the deterministic processes always having been preempted, we see no good reason to hold that the presence of those deterministic processes deprives him of moral responsibility (1998: 110).

This is a provocative case. How are we to represent it? Figure 13.2 depicts the way in which, I believe, Mele and Robb would like us to envision the global Bob scenario.

But how could it be that, in the global Bob case, as Mele and Robb claim, "Bob could never have done otherwise than he did," yet "he did everything on his own" (ibid.)? To say that Bob did something "on his own" is to say that he did it as the outcome of an unmanipulated, indeterministic deliberative process. Recall the definition of an indeterministic cause. An indeterministic, or non-necessitating, cause is one that can fail to produce its effect, even without the intervention of anything to frustrate it. Notice that, given the description of the global Bob scenario, including the counterfactual truth concerning the deterministic process P, assuming that Bob is still alive and capable of making decisions, there is *no chance* that e_c will not occur, following e_a. That is, e_a together with the circumstances, *cannot fail* to produce e_c, without the intervention of an event that kills Bob or makes him incapable of action or decision. Given the occurrence of e_a and given the setup of the scenario and the laws governing it, in the absence of a frustrating event, the probability is equal to 1 that e_c will occur following e_a. And by the same reasoning, the same applies for each event in process x, that is, for e_e, e_g, e_i, and e_k. For each event, whether it is caused by the previous event in process x or by the counterfactually intervening process, it *will* occur: the probability is equal to 1 that it will occur, on the assumption of no frustrating event.

So the *correct* depiction of the global Bob case occurs in figure 13.3. Let a heavy wavy line represent the blockage of the alternative possibility by the presence of the counterfactually intervening process.

In the global Bob case, e_k is *not* the result of an indeterministic process but occurs rather of physical necessity.[6] It is not the case that, given the occurrence of event e_a, event e_c might or might not follow, even in the absence of anything

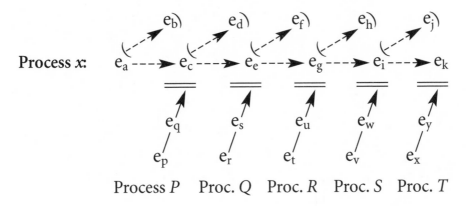

Fig. 13.2

to frustrate e_a. And it is not the case that, given the occurrence of e_c, event e_e might not occur, even in the absence of anything to frustrate e_c. The same is true of each of the events constituting process x: not one of them is an indeterministic cause of the subsequent event. Process x, that is, is a sequence of events connected entirely by deterministic causal relations. Therefore, Mele and Robb's description of the global Bob case should be rejected as incoherent. It cannot be the case that Bob "indeterministically decided on his own," given the details of the case. Since e_k is the result of a deterministic causal process, there is no reason for a libertarian to grant that Bob is morally responsible for e_k. Thus the global Bob case does not show that moral responsibility is consistent with a complete lack of alternative possibilities and thus it does not help to settle Issue 2.

3. THE LIBERTARIAN'S BURDEN

Libertarians need not accept compatibilist attempts to push them into focusing on a new and quite difficult task: that is, proving that causal determinism threatens moral responsibility for reasons *other than* its negation of all alternative possibilities to choice and action. On the basis of an argument from Frankfurt-type scenarios, Fischer, for instance, alleges that the incompatibilist must demonstrate that causal determinism undercuts moral responsibility *"in itself and apart from ruling out alternative possibilities"* (Fischer, this volume, chapter 12). In other words, libertarians allegedly must provide what Fischer calls "a direct argument" for responsibility-determinism incompatibilism, one not dependent upon the truth that causal determinism rules out alternative possibilities (Fischer forthcom-

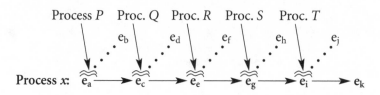

Fig. 13.3

ing). However, as we have seen, the use of Frankfurt-type scenarios to support this conclusion is unsuccessful.

The libertarian certainly does need to show that the state of affairs of an agent's having no alternative possibilities for action at a certain time and her *never* having had alternative possibilities for choice or action in her lifetime is inconsistent with that agent's being morally responsible for what she does. What reasoning underlies the appeal of this position? Perhaps, the following. If determinism is true, then everything that happens *must* happen—every thought and every action occurs of physical necessity. It is not that everything one does is somehow *fated* to occur no matter what else happens. It is not that everything one does one is *manipulated* into doing by some person outside of oneself. Rather, if determinism is true, then given what has come before and the laws governing the universe, at every instant there is exactly one way the world must be at the next instant.

Ordinarily, the causal sequences leading to persons' acts are concealed. We have little knowledge of why a person does what he does, in the usual case, and even less do we know whether the causes preceding his decisions and acts necessitate or only make probable their effects. This cloaked nature of the typical causal sequence helps to explain the fact that our intuitions concerning individuals' moral responsibility are often hasty and misled. In inscrutable causal contexts, we tend to *assume* that individuals had options—genuinely available alternative courses of action at some point along their paths—perhaps as a projection of our own introspectively certified conviction of an open future (Ekstrom 1998a, 2000).

But consider what happens to our intuitions when the deterministic sequence leading to an act is exposed. Suppose you lie on your couch looking at your feet, and you decide to flick your right foot rather than the left one just to exercise your ability to choose. *There*, you say to yourself, *that shows that I am a free agent.* Suppose you then decide—to drive home the point and to be a nuisance—deliberately to flick your right foot hard enough to knock over a glass of tea on the coffee table. Suppose we ask whether you ought to be blamed for knocking over the glass (and perhaps for thereby chipping the glass and staining the carpet). Testing our intuitions about this question in a deterministic setting is complicated by our tendency, again, to cling to a belief in the availability of alternative possibilities. In this case, it is natural to assume that you could have refrained from kicking over the glass.

But suppose we assume and hold vividly in our minds the truth of causal determinism in this scenario. Then your decision to kick over the glass was the only decision that could have occurred at the time, given the events that preceded it and the laws governing the universe. *But surely I am responsible for kicking over the glass,* you may think. *I did it deliberately; no one forced me; I chose and I acted on my choice.*

Do you really maintain this judgment when appreciating that your choice could not have been anything other than what it was? Due to the events that led up to your decision and due to the reigning natural laws, at the moment of decision you could not have chosen to refrain from kicking over the glass with your right foot. As you briefly deliberated over what to do, there were no forking paths in front of you. There was, instead, exactly one physically possible outcome. The events of the past led inevitably to your kicking over the glass. Furthermore, the events of the past have led inevitably to your *every* decision and action. You have never been in a position of being able to take the path to the right and being able to take the path to the left, for there has always been exactly one available pathway into your future. Do you, then, deserve blame for kicking over the glass?

Perhaps one's intuitions concerning this case are unclear. Consider instead, as in Ridley Scott's *Blade Runner,* the case of a replicant: a being artificially constructed to look and act like a human person. Suppose that our replicant—call her "RP3"—is designed to appear as a twenty-year-old female human being. She is implanted with memories of a childhood, given political opinions and preferences and mathematical, religious, and other beliefs. From the moment she is operational, all of RP3's decisions and all of her actions are deterministic outworkings of her initial state. Although her actions seem to RP3 to be fully up to her, we are aware of precisely what RP3 will do in each instance, as her initial genetic code and the laws governing her behavior are, to us, transparent. Despite RP3's subjective perception of an open future, the singular nature of the path before her is to us perfectly plain. Does this fact cause suspension of our tendency to assign moral responsibility status to RP3?

One might find this question difficult to answer. One might agree that it is inappropriate to praise or blame RP3 but maintain that the explanation of this judgment remains unclear. Does the deterministic nature of the causal sequence preceding RP3's behavior undermine responsibility or is it, rather, the fact that she is an artificial being with imposed preferences and beliefs? The manipulation by a human agent in the past of RP3 clouds her case as a test of our responsibility intuitions in an exposed deterministic causal context.

So consider a case without such objectionable coercion or human interference. It is difficult, of course, to *tell* a full deterministic story of a human life in all its details, which feeds our skepticism that there in fact ever is one. But suspend for a moment this doubt and reflect on a life the path of which through time is a singular line without any forking paths. One could attempt to provide a lengthy account of each of the deterministically linked events in the person's life beginning at the stage of an embryo. But here is a shortcut, a way of suggesting that there *is* such a story, without the tedium of telling it. It is a familiar device: your mother gave birth to both you and an identical twin. At birth, she gave your twin to a family the most like yours in economic class, ethnic background, religion, educational credentials, moral and political beliefs and so on, that she could find. You grew, unaware of your twin, until the day that you met, when you discovered that, just as you were graduating from Harvard, he was graduating from Stanford; just at the point when you developed an embarrassing addiction to pornography, so did he; you have the same habits of smoking, kayaking, and voting independent; as you founded a successful Internet company, so did he; you like the same wines and enjoy impressionist art; and when you blush confessing your cheating on a college entrance exam, he does the same. Although your childhood environments and experiences were not identical in all their details, you suspect based on your similarity with your twin that if they had been, the behavior of the two of you would have been identical in all its details.

Such a scenario gives one pause in assigning the praise and blame one ordinarily would to one's acts. Here is the annoying thought: I agonized over my decisions, I mentally beat myself up over my flaws, I took pride in my accomplishments, and now, given my acquaintance with this twin, it appears that my actions were all along inevitable. I took the course of my life to be up to me, but now I see that there is a full account for what I have done and who I have become.

Hesitancy in fully freeing oneself of responsibility may be ascribed to doubt that there really is a deterministic story explaining the entire course of one's life. But if one becomes convinced that there is a complete story—either by discovering one's identical twin or by having the true, complete deterministic causal account revealed to one by a scientist or a deity—then one is left in the odd position of viewing oneself as an object. Under the assumption of determinism, it is as if one is a pinball, bounced from one location to the next from the initial conditions by natural momentum. Or, perhaps better, it is as if one is a windup toy, marching to and fro from the moment the key at one's back is released, thinking to oneself, *"Maybe I'll march straight ahead and then turn to the right; no, perhaps I'll spin on my heel to the left,"* when all the while one's course is perfectly prescribed as the physically necessary outcome of prior events.

Such analogies for human life under the assumption of determinism—that it would resemble being a pinball or a windup toy—appear simplistic the compatibilist, and the reasoning supporting responsibility-determinism incompatibilism seems feeble-minded. Yet the incompatibilist is surely not so feeble-minded as not to notice disanalogies between ourselves and pinballs and windup toys. Of course, we are more complex; of course, we reason, have emotions, and form values and preferences. Of course, we are able to guide our behavior in that we act to accomplish our purposes.

But when we ask for a causal explanation of what we do and when a fully deterministic causal sequence preceding each decision and every action is exposed, the result is a baffling pause, an almost painful because so momentous suspension of our everyday practice of assigning praise and blame to everyone we encounter, including ourselves. If we must use simple analogies, the reason is that the insight is so powerful and difficult to convey.

The intuition is that it is unfair, and hence inappropriate, to blame a person for acting from, or in expression of, a self that could not have been different from what it is. If determinism is true, then one's character is exactly what it is of physical necessity, and the entire course of one's life proscribes a single path along which the past pushes one. A fundamental libertarian intuition is that we need alternative possibilities in the construction of the self, so that there is some chanciness in who we are and some openness in who we become.[7]

4. CONCLUSION

No amount of psychological complexity is sufficient for free will. We have the power to act freely only if at some time we are able to act otherwise than as we do. I conclude that the literature on Frankfurt-style scenarios has not overturned traditionalism concerning the necessity of free will for moral responsibility.

NOTES

1. In outlining his response to libertarian challenges to arguments from Frankfurt-type cases, Fischer claims that "the first step is to argue—based on the Frankfurt-type examples—that intuitively it is plausible that alternative possibilities are irrelevant to ascriptions of moral responsibility" (ch. 12, p. 292). But this statement is too incautious. Fischer might rather say that in deterministically specified Frankfurt-type scenarios, intuitively it is plausible that if the agent is not morally responsible for his action, then the reason is not the lack of alternative possibilities *to the target action*. The logic is apparently this: the agent *seems* to be morally responsible for his act, given the nonintervention of the counterfactual intervener; but if he is not morally responsible, then his nonresponsibility must be attributable to some factor other than the absence of an alternative possibility to the target action. I am not sure why Fischer thinks this first argu-

ment is persuasive. As I argue in the body of this chapter, it is illicit to hold on to an unreflective judgment that the agent is responsible once the context of determinism is made explicit.

2. There are other ways of specifying the Bob scenario consistent with the general description of it given by Mele and Robb. I fill in the example in the way that I think is most helpful to its effectiveness in showing Mele and Robb's point—that is, in a way that makes it most plausible that Bob is morally responsible for forming at *t2* the intention to steal Ann's car, even though at the time he could not do otherwise due to the preempted deterministic process *P*. Mele and Robb suggest other ways of construing the case such that process *x* is indeterministic: it may be, for instance, that at a time prior to *t2*, Bob could have decided not to steal the car, yet he decided at that prior time to steal it; and *P* would cause Bob to decide again at *t2* to steal the car *unless* he decided again on his own at *t2* to do this (as might happen if Bob were especially forgetful or if he had in the meantime reconsidered the matter, perhaps out of fear) (Mele and Robb 1998: 102n. 11). The authors claim that nothing about the Bob case assures that Bob's deciding at *t2* to steal Ann's car is inevitable since, for instance, Bob might be dead at *t2*. They emphasize that, given the details of the scenario, any future open to Bob *in which he is capable at t2 of making a decision* includes Bob's deciding at *t2* to steal Ann's car (or, as I have put it, Bob's forming at *t2* the intention to steal Ann's car).

3. Mele and Robb do not take the case to demonstrate that libertarianism is false.

4. Mele and Robb (1998: 109). The authors present but do not defend *PAPh;* they go on to argue against it.

5. Ibid. This statement is mistaken because in the original Bob case, process x can count as an indeterministic process by virtue of its indeterministic causal links early on in the process, prior to the causal relation between e_g and e_i. But in the global Bob case, process x cannot be an indeterministic process, given the description of the scenario, as I argue in the body of this essay.

6. It occurs of physical necessity given that process x is a *deliberative* process. Mele and Robb might claim that e_k is not inevitable since after e_g, say, Bob *might have* died or become incapacitated. But Bob's stealing Ann's car "on his own" is not satisfied by his having done it as the result of a process that is indeterministic only in this sense: that he might have died (or become incapacitated) at some point along the way. For Bob to have acted from an indeterministic deliberative process, he would have to have been in a position at some point(s) such that his deliberations might have proceeded one way and they might have proceeded in another way instead. But Bob in the global Bob scenario is never in such a position.

7. Compare Kane (1996a), Ekstrom (2000).

....

CHAPTER 14

RESPONSIBILITY AND FRANKFURT-TYPE EXAMPLES

....

DAVID WIDERKER

A widely accepted moral intuition states that

(PAP)   An agent is morally responsible for performing a given act A only
if he could have avoided performing it.[1]

In his seminal article "Alternate Possibilities and Moral Responsibility," Harry
Frankfurt (1969) has attacked this principle.[2] Central to his argument is the following assumption:

(FR)   There may be circumstances in which a person performs some action which, although they make it impossible for him to avoid performing that action, they in no way bring it about that he performs
it. (Frankfurt 1969: 830, 837)

Frankfurt contends that in a situation of the sort described in FR (call it "FR-
situation") the agent is morally responsible for what he did even though he could
not have refrained from so acting. Hence, according to him, PAP is false. To
establish FR, Frankfurt appeals to an example of the following sort[3]:

Jones is deliberating whether or not to keep a certain promise he made. Unbeknownst to Jones, there is another person, Black, who for some reason does not want Jones to keep his promise. Black has the power and the means to force Jones to break the promise. But wishing to avoid showing his hand unnecessarily, he has made up his mind to intervene if and only if Jones does *not* show a sign of going to decide to break the promise. Call that sign "S1." If Jones does show that sign, then Black does nothing, knowing that in this case Jones will act as he (Black) wants him to act. (It is assumed that Black knows Jones very well in this regard). Finally, suppose that Jones decides to break the promise for reasons of his own.

It seems that in this situation Jones acts freely without Black's intervention and is therefore morally responsible for what he does. But, given Black's presence, it would appear that he cannot avoid deciding to break the promise. Call this example the "Promise Example."

Libertarians[4] who hold that moral responsibility requires the power to avoid acting as one did have responded to Frankfurt's attack on PAP by objecting that examples such as the Promise Example fail to establish FR, and therefore a central assumption of his argument against PAP is unwarranted. Most important, such examples fail to establish FR when applied to simple mental acts such as deciding, choosing, undertaking, or forming an intention, that is, acts that for the libertarian constitute the loci of moral responsibility.[5] Their objection may be expressed as follows:

Consider the relation between the sign S1, which Black employs as a sign for not intervening and Jones's decision to break the promise. Either the occurrence of S1 is (or indicates) a condition that, under the circumstances, is causally sufficient for Jones's decision at T to break his promise or it is not. If it is, then the example does not describe an FR-situation, since the latter requires that the decision must not be causally determined. On the other hand, if S1 is not so associated with Jones's decision to break the promise, if S1 is merely a reliable indicator of it, then there is no reason to think that Jones's decision was unavoidable. In either case, the truth of FR has not been established.[6]

Recently, there have been a number of attempts to strengthen Frankfurt's argument against PAP by providing better examples of FR-situations. In what follows, I examine some of these examples from a libertarian viewpoint and argue that they do not succeed either. I then go farther and claim that, even if at one point a defender of Frankfurt might be able to come up with a genuine example of an FR-situation, avoidability would still remain a necessary condition for at least one important type of moral responsibility—that of moral blameworthiness. In the course of my defense of this last claim, I defend a more comprehensive constraint on moral blameworthiness than avoidability and then apply this constraint to meet a well-known recent objection to PAP by John Fischer.

1. The Examples

I shall not survey here all the recent attempts to provide a successful example of an FR-situation. In particular, I shall not discuss Alfred Mele and David Robb's interesting example (Mele and Robb 1998), as it has already been treated by two other contributors to this volume, John Fischer and Laura Ekstrom.[7] For my criticism of it, see Widerker (2000a, 183–85).

1.1. The Stump Example

Consider the following example proposed by Eleonore Stump:

> Suppose that a neurosurgeon Grey wants his patient Jones to vote for Republicans in the upcoming election. Grey has a neuroscope which lets him both observe and bring about neural firings which correlate with acts of will on Jones's part. Through his neuroscope, Grey ascertains that every time Jones wills to vote for Republican candidates, that act of his will correlates with the completion of a sequence of neural firings in Jones's brain that always includes near its beginning, the firing of neurons a,b,c (call this sequence 'R'). On the other hand, Jones's willingness to vote for a Democratic candidate is correlated with the completion of a different neural sequence that always includes near its beginning, the firings of neurons x, y, z, none of which is the same as those in neural sequence R. (Call this neural sequence 'D'.) For simplicity's sake, suppose that neither neural sequence R nor neural sequence D is also correlated with any further set of mental acts. Again for simplicity's sake, suppose that Jones's only relevant options are an act of will to vote for Republicans or an act of will to vote for Democrats. Then Grey can tune his neuroscope accordingly. Whenever the neuroscope detects the firing of x, y, and z, the initial neurons of sequence D, the neuroscope immediately disrupts the neural sequence so that it is not brought to completion. The neuroscope then activates the coercive neurological mechanism which fires the neurons of neural sequence R, which is correlated with the act of will to vote for Republicans. But if the neuroscope detects the firings of neurons a, b, and c, the initial neurons of sequence R, the neuroscope does not interrupt that neural sequence. It does not activate that coercive neurological mechanism, and neural sequence R continues, culminating in Jones's willingness to vote for Republicans, without Jones's being caused to will in this way by Grey.
>
> And suppose that . . . Grey does not act to bring about the neural sequence R, but that Jones wills to vote for Republicans without Grey's coercing him to do so. (Stump 1996a: 76–77, 1999a)

This example certainly fails to provide a successful illustration of an FR-situation, at least as it stands, because in Stump's story Jones's act of will to vote for a

Republican candidate (henceforth "W[R]") turns out to be causally determined by the neural firings a, b, c. This is so, since these events cause the completion of neural sequence R, which, Stump assumes, is an event (process) that is correlated with W(R). For if a, b, c cause the completion of R, and the latter is correlated with W(R), then they also cause W(R). The reason a, b, c must causally determine the rest of the neuron firings belonging to R is rooted in Stump's assumption that in her example Jones must decide to vote either for Republicans or for Democrats, lacking the option of remaining undecided. Were a, b, c not to determine the rest of R, there would be the distinct possibility of R being spontaneously interrupted after the occurrence of a, b, c, in which case Jones would have made no decision at all at T (T = the exact time at which he decided to vote for Republicans).

If she admits that her example needs modification, Stump might explain that another way of conceiving the relation between W(R) and the neural sequence R is to say that W(R), rather than being correlated with the *completion* of the neural sequence R, is correlated with that very sequence itself. On this account, a decision or act of will such as W(R) is a temporally extended process which is correlated with a neural sequence whose initial members causally determine the rest of the sequence. Furthermore, W(R) and R are assumed to occur simultaneously.[8] My previous objection does not apply, since now W(R) is not causally determined by a, b, c, whose occurrence, Stump assumes, is also not causally determined.

Although I do not find this account of a decision plausible, I will not argue against it here. Fortunately, there is a simple and forceful argument that shows that even if one grants Stump's alternative notion of an act of will or a decision, the agent in her story still maintains the power to refrain from his decision.

To see this, consider a scenario like the one described by Stump, except that it does not feature a counterfactual intervener like Grey. In that scenario, there would be no reason to think that Jones could not have decided otherwise or that he could not have refrained from the decision he made. Now recall that, on Stump's alternative account of decisions, once the neural firings a, b, c occur, Jones is bound to make W(R), that is, he is bound to decide to vote for a Republican candidate. This means that the only way in which Jones could have refrained from his decision in that scenario, is by having the power to bring about the nonoccurrence of a, b, c, a power that he would have before the occurrence of a, b, c and not after that. But if he has that power in the said scenario (as he surely does), he must also have it in the scenario featuring Grey. That the latter scenario includes a potentially coercive neuroscope does not change this fact, since its coercive influence would come into play only after the possible occurrence of x, y, z, that is, at a time later than the occurrence of a, b, c. Hence, it does not affect Jones's power to bring about the nonoccurrence of a, b, c. Now, if Jones has the power to bring about the nonoccurrence of a, b, c in the scenario featuring Grey, then he also has it within his power in that scenario to refrain from his actual decision to vote for a Republican candidate.[9] For by having the former power, he also has the power to bring about the non-occurrence of R. And as his decision to vote for a Republican candidate is correlated with R, he also has the power to bring about the nonoccurrence of that decision. Thus, Stump's example fails to establish FR.[10]

The next two examples, which I will treat together, are attempts to construct an FR-scenario by bringing in an essentially omniscient agent such as God.[11]

1.2. The Hunt Example

Consider a possible world in which Jones's decision to break the promise (D[B]) is foreknown by God. Hunt argues that this is an FR-situation, because in these circumstances the decision is both unavoidable and causally undetermined. To establish its unavoidability, Hunt appeals to an influential argument for theological fatalism. According to this argument, if Jones were able to refrain from D(B), there would be a time T1 prior to the occurrence of D(B) and a possible future relative to T1, in which D(B) does not occur. But if divine foreknowledge exists, then the past relative to T1 contains God's infallible belief that D(B) will occur. And this implies that *every* possible future relative to T1 contains D(B). Hence, D(B) is unavoidable.[12]

1.3. Another Omniscient Agent Example

In this example, God is said to employ the following strategy to ensure the unavoidability of D(B) without violating the constraints on an FR-situation specified in FR: Before Jones makes his decision, God considers the following two conditionals:

(a) If Jones is in circumstances C, then provided no one intervenes, Jones will not decide at T to break his promise.
(b) If Jones is in circumstances C, then provided no one intervenes, Jones will decide at T to break his promise. (C represents the circumstances in which Jones deliberates whether or not to break his promise to his uncle.)

Being essentially omniscient, God knows which of these two conditionals is true. Now, if He foreknows that (b) is true, he does nothing. On the other hand, if He foreknows that (a) is true, then shortly after Jones's deliberation process has begun, He intervenes and forces Jones to decide to break his promise. Suppose now that Jones is in C and (b) is true. It is not difficult to see that in these circumstances Jones does not have it within his power *not* to decide to break the promise. For suppose he had that power. Then there would be a possible world W sharing its past with the real world up until shortly before T, in which he exercises that power. Furthermore, this would be a world in which God abandons his policy to intervene iff he knows that (b) is true. But whether or not God abandons this policy is not up to Jones. Hence, though W is a causally possible world, whether or not it is actualized is not up to Jones. Hence, Jones does not have the power not to decide to break the promise.[13]

Again, I am not convinced that these examples provide noncontroversial cases of an FR-scenario. To see this, let us recall the dialectical situation between Frankfurt and the libertarian. Frankfurt wanted to show that (1) the freedom pertinent to moral responsibility is an agent's acting of his own accord, and that (2) this freedom cannot be identified with that of an agent's having the power to act otherwise. His attempt to prove FR was meant to establish precisely these two points. Examining now the previous examples from this point of view, it is not at all clear to me that they describe situations in which Jones can be said to be acting on his own. Since in them God is assumed to be infallible, the fact D(B) occurs at T is entailed (in the broadly logical sense) by the prior fact of God's believing at T' that D(B) occurs at T (T' is earlier than T). In this sense, D(B) can be said to be *metaphysically necessitated* or metaphysically determined by that belief of God.[14]/[15] Now, if a libertarian rejects as an instance of an agent's acting on his own a scenario in which an agent's decision is *nomically* necessitated[16] by a temporally prior fact (or a conjunction of such facts), why wouldn't he reject one in which the decision is metaphysically necessitated by a prior event? What, in my opinion, is crucial to the libertarian's conception of a free decision is that such a decision is not necessitated or determined in any way by an antecedent event or fact.[17] This condition is not satisfied in the examples under consideration. Now, one might object that metaphysical necessitation is not *nomic* necessitation. But why should this difference be relevant? If a decision is rendered unfree by the fact that its occurrence at T is entailed by the conjunction of some temporally prior facts together with the laws of nature, then why would it not be rendered unfree if its occurring at T is entailed by God's prior belief that it will occur at T? If the critic still thinks that there is a difference between the two cases, it is incumbent upon him to explain why.[18]

2. GLIMPSES BEYOND

I thus conclude that it is unclear whether one can produce an unproblematic example of an FR-situation. However, for the sake of discussion, let us assume that such an example can be provided. I shall now show that even then avoidability remains a necessary condition for one important type of moral responsibility—that of moral blameworthiness. In other words, I wish to defend the principle:

> (PAPB)   An agent is morally blameworthy for performing a given act A only if he could have avoided performing it.

First we need to convince ourselves that its proponent has an adequate reply to Frankfurt's claim that PAPB is false, as in an FR-situation (in which the agent acts in a morally wrong way) the agent is morally blameworthy for his act. To see this, let us focus on an allegedly successful example of an FR-situation, say some variation on the Promise Example mentioned earlier. Now consider the following reply by the proponent of PAPB:

> I understand that you, Frankfurt, wish to say that in this situation Jones is morally blameworthy for his decision to break the promise. If so, tell me *what, in your opinion, should he have done instead?* Now, you cannot claim that he should not have decided to break the promise, since this was something that was not in Jones's power to do. Hence, I do not see how you can hold Jones blameworthy for his decision to break the promise.

Call this defense the "What-should-he-have-done defense" or for short the "W-defense."[19]

The W-defense points to an important reason why it would be unreasonable to judge an agent morally blameworthy in an FR-situation. When we judge someone morally blameworthy for a certain act, we do so because we believe that morally speaking she should *not* have done it. This belief is essential to our moral disapproval of her behavior as blameworthy.[20] Sometimes, however, such a belief may be unreasonable. This happens in a situation in which it is clear to us that the agent could not have avoided acting as she did. To expect in that situation that the agent should not have done what she did is to expect her to have done the impossible. By implication, considering her blameworthy because she has not fulfilled this unreasonable expectation would be unreasonable.

The W-defense thus suggests the following general constraint on ascriptions of moral blame:

> (PAE)   An agent S is morally blameworthy for doing A only if under the circumstances it would be morally reasonable to expect S not to have done A.[21]

This principle enables PAP-defenders to formulate an intuitive argument for PAPB.

1. An agent S is morally blameworthy for doing A only if under the circumstances it would be morally reasonable to expect S not to have done A.
2. If S could not have avoided doing A, then on pain of expecting him to have done the impossible, it would be morally unreasonable to expect him not to have done A.
3. Hence, if S could not have avoided doing A, then S is not morally blameworthy for doing A.[22]/[23]

Note that PAE is a more general principle than PAPB, since it can be used to explain cases in which we exonerate an agent when his wrongful behavior was avoidable. These, for example, may be situations in which that behavior resulted from his unawareness of the causal consequences of some act of his, or from insufficient moral knowledge on his part. In these cases, there is no reason to assume that the agent could not have avoided acting wrongly.[24]

If PAE is correct, it enables the libertarian to answer an important recent objection to PAPB by John Fischer (1994: 140). Fischer argues that there are situations in which an agent makes a certain moral decision on his own, has a way (or ways) of not making that decision, and yet none of the alternatives open to him is significant or robust enough to attribute to him responsibility for his decision. A case in point is a scenario in which the agent's only way to avoid the decision he makes is by becoming unconscious at the moment of the decision, or by allowing himself to get distracted and forgetting about the decision altogether.[25] It is assumed that the agent does not know all this. He himself believes that he can avoid the decision simply by deciding otherwise. In such a scenario it would be unreasonable to base the agent's blameworthiness for his decision on the fact that he did not avail himself of the said options. We thus have a scenario that seems to be morally equivalent to an FR-situation, For in that scenario the agent is morally responsible for his decision (having made it on his own), and yet he had no morally relevant alternative open to him. According to Fischer, such scenarios show that avoidability should not be regarded as a bona fide necessary condition for moral responsibility, and therefore PAPB ought to be rejected.

Fischer's objection is ingenious. However, it is not difficult to anticipate the PAPB-proponent's response to it. Fischer assumes that in the situation he is envisaging it is intuitively clear that the agent is blameworthy for the decision he made. But this assumption would be contested by the proponent of PAPB. He would contest it for the same reason he contests Frankfurt's assumption that the agent is blameworthy in a regular FR-situation. After all, what should Fischer's agent have done instead, or what should he have done to avoid moral blame? He could not have decided otherwise, and it would be silly to expect him to have availed himself of those alternatives by which he might have refrained from his decision. Hence, he cannot be deemed blameworthy for what he did. The W-defense, then, applies to Fischer's scenario no less than to an FR-scenario.

It should also be noted that the earlier stated argument for PAPB does not amount to a *proof* that Frankfurt's position is mistaken. Frankfurt may argue that he is more convinced that in an FR-situation the agent is blameworthy for what he did than he is convinced of the plausibility of a principle such as PAE. He may want to ground this conviction in the intuition that in the said situation the agent acted wrongly and did so freely in the sense that he acted for reasons of his own and without interference.[26] Limitations of space prevent me from exploring this issue further. One thing, however, seems clear. PAPB rests on a much firmer ground than Frankfurt seems to realize. And so we see that the dispute between him and the proponent of PAP concerns not only the question whether FR-situations are conceptually possible but also a much deeper disagreement about the very notion of moral blameworthiness.

3. CONCLUSION

Despite various recent attempts to strengthen Frankfurt's argument against PAP, one important assumption of it, FR, remains unwarranted. Moreover, we have seen that, even if that assumption is granted, a strong case can be made for PAP where it applies to moral blame. Both these results call into question Frankfurt's contention that avoidability is irrelevant to moral responsibility.

NOTES

I would like to thank Bob Kane, Dovid Gottlieb, Michael McKenna, and Michael Morreau for excellent comments and discussions on an earlier version of this essay.

1. I am assuming a fine-grained account of action individuation, according to which an action is a dated particular consisting at least in part of an agent's exemplifying an act-property at a time. I use *act-property* in Goldman's sense, according to which, an agent's having exemplified such a property does not entail that he performed an ac-

tion, or that he acted intentionally. See Goldman (1970: 15–17). Although I adopt Goldman's use of *act-property*, I do not endorse his account of action.

2. The version of the principle of alternative possibilities (PAP) in the text is broader than Frankfurt's original formulation of it: "An agent is morally responsible for what he has done only if he could have done otherwise (Frankfurt 1969: 829)." Unlike the latter, it covers also the alternative possibility of the agent's not performing any act at all. This difference does not affect the dialectical situation between Frankfurt and the defender of PAP. If sound, Frankfurt's argument against PAP would be equally effective against the version of PAP under consideration.

3. See Frankfurt (ibid.: 835–36).

4. By libertarians I mean those who believe that an agent's decision (choice) is free in the sense of freedom required for moral responsibility only if (1) it is not causally determined, and (2) in the circumstances in which the agent made that decision (choice), she could have avoided making it. By a causally determined decision, I shall understand a decision D occurring at time T which is either caused by another event or is nomically necessitated in the sense that the proposition that D occurs at T is entailed by some conjunction of true propositions describing the laws of nature and state of affairs obtaining prior to T. Some libertarians regard a decision as free even though it was caused, provided it was caused in an appropriate way by an act of the agent that the agent could have avoided. Such decisions would be free at best in a derivative sense, one that I do not intend here.

5. These acts are simple in that they do not contain another act as a part.

6. See Widerker (1995a, 250–52), where I present an elaborate version of this argument. For similar responses to Frankfurt's argument against PAP, see Ginet (1996), Kane (1985: 51) and (1996a: 142–43), Lamb (1993), and Wyma (1997). For a libertarian response to Frankfurt of a Reidian type, see Rowe (1991: 82–85). Among supporters of Frankfurt's position are Fischer (1994: ch. 7), Mele and Robb (1998), Hunt (2000), Stump (1996a) and (1999a), and Pereboom (2000).

7. I am skipping the discussion of their example at the request of the editor. Another new Frankfurt-type example that I shall not discuss is Derk Pereboom's (2000).

8. That this seems to be her view is strongly suggested by Stump (1999a: section 2 and nn. 21 and 22 and *passim*). Note that the neural sequence *must* be simultaneous with W(R). Otherwise, if R begins before the occurrence of W(R), then W(R) is causally determined by a, b, c, in which case Stump's story would again fail to describe an FR-situation. Stump does not seem sufficiently aware of this fact. See Stump (1999a: n. 20).

9. Note that one cannot resist this conclusion by the claim that, because in the counterfactual scenario Jones is forced to decide to vote for a Republican, W(R) occurs in that scenario as well, in which case he would not have avoided making that decision. For Jones's decision in that scenario is not identical to W(R), since it occurs after the occurrence of the neural firings x,y,z, that is, later than the time at which W(R) occurs in the actual world. Here I am assuming that the (exact) time at which an act or event occurs is essential to it. An even simpler response is to say that, although in the said scenario Jones decides to vote for a Republican candidate, he does *not* decide to do so at T, the exact time at which W(R) occurs in the actual world. Surely it is the avoidability of his deciding *at T* to vote for a Republican candidate that is at issue here, since it is that for which he is held responsible.

10. For a different and illuminating criticism of Stump's example that also addresses other problematic aspects of it, see Goetz (1999) and idem (forthcoming).

11. My discussion of these examples is adapted from (Widerker 2000b). By an essentially omniscient agent, I mean an agent who is infallible in the sense that it is impossible for him to believe a false proposition, and who is essentially all-knowing in the sense that he cannot fail to believe any true proposition.

12. See Hunt (1996a and 2000: 219–20). For precursors of this example, see Fischer (1986a: 55 and Zagzebski 1991: ch. 6).

13. A version of this example was suggested to me in discussion by William Alston and Jerome Gellman. The difference between it and the previous example is that its proponent need not assume that God's foreknowing an agent's decision is incompatible with its being avoidable. Thus, he need not see himself committed to the argument for the unavoidability of D(B) employed by Hunt. As I shall argue soon, this difference does not make much of a difference.

14. Put more generally, an event E occurring at a time T is metaphysically necessitated by an event F occurring at time T' iff T' is earlier than T, and the fact that F occurs at T' entails the fact that E occurs at T.

15. Some think that, given God's essential omniscience, the fact that D(B) occurs at T is not only entailed by the fact that God believes at T' that D(B) occurs at T, but that it *also* entails the latter. But this is a mistake. What it entails is merely that the conditional fact that, if T' exists, then God believes at T' that D(B) occurs at T'. For there might be possible worlds in which a time such as T' does not exist.

16. A fact X is nomically necessitated by a temporally prior fact Y just in case X is entailed by the conjunction of Y and some laws of nature, and is not entailed by either conjunct alone.

17. For a constraint on libertarian freedom along precisely these lines, see Alston (1989: 164–65).

18. The second theological example is also open to another problem that, however, I shall not discuss here. The example assumes that "conditionals of freedom" such as (a) and (b) have a truth value. This assumption is very controversial. In this connection, see Adams (1977), Hasker (1989a: ch. 2), and Van Inwagen (1997b).

19. One may obtain a different version of the W-defense if in lieu of pressing the question, "What should he have done instead?" one insists on the question, "What should he have done to avoid being blameworthy for the act he performed?" These two questions yield different answers in certain cases of unavoidable acts for which the agent may be held derivatively responsible.

20. See Wallace (1994: ch. 4).

21. By "morally reasonable" I mean morally reasonable for someone who is aware of *all* the relevant moral facts pertaining to S's doing A. Note also that PAE, like PAP, is not meant to apply to cases of *derivative* responsibility, for example, cases where the agent is responsible for an act she could not have avoided partly by virtue of being responsible for the causal conditions that led to it. Obviously, PAE would be false if it were meant to cover such cases as well.

22. This argument for PAPB differs importantly from the argument for PAPB I give in Widerker (1991a), where the argument does not employ the notion of a morally reasonable expectation.

23. For a different defense of PAPB, see also David Copp's illuminating essay in Copp (1997).

24. For a more elaborate defense of PAE, see Widerker (2000a).

25. This particular example is mine.

26. Cf. Frankfurt (1999: 370). For another way of explaining Frankfurt's conviction that in a FR-situation the agent is blameworthy for his act, see Widerker (2000a).

PART VI

LIBERTARIAN PERSPECTIVES ON FREE AGENCY AND FREE WILL

LIBERTARIAN VIEWS: DUALIST AND AGENT-CAUSAL THEORIES

TIMOTHY O'CONNOR

THIS essay will canvass recent philosophical accounts of human agency that deploy a notion of "self" (or "agent") causation. Some of these accounts try to explicate this notion, whereas others only hint at its nature in contrast with the causality exhibited by impersonal physical systems. In these latter theories, the authors' main argumentative burden is that the apparent fundamental differences between personal and impersonal causal activity strongly suggest mind-body dualism. I begin by noting two distinct, yet not commonly distinguished, philosophical motivations for pursuing an agent-causal account of human agency. In the course of discussing the accounts developed by some philosophers in response to these considerations, I reconsider both the *linkage* of agent causation with mind-body dualism and its sharp *cleavage* from impersonal (or "event") causation.

1. MECHANISM, TELEOLOGY, AND AGENCY

A central motivation for many philosophers who espouse an agent-causation-based account of human action is the thesis that *mechanistic* explanations of a sort found in the physical sciences and *purposive* explanations of the sort typically applied to human action are in general mutually exclusive: it could not be true, say, that a neurophysiological account (referring only to electrochemical and biological properties) and a purposive account (referring to an agent's beliefs, desires, and intentions) are complementary, true accounts of the very same phenomena—say, the agent's picking up a book.

One indirect line of argument for this thesis is suggested by the "explanatory exclusion problem" developed over numerous articles by Jaegwon Kim. (For a recent statement, see Kim 1998.) Kim directs his argument against the nonreductionist-physicalist position that mental events and processes are distinct from, yet wholly "realized by," physical processes. He tries to show that such a view cannot coherently account for the causal efficacy of the mental, assuming (as is plausible on the view) that there are no causal factors beyond the physical (the "causal closure of the physical") and that mental causes do not systematically overdetermine events caused by physical factors. Kim's argument, if successful, forces one to either assume an outright identity of sorts between mental events and specific physical events—something many philosophers regard as highly implausible—or to move toward a more robust sort of dualism, entailing the falsity of the closure of the physical. While taking the latter option concerning the ontology of mental states does not favor any specific account of agency, it does open up the possibility of supposing that the explanation of actions in terms of mental factors differs from the general mechanistic form of explanation universally applied in the purely physical domain.

An argument directly for the distinction in form between these two sorts of explanation that was popular in the 1960s was articulated by Norman Malcolm (1968): mechanistic forms of explanation posit merely contingent lawful connections between events, whereas purposive explanations posit necessary connections between desires or intentions and actions. Therefore, instances of the latter cannot be explained by instances of the former, conceived as more fundamental in both ontological and explanatory terms. It is concluded that since purposive explanations are not illusory, mechanistic explanations are insufficient for the understanding of human agency.

A second direct line of argument that purposive explanations differ in kind from mechanistic ones is of special interest here, as it aims to show the necessity of a specifically agent-causal account of purposive action. In brief, the argument is this: the only plausible way to make out purposive explanations as special cases of mechanistic ones is to hold that desires, intentions, and beliefs are important and salient antecedent *causes* of action. However, this "causal theory of action," championed by Donald Davidson in his influential (1963), faces the problem of wayward causal chains: possible scenarios that satisfy the causal theory's requirement, but that seem not to exemplify purposive actions, due to the wayward or deviant way in which the agent's motivational states generate the action. For example, suppose David desires to kill Ser-Min by poisoning his tea. His desire to do so makes him very nervous, so much so that it causes him to *spill* the poison into the tea. Here, David's desire causes an action of the intended sort, but he did not act intentionally, or with the purpose of poisoning the tea. Such examples show that the causal theorist must refine her account, specifying the way that motivating factors cause actions that are genuinely intentional. This has proved difficult, prompting Roderick Chisholm (1966), John Bishop (1983, 1986), and especially Richard Taylor (1966) to contend that any adequate account of intentional action must include the *agent's* causing the action as a primitive notion. Not many have been convinced by this pessimism, however, because a small cottage industry has sprung up to remedy the defects in the simple causal account. To date, the most sophisticated attempts by causal theorists are Bishop himself (1989) and Alfred Mele (1992a).

2. Mechanism and Freedom of Action

People act intentionally throughout their waking lives. Whether or not they do so freely is a further substantive matter, one that depends on the nature of their control over their own actions. The concept of action is distinct from that of free action, and it is not obvious that a good way to understand freely performed action is to develop a set of plausibly sufficient conditions for action and then to add a further freedom condition. For perhaps there are more than one interestingly different ways that the concept of intentional action might be satisfied, but some of these do not admit of freedom variants. To speak more concretely: many theorists of action have found it plausible (*pace* Taylor and the early Bishop) that a suitably nuanced causal theory can provide a set of conditions sufficient for intentional action. (Some have also thought that their favored accounts provide necessary conditions as well, but that is rarely argued with any care.) Suppose that they are right. It may be, however, that a picture of actions as causal products of appropriate motivational states of the agent cannot provide an account of the sort of freely chosen activity we typically ascribe to ourselves, a sort that grounds moral responsibility and the significance we accord to some of our achievements.

Some agent causation theorists are best interpreted in this manner. Agent causation is a necessary feature of *freely* chosen activity, even though there may be possible forms of intentional activity that lack it altogether. (C. A. Campbell 1967; John Thorp 1980; Alan Donagan 1987; Randolph Clarke 1993, 1996a; and T. O'Connor 1993a, 1995a, and 2000 explicitly take this view, while Chisholm vacillates in his early essays. Taylor, as already noted, propounded agent causation as a feature of all intentional action, as do Godfrey Vesey [in Flew and Vesey 1987], William Rowe 1991, and Richard Swinburne 1986, assuming Swinburne is in fact an agent causationist—on which question see note 2 of this chapter.) Indeed, it may be that while some of our own actions are agent-causal in character, others are not. For the remainder of this essay, I will focus solely on this freedom-based motivation for developing an agent-causal account of agency.

Agent causationists have generally also been *incompatibilists*, holding that freedom of action and causal indeterminism are incompatible. Now a causal theorist of action can likewise endorse incompatibilism. While an intentional action, on her account, involves one's reasons causing one's actions, the causal connection need not be deterministic. So she might suppose that a freely performed action is one in which the agent's reasons are salient parts of an indeterministic causal condition generating the action. The condition causes the action, but it need not have done so. It might have been, under those very circumstances, that one of the agent's competing desires (and corresponding belief) had caused a different action altogether. (See the essays by Clarke and Kane in this volume, ch. 16 and 18, respectively.)

Agent causationists typically hold that this is not enough for freedom, or at least for the sort of freedom that can directly ground ascriptions of responsibility. And what this causal indeterminist scenario lacks is precisely the agent's directly controlling the outcome. The agent's internal states have objective tendencies of some determinate measure to cause certain outcomes. While this provides an *opening* in which the agent might freely select one option from a plurality of real alternatives, it fails to introduce a causal capacity that fills it. And what is better here than a scenario in which the agent himself causes the particular action that is to be performed?

Such is the intuitive pull in favor of an agent-causal account. But pursuing this suggestion leads to a number of theoretical questions: What kind of thing is the "agent"? What precisely is it that the agent causes? How are agent causation and event causation related? How do the agent's reasons figure into the equation? (Surely they must somehow govern instances of agent causation—but how?) And under what circumstances might agent causation occur? Unsurprisingly, agent causationists (AC) have answered these questions in different ways.

2.1. Some Ontological Requirements

All AC theorists require that we think of agents as things which endure through time, such that they are wholly present at each moment of their existence. This is in contrast to a now popular "temporal parts" ontology, according to which things are supposed to be composed of temporal parts, in much the way that they have spatial parts. According to this view, just as my left foot is but a spatial part of me (and when we say that I exist there, we actually mean that a part of me is there, that I overlap that region), so also the present stage of my existence is a temporal slice of my whole being, a component of the four-dimensional object spanning some eighty (?) years that, speaking tenselessly, *is* me.[1] Clearly, such a temporally extended object is not suited to play the role of an agent cause of ever so many particular episodes in its own life. But nor are any of the momentary stages suitable, in that these are not distinct from total states of the object at a particular time, and agent causation is supposed to be different from causation by states or events within the agent. Hence, there is nowhere to "put" agent causation in the temporal parts theorist's ontology.

More is required, however, than a rejection of the doctrine of temporal parts. For suppose a contrary view ("presentism") on which all that exists *simpliciter,* exists at the present moment. Some have supposed, consistent with this, that the general category of objects or substances is somehow reducible to that of events, conceived as localized property instantiations. Again, if this were so, the notion of a distinctively personal causality could not be made out, since its distinctiveness from event causation rests in part on the assumption that agents belong to a distinct ontological category (that of substance).

Finally, even on views that admit enduring substances, many suppose a kind of reductionism concerning composite substances. The being and activity of such composites, they aver, is wholly constituted by the being and activity of their fundamental constituents. If I am a composite biological organism, my activity now—I here speak of the concrete "token" process embedded in the world, as opposed to any abstract type to which this process belongs—is simply and entirely a structured, logical consequence of the mechanistic activity of my present constituents. And so, once more, there should be no room for a distinctive kind of agency exhibited by me and other persons. So the agent causationist requires an ontology on which persons are enduring, ineliminable substances that are in *some* robust sense more than the sum of the constituents of their bodies.

2.2. Does Agent Causation Require Substance Dualism?

It has often been supposed that the only way the requirement that agents not be *mere* composites can be satisfied is for agents to be *wholly* distinct substances from their bodies. However, this is not typically argued with any care. Chisholm did hold that agents were simple substances, but the reason he gave for this had to do with his very demanding view on what it takes for any object to endure through time.[2] He was a "mereological essentialist," believing that objects have all of their parts essentially. Given that human bodies are like every other composite physical objects in losing parts over time, this implies that an individual human body does not exist for a substantial length of time—or if it does, it is only as a "scattered object" that cannot be identified with a human person, much less with someone having an irreducible agent-causal capacity. By contrast, Richard Taylor (1966: 134–38) is quite emphatic that human persons are simply living animals, having no immaterial parts, and Randolph Clarke suggests the same (1993: 201 n.14).

Is there a special reason for the agent causationist to be a dualist? Clearly, agent causal power and its exercise cannot be constituted by underlying event-causal processes, on pain of giving up the claim that it is an ontologically irreducible power. (John Bishop 1983, 1986 held for a time that agent causation was conceptually, but not ontologically, irreducible to event-causal processes. But this would render agent causation useless for the purpose of solving the metaphysical problem of freedom.) It may be enough, though, that one suppose that agent causal power and its allied properties are ontologically emergent, while still being powers and properties of the biological organism. That is, one might embrace a strong form of property dualism, consistent with substance monism. Note that this requires a metaphysical, not merely epistemological, understanding of emergence, and so something rather more ambitious than what is contemplated when the term *emergence* is used in some contemporary theories of mind in philosophy and cognitive science.

O'Connor (2000: ch. 6) defends just such a position. On that account, a state of an object is emergent if it instantiates one or more simple, or nonstructural, properties and is a causal consequence of the object's exhibiting some general type of complex configuration (whose complexity will probably be a feature of both its intrinsic and functional structure). A property is "nonstructural" just in case its instantiation does not even partly consist in the instantiation of a plurality of more basic properties. An emergent state is a "causal consequence" of the object's complex configuration in the following way: in addition to having a locally determinative influence in the manner characterized by physical science, fundamental particles or systems also naturally tend (in any context) toward the generation of such an emergent state. But their doing so is not discernible in contexts that do not exhibit the requisite macro-complexity, because each one tending on its own is "incomplete." It takes the right threshold degree of complexity for those tendings, present in each micro-particle, to jointly achieve their characteristic effect, which is the generation of a specific type of holistic state.

Note that agent causation would require the emergence of a very different *sort* of capacity altogether, one that is distinctive in kind (a fundamentally intentional form of causality) and whose indeterminacy may well not be characterizable in a manner suitable to any quantum indeterminacy. As Jan Cover and John O'Leary-Hawthorne (1996) note, in criticizing this emergentist approach to an agent-causal theory, we are forced to posit a sharp break somewhere in the seemingly smooth difference of degree between organisms of increasing complexity. They also suggest that such a theorist is going to have a difficult time saying just what *exactly* the agent who is doing the causing is. The official answer is the whole living organism, but one might suppose that this is too inspecific. For presumably the agent-causal capacity emerges from the right kind of neural structure. (A brain in a vat would have this capacity, too, one assumes.) But perhaps this is too general still. Might it not strictly be some part of the brain? Or perhaps the capacity is associated with different particular parts under different particular circumstances? They worry that one's answer will either attribute (implausibly) some degree of arbitrariness to the basic workings of nature or will require us to suppose (again implausibly) that the kind of thing that is the subject of agent causal power is determined *extrinsically*. (It is the whole organism where there is one, but a brain where it is envatted and disembodied.) Along similar lines, William Hasker (1999) contends that the kind of unity of the agent that is presupposed by the thesis of agent causation directly entails that the agent is a mereological simple.

I will not try to sort through possible replies to this last worry, involving as it does difficult questions about the metaphysics of composites. (Can there be an individual who is composed of many things yet whose individuality is not a function of—not grounded in—the individuality of those parts, and who indeed can persist in the face of a complete changeover of those parts over time? Would the holistic emergent properties of systems as characterized here suffice for such distinctive individuality? How would one distinguish this kind of emergent *composite* individuality from an emergent substance dualism, on which the bodily system is wholly non-overlapping the mental substance?) But I note that the other worries, concerning the strong assumptions necessary regarding the dramatic difference emergence can make, are likely to be faced by the substance dualist as well. For it is plausible that if substance dualism is true, it will involve the *emergence* of mental substances.

Suppose a substance dualist picks up the argument at this point and claims that we have philosophical motivation to want this even stronger kind of emergence: Agents seem too ontologically superficial on the emergent-capacity-only view, on which, the emergence of free choices by highly complex systems of matter was foreordained long ago, a direct product of the microphysical fabric of things.[3]

Why not go for the "whole hog," then, and embrace an emergentist form of substance dualism, according to which agents themselves are radically distinct things? Probably the main objection to this is that the causal generation of mind stuff amounts to creation ex nihilo. What some refuse to contemplate even for God is now being contemplated for bits of matter! Note that the kind of "tending towards the generation of an emergent property or capacity" ascribed to fundamental particles according to the more modest emergentist picture does not differ from garden variety tendencies. It is a tendency to qualify a system in a certain way, to induce a change in the system's properties. The substance emergence view, by contrast, involves a tendency to generate new stuff. Hasker (1999) denies that this amounts to creation ex nihilo, but his reason is unclear. It may be that, as a theist, he regards the exercise of causal power by any created thing as inherently dependent on God's constant activity of sustaining things in existence. But it would seem that for this to suffice to ward off the charge, one will have to further suppose that God directly plays a further, ineliminable role in the very producing of the emergent substance, so that while it is creation ex nihilo, it is not (entirely) an accomplishment of the physical system.

Others will question the sharpness of the contrast between substance and property emergence by rejecting traditional views of the ontology of substances and their properties on which the contrast is based. The dualist Karl Popper, for example, would not see a sharp difference between the two forms of emergence. If the "property emergence" view posits rich and *enduring* psychological structures of an emergent sort—as argued in Eccles and Popper (1977)—then, says Popper, one has *thereby* described a self or person that is distinct from the physical organism.

2.3. What Is the Relation between Agent and Event Causation?

I now turn to the idea of causation at work in various agent causationist accounts and the consequent similarity or dissimilarity between agent and event causation. Agent causationists universally reject theories that purport to reductively analyze the concept of causation to noncausal notions, such as certain patterns of actual similarity among event types, as in the traditional Humean analysis, or of counterfactual similarity, as exemplified by David Lewis's more recent view (1986b). This rejection is unsurprising, since agent causation, understood as a kind of control functioning more or less independently of the agent's dispositional states, clearly cannot be understood in any such terms. Thomas Reid (1769) and George

Berkeley (1998a and 1998b), the two most prominent defenders of agent-causal theories in early modern philosophy, went so far as to hold that agent causation is the only form of causation properly named. The regular patterns exhibited in our experience among sensible objects are directly produced by God, the supreme agent cause. (For a fine exposition of Thomas Reid's views on agent and event causation that situates Reid's views alongside more recent accounts, see William Rowe 1991. Also see O'Connor 1994 and 2000: ch. 3).

Contemporary agent causationists have instead held that agent and event causation are equally basic, related features in the natural order of things, although Chisholm and Taylor betray a lingering tendency to think of event causation as ontologically second-class.[4] In emphasizing differences between event and agent causation, they naturally opened themselves to the charge that the sole similarity was in the term *causation*. They were far from hostile to this—Taylor (1966: 262) says as much—but their critics saw this as casting suspicion on the idea of *agent*, not event, causation.

In various writings (for example, 1971 and 1979), Roderick Chisholm contended that the correlated notions of physical necessity and law of nature are primitives in terms of which event causation is to be understood. Roughly speaking, an event A causally contributes to event B just in case it is part of a minimally sufficient condition for B or is essential to *preventing* a sufficient condition for not-E. (This last case allows for indeterministic event causation. I note that in his various writings on this matter, (for example, 1966, 1976a and b), Chisholm did not always include such a condition.) By contrast, the core agent-causal event, which Chisholm termed an "undertaking (or endeavoring) to make [state of affairs] A happen," is understood apart from the concept of law of nature as an essentially intentional form of direct control by an agent (1967: 413). So in the event-causal case, causality is reductively definable in terms of a modal concept (albeit a primitive one, distinct from the fundamental notion of absolute necessity), whereas in the agent-causal case, it is a primitive intentional concept, also intended to carry a primitive causal sense (see ibid: n. 6.)

Richard Taylor (1966) also supposed that a primitive, logically contingent form of necessity figures into our understanding of event causation. On his view, event or condition A was the total cause of event B only if each was a "necessary and sufficient condition" for the other under the circumstances. But in contrast to Chisholm's reductive analysis, he added the requirement that A made B happen by virtue of its power to do so (p. 38). This forges a link between agent and event causation: both are manifestations of primitive powers or capacities. The difference between them consists in the different types of entities that are causes and the modal feature that event causes, but not agent causes, necessitate their effects. Indeterministic event causation is a conceptual impossibility for Taylor; if our best fundamental physical theories posit merely statistical regularities, then they imply a lack of causality. But the existence of the agent with his distinctive capacities does not necessitate any particular effects. Taylor does allow that circumstances might necessitate the causally complex event of the agent's *causing* some event B, in which case the agent would not be acting freely. (He denies, however, that this is typically the case.) This idea is problematic, as it implies that a condition might directly make happen the obtaining of a causal relation (see O'Connor 1996, 2000). But it is quite independent of the rest of what Taylor says and is not of central interest here.

More recently, I have defended a conception of the relation of agent and event causation that is a hybrid of these accounts (see O'Connor 1995a and 2000). With Chisholm, I hold that agent causation alone is essentially intentional and purposive. The fundamental locution I employ is "an agent's causing an intention for a reason."[5] (Taylor, by contrast, holds that an agent might cause an event for no reason at all.) But I also agree with Taylor that event causation, too, involves the exercise of primitive capacities, though I deny that all such capacities must be structured in such a way that event causes invariably necessitate their effects. Deterministic propensities are but the limiting cases of probabilistic tendencies. In saying this, we should not suppose with some (for example, Paul Humphreys 1989) that an indeterministic tendency is something that merely structures what is a "chance" outcome. Whatever happens is made to happen by its cause. That the cause operated indeterministically implies only that it might not have produced that outcome—it had a positive tendency in the total circumstances toward more than one type of outcome.

A final and markedly different understanding of agent and event causation and their relationship has recently been proposed by Randolph Clarke, whose point of departure is the novel analysis of event causation proposed independently by Fred Dretske (1977), David Armstrong (1983), and Michael Tooley (1977, 1987). This view eschews primitive dispositionality in favor of a primitive type of relation. In basic outline, the view identifies *laws of nature* with certain primitive, contingent, and second-order relations among universals, ones that are specified as satisfying certain theoretical requirements associated with our concept of scientific law. The event-causal relation, conceived as a type, is a special subset of these and is instanced between first-order events.

Clarke suggests that the very relation of causation that is thus theoretically identified within the domain of complex universals also holds between agents and their actions in instances of freely performed action. (The agent causationist can ride piggyback on the proposed understanding of the causal relation discernible in its role in structuring patterns among events.) The sole differences between event and agent causation are the causal relata and the contingent fact that event causings are structured by probabilistic or deterministic laws. (But see later in this chapter for more on Clarke's view on agent causation and causal laws.)

Now the second-order relation view of the causal relation is not without its problems. Bas van Fraassen (1988: ch. 5) has challenged the relevance of the posited relation to the *explanation* of any particular causal sequence: How does the existence of a second-order relation among pairs of complex universals explain why *particular* event A brought about *particular* event B? After all, not all properties of types, including relational properties, carry over to their tokens. Van Fraassen calls this "the Inference Problem": the problem of explaining why we are entitled to infer from the posited second-order relation among pairs of universals that this particular event or state of affairs, instantiating the first member of one of the pairs, will *cause* an instantiation of the corresponding member.

My purpose in drawing attention to this problem for the general view is to note a certain direction within the responses of the view's proponents. David Armstrong (1997) has come to hold that causation is manifested in our world as simply and solely a relation among *types* of states of affairs. (So when I experience the causal force, say, that is exerted on my toe by a heavy object, what I am experiencing is nothing particular, but rather causation in general, or nomicity.) And Michael Tooley's "speculative proposal" in response to the Inference Problem is to posit unusual features in the mereology of transcendent universals. If it is a law of nature that all things having property P have property Q, then, he says, we might suppose that P "exists only as part of the conjunctive universal, P and Q" (1987: 124). It would then follow that *any*time P is instantiated, Q is as well, thus grounding the inference from the observation of a P-type event. Both of these responses challenge the official view that the second-order relations by means of which we specify the causal relation are only contingently associated with it (as clearly is true when we use the contingent fact about Socrates that he was the teacher of Plato as one means of identifying him).

The present significance of this is that by supposing such associations to be *essential* to the causal relation, as I myself think proponents of the general program should, one will also require that agent causation be law-governed. Now Clarke suggests that will be so, in any case. We might suppose laws of nature to the effect that the causal relation obtains between agents and certain events only where agents have properties requisite to reflective practical reasoning and the caused events are instances of acting for reasons. Further, it might be a law of nature that whenever agents with such capacities do act on reasons, the causal relation obtains between the agent and the action (though the laws and antecedent circumstances do not imply *which* action will be so caused.) But if this is so, the explanation for there being a causal relation now between me and my action appears to reside in these general lawlike facts about agents in general, not me in particular. That is, it is not clear that I am fundamentally responsible for this result. Bear in mind that on the general causal view in question, there are no primitive, single-case dispositions at work. The significance of calling the posited relation "causal" instead lies in the higher order, completely general facts about how this relation structures patterns of property instantiation in the world. One worries, then, that this general view is less hospitable than Clarke supposes to the agent-causalist's motivation to attribute fundamental responsibility for certain outcomes to agents.

2.4. What Does the Agent Cause?

As a rule, agent causationists are surprisingly vague on the basic question of just what agents cause. Chisholm and Taylor both repudiate choices or volitions as a basic mental category. Taylor says that agents cause their behavior (the whole sequence?) and Chisholm says that in trying to bring about some state of affairs, the agent makes happen some more immediate state of affairs, which he supposes is neurophysiological in character. This neurophysiological event is not identified with any intentional state, though, as we have seen, the agent's causing it is intentional. Finally, while Clarke does speak of agents as making choices, he consistently says that agents cause their actions and so seems to have a view similar to Taylor's on this score (though they differ on what features warrant characterizing the behavior as an "action"). C. Campbell (1967), by contrast, speaks of the self as directly determining a decision, and Michael Zimmerman (1984), of the agent's directly effectuating a volition.[6] Along similar lines, Donagan (1987) and O'Connor (1995a, 2000) hold that the agent causes an immediately executive, or action-triggering, intentional state. (Strictly speaking, the agent's causing such an intentional state is what they term the agent's "choice," and it is also the agent's basic action, which typically constitutes the initial segment of more extended event-causal processes that result from such choices.)

3. AGENT CAUSATION AND REASONS EXPLANATION

C. Campbell (1967) held that self-causality is conceivable only in the special circumstance where our "desiring nature" is opposed to our perception of moral duty (p. 46). In all other cases, he supposed, our formed character will inevitably result in some particular outcome, even if it is not immediately apparent to us which outcome that will be. But in this special situation of moral temptation, *nothing* other than the agent or self determines what happens. If one asks why the agent acts as he does on a given occasion—now succumbing to temptation, now doing what he ought—the correct answer, Campbell insists, is that there is no explanation. (Seemingly at odds with this, however, he does allow that some situations of temptation are more difficult than others, and that consequently we may reasonably expect resistance to temptation to occur less frequently in such cases.) Though this view is implausibly restrictive of the scope of free action, it does have the advantage of evading the difficult matter facing most agent causationists of how reasons guide and thereby explain the agent's exertion of causal power.

Chisholm suggested that reasons are necessary causal conditions on agent's causing their actions. I am always acting with some purpose, and my desiring to attain that end and having appropriate beliefs about how to do so thereby contribute to my doing so, not by forming part of a sufficient condition for the action, but by their being essential to *preventing* the occurrence of a sufficient condition for my *not* causing the action. (Had those factors not obtained, there would have been a sufficient condition for my not causing that particular action.) One problem with this way of understanding the role of reasons is that we can envision cases where my having reason A and my having reason B each guide my performing an action but neither of which is such that, had that state not obtained, I would have been precluded from performing the action. (As should be apparent, this is most directly a problem for Chisholm's modal analysis of event causation.)

Taylor had a different view. According to him, explanations in terms of reasons or purposes are entirely different from explanations in terms of causes (1966: 142).[7] When we recall that Taylor repudiates any intentional event that triggers and guides the completion of the action, it becomes puzzling how the agent's having a purpose guides his causing the action. The action's initial segment will be constituted by enormously complex neuronal events, none of which the agent is consciously aware of. So how does he effortlessly "get it right," causing just the right complex sequence for an action that will carry out his purpose? (We cannot suppose, for example, that the agent's having the purpose is a state that is governed by causal laws that map it onto the appropriate outcomes.) Furthermore, it is not clear how Taylor can meet Davidson's famous challenge to noncausal understandings of reasons explanations: Among cases where the agent has more than one reason for performing an action, it is plausible to suppose than in some of them only one reason actually prompted the action, while in others a plurality of factors did so. In what does this difference consist?

In O'Connor (1995a), I follow Taylor in construing reasons explanations as noncausal. However, I contend that a satisfactory answer to Davidson's challenge requires (what is independently plausible on introspective grounds) the agent causationist to suppose that agents cause executive states of *intention* of a particular sort. The content of these intentions is not merely that I perform an action of type $\emptyset$, but that I perform an action of type $\emptyset$ *in order to satisfy desire D* (or prior intention I). If intentions have this rich sort of content, then the difference between acting to satisfy desire D1 and acting to satisfy D2 and acting to satisfy both, will be a function of the content of the intention that I cause to occur. When Davidson asks what accounts for my acting on reason R1 and not R2, given that I was aware of both at the time of acting, the answer will be that we must look to the content of the intention I cause; this will have the form, that I do A for in order to satisfy reason ————. In a given case, the blank will be filled by either or both of R1 and R2. In actively deciding which action I will undertake, I am *inter alia* deciding which reason I am aiming to satisfy.

Note that it is also required that this intention, once generated, causally sustains the completion of the action in an appropriate manner. We thereby avoid the sort of counterexample Alfred Mele (1992a) raises against purely noncausal accounts of reasons explanations, such as that of George Wilson (1989), in which a causal process is independent of the intention that generates the action.

Randolph Clarke (1996a) objects that since the intention refers to the action, it must be causally or explanatorily posterior to the action, and so the account absurdly implies that what explains the action depends on the outcome of something posterior to it in this way. But this rests on a misunderstanding. On the proposed account, the agent directly causes (the coming to be of) a state of intention. This constitutes the "core" action. The intention refers not to some independent process that is the action, but to an action sequence of which it is the initiating segment.

Finally, Galen Strawson (1986: ch. 2, 1994) has objected to indeterministic theories of free action generally that they (unwittingly) entail an infinite regress of choices corresponding to every indeterministic choice of a course of action. Since the way one acts is a result of, or explained by, "how one is, mentally speaking" (M), for one to be responsible for that choice one must be responsible for M. To be responsible for M, one must have *chosen to be M* itself—and that not blindly, but deliberately, in accordance with some reasons R1. But for that choice to be a responsible one, one must have chosen to be such as to be moved by R1, requiring some further reasons R2 for such a choice. And so on, *ad infinitum*. Free choice requires an impossible regress of choices to be the way one is in making choices.

What should one say to this? Alfred Mele (1995: 221ff.) argues that Strawson misconstrues the locus of freedom and responsibility, as that is understood by just about any free will theorist (including compatibilists). Freedom is principally a feature of our actions, and only derivatively of our characters from which such actions spring. The task of a free will theorist, then, is to show how one is in rational, reflective control of the choices one makes, consistent with their being no freedom-negating conditions. This seems right, although the agent causationist is likely to add that since compatibilist theories and even some incompatibilist theories make one's free control to directly reside in the causal efficacy of my reasons, it is entirely appropriate in that context to worry about how I got that way in the first place. (Which is just to say, Strawson's argument when directed against such accounts is best understood as challenging the adequacy of its understanding of free control over one's choices.)

But let us consider what the agent causationist might reply to Strawson, on the agent-causal account I have sketched. Aware of certain reasons pro and con, I cause an action-initiating intention *to A for reason R1*. This is explained by my having been aware of reason R1 while deliberating and as I completed the action. I did not directly choose to be in a state of being aware of and motivated by R1. I simply found myself in that state, among others, and proceeded to deliberate. Being in that sum total of rational states circumscribed the range of possibilities for me, and also presumably the scope of responsibility *directly* connected to my free choice. But that choice was neither fully causally determined by those states nor merely a "chancy" outcome of tendencies of those states. Instead, *I* directly determined which choice within the available range would be made, a choice *explained by* "how I was, mentally speaking," at that time, although it is not fully a *result of* that state. These two factors are treated separately, on agent causal accounts (as Clarke 1997 observes, in discussing Strawson 1994a), permitting direct control of an action that is not "blind." I chose for certain reasons, but I was not constrained to do so; given that this is so, there is no need for me to have first freely chosen which reasons I would act upon.

Of course, there is a residual worry hinted at by Strawson's argument. We enter the world with powerful and deep behavioral and attitudinal dispositions. Long before we mature to the point of making sophisticated, reflective choices, we are placed in environments that mold and add to those dispositions. Such factors heavily influence our early choices, even if they do not causally determine all of them. They certainly do determine that Billy will choose from only a very limited range of options in any given situation, a range that will differ quite a bit from that open to Susie under similar circumstances. These choices and continuing contingencies of circumstance, in turn, will sharply circumscribe the options Billy considers at a more reflective stage, when we begin to hold Billy accountable for his actions. The worry, then, is that factors unchosen by Billy largely account for the kinds of deliberation and the overall pattern of outcomes of Billy's mature choices. Even if an agent-causal capacity is at work in these choices, Strawson might ask, is it autonomy enough?

Surely one must concede in response that responsibility for "shaping who I am" and for the choices that ensue from this comes in degrees and, indeed, can only sensibly be measured within a limited scope of possibilities. We cannot hold Billy responsible for failing to consider an option entirely outside the range of his experience. And his responsibility for passing by options that are within the range of his experience but that he has had precious little opportunity to consider as attractive is attenuated. In concrete cases, given limited information, we hazard rough guesses on these matters. When we are confronted with an individual who quite deliberately and unhesitatingly makes a grossly immoral choice—indeed, who seems not to even consider the obvious moral alternative—the question we need to ask is, Was there a point earlier in her life when paths were open to her (ones for which at each step of the way she had some significant motivation to pursue, and which she recognized as having moral significance) such that had she taken them she would now be in a position to see the force of the moral considerations at hand? How "difficult" would it have been for her to pursue such a path? Our guesses about such matters are exceedingly rough, relying on the assumption that most mature individuals possess a certain measure of rough moral sensitivity. Lacking compelling information to the contrary, then, we deem it appropriate to hold individuals responsible for their own moral indifference.

Perhaps the important point to emphasize here is that the agent causationist can consistently allow for the existence of individuals whose basic choice-making capacities are just like ours, but who lack sensitivity to a variety of forms of basic human decency through no fault of their own. Furthermore, he can also accept (what may also be behind Strawson's argument) that perfect responsibility for one's choices and character is not just contingently lacking in human beings but is impossible: it would require perhaps perfect indifference at the outset, or at least an openness to all possible courses of action. The coherence of *that* idea is very doubtful.

4. MECHANISM AND AGENT CAUSATION: NARROWING THE GAP?

In the preceding discussion, I frequently adverted to the boringly familiar thought that our motivation to pursue courses of action varies considerably. Evident as this is, one might well suppose that some agent causationists have not sufficiently taken this fact to heart in their accounts of the way reasons explain actions. Taylor (1966) and O'Connor (1995a), for example, both lack any account of strength of desire and settled preferences. This doubtless figures into Taylor's rejection of any causal role for reasons (see 1966: 250) and into the very attenuated role O'Connor (1995a) assigns, in which my now having a reason to A is a necessary causal condition on my now causing the intention to A.

Randolph Clarke (1993, 1996a) develops his account of agent causation with the explicit goal of remedying this defect in the traditional picture. In the early version, when an agent acts freely, her coming to have reasons to so act (R_A) indeterministically causes her action (A). The agent figures into the picture by causing, not the action *simpliciter*, but the action's being done for those reasons. If we let "→" stand for the causal relation, we may diagram Clarke's basic picture thus:

$$|R_A \rightarrow A|$$
$$\uparrow$$
AGENT

One worry with this picture is that while it allows that reasons have varying strength—now explicated as a measurable causal tendency to produce an action—it is not clear that their having such strengths influences the agent's activity. To be sure, Clarke says that the reasons indeterministically cause the *action* itself. But this, for him, does not include the agent's causal activity. And this seems odd: is not my directly causing some outcome something I do? And in any case, do we not want to say that my reasons have varying degrees of influence over this causality, whether or not we conceive it as part of my action? The above account does not make clear how this might be.

In Clarke (1996a), the author maintains instead that the agent and the agent's indeterministic state of having reason R_A *jointly* produce A. The agent's causal capacity consists in the ability to make effective an indeterministic propensity of one's reason to bring about A, not by directly producing a causal relation between two events, but in the sense of "acting alongside" or bolstering the tendency (whether it be of a low or high probability measure), ensuring that it will achieve its characteristic effect.

Does this achieve the desired integration of my tendency-conferring reasons and my agent causality? It may seem not. In any given instance, the action has some chance of occurring (and on occasion does occur) apart from the agent's activity. Otherwise, what is meant by saying that the reason has a tendency to produce the action? This would be to conceive reasons as actively *competing* with the agent, qua agent. But Clarke says something further here: "[s]uppose that, under the circumstances, whichever of the available actions the agent performs, that action will be performed, and it will be caused by the reasons that favor it *only if* the agent causes that action" (ibid. 1996a: 25, emphasis added).

Clarke does not elaborate on this hegemony of the agent's causality over the tendencies conferred by one's reasons, but it seems to me to be a promising way to achieve the desired integration. In O'Connor (2000), I suggest that my coming to recognize a reason to act induces or elevates an objective propensity for me to initiate the behavior. That is to say, agent causation is a probabilistically *structured* capacity. It will be structured not only by tendency-conferring states of having reasons to act in specific ways but also by more enduring states of character, involving relatively fixed dispositions and long-standing general intentions and purposes around which my life has come to be organized. I am the sole causal factor directly generating my intention to A (not a co-cause along with my reasons, as in Clarke's view), but my doing what I do is shaped, causally, by my total motivational state.

Embracing this causal-propensity account of the relative *strength* of reasons—and perhaps even supposing it to be required to make sense of the very idea that reasons in general motivate actions—need not lead one to abandon the noncausal link suggested earlier between actions and the reasons that explain them. For the mere fact that a reason I had gave me some tendency in this sense to act as I did does not explain my action. Maybe I did not act for that reason, despite my recognition that it was a relevant reason. (I wanted to spare Charles pain, but that is not, even in part, why I pulled the plug.) Within the framework of an agent-causal account, this is still to be determined by the content of the agent's intention in acting.

Or so it seems. Randolph Clarke (1996a: 47n.37) challenged the original content-of-the-intention approach to reasons explanation in a way that might be transposed as follows to apply to the present, more complicated picture: The account appears to allow that the purpose-identifying content of my intention might not refer to a motivational state generating a very high propensity for me to cause the type of action I did cause. But surely, he objects, such a state must figure into the true explanation of my acting as I did. I cannot declare by fiat in my intention that guides my action what *had been* my motivation in so acting. My reply is that this last is surely so, but I do *form* the intention, and this is not an accompanying declaration of some kind, possibly mistaken, but the initiating core of what I do, and its content guides the completion of the action. The fact that a particular reason gave me a strong propensity to act in a particular way certainly explains in part my considering that possibility while deliberating; but if I cease to consider this factor when I cause my intention to act in this way—an odd scenario, to be sure, but seemingly possible—and actively form an action with the intentional content of satisfying another reason, then that alone explains why I acted just as I did.

(Are we then saying as a general thesis about action explanations that reasons that are referred to in the content of any agent's intentions automatically explain? Surely we can conceive an external manipulation of one's choice formation such that one is caused to do A with the intention of doing A for reason R, although R is in no way explanatory. But the agent causationist need make no such general claim. The agent-causal origin of the intention is a necessary ingredient of this sort of explanatory framework. It makes the coming to be of the content of the intention something I am directly responsible for *and* [if the argument of O'Connor 1996 and 2000 is correct] it precludes an independent causal explanation.)

NOTES

1. For accounts and defenses of temporal parts ontology, see David Lewis (1986b) and Mark Heller (1990). The view is criticized by Peter van Inwagen (1990b).

2. Richard Swinburne (1986) *may* be advocating agent causation with his notion of active "purposings," although he is not explicit on this point. Purposings are likened to volitions in some other accounts, though Swinburne emphasizes that purposings (1) may merely consist in allowing certain actions to occur, rather than consciously choosing them and (2) are intrinsically active and have content that points to the result sought. But these claims are accepted, for example, by Hugh McCann (1998)—discussed in Clarke's contribution to this volume—and McCann is not an agent causationist. Swinburne is also a dualist, but like Chisholm, his motivations concern problems with identity over time rather than reasons specific to freedom of action.

3. In correspondence, Peter Unger has advanced this argument in favor of substance dualism over softer varieties. He discusses this matter in Unger (forthcoming).

4. Jennifer Trusted (1984) appears to defend an agent-causal account of human agency, the capacity for which emerges from event-causal physical activity. But I am not at all confident in interpreting her final view, developed over the course of a wide-ranging discussion, much of which exposits the views of others.

5. William Rowe (1991), in interpreting Thomas Reid's view, speaks of an agent's "exerting active power." But he wishes to *contrast* this with an allegedly mysterious view on which there is an "irreducible relation" between the agent and his act of willing, a view he sees in Chisholm and Taylor (see pp. 156–57). I myself am unclear on what an exertion of active power is, if it does not consist precisely of an event in which an agent causes some event, and this is how I understand Reid himself. Perhaps all that Rowe's remarks on this point amount to is an insistence that an agent's exerting active power is something he *does*, a point on which Rowe may find Chisholm and Taylor to be unclear. If this is correct, then my earlier (1994) understanding of Rowe's account, on which Reid is read as a noncausal theorist of the sort discussed in Clarke's contribution to this volume (ch. 16), is mistaken and the consequent criticisms misplaced.

6. John Thorp (1980: 102) writes: "Now presumably we shall want to say that the agent's causing the event is also an event. We seem then to have two events, the decision which is an alteration in the agent, and the agent's causing that alteration. At once there looms a vicious regress. It can be forestalled only by saying that these apparently two events, the decision and the agent's causing the decision to itself, are in fact one and the same. . . . We do not require that an event be the same as its cause, but that an event be the same event as its being caused." It is not clear to me from the wider text whether this is a (misleading) way of saying that an agent's causing an event is not itself an event or whether he is effectively reducing agent causation to simple indeterminism.

7. Indeed, he held the puzzling thesis that there might be completely independent purposive and causal explanations for the very same action (1966: 144).

CHAPTER 16

LIBERTARIAN VIEWS: CRITICAL SURVEY OF NONCAUSAL AND EVENT-CAUSAL ACCOUNTS OF FREE AGENCY

RANDOLPH CLARKE

SOME libertarian accounts require that a free decision or other free action have no cause at all; some require that it either have no cause or be only nondeterministically caused by other events. Since both such views place no positive causal requirements on free action, we may call them "noncausal accounts." (They are sometimes called "simple indeterminist views.") Accounts of another type require that a free action be nondeterministically caused by events of certain sorts involving the agent, such as her having certain beliefs and desires or a certain intention; call these "event-causal accounts." (They are also called "causal indeterminist views.") This essay will examine and evaluate some of the most fully developed recent noncausal and event-causal libertarian accounts. The focus in the first two sections will be on the question whether, if one or another of these accounts is true, that suffices for our having free will. The third section will assess the evidence we have bearing on the truth of these views.

1. NONCAUSAL ACCOUNTS

Proponents of noncausal accounts of free action hold (quite obviously) noncausal views of action. Generally, the view is that every action is or begins with a basic mental action. A decision or a choice is typically held to be an example of such a basic action. An overt bodily action, such as raising one's arm, is held to be a nonbasic, complex action constituted by a basic mental action's bringing about certain other events, culminating in the rising of the arm. The basic action here is often called a volition, which is said to be the agent's willing, trying, or endeavoring to move a certain part of her body in a certain way.

Carl Ginet (1990) and Hugh McCann (1998) have set out the most fully developed recent noncausal libertarian accounts. Less detailed views of this type have been advanced by Stewart Goetz (1988 and 1997) and Storrs McCall (1994: ch. 9).[1]

Both Ginet and McCann maintain that an event is a basic action in virtue of its possessing some noncausal intrinsic feature. On Ginet's view, the feature in question is a certain "actish phenomenal quality," which he describes (1990: 13) as its seeming to the agent as if she is directly producing, making happen, or determining the event that has this quality. McCann holds that basic actions are characterized by intrinsic intentionality. For example, in making a decision, he maintains (1998: 163), one intends to decide—indeed, one intends to decide exactly as one does. (That is, when one decides to A, one intends to decide to A.) One's so intending, though intrinsic to the decision, is not a matter of the content of the intention that is formed in deciding, nor is it a matter of one's having any further intention in addition to that formed in making the decision. Rather, McCann holds, it is simply a matter of the decision's being, by its very nature, an act that the agent means to be performing.

Most libertarians accept, as do compatibilists, that some event may be an action but unfree.[2] If this is correct, then we may ask what more, besides what is required for action, is required for a decision or other action to be free. As is characteristic of proponents of noncausal accounts, Ginet and McCann place no additional positive requirements on freedom; the further requirements are instead that certain conditions be absent. Both require that the action not be causally determined. Ginet requires, further (1990: 121), that in performing the action the agent not be subject to irresistible compulsion.

Two (related) main problems arise for libertarian accounts of this sort; both are problems, in the first instance, for noncausal accounts of action. The first concerns control. Performing an action, even acting unfreely, is exercising some variety of active control over one's behavior; acting freely is exercising an especially valuable variety of active control. A theory of action, whether of specifically free action or not, ought to say what the pertinent variety of control is or in what it consists. It is questionable whether noncausal views have an adequate account to offer on this point.

The second main problem concerns rationality. Acting freely is acting with a capacity for rational self-governance and determining, oneself, whether and how one exercises that capacity on a given occasion. Hence it must be possible for a free action to be an action performed for a certain reason, an action for which there is a rational explanation. Again, it is questionable whether noncausal views can provide adequate accounts of these phenomena.

1.1. Control

Consider first the matter of control. An obvious candidate for an account here is that an agent's exercising active control consists in her action's being caused, in an appropriate way, by her, or by certain events involving her, such as her having certain beliefs and desires or a certain intention. Since noncausal accounts reject this type of view, what alternatives are available?

On Ginet's view, the single positive characteristic present in every basic action is the actish phenomenal quality, its seeming to the agent as if she is directly producing that event. But Ginet rejects the possibility of causation by agents, where this is taken to be something other than event causation; and, as we have seen, he holds that when agents act, it need not be the case that any events involving those agents cause their actions. David Velleman (1992: 466, n.14) consequently objects that, on this view, the actish phenomenal quality is misleading, illusory. However, Ginet stresses that his description of this quality is metaphorical; the experience does not literally represent to the agent that she is bringing about the event in question.[3]

Whatever the correct characterization of this phenomenal quality may be, it is highly doubtful that the mere feel of a mental event, the way it seems to the individual undergoing it, can itself *constitute* the individual's active control over that event, rather than being a (more or less reliable) sign of that control (compare O'Connor 2000: 25–26). The doubt is reinforced by the fact that, on Ginet's view (1990: 9), an event with this quality could be brought about by external brain stimulation, in the absence of any relevant desire or intention on the part of the "agent." An event produced in this way and in these circumstances hardly seems to be an exercise of agency at all.

McCann holds that the control that is exercised in acting has two aspects:

> One has to do with ontological foundations. An exercise of agency has to be spontaneous and active; it is a creative undertaking on the agent's part, to be accounted for in terms of its intrinsic features, not via the operations of other denizens of the world. Second, exercises of agency must be intentional; they

have to be undertaken for the sake of some objective the agent deems worthy of attainment. (McCann 1998: 180)

These two aspects are said to be inseparable in fact, though capable of independent consideration.

As indicated earlier, McCann views the intentionality of basic actions as intrinsic to those events. He observes (for example, 1986: 265–66 and 1998: 163) that it is impossible for a decision to be unintentional, and he concludes that the intentionality must then be intrinsic to the decision.[4] But an alternative explanation is possible (Mele 1997c 240–43 and 2000: 89–93). For something to count as a decision, it may be said, one's acquisition of an intention (to pursue some more or less specific course of action) must be caused, in an appropriate way, by one's having an intention to make up one's mind about what to do. Given the requirement of such a causal history, the alternative continues, necessarily any event that is a decision is intentional. But this fact implies nothing about the intrinsic features of decisions (any more than the fact that nothing counts as sunburn unless it is caused by the sun implies anything about the intrinsic features of the burns that are so caused). However, let us accept, for the sake of the discussion of control, that certain events can have an intentionality that is not at all a matter of how these events are brought about. By itself, such intentionality would not seem to constitute any exercise of active control.[5]

The other aspect of the control that is exercised in basic action, the spontaneity or activeness of such an occurrence, thus appears to be the crucial one. (McCann agrees that this dimension of agency "constitutes its core"; 1998: 185.) This aspect, too, according to McCann, is intrinsic and essential to basic actions, and he maintains that "it has a certain *sui generis* character that renders it incapable of being reduced to anything else" (ibid.). Reducible or not, however, activeness is a phenomenon that stands in need of explication. McCann rejects causal construals of it, but since he offers no substantive alternative, the exercise of active control is left something of a mystery. The resulting view, in my judgment, falls short as an account of action (and hence of free action) because it provides no positive account of the crucial phenomenon.

1.2. Rational Explanation

When it comes to acting for certain reasons and to rational explanation, again obvious candidates for accounts of the phenomena invoke causation: an agent acts for a certain reason only if the agent's having the corresponding reason-state (such as a desire) causes, in an appropriate way, the agent's behavior, and citing a reason-state contributes to a rational explanation of an action only if the agent's having that reason-state caused, in an appropriate way, the action. Proponents of noncausal libertarian views reject such proposals. Let us consider the alternatives that are offered.

Suppose that an agent, Sue, wants her glasses, which she has left in her friend Ralph's room, where he is now sleeping. Sue also wants to wake Ralph, because she desires his company, but she knows that Ralph needs sleep right now, and hence she desires, too, not to wake him. Sue decides to enter Ralph's room and does so, knowing as she does that her action will satisfy her desire to wake Ralph. (The example is from Ginet 1990: 145.) What further facts about the situation could make it the case that, in entering the room, Sue is acting on her desire to get her glasses, and that citing that desire provides a true rational explanation of her action, while she is not acting on her desire to wake Ralph, and citing this latter desire does not give us a true rational explanation of what she is doing?

Ginet maintains that the following conditions suffice for the truth of the explanation that cites Sues's desire to get her glasses:

(a) prior to entering the room, Sue had a desire to get her glasses, and
(b) concurrently with entering the room, Sue remembers that prior desire and intends of her entering the room that it satisfy (or contribute to satisfying) that desire. (ibid.: 143)

Citing Sue's desire to wake Ralph will fail to give us a true rational explanation, Ginet holds (ibid.: 145), just in case Sue does not intend of her action that it satisfy (or contribute to satisfying) that desire.

It is questionable whether Ginet's conditions are sufficient. Suppose that Sue's desire to get her glasses plays no role at all in bringing about (causing) her action, while her desire to wake Ralph, of which she is fully aware when she acts, does play such a role. Here, I think, we have a clash of intuitions between causalists and noncausalists, with the former denying that Sue is really acting on her desire to get her glasses and that citing it truly explains her action.[6]

Further problems with Ginet's proposal tell more decisively against it. The memory condition is, it seems, unnecessary.[7] If Sue's desire to get her glasses is retained and remains fully conscious while she acts, there is no need for her to remember it in order for her to be acting on it. And several problems attend the concurrent intention that is required. First, it is a second-order attitude, an attitude about (among other things) another of the agent's own attitudes (a certain desire of hers). But it seems plain that one can act for a certain reason, and citing a desire can rationally explain one's action, even if when one acts one does not have any such second-order intention.[8] Sue, for example, might act on her desire to get her glasses even if her only intention when she enters the room is to retrieve her glasses. Second, the concurrent intention to which Ginet appeals is said to make direct (or demonstrative) reference to the action, and Ginet (1990: 139–40) suggests that such direct reference requires that the intention be caused by the action (or at least by some initial segment of it). If that is so, then at least some part of the action has occurred before the concurrent intention is acquired. It does not seem, then, that the acquisition of that intention can figure in an account of what, if anything, rationally explains that part of the action.[9] Finally, intention-acquisitions themselves can be explained by citing reasons or reason-states. Since Ginet's account of the rational explanation of an action appeals to an intention, the question arises what can be said about the rational explanation of the acquisition of that intention. Obviously, repeating the same sort of account here would generate a regress. Some other account would have to be offered, but it is not clear what that account could be.[10]

McCann takes a different approach. (See especially his 1998: ch. 8.) On his view, an agent decides for a certain reason, and citing that reason rationally explains the decision, just in case, in cognizance of that reason, and in an intrinsically intentional act of intention formation, the agent forms an intention the content of which reflects the very goals presented in that reason. When Sue decides to enter Ralph's room, for example, she decides for the reason of getting her glasses only if the intention that she forms in making that decision is an intention to enter for the sake of getting her glasses. (McCann takes reasons to be not token mental states but rather the contents of such states.) We have already considered some doubts about the intrinsic intentionality to which the account here appeals. A further problem is that the correspondence between the reasons for which one decides and the content of the decision seems too much to require. Sue may want her glasses so that she can finish reading a certain novel, which she may want to do so that she can contribute to the discussion in her book club tomorrow. Finishing the novel and preparing for tomorrow's discussion may be among the reasons for which she decides to enter the room even if they are not included in the content of her decision.[11] Finally, there will again be a clash of intuitions here between causalists and noncausalists, with the former maintaining that if Sue's desire to get her glasses plays no role at all in bringing about her decision, then even if the content of her decision is to enter for the sake of getting her glasses, she does not really decide for that reason and citing it does not truly explain her decision. (One does not, the objection goes, make it so just by intending it to be so, not even by intrinsically intentionally intending it to be so.)[12]

I have focused on problems for noncausal accounts of action. However, since the noncausal libertarian views under review place no positive requirements on free action beyond those that are placed on action, if they fail as adequate accounts of action, then a fortiori they fail as adequate accounts of free action. The problems are, in my view, severe enough to warrant a turn to causal accounts of action and free action.

2. EVENT-CAUSAL ACCOUNTS

Compatibilist accounts of free action are typically event-causal accounts, invoking event-causal accounts of action. The simplest event-causal libertarian view takes the requirements of a good compatibilist account and adds that certain agent-involving events that cause the action must nondeterministically cause it.[13] When these conditions are satisfied, it is held, the agent exercises in performing his action a certain variety of active control (which is said to consist in the action's being caused by those agent-involving events), the action is performed for reasons, and there was a chance of the agent's not performing that action. It is thus said to have been open to the agent to do otherwise, even given that (it is claimed) its being so open is incompatible with determinism.

A common objection against such a view is that the indeterminism that it requires is destructive, that it would diminish the control with which the agent acts. There are several importantly different forms that this objection takes; I shall examine some of them later. First, I shall consider a type of event-causal libertarian view that is advocated by writers who accept a qualified version of this objection.

2.1. Deliberative Indeterminism

Some writers on free will accept that indeterminism located in the immediate causal production of a decision or subsequent action would diminish control but hold that indeterminism confined to earlier stages in the process leading to decision need not do so. Alfred Mele (1995, 1996, and 1999a; see also his contribution to this volume, ch. 24) and Laura Ekstrom (2000) have advanced the most fully developed recent event-causal libertarian accounts of this sort. Daniel Dennett (1978) and John Martin Fischer (1995) have also sketched libertarian views of this sort, though neither endorses such a view.[14]

Overt action is often preceded by a decision, and decision is often preceded by a deliberative process in which the agent considers reasons for and against alternatives and makes an evaluative judgment concerning which alternative is best (or better or good enough). Focusing on decisions that follow such deliberation, Mele (1995: ch. 12) argues that libertarians should accept a compatibilist account of the relation between a deliberator's evaluative judgment and her decision (and of that between decision and subsequent action); that is, libertarians should allow but not require deterministic causal relations here. Indeterminism should be required, he argues, only at an earlier stage in the deliberative process. His account may be satisfied, for example, if it is undetermined which of a certain

subset of the agent's nonoccurrent beliefs come to mind in the process of deliberation, where their coming to mind combines with other events to bring about
the agent's evaluative judgment (ibid.: 214).[15] The subset in question consists of
"beliefs whose coming or not coming to mind is not something that one would
control even if determinism were true" (ibid.: 216).

Mele argues that the indeterminism required by his view does not diminish,
at least not to any significant extent, "proximal control," a variety of control that
is compatible with determinism. The required indeterminism nevertheless suffices,
he holds, to provide the agent with "ultimate control" over her decision, which
an agent has only if at no time prior to the decision is there any minimally causally
sufficient condition for the agent's making that decision that includes no event or
state internal to the agent. The resulting libertarian view is thus said to secure a
variety of control that is incompatible with determinism without sacrificing (to
any significant extent) the type of control that is so compatible.

Ekstrom offers an account in which the notion of preference, rather than that
of evaluative judgment, plays a prominent role. A preference, as she understands
it, is a desire "formed by a process of critical evaluation with respect to one's
conception of the good" (2000: 106). The formation of such a preference, she
maintains, is an action.[16] She requires indeterminism only in the production of
these preferences, allowing that free decisions be causally determined by
preference-formations favoring those decisions. A decision or subsequent action
is free, on her view (ibid.: 109 and 114), just in case it is nondeviantly caused by
an active formation of a preference (favoring that decision or action), which
preference-formation is in turn the result of an uncoerced exercise of the agent's
evaluative faculty, the inputs to which (the considerations taken up in deliberation) nondeterministically cause the preference-formation.[17]

Ekstrom holds that an agent *is* her preferences and acceptances (reflectively
held beliefs), together with her faculty of forming these by reflective evaluation.[18]
When a preference-formation is nondeterministically caused and it deterministically causes a decision and subsequent action, then, the formation of an attitude
that partly constitutes the agent, which is generated by an evaluative faculty that
partly constitutes the agent, and which the agent could have prevented (by not
forming that preference) causally determines that decision and subsequent action.
What the agent does is then, Ekstrom maintains (ibid.: 116), up to her.

I shall argue in section 2.2 that no compelling argument has been offered for
the view that indeterminism in the direct production of a decision would diminish
control. If that is correct, then Mele's and Ekstrom's rejection of a requirement
of such indeterminism may be unwarranted.[19] For the present, let us consider the
costs incurred by the rejection.

Given this rejection, Mele and Ekstrom must allow, on pain of regress, that
a free decision or other free action may be causally determined by events none
of which is a free action and to none of which the agent has contributed by his

performance of any free action.[20] Libertarians do not typically allow such things. Some hold that any action that is causally determined is unfree; others (see the discussion of Kane's view in section 2.3) allow that a determined action may be (indirectly) free, but only if any determining cause of it either is or results (at least in part) from some other free action by that agent.

A weaker requirement might be considered here. It might be allowed that a causally determined decision or other action may be free, but only if either (1) any determining cause of it either is or results (at least in part) from some other free action by that agent, or (2) the agent was able, by performing some free action, to prevent any determining cause of the action in question. A decision satisfying other requirements of Mele's and Ekstrom's views will be held to be free, then, if it is causally determined by a judgment or a preference-formation that the agent had not actually influenced by performing any free action but which he could have prevented by performing some earlier free action. The requirement may strike many libertarians as too weak, but it will at least ensure a preventability of any determining causes of free actions.

Note that if Mele and Ekstrom reject even this weaker preventability requirement, then they will allow that a free decision or other free action may be causally determined by events none of which was a free action, to none of which the agent contributed by any other free action, and none of which the agent was able to prevent by performing any free action. Such events may fairly be said not to be up to the agent in question. And it would be a curious libertarian view that allowed that an action may be free even if it is causally determined by events none of which was up to the agent. Libertarians are, in the first place, incompatibilists.[21] The most widely accepted arguments for incompatibilism stem from the Consequence Argument (van Inwagen 1983: 16), which finds actions to be unfree if they are the consequences of the laws of nature and events that are not up to us—if they are determined by events that are not up to us. The Consequence Argument, then, gives libertarians a reason to impose at least the weaker requirement of preventability.[22]

2.2. Indeterminism and Control

Event-causal libertarians who find the preventability requirement too weak should favor a view on which for at least some free actions, it is required that there be nondeterministic causation of the free actions themselves. Such views need not require the occurrence of any event that would not figure in a good compatibilist account of free action. They need not, for example, require that some additional undetermined event intervene between the agent's having certain reasons and her performing the action.[23] Nor need they require any literal gaps or breaks in the causal process leading to the action. What is required is just that the direct causation of the action be governed by a nondeterministic rather than a deterministic law.[24] This requirement, moreover, does not obviously imply that the causal relation between antecedent events and action is any weaker than that involved in deterministic causation. On a Humean, regularity view, there is no irreducible relation here anyway; the nondeterministic nature of the law is just a matter of similar agents' elsewhere behaving differently, something that does not obviously imply any weakening of any relation between token events involving this agent and her token action. And on some nonreductive views (for example, Armstrong 1983: 131–35), the irreducible relation between cause and effect is the same whether the governing law is deterministic or nondeterministic.

Still, even if the difference is just a matter of the nature of the governing law, where the law governing the causation of a certain action is nondeterministic, there was a chance of the agent's not acting as she did, and it may be objected that, because there was such a chance, the agent's control over her behavior was diminished. The objection takes a variety of forms.[25]

It is often objected that an action that was not deterministically caused could not be explained, or that such an action could not be fully explained, or that it could not be explained (contrastively) why the agent performed that action rather than some other that remained open to him until he performed that action. (See, for example, Ayer 1954: Double 1991: 203–9; and Nagel 1986: 113–17.)[26] If this objection is intended to raise the problem of control (and it often seems that it is), it is at best a clumsy way of doing so. Control is a metaphysical phenomenon. Explanation requires some real relation between explanans and explanandum, but explanation involves an epistemological element as well. And as a result, solutions to a problem about explanation, or the absence of such solutions, may not reveal anything about a problem concerning control.

Contrary to the claims of some who raise an objection concerning explanation, events that are nondeterministically caused, even events that remain quite unlikely until they occur, may be explained by citing their causes. (See Clarke 1992b and 1997, and sources cited there.) Indeed, often when an event is nondeterministically caused, it is possible to explain why it occurred rather than some alternative that remained open until the occurrence of the event in question; and this may be so even for events that remained unlikely until they occurred. (See Clarke 1996a, and sources cited there.) This holds for nondeterministically caused events that are not actions, and since, on an event-causal libertarian view locating indeterminism in the production of free actions, free actions are nondeterministically caused, this applies also to free actions. On an event-causal libertarian view, there will be available explanations of free actions that cite reason-states of the agent which caused the action; such explanations will be rational explanations, simple as well as contrastive. Free actions will, then, be adequately explicable. But obviously this observation does not solve the problem of control.[27] (By the same token, in cases where a nondeterministically caused action cannot be contrastively explained, that shows nothing about a lack of control.)

Better arguments alleging a problem of control are couched in terms of ensurance and luck. Here is an example of the former. Consider two agents, Sam and Dave. Suppose that both are considering whether to A or to B, and both reach a rational judgment about which thing it would be better to do. Suppose that it is causally determined that, whichever alternative Sam judges better, he will decide in accord with that judgment, whereas it is causally open that whichever alternative Dave judges better, he will decide contrary to that judgment. Sam has a power to ensure what he will decide by making a better judgment, while Dave does not. It is thus concluded that Dave has less control over his decision than Sam has over his. (See Mele 1995: 212.)

The argument from luck is often stated in terms of identical agents in different worlds, or in terms of an agent and her counterparts. (See Haji 1999a; and Mele 1998b, 1999a, and b.)[28] Suppose that a certain agent, Peg, is deliberating about whether to keep a promise or not. She judges that she (morally) ought to keep it, though she recognizes and is tempted to act on reasons of self-interest not to. She decides to keep the promise, and her decision is nondeterministically caused by her having certain reasons for doing so, including her making the moral judgment. Until she decided to keep the promise, there was a chance that her deliberative process would terminate in a decision not to keep the promise, a decision nondeterministically caused by her having reasons of self-interest. Everything prior to the decision, including everything about Peg, might have been exactly the same and yet she have made the alternative decision. Peg in some other possible worlds, or some of her counterparts, are exactly the same up to the moment of decision but decide not to keep the promise. There, but for good luck (it is said), goes she. It is a matter of luck, it is said, that Peg decides to do what she judged to be morally right. To the extent that some occurrence is a matter of luck, the argument continues, it is not under anyone's control. The indeterminism in the production of her decision is thus said to diminish Peg's control over the making of her decision.

Certainly these arguments have some allure; but I do not find either very convincing. With respect to the ensurance argument, note first that the power to ensure that Dave is said to lack is not required for the control that constitutes acting freely. In akratic or weak-willed decision, an agent may decide contrary to his better judgment. Such an agent does not ensure, by making a better judgment, what he will decide, and in an ordinary case of akratic decision, the agent may lack the power to ensure this just by making the judgment. He may nevertheless act freely and be responsible for what he does.[29]

Nor is it clear that Dave's lacking the indicated power constitutes some diminution of his active control, even if not enough to render his decision unfree. What Dave lacks is a power to ensure what *action* he performs (for a decision is a mental action) by first undergoing some *nonactive* change (over which, we may suppose, he has no active control). Now consider significantly different case: Chuck lacks a power to ensure what emotion he will experience by trying to feel a certain way. Chuck's lacking this power does diminish his indirect active control over what he experiences, control that he might be able to exercise just by trying to feel a certain way. This is true because what Chuck lacks is a power to ensure what *nonactive* change he will undergo by first *actively* trying to bring about a certain change. But this is very different from lacking a power to ensure what *action* one will perform by first undergoing some *nonactive* change. If Dave's lacking the power that he lacks constitutes any diminution of active control, the explanation of why it does so has to be different from the explanation of why Chuck's lacking the power that he lacks constitutes a diminution of his active control. We have an explanation of why there is a diminution of active control with Chuck; the ensurance argument gives us no explanation of why the analogous thing is so with Dave.

Active control is exercised in acting, not in undergoing nonactive changes prior to action. To hold this is consistent with holding, as will any event-causal theorist, that Dave's exercise of active control consists in his decision's being caused, in an appropriate way, by his being in certain mental states. His being in these states begins prior to his decision, but their causing the decision occurs when the decision is made. He exercises control not when he enters into these states, but when he makes his decision.[30]

Turning to the argument from luck, it should be noted, first, that Peg's decision is not *just* a matter of luck. Her decision is caused (we may suppose in a nondeviant way) by her having certain reasons, including her judgment that it would be morally better to keep the promise. And, compatibilists should agree, her decision's being so caused constitutes her exercising some degree of active control in making it. It is not, then, due *only* to good luck that Peg decides to keep the promise. It is due to her exercise of active control.

Further, if by *luck* is meant "*control-diminishing* luck," then, for a reason analogous to that offered in reply to the ensurance argument, it is just not clear that Peg's decision is at all a matter of luck. Here, we need to distinguish the following two significantly different varieties of case: those in which there is in-determinism between a basic action and an intended result that is not itself an action, and those, like Peg's, in which the indeterminism is in the production of a basic action itself. For the first sort of case, suppose that you throw a ball attempting to hit a target, which you succeed in doing. The ball's striking the target is not itself an action, and you exercise control over this event only by way of your prior action of throwing the ball. Now suppose that, due to certain prop-erties of the ball and the wind, the process between your releasing the ball and its striking the target is indeterministic. Indeterminism located here inhibits your success at bringing about a nonactive result that you were (freely, we may suppose) trying to bring about, and for this reason it clearly does diminish your control over the result—it constitutes control-diminishing luck.[31] But the indeterminism in Peg's case—and the indeterminism required by the sort of event-causal libertarian view at issue here—is located differently. It is located not between an action and some intended result that is not itself an action, but rather in the direct causation of the decision, which *is* itself an action. The control that an agent exercises in making a decision does not (typically) derive at all from any prior attempt on her part to bring about that decision.[32] In the ball-throwing case, the indeterminism constitutes control-diminishing luck because it inhibits the agent from bringing about a nonactive result that she is actively trying to bring about. But that explanation is not available in the second kind of case. Unless the argument from luck offers some alternative explanation, that argument is at best inconclusive.

The argument is sometimes supplemented with the claim that, where an agent's decision is nondeterministically caused, and where she (or her counterpart) in another world makes an alternative decision despite being exactly the same until the decision is made, nothing about the agent prior to the decision explains this difference. (See, for example, Haji 1999a: 48 and 53; and Mele 1999b: 100.) If the claim is that a certain contrastive explanation is unavailable, then, as noted earlier, this is often not so. If, on the other hand, the claim is that nothing about the agent prior to the decision *makes it the case* that one rather than the other decision is made, where this just means that the decision is not causally determined (and what else could it mean), then this will of course be granted. But this claim simply restates what is stipulated in the event-causal libertarian account without adding any argument that the feature remarked upon constitutes any diminution of active control. Finally, it is sometimes claimed that, in the sort of case we are considering, the agent does not determine which set of reason-states is causally effective. (See, for example, Russell 1984: 168.)[33] But the agent does exercise a certain degree of active control over this; she exercises such control by making a certain decision, which, if made, is caused by the reason-states (or her being in those states) that favor it.[34]

Proponents of event-causal libertarian accounts that locate indeterminism directly in the causation of a free decision (or other free action) hold, with compatibilists, that the active control that is exercised by the agent consists in the decision's being caused by certain agent-involving events. The libertarian here may hold that the control that is actually exercised is a matter of what actually causes what, not of what might have caused what. There having been a chance of the decision's not being caused by those events may be there having been a chance of the agent's exercising less control; it need not constitute the agent's actually having exercised less control. The ensurance and luck arguments contradict this claim. But as they have been developed, these arguments fail to establish that the claim is false. Perhaps some find it obviously false. But those who find that the issue can be settled only by argument should regard it as remaining unsettled.[35]

2.3. Efforts and Wanting More

The most fully developed recent event-causal libertarian account locating indeterminism in the production of free actions themselves is that advanced by Robert Kane (1996a, 1999a and b, and 2000a; see also his essay in this volume ch. 18). A free decision or other free action, Kane holds, is one for which the agent is "ultimately responsible" (1996a: 35). Ultimate responsibility for an action requires either that the action not be causally determined or, if the action is causally determined, that any determining cause of it either be or result (at least in part) from some action by that agent that was not causally determined (and for which the agent was ultimately responsible).[36] Thus, on Kane's view, an agent may be ultimately responsible for a decision that is causally determined by his possessing certain character traits. Indeed, it may even be that all of his actions that directly contributed to his having those traits were causally determined as well. But somewhere in the history of events that contributed to those traits, and thus to his decision, there must have been some actions by him that were not causally determined. Kane calls such "regress-stopping" actions "self-forming actions" (ibid.: 74). All self-forming actions, he argues, are acts of will; they are mental actions. He thus calls them "self-forming willings" (ibid.: 125), or SFWs. Kane identifies six different types of SFWs, giving the most detailed treatment to what he calls moral choices or decisions and prudential choices or decisions.[37] I shall focus here on the former; since the two types of case are analogous, my points can be easily transferred to the latter.

In a case of moral choice, there is a motivational conflict within the agent. She has a belief that a certain type of thing (morally) ought to be done (and she is motivated to do that), but she also has a self-interested desire to perform an action of a type that is, in the circumstances, incompatible with her doing what she believes she ought to do. She is committed to her moral belief and makes an effort of will to resist the temptation that threatens this commitment, an effort "to get [her] ends or purposes sorted out" (ibid.: 126). If the choice is to be a SFW, then the strength of this effort must be *indeterminate;* Kane likens its indeterminacy to that of the position or momentum of a microphysical particle (ibid.: 128). The indeterminacy of the effort, he speculates, might be due to some microlevel physical indeterminacies in the brain, which are amplified by the chaotic behavior of networks of neurons (ibid.: 128–30). "[I]ndeterminate processes in the brain . . . ," he suggests, "are . . . physical realizations of the agents' efforts of will . . ." (ibid.: 131). Such indeterminacy is held to be the source of the required indeterminism in the causal production of the choice. Again, an analogy is drawn from microphysics. Just as whether a particle will penetrate a barrier may be undetermined because the particle's position and momentum are not both determinate, so "[t]he choice one way or the other is *undetermined* because the process preceding it and potentially terminating in it (i.e., the effort of will to overcome temptation) is *indeterminate*" (ibid.: 128).

Kane further requires that any choice that is a SFW satisfy three plurality conditions, which require plural rationality, plural voluntariness, and plural control. When moral choices are plural-rational, he holds,

> the agents (r1) will in each case have *had* reasons for choosing as they did; (r2) they will have chosen *for* those reasons; and (r3) they will have made those reasons the ones they wanted to act on more than any others *by* choosing for them. (ibid.: 135)

Moreover, in each case there must have been at least one alternative choice open to the agent that would have met these conditions as well, had it been made.[38] An agent's making a choice for certain reasons, on Kane's view, consists partly in that choice's being caused by the agent's having those reasons.

An agent acts voluntarily (or willingly), he holds, "just in case . . . the agent does what he or she wills to do . . . , for the reasons he or she wills to do it, and the agent's doing it and willing to do it are not the result of coercion or compulsion" (ibid.: 30). And "[a]n agent *wills* to do something at time t just in case the agent has reasons or motives at t for doing it that the agent wants to act on more than he or she wants to act on any other reasons (for doing otherwise)" (ibid.: 30). A choice is plural-voluntary just in case it was made voluntarily, in the sense just described, and there was at least one alternative choice open to the agent that would have been voluntary had it been made.

Finally, a choice is made with plural control just in case there was open to the agent a set of options such that the agent was "able to *bring about* any one of the options (to go more-than-one-way) *at will* or *voluntarily* at the time" (ibid.: 111). Here, too, voluntariness is to be understood in terms of an agent's wanting more to act on certain reasons than she wants to act on any others.

Wanting more, then, figures crucially in all three plurality conditions. An agent wants more to act on certain reasons, according to Kane, just in case her desire to act on these reasons has greater motivational strength than have any desires she has to act on other reasons and, further, it is settled in her mind that these reasons, rather than her reasons for doing otherwise, are the ones she will now and in the future act on (1999b: 118).

Kane maintains that in a situation of moral conflict, the requirements for being a SFW may be satisfied by either choice that is made—the choice to do what one believes one ought to do or the choice to do what one is tempted to do. Where this is so, whichever choice the agent makes, he has chosen for the reasons that he wants more to act on, free from coercion and compulsion. If he has chosen to do what he believes he ought to do, then that choice is the result of his effort. If he has chosen to do what he was tempted to do, then he has not allowed his effort to succeed (Kane 1996: 133). Whichever choice he has made, he could have made the other. He is then ultimately responsible for the choice he has made.

The notions of wanting more and of indeterminate efforts are prominent in Kane's account and perhaps what is most distinctive about it. However, I do not find that either of these notions helps to address the problem of control considered in the preceding section.

An agent's wanting more to act on certain reasons is, on Kane's view, brought about *by* her performing a SFW, by, for example, her making a certain choice. Hence it cannot contribute to the active control that the agent exercises, for this (supposing that an event-causal view is on the right track) is a matter of what brings about the choice or other action, not of what the choice or other action brings about.[39]

Kane appeals to two features of the required efforts of will in response to the problem of control. Recall that, in the argument from luck, it is said that Peg in other worlds, or Peg's counterparts, may be exactly like her up to the moment of decision but make a different decision. This can't be so, Kane claims, when decisions (or choices) result from indeterminate efforts of will.

> If the efforts are indeterminate, one cannot say the efforts had exactly the same strength, or that one was exactly greater or less great than the other. That is what indeterminacy amounts to. So one cannot say of two agents that they had exactly the same pasts and made exactly the same efforts and one got lucky while the other did not. . . . Exact sameness (or difference) of possible worlds is not defined if the possible worlds contain indeterminate efforts or indeterminate events of any kinds. (ibid.: 171–72)

Kane distinguishes two kinds of indeterministic worlds: Epicurean and non-Epicurean. In the former there is chance but not indeterminacy; in the latter there are both, with the chance stemming from the indeterminacy. Free will, he argues, can exist only in a non-Epicurean world. The chance in an Epicurean world, he implies, constitutes control-diminishing luck.

This appeal to indeterminacy in response to the argument from luck appears unsuccessful. First, in a straightforward sense, there can be exact sameness of one world to another even if there is indeterminacy. In physics, the indeterminate position of a particle may be characterized by a wave function (one specifying the probabilities of the particle's being found, upon observation, in various determinate positions), and the particle (or its counterpart) in a different world may be correctly characterized by exactly the same wave function. (Exactness and determinacy are not the same, (compare O'Connor 1996: 156.)

Second, even if there could not be exact sameness where there was indeterminacy, that would not disarm the argument from luck. Haji (1999a: 53) and Mele (1999a: 279–80 and 1999b: 98–99) advance versions of the argument that consider agents (in different worlds) who are as similar as possible, given the indeterminacy of their efforts. More fundamentally, any claims comparing one world to another seem incidental to the argument; it can be restated without them, to roughly the same effect.[40]

The second feature of the required efforts of will that is intended to address the problem of control is their active directedness: they are active attempts to produce certain outcomes. In a case of moral conflict, Kane holds, the agent makes an effort to choose to do the thing that she believes she morally ought to do. When the effort succeeds, it is by performing an action (making the effort) aimed at bringing about the moral choice that the agent brings about that very choice. The agent then succeeds, despite the indeterminism, at doing something that she was (actively) trying to do. And Kane points out that typically, when this is so, the indeterminism does not undermine responsibility (and hence it does not so diminish active control that there is not enough for responsibility). He draws an analogy with a case (1999a: 227) in which a man hits a glass tabletop attempting to shatter it. Even if it is undetermined whether his effort will succeed, Kane notes, if the man does succeed, he may well be responsible for breaking the tabletop.

If left here, this reply would fail to address the problem of control in a case where the agent chooses to do what she is tempted to do rather than what she believes she ought to do.[41] In response to this shortcoming, Kane (1999a and b, and 2000a) has recently proposed a "doubling" of effort in cases of motivational conflict. In a case of moral conflict, he now holds, the agent makes two simultaneous efforts of will, both indeterminate in strength. The agent tries to make the moral choice, and at the same time she tries to make the self-interested choice. Whichever choice she makes, then, she succeeds, despite the indeterminism, at doing something that she was trying to do.

This doubling of efforts of will introduces a troubling incoherence into cases of moral (and prudential) choice. There is already present, in such a case, an incoherence in the agent's motives. This type of conflict is common and no apparent threat to freedom. Indeed, libertarians often maintain (as does Kane (1996a: 231 n.3)) that such motivational conflict is *required* for freedom. However, to have the agent actively trying, at one time, to do two obviously incompatible things raises serious questions about the agent's rationality. This additional incoherence may thus be more of a threat than an aid to freedom.

But there is a more fundamental problem in this second appeal to efforts to address the problem of control. In the case of the man who breaks the tabletop, we accept that he acts with the control that suffices for responsibility because we presume that his attempt to break the tabletop is itself free. If, on the contrary, we suppose that the attempt is not free, then we will judge that he does not freely break the tabletop. An effort to make a certain choice can contribute in the same way to that choice's being free, then, only if the effort itself is free.[42] What is needed, then, is an account of the freedom with which the agent acts in making these efforts. (Compare O'Connor's discussion in 1993a: 521–22 of an earlier version of Kane's view.)

Kane maintains that, although the effort of will that precedes a choice that is a SFW must be an action for which the agent is ultimately responsible, the effort need not itself be a SFW; it is allowed that the effort be causally determined.[43] However, in order for an agent to be ultimately responsible for a causally determined effort, on Kane's view, the agent must have performed at least one earlier SFW that either was or contributed to any determining cause of the effort in question. Since, on Kane's view, all SFWs either are efforts of one sort or another or must be preceded by efforts,[44] the task of providing an account of the freedom of an effort cannot be avoided.

Kane faces the following dilemma in providing such an account. If the account of the freedom of an effort of will requires that the effort itself result from a prior free effort, then a vicious regress looms. On the other hand, if the account of the freedom of an effort of will need not appeal to any prior free efforts of will, then it would seem that the account of a regress-stopping free choice can likewise dispense with such an appeal. At any rate, Kane has provided no reason to think that the latter account must differ in this respect.[45]

An event-causal libertarian needs a solution to the problem of control that makes no appeal to prior free actions. But if there is such a solution, it is not clear why it cannot be applied directly to decisions or choices (and perhaps to overt actions as well). Hence it has not been shown that the appeal to indeterminate efforts of will, and that to non-Epicurean indeterminism, is required or helps to address the problem of control.[46]

2.4. This Freedom's Worth

A relatively simple view, of the sort alluded to in the first paragraph of section 2, may be as good as any (and better than many) available to an event-causal libertarian. Although such a view faces the objection that the indeterminism it requires diminishes control, we have seen no convincing argument to support of that charge.

But now the view faces a second type of objection. Even if the required indeterminism does not diminish control, the objection goes, neither does it augment control. It introduces mere chance, which, it may be said, is at best superfluous. And perhaps worse. In a case where an agent decides rationally, and where any alternative decision would have been irrational, if there was a chance that the agent make an alternative decision, that was a chance of something's happening that would have been worse that what actually happened, and it may be said that such a chance is itself a bad thing (even if it does not constitute a diminution of control). The chanciness required by an event-causal libertarian view, then, is said to be at best superfluous and arguably a bad thing. There is, the objection concludes, no reason for requiring it in an account of free will.

This objection raises a serious challenge, a problem of gratuity for event-causal libertarian accounts. The question that must be addressed is whether anything of value is offered by an event-causal libertarian view that might make such chanciness worth having in the production of our decisions and other actions.

Here we need to reflect on why freedom is important to us. Deciding and acting freely is, many think, partly constitutive of human dignity. Only when an agent acts with a certain variety of active control are her actions attributable to her in such a way that she may be morally responsible for what she does, deserving of praise or blame, reward or punishment, depending on the moral qualities of her decisions and other actions. Moreover, we want it to be the case that by exercises of active control, we are making a difference to what happens in the world, including what kinds of persons we become. And when we deliberate, it generally seems to us that more than one option is open to us and we are free to pursue each of the alternatives we are considering; if this impression is systematically mistaken, then we are routinely subject to an undesirable illusion.[47]

We can distinguish two aspects of the freedom that is important to us in these respects: a kind of leeway or openness of alternatives, and a type of control that is exercised in action. It may be (it has been argued) that the freedom that is required for certain of the things just mentioned involves one but not the other of these aspects.[48] With regard to the question before us here, it may be argued that what is gained with the indeterminism required by an event-causal libertarian view has to do with one of these aspects but not the other.

An agent's exercise of control in acting is his exercise of a positive power to determine what he does. We have seen reason to think that this is a matter of the action's being caused by the agent, or by certain events involving him, such as his having certain reasons and a certain intention. An event-causal libertarian view adds no new types of causes to those that can be required by a compatibilist account, and hence the former appears to add nothing to the agent's positive power to determine what he does. As far as this aspect of freedom is concerned, the requirement of indeterminism does indeed appear (at best) superfluous.

But not so with regard to the other aspect, the openness of more than one course of action. If incompatibilists are correct, there is never any such openness in a deterministic world. The indeterminism required by an event-causal libertarian account suffices to secure this leeway, and this may be important to us for several reasons.

When an agent is deliberating about whether to A or to B, it generally seems to her as though, in some sense, it is open to her to A and open to her to B. Even if it is possible for us, on occasion, to deliberate without explicitly believing of each alternative that we can pursue that alternative,[49] the presumption of openness is so much a part of our nature, or our second nature, that it may be practically impossible for us always or even generally to deliberate without so presuming. Now, it is no straightforward matter to say what sort of openness is presumed here. But an individual may reasonably believe that it is something at least very like that secured by an event-causal libertarian view—a sort that cannot be present in any deterministic world—that *she* commonly presumes, or that such an account, unlike an otherwise similar compatibilist view, provides an at least roughly faithful articulation of the rather vague idea that she commonly presumes.[50] Such an individual, then, may reasonably hold that if determinism is true, then whenever she deliberates (or at least generally when she deliberates) she is subject to an illusion. She may grant that the illusion is occasionally avoidable; but she may find, as I think we do find, that it is practically impossible consistently to deliberate without the presumption of openness. And since it is practically impossible for us never to deliberate, she may reasonably hold that if determinism is true, then she is routinely subject to a practically unavoidable illusion.

The leeway secured by an event-causal libertarian account, then, may be reasonably valued as partly constitutive of the nonillusoriness of deliberation, which is a property making for goodness. This is one consideration that can provide a justification for the account's requirement of indeterminism. It is one consideration that can be balanced against any cost occasioned by the required chanciness.

Similarly, some individuals may reasonably judge that if things are as presented in an event-causal libertarian view, that is better with regard to our decisions' and other actions' making a difference to how the world goes. Of course, even if the world is deterministic, there is a way in which our actions generally make a difference: had we not performed them, things would have gone differently. If things are as required by an event-causal libertarian account, our actions still generally make a difference in this way. But some of them, at least, may make a difference in a second way as well: in performing them we may initiate, by the exercise of active control, branchings in a probabilistic unfolding of history. There may have been a real chance that things would not go in a certain way, and these actions may be what set things going that way. One may reasonably judge that it is better to be making a difference in this second as well as in the first way with one's actions. Since we cannot be making a difference in this second way if the world is deterministic, some individuals may have reason to find that the indeterminism required by the event-causal libertarian view is not superfluous but adds something of value, something to be balanced against whatever cost that indeterminism might carry.

I find less reason to think that an event-causal libertarian view improves upon a comparable compatibilist account when it comes to moral responsibility. If determinism is true, misdeeds may still be willful and deliberate, exercises of a capacity to consider reasons and act on one's appreciation of them. There may consequently still be a type of justification for praise and blame, reward and punishment. Such reactions may be appropriate expressions of our feelings and our judgments about past behavior; they may contribute to moral education and may encourage good behavior and discourage bad; and they may help protect us from miscreants. Incompatibilists typically hold, however, that a very important type of justification would always be lacking: none of these reactions would ever be deserved. Less categorically, some incompatibilists allow that, in a deterministic world, there might be a type of desert of these kinds of reactions or of some version of these reactions, or that they may be deserved to a degree. But it is then said that there would be an important type of desert missing, or that an important version of these reactions would not be deserved, or these reactions would not be fully deserved. (Compare Honderich 1988: ch. 10; Pereboom 1995; Smilansky 2000; and the essays by these writers in this volume, chs. 20, 21, and 22, respectively.)

Whatever the implications of determinism for desert really are, the implications for desert of our having just the variety of active control that is characterized by an event-causal libertarian view are, it seems, the same. Such a view secures a type of leeway or openness not available in a deterministic world, but the view provides the agent with no additional positive power to determine what he does; it does not secure any greater degree of active control. And this is what seems to be needed if there is to be a different verdict concerning desert and hence responsibility.[51] If responsibility of a full-blooded variety is incompatible with determinism, then it may also be incompatible with the truth of an event-causal libertarian view.

In sum, it may be reasonably held that an event-causal libertarian account secures something more, but not a whole lot more, than can a good compatibilist view. Is the little more that is provided more than enough to compensate for the cost of the chanciness? That is hard to judge. It seems that reasonable, well-informed people may come down, after careful consideration, on either side of this question.[52]

3. THE EVIDENCE

I turn now to the question whether we have good evidence that either a noncausal or an event-causal libertarian view is true. The answer seems to be negative.

Both types of account require, first, that determinism be false. But more than this, each requires that there be indeterminism of a certain sort (with some events uncaused, or nondeterministically caused) and that this indeterminism be located in specific places (in the occurrence of decisions or other actions, or at certain earlier stages in the deliberative process). What is our evidence with regard to the satisfaction of these requirements?

It is sometimes claimed that our experience when we make decisions and act constitutes evidence that there is indeterminism of the required sort in the required place.[53] We can distinguish two parts of this claim: one, that in deciding and acting, things appear to us to be the way that one or another libertarian account says they are, and two, that this appearance is evidence that things are in fact that way. Some (for example, Mele 1995: 135–37) deny the first part. But even if this first part is correct, the second part seems dubious. If things are to be the way they are said to be by some libertarian account, then the laws of nature—laws of physics, chemistry, and biology—must be a certain way.[54] And it is incredible that how things seem to us in making decisions and acting gives us insight into the laws of nature. Our evidence for the required indeterminism, then, will have to come from the study of nature, from natural science.

The scientific evidence for quantum mechanics is sometimes said to show that determinism is false. Quantum theory is well confirmed. However, there is nothing approaching a consensus on how to interpret it, on what it shows us with respect to how things are in the world. Moreover, there are deterministic as well as indeterministic interpretations of the theory, and in the view of many, the evidence we have does not decisively rule out the former. Perhaps the best that can be said for libertarianism here is that, given the demise of classical mechanics and electromagnetic theory, there is no good evidence that determinism is true. (For further discussion of these issues, see Loewer 1996 and the essays by Bishop and Hodgson in this volume, chs. 4 and 5, respectively.)

The evidence is even less decisive regarding the presence of the kind of indeterminism in exactly the places required by one or another of the libertarian accounts we have considered. Unless there is a complete independence of mental events from physical events, then even for free decisions there has to be indeterminism of a specific sort at specific junctures in certain brain processes. There are some interesting speculations in the works of some libertarians about how this might be so (see Kane 1996a: 128–30 and 137–42, and the sources cited there); but our current understanding of the brain gives us no solid evidence one way or the other on this question. At best, it seems we must remain, for the time being, agnostic.

If our beliefs on the issue are to be (as I think they should be) guided by the evidence, then we will leave the question open whether we have what is characterized by any libertarian view. We will accept, then, that perhaps we never have more than one course of action open to us at any given time and we never exercise any greater degree of active control than what can be characterized by a compatibilist account. If this is in fact so, then we have never actually possessed something that many of us thought we had, and something that we may reasonably value. Though not the end of the world, neither is that a matter of indifference.[55]

NOTES

I am grateful to Carl Ginet, Ishtiyaque Haji, Robert Kane, Hugh McCann, and Alfred Mele for comments on a draft of this essay. Charles Cross also provided helpful discussion.

1. Goetz (1997) argues that a choice is an exercising of a mental power and that an exercising of a mental power is essentially an uncaused event. Choices, he holds, are essentially made for reasons, and their explanations are teleological and noncausal. McCall's account is set out in the context of a branching model of space-time. Open alternatives constitute what he calls a choice-set. McCall distinguishes between deliberation-reasons—those weighed while deliberating—and explanation-reasons—those for which a decision is made. A free decision, he holds, is uncaused, and its explanation in terms of explanation-reasons is noncausal.

2. Goetz apparently rejects such a view when it comes to decisions. And McCann may not accept it at all. He says (1998: 173), "The concept of agency has it that the operations of my will are fully my responsibility." However, if, as it seems, dogs and cats are agents, then there is a concept of agency that does not imply freedom or responsibility.

3. He has so indicated in correspondence.

4. McCann's argument for this conclusion relies on the stronger claim that, necessarily, when an agent decides to do a certain thing, she intends to decide to do that thing (and on the further premise that if an agent intends to decide to do a certain thing, then she has already decided to do that thing). For a brief rebuttal of this stronger claim, as well as references to further discussion of a principle on which it rests, see Mele (1997c: 242–43).

5. Considering an act "whose origin lies elsewhere," McCann acknowledges (1998: 180) that its intentionality would be "hollow."

6. Causalist objections to Ginet's account of rational explanation are developed in Mele (1992a: ch. 13).

7. Ginet presents his account as providing *sufficient* conditions, but he also claims

(1990: 143–44) that any anomic account of rational explanation (any account that does not appeal to laws of nature connecting prior conditions to the action) that cites an antecedent desire will *require* that the agent remember that prior state.

8. Again, although he presents his view as providing sufficient conditions for the truth of an explanatory claim, he appears to hold also that the concurrent, second-order intention is necessary. He claims that a desire that is a reason for doing what an agent has done fails to be a reason for which the agent performed that action if "the agent has no such intention concurrent with the action despite being aware of the desire and of the fact that it is a reason for acting as she did (given her beliefs)" (Ginet 1990: 145).

9. In his contribution to this volume (ch. 17), Ginet responds to an objection of this sort by arguing against a requirement of causation for direct reference.

10. Objections similar to those raised here concerning the appeal to a concurrent intention are advanced by McCann (1998: 162–63).

11. McCann denies this, but what reason is there to support the denial? Certainly we do not see by introspection that the reasons for which we make a decision are always enshrined in the content of the decision; on the contrary, self-reflection seems to tell us (at least it tells me) that this is not always so. What reasons there are, then, must be theoretical. But if there is a rival account of acting for reasons and of rational explanation that does not require this correspondence and is in other respects at least as plausible, theoretical reasons, too, are lacking. The dispute here turns, then, on the adequacy of alternative accounts—including causal accounts—of acting for reasons and of rational explanation, a question that cannot be settled in this essay.

12. The requirement that one be cognizant of one's reasons may also be excessive. One can act on reasons of which one is not consciously aware. However, McCann says little about this requirement; he may not intend it to require conscious awareness.

13. There is an early suggestion of such a view in Wiggins (1973).

14. Dennett recommends a view of this type as the most promising libertarian account but argues that it is in no way preferable to a compatibilist account. Fischer discusses it as a view that might satisfy some libertarians. Kane (1985) incorporates some of the features of this type of view into a more comprehensive account.

15. This "doxastic" indeterminism is presented as just one illustration of a type of process that may be conducive to libertarian freedom. Mele notes:

> Other indeterministic scenarios may also be considered. For example, one may explore the benefits and costs of its being causally undetermined which of a shifting subset of *desires* come to mind at a time, or which of a changing segment of beliefs an agent actively *attends* to at a given time, or exactly *how* an agent attends to various beliefs or desires of his at certain times. (Mele 1995: 221)

16. Ekstrom (2000: 135. n.46) argues that the formation of a preference as a result of reflection on what it would be good to do counts as an action in virtue of its resulting from an intention to decide what to prefer. I find this unconvincing. A preference, as she understands it, is a desire, and "forming" a desire is no more active than is "forming" a belief. The fact that I can come to a belief about, say, whether God exists as a result of intending to make up my mind about this issue does not suffice to show that

forming a belief in such a case is acting. The objection I shall raise in the text applies, however, even if I am wrong about the point here.

17. Ekstrom (2000: 118) denies that action contrary to one's preference can be free. This seems a shortcoming of the view. An agent may have a power to act in accord with his preferences and be able, on a certain occasion, to exercise that power but simply not exercise it on that occasion. Such perversity need not be unfreedom.

18. I find this not literally true. A human agent is a human animal, constituted by whatever parts, states, and capacities constitute that animal. (For a cogent defense of such a view, see Olson 1997.) Certainly the agent's mental attitudes and capacities are relevant to whether she acts freely. But they do not, in a literal sense, constitute her any more than do the states and capacities of her circulatory system.

19. On the other hand, if Mele and Ekstrom are right in thinking that indeterminism in the direct production of a decision would diminish control, then the indeterminism required by their views may also diminish control. Ekstrom contends that if there remains, until a decision is made, some chance that it will not accord with the agent's preference, then even if the decision does so accord, the decision "seems a lucky accident" (Ekstrom 2000: 105). However, a similar objection appears equally forceful against the view that she favors. On that view, when a decision is freely made, the reasons considered in deliberating nondeterministically cause the formation of a preference. Consider a case where an agent recognizes a strong reason to A and a weak reason to B, and no other relevant reasons. If there remains, until the agent forms a preference, a chance that she will form a preference to B, then even if she forms a preference to A, the formation of this preference may with equal warrant be said to be "a lucky accident."

It is less clear that the indeterminism required by Mele raises a parallel problem. He confines chance to the occurrence of certain events in deliberation, such as the coming-to-mind of certain beliefs, that we do not control even if determinism is true. However, even if we do not actually control such events, we could, in an ideal scenario, have a type of nonactive rational control over them. It could be that, when an agent sets out to make up his mind about which of several alternatives to pursue, all and only the most relevant considerations, or all and only those that he has time to consider, come promptly to mind and then figure rationally and efficiently in the production of an evaluative judgment. In a deterministic world in which our deliberations always ran in this ideal fashion, we would exercise a valuable type of nonactive rational control in deliberating. If chance at a later stage of deliberation would diminish active control, then chance of the sort required by Mele's view would seem to diminish this nonactive rational control. We might then prefer a deterministic world in which our deliberative processes ran in this ideal way to a world in which Mele's libertarian view was true.

Note, however, that these criticisms of Mele's and Ekstrom's views are conditional, forceful only if (what I think we do not have conclusive reason to believe) the indeterminism that Mele and Ekstrom reject would diminish control.

20. A free decision or other free action is preceded, on Mele's view, by an evaluative judgment or, on Ekstrom's account, by a preference-formation. An infinite regress would be generated if, in order for a decision or other action to be free, it were required that the prior evaluative judgment or preference formation either itself be a free action or have resulted from some other free action.

21. In fact, Mele, unlike Ekstrom, does not reject compatibilism. He remains non-committal about whether determinism is compatible with the freedom required for responsibility (Mele 1995: 251–54). And he suggests (1996 and 1999a) that one may hold that these two are compatible and still (reasonably) prefer the sort of freedom characterized by the libertarian view that he advances. Such freedom, it appears, would not be preferable for the reasons that move most libertarians.

22. For my discussion in this section, I have drawn from Clarke (2000).

23. Mele (1995: 201–2) describes the following scenario:

> Suppose that [a] thief has a little mechanical device in his head that works as follows. His having a reason (R_1) to refrain from stealing then while also having a reason (R_2) to steal then . . . activates the device, which then goes into either state 1 or state 2. The device is indeterministic and is so constituted that it goes into state 1 on about half the occasions on which it is activated and into state 2 on the others. The immediate result of the device's going into state 1 is that R_1 is "enhanced" in such a way that R_1 (together with any other causally relevant factors) immediately causally determines a proximal decision to refrain from stealing; the device's going into state 2 has an exactly parallel result involving R_2.

Even if we substitute for the mechanical device some natural part of the thief's brain, what is described here is significantly different, in the way indicated in the text, from what is required by the sort of event-causal libertarian view under consideration.

24. When one event brings about another, that instance of causation may be (on some views of causation, it must be) governed by a causal law. But causal laws may be either deterministic or nondeterministic. Statements of the former imply that events of one type always cause events of a second type. Statements of nondeterministic laws imply that events of one type might cause events of a second type. Nondeterministic laws may be probabilistic, with their statements implying that events of one type probabilify (to a certain degree) events of a second type, or that when there occurs an event of the first type, there is a certain probability that it will cause an event of the second type. When one event nondeterministically causes another, the first produces the second, though there was a chance that it would not bring about that event. For a variety of accounts of nondeterministic causation, see Lewis (1973b [1986a]: Vol. 2, postscript B), Eells (1991), and Tooley (1987: 289–96).

25. Van Inwagen (1983: 142–50) considers an objection that, if indeterminism is located as required by the view we are now considering, then the agent "has no choice about" which decision she makes or which action she performs. (He calls the argument for this claim "the third strand of the *Mind* Argument.") Having a choice about what one does is, in van Inwagen's terms, acting freely. Nevertheless, the objection he discusses is not the objection we are considering in the text here. We are considering the claim that the required indeterminism leaves agents with less control than they would have in an otherwise similar deterministic world. We might reject this claim and yet accept that, on the type of event-causal libertarian view under consideration, agents do not act with *more* control than do their deterministic counterparts and hence do not act with sufficient control to count as acting freely. Indeed, van Inwagen construes acting freely to be acting with enough control to be morally responsible for what one does,

and I shall suggest later that this type of event-causal libertarian view does not secure enough control for moral responsibility.

26. Sometimes (as with Ayer) the denial of explicability stems from a view that all causation is deterministic. More restricted denials are made by some authors who do not hold this view of causation. Double argues that a choice that was improbable given the preceding deliberative process cannot be rationally explained. Nagel argues that it is not possible to provide for an undetermined choice a contrastive explanation (an explanation of why this choice rather than some alternative was made) that is either causal or "intentional," where the latter is "comprehensible only through [the agent's] point of view" (Nagel 1986: 115). Libertarians themselves sometimes grant the unavailability of certain types of explanation of free actions. Kane (1996a: 145) concedes that "free choices are arbitrary in the sense that they are not fully explicable in terms of the past." And Sorabji (1980: 31), discussing an indeterministic view that he finds adequate, agrees that, when an action is nondeterministically caused, there will not be available a contrastive explanation of why the agent performed that alternative rather than another open alternative that he was considering.

27. Nozick (1981) sets out an event-causal indeterministic account that focuses on securing the explicability of free decisions. I do not think that his view secures the sort of explanation relevant to the rationality of decisions. These would be explanations in terms of the reasons for which an agent makes a certain decision, whereas the explanations his view is said to provide stem from weightings of reasons that come about when the decision is made. In any case, it is clear that the availability of this latter sort of explanation is quite irrelevant to the problem of control.

28. All these arguments are directed against Kane's view (discussed in section 2.3), which requires that certain free choices be preceded by efforts to make specific choices. No such efforts play a role in the simpler event-causal view under consideration in this section, and hence the version of the argument from luck that I present here differs slightly from those presented by Haji and Mele.

What is called the "rollback argument" resembles the argument from luck. We are invited to imagine that the world is repeatedly rolled back to its state just before the agent makes the nondeterministically caused decision and then allowed to unfold each time into the future. In some unfoldings, a certain decision is made; in others, some alternative decision is made. Since everything prior to the decision is the same in every unfolding, it is said that the agent lacks control over (or is not responsible for) the decision that is made. This device is introduced by van Inwagen (1983: 141) in his discussion of the *Mind* Argument (see 25); he employs it again in his essay in this volume (ch. 7). For discussion of the rollback argument, see Fischer (1999b: 100–103) and Mele (1995: 196–203).

Additional arguments that indeterminism either diminishes control or fails to secure enough control for responsibility (but without explicit appeal to luck) are advanced in Bernstein (1995), Double (1991: 198–99), Strawson (2000), and Waller (1988).

29. Such an agent may have a different power to ensure that he will decide in accord with, and on the basis of his better judgment. He may be able to perform certain mental actions—acts of attention, for example—that would so alter the relative strengths of his various motivations that it would then be ensured that he would decide to do what he has judged best. But even an indeterministic agent such as Dave (who decides nonakratically) can have this power. As things stand, it is causally open that he

decide contrary to his better judgment. But he may be able to close this off. He cannot ensure what he will decide *just* by making his evaluative judgment; but he may be able to ensure what he will decide by performing certain mental actions that he is able to perform.

30. Consider a case where an agent deliberates, judges that a certain alternative is best, and then makes her decision about what to do. Ekstrom (2000: 105) objects that, if the decision is nondeterministically caused, then, after making the evaluative judgment, the agent must "wait to see whether the corresponding intention to act will or will not be formed." Since Ekstrom allows nondeterministic causation at this juncture in the view that she favors, it does not appear that she intends to deny that the intention-formation in this case is an action—a decision. And if that is granted, then surely we may correctly say that, having made the judgment, the agent must make up her mind (decide) what to do. She must, that is, exercise active control, not merely wait upon and observe some nonactive occurrence.

31. The contrast, of course, is with a ball-throwing case in which your throwing the ball causally determines its hitting the target.

32. What is claimed here is denied by one prominent event-causal libertarian; see the discussion of Kane's view in section 2.3.

33. Russell argues not that the sort of indeterminism we are considering diminishes control but that it does not increase it, and hence that a view that requires such indeterminism does no better than a compatibilist view at securing moral responsibility.

34. In discussing the third strand of the *Mind* Argument, van Inwagen (1983: 149) wonders how, on an event-causal libertarian account, an agent has a choice about whether her being in certain reason-states is followed by her making a certain decision. If the question is how such an agent might have *more* control over this sequence than would a deterministic counterpart, then, as indicated earlier, I am not inclined to think he would. My contention is just that we have seen no compelling reason to hold that the agent has *less* control over this sequence than would a deterministic counterpart.

35. Here I have drawn from Clarke (2000 and forthcoming).

36. Kane states his condition UR as follows:

> An agent is *ultimately responsible* for some (event or state) E's occurring only if (R) the agent is personally responsible for E's occurring in a sense which entails that something the agent voluntarily (or willingly) did or omitted, and for which the agent could have voluntarily done otherwise, either was, or causally contributed to E's occurrence and made a difference to whether or not E occurred; and (U) for every X and Y (where X and Y represent occurrences of events and/or states) if the agent is personally responsible for X, and if Y is an *arche* (or sufficient ground or cause or explanation) for X, then the agent must also be personally responsible for Y. (Kane 1996a: 35)

37. The other types of SFWs are "(3) efforts of will sustaining purposes, (4) attentional efforts directed at self control and self modification, (5) practical judgments and choices, and (6) changes of intention in action" (Kane 1996a: 125).

38. Kane (ibid.: 156) notes that one alternative that may be open is simply not making any choice.

39. Nor does it seem that wanting more, as Kane construes it, contributes to the rationality, plural or otherwise, of free choices or other free actions. First, wanting more

is a matter of motivational strength and of settling on which reasons will prevail, not a matter of normative strength—of which reasons are normatively better or ought to prevail—and only the latter, it seems, is relevant to the rationality of an action. Second, as previously noted, on Kane's view, the agent's wanting more is brought about *by* performing a SFW. But the rationality of a choice is a matter of the normative strength of the reasons *for which* the agent makes the choice; and these, if an event-causal view is correct, are the reasons the agent's having which (nondeviantly) brings about the choice.

40. Indeed, the very similar rollback argument (see n.28) makes no appeal to other worlds.

41. The problem of control is raised with respect to such cases by Mele (1998a: 582–83; 1999b: 98–99; and 1999a: 279)

42. I shall consider later the view that the effort need not be directly free, that the choice might be free so long as the effort results from some earlier action that was free. Might the effort contribute to the freedom of the choice even if the effort is not even indirectly free? I do not see what contribution made here by a not-even-indirectly free effort could not also be made by a nonactive event, such as the agent's having (or acquiring) a certain reason.

43. He has so indicated in correspondence.

44. Efforts of will are required to precede SFWs that are moral or prudential choices, practical judgments or choices, or changes of intention in action. All the remaining types of SFWs are themselves efforts of one sort or another.

45. Although Kane holds that certain types of efforts can themselves be SFWs, I find in his work no clear account of the freedom of such efforts. In order to be SFWs, it is required that they not be causally determined. But surely that does not suffice for their freedom, and it is not clear why something that would suffice would not suffice also for the freedom of a choice.

46. Here I have drawn from Clarke (1999 and forthcoming-a).

47. I have not tried to be complete here. For more extended discussion of the importance of free will, see Clarke (2000), Honderich (1988: chs. 7–10), and Kane (1996a: ch. 6).

48. Frankfurt (1969) and others argue that an agent may be morally responsible for doing something even if she could not have done otherwise. For discussion, see the essays by Ekstrom, Fischer, Widerker, and Haji in this volume (chs. 15, 12, 14, and 9 respectively).

49. I argue in Clarke (1992b) that this is indeed possible. There I contest claims by Richard Taylor (1964), van Inwagen (1983: 153–61), and others to the effect that one cannot deliberate about whether to perform a certain action unless one believes that one can perform that action.

50. Some individuals believe that the sort of openness that seems to them to lie ahead in deliberation is a sort that could be there even if determinism were true. (See, for example, Mele 1995: 135–37.) I do not claim that they are mistaken, nor that they are not rationally justified in holding that belief. My claim is the some other individuals may reasonably hold a contrary belief.

51. This suggestion fits with Frankfurt's argument that the ability to do otherwise is not required for moral responsibility. The suggestion here, however, does not imply that responsibility is compatible with determinism, nor that it cannot be secured by a libertarian view that provides, in addition to leeway, further positive agential powers.

52. Here I have drawn from Clarke (2000).

53. O'Connor (1995b: 196–97 and 2000: 124) claims that our experience in acting provides us with evidence that we have libertarian free will, though he takes this to be evidence for the truth of an agent-causal libertarian account rather than either of the types examined in this essay.

54. This is so for overt bodily actions regardless of the relation between mind and body, and it is so for mental actions (including decisions) barring a complete independence of mental events from physical, chemical, and biological events. Such independence itself seems quite unlikely on the evidence available to us.

55. Here I have drawn from Clarke (forthcoming).

CHAPTER 17

REASONS EXPLANATIONS OF ACTION: CAUSALIST VERSUS NONCAUSALIST ACCOUNTS

CARL GINET

SUE opened the door to the bedroom and walked in. Why did she do that? In order to see whether her glasses were on the dresser. That is, she entered the room because she thought that by looking on the dresser she would satisfy her desire to either find her glasses or at least narrow down the number of places where they might be.

This paradigmatic explanation tells us why an action occurred by revealing the agent's reason for performing the action. The principal philosophical question about such explanations—and the question to be discussed here—is, What makes such an explanation true? What informative specification of truth-conditions for such an explanation can we give?

The chief controversy about this has focused on the question whether it is necessary for the truth of such an explanation for a *causal* connection to exist between the explanans—the desire(s), belief(s), or intention(s) of the agent that, according to the explanation, do the explaining—and the explanandum—the action that they explain. The position that this is necessary we can call *causalism* regarding reasons explanations; the position that there need not be a causal connection, that there is at least one sufficient condition for the truth of such an explanation that does not entail any causal connection, we can call *noncausalism*.

Those who advocate noncausalism usually also maintain that the existence of free and responsible action is incompatible with the truth of determinism; and so they are concerned to show that this view, that free and responsible actions are not causally necessitated, does not commit them to the absurd conclusion that such actions must lack reasons explanations.

1. Davidson's Challenge

Before the publication of Donald Davidson's defense of causalism in "Actions, Reasons, and Causes" (1963[1]), the dominant attitude among analytic philosophers was anticausalist—but not since then. Davidson's article turned the tide. He gave effective rebuttals to various arguments that purported to show that the explanatory connection in a reasons explanation is not causal.[2]

Davidson also offered an argument *for* causalism. He pointed out that an agent's *having had* a reason to perform a certain action she performed does not entail that she performed it *for* that reason. There are two essential aspects to a reasons explanation: (1) the set of the agent's propositional attitudes offered as explanans must constitute a rationale for acting in the way the agent acted, and, *in addition*, (2) that rationale must be the reason (or one of the reasons) for which the agent acted in that way; and the first does not entail the second.

> [A] person can have a reason for an action, and perform the action, and yet this reason not be the reason why he did it. Central to the relation between a reason and an action it explains is the idea that the agent performed the action *because* he had the reason. (Davidson 1980: 9)

To illustrate, suppose Sue had a second desire that was a reason for her entering the bedroom: she wanted Sam who was sleeping in the room to wake up and give her some company, and she believed that her opening the door to the room might well cause Sam to wake up. Compatibly with this, we can suppose further, however, that Sue did *not* enter the room for that reason: although she was aware that waking Sam was an outcome toward which she had a "pro-attitude" and that her entering the room might produce that outcome, it was not the case that she entered the room in order to produce it (not even in order to produce it among other things).

Davidson writes (ibid.: 11–12) that what must be added to "S did A and S had reason R for doing A" to get "S did A because S had reason R for doing A" is that S's having R caused S's doing A. The *explanatory connection* between the reason and the action that is implied by saying that S did A *for* reason R must be constituted, he believes, by a causal connection between them. "Failing a satisfactory alternative," he says, "the best argument for [causalism] is that it alone promises to give an account of the [explanatory] connection between reasons and action" (ibid.: 11).

2. A NONCAUSALIST ALTERNATIVE

But there is a satisfactory alternative. For any true reasons explanation, we can formulate a condition that, if it obtains, is sufficient for its truth but that does not entail that the propositional attitudes of the explanans caused the action explained.

Reasons explanations take many different forms, not all of which can be discussed here. Let us focus on just the following two forms:

(1) S A-ed in order to B.
(2) S A-ed because she had promised to B and she believed that by A-ing she would B.

(1) could be paraphrased by "S's purpose/intention/aim in A-ing was to B." (2) could be paraphrased by, for example, "What led S to A was her remembering her promise to B and her belief that by A-ing she would (or might) keep that promise."

(1-C) and (2-C) state sufficient conditions, respectively, for the truth of (1) and (2):[3]

(1-C) Concurrently with her A-ing S intended of that A-ing that by it (and in virtue of its being an A-ing) she would B (or would contribute to her B-ing).[4]
(2-C) Before her A-ing, S had promised to B, and concurrently with her A-ing S intended of that A-ing that by it she would keep that promise.

One could not consistently affirm (1-C) and deny (1) that S A-ed in order to B; nor could one consistently affirm (2-C) and deny (2) that S A-ed because she believed that by A-ing she would keep her promise to B. The truth of those propositions guarantees the truth of those reasons explanations. Those propositions do not, however, give causal conditions. (1-C) does not entail that the accompanying intention it mentions caused the action. (2-C) does not entail that the desire-plus-belief it mentions caused the action. Neither entails anything at all about what, if anything, caused the action or any of the events, physical or mental, ingredient in the action. Yet each is sufficient for the truth of the corresponding reasons explanation.

3. A Causalist Objection

There are some who would disagree with this claim. They think that the truth of (1-C) cannot be sufficient for the truth of (1) unless a causal requirement is added, so that (1-C) is revised as follows:

(1-C, rev)   Concurrently with her A-ing S intended of that A-ing that by it she would B (or would contribute to her B-ing) *and* that intention caused her A-ing.

Alfred Mele is one of those who advocate this addition. He supports his view by imagining an agent S who opens a window and has two concurrent intentions in doing so: intention N is to let in some fresh air and intention O is to gain a better view. He writes: (Mele 1992a: 253)

> [S]uppose that a mad scientist, without altering the neural realization of N itself, renders that realization incapable of having any effect on S's bodily movements . . . while allowing the neural realization of O to figure normally in the production of movements involved in S's opening the window. Here, it seems clear, O helps to explain S's opening the window, and N does not. Indeed, N seems entirely irrelevant to the performance of that action. And if that is right, Ginet is wrong; for on his view, the *mere presence* in the agent of an intention about her [action] is sufficient for that intention's being explanatory of her action.

Mele's argument here seems to boil down to this: If we imagine that the neural realization of a particular concurrent *de re* intention plays no causal role in the production of the voluntary movements it is about—instead of supposing that it figures normally in the production of them—then we have imagined a situation in which the presence of the intention obviously does not contribute to explaining the action.

There is a whiff of question-begging about this argument. The argument assumes that, as things actually are, the neural realizations of such concurrent intentions normally do play a causal role in producing the relevant voluntary exertions. It is possible that this is true, but it is not something we know. We do not know nearly enough about how the relevant mental states are realized. For all we know, the neural realizations of our accompanying intentions about our voluntary exertions do *not* normally play a causal role in producing them (in producing, that is, the central volitional neural processes and thereby the bodily exertions they cause). But our ignorance on this point does not mean that we are therefore ignorant as to whether the reasons explanations we so confidently give, of our own and others actions, are true. If we were to discover, or somehow become convinced, that the neural realizations of intentions and volitional motor impulses are not causally connected in the way Mele assumes they are, we would not be obliged on that account to abandon giving reasons explanations, to say that concurrent *de re* intentions with the sorts of contents specified in my sufficient conditions do nothing to explain the actions they concern.

4. What Is the Noncausal Explanatory Connection?

If the explanatory connection between action and reasons provided by (1-C) and (2-C) is not causal, what is it? In the case of (1-C), the concurrent intention explains the action simply in virtue of the fact that it is an intention *of* that action that by it one will B, that is, in virtue of being that sort of propositional attitude with that content. Aside from the extrinsic relation required for the content's direct reference to the action, the explanatory connection is an *internal* relation between the explaining intention and the action explained: it follows from *intrinsic* properties of the relata (plus the direct reference). The explanatory connection is made, not by a causal relation, but simply by the direct reference and the internal relation.

In the case of (2-C) the explanatory connection between the prior promise and the action has two links. The first link is from the prior promise to the concurrent intention and the second link is from that concurrent intention to the action. The concurrent intention is the linchpin where the two links connect. The first link requires a concurrent memory of the prior promise and consists in the fact that the concurrent intention refers to *the remembered promise* and says of *it* that the action is to keep it (that is, to bring about what is specified in the content of that promise). The second link consists in the fact that the concurrent intention's content directly refers to *the action* and says of *it* that it is to keep the prior promise.

Note that the first link, in requiring that S concurrently remember the prior event (which is necessary if the concurrent intention is to be about the prior event), does imply a causal connection between the prior event and the memory part of S's concurrent state. But this memory link obviously does not imply that the prior event causes the concurrent intention, even on the assumption that the prior event does cause the memory of it. The memory of the prior event is a condition that enables the concurrent *de re* intention to refer directly to the prior event—if S did not remember the prior promise, S could not intend of it that the current action keep it—but of course this does not mean that the memory causes the intention.

The direct reference of the concurrent intention to the action *may* require a causal link between the action and the intention. Since the subject is directly aware of at least the initial conscious volitional part of the particular action her intention concerns, it seems that she can take advantage of that and refer directly to that action, in a demonstrative fashion—"*this* action." Perhaps this requires that something intrinsic to the intention-state is caused by part of the action. But even if such a causal connection is required, it is obvious that this will not entail that the intention cause any part of the action: the causation is in the opposite direction.

But there may be a difficulty in supposing that such a causal connection is required. If (a) the direct reference requires that what is referred to, the action, cause (or contribute to causing) what refers to it, the intention, and if (b) causes must always precede their effects, then there will be a small period at the beginning of the action during which the concurrent directly referring intention will not be in place, a gap during which the agent will have *no* intention about the action already begun, during which it will not be the case that she intends anything *of* that action. This is an unpalatable consequence.

Perhaps it can be avoided by denying one of the two premises, (a) and (b), from which it is deduced. In fact, neither one seems obvious to me. Consider (b) first. Why not an effect that is simultaneous with its cause? Suppose I push a button. My exerting force against the button with my finger causes the button to move. Does the button not begin to move as soon as I begin exerting force against it? Must there be any delay? (Whether or not there is in fact any delay, is a delay required by the very notion of a causal relation between the two?)

Consider (a), the claim that direct reference to one's action in the content of one's intention requires that the action cause the feature of one's intention-state that does the referring. Now, there is no doubt that direct reference often does involve the referent's entering into causing that which does the referring. When the representation given in my visual experience directly refers to a particular car, it does so because that car played a part in causing the relevant features of my visual experience; and when my utterance of "That car" directly refers to that car, the reason is that the car played a part in bringing about my utterance (via its role in bringing about features of my visual experience). But I think that not all direct, demonstrative reference requires such a causal relation. Consider the following counter-examples:

- The demonstrative reference of an utterance to itself: "This utterance will have more than ten words in it by the time it is finished."
- Suppose I know that my pressing a certain key will more or less instantaneously produce a brief flash on the computer screen. As I press the button, I utter, "Look at that flash [pointing to a place on the screen]," timing it so that my utterance of "that flash" coincides exactly with the occurrence of the flash.
- Suppose I voluntarily lift my arm and at exactly the same time as I begin willing the movement I begin an utterance of "This is a voluntary movement."
- Suppose I voluntarily move my right leg a little and at exactly the same time as I begin willing the movement I begin an utterance of "This movement I intend to bring me into a more stable stance."

If, as in the last example, I can simultaneously begin *uttering an expression* of an intention that directly refers to a concurrent voluntary movement, without any part of the movement's causing any part of the utterance, then surely I can simultaneously begin *having* an intention that refers to the movement without any part of the movement's causing any part of the intention.

We must suppose, of course, that the conscious beginning of the action and the accompanying intention that directly refers to the action occur within the same unified consciousness, that a single conscious subject is simultaneously aware of both mental items and the aboutness relation between them. This means, no doubt, that these items cannot belong to separate streams of events that are completely isolated causally from each other. But it does not entail that the accompanying intention causes the action.

5. Another Noncausalist View: Intention in the Action

Some (for example, Searle 1983, Wilson 1989, and O'Connor 2000) have suggested a sufficient condition for the truth of (1) that is much like (1-C); however, they regard the required intention as quite literally *in* the action, as a constituent or intrinsic property of it rather than a mere accompaniment. They would revise (1-C) in something like the following way:

(1-C*)   It was a constituent or intrinsic property of her A-ing that S intended of it that by it she would B (or contribute to her B-ing).

A subscriber to (1-C*) who also holds that the part that an intention-in-action plays in the action is to cause and sustain the bodily movements involved in it[5] must allow that (1-C*) does imply something about how some of the constituents of the action were caused: it implies that the intention in the action caused the bodily movement(s) ingredient in it. But even so, (1-C*) does not entail any causal connection between the action and anything outside the action.

(On O'Connor's agent-causation view, an action consists in the agent's causing an intention to move her body in a certain way *immediately*, which intention causes and sustains the bodily movement (O'Connor 2000: 72, 86). He suggests (ibid.: 88–89) that his view introduces a causal element into a reasons explanation, and even that agent-causation is somehow required for a satisfactory account of reasons explanations. He says that the agent's exercise of active power

> provides a necessary link between reason and behavior without which the reason could not in any significant way explain the behavior. It allows the reason to influence the agent's *producing* the outcome while not (directly and independently) causing it. Were nothing to have caused this [the behavioral outcome, I take him to mean], then noting that the agent had a reason that motivated acting in that way would not suffice to explain it.

This last sentence sounds like a commitment to Davidson's claim that the only thing that can make a reason the agent *has* a reason *for* which she acted is a causal connection; but it is hard to see how such a causalist view can square with O'Connor's claim (ibid.: 52–55) that an event consisting of an agent's causing something cannot be caused at all. To claim that, it seems to me, is to deny that the explanatory connection between an agent's causing something and the reason for which he did so can be a causal connection of any sort (whether direct or indirect, deterministic or indeterministic).[6])

Those who go for (1-C*) do so, perhaps, because they fail to see any other way, than by positing such an intention in the action, to make the bodily movements part of an *action* rather than just involuntary movements. They overlook, however, the fact that one can perform a voluntary movement, and therefore act, without intending to perform a voluntary movement and therefore without intending the movement or any consequence of it. This would happen, for example, if one believed falsely that one's arm was paralyzed, tried nevertheless to raise it, and, to one's surprise, did raise it. The sort of thing sufficient for such a voluntary movement when it is thus unintentional is also present when a voluntary movement is intentional (I would say that this is a certain sort of mental activity, volition, which causes the movement).[7] So in all voluntary movements, intentional or not, we have ingredients sufficient to make an action that do not include any intention about the movement or its consequences. So in a case where the agent does intend her voluntary movement, the intention should be thought of, not as a constituent of the action, but as an accompaniment.

6. An Objection to Deterministic Causalism

One objection to causalism that Davidson mentioned (Davidson 1980: 12–13) but did not deal with effectively is this: The explanans in reasons explanations often include only more or less enduring *states* of the agent—beliefs, desires, intentions, and so on. But a causal explanation of an event, says Davidson, requires that there be an antecedent *event* among the totality of relevant causal factors. Presumably he requires this because, on his view, causal laws are deterministic, specifying that when a certain collection of factors obtain at a time there immediately ensues as a result a certain effect. So not only must the totality of relevant causal factors explain why a certain sort of event occurred, but the timing of those factors—their coming to obtain precisely when they did—must also explain why the effect occurred precisely when it did. The objection is that, for at least many reasons explanations, no relevant event seems to play that role. There is only a certain combination of reasons-states that obtained for some interval and that could have led to the explained action at any of several times during that interval. In response Davidson writes:

> In many cases it is not difficult at all to find events very closely associated with the [reason states]. States and dispositions are not events, but the onslaught of a state or disposition is. A desire to hurt your feelings may spring up at the moment you anger me; I may start wanting to eat a melon just when I see one; and beliefs may begin at the moment we notice, perceive, learn, or remember something. [In the case of a driver who signals a turn by raising his arm] there is a mental event; at some moment the driver noticed (or thought he noticed) his turn coming up, and that is the moment he signalled. (Davidson 1980: 12)

But the point of the objection seems to be missed here. The moment the driver noticed his turn coming up might *not* have been the moment he signaled. He might have been aware that his turn was coming up, and have been intending to signal before getting there, for some time before he actually signaled; and he might have signaled at any of many different moments between that moment and the moment his turn came up, and the reasons explanation of his raising his arm have been the same, namely, that he wanted thereby to let others know that he would be turning at the next intersection and believed that raising his arm would do that. (It is surely implausible to suggest that, as a matter of causal law, his becoming aware that his turn is coming up (or some neural realization of this event) would, in sufficiently similar circumstances, always produce his signaling after exactly the same interval as occurred in this case.)

Davidson acknowledges that [there]

> seem to be cases of intentional action where we cannot explain at all why we acted when we did. In such cases, explanation in terms of primary reasons parallels the explanation of the collapse of the bridge from a structural defect: we are ignorant of the event or sequence of events that led up to (caused) the collapse, but we are sure there was such an event or sequence of events. (ibid.: 13)

Supposing Davidson is right about the bridge case; it is not at all evident that the reasons case is parallel, that the truth of the reasons explanation requires some event to explain the precise timing of the action (whether or not we know what that event is). We certainly have nothing like the empirical reasons for believing this about reasons explanations that we have for believing the parallel that applies to the bridge-collapse explanation. And if we were to come to have empirical reason to doubt, with respect to lots of cases where I would have sincerely reported that I raised my arm in order to signal a turn, that there was an event that explains why I raised my arm precisely when I did (rather than a moment or two earlier or later), we would not, I submit, have come to have reason to doubt that I did raise my arm in order to signal a turn. It seems that one could have the conviction about reasons explanations that Davidson expresses in the last sentence of the remarks just quoted only if one were already convinced that reasons explanations must be deterministic causal explanations.

7. INDETERMINISTIC CAUSALISM

A causalist who did not hold that all causal explanation is deterministic would not face the difficulty that Davidson struggled with here. A causalist who allows that causation can be indeterministic—that is, that the laws of nature governing causation, the laws that determine what sorts of thing cause what other sorts of things, can be indeterministic—can say that, where a reasons explanation can cite only states and no event that explains the precise timing of the explained act, the indeterministic law governing the causation here says that at any time at which that combination of states is present (and other conditions are right) there is a certain chance but no certainty that it will cause the result. Thus at each moment after I began both to believe that my turn was coming up and to intend to signal before reaching the turn, there was a chance but no certainty that those states would cause my signaling then. And there is no difference between conditions at the moment I do signal and those at the earlier moments that explains why it was at that moment and not an earlier one that the states caused the result. Of course, there is a chance that they will not cause me to signal at all; and, if the causation involved is indeterministic, there need be no difference between a case where they do cause me to signal and one where they do not that explains why they caused the signaling in one case and failed to cause it in the other (though I think that, if I end up not signaling at all, we will have to say that I either abandoned my intention to signal or forgot about it: it is not a conceptual possibility that all of the following should have obtained: nothing rendered me unable to signal, I continued to intend to signal, I remembered that intention throughout the relevant interval, and yet I did not signal).

Now that we have mentioned causal laws, let us note that how one conceives of the relation between such laws and particular instances of causation depends on which of two fundamentally different ways of thinking of causation one adopts. On a strictly Humean view, the causal relation is definable in terms of (reducible to) generalizations or laws: to say that the occurrence of a certain combination of states or events at a particular time caused a certain particular event to occur is to say that there is a description "C" of the causal factors and a description "E" of the effect event such that it is a law of nature that in a certain percentage of cases occurrences of sort C will be accompanied by events of sort E. (For deterministic laws, this percentage is 100; for indeterministic laws it is less.) On the other conception, causation is not definable in any such way: the concept of the causal relation is primitive. This does not mean, however, that on this conception there cannot be true laws about causation, for example, ones of the form "Whenever an event of sort A occurs in circumstances of sort C, this will cause (or have a propensity to cause) an event of sort E." Nor does it mean even that on this conception one cannot say that wherever there is causation a true causal law must cover the case.

Some have proposed that the explanatory connection in reasons explanation should be thought of as indeterministic causation. Call this view about reasons explanation "indeterministic causalism." (Davidson's view is deterministic causalism.) Indeterministic causalists, like noncausalists (those who think that the connection need not be causal at all), think that the truth of determinism is incompatible with the existence of free action and wish to show how their incompatibilism does not entail the absurd conclusion that no free action has a reasons explanation, that no one can act freely and responsibly and at the same time act for a reason.

Robert Kane is an indeterministic causalist, holding that "[w]hen agents choose for reasons . . . [t]he reasons play a role in the causal etiology of the choice (though they need not determine it) . . ." (Kane 1996a: 136); he holds (ibid.: 192–95) that nondeterministic event-causation of an action by the agent's "self-network" (her plans, aspirations, ideals, and motivational structures [ibid.: 139]) is essential if the action is to be something that the agent produces or does, instead of something that just happens to her.

He gives no argument for this claim and, as far as I can see, it is no more evident than is "the pernicious assumption," which Kane rejects, that an agent's control over an action requires that the action have an antecedent determining cause. It may be, as Kane appears to think, that the speculation as to how decisions or actions for reasons could be undetermined that is most conformable to science's present understanding of basic physical processes is that (the neural realizations of) such decisions are resolutions of indeterminate processes. But even if this is true, it does not follow that such a feature is entailed by the nature of decision or action for reasons. And it is unclear why an account of the truth conditions for reasons explanation that simply leaves open the question of whether there is any causal relation between reasons and the actions they explain is not just as compatible with the best scientific understanding of the natural order as an account that requires a probabilistic causal relation. Further, it is clear—and here I echo Kane's argument against the "pernicious assumption"—that, even if we were to discover that the brain-processes underlying our deliberated decisions offer no basis for saying that the decisions are caused (either deterministically or probabilistically) by what we take to be our reasons for them, this would not be a ground for thinking that we do not after all make those decisions *for* those reasons.

Randolph Clarke (1993 and 1996a) combines indeterministic causalism with agent-causation. He thinks that free and responsible actions are directly caused by the agent, but also that a satisfactory account of reasons explanation requires that the agent's reasons probabilistically cause the action (a form of event-causation). He favors the irreducibility (anti-Humean) conception of the event-causal relation.

The difficulty with this view is that it threatens to make every reasons-explained action over-determined. If an action-event of type A was caused by an antecedent reasons-event of type R (which includes all the propositional-attitudes that at the time the agent took to bear on her choice of action, including competing reasons for alternative actions, so that R might have indeterministically produced a different action instead of A), then it seems that the agent's own agent-causal effort was not really needed to bring about A, was instead otiose.

I think it is no answer to this to say that R only indeterministically caused A. To say this is *not* to say that R was only part of the cause of A or was only a causally necessary condition of A; it is to say that R did in this instance bring about A but the relevant event-causal laws leave it naturally possible that R might not have caused A (the laws of nature give the occurrence of R less than a 100 percent propensity, but greater than a 0 percent propensity, to cause A), that it might have caused a different action-event or perhaps nothing at all. Thus, it would seem, to say that this particular instance of R indeterministically caused this instance of A is not to imply that it needed help from something else, such as the agent, in order to do so. It is, rather, to say that while it might not have caused A, it did in fact cause A.

Nor will it help, it seems to me, to suggest (as Clarke 1993 does) that by exercising his agent-causal power the agent determines which of the several alternative sorts of action-events R *could* cause it does cause, to say that the agent causes R's causing A (and had it in his power to instead cause R's causing some alternative sort of event in place of A). The difficulty is still there: if R needed help from the agent's agent-causal power in order to cause A, if something other than R was a nonredundant part of what made it the case that A was caused, then we cannot say that R indeterministically caused A. Indeed, Clarke gives this objection additional purchase when he suggests (Clarke 1996a: 29) that when A, the action-event, is in a subject of the right sort—one with the power to cause it (and the capacity to act for reasons)—then it is nomologically necessary that, if A occurs, it is caused by the agent. If this is true, then it is hard to see how it can be said of R that it indeterministically causes A: R may be a necessary condition of the agent's causing A, but if it is nomologically necessary that A does not occur unless caused by the agent, then R does not indeterministically cause A.

To see this, let R+ be a complex state of affairs that includes the agent's having reasons R1 for doing A1 and reasons R2 for doing A2, plus the agent's having the power to cause A1 and the power to cause A2, and a situation of which Clarke would say that if the agent does A1 for reasons R1, then R1 indeterministically caused A1 and it is nomologically necessary that the agent caused A1. Think of R1 and R2 as like springs, each of which, if released, will produce a particular action-event; and think of the agent's causing A1 as her releasing the energy in R1. Now it sounds correct to say that R+, in virtue of containing the tensed springs R1 and R2, has a "propensity" to cause A1 and a "propensity" to cause A2 and that the agent determined which propensity of R+ issued in actual causation. But is it right to say that R+, or its component R1, *indeterministically caused* A1? No. Here R+'s propensity to cause A1 cannot be what we mean in talking of indeterministic causation. For there is not here a probabilistic causal law stating that in a certain percentage of the cases when R+ obtains it (or its component R1) will cause A1, and whether it does so or not is not dependent on some difference between the cases where it does so and those where it does not. What we have here rather is more like a deterministic law that says that when R+ obtains *and* the agent releases R1, then that causes A1. [8]

8. COUNTERFACTUALS

Some have suggested that causalism is supported by the (alleged) fact that reasons explanations support counterfactual conditionals of a sort whose truth has to be underwritten by the obtaining of a causal connection (Hornsby 1993: 165 n.5).[9] It is true that very often when an explanation of the form "S did A in order to satisfy her desire D (carry out her intention I)" is true there is also true a corresponding counterfactual of the form "S would not have done A if S had not had the desire D (or the intention I)."

But when such a counterfactual is true, the reason is not that the truth of the explanation requires it: it is not that the explanation entails the counterfactual. There are cases where such an explanation is true but the counterfactual is not. Consider our earlier example of Sue's entering the bedroom in order to find her glasses, while harboring a desire for Sam to wake up and believing that her entering the room might cause that awakening. Change the example and make it the case that Sue intended of her action *both* that it would help her find her glasses *and* awaken Sam. Then it could be true that she entered the room in order to look for her glasses but false that had she not had the desire to look for her glasses she would not have entered the room: it might be that she would still have entered in order to wake Sam; it might be, that is, that her attitude toward her two reasons was that either one by itself was a sufficient reason for the action.

But, the causalist might say, suppose (as we did earlier) that Sue did *not* enter in order to wake Sam, that, although she had that reason for entering, it was not a reason *for* which she entered: it was not because she had that reason that she entered. Then surely (the causalist continues) both of the following counterfactuals are true:

(a) If S had not had a desire to look for her glasses, she would not have entered;

(b) If S had not had a desire to wake Sam, she would still have entered;

and surely the truth of these counterfactuals must be underwritten by facts about a causal connection between the desire S acted to satisfy and the action explained. Surely what we must say (the causalist concludes) is that S's desire to wake Sam was, under the circumstances insufficient to cause her to enter, but the desire to find her glasses was.

In fact, it seems that the truth of these counterfactuals can be guaranteed by something other than a causal connection. It can be guaranteed in the way that the truth of a statement of conditional intention is guaranteed. Suppose Henry decides that, if he does not receive a call from Pam in the next ten minutes, he will call her. His forming and maintaining that intention until she calls (together with there being no obstacle to his carrying it out) is enough to make true Henry's later counterfactual statement to Pam, "If you hadn't called, I would have called you." Henry can know that this conditional is true just by knowing that he was committed to making it true. But, the causalist protests, does not his commitment to making it true entail that there is true a causal law linking his having that intention plus his believing its antecedent to be satisfied, with his making (or trying to make) its consequent true? No. He can know that he was committed to making the conditional true without having any idea whether such a causal law holds.

It does seem that counterfactuals (a) and (b) must be true *if* it is true that Sue entered only in order to satisfy her desire to look for her glasses and not in order to satisfy her desire that Sam awaken. But this is true not, as causalists think, because the first desire, but not the second, was causally sufficient for her action whether or not the other desire was present. It is true, rather, because Sue's commitment to these conditionals—as a matter of her intention—is conceptually necessary for her to have at the time of the action the intention thereby to look for her glasses while lacking the intention thereby to wake Sam.

Consider counterfactual (a). It would be incoherent for Sue to say, "(1) I intended by entering the room to look for my glasses, but (2) I did not intend thereby to wake Sam; however, (3) had I not wanted to look for my glasses, I would [contrary to (a)] still have entered, in that case in order to wake Sam." Statements (1) and (3) indicate that Sue acted for both reasons, which clashes with what statement (2) says.

Consider counterfactual (b). Sue's having in the action the intention to satisfy her desire to look for her glasses but not the intention to satisfy her desire to wake Sam commits her to having the conditional intention regarding the latter desire that, had she not had it, she would still have entered the room. Sue could not consistently say, "(1) I did not intend my action to wake Sam, but (2) had I not had the desire to wake Sam, I would [contrary to (b)] not have entered the room."

What about the example, considered a few paragraphs back, in which Sue entered the room in order *both* to look for her glasses and to wake Sam? In that case it might or might *not* be true that, had she lacked the one desire, she would still have entered the room in order to satisfy the other. Her attitude when she decided to enter might have been that neither reason by itself was sufficient but that together they were jointly sufficient. That is, her attitude was a conditional intention: "If entering the room will both help me find my glasses and wake Sam, then I'll do it; otherwise I won't." In that case, it would be true of neither desire that, had she lacked it, she would have entered the room in order to satisfy the other. Or her attitude might instead have been that each reason was by itself sufficient reason to enter the room. In that case it would (as a matter of her intention) be true of each desire that, had she lacked that desire she would still have entered in order to satisfy the other.

9. Intention Guides Action

Let us consider one more argument for causalism. This one has to do with the idea that intention *guides* action. Sue entered the bedroom by voluntarily making certain exertions with her body and she intended of those bodily exertions that they would bring about her entering the bedroom. In general, when an intentional action involves voluntary exertion of the body, the agent intends of the voluntary exertion, under some description of it, that it will accomplish the intended action. So the agent's propositional attitudes contain a fully adequate reasons explanation of the action only if they contain a rationale for making the particular sort of voluntary bodily exertion that she made in order to perform that action—only if they contain, that is, a belief that by exerting her body in that way she will (or might) perform the intended action.

The content of the intention accompanying the voluntary exertion specifies of it that it should have certain intrinsic features—for example, that it should be an exertion of force forward with arm and hand—and, typically, also that it should bring about a certain thing—for example, that it should push against a door and continue until it has caused the door to open a certain distance. It seems right to say that the intention, in virtue of having this content, *guides* the course of the voluntary exertion, or rather that the agent is guided by it in making the exertion so as to conform to its content. If this is right, then, it might be urged, there is a causal connection involved in the truth-maker of a reasons explanation after all, for surely guidance is a causal notion.

Sometimes guidance is a causal notion, but here it is not. Here what makes it the case that an antecedent intention guides a voluntary exertion is, not its causing the exertion, but rather this: the agent's concurrently intending of the voluntary exertion that it conform to the content of the antecedent intention. The only causal relation this requires is whatever causation is involved in the agent's currently remembering the antecedent intention and its content; it does not entail that the antecedent intention cause either the voluntary exertion or the concurrent intention about it.

What about a case where an intended voluntary movement takes more than just a moment, where it requires a more or less extended course of voluntary exertion—for example, a dance movement, the movement involved in a tennis serve, the movements involved in playing a scale on the piano, the movements involved in writing or typing a longish word—and where the agent is not practiced in the movement? Here, surely, the agent's concurrent intention to be making a movement of the sort in question guides the development of the movement in a sense that is not exhausted by saying merely that this intention accompanies the movement throughout. This is true, but still no causing of the movement by an intention need be involved.

Consider a simple example. I am, let us suppose, just beginning to learn to play the chimes. I am practicing and I wish to produce a certain pattern of three successive notes, as prescribed on the exercise sheet before me. This will involve, I realize, a certain complex movement of my arm and hand (which grasps a mallet), consisting of three successive stages. So I form the intention to make such a movement and then carry out that intention, attending carefully to the successive movements as I make them. A causalist picture of what happens here might be something like this: my initial intention to make the three-stage movement of my arm and hand beginning now causes the movement involved in striking the first note; and as I go along, the accompanying intention to complete such a movement together with realization of where I currently am in it causes the next phase of the movement involved in striking the next note.

My alternative picture is this: as I make each voluntary exertion involved in striking a note, I recall my antecedent intention to produce the three-note pattern and I intend of the concurrent exertion that it be what is needed *at this point* to contribute to making a whole movement that conforms to that prior intention; and, of course, as I begin each successive voluntary exertion, I am aware of what I have done so far toward completing the intended three-part movement and thus of what is needed next to contribute to its completion. This series of concurrent intentions makes the explanatory link between the antecedent intention and the whole movement. (And, of course, it could be broken down further into a series of many more intentions, each about a more limited current phase of the exertion; or we could think of it as a single continuing intention with a continuously changing content.) But these concurrent intentions provide that explanatory link without its being the case that they causally produce the voluntary exertions they accompany. The explanatory link is made simply by the content of the concurrent intentions, including their direct references to the prior intention and to the concurrent actions. A similar account can be given for extended movements, like a basketball player's drive to the basket for a layup, where the agent needs in later phases of the movement to take account of how well the earlier phases have gone and of how relevant circumstances have changed.

10. CONCLUSION

I have defended noncausalism about reasons explanations. Specifically, I have argued that it is sufficient for the truth of an explanation of the form "S A-ed in order to B" that, concurrently with her A-ing, S intended of that A-ing that by it she would B; and that it is sufficient for the truth of an explanation of the form "S A-ed because she had a desire to B" that before her A-ing S had a desire to B and concurrently with her A-ing S intended of that A-ing that by it she would satisfy that desire. I have argued that these sufficient conditions entail nothing about how the action was caused.

But I have *not* argued—and I see no good reason to believe—that these sufficient conditions *rule out* the possibility that the action was caused either by factors that include the intention or desire cited in the reasons explanation or by something else (for example, external manipulation of the subject's neural processes). Thus, as far as I can see, if our universe were one where every event is caused, or where every event is deterministically caused, our actions could still have the sort of reasons explanations we are accustomed to think they have.[10]

NOTES

1. Reprinted in Davidson 1980: 3–20.

2. Earlier works mentioned by Davidson which took noncausalist or anticausalist positions, include Anscombe (1958), Dray (1957), Hart and Honore (1959), Kenny (1963), Melden (1961), Peters (1960), Ryle (1949), and Winch (1958). Somewhat later works in this same category include Charles Taylor (1964), Richard Taylor (1966), and von Wright (1971).

3. I give noncausalist sufficient conditions for a few other forms of reasons explanations in Ginet (1990: ch. 6).

4. I take "S intended of this A-ing that by it she would B" to entail that S believed that by this A-ing she would or might B.

5. As do, for example, Searle (1983) and O'Connor (2000).

6. Thus despite those misleading remarks, O'Connor's view is best seen as combining agent-causation with noncausalism about reasons explanation. On his view, agent-causation is needed, not to account for how reasons explain action, but rather to account for how agents *control* or *determine*, and are responsible for, which action they perform.

On my view, agent-causation is not needed for that either. The question we incompatibilists face is this: if an action is uncaused, then what makes it the case that the agent is responsible for it, that its occurrence was up to her, something she determined? O'Connor and I agree that the answer to this must lie at least partly in the intrinsic nature of an action event: it has to be intrinsically a sort of event of which it is plausible to say that, given that such an event was not causally necessitated by antecedents, the subject of it is responsible for it. O'Connor thinks that agent-causings are events of this sort (and I agree that they are, or would be if any such events existed). I think (but O'Connor does not) that another sort of event, namely, a causally simple mental event possessing an 'actish' phenomenal quality—one that "feels" to the subject like an action, like something she does—such as a volition, is an event of this sort. In support of his intuition that an agent-causing event has intrinsically what makes for agent control of the event, but a causally simple volition does not, O'Connor (2000: 59) writes:

> [T]here is *internal* causal structure to the agent-causal event that is lacking in a volition. This difference in causal structure bears directly on the issue of agent control. An agent-causal event is intrinsically a doing, an *exercise* of control. Ginet claims that this is true of uncaused volitions as well, in view of their "active phenomenal quality." However, "control," "determination," and allied notions cannot be grounded in intrinsic, phenomenal characteristics alone— they require causal elucidation. It is just this missing feature in simple indeterminism that the agency theory captures.

I cannot see that the *internal* causal structure of an agent-causal event provides a special basis for saying that the agent controls that event, a basis that is lacking in a causally simple volition for saying the corresponding thing about it. To say that in an uncaused agent-causal event the agent controls *what he causes* is not to say that he controls *his causing* it. O'Connor says that " 'control,' 'determination,' and allied notions require causal elucidation." What does this mean? It cannot mean that any event an agent controls must have internal causal structure, for, as O'Connor would surely allow, an agent can control and be responsible for a causally simple event that she causes. But if it means that any event that an agent controls must be either one the agent causes or itself an agent-causal event, then it is just asserting what needs to be proved.

I suspect that the terms "*control*" and "*determine*" may cause mischief here. In the ordinary senses of these words, to say that a person determined or controlled the occurrence of some event is to imply that she caused it, but that is not implied by saying that an agent was responsible for an event, that it was up to her whether it occurred or not. And what is required for the latter is the issue. What I find evident is that, if any intrinsic feature of an uncaused event will make it one an agent is responsible for, it is either its being an agent-causal event or its having the actish phenomenal quality. The only thing that should make us doubt with respect to either of these features that it makes the agent responsible for the event would be some reason to think that *no intrinsic* feature of an uncaused event could guarantee the agent's responsibility for it, that only some-extrinsic relation of the event to the agent could do that.

7. For more on my account of voluntary exertion of the body see Ginet (1990: ch. 2).

8. For further discussion of Clarke's view see O'Connor (2000: 76–79).

9. This suggestion is discussed and disputed in Wilson (1997: 77–80), and in Sehon (1994: 65–67).

10. Though, in my view (which I have not argued for here), in a deterministic universe they would not be freely chosen actions for which the agents are morally responsible.

CHAPTER 18

....

SOME NEGLECTED PATHWAYS IN THE FREE WILL LABYRINTH

....

ROBERT KANE

IT was often said in the twentieth century that the free will issue is a "dead issue." All the passages in the labyrinth had been traveled and retraveled. Since I first began thinking about this topic thirty years ago, my conviction, to the contrary, was that whole passages in the labyrinth of free will remained unexplored or others were too lightly explored. People preferred familiar pathways, many of which had indeed reached dead ends. My goal in the thirty years since has been to point current debates about free will in new directions by exploring some of these unfamiliar pathways, especially with regard to incompatibilist or libertarian views of free will, which I defend. In this essay, I describe some of these new directions and explain why I think they are important.

1. THE COMPATIBILITY QUESTION: ALTERNATIVE POSSIBILITIES AND ULTIMATE RESPONSIBILITY

Consider first the Compatibility Question ("Is free will compatible with determinism?"), which has been the focus of much of the attention in contemporary free will debates. Almost all contemporary (and most historical) debates about compatibility have focused on the question of whether determinism is compatible with "the condition of alternative possibilities" (AP, as I shall call it)—the requirement that the free agent "could have done otherwise." Incompatibilists have codified their belief that determinism is not compatible with this AP condition in various versions of the Consequence Argument. Compatibilists, by contrast, have tried to show that the power to do otherwise does not conflict with determinism, or (more frequently in recent years) that freedom and responsibility do not require AP at all. But on both sides of these debates, which are amply surveyed in this volume, the focus has been almost exclusively on the power to do otherwise or alternative possibilities.

I have argued for two decades that this exclusive focus on alternative possibilities in debates about compatibility is a mistake. The fact that these debates have tended to stalemate over differing interpretations of *can, power, ability,* and "could have done otherwise"[1] is a symptom of a deeper problem—namely, that AP alone provides too thin a basis on which to rest the case for incompatibilism: the Compatibility Question cannot be resolved by focusing on alternative possibilities alone. This does not mean that alternative possibilities have no role to play in free will debates, as some compatibilists would have us believe. But it does mean that their role is more complicated than is generally recognized. To see this, however, one has to look more deeply into the situation. (Here we enter one of those less explored parts of the labyrinth.)

Fortunately, there is another place to look for reasons that free will might conflict with determinism. I have argued that in the long history of free will debate, one can find a second criterion fueling incompatibilist intuitions even more important than AP, though comparatively neglected. I call it Ultimate Responsibility, or UR (Kane 1996a: 35).[2] The idea is this: to be ultimately responsible for an action, an agent must be responsible for anything that is a sufficient reason (condition, cause, or motive) for the occurrence of the action. If, for example, a choice issues from, and can be sufficiently explained by, an agent's character and motives (together with background conditions), then to be *ultimately* responsible for the choice, the agent must be at least in part responsible, by virtue of choices or actions voluntarily performed in the past, for having the character and motives he or she now has. Compare Aristotle's claim that if a man is responsible for wicked acts that flow from his character, he must at some time in the past have been responsible for forming the wicked character from which these acts flow.[3]

This UR condition does not require that we could have done otherwise (AP) for every act performed "of our own free wills"—thus *partially* vindicating philosophers such as Frankfurt (1969), Dennett (1984), and Fischer (1994), who insist that we can be held morally responsible for many acts even when we could not have done otherwise. But the vindication is only partial. For UR does require that we could have done otherwise with respect to *some* acts in our past life histories by which we formed our present characters. (I call these "self-forming actions," or SFAs, or sometimes SFWs, "self-forming willings."[4]) Consider Dennett's much-discussed example of Martin Luther (1984: 131–33). When finally breaking with the Church at Rome, Luther said "Here I stand, I can do no other." Suppose Luther was literally right about himself at that moment, says Dennett. Given his character and motives, he literally could not then have done otherwise. Does this mean he was not morally responsible? Not at all, Dennett answers. In saying "I can do no other," Luther was not disowning responsibility for his act, but taking full responsibility for it; and thus "could have done otherwise," or AP, is not required for free will in a sense demanded by moral responsibility.

My response is to grant that Luther could have been responsible for this act, even *ultimately* responsible in the sense of UR, though he could not have done otherwise then, and even if his act was determined. But this would be so, I would argue, to the extent that Luther was responsible for his present motives and character by virtue of earlier struggles and self-forming choices (SFAs) that brought him to this point where he could do no other. Often we act from a will already formed, but it is "our own free will," by virtue of the fact that we formed it by other choices or actions in the past (SFAs) for which we could have done otherwise (which did satisfy AP).[5] If this were not so, there would have been nothing we could have *ever* done to make ourselves different than we are—a consequence, I believe, that is incompatible with being (at least to some degree) ultimately responsible (UR) for what we are.[6]

If the case for incompatibility cannot be made on AP alone, it can be made if UR is added; and thus, I suggest that the too-often neglected UR should be moved to center stage in free will debates. If agents must be responsible to some degree for anything that is a sufficient reason (cause or motive) for their actions, an impossible infinite regress of past actions would be required unless some actions in the agent's life history (SFAs) did not have sufficient causes or motives (and hence were undetermined). What is noteworthy about this argument, however, is that it *does not at any point invoke alternative possibilities* (AP). It focuses rather on the *sources* or *grounds* (*archai*)—conditions, causes, or motives—of what we actually do rather than on the power to do otherwise.[7] Where did our characters, motives, and purposes come from? Who produced them, and who is responsible for them? Was it we ourselves who are responsible for forming them, or someone or something else—God, fate, heredity and environment, nature or upbringing, society or culture, behavioral engineers or hidden controllers? Therein, I believe, lies the core of the traditional "problem of free will."

But if one can arrive at incompatibilism directly from UR, why is AP needed at all? Incompatibilists might be tempted to think at this point that they could dispense with AP altogether.[8] This, I think, would be a mistake. But understanding why it is a mistake leads us to yet other neglected pathways in the free will labyrinth. To access these, one must begin by focusing on different reasons for thinking that alternative possibilities cannot be the whole story about the Compatibility Question.

2. PLURALITY CONDITIONS

It is normally assumed that what incompatibilists need for free will are alternative possibilities (AP) *plus* indeterminism. But these two conditions are not jointly sufficient for free will, even if each should be necessary. One can see this by paying greater attention to a significant class of actions for which the agents could have done otherwise (had AP) *and* the actions are undetermined—and yet the agents lack free *will*. Reflection on actions of this kind leads to the other neglected pathways in the labyrinth just mentioned.

The actions I have in mind go back to examples put forward thirty or more years ago in debates about "could have done otherwise" by J. L. Austin (1961), Phillippa Foot (1957), Michael Ayers (1968), G. E. M. Anscombe (1971), and others. These "Austin-style examples," as I shall call them, were originally conceived for purposes having to do with the analysis of *can* and *could*. (Bernard Berofsky's essay in this volume [ch. 8] discusses their original uses.) But it is rarely noticed that examples of this sort have a significance well beyond what was originally envisaged for them. Here are three such examples, the first from J. L. Austin's celebrated "Ifs and Cans" (1961). Austin imagined that he must hole a three-foot putt to win a golf match, but owing to a nervous twitch in his arm, he misses. The other two examples are ones I have used on other occasions. An assassin is trying to kill the prime minister with a high-powered rifle when, owing to a nervous twitch, he misses and kills the minister's aide instead. I am standing in front of a coffee machine intending to press the button for coffee without cream when, owing to a brain cross, I accidentally press the button for coffee with cream. In each of these cases, we can further suppose, as Austin suggests, that an element of genuine chance or indeterminism is involved (perhaps the nervous twitches or brain crosses are brought about by undetermined quantum events in the nerve pathways). We can thus imagine that Austin's holing the putt is a genuinely un-determined event. He might miss it by chance and, in the example, does miss it by chance.

Now Austin's inspired question about his example was this: Can we say in such circumstances that "he could have done otherwise" than miss the putt? His answer is that we can indeed say this. For he had made many similar putts of this short length in the past (he had the *capacity* and the *opportunity*); and since the outcome of this one was also undetermined, he might well have succeeded in holing it, as he was trying to do. But this means we have an action (missing the putt) that is (1) undetermined and (2) such that the agent could have done oth-erwise. Yet missing the putt is not something that we regard as *freely* done in any normal sense of the term because it is not under the agent's voluntary control. The same is true of the assassin's missing his intended target and my accidentally pressing the wrong button on the coffee machine.

One might be tempted to think these occurrences are not *actions* at all because they are undetermined and happen by accident. But Austin rightly warns against such a conclusion. Missing the putt, he says, was clearly something he *did*, even though it was not what he wanted or intended to do; similarly, killing the aide was something the assassin did, though unintentionally; and pressing the wrong button was something I did, even if only by accident or inadvertently. The point is that many of the things we do *by accident* or *mistake, unintentionally* or *inad-vertently*, are things we *do*. We may sometimes be absolved of responsibility for doing them (though not always, as in the case of the assassin). But it is for *doing* them that we are absolved of responsibility; and this can be true even if the accidents or mistakes are genuinely undetermined.

To see what this implies about free will, consider the following scenario. Sup-pose God created a world in which there was a considerable amount of genuine indeterminism or chance in human affairs as well as in nature. In this world, people set out to do things—to kill prime ministers, hole putts, press buttons, thread needles, punch computer keys, scale walls—usually succeeding, but some-times failing by mistake or accident in the Austinian manner. Now further imagine that all actions in this world, whether the agents succeed in their purposes or not, are such that their reasons, motives, and purposes for trying to act as they do are always predetermined or pre-set by God. Whether the assassin misses the prime minister, his *intent* to kill is predetermined by God. Whether Austin misses his putt, his wanting and trying to make it are preordained by God. Whether I press the button for coffee without cream, my wanting to do so because of my dislike of cream is predetermined by God; and so it is for all persons and all actions in this imagined world.

I would argue that persons in such a world lack free *will*, even though it is often the case that they have *alternative possibilities* and their actions are *undetermined*. (This is one of many reasons why the "will" cannot be taken out of "the free will issue.") They can do otherwise, but only in the Austinian manner—by mistake or accident, unwillingly or inadvertently—and this is a limited kind of freedom at best. What they cannot do in any sense is *will* otherwise; for all of their reasons, motives, and purposes have been pre-set by God. We may say that their wills in every situation are already "set one way" before and when they act, so that if they do otherwise, it will not be "in accordance with their wills."

When we wonder about whether the wills of agents are free, it is not merely whether they could have done otherwise that concerns us, even if the doing otherwise is undetermined. What interests us is whether they could have done otherwise *voluntarily* (or *willingly*), *intentionally*, and *rationally*. Or to put it more generally, we are interested in whether they could have acted voluntarily, intentionally, and rationally in *more than one way*, rather than in only one way, and in other ways merely by accident or mistake, unintentionally, inadvertently, or irrationally. (*Voluntarily* and *willingly* here mean acting "in accordance with one's will [character plus motives]"; *intentionally* means "knowingly" [as opposed to "inadvertently"] and "on purpose" [as opposed to "accidentally"]; and *rationally* means "having reasons for so acting and acting for those reasons.")

I have called such conditions—of more-than-one-way, or *plural,* voluntariness, intentionality, and rationality—"plurality conditions" for free will (Kane 1996a: 107–11). They seem to be deeply embedded in our intuitions about free choice and action. Most of us naturally assume that freedom and responsibility would be deficient if it were always the case that we could *only* do otherwise by accident or mistake, unintentionally, involuntarily, or irrationally. But why do we assume this so readily; and why are these plurality conditions so deeply embedded in our intuitions? It is surprising how rarely philosophers have asked these questions, given the importance I think they have for free will. (Again we are at this point traversing too-often neglected pathways in the labyrinth.) If free will involves more than alternative possibilities and indeterminism, the plurality conditions appear to be among the additional requirements. Philosophers would do well to focus more attention on these conditions rather than on alternative possibilities alone.

3. WILL-SETTING

To understand the importance of plurality conditions, we have to consider another neglected topic in free will debates that I call "will-setting" (Kane 1996a: 113–15;

1996b). In the imagined world of section 2, all of the motives and purposes of agents in every situation were already "preset" or "set one way" by God. Another way to put this is to say that all the "will-setting" in this imagined world was done by God, rather than by the agents themselves—even though the agents could sometimes have done otherwise. Actions are "will-setting" when the wills of agents (their motives and purposes) are not already "set one way" *before* they act (as the assassin's will is set on killing the prime minister), but rather the agents set their wills one way or the other in the performance of the actions themselves. Choices or decisions are will-setting when they do not result from the agents' merely discovering during deliberation what they (already) favored, but when the agents make the reasons for preferring one option prevail at the moment of choice *by* choosing or deciding. Will-setting actions are in this sense "will-settling," not already "will-settled."

The imagined world in which all the motives and purposes of agents are set one way by God provides a clue to the deep connection between will-setting, UR, free will, and the plurality conditions. According to UR, if agents are to be ultimately responsible for their own wills, then if their wills are already set one way when they act, *they* must be responsible for their wills having been set that way— not God (as in the imagined world) or fate or society or behavioral engineers or nature or upbringing. And this means that some of their past voluntary choices or actions must have played an indispensable role in the formation of their present purposes and motives.[9]

But it is easy to see that this requirement would lead to a vicious regress unless there were some choices or actions in the agents' pasts that were voluntarily performed, but such that the agents' wills were not *already* set one way when they performed them. These actions would be "will-setting": the agents would be faced with motivationally viable options until the moment of choice or action and would set their wills one way or the other by choosing or acting. But then it follows that these actions would be more-than-one-way voluntary. When the will is already set one way (as in the case of the assassin), the action is "one-way" voluntary; the agent does otherwise only by accident or mistake (unwillingly). In the case of will-setting, it is voluntary either way. Will-setting actions are also plural rational, since the agents make the reasons for preferring one of the options prevail by deciding or acting. And if we assume for genuine cases of will-setting, as I think we should, that the agents know what they are doing and are doing it on purpose, then will-setting actions will be plural intentional as well. We thus have an answer to the question of why the plurality conditions are important for free will. They follow from the requirement that, if we are to be to any degree *creators of our own wills*, some actions in our lifetimes must be will-setting and not already will-settled. At those moments, we must be able to go in different directions willingly.

We now have a sequence of connected notions—from (1) acting "of one's own free will" to (2) being ultimately responsible for the will one has (UR), to (3) "will-setting," to (4) the "plurality conditions." Each notion implies the next and all, I believe, are required to account for freedom of *will* as well as for freedom of action. And we can now add another notion to the sequence, for the plurality conditions (4) immediately imply (5) "could have done otherwise" (that is, AP), since a fortiori, if you are able to do otherwise voluntarily, intentionally, or rationally, you are able to do otherwise.

But note that such an argument for AP is indirect. Unlike most other philosophers who debate these issues, I think the connection between (1) free will and (5) the power to do otherwise is not direct, but goes through other notions, namely, (2) ultimate responsibility, (3) will-setting, and (4) plurality. You have to travel some usually neglected passages in the free will labyrinth to get from one to the other. That is why trying to go directly from (1) to (5), which is the normal pattern, leads to unresolvable debates about whether "could have done otherwise" *really* requires incompatibilism or whether free will really requires "could have done otherwise." Intuitions will inevitably conflict on these matters, so long as other notions are not taken into account.

4. THE DUAL REGRESS OF FREE WILL

It would appear that AP is needed for free will after all. Yet we saw earlier that one could argue for incompatibilism from UR alone without appealing to AP. How are we to make sense of this? The answer lies in UR. Both (5) AP and (6) indeterminism follow from UR, but *by different argumentative routes*. I call this "the dual regress of free will" (Kane 2000b). In sections 2 and 3, we encountered two separate regresses associated with UR. The first began with the requirement that agents be responsible by virtue of past voluntary actions for anything that is a sufficient ground (*arche*) or reason for their actions in the sense of a *sufficient cause*; and it led to the conclusion that some actions in the life histories of agents must be undetermined (lack sufficient causes). The second regress began with the requirement that agents be responsible for anything that is a sufficient ground (*arche*) or reason for their actions in the sense of a *sufficient motive*; and it led (by way of will-setting and plurality) to the conclusion that some actions in the life histories of agents must be such that they could have done otherwise—that is, to AP.[10]

The first of these regresses results from the requirement that we be ultimate sources of our *actions,* the second from the requirement that we be ultimate sources of our *wills* (to perform those actions). If the second requirement were not added, we might have a world in which all the will-setting was done by someone or something other than the agents themselves (as in the imagined world in which God did all the will-setting). Agents in such a world might be unhindered in the pursuit of their purposes and their actions might sometimes be undetermined, but it would never be "up to them" what *purposes* they pursued. They would have some freedom of action, but not freedom of will.

In such manner, the requirements of indeterminism and alternative possibilities have a common origin in the idea that we must be the ultimate sources or grounds (archai) of our willed actions, though the two requirements are reached by different routes. Do the two regresses converge? Are the undetermined actions needed to stop one regress the same actions as the will-setting and plural actions needed to stop the other? The answer is yes, but the reasons for it are not trivial and I forgo the argument here for reasons of space (see Kane 1996a, 2000b). The convergent actions that result are the SFAs needed to satisfy UR. They must be (6) undetermined, (5) such that the agents could have done otherwise, (3) will-setting, and (4) satisfy the plurality conditions—a formidable set of conditions, but all required, I believe, for free will.

5. THE INTELLIGIBILITY QUESTION

It is one thing to argue that free will is incompatible with determinism, quite another to say positively what an incompatibilist or libertarian free will would look like. Many thinkers in the past century have believed that the traditional idea of being an ultimate source or ground of one's will is unintelligible and leads to insoluble puzzles and paradoxes. They argue that such a notion is outdated and cannot be fitted to modern images of human beings in the natural and social sciences. Many essays of this volume testify to the persistence of such skeptical attitudes about the intelligibility of libertarian free will in the latter half of the twentieth century.[11] Most of my work on free will over the past thirty years has been directed at this problem—at answering what I call the Intelligibility Question for free will. Can we make sense of a free will that is incompatible with determinism? Is such a freedom coherent or intelligible, or is it, as many critics claim, essentially mysterious or terminally obscure? Can it be fitted to modern scientific pictures of the world?

The threat to free will posed by this Intelligibility Question does not come from determinism, but from its opposite, *indeterminism*: if free will is not compatible with determinism, it does not seem to be compatible with indeterminism either. An event that is undetermined might occur or not occur, given the entire past. So whether or not it actually occurs, given its past, would seem to be a matter of chance. But chance events are not under the control of anything, hence not under the control of the agent. How then could they be free and responsible actions? If a different choice might have occurred given exactly the same past, then exactly the same deliberation, the same thought processes, the same prior beliefs, desires, and other motives—not a sliver of difference—that led to an agent's favoring one option (say, choosing to vacation in Hawaii rather than Colorado), might by chance have issued in the opposite choice instead. If such a thing happened, it would seem a fluke or accident, like an uncontrolled quantum jump in the brain, not a rational, free, or responsible action.

Reflections such as these (and many other related objections) have led to repeated charges that undetermined choices or actions would be "arbitrary," "capricious," "random," "irrational," "uncontrolled," "inexplicable," or merely "matters of luck or chance," not really free and responsible actions. It appears that the indeterminism that libertarians demand for free will would in fact undermine freedom rather than enhance it.

What prompted me to begin thinking about free will issues thirty years ago was a growing dissatisfaction with the standard responses to this intelligibility problem on the part of defenders of incompatibilist or libertarian free will. Libertarian responses invariably followed a certain pattern. Since agents had to be able to act or act otherwise, given exactly the same prior psychological and physical history (as indeterminism seems to require), some "extra (or special) factors" had to be introduced over and above the normal flow of events in order to explain how and why agents acted as they did. These extra or special factors postulated by libertarians have been various. They have postulated noumenal selves (Kant) or immaterial egos (Cartesian dualists) or "transempirical power centers" that intervene in the brain (Nobel physiologist Sir John Eccles). Some philosophers reified the Will as a mysterious homunculus within the agent or appealed to *sui generis* acts of volition or attention that could not in principle be determined by other events.[12] Still other thinkers have appealed to a special kind of "agent-" or "immanent" causation that cannot be explained in terms of ordinary modes of causation by events or occurrences. Views of the latter kind—so-called agent-causal or (AC) theories—are the most popular variants of this extra factor pattern in recent free will debates.[13]

But, whatever form they have taken, extra factor strategies have tended to reinforce the widespread view that notions of free will requiring indeterminism are mysterious and have no place in the modern scientific picture of the world. More important, as I see it, extra factor strategies give only the appearance of solving the problems of indeterminism, while creating further problems of their own. This marks another place in free will debates where exclusive focus on one line of argument—in this case on extra or special factor strategies, and especially on AC theories—has diverted attention from other promising possibilities and left important pathways in the free will labyrinth unexplored. In my writings, I disavow all such traditional appeals to special forms of agency or causation in order to explore alternative ways of making sense of libertarian free will without them.

To make this clear, in an earlier essay (Kane 1989), I distinguished two kinds of contemporary incompatibilist theory—agent-cause or AC theories, which "postulate a sui generis form of causation between an agent and an action" (O'Connor 1995a: 7), and "teleological intelligibility" or TI theories, which try to make undetermined free actions intelligible in terms of reasons and motives, intentions and purposes, without invoking extra entities or special forms of causation. My own view is of this TI kind. More specifically, it is a TI theory of a "causal indeterminist" (or "event-causalist") kind because, unlike some other TI theories, it also does not rely on claims that reasons or motives for action cannot be causes of action or that reasons explanations are noncausal.[14] The idea is to see how far one can go in making sense of libertarian freedom without appealing either to sui generis kinds of agency or causation or to claims that reasons explanations might somehow escape being subject to causal laws.[15]

This makes the task of answering the Intelligibility Question considerably more difficult, to be sure, but I think efforts in this direction are necessary if the free will issue is to be brought into more direct confrontation with modern science. I have always thought that by appealing to extra factors when the going gets tough, libertarians have chosen unearned extravagance over honest toil. Honest toil requires addressing the deep problems posed by indeterminism directly, rather than trying to circumvent them with extra factor strategies; and this means rethinking issues about indeterminism and responsibility from the ground up. To do this is to explore yet other neglected pathways in the free will labyrinth, to which I now turn.

6. INDETERMINISM AND RESPONSIBILITY

The first step is to note that indeterminism does not have to be involved in all acts done "of our own free wills," as argued earlier. Not all of them have to be undetermined, but only those choices or acts in our lifetimes by which we make ourselves into the kinds of persons we are, that is, the "will-setting" or "self-forming" actions (SFAs) discussed in earlier sections. Now I believe such will-setting or self-forming actions occur at those difficult times of life when we are torn between competing visions of what we should do or become; and they are more frequent in everyday life than we may think.

Perhaps we are torn between doing the moral thing or acting from ambition, or between powerful present desires and long-term goals, or we are faced with difficult tasks for which we have aversions. In all such cases, we are faced with competing motivations and have to make an effort to overcome temptation to do something else we also strongly want. At such times, there is tension and uncertainty in our minds about what to do, I suggest, that is reflected in appropriate regions of our brains by movement away from thermodynamic equilibrium—in short, a kind of stirring up of chaos in the brain that makes it sensitive to micro-indeterminacies at the neuronal level (Kane 1996a: 130ff.). The uncertainty and inner tension we feel at such soul-searching moments of self-formation would thereby be reflected in the indeterminacy of our neural processes themselves. What is experienced personally as uncertainty corresponds physically to the opening of a window of opportunity that temporarily screens off complete determination by influences of the past.[16] (By contrast, when we act from predominant motives or settled dispositions, the uncertainty or indeterminacy is muted. If it did play a role in such cases, it *would* be a mere nuisance or fluke, as critics suggest, like the choice of Colorado when we favored Hawaii.)

When we do decide under such conditions of uncertainty, the outcome is not determined because of the preceding indeterminacy—and yet it can be willed (and hence rational and voluntary) either way because, in such self-formation, the agents' prior wills are divided by conflicting motives. Consider a business-woman who faces a conflict of this kind. She is on the way to a meeting important to her career when she observes an assault taking place in an alley. An inner struggle ensues between her moral conscience, to stop and call for help, and her career ambitions that tell her she cannot miss this meeting. She has to make an effort of will to overcome the temptation to go on to her meeting. If she overcomes this temptation, it will be the result of her effort, but if she fails, it will be because she did not *allow* her effort to succeed. And this is due to the fact that, while she wanted to overcome temptation, she also wanted to fail, for quite different and incommensurable reasons. When agents, like the woman, decide in such circumstances, and the indeterminate efforts they are making become determinate choices, they *make* one set of competing reasons or motives prevail over the others then and there *by deciding* (Kane 1996a: 126ff.). Their acts are "will-setting."

Now let us add a further piece to the puzzle. Just as indeterminism does not necessarily undermine rationality and voluntariness, so indeterminism, in and of itself, does not necessarily undermine control and responsibility. Suppose you are trying to think through a difficult problem, say a mathematical problem, and there is some indeterminacy in your neural processes complicating the task—a kind of chaotic background. It would be like trying to concentrate and solve a problem with background noise or distraction. Whether you are going to succeed in solving the mathematical problem is uncertain and undetermined because of the distracting indeterministic neural noise. Yet, if you concentrate and solve the problem nonetheless, we have reason to say you did it and are responsible for it even though it was undetermined whether you would succeed. The distracting neural noise would have been an obstacle that you overcame by your effort.

There are numerous examples supporting this point, where indeterminism functions as an obstacle to success without precluding responsibility. The Austinian examples considered earlier are of this kind. The assassin might fail to kill the prime minister because of undetermined events in his nervous system that might have led to a wavering of his arm. But if he does succeed in hitting his target, despite the indeterminism, can he be held responsible? The answer is obviously yes because he voluntarily and intentionally succeeded in doing what he was *trying* to do—kill the prime minister. Yet his action, killing the prime minister, was undetermined. One might even say "he got lucky" in killing the prime minister, since there was a chance he might have missed. Yet, for all that, he *did* kill the prime minister and *was* responsible for it.

Here is another example: a husband, while arguing with his wife, in a fit of rage swings his arm down on her favorite glass-top tabletop, intending to break it. Again, we suppose that some indeterminism in the nerves of his arm makes the momentum of his swing indeterminate so that it is literally not determined whether the table will break right up to the moment when it is struck. Whether the husband breaks the table or not is undetermined and yet he is clearly responsible if he does break it. (It would be a poor excuse for him to say to his wife, "Chance did it, not me" or "It wasn't my doing; it happened by chance." She would not be impressed.)

Such examples, to be sure, do not amount to genuine exercises of free will in SFAs, such as the businesswoman's, where the wills of the agents are divided between conflicting motives. The businesswoman wants to help the victim, but she also wants to go on to her meeting. By contrast, the will of the assassin is not equally divided. He wants to kill the prime minister but does not also want to fail. Thus, if the assassin fails to hit his target, it will be merely by chance or as a fluke, not voluntarily (and so also for the husband, and mathematical problem-solver). So cases like the assassin, husband and mathematical problem-solver are not all that we want. Yet they are a step in the right direction because they show that indeterminism does not necessarily rule out action and responsibility, any more than it necessarily rules out rationality and voluntariness. To go farther, we have to dig more deeply into the situation and add some further ideas.

7. DOUBLING OR PARALLEL PROCESSING

Let us imagine, in cases of SFAs like the businesswoman's, where the agents' wills are conflicted, that the indeterministic noise which is obstructing her will to overcome temptation (and do the moral thing) is not coming from an external source, but from her own will, since she also deeply desires to do the opposite (go on to her meeting). Imagine that in such conflicting circumstances, two competing (recurrent) neural networks are involved. (These are complex networks of interconnected neurons in the brain circulating impulses in feedback loops of a kind generally involved in high-level cognitive processing.[17]) The input of one of these networks is coming from the woman's desires and motives for stopping to help the victim. If the network reaches a certain activation threshold (the simultaneous firing of a complex set of "output" neurons), that would represent her choice to help. For the competing network, the inputs are her ambitious motives for going on to her meeting, and its reaching an activation threshold represents the choice to go on.

Now imagine further that these two competing networks are connected so that the indeterministic noise that is an obstacle to her making one of the choices is coming from her desire to make the other. Thus, as suggested for SFAs generally, the indeterminism arises from a tension-creating conflict in the will. Under such circumstances, when either of the pathways "wins" (that is, reaches an activation threshold, which amounts to choice), it will be like the agent's solving the mathematical problem by overcoming the indeterministic background noise generated by the other. And as in the instance when you solved the mathematical problem by overcoming the distracting noise through your effort, we could say you did it and are responsible for it, so one can say this as well, I would argue, in the present case, *whichever one is chosen*. The neural pathway through which she succeeds in reaching a choice threshold will have overcome the obstacle in the form of indeterministic noise coming from the other.

Note that, under these circumstances, the choices either way will not be "inadvertent," "accidental," "capricious," or "merely random," because they will be *willed* by the woman either way, when they are made, and done for *reasons* either way (moral convictions if she turns back, ambitious motives if she goes on) which she then and there endorses. And these are the conditions usually required to say something is done "on purpose," rather than accidentally, capriciously, or merely by chance. Moreover, if we also assume (as we can in the woman's case) that the agent is not being coerced (no one is holding a gun to her head), nor physically constrained or disabled, nor forced or controlled by others, then these conditions (that she wills it, does it for reasons, and could have done otherwise willingly and for reasons), rule out each of the normal reasons we have for saying that agents act but lack control over their actions (coercion, constraint, incapacity, inadvertence, involuntariness, mistake, or control by others; Kane 1996a: 137–50). We could of course have imagined cases in which one or another of these conditions was not absent (for example, cases where she is being coerced), and then the acts in question would not be free and would not be SFAs.[18] But the point is that there is nothing inconsistent in imagined cases, like the businesswoman's, in which all of these undermining conditions are absent; and these would be examples of SFAs.

To be sure, with such "self-forming" choices, agents cannot control or determine which choice outcome will occur *before* it occurs, or else the outcomes would be predetermined after all. But it does not follow, because one does not control or determine which of a set of outcomes is going to occur before it occurs, that one does not control which of them occurs, *when* it occurs (Kane 1996a: 134–36). When these conditions for self-forming choices are satisfied, agents exercise control over their future lives *then and there* by deciding. Indeed, they have what I have called "plural voluntary control" in the following sense: agents have plural voluntary control over a set of options (stopping to help or going on to a meeting) when they are able to bring about *whichever* of the options they will, *when* they will to do so, for the *reasons* they will to do so, *on purpose* rather than by mistake or accident, without being coerced or compelled in doing so, or otherwise controlled by other agents or mechanisms. Each of these conditions can be satisfied in cases like the businesswoman's, despite the indeterminism involved, as I have argued here and at greater length elsewhere (Kane 1996a: 133–48, 1999a). Satisfying them amounts in common parlance to the claim that the agents can choose either way "at will."

Note also that this account of self-forming choices amounts to a kind of "doubling" of the mathematical problem. It is as if an agent faced with such a choice is *trying* or making an effort to solve *two* cognitive problems at once, or to complete two competing (deliberative) tasks at once—in our example, to make a moral choice and to make a conflicting self-interested choice (corresponding to the two competing neural networks involved). Each task is being thwarted by the indeterminism coming from the other, so it might fail. But if it succeeds, then the agents can be held responsible because, as in the case of solving the mathematical problem, they will have succeeded in doing what they were knowingly and willingly trying to do. Recall the assassin and the husband once again. Owing to indeterminacies in their neural pathways, the assassin might miss his target or the husband fail to break the table. But if they *succeed*, despite the probability of failure, they are responsible, because they will have succeeded in doing what they were trying to do.

And so it is, I suggest, with self-forming choices, except that in their case, *whichever way the agents choose*, they will have succeeded in doing what they were trying to do because they were simultaneously trying to make both choices, and one is going to succeed. Their failure to do one thing is not a *mere* failure, but a voluntary succeeding in doing the other. Does it make sense to talk about the agent's trying to do two competing things at once in this way, or to solve two cognitive problems at once? Well, we know that the brain is a parallel processor; it can simultaneously process different kinds of information relevant to tasks such as perception or recognition through different neural pathways. Such a capacity, I believe, is essential for free will.[19]

In cases of self-formation (SFAs), agents are simultaneously trying to resolve plural and competing cognitive tasks. They are, as we say, of two minds. Yet they are not two separate persons. They are not dissociated from either task. The businesswoman who wants to go back to help the victim is the same ambitious woman who wants to go to her meeting and make a sale. She is a complex creature, torn inside by different visions of who she is and what she wants to be, as we all are from time to time. But this is the kind of complexity needed for genuine self-formation and free will. And when she succeeds in doing one of the things she is trying to do, she will endorse that as *her* resolution of the conflict in her will, voluntarily and intentionally, not by accident or mistake.

8. Responsibility, Luck, Chance

Yet it remains difficult to shake the intuition that if the choices are undetermined, their outcomes must be merely "random," "capricious," or matters of "luck" or "chance." Such intuitions are deep-seated. But one thing we learn from debates about free will is that common intuitions should not be taken at face value without being questioned; and I believe that common intuitions about indeterminism are as much in need of deconstructing as any others.

The first step in doing this is to question the intuitive connection in people's minds between "indeterminism's being involved in something" and "its happening merely as a matter of chance or luck." *Chance* and *luck* are terms of ordinary language that carry the connotation of "its being out of my control." So using them already begs certain questions, whereas "indeterminism" is a technical term that merely precludes *deterministic* causation, not causation altogether. Indeterminism is consistent with nondeterministic forms of causation, where outcomes are caused, but not inevitably. It is a mistake to assume that *undetermined* means "uncaused."

Another source of misunderstanding is this. Since the outcome of the businesswoman's effort (the choice) is undetermined up to the last minute, we may imagine her first making an effort to overcome temptation (to go on to her meeting) and then at the last instant "chance takes over" and decides the issue for her. But this image is misleading. On the view just described, one cannot separate the indeterminism and the effort of will, so that *first* the effort occurs *followed* by chance or luck (or vice versa). One must think of the effort and the indeterminism as fused; the effort *is* indeterminate and the indeterminism is a *property* of the effort, not something separate that occurs after or before the effort. The fact that the effort has this property of being indeterminate does not make it any less the woman's *effort.* The complex recurrent neural network that realizes the effort in the brain is circulating impulses in feedback loops and there is some indeterminacy in these circulating impulses. But the whole process is her effort of will and it persists right up to the moment when the choice is made. There is no point at which the effort stops and chance "takes over." She chooses as a result of the effort, even though she might have failed. Similarly, the husband breaks the table as a result of his effort, even though he might have failed because of the indeterminacy. (That is why his excuse, "Chance broke the table, not me" is so lame.)

And just as expressions like "she chose *by* chance" can mislead in such contexts, so can expressions like "she got lucky." Recall that in the cases of the assassin and the husband, one might say "they got lucky" in killing the prime minister and breaking the table because their actions were undetermined. Yet, as we noted, it does not follow that they were not responsible. So ask yourself this question: Why does the inference "He got lucky, *so he was not responsible?*" fail when it does fail, in the cases of the husband and the assassin? The first part of an answer has to do with the point made earlier that *luck,* like *chance,* has question-begging implications in ordinary language that are not necessarily implications of *indeterminism* (which implies only the absence of deterministic causation). The core meaning of "he got lucky" in the assassin and husband cases, which *is* implied by indeterminism, I suggest, is that "he succeeded *despite the probability or chance of failure*"; and this core meaning does not imply lack of responsibility, if he succeeds.

If "he got lucky" had further meanings in the husband and assassin cases that are often associated with *luck* and *chance* in ordinary usage (for example, the outcome was not his doing, or occurred by *mere* chance, or he was not responsible for it), the inference would not fail for the husband and assassin, as it clearly does. What the failure of the inference shows is that these further meanings of *luck* and *chance* do not follow *from the mere presence of indeterminism.* The second reason why the inference "He got lucky, so he was not responsible" fails for the assassin and the husband is that *what* they succeeded in doing was what they were *trying* and *wanting* to do all along (kill the minister and break the table, respectively). The third reason is that *when* they succeeded, their reaction was not "Oh dear, that was a mistake, an accident—something that *happened* to me, not something I *did*." Rather, they *endorsed* the outcomes as something they were trying and wanting to do all along, that is to say, knowingly and purposefully, not by mistake or accident.

But these conditions are satisfied in the businesswoman's case as well, *either way* she chooses. If she succeeds in choosing to return to help the victim (or in choosing to go on to her meeting), (1) she will have "succeeded *despite the probability or chance of failure*," (2) she will have succeeded in doing what she was trying and wanting to do all along (she wanted both outcomes very much, but for different reasons, and was trying to make those reasons prevail in both cases), and (3) when she succeeded (in choosing to return to help), her reaction was not "Oh dear, that was a mistake, an accident—something that happened to me, not something I did." Rather, she endorsed the outcome as something she was trying and wanting to do all along; she recognized it as her resolution of the conflict in her will. And if she had chosen to go on to her meeting, she would have endorsed that outcome, recognizing it as her resolution of the conflict in her will.

Let us consider some other possible objections. Are we perhaps begging the question by assuming that the outcomes of the woman's efforts are *choices* to begin with? One might argue that if an event is undetermined, it must be something that merely "happens" and cannot be someone's choice or action. But to see how question-begging such a claim is, one has only to note what it implies: if anything is a choice or action, it is determined ("all choices and actions are determined"). Are we to assume that this is necessarily true or true by definition? If so, the free will issue would be solved by fiat. But, aside from its being question-begging, there is no good reason to believe such a claim anyway. A choice is the formation of an intention or a purpose to do something. It resolves uncertainty and indecision in the mind about what to do. Nothing in such a description implies that there could not be some indeterminism in the deliberation and neural processes of an agent preceding choice corresponding to the agent's uncertainty about what to do. Recall from preceding arguments that the presence of indeterminism does not mean the outcome happened merely by chance and not by the agent's effort. Once again we must be wary of confusing *undetermined* with *uncaused*.[20] Self-forming choices are undetermined but not uncaused; they are caused by the agent's efforts.

If indeterminism does not undermine the idea that something is a choice, perhaps it undermines the idea that it is *the agent's* choice. But again, why must it necessarily do that? What makes the woman's choice her own is that it results from her efforts and deliberation, which in turn are causally influenced by her reasons and intentions (for example, to resolve indecision in one way or another). And what makes these efforts, deliberations, reasons, and intentions *hers*, as I have elsewhere argued, is that they are embedded in a larger motivational system realized in her brain in terms of which she defines herself as a practical reasoner capable of responding to and acting on reasons. (I call this system the "self-network" in Kane 1996a: 137–41). Such a motivational system or self-network is needed to account for rational agency, no matter what position one takes on free will, whether compatibilist or incompatibilist, as Fred Dretske (1988) and David Velleman (1992) have persuasively argued. A choice is the agent's doing when it is produced intentionally by efforts, deliberation, and reasons that are part of the agent's self-network and in addition when the agent *endorses* the new intention or purpose that the choice creates (for example, to help the assault victim) as an additional part of the self-network capable of guiding future practical reasoning and action.[21] This is what happens in the businesswoman's case when she chooses (either way).

Perhaps the issue then is not whether the result of the woman's effort was a *choice*, or even whether it was *her* choice, but rather how much *control* she had over it. I have already argued (in earlier discussions of voluntariness and control) that the presence of indeterminism need not eliminate control altogether. But would not the presence of indeterminism at least *diminish* the control persons have over their choices and other actions? Is it not the case that the assassin's control over whether the prime minister is killed (his ability to realize his purposes or what he is trying to do) is lessened by the undetermined impulses in his arm—and so also for the husband and his breaking the table? And if so, would it not be the same for self-forming choices, like the businesswoman's? Moreover, this limitation is connected with another often noted by critics—that indeterminism, wherever it occurs, appears to be a *hindrance* or *obstacle* to the realization of our purposes and hence an obstacle to our freedom.

There is some truth in these claims, but I think it is a truth that reveals something important about free will. One should concede that wherever it occurs, indeterminism *does* diminish control to some degree over what we are trying to do and *is* a hindrance or obstacle to the realization of our purposes. But recall that in the case of the businesswoman (and SFAs generally), the indeterminism that is admittedly diminishing her control over one thing she is trying to do (the moral act of helping the victim) *is coming from her own will*—from her desire and effort to do the opposite (go to her business meeting), and vice versa. Thus, in each case, while the indeterminism is indeed functioning as a hindrance or obstacle to the realization of one of her purposes, it is doing so in the form of resistance within her will which has to be overcome.

If there were no such hindrance, no resistance in the will, she would indeed have "complete" control over one of her options in the sense that no competing motives would stand in the way of her choosing it. But then also she would not be free to rationally and voluntarily choose the other purpose because she would have no good competing reasons to do so. Thus, indeterminism, by hindering the realization of *some* of our purposes, paradoxically opens up the genuine possibility of pursuing other purposes—doing otherwise—voluntarily and rationally. To be genuinely self-forming agents (creators of ourselves), to have free will, there must at times in life be such obstacles and hindrances in our wills that must be overcome.

Let me conclude with one final objection that is perhaps the most telling and has not yet been discussed. Even if one granted that persons, such as the businesswoman, could make genuine self-forming choices that were undetermined, is there not something to the charge that such choices would be *arbitrary*? A residual arbitrariness seems to remain in all self-forming choices, since the agents cannot in principle have sufficient or overriding *prior* reasons for making one option and one set of reasons prevail over the other. There is also some truth to this charge, but again I think it is a truth that reveals something important about free will. I have argued elsewhere (Kane: 1996a: 145–46) that such arbitariness relative to prior reasons tells us that every undetermined self-forming choice is the initiation of what might be called a "value experiment" whose justification lies in the future and is not fully explained by the past. In making such a choice we say, in effect, "Let's try this. It is not required by my past, but is consistent with my past and is one branching pathway my life can now meaningfully take. Whether it is the right choice, only time will tell. Meanwhile, I am willing to take responsibility for it one way or the other."

It is worth noting that the term *arbitrary* comes from the Latin *arbitrium*, which means "judgment"—as in *liberum arbitrium voluntatis*, "free judgment of the will" (the medieval designation for *free will*). Imagine a writer in the middle of a novel. The novel's heroine faces a crisis and the writer has not yet developed her character in sufficient detail to say exactly how she will act. The author makes a "judgment" about this that is not determined by the heroine's already formed past, which does not provide unique direction. In this sense, the judgment (*arbitrium*) of how she will react is "arbitrary," but not entirely so. It had input from the heroine's fictional past and in turn gave input to her projected future.

In a similar way, agents who exercise free will are both authors of and characters in their own stories at once. By virtue of "self-forming" judgments of the will (*arbitria voluntatis*), they are "arbiters" of their own lives, "making themselves" out of past that, if they are truly free, does not limit their future pathways to one. If we should charge them with lacking a sufficient or *conclusive* prior reason for choosing as they did, any one of them might reply: "True enough. But I did have *good* reasons for choosing as I did, which I'm willing to endorse and take responsibility for. If they were not sufficient or conclusive reasons, that's because, like the heroine of the novel, I was not a fully formed person before I chose (and still am not, for that matter). Like the author of the novel, I am in the process of writing an unfinished story and forming an unfinished character who, in my case, is myself."

9. Agent Causation

When I began discussing the Intelligibility Question in section 5, I said the goal would be to see how far one could go in making sense of incompatibilist free will without appealing to "extra factor" strategies in the form of special forms of agency or causation (noumenal selves, transempirical power centers, agent- or non-occurrent [AC] causes, and the like). In short, the goal was to pursue a TI or teleological intelligibility strategy, attempting to make libertarian free will purposively intelligible without appeals to extra factors or sui generis forms of causation that cannot be spelled out in terms of events, occurrences, or states of affairs.

The preceding account of libertarian free will makes no such appeals. It does appeal to a notion of *mental causation.* It assumes that choices and actions can be caused or produced by efforts, deliberations, beliefs, desires, intentions, and other reasons or motives of the agent.[22] (Hence it is also a causalist or causal indeterminist TI strategy.) But this is causation by events, occurrences, or states of affairs involving the agent; it is not a special kind of nonoccurrent causation by an agent such as AC theories require. Moreover, mental causation of this sort is not a specifically incompatibilist or libertarian assumption. Compatibilist and determinist accounts of free agency also assume that choices and actions can be caused by efforts, beliefs, desires, intentions, and the like; and it is hard to see how they could avoid doing so. The only added assumption I have made to account for libertarian free agency is just the one you would expect—that some of the mental events or processes involved may be *undetermined,* so that the causation by mental events may be nondeterministic or probabilistic as well as deterministic.

The question I want to ask in this concluding section is this: what is missing in the TI and causal indeterminist account of libertarian freedom presented in earlier sections that an added postulate of nonoccurrent or nonevent agent-causation is supposed to provide? Analogous questions could be posed for other extra factor strategems, such as noumenal selves, transempirical power centers, and the like. But since these have fallen out of favor among contemporary philosophers, I choose to concentrate on extra factor theories that have played the most prominent role in recent philosophy, theories of agent- or nonoccurrent or nonevent, causation, that is, AC theories.

Let it be clear at the outset that the TI theory presented in earlier sections *does* postulate *agent causation.* Agents *cause* or bring about their undetermined self-forming choices (SFAs) by making efforts to do so, voluntarily and intentionally; and agents cause or bring about many other things as well by making efforts or by performing other actions—they cause deaths (of, say, prime ministers), broken tables, messes, accidents, pain, fires, and so on. Agent causation in general is not the issue here. TI theorists can also believe in agent causation and I certainly do, even for undetermined free choices (SFAs). What is at issue is agent-causation (hyphenated)—a sui generis form of causation that cannot be spelled out in terms of events, occurrences, or states or affairs involving agents. It is misleading to frame this debate in such a way that AC theorists believe in agent causation while TI theorists do not (presumably because the latter believe only in event causation). They both can and should believe in agent causation. The issue is how it is to be spelled out.

A related point is this: just as we can say, on the theory I have proposed, that agents *cause* their self-forming choices (SFAs) by making efforts to do so, and cause other things such as broken tables and messes, so we can say that agents *produce* or *bring about* their self-forming choices by making efforts to do so and produce many other things by their efforts and other actions. Of course, the causation or production in the case of SFAs is nondeterministic or probabilistic, since they are undetermined. But so it is also in the case of the assassin or the husband who breaks his wife's table. And the burden of my argument was that nondeterministic or probabilistic causation can support claims that agents really do *produce* or bring about what they nondeterministically or probabilistically cause by their voluntary efforts and can be held responsible for doing so.[23] This is true of the asssassin, the husband, the mathematical problem-solver, and those who make SFAs, like the businesswoman.

This point is worth emphasizing, because it is often claimed by AC theorists that what TI theories (including causal indeterminist theories) lack—and what nonoccurrent agent-causation is supposed to provide—is a conception of agents *producing* or *bringing about* their undetermined actions rather than those actions occurring merely by chance. But I have repeatedly argued in earlier sections—without invoking nonoccurrent agent-causation—that the mere presence of indeterminism does not imply that SFAs and other actions (such as the assassin's or the husband's) must occur *merely* by chance and not as a result of the agent's voluntary and intentional efforts. The mistake here lies in assuming that if something is undetermined by prior reasons or efforts of an agent, it must be uncaused by prior reasons or efforts of the agent (which is a special case of the mistaken assumption that what is undetermined must be uncaused).

I also argued in previous sections that nondeterministic causation by efforts and reasons supports ascriptions of responsibility when one also considers that the efforts are voluntarily and intentionally made for reasons and that the results of the efforts (such as choices) are endorsed by the agents as successful outcomes of what they were trying to do. This is so in the assassin and husband cases; and it is doubly so for SFAs, like the businesswoman's, where the failure of one effort is not a mere failure, but a voluntarily succeeding in doing something else.

So we are still looking for what the postulation of nonoccurrent agent-causation is supposed to add to the picture. In his perceptive survey of contemporary AC theories in an essay of this volume (ch. 15), Timothy O'Connor provides some further clues about this matter that are worth considering. Speaking to the issue of what causal indeterminist theories like mine lack that nonoccurrent agent-causation is supposed to provide, O'Connor writes: For causal indeterminist theories, "the agent's internal states [including reasons, motives, and so on] have objective tendencies of some determinate measure to cause certain outcomes. While this provides an *opening* in which the agent might freely select one option from a plurality of real alternatives, it fails to introduce a causal capacity that fills it. And what better here than it's being the agent himself that causes the particular action that is to be performed?"[24] The missing element suggested in this quote is the "causal capacity" to "freely select one option from a plurality of real alternatives" that are left open by the (causal) indeterminism of prior events.

Now such a causal capacity is surely important. But why do we have to suppose that agent-causation of a nonevent kind is needed to capture it? The fact is that, on the causal indeterminist theory I have presented, the agent *does* have such a causal capacity. Not only does the businesswoman facing an SFA have a plurality of real alternatives from which to choose, she has the *capacity* to make either choice by making an effort to do so. The conflicting motives in her will and the consequent divisions within her motivational system make it possible for her to choose either way for reasons, voluntarily and intentionally. And this is clearly a *causal* capacity since it is the capacity to *cause* or *produce* either choice outcome (nondeterministically, of course) as a result of her effort against resistance in her will.

This is a remarkable capacity to be sure; and we may assume that it is possessed only by creatures who attain the status of *persons* capable of self-reflection and having the requisite conflicts within their wills. (So O'Connor's calling it a form of "*personal* causation" is altogether apt.) But there is no reason to suppose we need to postulate a nonevent form of causation to account for it.[25] The *capacity* itself (prior to its exercise) is a complex dispositional *state* of the agent; and its *exercise* is a sequence of *events* or *processes* involving efforts leading to choice or formation of an intention, which intention then guides subsequent action (of going back to help the victim or going on to a meeting.) It is a capacity *of* the agent, to be sure, but both the capacity and its exercise are described in terms of properties or states of the agent and in terms of states of affairs, events, and processes involving the agent, as I have done in the preceding paragraph and earlier in the paper.

Is there a residual fear functioning here that the "agent" will somehow disappear from the scene if we describe its capacities and their exercise, including free will, in terms of states and events? Such a fear would be misguided at best. A continuing substance (such as an agent) does not absent itself from the ontological stage because we describe its continuing existence—its *life*, if it is a living thing—including its capacities and their exercise, in terms of states of affairs, events, and processes involving it. One needs more reason than this to think that there are no continuing substances, or no agents, but only events, or that agents do not cause things, only events cause things. For my part, I should confess that I am a substance ontologist and indeed something of an Aristotelian when it comes to thinking about the nature of living things and the relation of mind to body. Agents are continuing substances with both mental and physical properties. But there is nothing inconsistent in saying this and being a TI theorist about free will who thinks that the *lives* of agents, their capacities, and the exercise of those capacities, including free will, must be spelled out in terms of states, processes, and events.

Similar remarks are in order about O'Connor's comments on "emergence" in chapter 15 of this volume. Issues about the existence of emergent properties (like issues about continuing substances) must also be distinguished from issues about nonevent causation. Indeed, I also believe that emergence of a certain kind (now recognized in self-organizing systems) is necessary for free will, even of the TI kind that I defend. Once the brain reaches a certain level of complexity, so that there can be conflicts in the will of the kind required for SFAs, the larger motivational system of the brain stirs up chaos and indeterminacy in a part of itself which is the realization of a specific deliberation. In other words, the whole motivational system or self-network has the capacity to influence specific parts of itself (processes within it) in novel ways once a certain level of complexity of the whole is attained. This is a kind of emergence of new capacities and indeed even a kind of "downwards causation" (novel causal influences of an emergent whole on its parts) such as are now recognized in a number of scientific contexts involving self-organizing and ecological systems (Kuppers 1992, Kauffman 1995, Gilbert and Sarkar 2000).

But this kind of emergence characteristic of self-organizing systems does not, in and of itself, imply causation of a nonoccurrent or nonevent kind, since the wholes and parts involved are states and processes of the organism of various levels of complexity. Of course, O'Connor would like a stronger form of emergence than this, which would require nonoccurrent causation. But his argument—that some kind of emergence of capacities for holistic or downward causation of wholes on parts is required for free will—does not prove the need for a *nonevent* kind of causation. Such emergence, which I agree is important for free will, can be accommodated within a teleological intelligibility theory.

O'Connor offers yet another argument when he says that what non-agent-causal theories lack and what agent-causation supplies is "the agent's directly controlling the outcome" of an undetermined choice. This is the other side of the AC equation. AC theorists usually focus on one or both of two things when asked what is missing in non-AC theories: *production* and *control*. We have just considered production. Let us now turn to control, a topic that I have said a great deal about earlier in this chapter. What is it for an agent to have direct *control* at a given time over a set of choice options (for example, to help the assault victim or go on to a meeting)? The account I have given of this idea is embodied in the notion of plural voluntary control. To state it more precisely for present purposes, agents have plural voluntary control over a set of options at a time when they have the (1) *ability* to (2) *bring about* (3) at that time (4) *whichever* of the options they will or want, (5) for the reasons they will to do so, (6) on purpose or intentionally rather than accidentally, by mistake or merely by chance (as when by mistake I press the wrong button on the coffee machine), hence (7) voluntarily (in accordance with their wills rather than against them), (8) as a result of their efforts, if effort should be required, (9) without being coerced or compelled, or (10) otherwise controlled or forced to choose one way or the other by some other agent or mechanism. Agents *exercise* such control directly when they voluntarily and intentionally *produce* one of the options (a particular self-forming choice or SFA) *then and there* (at the time in question) under these conditions.

I have argued that every one of these conditions can be satisfied for SFAs of the type exemplified by the businesswoman, even when the choice options are undetermined—without appealing to nonevent causation. It is true that, with undetermined SFAs, agents do not have control over which choice outcome will occur before it occurs; otherwise the outcomes would be predetermined. But, as also argued earlier, it does not follow from this fact that one does not have control over which of the outcomes occurs *when* it occurs.[26] Moreover, these conditions of plural voluntary control are the kinds we look for when deciding whether persons are or are not *responsible* for their choices or actions (for example, when they produce something voluntarily and intentionally as a result of making an effort to do so). Thus, *control* in a responsibility-entailing sense can be accommodated within a TI theory just as *production* can be. Indeed, it is worth noting that control and production are related: *control* (over x) at a time t is the *ability* at t to *produce* (x) at t; *voluntary* control is the ability at t to produce (x) at t "at will"; and *plural* voluntary control is the ability at t to produce (x) at t at will and to do otherwise than produce (x) at t at will.

I turn finally to some criticisms in this volume (chapter 16) of my TI and causal indeterminist view by another AC theorist, Randolph Clarke. Clarke is an unusual AC theorist because he takes nondeterministic causation by reasons more seriously than do other AC theorists and has argued persuasively for the role of such causation in libertarian accounts of free will (Clarke 1992a, 1996b, 1997). Indeed, I agree with much of what Clarke says about this topic and have learned much from his writings on it. For example, in his essay (ch. 16) for this volume, when discussing an event-causal or causal indeterminist view like mine, Clarke says that, on such a view, "there will be available explanations of free actions that cite reasons-states that caused the action; these explanations will be rational explanations, simple as well as contrastive. Free actions will then be adequately explicable" by such theories.[27] Of course, as Clarke also notes, issues of explanation are not the same as issues of control. Yet, he also argues in chapter 16 that many objections to the effect that causal indeterminist theories cannot account for agent control also miss the mark. For example, Clarke considers the so-called "luck objection"—the objection that, on causal indeterminist views, it would merely be a matter of luck which of a set of undetermined choices occurred—and finds this objection unconvincing. Needless to say, I agree with Clarke on all these points. (See my arguments on *luck* and *chance* in sections 7 and 8 of this essay.)

Where then does Clarke think event-causal, or causal indeterminist, TI theories fall short, so that some further nonevent causation is needed? The reason (so far as I understand it) emerges toward the end of his essay: "[A]n event-causal libertarian view adds no new types of causes to those that can be required by a compatibilist account, and hence the former appears to add nothing to the agent's positive power to determine what he does."[28] Causal indeterminist theories provide "leeway" for choice, Clarke says, but no more control over actions than compatibilists offer; and more control than compatibilists offer is needed to account for the genuine responsibility and desert in libertarian senses.[29]

I agree that something more in the way of control than compatibilists offer is needed to account for genuine responsibility in the libertarian sense. But I think the "more" control libertarians need is not more of the same *kind* of control compatibilists offer, but rather another kind of control altogether. The kind of everyday control that usually concerns compatibilists is what I call "antecedent determining control" (Kane 1996a: 144)—the ability to guarantee or determine beforehand which of a number of options is going to occur.[30] This kind of control is clearly important in everyday life. But it is not the only kind of control that must matter for libertarians. If free choices are undetermined, we cannot have antecedent determining control over them, for exercising such control would mean *pre*determining them (determining beforehand just which choice we are going to make). What libertarians must require for undetermined SFAs, I believe, is another kind of control altogether (that compatibilists cannot obtain)— namely, *ultimate* control—the originative control exercised by agents when it is "up to them" which of a set of possible choices or actions will now occur, and up to no one and nothing else over which the agents themselves do not also have control. One can show that this kind of control, which is required by ultimate responsibility (UR), entails indeterminism (as I have shown earlier in this chapter). So it is not something that can be captured by compatibilist accounts of freedom; but neither does it require nonoccurrent causation, as I have also argued. It does require the ability to cause or produce any one of a set of possible choices or actions each of which is undetermined (hence nondeterministically)— and to do so "at will" (that is, rationally (for reasons), voluntarily, and intentionally).

Moreover, there is a trade-off between such ultimate control required for incompatibilist freedom and the antecedent determining control that compatibilists can get. To have some ultimate control over our destinies, we have to give up antecedent determining control at crucial points in our lives. We have to accept a measure of uncertainty and genuine indeterminacy in our deliberative lives right up to the moment of decision. Indeterminism does not leave everything unchanged, for it implies "the probability or chance of failure"—though with genuine free will, every failing is also a succeeding, so we are responsible either way. If libertarians were after the same kind of control that compatibilists have to offer, only more of it, then I would agree with Clarke. But I think that what motivates the need for incompatibilism is an interest in a different kind of "control over our lives" altogether—a control related to our being to some degree the ultimate creators or originators of our own purposes or ends and hence ultimate "arbiters" of our own wills. We cannot have that in a determined world.

NOTES

1. See Berofsky's essay in this volume (ch. 8) for an overview of recent debates about *can, power, ability,* and "could have done otherwise." Aspects of the debates are also discussed in essays by Kapitan, van Inwagen, Russell, Taylor and Dennett, Fischer, Ekstrom, and Widerker—chs. 6, 7, 11, 12, 13, and 14, respectively.

2. The formal statement of the condition is,

> (UR) An agent is *ultimately responsible* for some (event or state) E's occurring only if (R) the agent is personally responsible for E's occurring in a sense which entails that something the agent voluntarily (or willingly) did or omitted . . . either was, or causally contributed to, E's occurrence and made a difference to whether or not E occurred; and (U) for every X and Y (where X and Y represent occurrences of events and/or states) if the agent is personally responsible for X, and if Y is an *arche* (or sufficient ground or or explanation) for X, then the agent must also be personally responsible for Y (Kane 1996a: 35)

R is the "responsibility condition" and U the "ultimacy condition" of UR. My first formulation of a condition of this sort was in Kane 1985: ch. 3. I have since dropped the phrase "for which the agent could have voluntarily done otherwise" from the statement of R in Kane 1996a because it is not needed (see Kane 2000a, particularly the response to Fischer 2000); it turns out that what this phrase says follows from U for reasons discussed later in this chapter. Other philosophers, such as Galen Strawson (1986) and Martha Klein (1990), have also noted the importance of an ultimacy condition for free will, though neither believes such a condition can be satisfied; and so they reject libertarian free will. See Strawson's essay in this volume (ch. 19) and the discussion of Klein in Paul Russell's essay (ch. 10 of this volume).

3. Aristotle (1915: 1114a13–22). Also see Richard Sorabji (1980: 234–38) for a perceptive discussion of this condition in Aristotle's writings.

4. Kane (1996a: 74–78, 125ff).

5. An interesting religious use of this idea is made by Sennett (1999) regarding the freedom of creatures in heaven. If they have reached a state where their wills are determined to do the good, in what sense, if at all, would they be free and responsible? Sennett argues that one can make sense of this religiously if they have a history of actions that were free in an incompatibilist sense at some point in their earthly lives and through which they have arrived at this state. In a footnote, he correctly suggests that my view of free will would support such an account (ibid.: 81). Though I do not usually engage in heavenly speculation, were I to do so, I would put it this way (compare Kane 1996a: 179–81): [C]reatures in an orthodox heaven, if they acted at all, would continue to act "of their own free wills" in the sense of "wills of their own free making."

6. A proof that UR does indeed entail AP for self-forming actions (SFAs) comes later. The complete version is in Kane (1996a: chs. 5, 7).

7. Klein (1990: ch. 2) also notes that worries about ultimacy are distinct from worries about alternative possibilities, as does Strawson in this volume (ch. 19). As we shall see, however, I argue that the two conditions are connected in surprising ways.

8. Some libertarians such as Eleonore Stump (1990, 1996a) and Linda Zagzebski (1991), influenced also by Frankfurt-style examples, have argued that while free will is incompatible with causal determinism, it does not necessarily require alternative possibilities or AP. Such a view has been called "hyperincompatibilism." Why might free will require indeterminism if not for AP? Stump (1999b) has suggested that something like my UR might be the reason. I think she is right about this, but it does not follow that AP is entirely out of the picture, as we shall see.

9. Not as sole causes, of course, but as necessary or indispensable parts of the actual web of causes or conditions that produced these purposes and motives (compare Kane 1996b).

10. It is worth noting that one might have a sufficient motive without a sufficient cause, and vice versa. There is a sufficient motive when the agent's will is "set one way" on performing an action so that the agent will act in only one way voluntarily. The Austinian examples show that this can be the case even in the absence of sufficient causes. The opposite cases of sufficient causes without sufficient motives are more obvious. My pressing the button for coffee with cream by mistake might have been determined, in which case it would have a sufficient cause, but no sufficient motive, since I wanted and intended to press a different button.

11. For extended discussions of the arguments behind this widespread skepticism, see the essays of Strawson, Honderich, and Taylor and Dennett in this volume (chs. 19, 20, and 11, respectively). Other essayists of this volume who endorse the scepticism include Berofsky, Russell, Pereboom, Smilansky, Double, and Walter (chs. 8, 10, 21, 22, 23, and 26, respectively).

12. Kant (1959), Eccles (1970, 1994); among the Cartesians, see Price (in Priestley and Price 1778) and Mansel (1851). The views of Duns Scotus on free will are complex, but he expresses a common, though not univeral, medieval theme when he says, "[N]othing other than the Will is the total cause of volition in the will" (Scotus 1962: 38).

13. See O'Connor's essay in this volume (ch. 15) for an overview of AC theories. For criticisms of AC theories by libertarians, see the essays of van Inwagen (ch. 7) and Ginet (ch. 17) as well as section 9 of this chapter. Also see O'Connor (1995) for defenses of agent-causal positions by various authors, including William Rowe, Randolph Clarke, and Timothy O'Connor.

14. See Randolph Clarke's essay in this volume (ch. 16) for a general critical survey of TI theories of the noncausalist as well as causal indeterminist varieties. David Wiggins (1973), Richard Sorabji (1980), and Roderick Chisholm (1995) express sympathy for a causal indeterminist TI approach though they do not work out detailed theories. (Chisholm's 1995 amounts to a repudiation of his earlier commitment to an agent-causation or AC view, 1982b). See Ginet's essay in this volume (ch. 17) for a discussion of the differences between noncausalist and causalist theories.

15. There are three other libertarians with whom I agree on many points though I am not sure exactly how to classify their views or whether they share the commitments of this footnoted statement. They are David Hodgson (1991, 1999), Storrs McCall (1987, 1994, 1999), and James Felt S.J. (1994). In his essay for this volume (ch. 4) and in (1999), Hodgson accurately points out a number of similarities between his view and mine. My uncertainty about the relation of our views focuses on how to classify his notion of "volitional causation." It seems not to be a form of nonevent causation, which suggests a TI approach. Yet it is not clear to me whether or not it constitutes an "extra" form of causation over and above those accepted in the sciences, and hence whether Hodgson's view really involves an "extra factor" strategy or not. Storrs McCall has been writing perceptively about free will for many years and I agree with much of what he says on the subject. It seems that his view is also a TI theory, but it is not clear to me whether his account of decision making is genuinely causalist or a more modest causal indeterminist account, like Mele's, or a stronger account like mine. (McCall and I are currently trying to figure out just how we differ.) Finally, James Felt puts forward a unique theory of free will that has many TI features. But he relies on a Bergsonian distinction between two notions of time in order to account for agency, on which I do not rely. Despite these differences and uncertainties, I do agree with much in the views of all three of these philosophers.

16. Whether the requisite indeterminacy is there in the brain is an empirical question of course. The question at issue here is what we could do with it to make sense of incompatibilist freedom, if it were present. I assume for the sake of argument that indeterminacy might enter the picture by way of chaotically amplified quantum indeterminacies of some sort. There is growing evidence that chaotic activity plays a significant role in cognitive processing in the brain (See Walter 2001: ch. 3.) But chaotic amplification is not the only possibility. It is conceivable that novel indeterminacy could arise at macrolevels, as suggested by Senchuk (1991), Prigogine (1997), and others. Dupré (1993 and 1996) also has interesting things to say on this topic. For discussion of the possibilities and issues in this area, see the essays by Hodgson and Bishop in this volume, chs. 4 and 5, respectively.

17. Accessible introductions to the role of neural networks in cognitive processing which bring out the relevant features of recurrent neural networks include P. M. Churchland (1996) and M. Spitzer (1999).

18. The sense in which coerced actions are not free is of course tricky, since even persons with a gun to their heads have some choices (for example, handing over their

money or serious bodily harm). I discuss the sense in which coerced actions are not free and how coercion fits into this picture of SFAs more fully in Kane (1996b).

19. Michael Bratman (1984) has shown that trying to do competing things can also make sense in ordinary terms—in his well-known example of the person playing two video games at once. As Bratmen points out, it does not make sense to say that the player *intends* to win both games (by analogy, make both choices), because he knows he cannot. He intends to win one or the other, but he can be *trying* to win both. Bratman also points out that when the agent does win one or the other, he does so *intentionally* even though he did not have the *prior* intention to win *that* particular game. It is not often noted that this is precisely the situation for deliberated choices generally. We intend, while deliberating, to choose one or another of the options but do not intend beforehand to choose this or that particular option. Yet when we do choose a particular option, we nonetheless do so intentionally, by virtue of our prior intention to choose *one or the other*.

20. I suspect that much of the plausibility of the statement, "If an event is undetermined, it must be something that merely 'happens,' it cannot be somebody's choice or action" comes from tacitly assuming that *undetermined* in the statement means "uncaused."

21. For further discussion of the idea of a self network in relation to agency in cognitive and neuroscientific literature, see Walter (2001: ch. 3), Flanagan (1992), A. Damasio (1994) and essays in A. Damasio, H. Damasio, and Christen, eds. (1996).

22. I am well aware that the nature of mental causation is itself the subject of considerable debate in contemporary philosophy and that there is no generally agreed upon account to it. But my point, in this paragraph and subsequent ones, is twofold: first, some account of mental causation is needed by any adequate theory of free agency, libertarian or nonlibertarian, so any problems with the idea do not attach only to libertarianism; second, causation by desires, beliefs, intentions, efforts, and other mental phenomena is causation by *states* or *events* of the agents and does not, in and of itself, imply nonoccurrent or nonevent agent-causation. I think both points are eminently defensible. With regard to the first, a few philosophers might dispute it, notably noncausalist libertarians such as Ginet, McCann, and Goetz, but my disagreements with them are not at issue here, since they also reject AC theories.

23. Compare Clarke (1995b).

24. This volume, p. 340.

25. Consider also the formula by which O'Connor positively characterizes agent-causation in his essay (ch. 15) for this volume and in his recent book (O'Connor 2000): "[A]n agent causes an intention for a reason (or for a desire)." This formula can also be accommodated by a teleological intelligibility (TI) theory of a causal indeterminist kind, if one gives, as I have done, an account of agents' causing or producing their undetermined self-forming choices without appealing to nonoccurrent causation. Thus the formula in and of itself does not distinguish agent-causal views from non-agent-causation views, unless one assumes (question-beggingly) that the causation involved *must* be nonoccurrent. What really distinguishes agent-causation is not any such formula taken by itself, but the negative requirement that it is a kind of causation that cannot be accounted for in terms of events, occurrences, and states of affairs involving the agents.

26. Might nonoccurrent agent-causation do something in addition to this, for example, might it antecedently raise the probability that one choice would be made with-

out antecedently determining that choice (as O'Connor also suggests at one point)? Antecedently raising the probability of one outcome rather than another during deliberation is certainly something that can happen and I accommodate it into my TI theory (see Kane 1996a: ch. 9). Such choice-preceding probabilities can be raised by focusing on certain considerations relevant to deliberation, entertaining new thoughts prior to choice, making practical judgments, and so on; and some of these earlier acts of attention, thinking, or judgment during deliberation may be undetermined self-forming actions understood along the lines suggested for other SFAs in this essay, as I show in Kane (1996a: 157–69). So while the ability to raise (or lower) the probability that certain choices will be subsequently made by earlier acts of attention, thought, or practical judgment is important to a complete account of free will, it is not something that we require nonoccurrent causation to explain.

27. This volume, p. 365.

28. This volume, p. 374.

29. Clarke makes some other more specific objections to my causal indeterminist theory in his essay for this volume (ch. 16) which are important, but which I have addressed in other places. (See Kane 1999b, which is a response to Clarke 1999.) There are several related objections he makes concerning efforts of will, however, that I would like to briefly address here because they bear on other things I have said. He focuses on the "efforts of will" that figure in my account of SFAs and asks whether these efforts in turn are causally determined. I indicated in correspondence that they would be, as Clarke notes, but that admission was a lapse that should have been significantly qualified as follows. The efforts agents make in SFA situations are *causally influenced* by their reasons or motives, to be sure. For example, if the businesswoman did not have moral motives, she would not make an effort to return to help the assault victim; she would have no reasons to do so. But while the efforts that precede SFAs are causally influenced by the agent's reasons, they are not strictly speaking determined by those reasons because the efforts themselves are indeterminate, which means that some indeterminism is involved in the complex neural processes realizing them in the brain. Thus, the reasons do not determine that an exact amount of effort will be made. As a consequence, it turns out that indeterminism enters into my theory in two stages, first, with the efforts, then with SFAs. One might say that, with the efforts, one opens a "window" of indeterminacy whose upshot is that the choice outcome (the SFA) will not be determined. But the primary locus of indeterminism is in the moment of choice itself, the SFA. The latter is undetermined in a way that allows for robust alternative possibilities (making a moral choice or an ambitious choice). Yet in order to prepare the way for these robust undetermined alternatives of SFAs, a measure of indeterminacy enters the picture earlier, in the preceding indeterminate efforts. These prior efforts in turn, though indeterminate, do not themselves represent robust alternative possibilities in the way that the resulting SFAs do, because the agents do not choose to make one or the other of the efforts. They make them both. Yet the efforts do open a window of indeterminacy whose full flowering in undetermined free choice occurs in the SFA. This means, in reference to Clarke's objection, that there is no UR-generated regress, because neither the effort, nor the reasons that cause it, are *sufficient* causes of the SFA. A related question about the efforts is this: do the agents *cause* these efforts? No, not in the way they cause their SFAs, because the efforts are basic actions. Agents *make* the efforts, they do not cause them by doing something else. And what it means to say they make the efforts was spelled out in sec-

tion 8: the businesswoman's effort to choose the moral action is causally influenced by reasons, is guided by her intention to resolve indecision by making a moral choice in accordance with those reasons, and the relevant reasons and intentions that influence her in this way are *hers* in the sense that they are embedded in, and subserve the aims of, the larger motivational system realized in her brain (the self-network) in terms of which she defines herself as practical reasoner. Finally, are the efforts *freely* made? I distinguish three senses of freedom, all of which I think are required for a complete account of free action and free will: (1) not being coerced, compelled, controlled, and so on; (2) acting "of one's own free will" in the sense of a will of one's own making (i.e., satisfying UR); and (3) being an undetermined self-forming, plural voluntary action (or SFA). Sense (1) is compatibilist (and I think it is necessary for free will, though not sufficient); senses (2) and (3) are incompatibilist. Efforts of will preceding SFAs are free in senses (1) and usually (2) also; SFAs (the full flowering of free will) are true in all three senses.

30. As when we say, "I am in control here," meaning "I am in a position to insure that a future desired outcome will occur."

PART VII

NONSTANDARD VIEWS: SUCCESSOR VIEWS TO HARD DETERMINISM AND OTHERS

CHAPTER 19

THE BOUNDS OF FREEDOM

GALEN STRAWSON

ARE human beings ever really—without qualification—responsible for their actions? Are they ever really *morally* (and not just causally) responsible for their actions? Are they ever *ultimately* responsible for their actions? Are they ever *ultimately morally* responsible for them? Are they ever responsible for their actions in such a way that they are, without any sort of qualification, morally deserving of praise or blame or punishment or reward for them?

This question, with its various strengths, is the only really troublesome question when it comes to the problem of free will, and it is the only one I will consider here. The difficulty with it is simple and well known: there appear to be powerful reasons for answering yes and powerful reasons for answering no. One might say that there are frames in which the answer is yes and frames in which the answer is no. I want to draw attention to the fundamental frame in which the answer is no. The point I have to make is old and simple and a priori and I will articulate it in more than one way, as a kind of exercise.

There are also powerful a posteriori reasons for answering no. No seems unavoidable if Einstein's theory of special relativity is anything close to correct, for example—a fact little discussed in recent debate about free will. Einstein reckoned that "a Being endowed with higher insight and more perfect intelligence, watching man and his doings, would smile about man's illusion that he was acting according to his own free will."[1] Here, however, I will stick to the a priori point.

Being a priori, it holds good whether determinism is true or false: the issue of determinism is irrelevant to the present discussion.[2] For the record, though, determinism is the view that the history of the universe is fixed in such a way that everything that happens is necessitated to happen by what has already gone before in such a way that nothing can happen otherwise than it does. It can also be expressed, more simply, as the view that every event has a cause.[3]

1. SOME SYMBOLS

In speaking of actions I will restrict attention to fully intentional and consciously deliberated actions (as opposed to reflex actions, say, or habitual or otherwise undeliberated actions); not because these are the only ones for which we judge people to be morally responsible, but because any successful case for the view that people can (without qualification) be morally responsible for their actions must cover these cases, and the other cases raise no fundamentally different questions. I will use "R" to abbreviate "truly and without qualification responsible" and the corresponding noun, "D" to abbreviate "truly and without qualification deserving of praise or blame or punishment or reward" and the corresponding noun, "U" to abbreviate "ultimate" when prefixed to a noun and "ultimately" when prefixed to an adjective, "M" to abbreviate "moral" and "morally," and "[$\varphi \to \psi$]" to represent "φ entails ψ." I will take it that R and D can be fused to form a single notion—true, unqualified responsibility-and-deservingness or "RD," for short—in the present context of debate, and I will also use "RD" as an adjective, meaning "(truly and without qualification) responsible and deserving of praise or blame or punishment or reward."[4]

With these provisions, the opening question is

Are human beings ever RD for their actions? Are they ever URD for their actions? Are they ever UMRD for their actions?

But one of these letters is not needed: with one exception, I will only consider questions of *moral* responsibility and deservingness in what follows, so 'M' can be dropped and taken as read.[5] The question, then, is

Are human beings ever really RD? Are they ever really URD?[6]

This question raises several others: What exactly is URD? Is there really any interesting distinction to be drawn between RD and URD? Given that [URD →

RD], is it also true that [RD → URD]? I will consider these questions in sections 3 and 4. Until then I will rely on the reader's prereflective understanding of RD and URD and give four versions of the argument—the *Basic Argument*—for answering No to the key question: Are we ever really RD, or URD?

2. THE BASIC ARGUMENT

The Basic Argument has various expressions, but its core is simple and can be quickly stated as follows:

Version 1

   1.1 When you act, you do what you do—in the situation in which you find yourself[7]—because of the way you are.

   1.2 If you do what you do because of the way you are, then in order to be URD for what you do you must be URD for the way you are.

But

   1.3 You cannot be URD for the way you are.

So

   1.4 You cannot be URD for what you do.

Version 1 of the Basic Argument has three premises, 1.1, 1.2, and 1.3. I take premise 1.1 to be obvious and will not defend it. I think that 1.2 and 1.3 are also obvious, but I will give them—or close cousins of them—some explicit defense in due course.

The Basic Argument can be restated as follows.

Version 2

   2.1 One cannot be *causa sui*—one cannot be the cause of oneself.

But

   2.2 One would have to be *causa sui*, at least in certain crucial mental respects, in order to be URD for one's thoughts and actions.

It follows that

2.3 One cannot be URD for one's thoughts or actions: one cannot be ultimately morally deserving of praise or blame for one's thoughts or actions or one's character or indeed for anything else.

But

2.4 [RD → URD]; *unqualified* responsibility and deservingness requires *ultimate* responsibility and deservingness.

So

2.5 One cannot be RD: one cannot be (truly and without qualification) morally deserving of praise or blame: not for one's thoughts, or actions, or character, or anything else.

This argument goes through whether determinism is true or false, for we cannot be URD either way. Nor, therefore, can we be RD. Even if the property of being *causa sui* is allowed to belong (entirely unintelligibly) to God, it cannot be plausibly supposed to be possessed by ordinary human beings: "*No one is accountable for existing at all, or for being constituted as he is, or for living in the circumstances and surroundings in which he lives,*" as Nietzsche remarked:[8]

> [T]he *causa sui* is the best self-contradiction that has been conceived so far; it is a sort of rape and perversion of logic. But the extravagant pride of man has managed to entangle itself profoundly and frightfully with just this nonsense. The desire for "freedom of the will" in the superlative metaphysical sense, which still holds sway, unfortunately, in the minds of the half-educated—the desire to bear the entire and ultimate responsibility for one's actions oneself, and to absolve God, the world, ancestors, chance, and society—involves nothing less than to be precisely this *causa sui* and, with more than Baron Münchhausen's audacity, to pull oneself up into existence by the hair, out of the swamps of nothingness.[9]

Version 2 of the Basic Argument has three premises, 2.1, 2.2, and 2.4. Few would dispute 2.1, but 2.2 and especially 2.4 can be challenged. I will consider these challenges after setting out a third, longer version of the Basic Argument.[10]

Consider a particular action or piece of deliberation in which you engage, and consider everything about the way you are when you to engage in it that leads you to engage in it in the way you do. I will call the particular action or piece of deliberation that you engage in "*A*," and I will call everything about the way you are mentally when you engage in it that leads you to engage in it in the way you do "*N*." I will use URD$A(t)$ and URD$N(t)$ to mean URD for A at time t and URD for N at time t, respectively.

Version 3

> 3.1 When you act or deliberate, at t_1—when A occurs, at t_1—you do what
> you do, in the situation in which you find yourself, because of the way
> you are—because you are N, at t_1.

This is the first premise of the argument. I take it to be incontrovertible, quibbles
aside, and will not defend it.

It appears to follow immediately that

> 3.2 If you are to be URDA(t_1)—URD for what you *do*, at t_1, then you must
> be URDN(t_1)—URD for the way you *are*, at t_1, at least in certain cru-
> cial mental respects.

(Comment: I take the qualification "at least in certain mental respects" for granted
from now on. Obviously you do not have to be responsible for the way you are
in all respects. You don't have to be responsible for your height, age, sex, and so
on. But it does seem that you have to be responsible for the way you are mentally,
at least in certain respects. After all, it is your overall mental makeup that leads
you to do what you do when you act or deliberate.)

The move from 3.1 to 3.2 can be set out as an explicit premise:

> 3.3 [3.1 → 3.2]: if, when A occurs, you do what you do because you are N,
> because of the way you are, then if you are to be URDA(t_1) you must
> somehow be URDN(t_1).

(Comment: 3.3 has deep intuitive plausibility, and I will take it for granted for the
moment. Note that 3.2 follows from 3.1 and 3.3, so that we only have two premises
so far.)

But

> 3.4 You can't be URDN(t_1)—you can't be URD for the way you are in any
> respect at all, or at any time.

So

> 3.5 You certainly can't be URDA(t_1)—for what you do, at t_1.

This completes the first stage of Version 3. It has three premises, 3.1, 3.3, and 3.4.
I take 3.1 to be incontrovertible, like 1.1 and 2.1. The second stage of Version 3 is
devoted to establishing 3.4. 3.3 is reserved for discussion in section 3.

So far, perhaps, so good. But why is 3.4 true? Why can't you be URDN, at
least in certain mental respects? Well,

> 3.6 If it is true that you are URDN(t_1)—URD for the way you are, at t_1, in
> certain mental respects, then it must be true that you have somehow

intentionally brought it about that you are N at some time t_0 prior to t_1.

(Comment: 3.6. is another premise I will not defend, on the grounds that it is evident on reflection. It does not just state that you must have caused yourself to be the way you are, mentally speaking, at least in certain mental respects; that is certainly not enough for ultimate responsibility. It states that you must have consciously and explicitly decided on a way to be and—roughly—must have acted on that decision with success.)

Is it possible for you to have intentionally brought it about that you are N at some time t_0 prior to t_1, as 3.6 requires? Well, let us assume that it is. Let us simply assume, for the sake of argument, that

> 3.7* You have somehow intentionally brought it about that you are N at t_0 prior to t_1.

Or rather, more richly, let us simply assume that

> 3.7 You have somehow intentionally brought it about that you are N, at t_0, in such a way that you can now be said to be URD for being N, at t_1

without enquiring into how exactly this might have come about.[11] Clearly, for 3.7 to be true

> 3.8 You must already have had a certain mental nature—call it M—at t_0, in the light of which you intentionally brought it about that you now have nature N.

Why? Because

> 3.9 If you did not already have a certain mental nature, at t_0, then you cannot then have had any intentions or preferences at all; and if you did not then have any intentions or preferences at all, you cannot be held to be RD, let alone URD, for intentionally bringing anything about, at t_0.

(Comment: I take this premise too to be evident.)

So 3.8 is true. But there is more to say, because

> 3.10 For it to be true that you and you alone are RDN or URDN, at t_1, you must have been RDM or URDM at t_0—RD or URD for your having had that nature M in the light of which you intentionally brought it about that you now have N.

(Comment: I take it that this follows from 3.3, and leave aside the difficulties about the nature of time raised by the work cited in note 1.)

But

3.11 For you to have been RD*M* or URD*M* you must have intentionally brought it about that you had *M*.

(Comment: This is a version of 3.6.)
So

3.12 You must have intentionally brought it about that you had *M*.

But in that case

3.13 You must (given 3.9) have existed already with a prior nature, *L*, in the light of which you intentionally brought it about that you had that nature, *M*, in the light of which you intentionally brought it about that you now have nature *N*.

3.14 And so on.

Here one is setting off on a potentially infinite regress: it seems, quite generally, that if one is to be URD*N*, URD for *how one is*, in such a way that one can be URD*A*, URD for *what one does*, something impossible has to be true. There has to be, but there cannot be, a starting point in the series of acts or processes of bringing it about that one is a certain way, or has a certain nature, a starting point that constitutes an act or process of ultimate self-origination. It follows that 3.7 is impossible; in which case 3.4 is true, given 3.6.

This completes the second stage of Version 3 of the Basic Argument. It assumes 3.7 for reductio and has two premises, 3.6 and 3.9, both of which seem evident. As a whole, Version 3 sets out in more detail the claim of Versions 1 and 2—the claim that URD requires the occurrence of processes of ultimate self-origination of a kind that are impossible. Hardly any of those who appear to believe in URD—nearly all human beings[12]—have ever had any conscious thought to the effect that it requires some such ultimate self-origination, but that is beside the point.[13]

In 3, the next section, I will look at two of the premises (or premise-groups) of the various versions of the Basic Argument. In 4 I will say something more about what URD is meant to be. In 5 I will consider a different challenge to one of the premise-groups of the Basic Argument. I will end this section with a more everyday version of the Basic Argument.

Version 4

4.1 Initially—early in life—one is the way one is as a result of one's heredity and experience.[14]

4.2 One's heredity and early experience are *obviously* things for which one cannot be held to be in any way RD or URD.[15]

4.3 One cannot at any later stage of one's life hope to accede to URD for the way one is, and, in particular, for the way one is morally speaking, by trying to change the way one already is as a result of one's heredity and previous experience.

4.4 There is no other way in which one could hope to accede to URD for the way one is.

So

4.5 One cannot be URD for the way one is in any respect at all.

And if

4.6 [RD → URD]

as supposed on page 444, then

4.7 One cannot be RD for the way one is in any respect at all.

I take 4.1 and 4.2 to be evident, assume 4.4, and discuss 4.6/2.4 in section 3. I will now defend 4.3.

4.8 The reason 4.3 is true is not that one cannot try to change the way one is as a result of one's heredity and previous experience, or that one cannot succeed if one does try. One can both try and succeed. The reason 4.3 is true is simply that if one does try to change oneself then one aims at the particular changes one does aim at, and takes the particular steps one does take in the attempt to bring them about, and succeeds in bringing them about to the extent that one does, in the situations in which one finds oneself, wholly because of the way one already is as a result of one's heredity and previous experience—which is something for which one is in no way URD.

4.9 There may be certain further changes that one can bring about only after one has brought about certain initial changes, and one may succeed in bringing about some of these further changes too. But the point made in 4.8 simply reapplies.

Note that once again it makes no difference whether determinism is true or false. If determinism is false, it may be that some changes in the way one is are traceable to the influence of indeterministic or random factors. It is even possible that difficult decisions or efforts to change oneself may trigger indeterministic events in the brain.[16] But indeterministic or random factors, for whose particular character one is *ex hypothesi* in no way responsible, cannot contribute in any way to one's being URD for the way one is.[17]

The claim is not that people cannot change the way they are. They can, in certain respects. It is only that people cannot be supposed to change themselves in such a way as to be or become URD for the way they are, and hence for their actions. One can put the point by saying that the way you are is, ultimately, in every last detail, a matter of luck—good or bad.[18]

"Character is fate: your character determines your fate. So radical freedom is excluded," say Heracleitus, Novalis, George Eliot, and others. "Not so fast," say the Sartreans: "Character may determine fate, but character is choice. Character is a product of choice, so you can choose your fate. Radical freedom is possible after all." "Maybe character is choice," reply proponents of the Basic Argument, taking the side of Heracleitus, "but choice is character: character determines choice, even choice of character. And character is fate. So radical freedom is excluded after all."

3. Two Premises, Three Positions

So much for the Basic Argument. I want now to consider two of its premises. First, 2.4/4.6. Is it true, or even plausible, that [RD → URD]?

Some say no. Faced with arguments like those just given, they take the following position:

3.1. Position 1

There is indeed an ineliminable sense in which human beings cannot be URDN, and it does indeed follow that there is an ineliminable sense in which they cannot be URDA. But who needs the "U," the "ultimate"? Even if these sorts of ultimacy are unavailable, human beings can be truly RDA—wholly proper objects of moral praise and blame and punishment and reward.

One popular version of this position runs as follows:

3.2. Position 2

Being RDA, *fully*, *wholly*, and without qualification responsible for some action *A*, is just a matter of being a responsible (as we naturally say) adult, a fully responsible adult: a normal, self-conscious, adult human being who is not subject to any compulsion, so far as *A* is concerned. That is all. Being a normal self-conscious adult human being is already sufficient for RD*A*, whatever else is or is not necessary for it, and since we know such adult human beings exist, we know that RD*A* is possible and actual. No metaphysical issues need be considered. Philosophers can distinguish URD*A* from RD*A* if they like. They can raise complicated questions about whether one can be URD*N* or RD*N*—URD or even merely RD for how one is. Let them. RD*A* is possible and actual whatever scintilla-loving philosophers choose to say about RD*N* and URD*N*. Have they defined URD*A* in such a way that it is neither actual nor possible? Let them. RD*A* is possible and actual for all that.

Some go farther and reject the possibility of any gap between RD*A* and URD*A*.

3.3. Position 3

Look, anything that really counts as *genuine* or *full* or unqualified RD*A* just is URD*A*. The adjective "U" or "ultimate" adds nothing. RD*A* certainly exists, and RD*A* is RD*A* is URD*A*. Suppose there is a clear and undeniable sense in which human beings cannot be URD*N*; it just does not follow that they cannot be URD*A*. RD*A* exists and RD*A* = URD*A*. The idea that there might be some further kind of radical, "ultimate" responsibility for action over and above the kind of straight-up responsibility possessed by a normal self-conscious adult human being is moonshine.

I disagree. It is possible to characterize a notion of URD*A* that is importantly distinct from any notion of RD*A* truly applicable to human action; I will do so in section 4. And yet I agree that there is a way of understanding the notion of RD according to which it is true that human beings can—rightly and without reservation—be held to be fully RD for their actions. And I agree that this notion of RD allows us to say that human beings can be fully RD for their actions even if they are not URD either for how they are or for their actions. This notion of RD is a *compatibilist* notion. Compatibilists have laid out its structure and variants with great ingenuity and devotion over many years,[19] and I have nothing to add to what has been said about it. My present task is simply to provide a reminder of what compatibilism is not and cannot be, in case anyone should have any tendency to forget: a reminder that compatibilism is nothing more than a "wretched subterfuge . . . , a petty word-jugglery,"[20] "so much gobbledegook,"[21] when it is taken to be more than it is.[22]

I will return to the question whether [RD → URD] in various ways. First, I want to mention the second premise (the 1.2, 2.2, 3.2–3.3 group), which can be expressed as [URD*A* → URD*N*]. I have endorsed it, argued that URD*N* is impossible, and concluded that URD*A* is impossible. I do not really think that it needs defense, but the characterization of URD in section 4 can be taken as a defense if one is felt to be needed.

Robert Kane endorses the [URD*A* → URD*N*] premise, but he argues that there is a sufficient sense in which URD*N* is possible, and that there is (therefore)[23] also a sufficient sense in which URD*A* is possible. He further holds that URD*N* is possible only if determinism is false, adopting an explicitly incompatibilist—libertarian—position.

Immanuel Kant agrees with Kane and me in accepting that [URD*A* → URD*N*], and he agrees with Kane, but not me, in asserting that URD*A* is possible. He goes farther than both of us in asserting that it is knowably actual. Unlike Kane, however, he does not think that one can give any substantive account of how URD*N* is possible.[24]

Other positions are of course possible.[25] Most, though, are likely to protest that questions about whether or not we are or can be responsible for how we are are simply (even magnificently) irrelevant to any and all assessments of RD that actually concern us.[26]

Could this be true? It is certainly true that such questions seem irrelevant in most ordinary moral discussions, and if they are irrelevant then the whole issue of whether or not the [URD*A* → URD*N*] premise is true is equally irrelevant.

I will reject the charge of irrelevance in section 5, and make three suggestions about what motivates it in section 6. First, though, I must say something more about what I take URD to be.

4. ULTIMATE RESPONSIBILITY

What exactly is URD, this "ultimate" responsibility that is meant to be impossible? One simple and dramatic way to characterize it is by reference to the story of heaven and hell. URD is *heaven-and-hell* responsibility: if we have URD, then it makes sense to propose that it could be just—without any qualification—to punish some of us with (possibly everlasting) torment in hell and reward others with (possibly everlasting) bliss in heaven. The proposal is morally repugnant, but it is perfectly intelligible because if we really have URD then what we do is wholly and entirely up to us in some absolute, buck-stopping way.

One does not have to believe in the story of heaven and hell in order to understand the notion of URD it is used to illustrate. Nor does one have to believe in the story of heaven and hell in order to believe in URD (many atheists have believed in URD). One does not even have to have heard of the story, which is useful here simply because it illustrates the *kind* of absolute or ultimate responsibility—URD—that many suppose themselves to have. And the core notion of URD has no essential connection with moral matters. If we momentarily drop the "M" for *moral* that is implicit in "URD" (p. 626), we may observe, first, that self-conscious agents that face difficult life-determining choices but that have no conception of morality at all can have a sense of UR—of radical, absolute, buck-stopping (buck-printing) "up-to-me-ness" in choice and action—that is just as powerful as ours, and, second, that the story of heaven and hell can be used to convey the absolute character of this supposed *non*moral URD just as well as it conveys the absolute character of any supposed moral URD.

So much for the notion of URD. There is a sense in which it is not coherent, but it does not follow that it is unintelligible or has no genuine content. That could not be, for it is a notion that is central to common moral consciousness, at least in the West, and certainly not just in the West. I have conveyed its content by reference to the story of heaven and hell, but it can also be conveyed less colorfully: URD is responsibility and desert of such a kind that it can exist if and only if punishment and reward can be fair or just without having any pragmatic justification, or indeed any justification that appeals to the notion of distributive justice.[27]

Whichever characterization one prefers, it is precisely (only) because one has a grasp of the content of the notion of URD that one can see, or can be brought to see, that it is incoherent. It is the same with the notion of a round square. Some may say that they don't really know what the content of this notion is, but it is easy to specify. A round square is an equiangular, equilateral, rectilinear, quadrilateral closed plane figure every point on the periphery of which is equidistant from a single point within its periphery. It is because we know the content of the notion that we know that there cannot be such a thing as a round square, and the same is true of the notion of URD. Many say that statements or concepts that are self-contradictory are meaningless, but meaningfulness is a necessary condition of contradictoriness.

—*"You are not making any progress in offering these characterizations because both of them make use of some notion of 'ultimate' justice, and exactly the same sort of commonsense move that was made in response to the qualification of responsibility by* ultimate *can be made in the case of the qualification of justice by* ultimate. *Human beings cannot be URDA given your characterization of URD, but praise and punishment of, and reward and blame for, human action can nonetheless be just, just* tout court, *just without any qualification. Other things be-ing equal, to be capable of being justly punished, justly punished* sans phrase, *is simply a matter of being a normal self-conscious adult human being who is not subject to any relevant compulsion. Your attempt to characterize URD in terms of justice does not work."*

This objection simply restates positions 1 and 2 (pp. 449–50) in terms of jus-tice instead of RD. It allows the sense in which we are not URDA but claims that punishment on moral grounds can nonetheless be just *sans phrase*, heaven-and-hell just, just without any qualification or appeal to pragmatic considerations or considerations of distributive justice. I disagree. We may have reached the end of argument.

5. The Relevance View

"References to RDN and URDN—I will use '/RDN/' to refer to them jointly when the distinction between them is not at issue—disappeared from the discussion in section 4. References to URDA and RDA—'/RDA/' for short—did not. Doesn't this strongly confirm the view that questions about /RDN/ are irrelevant to any of the issues about /RDA/ that actually concern us in everyday life? And aren't such ques-tions equally irrelevant to sensible moral philosophy? And aren't they irrelevant to sensible moral philosophy precisely because they're irrelevant to the issues about RDA that actually concern us in everyday life?"

No, to all these questions.

—*"But even if questions about /RDN/ aren't irrelevant to the issues about RDA that concern us in everyday life, they're generally thought to be irrelevant. The* Irrelevance View, *as one might call it, lies deep in ordinary moral thought and feeling."*

This is an important fact, and I will try to explain it in section 6. But it is equally important that the directly contrary view—the *Relevance View*, according to which /RDA/ does somehow involve /RDN/, so that questions about /RDN/ are profoundly relevant to issues of moral responsibility—also lies deep in ordi-nary moral thought and feeling, constantly ready to precipitate out into con-sciousness in ways I will consider now.[28]

One way in which the Relevance View manifests itself is in the sense that many have that they are somehow or other responsible for, answerable for, how they are mentally, or at least for certain crucial aspects of how they are mentally. Certainly we do not ordinarily suppose that we have actually gone through some sort of active process of self-determination at some particular past time. And yet it seems accurate to say that we do unreflectively experience ourselves, in many respects, very much as we would experience ourselves if we did think we had engaged in some such process of self-determination, or had at least engaged in some process of scanning and ratification of how we are mentally that we had undertaken from a position of power to induce change. Many, perhaps, feel that it is just a fact about growing up that one comes to be such that one is /RDN/.

Some find traits in themselves that they regret, or experience as foreign, and feel powerless to change. This, however, does not put the present point in doubt, for traits can appear as regrettable or foreign only against a background of character traits that do not seem regrettable or foreign, but are, rather, identified with. In general, people have a strong sense of general identification with their character (it may well be strengthened, not weakened, by the experience of some tendency as alien), and this identification seems to carry within itself a powerful implicit sense that one is, generally, somehow in control of, and in any case answerable for, how one is.[29]

So /RDN/ does not always appear irrelevant in ordinary moral thought. And the idea that /RDN/ is necessary for /RDA/ arises with intense naturalness, and in an explicit form, when people begin to reflect about the nature of moral responsibility, as they quite often do. Many who feel certain that they are URDA also explicitly hold that [URDA → URDN] and are accordingly sure that they are URDN.[30] John Patten, British minister for education in the 1980s, a nonphilosopher and a Roman Catholic, thinks it "self-evident that as we grow up each individual chooses whether to be good or bad." E. H. Carr, a historian, holds that "normal adult human beings are ultimately responsible for their own personality." Among professional philosophers, Jean-Paul Sartre speaks of "the choice that each man makes of his personality" and holds that "man is responsible for what he is," and Robert Kane is explicit about the point that one must show that URDN is possible in order to show that URDA is possible. Immanuel Kant puts the view very clearly when he claims that

> man *himself* must make or have made himself into whatever, in a moral sense, whether good or evil, he is to become. Either condition must be an effect of his free choice; for otherwise he could not be held responsible for it and could therefore be *morally* neither good nor evil,

and since he is committed to belief in URDA, he takes it that such self-creation does indeed take place, writing accordingly of "man's character, which he himself creates" and of the "knowledge [that one has] of oneself as a person who . . . is his own originator." Aristotle also seems to take this view for granted.[31]

6. THE IRRELEVANCE VIEW AND THE AGENT-SELF

So much for the Relevance View. How does the contrary view (that URD*N* is irrelevant to URD*A*) manifest itself? The primary fact is this: it seems that we naturally take it that our capacity for fully explicit self-conscious deliberation in a situation of choice—our capacity to be explicitly aware of ourselves as facing choices and engaging in processes of reasoning about what to do—suffices by itself to constitute us as /RD*A*/ in the strongest possible sense. Should the issue of /RD*N*/ be raised—and it standardly is not—one is likely to feel that one's full self-conscious awareness of oneself and one's situation when one chooses simply vaporizes any supposed consequences of the fact that one neither is nor can be URD*N*. It seems as if the mere fact of one's self-conscious presence in the situation of choice confers radical, total /RD*A*/ on one—it seems obvious that it does so. One may in the final analysis be wholly constituted as the sort of person one is by factors for which one is not and cannot be in any way URD, and one may acknowledge this, but the threat that this fact is alleged to pose to one's claim to /RD*A*/ seems to be annihilated by the simple fact of one's full self-conscious awareness of one's situation.[32]

I think this correctly describes one of the forms taken by our powerful belief in URD*A*. It is not, however, an account of anything that could really constitute URD*A*, for reasons already given: when one acts after explicit self-conscious deliberation, one acts for certain reasons. Which reasons finally weigh with one is wholly a matter of one's mental nature *N*, which is something for which one cannot be in any way URD.

The conviction that fully explicit self-conscious awareness of one's situation can be a sufficient foundation of URD*A* in spite of this is *extremely* powerful; it runs deeper than rational argument and seems to survive untouched, in the everyday conduct of life, even after the validity of the argument against URD*A* has been admitted; but that is no reason to think that it is correct.

Suppose you arrive at a shop on the evening of a national holiday, intending to buy a cake with your last ten-pound note to supplement the generous preparations you have already made.[33] Everything is closing down. There is one cake left; it costs ten pounds. On the steps of the shop, someone is shaking an Oxfam tin. You stop, and it seems clear to you that it is entirely up to you what you do next—in such a way that you will be RD*A* and indeed URD*A* for whatever you do do. The situation is in fact *utterly* clear: you can put the money in the tin, or go in and buy the cake, or just walk away. You are not only completely free to choose in this situation. You are not free not to choose. You are condemned to freedom, in Sartre's phrase. You are already in a state of full consciousness of what is (morally) at stake and you cannot prescind from that consciousness. You cannot somehow slip out of it. You have to choose. You may be someone who believes that determinism is true: you may believe that in five—two—minutes time you will be able to look back on the situation you are now in and say, of what you will by then have done, "It was determined that I should do that." But even if you do fervently believe this, it does not check your current sense of your URDA in any way.[34]

One diagnosis of this phenomenon is that one cannot really accept or live the rather specific and theoretical thought that determinism may be true, in such situations of choice, and cannot help thinking that the falsity of determinism might make URDA possible. But this is too complicated: most people do not think about determinism at all; still less do they think that its falsity might be necessary for URDA.[35] In situations like this one's URDA seems to stem simply from the fact that one is fully conscious of one's situation, and knows that one can choose, and believes that one action is morally better than the other. This full awareness seems to be immediately enough to confer URDA. And yet it cannot really do so, as the Basic Argument shows. For [URDA → URDN] and URDN is provably impossible.

This raises an interesting question: Must *any* cognitively sophisticated, rational, self-conscious agent that faces choices and is fully aware of the fact that it does so experience itself as being URDA, simply because it is a self-conscious agent (and whether or not it has a conception of moral responsibility)? It seems that we human beings cannot help experiencing ourselves as URDA, but perhaps this is a human peculiarity or limitation, not an inescapable feature of any possible self-conscious agent.[36] And perhaps it is not inevitable for human beings. Krishnamurti is categorical that "you do not choose, you do not decide, when you see things very clearly.... Only the unintelligent mind exercises choice in life." A spiritually advanced or "truly intelligent mind simply cannot have choice," because it "can . . . only choose the path of truth." "Only the unintelligent mind has free will"—by which he means experience of radical free will.

A related thought is expressed by Saul Bellow in *Humboldt's Gift*: "In the next realm, where things are clearer, clarity eats into freedom. We are free on earth"—that is, we experience ourselves as radically free—"because of cloudiness, because of error, because of marvellous limitation." And Spinoza extends the point to God. God cannot, he says, "be said . . . to act from freedom of the will," and if this is so, then (being omniscient) he cannot think that he does so.[37]

This is one way in which ordinary thought moves in support of the view that questions about /RDN/ are irrelevant to the issue of /RDA/. But it is also very tempted by the idea that /RDA/ is possible because one's *self*—that is, *the* self, the *agent-self*, the thing that one most fundamentally is, both morally speaking and in general—is in some crucial way independent of one's general mental nature N, one's overall character, personality, motivational structure. What happens when one faces a difficult choice between X, doing one's duty, and Y, following one's nonmoral desires? Well, given N, one responds in a certain way. One is swayed by reasons for and against both X and Y. One tends toward X or Y, given N. But one is as an agent-self independent of N, and one can be /RDA/ in a situation like this even if (even though) one cannot be /RDN/, because although one's nature N certainly *inclines* one to do one thing rather than another, it does not thereby *necessitate* one to do one thing rather than the other.[38] As an agent-self, one incorporates a power of free decision that is independent of all the particularities of N in such a way that one can after all count as URDA even though one is not ultimately responsible for any aspect of N.[39]

That, at least, is the story. The agent-self decides in the light of N but is not determined by N and is therefore free. But the following question arises: *Why* does the agent-self decide as it does? And the general answer is clear. Whatever the agent-self decides, it decides as it does because of the overall way it is; it too must have a nature—call it N^*—of some sort. And this necessary truth returns us to where we started. Once again it seems that the agent-self must be responsible for N^*—URD N^* or RD N^*—in order to be URDA. But this is impossible, for the reasons given in section 2: nothing can be *causa sui* in the required way. Whatever the nature of the agent-self, it is ultimately a matter of luck (or grace, as some would have it) that it is as it is.

It may be proposed that the agent-self decides as it does partly or wholly because of the presence of indeterministic occurrences in the decision process. But this is no good because it is as clear as ever that indeterministic occurrences can never be a source of URDA. The story of the agent-self may add another layer to the description of the human decision process, and it may have a certain phenomenological aptness, considered as such a description, but it cannot change the fact that human beings cannot be /RDN/ in such a way as to be /RDA/.[40]

It cannot, in other words, change the fact that human beings can never be truly or without qualification morally responsible for their actions, responsible for them in such a way that they are flat-out deserving of moral praise or blame or punishment or reward for them. This is, in a sense, a quite bewildering fact, but it is a fact nonetheless. We are what we are, and we cannot be thought to have made ourselves *in such a way* that we can be held to be free in our actions *in such a way* that we can be held to be RD for our actions *in such a way* that any punishment or reward for our actions is ultimately just or fair. Punishments and rewards can seem intrinsically appropriate or profoundly fitting to us in spite of this, and many of the various institutions of punishment and reward in human society seem both beneficial and practically indispensable. But if one takes the notion of justice that is central to our intellectual and cultural tradition seriously, the evident consequence of the Basic Argument is that there is a fundamental sense in which no punishment or reward is ever ultimately just. It is *exactly* as just to punish or reward people for their actions as it is to punish or reward them for the (natural) color of their hair or the (natural) shape of their faces.

There is much more to say about free will, and the point made in this essay is just the beginning. But it is the beginning. It is important to be clear about it, and to try not to avoid or occlude it in any way.

NOTES

1. Einstein (1931). For an excellent presentation of the a posteriori point, see Putnam (1967) and especially Lockwood forthcoming, who effectively rebuts Putnam's critics.

2. Actually, it is also irrelevant on the terms of the a posteriori argument just mentioned: the generality of the argument from special relativity is such that it makes no difference whether determinism is true or false.

3. Some think that this simple formulation will not do; they think it better to say that determinism is the view that every event *and every aspect of every event* has a cause. But this adjustment is unnecessary, because anything that is characterized as an aspect of an event given one way of individuating events can itself be characterized as an event given another equally good way of individuating events.

4. Some actions are neutral in such a way that their performers are not D even if they are R. The idea behind the single notion of RD is that if one is RD then if one is R for some action A then one is also and ipso facto D for A *if* any praise or blame attaches to A-type actions—which it may not.

5. I will also regularly omit the phrase "for their actions."

6. The notion of URD is cognate with Kane's notion of UR; see Kane Ch 18 of this volume.

7. I will take this qualification for granted.

8. (1886: §21).

9. Nietzsche (1889:"The Four Great Errors," §8). For an outstanding discussion of Nietzsche's views on fate and the possibility of self-creation, see Leiter (1998).

10. For variants, see for example, G. Strawson (1986: 28–30, 1994a: 6–7, 12–14, 1998: 746–47).

11. The limiting case of this, presumably, would be the one in which you simply endorsed your existing mental nature *N* from a position of power to change it.

12. For a recent exposition of this point, see Smilansky (2000) and section 6.

13. Some of course do have the conscious thought. See section 5.

14. I take experience to include all impacts or effects on the mind, where this includes internal bodily impacts as well as external environmental impacts.

15. This might not be true if there were reincarnation, but reincarnation would just shift the problem backward—we would be off on another regress.

16. See Kane (1996a: 130).

17. Compare Kane (1989 and 1996a). I state my differences with Kane in Strawson (1994a: 17–21 and 2000: 149–55).

18. There is a sense in which talk of luck is odd in this context (see Hurley: forthcoming), but it makes the point clearly.

19. Compare, for example, Hobbes (1958, first published 1651), Locke (1959, first published 1690), Hume (1955, first published 1948), Hobart (1934), Schlick (1966), Frankfurt (1971), Watson (1975), Fischer (1994)—and many others. For discussions of compatibilism, see chapters 6, 8, 9, 10, and 11 of this volume.

20. Kant (1788: Ak. V. 97).

21. Anscombe (1971: 146).

22. On this issue, see Smilansky (2000: esp. part 2).

23. This "therefore" also requires [URDN → URDA], the converse of the premise on which Kane and I agree. But [URDN → URDA] is clearly very plausible. Nagel notes its plausibility explicitly (1987: 36) when commenting on a doubt that I raise about it in *Freedom and Belief* (1986: 299–301; I propose [1] that one must have a positive *sense* of oneself as URDA in order to be URDA *sans phrase*, (2) that one might conceivably lack any such sense of oneself as URDA even if URDN were possible and even if one were in fact URDN, concluding [3] that [URDN → URDA] is to that extent not true).

24. In various places he claims that we can know that URDA is actual even though we cannot even comprehend its possibility, and he would presumably take exactly the same line about URDN. (See, for example, Kant (1785: 127 [Ak. IV. 459]; 1788: 4 [Ak. V. 4]; 1793: 45 n [Ak. VI. 49–50].

25. Some, perhaps, may concede that we cannot be URDN while insisting that we can nonetheless be RDN in some robust way—so that we can be RDA even if [RDA → RDN].

26. Even those who reject all forms of compatibilism may take this view. C. Campbell (1957), for example, is a libertarian who takes it that URDA is possible even if URDN is not.

27. The qualification referring to distributive justice is strictly speaking unnecessary. Suppose X's deliberate and intentional action gives rise to a collective burden that can be alleviated only by imposing a special burden on some member of the community; or suppose the performance of the action has the consequence that someone must bear a burden whether anyone likes it or not. And suppose X knows that this will be so. Then even if it is thought to be intrinsically fair or just—in some absolute, wholly unqualified sense—to impose the burden on X, it does not follow that there is any way in which the burden can correctly be thought of as a fair or just *punishment*. I am grateful to Karin Boxer for discussion of this point.

28. It takes the distortions that arise from a philosophical training to doubt this obvious fact. It also takes a philosophical training to be confused enough—as some compatibilists have been—to suppose that it takes a philosophical training to think that this fact is obvious.

29. It is hardly surprising that there is some such sense of identification, because the subjects who contemplate their own character sets do so from the point of view of the very character sets they are considering. See Strawson (1986: 111–13).

30. One common progress of thought is from (1) an unquestioned conviction that

people have URDA to (2) the thought, after a little reflection, that URDA requires URDN, to (3), the conviction—whose examination is avoided—that URDN is possible, actual, and standard.

31. Carr (1961: 89); Sartre (1948: 29), and in the *New Left Review* (1969) (quoted in Wiggins 1973); Kant (1793: 40 [Ak. VI. 44], 1788: 101 [Ak. V. 98]); Patten in *The Spectator* (January 1992); Aristotle (1915) [*Nicomachean Ethics* V.3]). Among recent discussions, see, for example, Anglin (1990), Gomberg (1975), Honderich (1993), Klein (1990), Pereboom (1995), Smilansky (2000), and Sorabji (1980, on Aristotle).

32. "To observe a child of two fully in control of its limbs, doing what it wants to do with them, and to this extent fully free to act in the compatibilist sense of this phrase, and to realize that it is precisely such unremitting experience of self-control that is the deepest foundation of our naturally *in*compatibilistic sense . . . of URDA, is . . . to understand one of the most important facts about the genesis and power of our ordinary strong [incompatibilistic] sense of freedom" (Strawson 1986: 111).

33. I have told this story before in Strawson (1986: 242, 1998: 748).

34. Note that this description of the character of our experience gives further content or color to the characterization of URD offered in section 4.

35. It may be added that the feeling of URDA seems to be just as inescapable for someone who has been convinced by the Basic Argument against URDA given in section 3, which does not depend on determinism in any way: even clearheaded acceptance of the force of the Basic Argument seems to fail to have any impact on one's sense of one's URDA as one stands there, wondering what to do.

36. See, though, MacKay (1960) for a general argument that no self-conscious agent can truly experience its choices and actions as determined even if determinism is true. See also G. Strawson (1986: ch. 13 and pp. 281–84); Smilansky (2000: part 2).

37. Lutyens (1983: 33, 204); Bellow (1975: 140); Spinoza (1985, first published in 1677: part I, prop. xxxii, corolls. I and II).

38. The distinction is Leibniz's (1988; first published in 1686).

39. C. Campbell (1957) gives philosophical expression to this view.

40. Another a posteriori argument cuts in at this point: even if some notion of the agent-self is defensible, there are powerful neurophysiological reasons for thinking that the "conscious self" or "conscious I" cannot be supposed to be the author of decisions and initiator of actions. See Norretranders (1991: ch. 9), and, for the work on which Norretranders draws, Libet (1985, 1987). (See also idem this volume, ch. 25, a piece that contains considerable conceptual confusion.)

CHAPTER 20

DETERMINISM AS TRUE, BOTH COMPATIBILISM AND INCOMPATIBILISM AS FALSE, AND THE REAL PROBLEM

TED HONDERICH

An event is something in space and time, just some of it, and so it is rightly said to be something that occurs or happens. For at least these reasons it is not a number or a proposition, or any abstract object. There are finer conceptions of an event, of course, one being a thing's having a general property for a time, another being exactly an individual property of a thing—say my computer monitor's weight (19 kg) as against yours (also 19 kg). None of these finer conceptions can put in doubt that events are individuals in a stretch of time and space.

What is required for an event to have an explanation, in the fundamental sense, is for there to be something else of which it is the effect. That is, for there to be an answer to the fundamental question of *why* an event happened is for there to be something of which it was the effect. A standard effect is an event that had to happen, or could not have failed to happen or been otherwise than it was, given the preceding causal circumstance, this being a set of events. In more philosophical talk, the event was made necessary or necessitated by the circumstance.

Of course there are finer conceptions of what it is for an event's having been made necessary by a circumstance. Some say that *since* the circumstance occurred, *so* did the later event. They give a simple logician's account—disambiguate that to your taste, reader—of such a conditional statement. This reduces to David Hume's story of causation, where the particular causal circumstance and the particular event were just an instance of a constant conjunction. Others are impressed by the difference between a causal circumstance for an event and an invariable but non-causal signal of that coming event. To exclude the signal from being the causal circumstance they say, maybe in terms of possible worlds, that what a circumstance's necessitating an event came to is that since the circumstances occurred, whatever else had been happening, so did the event.

Evidently there is a little room for this difference of opinion—our conceptual and other experience does not immediately rule out one of these views. Our experience *does* rule out other contemplated accounts of what is needed for an event to have an explanation in the fundamental sense—of its being necessitated by a causal circumstance. Clearly we do not understand an event's having had to happen as being only that it was more probable, maybe just more probable than not, as a result of the circumstance. That is not what we believe either, you bet, when we say the event could not have failed to happen. It is yet clearer that we do not take an event's having had to happen as the fact that it might well not have happened despite there having been something on hand that was "enough" for it.

In my life so far I have never known a single event to lack an explanation in the fundamental sense, and no doubt your life has been the same. No spoon has mysteriously levitated at breakfast. There has been no evidence at all, let alone proof, of there being no explanation to be found of a particular event. On the contrary, despite the fact that we do not seek out or arrive at the full explanations in question, my experience and yours pretty well consists of events that we take to have such explanations. If we put aside choices or decisions and the like—the events in dispute in the present discussion of determinism and freedom—my life and yours consists in nothing but events that we take to have fundamental explanations. Thus, to my mind, no general proposition of interest has greater inductive and empirical support than that all events whatever, including the choices or decisions and the like, have explanations.

Offered as exceptions to the latter proposition, without begging the question, are certain items distinct from the ordinary or macro events of our lives. They are indeed spoken of as events. They are, we hear, a certain subclass of micro or atomic and subatomic events. They are the quantum events of quantum theory. They, like all micro events, are far below the level of spoon movements and, more importantly, far below the neural events associated with consciousness and conscious choices or decisions in neuroscience.

The first thing to be noted of these supposed quantum events, events of true chance, by anyone inclined to determinism, is that there is no experimental evidence in a standard sense that there are any. There is no such evidence within physics. There is no such evidence, moreover, three quarters of a century after Heisenberg and Schrodinger developed quantum theory. In that very long time in science, including the recent decades of concern with Bell's theorem, there has been *no direct and univocal experimental evidence* of the existence of quantum events.

A second thing to be noted of these items has to do with a prior issue of which you have had a hint from my skeptical usages. What are these items if they do exist? How are they to be conceived? How is the mathematics or formalism of quantum theory to be interpreted? How are we to think of these items that are supposed to turn up in our heads and, as some say, leave room for traditional free will? Well, standard accounts of them by physicists bravely say they are baffling, weird and wonderful, self-contradictory, inexplicable, etc., etc. These events so-called do not involve 'particles' as ordinarily understood and defined, and the special use of the term 'particle' within interpretations of the mathematics cannot be satisfactorily defined. So with uses of 'position' or 'location' and so on.

The situation can be indicated quickly by noting a well-known collection of physicists' own speculations as to what quantum events in general, this bottom level of all reality, comes to. It comes to observer-dependent facts, subjective ideas, contents of our consciousness of reality, epistemological concepts, ideal concepts, propositions, probabilities, possibilities, features of a calculation, mathematical objects or devices, statistical phenomena, measures and measurements, abstract particles, probability waves, waves in abstract mathematical space, waves of no real physical existence, abstract constructs of the imagination, theoretical entities without empirical reality, objects to which standard two-value logics do not apply.

It was remarked earlier that physics has not provided any direct and univocal experimental evidence of the existence of events that lack standard explanations, events that are not effects. The noted collection of speculations about the nature of quantum events shows more that that. It remains a clear possibility, indeed a probability, that physics has not started on the job, even seventy-five years late, of showing that there are events that lack explanations. This is so, simply, because it remains a probability that quantum events, so-called, are not events. They are not events in any of the senses gestured at in the first paragraph of this chapter. In brief, it is probable that they are not things that occur or happen, but are of the nature of numbers and propositions, out of space and time. They are theoretical entities in a special sense of that term, not events.

Someone inclined to determinism, and a little tired of a kind of hegemony of physics in a part of philosophy—the part having to do with determinism and freedom—may be capable of saying more. They may even remain capable after considering several relevant and admirable contributions by others to this very volume. As the above collection of speculations by physicists indicates, even without the addition of some wholly inconsistent and 'realist' speculations, the interpretation of the mathematics of quantum theory is not merely baffling, weird, and wonderful, and so on. It is *a mess*. That is what would be said of any such enterprise of inquiry that did not enjoy a general hegemony, in more than the mentioned part of philosophy. This is a matter to which we will revert briefly in the end.

What we have, then, is that the proposition that all events have explanations has unique inductive and empirical support in our experience, that there is no experimental evidence in a standard sense for quantum events, and that quantum theory's failure to provide experimental evidence for them may be the result of its confused concern with theoretical items other than events.

A fourth thing to be contemplated about the supposed quantum events goes flatly against all this, but not against determinism as often conceived for philosophical purposes, and as it is conceived here. Let it be assumed that quantum events so-called, despite the collection of speculations by physicists lately noted, *are* to be conceived as events. Let it be assumed, against our experience, that they *do* exist. They are right there among other micro events, at atomic and subatomic levels, as distinct from macro events. They are events that simply lack explanations, events of true chance.

These events of true chance may have been very probable, of course. They may have had a probability of 95 percent, whatever this talk of probability is taken to mean. But to the question of why they *actually occurred*, their having had a probability of 95 percent is clearly no answer at all. To assign them a probability of 95 percent is precisely not to claim they had to happen or could not have failed to happen. It is precisely to hold open the possibility that they might not have happened.

In fact, on the assumption about true chance being made, there is *no* answer to look for as to why in the fundamental sense they happened. To the question of why in the fundamental sense they actually occurred, there is no relevant fact to be known, no relevant fact of the matter at all. This is dead clear because, *ex hypothesi*, everything might have been just the same without their occurring at all. You can miss this little proof of the absolute exclusion of explanatory fact, but it is not a good idea to do so.

Let us understand by determinism the family of doctrines that human choices and actions are effects of certain causal sequences or chains—sequences such as to raise the further and separate question, as traditionally expressed, of whether the choices and actions are free. The choices and actions in this determinism, then, are not effects of special sequences beginning a little while before in what can be called *originations* or acts of free will. These are the stock-in-trade of libertarian philosophers. These items, whatever else they are, and you will be hearing some more about this, are not effects.

Determinism so conceived is a matter of only macro events. It remains so if it is developed, as certainly it ought to be, into explicit philosophies of mind that take into account the relation of choices and actions to the brain, to neural events. The latter, the stuff of neuroscience, as already remarked, are as much macro events as choices and actions themselves.

It is clear that anyone inclined both to the existence of true chance or quantum events and to determinism as defined is not at all forced to choose between them, but can have both. She is not stuck with the levitating spoons. Her essential idea will be that quantum events in our heads do not translate upwards into macro events that also lack explanations. The quantum events in this respect may cancel out one another—or something of the sort. Given the entire absence of events of real chance within standard neuroscience, this is perhaps the easiest theoretical position for those who want their philosophy, no doubt for some good reason, to be in accord with science as it is now rather than with whatever it will be, the paradigm now rather than the paradigm to come.

This macro determinism, determinism as defined, raises exactly the traditional problem of freedom despite being married to micro indeterminism. It leaves exactly where it was the question about determinism most attended to by philosophers, that of its consequences for our lives—our freedom in choosing and acting.

A fifth remark about determinism and denials of it is that physics, including quantum theory, as already implied, is deferred to by many as basic or ultimate science. This has importantly to do with its absolute generality, and the idea that all other science can somehow be reduced to it. Certainly this deference, despite difficulties raised by the rest of science, is open to anyone who simply denies that all events have explanations, and in particular denies determinism. However, there are other personnel to be considered: the libertarian philosophers, of whom there are some good examples to be found in this volume. They assert the existence of originations or acts of free will in their small philosophies of mind—these originations being non-effects, whatever else they are, and either causal predecessors of choices and actions or the choices themselves.

These philosophers take from physics the proposition that certain events are without explanations in the fundamental sense. They then add that these originations *have* other very different but real explanations that leave or put them and their effects within the control of the person in question, leave or make the person in question responsible for them and their effects in a certain way. This amounts to more than contradiction in just spirit.

Physics and in particular quantum theory as interpreted by physicists do not amount just to the proposition that certain events are not effects but in fact have or may have *other* explanations, mysterious but somehow just as real or good as standard explanations. Physics does not take itself as like a car dealer who needs to allow that there are other car dealers in town. Plainly physics does not tolerate the other real but mysterious explanations of choices and the like when the choices are taken, as they are by most contemporary philosophers of mind, to be just as physical as spoon-movements. Physics itself, whatever physicists on holiday or in retirement say, is no more tolerant of choices nonphysically conceived, along with conscious events generally, despite the blur of nonphysicality.

Thus the position of the philosophers of origination is exactly what is resisted or disdained by quantum theory's conventional defenders—a hidden variable theory, something that absolutely undercuts quantum theory as interpreted. The philosophers of origination cannot have it both ways, comfortably or uncomfortably.

Can this conclusion be resisted by supposing that there is some non-mysterious way, perhaps even consistent with quantum theory, in which originations as true chance events can nonetheless have explanations? Something to do with dark battleground of probability? Well, there can be no way in which it can consistently be asserted that the actual occurrence of an origination has a fundamental explanation. It is going to have to remain a total mystery—with no possible fact anywhere in existence to dispel the mystery.

But, it may be said, there is surely *some* sense in which an event is explained if it is established as having been very probable. This needs to be granted, but not for a reason that gives a helping hand to the philosophers of origination. What is it for event A to have made it 95 percent probable that event B would occur? If we put aside more mystery, and theories of probability that do not attempt to give its nature or reality, there seems to be only one answer to the question. It is of course that in 95 percent of the situations in which an event of the type of A occurs, there is precisely a causal circumstance for an event of the type of B. We have good evidence for that, even if we don't know, or know exactly, what is in the circumstance.

What this non-fundamental explanation of B comes to, then, in fact presupposes the possibility of a fundamental explanation of B. It presupposes precisely the existence of a causal circumstance, as yet unspecified, for B. It presupposes that B was a necessitated event. Non-fundamental explanations, as might have been expected, are dependent on exactly the existence of possible fundamental explanations. That is why non-fundamental explanations do indeed count as explanations of a kind. Whether or not these derivative explanations can be said to fit into interpretations of quantum theory, they evidently do not fit into the views of the philosophers of origination. To allow a derivative explanation of an origination would be precisely to deny that it is an event of real chance. (Cf. Kane 1996)

There is a seventh respect in which the philosophers of origination are in more than trouble. Their doctrine suffers from another inconsistency that must stick in the craw of anyone not also on a mission to rescue our freedom. Say my lover writes to ask if I have been to bed with someone else, and I then form the intention to lie, and then I do lie. In order to save my freedom and responsibility as understood by them, my rescuers insert a quantum event between the question and my intention. In order to complete the rescue, however, or rather to defend it from itself, they need to *exclude* a quantum event between the intention and the lie. Otherwise I shall be doing some random lying—neither freely nor responsibly.

How can they consistently do this? Does quantum theory as interpreted have some clause, hitherto unheard of, that its random events occur only in such places as to make us morally responsible in a certain sense? This objection of inconsistency, perhaps, is less effective with some uncommitted philosophers because they do not really take the philosophers of origination seriously. If it really *were* accepted as true that a random event could get in between the question and the intention, with great effect, then it would have to be accepted that one could get in between the intention and the lie, with as much effect. Any attempt to exclude the possibility is bound to be fatally ad hoc.

Let us now try to leave the question of the truth of the proposition that all events have fundamental explanations, and the truth of determinism in the narrower sense specified. Let us try to leave the question, at any rate, insofar as certain other things can be separated from them. One of these, which in fact should come first, is the question of the conceptual adequacy of determinism and of the opposed family of doctrines, those having to do with origination. It is possible to overlook or forget the fact, but both families do indeed and need to consist in philosophies of mind—accounts or anyway intimations of the nature of consciousness and mental activity, of how they come about, of mind and brain, and of the connection between mental activity and behavior or action.

It is a remarkable fact that when we put aside the little philosophies of mind expressly concerned with the further question of whether choices and actions are free—the literature on determinism and freedom—what we find is determinism and hardly anything else. That is, in the Philosophy of Mind itself, we find only philosophers who assume or explain that human choices and actions are effects of causal sequences or chains of the sort that are taken in the literature on determinism and freedom to raise the further question of our freedom. When philosophers are concerned with consciousness and mental activity and so on, in and for themselves, in the real Philosophy of Mind, they have nothing to say of origination.

Thus in the Philosophy of Mind's autonomous existence, its history since Gilbert Ryle's *The Concept of Mind* in 1949, there is nothing at all about what, if the philosophers of origination are right, is the *unique* fact of our consciousness and mental activity and so on. In monisms and dualisms, in Functionalism and in the Philosophy of Action, in assertions and accounts of our subjectivity, in conceptions of a person, and above all in various doctrines of the general explanation of our behavior—in all of this, at least half of it *not* scientistic or "materialistic," we find nothing of what is supposed by its supporters to be what actually sets us aside from the rest of the world: our originations.

Are a couple of qualifications in order? Well, there has been some support for the mysterious idea that reasons are not causes—what *are* they supposed to be, then?—but it has not gone so far as embracing origination. There is also Donald Davidson's Anomalous Monism, which denies the existence of lawlike or nomic connections between mental events, so-regarded, and physical events. There are no such connections between mental events and their physical antecedents—as there are no such connections between mental events and either simultaneous neural events or such later physical events as actions and their effects. Well, it is also part of this extraordinary doctrine that the mental events regarded as physical, which indeed they must be, *are* effects of their physical antecedents (Davidson 1980).

Of what relevance to the truth of determinism is the nearly complete absence of the opposing family of doctrines from the orthodox Philosophy of Mind? That particular question of truth has the interest of standing in connection with the matter of orthodox science and a certain presumption of truth—although not one into which I myself enter with full confidence. Let us leave it, and note instead that origination's absence from the Philosophy of Mind can indeed be taken to suggest that there is no *tempting* conception of origination in existence. Otherwise it would certainly have been made use of in general explanations of behavior.

Origination's absence from the Philosophy of Mind also reinforces the question of whether there is an *adequate* conception of it. What has been said so far, to recall, is that an act of origination (1) is not an effect, (2) is either a causal predecessor of a choice and action or the choice itself, and (3) has a special explanation such that it and therefore its effects are within the control of the person in question and such as to make her responsible in a certain sense for them. Is this *adequate*? That it is not has for some time been contemplated by the more-or-less determinist party in the philosophy of determinism and freedom. The idea was famously expressed by Peter Strawson when he spoke of panicky metaphysics (P. F. Strawson 1962).

It is indeed difficult to see what can be added to the conception we have so far of origination in order to have more to put in place of the standard account of the occurrence of choices and actions in terms of fundamental explanation and causation. It can be asked, certainly, how the special kind of explanation and thus personal control comes about. In answer, if talk of probability is given up, recourse may be had just to ordinary verbs of our human activity, such as "to give rise to" or indeed "to cause."

But these, as we understand them elsewhere, are a matter of fundamental explanation, of standard effects. "Give rise to," ordinarily used, is as much a matter of standard causality as "push." It is wholly obscure what remains of the verbs of human activity when their backbone of sense is taken out of them. They do not have a backbone put back in, either, when it is said that A's having caused B was just A's having been "enough" for B, which was consistent with B's not happening. No sense has ever been given to the "enough." (Cf. Ginet 1990)

Quite as plainly, there can be recourse to talk of *reasons* of a kind in trying to explain choices and actions without the aid of fundamental explanation. There can be recourse, that is, to logical or conceptual relations of an essentially normative kind. But that I had good reason eventually to confess to my lover, in terms of whatever value-system, including my own morality, gives no explanation of why I confessed. There may be the explanation that I was caused to confess by my good reason in a more robust and a standardly causal sense—where my reason clearly was something more than an abstract entailer or other premise—but this, of course, is exactly what origination is supposed to replace.

Let us leave open for a while the question of whether there is an adequate conception of origination—conceivably the question of whether we have one in what has been said already. Also the question of whether there is another use for what some will see as the irrelevance or indeed the philosophical low blow of pointing out that the stock-in-trade of origination-philosophers never gets attention in the Philosophy of Mind. Let us turn now to the question of what is taken to follow from determinism—the question not of its truth or the prior question of its conceptual adequacy, but its consequences. This does of course bring in the linked question of the consequences of origination.

Here we encounter those two traditions that began in the seventeenth century or before and are still with us, one with knobs of modal logic on it and the other encrusted with hierarchies of desire—the traditions of incompatibilism and compatibilism. The first is to the effect that if determinism is true we are unfree and are not morally responsible for our actions, since determinism and freedom are logically incompatible. The second is to the effect that even if determinism is true we remain free in many of our actions and hence morally responsible for them, since determinism and freedom are logically compatible. What the two traditions evidently agree about, and typically declare, is that our freedom is one thing, or would be one thing if we had it, and hence that we have this one concept of it—or at any rate one freedom or one concept of freedom is fundamental and somehow the only important one.

In the last couple of decades, a good deal of diligence has gone into a certain Incompatibilist line of thought. Plainly stated, it is that if determinism is true then my action today, perhaps of complying or going along again with my unjust society, is the effect of a causal circumstance in the remote past, before I was born. That circumstance, clearly, was not *up to me*. So its necessary consequence, my action of compliance today with my hierarchic democracy, is not up to me. Hence my action today is not free and I am not responsible for it (van Inwagen 1983).

This line of thought is dignified by having the name of the Consequence Argument for incompatibilism. It is worth noting in passing that in its essential content, its logic, the argument has nothing to do with our being unable to change the past. It is that the past had in it no act of origination and in particular no relevant act of origination. It had in it no act of origination that had the later action of compliance as content or object, so to speak, and as effect. Instead it had in that remote causal circumstance and a causal sequence from it leading up to the action of compliance. If the past *did* have such a relevant act of origination in it, although I still couldn't change it and the rest of the past, things would be OK. My action of compliance could be up to me.

It is also worth noting that the argument has nothing essential to do with a causal circumstance in the remote past. To repeat, what the incompatibilist supposes would make my action today up to me, make me free and responsible, is an act of origination relevant to today's action of compliance. Suppose that the act of origination for the action of compliance would have had to be in the last five minutes—originations wear out, so to speak, if they do not issue in actions within five minutes. If they are to work, they have to be renewed. We do indeed believe something like this. If so, for the incompatibilist, my action's having been the effect of a causal circumstance just over five minutes ago would make the action not up to me. Suppose on the other hand, absurdly, that a previous embodiment of me *did* perform a relevant act of origination. That might cheer up the incomatibilist, even if it was so remotely in the past as to be just after the Big Bang, and even if that event was immediately followed by a causal circumstance, certainly remote, for my later action of compliance.

Thus what is crucial for this line of thought is a relevant act of origination. And hence, to mention one thing, the argument has as much need of giving an adequate account of origination as any other argument of its ilk—any incompatibilism. What in fact has happened in connection with the line of argument, however, is a lot of reflection, aided by modal logic, on something else. We could transform it into reflection that makes the essential content or logic of the argument explicit, talk about a causal circumstance just over five minutes ago, but there is no need to do so.

The reflection has been on whether it does really follow, from the fact that a remote causal circumstance was not up to me, that its necessary consequence, my action today in going along with my society, is not up to me. The reflection has included variations on the plain version of the line of thought, and also objections to and supposed refutations of both the plain line of thought and the variations.

It is not easy for me to see that this has been philosophical time well spent. Does it not seem clear that in an ordinary sense of the words, it does indeed follow that if the remote causal circumstance was not up to me, neither was what was connected with it by an unbroken causal sequence—my action today? Will anyone say that there is *no* sense of the words in which it follows that if the remote circumstance was not up to me, neither was its necessary consequence? No fundamental or important sense in which lack of control is transitive? Might you join me in saying that if modal logic were to prove that there is no such sense of the words, or no important sense of the words, so much the worse for modal logic?

Now consider the other side in the traditional dispute—some compatibilist struggle in the last couple of decades, or rather two such struggles. Both are attempts to defend this tradition's fundamental conception of our freedom. That conception, at its simplest, is of a choice or action that is not against the desire of the person in question. Freedom consists in choice or action flowing from the desire of the person in question—or, a little less simply, from embraced rather than reluctant desire. Freedom is this absence of constraint or compulsion. Freedom is voluntariness—quite other than origination. An unfree decision or action, by contrast, is one made as a result of the bars of the prison cell, or the threat to one's life, or the compulsion of kleptomania.

Against this idea as to our freedom, it may be objected that we could be free in this way and yet not be in control of our lives. This voluntariness is not control. Exactly this was a complaint of incompatibilists. It gave rise to a struggle in response by our compatibilists. It is plainly a mistake, we still hear from them, to suppose that if I was free in this sense today in my action of social deference, I was *subject to control*. What control would come to would be my being subject to the desires of another person, or something akin to another person, maybe within me. Given this proposition, evidently, it is not the case that determinism, which is indeed consistent with the compatibilist idea of our freedom, deprives us of control of our lives (Dennett 1984).

So far so good, you may say, but clearly a question remains. Could what has been said by the compatibilists be taken as coming near to establishing that there is but *one* way in which we can conceive of *not* being in control of our lives, the way where we are subject to someone or something else's desires? To put the question differently, and more pointedly, does this come near to establishing that there is but *one* way, the compatibilist way, in which we can *be* in control of our lives, which is to say one way in which we conceive of being free? That all we think of or can care about is voluntariness?

There are rather plain difficulties in the way of this. There evidently is something very like another idea of self-control or freedom. Is it not against the odds, to say the least, that this dispute into which our compatibilist is seriously entering is between his own conceptually respectable party and a party that has *no different idea at all*, nothing properly called an idea or anyway no idea worth attention, of what our freedom does or may consist in? There *is* what has been said of origination.

Let me mention yet more quickly the effort by some compatibilists to make more explicit their idea of freedom. It is at bottom the effort to show why the kleptomaniac and other such unfortunates, on the compatibilist account of freedom, are in fact unfree. Certainly it could be thought there was a problem for the account here, since the kleptomaniac in walking out of the department store yet again without paying for the blouses presumably *is* somehow doing what he wants to do, presumably is *not* acting against desire.

Our compatibilist is indeed on the way to a solution if he supposes, a little bravely, that all kleptomaniacs not only desire to make off with the blouses but also desire not to have that desire. By means of this idea of a hierarchy of desires, that is, the compatibilist is indeed improving his conception of a free action—it is, at least in the first part of the conception, an action such that we desire to desire to perform it (Frankfurt 1971). Suppose more than that—that the whole philosophical enterprise, this hierarchical theory of freedom, works like a dream, with no difficulties about a regress or about identifying a self with a particular level of desires or about anything else.

Will that have come near to establishing that there is no other conception of a free action? Will it come close to establishing that we have operating in our lives only the hierarchic conception? Will it come close to establishing the lesser thing that this conception is fundamental or dominant or most salient or in any other way ahead of another one? Come to think of it, *how* could it actually do that? Are we to suppose that from the premise that one conception of freedom has now been really perfected it follows that there is no other conception of freedom or none worth attention?

So that you do not suppose I have been partial, let us glance back at the incompatibilist struggle. Think again of me today, acting again in compliance with my unjust society, and take the action to be the effect of a causal circumstance in the remote past, before I was born. It does indeed seem, as was maintained earlier, that there must be *some* proposition to the effect that if the remote circumstance was not up to me, neither was the action of compliance that was made necessary by the circumstance. But something else in surely quite as clear—and maybe more important than the previous point that the line of argument, like any incompatibilist line of argument, needs an adequate account of origination.

There *is*, isn't there, a clear sense in which my action, necessary consequence though it was, may well have been *up to me*—perfectly up to me. Suppose I was struck a month ago by Bradley's utterance that to wish to be better than the world is to be already on the threshold of immorality. Suppose I had then consciously determined after a month's serious reflection that henceforth I would consistently act on the side of my society. Suppose it had come about that a great desire drew me only to this—and of course that I desired to have the desire, and so on. In fact my whole personality and character now supported my action of deference. I could not have been more for it. Does not this conjecture, or any more restrained one you like, come close to establishing that it must be a *very* brave incompatibilist who maintains that there is no significant sense in which my action of compliance was up to me?

So much for recent activity in the two hoary traditions. There is yet more activity, in particular with respect to origination, in preceding essays in this book. I commend the activity to you—but also the idea that a yet more direct approach to the two traditions is possible (Honderich 1993: 80–106; 1988: 379–487).

We all have hopes for our lives—we all have a dominant hope in a particular stage of life, perhaps for more than one thing, perhaps a disjunctive hope. Like any hope, it is an attitude to a future possibility, at bottom a desire with respect to the possibility. Very likely indeed it is a desire with respect to our own future actions and their initiations in particular desires or whatever. To come to the crux quickly, such desires come in two sorts for all of us. One sort is for a future in which our actions will be voluntary, uncompelled and unconstrained. We won't be in jail or victims of our fearfulness. The other sort of desires is for a future in which our actions are also not fixed products of our natures and environments. We will not just be creatures of them. Each of us has the two sorts of desires, or at any rate each of us is more than capable of having them. One contains ideas of our future actions as our own in being voluntary. The other sort makes them our own in also containing at least an image of our future actions as originated.

There is the same plain truth, as it seems to me, with respect to the trampled ground of moral responsibility, of which incompatibilists in particular have had a too elevated notion. What determinism threatens here is also attitudinal. It is a matter of holding people responsible for particular actions and of crediting them with responsibility for particular actions. To do so is to approve or disapprove morally of them for the actions in question. We may do so on the contained assumption than an action was voluntary. Or we may do so, differently, on the contained assumption that the action was not only voluntary but originated. Different desires enter into the two sorts of attitudes—retributive desires are attached to the idea that the person in question, just as things had been and were, could have done other than the thing he did.

What is more, we act and have institutions or parts of institutions that are owed to one assumption rather than the other. One good example of a general fact is preventive punishment, depending only on a conception of actions as voluntary, and retributive punishment, depending on a conception of actions as also originated. There is thus a behavioral proof of the existence and indeed the pervasiveness of two attitudes and two conceptions of freedom.

What all this leads to is the real problem of the consequences of determinism—which is not the problem of proving something to be our one idea of freedom, or our only self-respecting one, or what you will along these lines. The real problem of the consequences of determinism is that of dealing with the situation in which we have both the idea of voluntariness and also the idea of voluntariness plus origination, and these two ideas run, shape, or at least color our lives, and the second conflicts with determinism. We may attempt to bluff and to carry on intransigently in the pretence that what matters is only the first idea and what it enters into, one family of attitudes. This is a response of intransigence. On the other hand we may respond with dismay to the prospect of giving up the second idea and what it enters into, the other family of attitudes.

It is at this point among others that the question of the adequacy of the idea of origination comes up. Some philosophers say there is no adequate idea of it. What it comes to is only some piece of nonsense, literally speaking, like the old nonsense of speaking of a thing's causing itself. Hence, for one thing, it does not matter if determinism is true or false. If it is true, there is no more problem than if it is false, since there is no serious idea with which it conflicts. Also, compatibilism has the field of discussion to itself, since incompatibilism comes to nothing. The question of truth does not arise. (Cf. Strawson 1986).

This is a curious position that prompts speculation. Suppose I have no idea of why the petunias on the balcony *need sun*, but am persuaded they do, no doubt by good evidence. Despite the evidence, I have no acquaintance at all with photosynthesis, not even any boy's own science of the matter. It does not follow, presumably, that I lack the idea that the petunias *need sun*. I could have the idea, too, in a prescientific society where news of the science of the thing would for a long time make no sense. Could I not also have the idea, in a later society, if all of many attempts to explicate the need had broken down in obscurity and indeed contradiction?

At first sight, certainly, those who suppose that there *is* an adequate idea of origination are in just this sort of position. They speak no nonsense when they assert or offer for contemplation a certain thing. It is that there occur originations, these being events that are not effects, are in the control of the person in question, and render the person responsible in a certain way for ensuing actions—his being held responsible can consist in an attitude having in it certain desires, notably retributive ones. The friends of origination speak no nonsense when they depend considerably for their characterization of the events of origination on these consequences. The friends still speak no nonsense when it transpires that they cannot in some way explain how it comes about that there is origination, or would come about if there were any. They still speak no nonsense in what went before if their attempts to explain are themselves pieces of nonsense.

No doubt more distinctions are needed here, but it remains my own view that determinism *does* threaten something important to us of which we have an adequate idea if not a tempting idea. The latter sort of thing, as you will expect, is an idea open to a kind of explanation, an idea of something along with an some explication of it. My untroubled view, too, until very recently, has been that the true problem of the consequences of determinism is the problem of giving up something of which we do have an adequate idea. It is not as if that problem does not arise for the clear-headed.

We can set out to try to deal with this problem of attitudes, at bottom desires. We can try to get away from the responses of intransigence and dismay, and oscillating between them, and make a response of affirmation. This, caricatured, is looking on the bright side. It is seeing the fullness and fineness of a life given much of its character by the attitudes consistent with determinism, and thus giving up the ones inconsistent with it. We can try this—but we may not succeed (Honderich 1993: 107–29, 1988, vol. 2: 488–612).

As it has seemed to me, what stands in our way, and in fact obstructs real belief in determinism despite all that can be said for it, is a great fact of our culture. We are so formed, first of all by mothers, those first agents of culture, as to be unable to escape the attitudes. We cannot dismiss one kind of our hopes, and we cannot escape other attitudes, such as those having to do with responsibility, notably when they are directed by ourselves onto ourselves.

Is this the only possible conclusion to the problem of determinism and freedom? For want of space, let me pass by some gallant work of originality and interest (Double 1991, 1996a) and come on to something else, an idea of another alternative.

Having lately engaged explicitly in autobiography, rather than the kind of it in which philosophy is sometimes said to consist, I have been newly taken aback by the strength and durability of my attitudes to myself seemingly inconsistent with determinism. Is the stuff about culture really enough to explain them? I have been taken aback too by a seeming fact about a further kind of explanation— picking out a cause within a causal circumstance and giving it special standing in connection with the effect. This has attitudes in it, all too evidently, but it also seems a business of truth. I do not mean that the attitudes direct and mislead explanation, but that they can seem somehow to enter into its constitution.

Thus a question has come up about attitudes seemingly inconsistent with determinism. Could they be owed not only to mothers and their successors in our culture but also have truth in them? Is *that* why they are so strong and durable? Will some dramatically different reconciliation of determinism and freedom one day be achieved? Certainly it will not be another appearance of that weary warhorse, compatibilism. Will it have something to do with a connection between desire and truth? Again the point is not about desires affecting our pursuit of truth or obscuring it, but about their entering into the constitution of it (Honderich 2000).

The point stands in connection with two remarks earlier. One was about quantum theory having a certain hegemony despite its interpretation being a mess. The other was about the stock-in-trade of origination-philosophers never getting noticeable attention in the real Philosophy of Mind. Can it be that attitude enters more into belief, some of it also knowledge, including quantum theory as inter-preted and free will philosophy, than we have thought is possible or proper to suppose?[1]

NOTE

1. If it had appeared in time, an essay on consciousness and freedom, Searle 2000, might have been mentioned here. It is fully considered in Honderich 2001.

....

LIVING WITHOUT FREE WILL: THE CASE FOR HARD INCOMPATIBILISM

....

DERK PEREBOOM

THE central thesis of the position I defend (Pereboom 1995, 2001) is that we do not have the sort of free will required for moral responsibility. My argument for this claim has the following structure: An agent's moral responsibility for an action depends primarily on its actual causal history, and not on the existence of alternative possibilities. Absent agent causation, indeterministic causal histories pose no less of a threat to moral responsibility than do deterministic histories, and a generalization argument from manipulation cases shows that deterministic histories indeed undermine moral responsibility. Agent causation is a coherent possibility, but it is not credible given our best physical theories. Consequently, no position that affirms the sort of free will required for moral responsibility is left standing. I also contend that a conception of life without this sort of free will would not be devastating to our sense of meaning and purpose, and in certain respects it may even be beneficial. Although this position is clearly similar to hard determinism, it does not endorse determinism itself, and thus I call it *hard incompatibilism*.

1. Outline of the Argument

I reject an alternative-possibilities type of incompatibilism and accept instead a type of incompatibilism that ascribes the more significant role to an action's causal history. My view is that an agent's responsibility for an action is explained not by the existence of alternative possibilities available to her, but rather by the action's having a causal history of a sort that allows the agent to be the source of her action in a specific way. Following Ted Honderich (1988, vol 1: 194–206) and Robert Kane (1996a: 35), the crucial condition emphasizes that an agent must be the origin of her action in a particular way. According to my version of this condition, if an agent is morally responsible for her decision to perform an action, then the production of this decision must be something over which the agent has control, and an agent is not morally responsible for the decision if it is ultimately produced by a source over which she has no control.

The grounding for this kind of incompatibilism includes the argument that certain Frankfurt-style cases rule out the notion that having alternative possibilities explains an agent's responsibility for action (Frankfurt 1969), and the argument that a deterministic causal history would make it impossible for the agent to be the source of her action in the way required. The best strategy for establishing the latter claim involves devising manipulation cases in which the agent is covertly induced to perform an action by some external cause and for that reason is not responsible for her action, and then generalizing to nonresponsibility in more ordinary deterministic cases. I contend that no relevant and principled difference can distinguish an action that results from responsibility-undermining manipulation from an action that has a more ordinary deterministic causal history (R. Taylor 1974: 43–44; Kane 1996a: 65–71). Moreover, exclusively event-causal indeterministic histories are no less threatening to moral responsibility than deterministic histories, and since deterministic causal histories undermine moral responsibility, so do such event-causal indeterministic histories (Clarke 1997). If the crucial indeterministic events were appropriately produced by a randomizing manipulator, then one would have the intuition that the agent is not morally responsible (van Inwagen 1983: 132–34; Mele 1999a: 277). But there is no relevant and principled difference between the manipulated action and one that is indeterministic in a more ordinary way. Among available models for agency, to my mind only agent causation allows for moral responsibility, but simply because it builds into the agent, as a primitive power, the capacity to be a source of action that is required for moral responsibility. The agent-causation model is coherent as far as we can tell, but given evidence from our best scientific theories, it is not credible that we are in fact agent-causes. We are therefore left with the view that we do not have free will of the kind required for moral responsibility.

2. Wrongdoing

Accepting hard incompatibilism demands giving up our ordinary view of ourselves as blameworthy for immoral actions and praiseworthy for those that are morally exemplary. One might argue that giving up our belief in moral responsibility would have very harmful consequences, or even that they would be so damaging that thinking and acting as if hard incompatibilism is true is not a practical possibility for us. Thus even if the claim that we are morally responsible turns out to be false, there may yet be a practical argument for continuing to treat ourselves and others as if we were. One might find this proposal attractive because acting as if people are at times blameworthy is typically required for moral reform and education. If we began to act as if people were not morally responsible, then one might fear that we would be left with insufficient leverage to change immoral ways of behaving.

It is nevertheless important to understand that this option would have the hard incompatibilist treating people as blameworthy—by, for example, expressing indignation toward them—when they do not deserve it, which would seem morally wrong. As Bruce Waller argues, if people are not responsible for immoral behavior, treating them as if they were would be unfair (Waller 1990: 130–35). However, it is possible to achieve moral reform and education by methods that would not suffer from this sort of unfairness, and in ordinary situations such practices could arguably be as successful as those that presuppose moral responsibility. Instead of treating people as if they were deserving of blame, the hard incompatibilist can draw upon moral admonishment and encouragement, which presuppose only that the offender has done wrong. These methods can effectively communicate a sense of what is right and result in beneficial reform. Similarly, rather than treating oneself as blameworthy, one could admonish oneself for one's wrongdoing and resolve to avoid similar behavior in the future.

But what resources does hard incompatibilism have for dealing with criminal behavior? Here hard incompatibilism would appear to be at a disadvantage, and if so, practical considerations might force us nevertheless to treat criminals as if they were morally responsible. Indeed, if hard incompatibilism is true, a retributivist justification for criminal punishment is ruled out, for it assumes that we deserve blame or pain or deprivation just for performing an immoral action, while hard incompatibilism denies this claim. Hard incompatibilism must therefore forswear retributivism—one of the most naturally compelling ways for justifying criminal punishment.

By contrast, the moral education theory of punishment is not challenged by hard incompatibilism specifically. Still, without strong empirical evidence that punishment of criminals would bring about moral education, it would be wrong to punish them for the sake of achieving this goal. In general, it is morally wrong to harm someone in order to realize some good if there is insufficient evidence that the harm can produce the good. Morreover, even if we knew that punishment could be effective in moral education, we should prefer nonpunitive methods for producing this result—whether or not we are morally responsible.

Although the two most prominent deterrence theories are not challenged by hard incompatibilism in particular, they are questionable on other grounds. The utilitarian version is dubious for well-known reasons—it would at times demand punishing the innocent, in some circumstances it would prescribe punishment that is unduly severe, and it would authorize using people merely as means. I contend that the type of deterrence theory that justifies punishment on the basis of the right to harm in self-defense is also objectionable (Farrell 1985). For at the time when a criminal is sentenced, he is typically not an immediate threat to anyone, and this fact about his circumstances distinguishes him from those who may legitimately be harmed on the basis of the right of self-defense.

A theory of crime prevention whose legitimacy is independent of hard incompatibilism draws an analogy between treatment of criminals and policy toward carriers of dangerous diseases. Ferdinand Schoeman (1979) argues that if we have the right to quarantine people who are carriers of severe communicable diseases to protect society, then we also have the right to isolate the criminally dangerous to protect society. Schoeman's claim is true independently of any legitimate attribution of moral responsibility. If a child is infected with the Ebola virus because it has been passed on to her at birth by her parent, quarantine may nevertheless be justified. By analogy, suppose that someone poses a known danger to society by having demonstrated a sufficiently strong tendency to commit murder. Even if he is not in general a morally responsible agent, society would nevertheless seem to have as much right to detain him as it does to quarantine a carrier of a deadly communicable disease who is not responsible for being a carrier.

One must note, however, that it would be morally wrong to treat carriers of a disease more severely than is required to defuse the threat to society. Similarly, given the quarantine model, it would be wrong to treat those with violent criminal tendencies more harshly than is needed to remove the danger to society. In addition, just as moderately dangerous diseases may only license measures less intrusive than quarantine, so tendencies to moderately serious crimes may only justify responses less intrusive than detention. Shoplifting, for example, may warrant merely some degree of monitoring. Furthermore, I suspect that a theory modeled on quarantine would never justify criminal punishment of the sort whose legitimacy is most in doubt, such as the death penalty or confinement in the worst prisons in our society. Moreover, it would require a degree of concern for the rehabilitation and well being of the criminal that would decisively alter current policy. Just as society has a duty to try to cure the diseased it quarantines, so it would have a duty to attempt to rehabilitate the criminals it detains. And when rehabilitation is impossible, and if the protection of society were to demand in-definite confinement, there would be no justification for taking measures that aim only to make the criminal's life miserable.

3. MEANING IN LIFE

Would it be practically impossible for us to live without a conception of ourselves as praiseworthy for achieving what makes our lives fulfilled, happy, satisfactory, or worthwhile—for realizing what Honderich has called our *life-hopes*? (Honder-ich 1988, vol. 2: 382) Honderich argues that there is an aspect of these life-hopes that is undermined by determinism, but that nevertheless determinism leaves them largely intact. I agree with this type of position, and develop it in the following way. It is not unreasonable to object that life-hopes involve an aspiration for praiseworthiness, which hard incompatibilism would undercut. For life-hopes are aspirations for achievement, and because it cannot be that one has an achievement for which one is not also praiseworthy, giving up praiseworthiness would deprive us of life-hopes altogether. However, achievement and life-hopes are not obviously connected to praiseworthiness in the way this objection supposes. If an agent hopes for success in some endeavor, and if she accomplishes what she hoped for, intuitively this outcome can be her achievement even if she is not praiseworthy for it—although the sense in which it is her achievement may be diminished. If an agent hopes that her efforts as a teacher will result in well-educated children, and they do, it seems clear that she achieved what she hoped for, even if, according to the truth of hard incompatibilism, she is not praiseworthy for her efforts.

Furthermore, one might think that acceptance of hard incompatibilism would instill an attitude of resignation to whatever one's behavioral dispositions together with environmental conditions hold in store. But this is not clearly true. In the hard incompatibilist view, given that we lack knowledge of how our futures will turn out, we can still reasonably hope for success in achieving what we want most even if we turn out to be creatures of our environments and our dispositions. It may sometimes be crucial that we lack complete knowledge of our environments and dispositions. Suppose that there is some disposition that an agent reasonably believes might be an obstacle to realizing a life-hope. However, because he does not know whether this disposition will in fact function this way, it remains epi-stemically possible for him to have a further disposition that will allow him to transcend the potential obstacle. For example, suppose that someone aspires to become a successful clinical psychologist but is concerned that his irritability will stand in the way. He does not know whether his irritability will in fact frustrate his life-hope, since it is epistemically possible for him that he will overcome this problem, perhaps due to a disposition for resolute self-discipline. As a result, he might reasonably hope that he will overcome his irritability and succeed in his aspiration. In the hard incompatibilist view, if he in fact does overcome his problem and becomes a successful clinical psychologist, his achievement will not be as robust as one might naturally have believed, but it will be his achievement in a substantial sense nevertheless.

But how significant is the aspect of our life-hopes that we must forgo if hard determinism or hard incompatibilism is true? Saul Smilansky argues that although determinism leaves room for a limited foundation for the sense of self-worth that derives from achievement or virtue, the hard determinist's (and also, by extension, the hard incompatibilist's) perspective can nevertheless be "extremely damaging to our view of ourselves, to our sense of achievement, worth, and self-respect," and in response we should foster the illusion that we have free will (Smilansky 1997: 94; also Smilansky 2000, and his essay in this volume, ch. 22). I agree with Smilansky that there is a type of self-respect that presupposes an incompatibilist foundation, and that it would be undermined if hard determinism (or hard incompatibilism) were true. I do question, however, whether he is right about how damaging it would be for us to find that we must give up this sort of self-respect, and thus whether his move to illusion would be justified.

One should note that our sense of self-worth, our sense that we are valuable and that are lives are worth living, is to a significant extent due to factors that are not produced by our volitions at all, let alone by free will. People place great value, both in others and in themselves, on beauty, intelligence, and native athletic ability, none of which are produced voluntarily. However, we also value voluntary efforts, hard work and generous actions, for example, and their results. But how much does it matter to us that the voluntary efforts are also freely willed? In my view, Smilansky overestimates how much we care.

Consider the formation of moral character. It is not implausible that good moral character is to a large extent the function of upbringing, and furthermore, the belief that this is so is common in our society. Parents typically regard themselves as failures if their children turn out to be immoral, and many take great care to raise their children to prevent this result. Accordingly, people often come to believe that they have a good moral character largely because they were brought up with parental love and skill. But I suspect that hardly anyone who comes to this realization experiences dismay because of it. We tend not at all to be dispirited upon coming to understand that our moral character is not our own doing, and that we deserve at best diminished respect for having this character. Rather, we feel fortunate and thankful for the upbringing we have enjoyed, and not that something significant has been lost.

Moreover, people typically do not become dispirited when they come to believe that success in a career depends very much on one's upbringing, opportunities in one's society, the assistance of colleagues, and good fortune. Realizations of this sort frequently give rise to a sense of thankfulness, and almost never, if at all, to dismay. Why then should we suppose that we would generally become dispirited were we to adopt a hard incompatibilist stance? We would then relinquish the view that character and accomplishments are due to free will and that we for this reason deserve respect, but given our response to the more commonplace beliefs in external determination, we have little reason to think that we would be overcome with dismay. But suppose that there are people who would become disheartened even upon coming to believe that moral character is largely due to upbringing. Then would it be justified or even desirable for them to sustain the illusion that they nevertheless deserve respect for producing their moral character? Most people are capable of facing the truth without incurring much loss, and those for whom it would be painful will typically have the psychological resources to cope with the new understanding. I suspect that the same would be true for those who come to accept hard incompatibilism.

4. Personal Relationships

P. F. Strawson (1962) contends that the justification for claims of blameworthiness and praiseworthiness terminates in the system of human reactive attitudes, and because moral responsibility has this kind of foundation, the truth or falsity of universal determinism is irrelevant to whether we are justified in holding agents morally responsible. These reactive attitudes, such as indignation, gratitude, forgiveness, and love are required for the kinds of relationships that make our lives meaningful, and so even if we could give up the attitudes—and Strawson believes that this is impossible—we would never have practical reason to do so. Accordingly, we would never have practical reason to give up on moral responsibility. On the other hand, if universal determinism did threaten the reactive attitudes, we would face the prospect of the "objective attitude," a cold and calculating stance toward others that would undermine the possibility of meaningful personal relationships.

Strawson is clearly right to believe that an objective attitude would destroy relationships, but I deny that we would adopt this stance or that it would be appropriate if we came to believe universal determinism (or hard incompatibilism) and it did pose a threat to the reactive attitudes. In my conception, some of the reactive attitudes would in fact be undermined by hard determinism, or more broadly by hard incompatibilism. For some of them, such as indignation, presuppose that the person who is the object of the attitude is morally responsible. I claim, however, that the reactive attitudes that we would want to retain either are not threatened by hard incompatibilism in this way or else have analogues or aspects that would not have false presuppositions. The complex of attitudes that would survive by no means amount to Strawson's objectivity, and they would be sufficient to sustain good relationships.

To a certain degree indignation is likely to be beyond our power to affect, and thus even supposing that a hard incompatibilist is thoroughly committed to morality and rationality, and that she is admirably in control of her emotional life, she might nevertheless be unable to eradicate this attitude. Thus, as hard incompatibilists, we might expect that people will become indignant under certain circumstances, and we would regard it as inevitable and exempt from blame when they do. However, we also have the ability to prevent, temper, and sometimes to dispel indignation, and given a belief in hard incompatibilism, we might attempt these measures for the sake of morality and rationality. Modifications of this sort, aided by a hard incompatibilist conviction, could well be good for relationships.

In response, one might contend that indignation is crucial to communication of wrongdoing in relationships, and if we were to diminish or eliminate this attitude, relationships would suffer as a result. But when one is wronged in a relationship, one typically experiences additional attitudes that are not threatened by hard incompatibilism, whose expression can play the communicative role at issue. These attitudes include feeling hurt, alarmed, or distressed about what the other has done, and moral sadness or concern for the other. Indignation, then, is not clearly required for communication in personal relationships.

Forgiveness might appear to presuppose that the person being forgiven is blameworthy, and if this is so, it would indeed be threatened by hard incompatibilism. But this attitude has central features that are unaffected by hard incompatibilism, and they are sufficient to sustain the typical role of forgiveness as a whole in good relationships. Suppose a friend repeatedly mistreats you, and because of this you have resolved to end your relationship with him. However, he then he apologizes to you, in such a way that (in harmony with hard incompatibilism) he thereby signifies his recognition of the wrongness of his actions, his wish that he had not mistreated you, and his sincere commitment to refraining from the offensive behavior. Because of this you decide not to terminate the friendship. The feature of forgiveness that is consistent with hard incompatibilism in this case is the willingness to cease to regard past immoral behavior as a reason to dissolve or weaken a relationship. In another type of case, independently of the other's repentance, you might simply dismiss the wrong as a reason to end or change the character of your relationship. This feature of forgiveness is also not jeopardized by a hard incompatibilist conviction. The only aspect of forgiveness that is undercut by hard incompatibilism is the willingness to disregard deserved blame or punishment. Having relinquished the belief in moral responsibility, however, the hard incompatibilist no longer needs the willingness to overlook deserved blame and punishment to have good relationships.

One might contend that hard incompatibilism also threatens the self-directed attitudes of guilt and repentance. There is much at stake here, one could argue, since these attitudes are not only necessary for maintaining good relationships for agents prone to wrongdoing, but are also required for sustaining their moral integrity. Without guilt and repentance, such an agent would not only be incapable of restoring relationships damaged because he has done wrong, but he would also be kept from restoring his moral integrity. For other than the attitudes of guilt and repentance we have no psychological mechanisms that can play these roles. But hard incompatibilism would seem to jeopardize guilt because it essentially involves a belief that one is blameworthy for something one has done. And if guilt is undermined by hard incompatibilism, the attitude of repentance might also be threatened, for it could well be that feeling guilty is required for motivating repentance. But suppose that you perpetrate some wrongdoing, but because you endorse hard incompatibilism, you deny that you are blameworthy. Instead, you agree that you have done wrong, you feel sad that you were the agent of wrongdoing, you deeply regret what you have done (Waller 1990). Also, because you are committed to doing what is right and to moral advancement, you resolve to forbear from wrongdoing of this kind in the future, and you seek the help of others in sustaining your resolve. None of this is threatened by hard incompatibilism.

Gratitude might well presuppose that the person to whom one is grateful is morally responsible for a beneficial act, and for this reason hard incompatibilism would imperil gratitude. Still, certain aspects of this attitude would be unaffected, and these aspects can play the role gratitude as a whole has in good relationships. Gratitude involves, first of all, thankfulness toward someone who has acted beneficially. True, being thankful toward someone often involves the belief that she is praiseworthy for an action. But at the same time one can also be thankful to a pet or a small child for some kindness, even though in these cases one does not believe that the agent is morally responsible. Given hard incompatibilism, the aspect of thankfulness could be retained even if the presupposition of praiseworthiness is relinquished. Gratitude also typically involves joy occasioned by the beneficent act of another. But hard incompatibilism fully harmonizes with being joyful and expressing joy when others are considerate or generous on one's behalf. Such expression of joy can bring about the sense of harmony and goodwill often occasioned by gratitude, and so in this respect hard incompatibilism is not at a disadvantage.

Is mature love endangered by hard incompatibilism? Consider first whether loving someone requires that she be free in the sense required for moral responsibility. Parents love their children rarely, if ever, because they possess this sort of free will, or because they choose to do what is right by free will, or because they deserve to be loved because of their freely willed choices. Moreover, when adults love each other, it is also seldom, if at all, for such reasons. Undoubtedly the kinds of reasons we have for loving someone are complex. Besides moral character and behavior, considerations such as intelligence, appearance, style, and resemblance to others in one's personal history all might have a part. But let us suppose that moral character and action are especially important in occasioning, enriching, and sustaining love. Even if there is a significant feature of love that is a deserved response to moral character and action, it is unlikely that love would be undermined if one came to believe that these moral qualities did not come about through freely willed decision. Moral character and action are loveable whether or not they merit praise. Love of another involves, fundamentally, wishing for the other's good, taking on her aims and desires, and a desire to be together with her. Hard incompatibilism threatens none of this.

One might argue that we very much want to be loved by others as a result of their free will—we want freely willed love. Against this, the love parents have for their children is typically engendered independently of the parents' will, and we do not find this love deficient. Kane agrees with this claim about parental love, and with a similar view about romantic love, but he nevertheless contends that there is a kind of love we want of which we would feel deprived if we knew that factors beyond the other's control determined it (Kane 1996a: 88; similar claims are made by G. Strawson in 1986: 309 and by W. S. Anglin: 20). The plausibility of this view might be enhanced by reflecting on how you would feel if you found out that someone you love was causally determined to love you by a benevolent manipulator.

Setting aside *free* will for now, when does the will play a role in producing love for another at all? When an intimate relationship is deteriorating, people sometimes make a decision to try to restore the love they once felt for each other. When a student finds herself at odds with a roommate from the outset, she may decide to attempt nevertheless to form an emotional bond. Or when one's marriage is arranged, one may choose to do whatever one can to love one's spouse. But first of all, in such situations we might want the other person to make a decision to love, but it is not clear that we would have reason to want the decision to be freely willed in the sense required for moral responsibility. A decision to love on the part of another might greatly enhance one's personal life, but it is not clear what value the decision's being free and therefore praiseworthy would supply in addition. Second, although under these kinds of circumstances we might desire that the other make a decision to love, we would typically prefer love that was not mediated by a decision. This is true not only when romantic love is at issue—when it is manifestly obvious—but also for friendships and for love between parents and children.

Suppose Kane's view could be defended, and we do want love that is freely willed in the sense required for moral responsibility. If we indeed desire love of this kind, then we desire a kind of love that is impossible if hard incompatibilism is true. Still, the kinds of love that are invulnerable to hard incompatibilism are surely sufficient for good relationships. If we can aspire to the sort of love parents typically have toward children, or the kind romantic lovers ideally have toward one another, or the type shared by friends who are immediately attracted to one another, and whose relationship is deepened by their interactions, then the possibility of fulfillment in personal relationships is far from undermined.

Hard incompatibilism, therefore, endangers neither relationships with others nor personal integrity. It might well jeopardize certain attitudes that typically have a role in these domains. Indignation and guilt would likely be theoretically irrational for a hard incompatibilist. But such attitudes are either not essential to good relationships, or they have analogues that could play the same role they typically have. Moreover, love—the reactive attitude most essential to good personal relationships—is not clearly threatened by hard incompatibilism at all.

5. THE BENEFITS OF HARD INCOMPATIBILISM

Furthermore, hard incompatibilism holds out the promise of substantial benefits for human life. Of all the attitudes associated with moral responsibility, anger seems most closely connected with it. It is significant that discussions about moral responsibility typically focus not on how we should regard morally exemplary agents, but rather on how we should consider those that are morally offensive. The kinds of cases most often employed in producing a strong conviction of moral responsibility feature especially malevolent actions, and the sense of moral responsibility evoked typically involves sympathetic anger. It may be, then, that our attachment to moral responsibility derives in part from the role of anger in our emotional lives, and perhaps we feel hard incompatibilism poses a serious threat because it challenges the rationality of anger.

The type of anger at issue is directed toward someone who is believed to have done wrong. Let us call this attitude *moral anger*. Not all anger is moral anger. One type of nonmoral anger is directed at someone because his abilities in some respect are lacking or because he has performed badly under some circumstance. Sometimes we are angry with machines for malfunctioning. On occasion our anger has no object. But still, by far most human anger is moral anger.

Moral anger forms an important part of the moral life as we ordinarily conceive it. Anger motivates us to resist oppression, injustice, and abuse. But at the same time expressions of moral anger frequently have harmful effects, and they fail to contribute to the well being of those against whom they are directed. Often expressions of moral anger are intended to cause physical or emotional pain. As a result, moral anger tends to damage or destroy relationships. In extreme cases, it can motivate people to torture and kill.

The sense that expressions of moral anger can be damaging gives rise to a robust demand that they be morally justified when they occur. The demand to morally justify behavior that is harmful to others is always strong, and expressions of moral anger are typically harmful to others. Moreover, this demand is made more pressing by the fact that we are often attached to moral anger; we often in a sense enjoy displaying it, and this is partly why we want these displays to be morally justifiable. Most commonly we justify expressions of moral anger by arguing that wrongdoers fundamentally deserve to endure them. If hard incompatibilism is true, however, this justifying claim is false. But even if we knew it was false, we might still have a strong interest in retaining the belief in moral responsibility to satisfy our need to justify expressions of moral anger.

Accepting hard incompatibilism is not likely to modify human psychology so that anger is no longer a problem for us. Nevertheless, anger is often nourished by the presupposition that its object is blameworthy for wrongdoing. Destructive anger in relationships is nurtured by the belief that the other deserves blame for immoral behavior. The anger that fuels many ethnic conflicts often derives from the conviction that a group of people deserves blame for some past evil. Hard incompatibilism advocates relinquishing these anger-sustaining beliefs because they are false, and as a result the anger might be weakened, and its expressions curtailed.

Would the benefits that result if anger were reduced in this way outweigh the losses? Moral anger does indeed motivate us to oppose wrongdoing. But even when the assumption that wrongdoers are blameworthy is withdrawn for hard incompatibilist reasons, the conviction that they have in fact done wrong could legitimately survive. Such a moral conviction could still engender a strong resolve to resist oppression, injustice, and abuse. Perhaps, then, the hard incompatibilist could retain the benefits that moral anger can also produce, while diminishing its destructive consequences.

CHAPTER 22

FREE WILL, FUNDAMENTAL DUALISM, AND THE CENTRALITY OF ILLUSION

SAUL SMILANSKY

THIS chapter presents, in outline, a novel position on the issue of free will and compares this position to other more familiar ones. It consists of two radical proposals, summarizing the main claims that I make in *Free Will and Illusion* (Smilansky 2000). The complexity of both the free will problem and my claims, and the fact that the latter appear at late stages of the complex train of arguments on the issue, mean that this brief essay is necessarily sketchy.

Part 1 presents, in a way that should not be controversial, the three questions composing the issue of free will and then briefly states reasons that libertarian free will is impossible, and hence reasons that we need to be concerned with compatibilism and hard determinism. Part 2 sets out the first of the two radical proposals just mentioned, a *Fundamental Dualism* according to which we have to be both compatibilists and hard determinists. Part 3 presents the second proposal, *Illusionism*, which claims that illusion on free will is morally necessary.

1. PRELIMINARIES

I believe that the best way to understand the problem of free will is as a conjunction of three questions:

1. Is there libertarian free will? This can be called the libertarian Coherence or Existence Question. Libertarians of course think that there is libertarian free will, compatibilists (typically) and hard determinists disagree. This first question is metaphysical or ontological, or perhaps logical.
2. If there is no libertarian free will, are we still in a reasonably good moral condition? This can be called the Compatibility Question; namely, are moral responsibility and related notions compatible with determinism (or with the absence of libertarian free will irrespective of determinism)? Compatibilism and hard determinism are opponents on the Compatibility Question. This question, in my opinion, is mostly ethical. The first proposal that I offer, Fundamental Dualism, relates to this second question, that of compatibility
3. I offer pessimistic answers to the first two questions. In response to question 1, I claim that there is no libertarian free will, and in response to question 2, that compatibilism is insufficient. This leads to a third question: What are the consequences of the undoing of *both* libertarianism and (in part) compatibilism? I call this the Consequences Question, and its nature turns out to be complex. My second proposal, Illusionism on free will, relates to this third question of consequences.

1.1. Why Not Libertarian Free Will?

The most ambitious conception of free will, commonly called *libertarian free will*, is the natural place to start exploring the issue of free will. For, as we have seen, if we have libertarian free will, then the free will problem is in effect solved—the Compatibility Question and the Consequences Question become unimportant. However, I believe that libertarian free will is impossible. The case against libertarian free will has already been well stated, and I have nothing substantially original to say about it (see, for example, G. Strawson 1994a and Strawson's essay in this volume, ch. 19; compare Smilansky 2000: ch. 4; also see the second half of van Inwagen's essay in this volume, ch. 7).

The reason that I believe that libertarian free will is impossible, in a nutshell, is that the conditions required by an ethically satisfying sense of libertarian free will, which would give us anything beyond sophisticated formulations of compatibilism, are self-contradictory and hence cannot be met. This is true irrespective of determinism or causality. Attributing moral worth to a person for her decision or action requires that it follow from what she is, morally. The decision or action cannot be produced by a random occurrence and count morally. We might think that two different decisions or actions can follow from a person, but *which* of them does, for instance, in the case of a decision to steal or not to steal, again cannot be random but needs to follow from what she is, morally.[1] But what a person is, morally, cannot be under her control. We might think that such control is possible if she *creates herself*, but then it is the early self that creates a later self, leading to vicious infinite regress. The libertarian project was a worthwhile attempt: it was supposed to allow a deep moral connection between a given act and the person, and yet not fall into being merely an unfolding of the arbitrarily given, whether determined or random. But it is not possible to find any way in which this can be done.

Libertarians will not of course be satisfied with this cursory treatment. For discussions of continuing attempts to make sense of libertarian free will, see the essays in this volume by O'Connor, Clarke, Ginet, and Kane (chs. 15, 16, 17, and 18, respectively). I am merely expressing here my conviction that these efforts to defend libertarianism cannot succeed and my reasons for this conviction. We shall proceed on the assumption that the conviction is correct from this point onward, and ask what the nonexistence of libertarian free will means.

2. THE FIRST PROPOSAL: THE FUNDAMENTAL DUALISM

2.1. The Assumption of Monism

It seems to me that a harmful Assumption of Monism has seriously impaired the debate about free will at this point, and this Assumption of Monism helps explain why an explicit dualism such as I am presenting has not been previously developed. The Assumption of Monism is the assumption that on the Compatibility Question (question #2 of the three I listed) one must affirm compatibilism or incompatibilism. In fact, there is no conceptual basis whatsoever for thinking that the Assumption of Monism is necessary. Compatibilism and incompatibilism are indeed logically inconsistent, but it is possible to hold a mixed, intermediate position that is not fully consistent with either. The Compatibility Question might be answered in a yes-*and*-no fashion, for there is no conceptual reason why it should not be the case that certain forms of moral responsibility require libertarian free will while other forms could be sustained without it. There is nothing to prevent incompatibilists and compatibilists from insisting that *real* moral responsibility does, or does not, require libertarian free will. But their case must be made in ethical terms, and it may well turn out that there is no single or exhaustive notion of moral responsibility.[2]

2.1.1. *An Economy of Intuitions*

Recognizing and rejecting the Assumption of Monism allows us to stay close to the deepest intuitions on the free will issue. The intuitive attraction of the Assumption of Monism is great, but once we cross this "intuitive Rubicon," we see that its parsimony is nothing but false economy. A true "economy of intuitions" cannot *afford* to sacrifice the strength of either our compatibilist or incompatibilist instincts, on the Compatibility Question. The initially counterintuitive step of rejecting the Assumption of Monism thus allows us to proceed along a new path that ultimately runs closer to the intuitive field than do either of the conventional monisms.

2.2. Why Not Compatibilism?

I will now say something about why I think that compatibilism, its partial validity notwithstanding, is grimly insufficient. First, compatibilism is a widely prevalent view, and hence it is necessary for me to show its inadequacy in order to defend my first proposal of Fundamental Dualism—the proposal that we should be, in a sense, both compatibilists and hard determinists. Second, I need to combat the complacency that compatibilism encourages if my second proposal of Illusionism is to be motivated.

We can make sense of the notion of autonomy or self-determination on the compatibilist level but, if there is no libertarian free will, no one can be ultimately in control, ultimately responsible, for this self and its determinations (on this topic, compare the essays in this volume by Strawson and Kane, chs. 19 and 18, respectively). *Everything* that takes place on the compatibilist level becomes on the ultimate hard determinist level "what was merely *there*," ultimately deriving from causes beyond the control of the participants. If people lack libertarian free will, their identity and actions flow from circumstances beyond their control. To a certain extent, people can change their character, but that which does or does not change remains itself a result of something. There is always a situation in which the self-creating person could not have created herself but was just what she was, as it were, "given." Being the sort of person one is and having the desires and beliefs one has, are ultimately something one cannot control, which cannot be one's fault; it is one's luck. And one's life, and everything one does, is an unfolding of this. Let us call this the "ultimate perspective," which connects to hard determinism, and contrast it with the "compatibilist perspective," which takes the person as a "given" and enquires about her various desires, choices, and actions.

Consider the following quotation from a compatibilist:

> The incoherence of the libertarian conception of moral responsibility arises from the fact that it requires not only authorship of the action, but also, in a sense, authorship of one's self, or of one's character. As was shown, this requirement is unintelligible because it leads to an infinite regress. The way out of this regress is *simply to drop* the second-order authorship requirement, which is what has been done here. (Vuoso 1987: 1681) [my emphasis]

The difficulty is that there is an *ethical basis* for the incompatibilist ("second-order authorship") requirement, and, even if it cannot be fulfilled, the idea of "simply dropping it" masks how *problematic* the result may be in terms of fairness and justice. The fact remains that if there is no libertarian free will, a person being punished for her determined but compatibilist-free actions *may suffer justly* in compatibilist terms for what is ultimately her luck. What follows from being what she is, was ultimately beyond her control, a state that she had no real opportunity to alter, hence neither her responsibility nor her fault.[3]

A similar criticism applies to other moral and nonmoral ways of perceiving and treating people. The compatibilist cannot maintain the libertarian-based view of moral worth or of the grounds for respect; what she has to offer is a shallower sort of meaning and justification for such notions. These two charges—of shallowness, and of a complacent compliance with the injustice of not acknowledging lack of fairness and desert (and in particular ultimate-level victimization)—form the backbone of my case against compatibilism. (Compare Wiggins 1973; Berlin 1980; G. Strawson 1986; Kane 1996a: chs. 2 and 6; Smilansky 2000: chs. 3 and 6.)

2.3. Why Not Hard Determinism?

If there is no libertarian free will and compatibilism is insufficient, should we not then opt for hard determinism, which denies the reality of free will and moral responsibility in any sense? In previous writings (for example, Smilansky 2000: ch. 3) I have favored certain hard determinist intuitions, along the lines of the previous section of this chapter, but I do not think we can go all the way with hard determinism either. Important distinctions made in terms of compatibilist free will need to be retained as well if we are to do justice to morally required "forms of life." These distinctions would be important even in a determined world, and they have crucial (nonconsequentialist) ethical significance. For example, the kleptomaniac and the alcoholic differ from the common thief and common drinker in the deficiency of their capacity for local reflective control over their actions (see, for example, Glover 1970; Fischer 1994). Here everyone should agree. But the point worth adding is that such differences are often morally significant.

A central concept in the free will problem is that of desert, and doing justice to this concept is the greatest challenge facing the compatibilist. For it seems that if people are in the end ultimately just arbitrarily "given" and have no ultimate control over the sources of their behavior, then they cannot truly deserve and, for example, merit no blame. This in any case is how a hard determinist would reason. But I think that this is too quick a judgment, and that we can defend a compatibilist-level sense even of desert. Consider the following:

Case of the Lazy Waiter

Take the example of a waiter working in a cafe. He is young and healthy, his pay is reasonable, the hours not too long. There is also a shortage of waiters, so he may feel reasonably certain that he can keep the job as long as he wishes. In short, our waiter has an agreeable job. Part of his earnings depend on tips, and let us assume that the level of tips is directly related to how he serves his customers. This waiter, however, usually does the minimum, is slow and inattentive to the customers, and makes little effort to be helpful or pleasant. There is nothing extreme in his behavior or in the motivation behind it, and he is quite capable of behaving differently, for example when his relatives come to the cafe or when a customer known to be particularly generous appears. But normally he is prepared to make no more than the very minimal effort required.

It seems to me that there is nothing wrong with a situation in which part of the waiter's pay depends on the tips of reasonable customers, and it is perfectly acceptable for those who have been badly served to make him "pay" for exercising his freedom, by reducing his tip. We can see from his varying daily behavior that it is within his control, and *no* deep moral concern is aroused if he receives part of his pay in accordance with his choices. He does not *deserve* the full tip. The intuitive strength of the compatibilist perspective in such a case does not seem to depend on actually seeing the waiter benefit from his laziness; it suffices that such behavior in normal cases is up to the person in question in any compatibilist sense that seems relevant. Moreover, if another waiter is more attentive but it is stipulated that tips cannot vary, then we may want to say that the effort-making waiter is not getting what he deserves.

This is not to deny that in many cases complex factors make it difficult to agree with compatibilist justice. Particularly with extremes of environmental deprivation, or when people's negative behavior does not seem to serve any obvious purpose, the reasons why some people make an effort and others do not will cause us to mitigate our judgment of people. Cases such as the lazy waiter, however, show that there is a legitimate compatibilist basis for talk about desert and justice.

In certain cases the compatibilist perspective is morally salient: the "givenness" of the initial motivation set is not so morally worrisome as long as the person can evaluate it and choose as he wishes. Respect for persons can be satisfied if they get the life they reflectively want in conditions of opportunity for the free exercise of compatibilist control.

We want to be members of a Community of Responsibility where our choices will determine the moral attitude we receive, with the accompanying possibility of being morally excused when our actions are not within our reflective control, for instance, when they result from a brain tumor. The exceptions and excuses commonly presented by compatibilism should continue to carry weight. For if people are to be respected, their nature as purposive agents capable and desirous of choice needs to be catered to. We have to *enable* people to live as responsible beings in the Community of Responsibility, to live lives based largely on their choices, to note and give them *credit* for their good actions, and to take account of situations in which they *lacked* the abilities, capacities, and opportunities to choose freely and are therefore not responsible in the compatibilist sense. (For an elaboration of the case for compatibilism and against hard determinism, see Smilansky 2000: ch. 5 and section 6.1.)

2.4. The Joint Perspective

The case for a Fundamental Dualism on the Compatibility Question follows from the partial validity of both compatibilism and hard determinism or, in what amounts to the same thing, from the partial inadequacy of both.

Many of the practices of a community based on compatibilist distinctions, a Community of Responsibility, would be *in one way* unjust, owing to the absence of libertarian free will, which implies that our actions are on the ultimate level not up to us. To hold us responsible for them is, therefore, in one deep sense morally arbitrary. Proper respect for persons requires that this be acknowledged. Nevertheless, working according to compatibilist distinctions might be just *in another way*, because they correspond to a sense of being up to us, which exists in many normal situations, but not in cases such as kleptomania or addiction. It would be unjust to treat these different cases in the same way. To *fail* to create a Community of Responsibility is also in one sense to fail to create a feasable nonarbitrary moral order, hence to fail to show the proper respect for persons. There is thus a basis for working with compatibilist notions of fault and moral responsibility, based on local compatibilist-level control, even though we lack the sort of deep grounding in the "ultimately guilty self" that libertarian free will was thought to provide. Moreover, we are morally required to work in this way. But doing so has often a "hard determinist" moral price in terms of unfairness and injustice. We must recognize both the frequent need to be compatibilists and the need to confront that price.

The immediate reaction of both compatibilists and hard determinists to such a dualistic account is likely to involve an attempt to discredit the other side. "Ultimate" hard determinist injustice does not matter, the compatibilist might say. After all, you yourself tend to admit that we can distinguish between the guilty and the innocent, and meet common intuitions about the way to treat various situations. Why care about "ultimate fantasies" when, if we only remain on the compatibilist level, we can see that people can have control of their lives, reform and even partly create themselves, and behave responsibly? The hard determinist is likely to attack my position from the other side, saying that all talk about moral distinctions and about desert is groundless. Do I not myself admit that everyone is not ultimately responsible for being whoever he or she happens to be and for the actions that result from this? What sort of control is it that is merely an unfolding of preset factors?

Both sets of arguments have a certain strength, which is why I think that any "monistic" position is inadequate. However, once we make a conscious attempt to rid our minds of the Assumption of Monism, we begin to see that there are aspects of the compatibilist case that the hard determinist cannot plausibly deny; and similarly, with the hard determinist case for the compatibilist. Since persons tend to be immediately inclined in one way or the other, and to be overly impressed with the side they are on, they will have to work on themselves *in order to see* the side they are blind to. One has to try to *conquer* one's blind side.

However deeply we might feel that all people are ultimately innocent, it is unconvincing to deny the difference between the control possessed by the common thief and that of the kleptomaniac, and to ignore the moral inadequacy of social institutions that would fail to take account of this difference. We have an intimate experience of control (or its lack). If a man believes that he is Napoleon, then he is deluded, and his belief is *false*. But a woman's belief that her decision to see a movie and not a play is up to her is, even in a deterministic world, well founded on the compatibilist level. True, she did not ultimately create the sources of her motivation, and this hard determinist insight is sometimes important. But her sense of local control is *not* illusory, although it is only part of the truth about her state. Irrespective of the absence of libertarian free-will, the kleptomaniac is simply not in a condition for membership in a Community of Responsibility in which most people, having the required control, *can be*, and *would want to be* members. The eradication of free will-related distinctions does not make the hard determinist more humane and compassionate, but rather morally blind and a danger to the conditions for a civilized, sensitive moral environment. We must take account of such distinctions and maintain the Community of Responsibility, in order to respect persons. That hard determinists are indifferent to such distinctions and ethical imperatives is morally outrageous.

Similarly, once we grant the compatibilist that his distinctions have *some* foundation and are partly morally required, there is no further reason to go the *whole* way with him. There is no reason to claim that the absence of libertarian free will is of no great moral significance and moreover to deny the fact that without libertarian free will even a vicious and compatibilistically free criminal who is being punished is in some important sense a victim of his circumstances. If we reflect upon the fact that many people are made to undergo acute misery while the fact that they have developed into criminals is ultimately beyond their control, it is hard to dismiss this matter in the way that compatibilists are wont to do. Similarly, any favorable compatibilist appreciation of persons is necessarily shallow for, in the end, it rests upon factors not under the person's control. One chooses and acts, but this follows from who one is, ultimately as a "given." Any factor for which one is appreciated, praised, or even loved is ultimately one's luck. That compatibilists are indifferent to such ultimate arbitrariness, shallowness, and injustice is morally outrageous.

I would emphasize that one need not follow my particular sort of dualism zealously: other varieties can be imagined, varieties that defend the compatibilist and hard determinist perspectives in somewhat different ways than mine. My main aim has been to illustrate the *possibility* of working within a dualistic framework, and even of looking at the same act or the same agent in dualistic ways. In fact, since the compatibilist and hard determinist cases have been well presented before, the point I would most like to stress is that we need to try out ways of combining them. We must overcome the temptation to say that there are two contrasting ways of looking at the Compatibility Question, and that is that. It is not as though we are *missing* something in order to appreciate that either the compatibilist or the hard determinist perspective is, in the end, the true one. Rather, to be entirely blind to the virtues of *either* of these two perspectives is to fail to see the case on free will. (For an elaboration of this joint "dualistic" position on the Compatibility Question, see Smilansky 2000: sections 6.1 and 6.4.)

3. Second Proposal: Illusionism

The Fundamental Dualism, according to which we must be both compatibilists and hard determinists, was my first proposal. Now let us move on to the second. Illusion, I claim, is the vital but neglected *key* to the free will problem. I am not saying that we need to induce illusory beliefs concerning free will or can live with beliefs that we fully realize are illusory. Both of these positions would be highly implausible. Rather, I maintain that illusory beliefs are in place, and that the role they play is largely positive.

3.1. The Problem: Examples

In order to see how illusion is crucial, we must deepen our understanding of the difficulties that (would) prevail without it. Why is there an urgent problem requiring illusion? I will give a number of illustrations.

3.1.1. *The Question of Innocence*

The danger concerning respect for moral innocence is serious. Even in a world without libertarian free will, the idea that only those who deserve to be punished in light of their free actions may be punished is a condition for any civilized moral order (see Hart 1970). "Punishment" of those who did not perform the act for which they are "punished" or did so act but lacked control over their action in any sense is the paradigm of injustice. Yet while the justification for these values does not require libertarian free will, in practice they might be at risk were the lack of libertarian free will internalized. Consider Anscombe's passionate remark, "[I]f someone really thinks, *in advance*, that it is open to question whether such an action as procuring the judicial execution of the innocent should be quite excluded from consideration—I do not want to argue with him; he shows a corrupt mind" (Anscombe 1981: 40). Surely, if a moral system that seeks to preserve and guard vigilantly the common conception of innocence is to function well, such a sentiment should be prevalent, almost instinctive. But if this is to be so, the worst thing one could do would be to point out that, ultimately, none of this makes sense—because the "guilty" are, ultimately, no more guilty than others.

3.1.2. *The Ultimate Conclusion as a Practical Threat to the Taking of Responsibility*

We cannot tell people that they must behave in a certain way, that it is morally crucial that they do so, but then, if they do not, turn and say that this is (in every case) excusable, given whatever hereditary and environmental influences have operated in their formation. Psychologically, the attribution of responsibility to people so that they may be said to justly deserve gain or loss for their actions requires (even *after* the act) the absence of the notion that the act is an unavoidable outcome of the way things were—that it is ultimately beyond anyone's control. Morality has a crucial interest in confronting what can be called the *Present Danger of the Future Retrospective Excuse*, and in restricting the influence of the ultimate hard determinist level. To put it bluntly: people as a rule ought not to be fully aware of the ultimate inevitability of what they have done, for this will affect the way in which they hold themselves responsible. The knowledge that such an escape from responsibility, based on retrospective ultimate judgment, will be available in the *future* is likely to affect the *present* view and hence cannot be fully admitted even in its *retrospective* form. We often want a person to blame himself, feel guilty, and even see that he deserves to be punished. Such a person is not likely to do all this if he internalizes the ultimate hard determinist perspective, according to which in the actual world nothing else could in fact have occurred—he could not strictly have done anything else except what he did do.

3.1.3. *A Sense of Value*

From the ultimate hard determinist perspective, all people—whatever their efforts and sacrifices—are morally equal, that is, there cannot be any means of generating a "real" moral value. There is a sense in which our notion of moral self-respect, which is intimately connected with our view of our choices, actions, and achievements, withers when we accept the ultimate perspective. From the latter any sense of moral achievement disappears, as even the actions of the "moral hero" are simply an unfolding of what he happens to be. *No matter how devoted he has been, how much effort he has put in, how many tears he has shed, how many sacrifices he has willingly suffered.* True appreciation, deeply *attributing* matters to someone in a sense that will make him worthy, is impossible if we regard him and his efforts as merely determined products. All that the compatibilist can offer us in terms of value, although important in itself, is meager protection from the cold wind that attacks us when we come close to reaching the luck-imbued ultimate level. There is an obvious practical danger here to our moral motivation, which can be named the "*Danger of Worthlessness.*" But the concern is not only to get people to function adequately as moral agents; it also has to do with the very meaning we can find in our lives. (See Nagel 1986: ch. 7; Kane 1996a: ch. 6; Smilansky 2000: sections 6.4, 7.3, 7.4 and chs. 8 and 9.)

3.1.4. *Remorse and Integrity*

If a person takes the ultimate hard determinist perspective, it is not only others who seem to disappear as moral agents—but in some way the person herself is reduced. In retrospect, her life, her decisions, that which is most truly her own, appear to be accidental phenomena of which she is the mere *vehicle*, and to feel moral remorse for any of it, by way of truly *owning up* to it, seems in some deep sense to be misguided. Feelings of remorse are inherently tied to the person's self-perception as a morally responsible agent (see G. Taylor 1985: 107).

It sharpens our focus not to dwell upon those happy to escape accountability, but rather upon those who have good will. Here we confront a third "danger," which can be termed the *Danger of Retrospective Dissociation.* This is the difficulty of feeling truly responsible after action. One can surrender the right to make use of the "ultimate level excuse" for normative reasons and yet perhaps not be able to hold oneself truly responsible (for instance, to engage in remorse), if one has no grain of belief in something like libertarian free will. One can, after all, accept responsibility for matters that were not up to one in any sense, such as for the actions of others, for normative reasons. But here we are dealing with a different matter: not with the acceptance of responsibility in the sense of "willingness to pay," but rather with feeling *compunction*. Compunction seems conceptually problematic and psychologically dubious when it concerns matters that, it is understood, ultimately one could not in fact help doing. But such genuine feelings of responsibility (and not mere acceptance of it) are crucial to being responsible selves! We see here the *intimacy* of the connection between moral and personal integrity and illusion about free will; hence the danger of realizing the truth also looms large. (For an elaboration of the "problem" requiring illusion, see Smilansky 2000: chs. 7–9.)

3.2. Illusion as a Solution

3.2.1. *What Is Illusionism?*

Illusionism is the position that illusion often has a *large and positive role* to play in the issue of free will. In arguing for the importance of illusion, I claim that we can see why it is useful, that it is a reality, and why by and large it ought to continue to be so. Illusory beliefs are in place concerning free will and moral responsibility, and the role they play is largely positive. Humanity is fortunately deceived on the free will issue, and this seems to be a condition of civilized morality and personal value.

The sense of "illusion" that I am using combines the falsity of a belief with some motivated role in forming and maintaining that belief—as in standard cases of wishful thinking or self-deception. However, it suffices that the beliefs are false and that this conclusion would be resisted were a challenge to arise. It is not necessary for us to determine the current level of illusion concerning free will.

The importance of illusion flows in two ways from the basic structure of the free will problem: first, indirectly, from the Fundamental Dualism on the Compatibility Question—the partial and varying validity of *both* compatibilism and hard determinism.[4] Second, illusion flows directly and more deeply from the meaning of the very absence of the grounding that libertarian free will was thought to provide.[5] We cannot live adequately with the *dissonance* of the two valid sides of the Fundamental Dualism, nor with a complete awareness of the deep *signifi-*

cance of the absence of libertarian free will. We have to face the fact that there are basic beliefs that morally ought not to be abandoned, although they might destroy each other, or are even partly based on incoherent conceptions. At least for most people, these beliefs are potentially in need of motivated mediation and defense by illusion, ranging from wishful thinking to self-deception.[6]

3.2.2. *Why Is There a Need for Illusion?*

Our previous results supply the resources for an answer to this question. Let us concentrate, for the sake of simplicity, on the concerns of a strictly "practical" point of view: if the basic ethical concern for free will is taken seriously, and the absence of libertarian free will is to some extent realized, then the ultimate-level (that is, hard determinist) conclusion might tend to dominate in practice. This might very well pose a danger—especially because of the human tendency to oversimplify—to the "common form of life" and to the strict observance of the corresponding moral order. Many people would find it hard to think that the partial compatibilist truth *matters*, as in fact it ethically does, if they realized the sense in which both the compatibilistically free and unfree were merely performing according to their mold. And this might lead them to succumb to "pragmatic" consequentialist temptations, or unprincipled nihilism. The ultimate hard determinist perspective does not leave sufficient moral and psychological "space" for compatibilistically defensible reactive attitudes and moral order. The fragile compatibilist-level plants need to be defended from the chill of the ultimate perspective in the hothouse of illusion. *Only if we do not see people from the ultimate perspective can we live in a way that compatibilism affirms*—blaming, selectively excusing, respecting, being grateful, and the like.[7]

Within these parameters, there is a prima facie case for a large measure of motivated obscurity regarding the objections to libertarian free will: if libertarian assumptions *carry on their back* the compatibilist distinctions, which would not be adhered to sufficiently without them, an illusion that defends these libertarian assumptions seems to be just what we need. The ethical importance of the paradigm of free will and responsibility as a basis for desert should be taken very seriously. But the ultimate perspective threatens to *present* it as a farce, a mere game without foundation. Likewise with the crucial idea of a personal sense of value and appreciation that can be gained through our free actions: this is unlikely to be adequately maintained by individuals in their self-estimates, nor warmly and consistently projected by society. A broad loss of moral and personal confidence can be expected. The idea of action-based desert, true internal acceptance of responsibility, respect for the efforts and achievements of others, deep ethical appreciation, self-respect, excusing the innocent—all these and more are threatened by the "leveling" or homogenizing view arising from the ultimate perspective. Illusion is crucial in pragmatically safeguarding the compatibilistically defensible elements of the "common form of life." *Illusion is, by and large, a condition for the actual creation and maintenance of adequate moral and personal reality.*

3.2.3. *How Does Illusion Function?*

When illusion plays a role, things can, in practice, work out. Two schematic answers can be given: first, it may be suggested that significant realization of the absence of libertarian free will, and concern about ultimate-level injustice, for example, can remain more or less limited to part of the population, say, those more concerned with policy-making (the "elitist solution"). This maintains the widespread intuition that, for instance, punishing the innocent is an abomination whereas criminals deserve "to pay," while permitting the amelioration of treatment, resulting from the recognition by some that ultimately things are not morally that simple. Complex patterns of self-and-other deception emerge with elitist solutions. But, in addition to all the general practical and moral difficulties with elitist solutions, which we cannot consider here, elitism can in any case be only a partial solution concerning free will. For, in the light of the reasons that we have already seen, people not under illusion would have great difficulty in functioning.

The major solution will be one where, since two beliefs are vaguely but simultaneously held, yet commonly not set side by side (often, I claim, due to the presence of a motivated element), their contrary nature is not fully noticed. When acting in the light of compatibilist insights, we suspend the insights of the ultimate hard determinist perspective (of which we in any case are likely to be only dimly aware). We *keep ourselves* on the level of compatibilist distinctions about local control and do not ask ourselves about the deeper question of the "givenness" of our choosing self; resisting threats to our vague, tacit libertarian assumptions. As Bernard Williams put it, "To the extent that the institution of blame works coherently, it does so because it attempts less than morality would like it to do . . . [it] takes the agent together with his character, and does not raise questions about his freedom to have chosen some other character" (Williams 1986: 194). The result is not philosophically neat, but that, after all, is its merit: the original reality was that we face practical dangers if we try to make our (incoherent or contradictory) conceptions *too clear*, but that we ought not to give any of them up entirely. Illusion, in short, allows us to have "workable beliefs."

Moreover, even those elements of our self-understanding that are solely illusory (and not compatibilistically grounded reality that is merely assisted by illusion) may nevertheless be very important in themselves. Illusion not only helps to sustain independent reality, but also is *in itself* a sort of "reality," simply by virtue of its existence. The falseness of beliefs does not negate the fact that they exist for the believer. This is the way in which the illusory libertarian beliefs exist.

In addition to supporting the compatibilist nonillusory basis, illusion also *creates* a mental reality, such as a particular sense of worth, appreciation, and moral depth associated with belief in libertarian free will, which would not exist without it. The effects of this illusory "reality" are sometimes positive. In a number of ways, then, illusion serves a crucial *creative* function, which is a basis for social morality and personal self-appreciation, in support of the compatibilist forms and beyond them. (For an elaboration of illusion as "a solution," see Smilansky 2000: section 7.4 and ch. 8.)

4. CONCLUSION

There is no libertarian free will: people can have limited forms of local control over their actions, but not the deep form of libertarian free will. Whether determinism is completely true or not, we cannot make sense of the sort of constitutive self-transcendence that would provide grounding for the deep sense of moral responsibility that libertarian free will was thought to supply. Our common libertarian assumptions cannot be sustained. All our actions, however an internalized and complex a form they may take, are the result of what we are, ultimately beyond our control.

The implications of the absence of libertarian free will are complex, and the standard assumption of the debate, the Assumption of Monism according to which we must be either compatibilists or hard determinists, is false. We saw why "forms of life" based on the compatibilist distinctions about control are possible and morally required but are also superficial and deeply problematic in ethical and personal terms. I claimed that the most plausible approach to the Compatibility Question is a complex compromise, which I called "Fundamental Dualism." The idea that either compatibilism or hard determinism can be adequate on its own is untenable.

There is then partial nonillusory grounding for many of our central free will-related beliefs, reactions, and practices, even in a world without libertarian free will. But in various complex ways, we require illusion in order to bring forth and maintain them. Illusion is seen to flow from the basic structure of the free will issue, the absence of libertarian free will, and the Fundamental Dualism concerning the implications. Revealing the large and mostly positive role of illusion concerning free will not only teaches us a great deal about the free will issue itself but also posits illusion as a pivotal factor in human life.

NOTES

I am very grateful to Robert Kane, Tomis Kapitan, Iddo Landau, Paul Russell and Daniel Statman, for helpful comments on drafts of this essay.

1. For example, in Robert Kane's sophisticated form of libertarianism (Kane 1996a), the agent's character stimulates effort resulting in a choice. However, crucially, *whether* this effort bears fruit in a given direction (goes one way or another) is in fact arbitrary and not under the agent's control.

2. There are, of course, other possibilities. For example, Richard Double presents a meta-ethical skepticism in the free will context, which would preclude moral responsibility altogether (see Double 1991 and his essay in this volume, ch. 23). A less extreme position, which would also preclude the need for the dualism proposed here, is Ted Honderich's "attitudinal-emotionalism," whereby the free will issue is not a matter of true or false belief but of emotional attitudes. On a different level, one could opt for utilitarianism and forsake inherent concern with free will as, for example, a condition for praise or blame, but rather praise and blame for the sake of the consequences. These positions do not seem plausible to me, but this cannot be taken up here (on Honderich, see his essay in this volume; Smilansky 2000: 25–27; on utilitarianism in the free will context, see ibid.: 27–33).

3. Compatibilists may argue at this point that if libertarian free will is incoherent, then it is not "worth wanting" in the first place, and we need not make such a fuss about the absence of the impossible (for example, Dennett 1984; Wolf 1987: 59–60; Frankfurt 1988: 22–23). This, however, is a red herring. The various things that free will could make possible, if it could exist, such as deep senses of desert, worth, and justification *are* worth wanting. They remain worth wanting even if something that would be necessary in order to have them is not worth wanting because it cannot be coherently conceived. It is just this, the impossibility of the conditions for things that are so deeply worth wanting, which makes the realisation of the absence of libertarian free will so significant. (See Smilansky 2000: 48–50) There are of course many compatibilist positions that would try to resist my criticism, but I cannot refer to the immense literature here.

4. The partial validity of compatibilism does not reduce the need for illusion so much as it complicates it and adds to it. This follows from the need to guard the compatibilist concerns and distinctions, in light of the contrast and dissonance with the ultimate hard determinist perspective.

5. This means that the Fundamental Dualism leads to Illusionism, but Illusionism does not depend on the dualism. Even a hard determinist, if she is not implausibly optimistic, should recognize the general case for Illusionism.

6. I consider the possibility for exceptions, which I call "Unillusioned Moral Individuals" (UMIs), in Smilansky 2000: section 10.2. See also the related discussion of the problematic role of philosophers in Smilansky 2000: section 11.4.

7. A number of distinct alternative positions conflict with my claim for the positive necessity of illusion: Honderich (1988), Waller (1990), and Pereboom (1995) explored some of the less pessimistic implications of hard determinism (see the essays of Honderich, Pereboom, and Russell in this volume, chs. 20, 21, and 10 respectively). Bok (1998) made a similar sort of contribution, although she would not agree to being characterized as a hard determinist. I claim that the possibility of living without belief in the actual

existence of free will and moral responsibility has been shown to be unreal and, due to the partial viability of compatibilism, it is also unnecessary. There is no substitute for the paradigmatic ethical requirement for control and responsibility as the central basis for moral life, a civilized social order, and self-respect. There is still room for revision of the sort that "optimistic" hard determinists propose, but this, I claim, would be only on the margins of our lives and hence would not seriously affect my claims. More problematic for me is the sort of "no need to worry" position proposed by P. F. Strawson in the seminal essay "Freedom and Resentment" (1981, originally published 1962). Strawson thinks that our natural "reactive attitudes" guarantee the status quo; there would thus be no need for illusion (see the discussion of his view in the essay by Haji in this volume, ch. 9). For all the importance of our natural proneness to free-will-assuming reactions, I think that there would be considerable room for worry if people became aware of the absence of libertarian free will, which they may do. I discuss Strawson's position in detail in Smilansky (2000: ch. 9) and Smilansky (2001). There are many good discussions of P. F. Strawson's position: see, for example G. Strawson (1986: ch. 5); Watson (1987a); Klein (1990: ch. 6); Russell (1992; 1995: ch. 5); and Haji's essay in this collection, ch. 9.

CHAPTER 23

METAETHICS, METAPHILOSOPHY, AND FREE WILL SUBJECTIVISM

RICHARD DOUBLE

THIS essay has four main divisions. In section 1, I describe a view that I call *free will subjectivism*. I show how this view and the free will problem in general are related to metaethical objectivism and subjectivism, and how free will debates are influenced by debates over metaphilosophy—our views about the nature of philosophy. In section 2, I explicate my version of free will subjectivism, demonstrating its connection to metaethical subjectivism and metaphilosophy. In section 3, I show how my view differs from those of several prominent thinkers: Bruce Waller, B. F. Skinner, Daniel Dennett, Galen Strawson, Peter Strawson, Thomas Nagel, Peter Unger, and Ted Honderich. In section 4, I consider reasons that philosophers endorse the theories they do.

1. Free Will Subjectivism and Metaethical Subjectivism

Anyone who argues for the *actual existence* of moral responsibility must make plausible the existence of a variety of free choice strong enough to underpin moral responsibility. Anyone who claims to vindicate the *possibility* of moral responsibility must show that such a variety of free choice is possible. Although there are other things philosophers care about when discussing free will (dignity, autonomy, genuine creativity, worthiness of love and friendship—Kane 1996a: 81–89), "the fundamental motor of the free will debate is the worry about moral responsibility" (G. Strawson 1998: 746). A handy reminder of the fact that free will is supposed to sanction assignments of moral responsibility is to define "free will" (the "faculty" of making free choices) in terms of "moral responsibility." I define "free choice" as "whatever degree of freedom of choice that, all other factors being equal, is necessary and sufficient for moral responsibility." Other thinkers emphasize the connection between moral responsibility and free will by using the term "moral freedom." A third way to cast the free will problem as a moral problem eliminates the term "free will" altogether: We could pose the problem this way: "Is it morally permissible to hold (determined, undetermined, naturalistic, supernaturalistic) persons morally responsible?"

Holding persons morally responsible encompasses a range of behaviors: expressed positive and negative reactive attitudes, verbal recrimination, praise and blame, retributive punishment, and just-deserts rewards, all the way to torment in hell and bliss in heaven. Philosophers disagree over how much of that range moral responsibility includes. But, because even the mildest of the adverse behaviors harms persons, assigning moral responsibility serves as a justificatory mantra that turns otherwise immoral treatment into just-deserts goods. Because of this justificatory role, I take "moral responsibility" to be a moral concept.

Believing the free will issue is a moral problem carries a little-noted implication. We may submit free will theories to metalevel analysis just as we do to theories in normative ethics. Making objectively true claims about what sort of choices underpin moral responsibility requires metaethical objectivism, just as does making objectively true claims about consequentialism or deontologism. So, if the claims of, for example, the compatibilists and incompatibilists can take objective answers, then there can exist objective (existing beyond subjective attitudes and opinions of individuals or groups) moral facts that reveal what sort of choices are needed to underpin persons' moral responsibility. Thus, *if* there are no objective moral facts, as metaethical subjectivists such as A. J. Ayer (1952) and J. L. Mackie (1977) aver, then logically there are no such facts regarding moral responsibility. I call this position "free will subjectivism."

Free will subjectivism is like metaethical subjectivism in important ways. Metaethical subjectivism does not claim that "X is wrong" means "I or my society approve of X" (as Ayer 1952: 104 observes), but that judgments assigning moral characteristics cannot be objectively true. Similarly, free will subjectivism does not hold that "S is morally responsible" means "I or my society hold S morally responsible," but that judgments assigning moral responsibility cannot be objectively true.

If we accept free will subjectivism, we may elect to be vitally concerned with lower-level accounts of persons' free will and moral responsibility. Subjectivists can take free will theories as explicating our important feelings and attitudes about free will and moral responsibility, just as Hume and J. L. Mackie (1977) take seriously their substantive normative theories despite their subjectivist metaethics. Nonetheless, espousing free will subjectivism does not leave everything as is. Concluding that there are no objectively true statements that assign moral responsibility is important to philosophers who are concerned with reaching the most plausible overall worldview. Moreover, for many subjectivists, accepting the theory may modulate the stridency of their free will theorizing.

In addition, uncovering the ambiguity of talk about the *incompatibility* (or compatibility) of moral responsibility and determined or undetermined choices can liberate metaethical subjectivists to engage in free will theorizing. There are at least three relevant kinds of incompatibility: analytic, factual, and moral. Examples of each category follow: *analytic incompatibility*: "S is a bachelor" and "S is married." *Factual incompatibility*: "S is in New York" and "S is in the Pacific time-zone." *Moral incompatibility*: "S is cruel to animals" and "S is morally exemplary." In principle, philosophers who talk about the incompatibility of moral responsibility and determinism (or indeterminism) might mean any of these three.

Compatibilists who think that the free will problem can be settled by linguistic analysis of *can, could*, and *free*, represent the first view. Other philosophers apparently believe the compatibility issue is not analytic, but perhaps synthetic a priori. Note that if one sees the incompatibility or compatibility at stake in either of these two ways, one must consider assignments of moral responsibility to be capable of being true. So, if these two groups of thinkers accept my view that assignments of moral responsibility are moral claims, then they are committed to holding that an important class of moral claims is capable of being true, and, ipso facto, accept moral objectivism.

Things are different if one takes the incompatibility at stake as *moral incompatibility*. This would amount to saying, "It is morally wrong to hold determined (undetermined) persons morally responsible." Metaethical objectivists *could* assert this, but so could metaethical subjectivists. For example, the metaethical subjectivist Bruce Waller (see his *Freedom without Responsibility*, 1990) is a moral incompatibilist who is stridently opposed to holding naturalistic persons morally responsible, whether they are determined or not. His subjectivist metaethics prevents him from saying that "S is a naturalistic being" and "S is morally responsible" have contradictory truth-values, but Waller believes the two judgments are morally incompatible. This means that it is wrong to hold naturalistic persons morally responsible. Waller is passionately opposed to the practice of blame and provides moral reasons for thinking we ought not blame, while admitting his position has no other grounding than the way he (and other like-minded persons) feel. So, interpreting the incompatibility at stake as moral brings metaethical subjectivists into the free will debate.

Metaethical subjectivists can also enter the free will debate through what I call "metaphilosophies." By a "metaphilosophy" I mean a view of what philosophy is and what philosophers should try to accomplish by philosophizing (Double 1996a). The metaphilosophy I hold is *Philosophy as Worldview Construction*, specifically, *Philosophy as Continuous with Science*. The former tries to construct a view of reality that is most likely to be accurate given our most reliable sources of epistemic justification. The latter takes science as the best model for philosophical theory construction, using methods of scientific theory construction such as inference to the best explanation and Occam's Razor. Philosophy as Continuous with Science accepts science as a Sellarsian measure "of what is that it is, and of what is not that it is not." Philosophy as Continuous with Science is a posteriori and defeasible. If another method is better able to reach the most accurate worldview, then some other species of Worldview Construction such as *Philosophy as Phenomenology,* or *Philosophy as Mysticism* would be better.

Philosophy as Praxis sees philosophy as an instrument to improve the world, as exemplified in Marx's claim in his eleventh thesis against Feuerbach that *the point* of philosophy is not to *interpret* the world, but to *change* it (Feuer 1959: 245). There are two ways for Praxis metaphilosophy to influence one's reasoning concerning philosophical problems. First, a Praxis thinker might think that moral urgency justifies giving nonepistemically justifying, Praxis considerations an important role in the picture of the world we construct. Second, a Praxis thinker might bend the objectivist's vocabulary by portraying a subjective theory as an objective one, or "objective enough" to serve the purposes that unobtainable objectivist theories are designed to serve.

Exemplifying the first type of Praxis argument, the metaethical objectivist David Brink argues:

> If . . . rejection of moral realism would undermine the nature of existing practices and beliefs, then the metaphysical queerness of moral realism may seem a small price to pay to preserve these practices and beliefs. I am not claiming that the presumption in favor of moral realism could not be overturned on a posteriori metaphysical grounds. I am claiming only that we could not determine the appropriate reaction to the success of this (Mackie's, R. D.) meta-

physical argument until we determined, among other things, the strength of the presumption in favor of moral realism. (Brink 1989: 173–74)

Here Brink pits the Praxis desirability of believing in metaethical objectivism against the argument against objectivism from ontological simplicity provided by Mackie and concludes that our overall ontological picture should contain objective moral truths. This reasoning is similar to the sort William James allowed regarding the existence of God and libertarian free will. I reject this kind of Praxis argument because it assigns weight in ontological theory construction to a factor that even its proponents admit does not increase the probability that the hoped-for entities exist. I do not support this appeal to wishful thinking in constructing a worldview, although I admit that in dire enough cases it is forgivable or, arguably, even morally obligatory.[1]

Exemplifying the second kind of Praxis argument are philosophers whom Stephen Darwall (1996) calls "constructivists" and "practical-reasoning theorists," who believe they can underpin morality without including objective moral truths within our theoretical worldview. Hobbes, Kurt Baier (1958), and David Gauthier (1986) all claim that although moral truth is not waiting to be found, we can build contractual systems of ethics on top of an egoistic foundation that suffices to underpin normative ethics. Kant, John Rawls (1971), and Thomas Nagel (1970) all argue that there are purely logical constraints on practical reasoning that make moral claims objectively true. In my view, constructivism and practical-reasoning theories are manifestations of Praxis metaphilosophy. If one sees the point of moral philosophy as providing an appealing theory of normative ethics, then, given the difficulties with *finding* moral truths, it is natural to try to *construct* them.

I regard constructivists and practical-reasoning theorists as metaethical subjectivists, because they portray moral truth as dependent upon features of humans' social arrangements and their psychological states. In this sense, these theories are just as subjective as "projectionist" theories (Mackie 1977; Blackburn 1993). Constructivism regarding postulated entities in scientific theories has a name: "scientific instrumentalism," which is a variety of subjectivism (nonrealism). If moral truth is created by human conventions or the putative nature of human reason, then logically there is nothing outside of those conventions or our minds to serve as the truth conditions of realistic moral truths. As a Worldview metaphilosopher, I treat *realism* and *true* as univocal for the moral and the nonmoral domains. Worldview Construction demands a correspondence theory of truth for moral judgments, as it does for nonmoral claims. The most coherent moral system— and I deny that any moral system can be *very* coherent anyway—logically cannot be sufficient for objective moral truth. So the second Praxis argument fails also. Neither it nor the first argument can be adapted to provide epistemic justification for free will objectivism.

Nonetheless, Praxis free will theorists are not left out of substantive free will theorizing. When I propound free will subjectivism, I take myself to be doing metaphysics on a scientific model. I do *not* say, "It is useless to construct theories for use in criminal justice and everyday life." My point is theoretical, that the traditional theorists cannot claim to have objective truth on their side, just as utilitarians and Kantians cannot claim metaethical truth on their side if metaethical subjectivism is true. I therefore have no objection to Praxis theorizing in ethics and free will. I merely criticize traditional theorists who purport to provide the real thing, when the real thing turns out to be logically impossible. Let us not confuse the issues of what practices are the most beneficial and what is the most likely to be a true worldview. There are other prominent metaphilosophies,[2] but the major ones for the purposes of this chapter are Worldview Construction and Praxis.

2. My View Defended

I endorse top-down and bottom-up strategies to argue for free will subjectivism. The *top-down argument* uses two premises. The first premise is the doctrine of metaethical subjectivism, and the second is the claim that *free will*, defined in terms of moral responsibility, is a moral term. Although I find this a powerful argument with the advantage of revealing the connection between lower level theorizing in normative ethics and free will, the top-down argument is weakened by its controversial first premise. Although I believe the general philosophical case for metaethical subjectivism is strong and have argued for it at length (Double 1991: ch. 7), in this essay I shall not press the top-down argument. The *bottom-up argument* does not rely on metaethical subjectivism but argues that free will subjectivism is the best explanation for our logically conflicting intuitions regarding the claims of compatibilists and incompatibilists.

The bottom-up argument faces a broadly metaphilosophical preliminary objection. Free will objectivists can criticize my appeal to intuitions about moral responsibility, just as some metaethical objectivists look askance at using moral intuitions to criticize normative theories. I emphasize that I do not view our intuitions concerning whether a person would be morally responsible in a certain thought-experiment as infallible or even as having great epistemic weight, but simply as providing thoughtful judgments about responsibility. Just as I do not see how we could evaluate egoism or relativism without appealing to our intuitive judgments of their implications, I do not see how to evaluate theories of moral responsibility without appealing to our intuitions.

Free will subjectivism of the kind I defend in this chapter entails two unfamiliar views regarding the free will problem. The first view is *metacompatibilism*, the doctrine that regarding persons we believe to be determined, logically we may hold them morally responsible *despite* our belief that they are determined (as compatibilists might) *and* we may fully exonerate them *because* we think they are determined (as incompatibilists would) (Double 1991: ch. 6). The second view is that because free will subjectivism holds that persons' "being" morally responsible is simply a matter of what attitudes persons hold toward them, subjectivists commit no error when they decide to hold strong views about moral responsibility *despite* their belief in free will subjectivism *or* to hold mild views *because* they believe their views are only subjective. I call these two options "strident subjectivism" and "sheepish subjectivism." Free will subjectivists might be stridently in favor of holding persons responsible (perhaps Peter Strawson 1962 is close to this view) or stridently opposed to holding persons responsible, as Waller (1990) is. Subjectivists might be sheepish, given their belief that their opinions about the assignment of moral responsibility has no grounding beyond their own feelings. Subjectivists might also vacillate between endorsing responsibility and exonerating all persons of responsibility, as I do myself.

Strident and sheepish subjectivist views in the free will problem are parallel to the two stances metaethical subjectivists might take regarding normative ethics. Strident metaethical subjectivists make judgments in normative ethics with full force despite their metaethical beliefs. J. L. Mackie (1977) would be an example. Sheepish metaethical subjectivists would take their metaethical positions as reason to assert normative claims with modulated or even no force. Perhaps some of the twentieth-century logical positivists came close to this position.

To clarify the free will vocabulary I use and to begin the bottom-up argument, I offer a taxonomy of five theories rather than the traditional dichotomy of compatibilism and incompatibilism. I arrive at the first four by distinguishing between the positive and negative answers to two questions: *Can determined choices be free (underpin moral responsibility)?* and *Can undetermined choices be free (underpin moral responsibility)?* I reach free will subjectivism by considering the first four claims from the perspective of metaethical subjectivism.

Here are the idealized positive and negative theses of traditional incompatibilists and compatibilists:

(IN) *Incompatibilism's Negative Claim*: "Determined choices cannot be free."
(IP) *Incompatibilism's Positive Claim*: "Indeterminism (suitably located) within our choice-making process can give rise to, or at least be consistent with, free choice."
(CN) *Compatibilism's Negative Claim*: "Undetermined choices cannot be free."

(CP) *Compatibilism's Positive Claim*: "Under certain conditions, determined choices can be free."

Here are the logical relations that hold between these four claims on the assumption that "free choice" is a univocal and logically coherent concept. The incompatibilists' claims (IN) and (IP) are logically consistent, though not equivalent; the compatibilists' claims (CN) and (CP) are consistent though nonequivalent also. There are two pairs of contradictories, namely, the negative and the positive claims of the respective theorists ([IN] contradicts [CP], and [IP] contradicts [CN]). Because there are four statements, each of which may be viewed as being true or false, there are sixteen mathematically possible results; but given the assumption about the contradictories, we can extract only four different theories (table 23.1).

Even if we prefer one of the first two theories, we have to admit the conceptual possibility of the latter two. Peter Strawson (1962) calls the third theory "moral skepticism" but does not examine it in that article. Waller (1990) and Derk Pereboom (2000) endorse the third position without using my term for it. The closest to the fourth theory is Alfred Mele's (1995: 253) conjecture which he calls "agnostic autonomism." (See the essays by Pereboom and Mele in this volume, chs. 21 and 24, respectively.)

Now consider what happens if we set aside the assumption that the pair (IN) and (CP) and the pair (IP) and (CN) are contradictories and instead try to evaluate each statement on its own merits.

I often feel inclined to accept (IN) ("Determined choices cannot be free") and (CN) ("Undetermined choices cannot be free"). Incompatibilists seem correct to disparage the freedom of determined choices (which categorically could not have been different than they were), and the compatibilist complaint that locating

Table 23.1. Theories regarding free will

	(IN)	*(IP)*	*(CN)*	*(CP)*
Classical incompatibilism	True	True	False	False
Classical compatibilism	False	False	True	True
No-free-will-either-way theory	True	False	True	False
Free-will-either-way theory	False	True	False	True

indeterminacy within our choices would lessen the control over our choices required for moral responsibility seems correct also. Nonetheless, I do not always find that the pessimism generated by (and contributing to) my acceptance of (IN) and (CN) carries over to my evaluation of (IP) ("Indeterminism can give rise to free choices") and (CP) ("Determined choices can be free"). Sometimes I do not hesitate to assent to the positive accounts (IP) and (CP).

By accepting all four statements I seem to have done something logically odd, but have I? The *rejection* of all candidates is not remarkable in philosophical disputes. For instance, many thinkers in normative ethics reject every normative theory that comes along, without concluding that there can be no true normative account. Such ethicists simply see their endeavor as forever trying to approximate a best account. Havoc occurs, though, when theorists *affirm* conflicting theories. Imagine what it would mean to say that Kantian and utilitarian theories are both true, instead of saying that they are both false. If we can show that these *apparently* contradictory theories are "equally true," then we have undone the claim of normative ethics to objective truth. Both theories could be "true" only if moral truth were subjectivized to individuals or groups of individuals, which is to say that the theories are not objectively true at all. By analogy, by accepting all four claims of the incompatibilists and compatibilists, I commit myself to the claim that "free choice" can have no objective reference, that free will and moral responsibility can exist only in the eye of the beholder.

There seem to be just three things to say about my acceptance of (IN), (IP), (CN), and (CP). Either (1) "free choice," in the sense I am using it, is unambiguous and logically coherent, in which case I have contradicted myself; or (2) I mean different things by "free choice" when I consider the four statements, and hence, there is no contradiction, only ambiguity; or (3) I am not guilty of contradicting myself and I have not used "free choice" ambiguously, in which case "free choice," when taken to have objective reference, logically cannot denote. I believe (3) is the most plausible.

Although various philosophers mean different things by "free will," it is easy to eliminate (2). I have defined "free will" (and "free choice") throughout as "whatever degree of freedom of choice that is necessary for moral responsibility." I find it easy to remember that I mean this responsibility-enabling sense of "free choice" when I consider (IN), (IP), (CN), and (CP). I do not claim that individuals always know what meanings they assign to words, but I am confident I know what I mean in this instance.

This leaves (1). I do not countenance the rebuttal that I *must* be contradicting myself because we know that "free choice" is coherent; that would be question-begging. Instead, we should investigate the question on its own merits. Here is my argument.

Our acceptance of (IN), (IP), (CN), and (CP) depends on our judgments concerning the conditions in which our choices can be "good enough" to warrant moral responsibility. As argued earlier, I believe these are moral judgments. So, if we are metaethical subjectivists, we have quick support for the bottom-up argument. But I have claimed that the bottom-up argument is independent of the top-down argument, so I cannot leave matters there. I believe that even metaethical objectivists can find reasons to accept free will subjectivism, and I propose these now.

To ask whether determined choices can be free frames the issue in a historical context. It prompts us to consider whether a choice can be good enough to count as free if we theoretically can trace its causes back to the laws of nature and events occurring before the chooser was born (van Inwagen 1983: chapter 1). When we frame the question with this historical perspective, it is tempting to assign determined choices a negative grade. When we assign this negative grade, we affirm (IN). On the other hand, to ask whether an *undetermined* choice can be free frames matters so that we think about the perils of indeterminism, bringing to mind the specter of choices that are not under the control of the chooser chronicled by Hobart (1934) and Ayer (1954). When we are in such a frame of mind, we are likely to be impressed that such cases are destructive to freedom, and we assent to (CN).

Nonetheless, having assented to (IN) and (CN), we have no reason—beyond self-imposed constraints that we might *think* are logical constraints—why we cannot give the high marks to certain choices that are implicit in (CP) and (IP). If we focus on the internal rationality of choices, as Harry Frankfurt (1971) does, the fact that they are determined, and, hence, theoretically predictable since before the chooser was even born, seems irrelevant to their freedom. This prompts us to affirm (CP). If we do not demand that free choices be so rigidly connected to what went before, as Robert Kane (1996a) tries to get us to do, we have little difficulty in giving up the claim that undetermined choices are unfree. This is to accept (IP).

I claim that the freeness of choices is not a characteristic that exists in the choices; all "freeness" amounts to is how we feel about or *grade* choices. The grades we give do not track a characteristic of choices but depend upon our opinions and feelings about the actual characteristics of choices. Such opinions and feelings are moved by a disorganized variety of factors that have little to do with the choices themselves. Instead, they involve such subjective factors as the context in which we consider the free will issue, our personal histories, our temperaments, philosophical schooling, ideologies, and other idiosyncratic elements. Also relevant in our judgments of the goodness of choices are the competing exemplars of freedom that philosophers use throughout the free will debate (Double 1991, chapter 5). Taken together, these considerations (as well as doubtless others that I have failed to list) explain why we *do* affirm (IN), (IP), (CN), and

(CP). This explanation creates a positive case for thinking that we are *correct* to do so.

This leaves (3) standing: If we take *free* to denote a characteristic of choices itself, that characteristic is contradictory. A free choice may be determined (CP) and cannot be determined (IN), can be undetermined (IP) and cannot be undetermined (CN). Such a "characteristic" cannot belong to a choice itself. Because the "freeness" of choices themselves is a logically impossible characteristic, it cannot—not only does not—exist. We are thus forced to understand talk about the freeness of choices in a subjectivized way. Speakers may give coherent senses to *free* in their own idiolects, just as we may for any subjective word. But this fact does not count against the claim that the meaning of "free choice" is idiosyncratic, with no possibility of denoting a class of choices that objectively underpin moral responsibility.

3. Other Views and How They Differ from Mine

3.1. Bruce Waller, B. F. Skinner, and Daniel Dennett

Bruce Waller (1990) argues for incompatibilism concerning moral responsibility and *naturalism*, which might be deterministic or indeterministic, and sees the world as devoid of nonphysical entities. Like the behaviorist psychologist and hard determinist B. F. Skinner (1948), Waller recommends surrendering the belief in retributive moral responsibility. Getting rid of what Waller calls "moral-judgment responsibility" allows persons to construct their social worlds without the baneful influence of traditional, theologically inspired ideas such as recrimination, vengeance, just deserts, guilt, and sin. At the same time, Waller argues that naturalism is compatible with a type of freedom that supports "role-responsibility" (tasks we have by virtue of our roles as, for example, parents, workers, bosses, and self-controlled persons) and "moral-act responsibility" (being causally responsible for moral and immoral acts). The naturalized freedom Waller believes we have is a compatibilist-style freedom, which allows full personhood and the ability to make moral judgments, with only moral responsibility excised. Thus, Waller teases apart those traits that most libertarians try to conjoin, keeping the desirable aspects of moral responsibility and jettisoning the undesirable ones.

Waller stands between the announced hard determinist Skinner and the announced compatibilist Dennett, being slightly closer to Skinner. Without saying so, Waller shows that these categories, at least as applied to Skinner and Dennett, are more verbal than substantive. When Skinner rejects libertarian free will and moral responsibility, he does so with studied hyperbole (witness the title of his book *Beyond Freedom and Dignity* 1971). Skinner never denies that persons act intelligently in a way that most compatibilists think instances freedom. Free will theorists can set aside as an idiosyncrasy Skinner's obligatory behaviorist use of scare quotes around the terms *belief, desire,* and *choice.* When Dennett writes that persons are morally responsible, he denies that he means that they are blame-worthy in "the eyes of God"; Dennett means instead that holding persons morally responsible is sound social policy:

> We simply hold persons responsible for their conduct (within limits we take care not to examine too closely). And we are rewarded for adopting this strategy by the higher proportion of "responsible" behavior we thereby inculcate. (Dennett 1984: 164)

Although Dennett apparently endorses negative reinforcement more than Skinner and Waller do, I believe the greatest difference between Skinner, Dennett, and Waller is over how best to *present* the antilibertarian view they share. Waller's position combines the most attractive selling points of the other two: Waller emphasizes Dennett's naturalized freedom, thereby avoiding the harsh sound of Skinner's denial of freedom, and eschews Dennett's talk about even a less severe form of moral responsibility, thereby emphasizing Skinner's insight that punishment, blame, and recrimination, that is, our typical ways to mete out negative reinforcement, are ineffective ways to inculcate desirable behavior.

I sympathize with Waller's compassionate rejection of the immorality of retributive moral responsibility, as I do with those of the hard determinist Skinner and the nonretributive compatibilist Dennett. I would rather live in a world populated by such soft-hearted theorists than a world of libertarians (Double n.d.). As a metaethical and free will subjectivist, I am slightly uncomfortable with Waller's talk about the incompatibility between moral responsibility and naturalism, because this claim is liable to misinterpretation. However, as discussed earlier, Waller is a metaethical subjectivist. The incompatibility Waller sees between naturalism and moral responsibility is not an incompatibility that holds between two truth-valued statements, but a *moral* incompatibility. In subjectivist terms, this amounts to the claim that it is morally wrong to hold naturalistic persons morally responsible.

I have one reservation. Waller is a subjectivist whose sympathies lie with traditional incompatibilists. In my terms, Waller is a strident subjectivist who thinks blaming is wrong. Although I appreciate his strident subjectivism, I also feel the pull of traditional compatibilism, which allows us to blame persons we believe to be determined. So, I also sympathize with subjectivists who blame, stridently or sheepishly. Waller thinks moral responsibility does not exist, and we must never blame. I think moral responsibility cannot exist as an objective property of persons, and we may blame depending on our psychological makeup and the way the facts of individual cases strike us.

3.2. Galen Strawson

Galen Strawson (1986: 28–29; 1998) gives an influential regress argument to show that being truly responsible for our behavior is logically impossible. I edit as follows:

1. To be responsible for our choices, we must be responsible for the psychological states that go into our choices.
2. To be responsible for these psychological states, we must choose them.
3. To choose our psychological states, we must use some principles for choosing them *and* we must be responsible for having those principles.
4. To be responsible for our principles of choice, we must consciously choose our principles by following some higher level principles of choice. And so on.
5. Therefore, to be responsible for our choices, we must complete an infinite regress of choices of principles of choice.

In my terminology, Strawson's view is a no-free-will-either-way theory. Although I am not sure in which premise or premises Strawson intends *responsible* to mean "causally responsible" and in which it means "morally responsible," he cannot prove what he wishes unless he connects causal and moral responsibility somewhere in the argument. At that point, subjectivists will find Strawson's crucial premise(s) to lack truth value and thus reject the argument. At the same point, compatibilists will reject the premise that to be *morally* responsible for our choices we must be *causally* responsible for the psychological states that go into them. Strawson disagrees because he requires deep responsibility or self-creation for his sense of "real" moral responsibility (as do incompatibilists like Kane 1996a), but compatibilists do not need to give ground here. Once again, the free will problem shows itself a standoff of intuitions about moral responsibility. Subjectivists explain this crucial disagreement between Strawson and the compatibilists in terms of the subjective nature of "moral responsibility." Both sides give a subjective term their idiosyncratic presuppositions and, thus, neither is right nor wrong. So, subjectivism both makes its own objection to Strawson's argument and explains the impasse between Strawson and his compatibilist critics. (For further defense of his position, see Galen Strawson's essay in this volume, ch. 19.)

3.3. Peter Strawson

Peter Strawson (1962) offers an argument, widely construed as compatibilistic, that is reminiscent of some speculations by Hume (1955: sec. 8, part 2). It consists of (1) the psychological premise that a belief in determinism would not *in fact* make us quit viewing persons as morally responsible, and (2) an inference that believing in determinism *should not* have that effect. For Strawson, we should accept (2) because "being" morally responsible just is belonging to a web of social interaction in which persons *do* hold each other responsible, by assigning praise and blame, and by feeling resentment, indignation, and gratitude, and other personal or reactive attitudes. In my terms, this is a subjectivist view. Objective moral responsibility does not ground reactive attitudes. Reactive attitudes, which are natural propensities of persons or culturally induced tendencies, "establish" moral responsibility, so far as it exists. This may reveal a pragmatic or Praxis motivation.[3]

I endorse Strawson's defense of the perseverance of our belief in moral responsibility despite our beliefs about determinism. I find this a valuable antidote to the oft-heard but little-supported, incompatibilist claim that common sense believes that determinism would destroy our belief in moral responsibility. And as a metacompatibilist and subjectivist, I endorse this part of Strawson's view.

Nonetheless, I find two reasons to resist Strawson's argument. First, if it involves no factual error for persons to assign moral responsibility despite their belief in determinism, it commits no factual error to make an incompatibilist response. Strawson's subjectivism guarantees the logical, factual, and psychological coherence of both options. If one uses subjectivism to derive one's conclusion, one is committed to the rest of subjectivism's repercussions. Instead, Strawson singles out his response to determinism as if it were the only one psychologically possible. But it is certainly not the reaction of Kane (1996a) and Peter van Inwagen (1983). Strawson uses subjectivism to support compatibilism, whereas it really supports meta-compatibilism, the view that we can both blame and exonerate from blame persons we believe to be determined.

Second, even for compatibilistic-minded subjectivists, (1) supports Strawson's conclusion only minimally. Most subjectivists demand justification. Strawson says that our human propensity toward reactive attitudes "grounds" moral responsibility. That *grounds* here cannot mean "justifies" is proved by asking, "Even if the propensity to hold persons responsible is universal, perhaps it is a barbaric evolutionary residue that anyone who believes in determinism should reject." Because punishing, blaming, and expressing negative reactive attitudes is to inflict evils, these activities require stronger justification than Strawson's speculated claim that humans would engage in them even if they accepted determinism. To the extent that I as a subjectivist would find the expressing of reactive attitudes as justified, I would want to hear substantive compatibilist reasons for doing so (for example, those given in Frankfurt 1971), not simply the assertion that reactive attitudes are part of human nature. (For further discussion of P. F. Strawson's view and other compatibilist views influenced by him, see the essays in this volume by Haji and Russell, ch. 9 and 10, respectively.)

3.4. Thomas Nagel

Thomas Nagel (1986) distinguishes between the objective, "scientific," third-person perspective for viewing ourselves and others and the subjective, "phenomenological," first-person perspective that each of us has only toward ourselves. Adopting the objective perspective regarding choices tends to lead us to accept determinism. If we do, we commit ourselves to the theoretical possibility of offering *contrastive explanations* of all human choices—explanations not only of our reasons for choosing as we do, but, in good Hempelian fashion, for failing to choose differently. If we consider the possibility of undetermined choices from the objective perspective, we find that those choices fail the contrastive explanation test and thus would be inexplicable. Although indeterminism might allow us to offer *intentional explanations* for whatever choices occur, such explanations "cannot explain . . . *why I did what I did rather than the alternative that was causally open to me*" (ibid. 1986: 116).

For Nagel, our belief in autonomy stems from our ability to take the subjective perspective ourselves and to impute a subjective perspective to others. For choices viewed from the subjective perspective, any individual's reason for performing an action "is the *whole* reason why it happened, and no further explanation is either necessary or possible" (ibid.: 115). All explanation begins and ends with the autonomous agent who selects between indeterministic open alternatives, for which the ultimate explanation is always that the agent wanted to choose in this way. Thus, the sense of autonomy we believe we experience from the first-person perspective is bound to the notion of intentional explanation. Unfortunately, when we examine our sense of autonomy from the third-person perspective, the legitimacy of the first-person perspective seems to vanish. We cannot coherently describe that subjective point of view, but we cannot dismiss it as illusory. We remain convinced that compatibilist views of free will leave out something we hope we have. Because Nagel thinks compatibilism and incompatibilism exhaust the free will options, he concludes, "[N]othing believable . . . has been proposed by anyone in the extensive public discussion of the subject" (ibid.: 112).

I find Nagel's perspectivalism extremely suggestive. I wish Nagel had couched his criticism of libertarianism by emphasizing the actual connections between persons and their choices instead of talking about explanation, the latter of which has tempted libertarian critics to respond, quite irrelevantly, that science is full of noncontrastive explanations (Clarke 1992a). The problem I see for any variety of libertarianism is that it loosens the connection between persons and their choices so that libertarian choosers would have less control of their choices than would deterministic choosers. Control is the problematic issue, not explanation.[4]

My primary objection to Nagel is that his perspectivalism has an incompatibilist bias. For Nagel, from the objective perspective, determined choices look unfree and undetermined choices look random. From the subjective perspective, undetermined choices seem free. Nagel evinces incompatibilist intuitions when he wishes that he could validate the libertarian view we receive from the subjective perspective. This wish corresponds to my claim above that libertarian choices look good to us when we do not worry about the looseness of the connection between persons and their choices (in Nagel's terms, when we reject the need for contrastive explanations). Taking perspectivalism one step farther, however, I think that adopting the subjective perspective can enhance our view of compatibilism also. If we focus solely on the rationality of our choices and not the number of physically possible choices available to us, as I argue that compatibilists would be wise to do (Double 1991: ch. 2), the fact that these choices are determined does not seem to count against their being free. From the subjective perspective, even a determined brain in a vat might have free will. So, I apply Nagel's perspectivalism within the subjective perspective itself. (I hold a similar opinion about the objective perspective, from which, both compatibilism and incompatibilism emerge as desirable options.)

I proffer a reason that incompatibilism and compatibilism appear both desirable and undesirable even from the same perspective: Our conflicting thoughts about free will are driven by merely psychological factors. Subjectivism explains Nagel's recognition of the perspectival nature of our thinking about free will and assuages his fear that no free will theory is remotely plausible.

3.5. Peter Unger

In *Philosophical Relativity* (1984) Peter Unger offers a general semantic view that he has applied to various philosophical debates, including those over skepticism (1986), normative ethics (1996), and free will (1984: 54–58). Very roughly, speakers may assign either a contextualist (context-sensitive) meaning or an invariantist (non-context-sensitive) meaning to the key terms of these philosophical debates. In contextualist semantics, the truth of debated statements (for example, "Smith knows there is milk on the rug," "Brown is immoral not to contribute to charity," or "Jones acted freely") varies according to the degree of leniency of justification speakers' contexts establish. Contextualism leaves open the possibility that disputed questions may take both "yes" and "no" answers depending on the contexts the interlocutors create. For example, when G. E. Moore establishes a lenient context for knowledge claims by claiming he knows he has a hand, his claim becomes true. When Descartes sets a stringent context by hypothesizing that he may be deceived by an evil genius, *his* skeptical denials of commonplace knowledge claims are true. According to invariantist semantics, the truth of such utterances does not vary according to context. So, in the skeptical debate, Moore or Descartes (or someone else) is correct and the others are wrong because *knowledge* has just one meaning that specifies the degree of justification anyone must have to possess knowledge.

Although in principle an invariantist may claim that the invariant meanings of key philosophical words portray lenient standards, in fact skeptics of many sorts tend to be invariantists, and nonskeptics tend toward contextualism. So, the skeptical Peter Unger of *Ignorance* (1975) was an invariantist who thought that "knowledge" entailed that knowers must have absolute certainty, and the compatibilist who claims we may choose freely despite being determined is a contextualist who relies on a commonsense belief that only untoward intrusions, not determinism per se, defeat our freedom. Unger completes the case for philosophical relativity by arguing that

> an invariantist can assign a semantics to the philosophically important terms that is comfortable to a skeptical view on the problem, and a contextualist can, with equal propriety, assign a semantics that is comfortable to the commonsense position on the problem, antithetical to the skeptic's problem.... [T]here is nothing to decide between the two assignments ... (1984: 46)

Unger's argument is similar to my bottom-up argument. Whereas Unger talks about the linguistic thesis of "semantic relativity," I call judgments about the disputed entities "subjective." Both views have the consequence that certain key philosophical debates are insoluble. I wish I had read his discussion of contextualism before I offered my bottom-up strategy in *The Non-Reality of Free Will* (1991). I prefer my dual approach, though, because I believe that two mutually supporting metaphysical arguments are more persuasive than one semantic argument. I believe that to successfully defend the claim that there is no reason to prefer contextualist or invariantist semantics for terms like *free will*, Unger would need to appeal to the metaphysical theory-construction considerations that support subjectivism. Semantic arguments alone do not strike me as powerful enough to establish ontological conclusions.

3.6. Ted Honderich

Ted Honderich (1993) proposes nine theses: (1) We have an image of ourselves as undetermined *originators* of actions in a cosmos with an open future. This image supports *life-hopes* that we may be able to overcome the influence of heredity and environment, which form the basis for incompatibilist theories of freedom. (2) Determinism, by definition, is logically inconsistent with the undetermined, open futures that we imagine when we attend to our incompatibilist life-hopes. (3) When we attend to (2), the thought that determinism might be true produces feelings of *dismay*. (4) We have another set of life-hopes that require only that our actions be voluntary, but not indeterministically originated. (5) Determinism is logically consistent with our actions being voluntary. (6) When we attend to (5), the thought that determinism might be true produces feelings of satisfied *intransigence*: "Everything is okay. Nothing changes" (ibid.: 86). (7) Adopting either attitude of dismay or intransigence in response to the possibility of determinism involves no intellectual error. (8) Attitudes are neither true nor false: "An attitude is an evaluative thought of something" (ibid.: 81), and "there don't seem to be logical relations of any kind between facts and values" (ibid.: 103). (9) There *are* consequences to determinism: "If we think determinism . . . is true, what we have to do is try to give up whatever depends on thoughts inconsistent with it. Above all we have to try to accept the defeat of certain desires" (ibid.: 110); "our attitudes involving voluntariness cannot really allow us to be intransigent, to go on as if determinism changes nothing. We can't successfully barricade ourselves in them" (ibid.: 111); "our retributive desires . . . are dependent on taking the other person's action as not only voluntary but also originated" (ibid.: 126). (Nicholas Nathan [1992] also sees the free will problem in terms of what we want to believe and what we are able to believe, recommending what philosophers can do to help when such conflicts arise.)

According to Honderich, a synthesis between compatibilism and incompatibilism is possible, because the attitudes of dismay and intransigence do not really conflict. Incompatibilists are dismayed because the sort of life-hopes they care about are undone by determinism. Compatibilists remain intransigent because the life-hopes they care about are unaffected by determinism. Honderich thinks that because both sides are concerned with different hopes, it is possible to find an answer that adjudicates their dispute by sorting out which attitudes can stand and which must be surrendered.

In Double (1996a) I claimed that according to the metaethical subjectivism both Honderich and I endorse, determinism has no logical, moral, or psychological consequences in any sense that I understand. Instead, it would be logically, morally, and psychologically possible to be dismayed and intransigent about the same fact. Honderich sees that we can adopt the attitudes of incompatibilistic dismay and compatibilistic intransigence when we view our choices as determined, provided we focus on *different* types of life-hopes. We should not take this as evidence that we cannot adopt compatibilistic intransigence toward determinism when we focus on the *same* life-hopes on which the incompatibilist focuses. Honderich replied to my argument with these words:

[N]either the proposition that facts do not entail values nor the proposition that an attitude as a whole does not have a truth-value comes close to (supporting) Double's third and most fertile mistake.

It is the simple mistake of ignoring that we *do* in fact share standard factual reasons having to do with voluntariness and origination for desires, evaluations, and behavior, despite the absence of entailments. . . . I have the human nature I have, not the nature of a Martian or a lunatic, despite the little truths about facts not entailing values and an attitude as a whole not having a truth-value. (1996: 859–60)

So far as I can see, Honderich has not shown that determinism has *consequences*. Rather he has claimed that he has the personality and views he has and has intimated that most nonlunatic earthlings agree with him. Even if this is true, I think the latter point cuts no ice. Philosophers can get readers to dislike the "consequences" of determinism by rehearsing, for example, van Inwagen's Consequence Argument (1983). Philosophers can also entice readers to regard determinism with equanimity by, for example, offering John Martin Fischer's (1994: 6–7) thought experiment: Would reading in next month's issue of *Science* that determinism has been shown true convince you that you never made a free choice? As Dennett (1984) says, we philosophers are adept at moving folks with our metaphors. The fact that we can worry ourselves and others about determinism is a merely psychological fact, not a *consequence*.

Honderich continues by reminding us:

[T]he desires and evaluations in an *attitude rest on its propositional content*. That the propositional content does not entail the desires and evaluations does not begin to put the fact in question. . . . [I]t is agreed on all hands that *some* factual belief about an action's having been free is required by us for holding an agent responsible. . . . If I lose the belief, I cannot persist in the attitude or behavior. Currently at any rate, that is a psychological impossibility. (Honderich 1996: 860–61)

I agree that propositional attitudes contain propositional contents. So, for example, if I resent you for purposely stepping on my toe, the propositional content is that you purposely stepped on my toe. My resentment misfires if you did not step on my toe. Presumably, by like reasoning, Honderich's application of blame requires that he believe that persons he blames are free in an undetermined sense, given that he has the psychology he has.

We can see, though, how different the two points are. It is clear why it is incorrect to blame persons for doing X when they do not do X: the attitude is misdirected. On an extensional reading of "for X," it is logically true that I may correctly blame you *for X* only if you *did X*. (On an extensional reading of "seeing the tree," I see the tree only if the tree exists.) But there is no similar logical presupposition that persons we blame must choose indeterministically before it is linguistically correct to hold them morally responsible. If there were, the debate between the compatibilists and incompatibilists would be solvable linguistically. But it is not.

Metaethical subjectivists acknowledge that most evaluative claims have presuppositions. To use Ayer's example, I make a factual mistake if I say that you were wrong to steal the money when you did not steal the money (1952: 107). Subjectivists sometimes call this the "descriptive meaning" of evaluative terms. Thus, subjectivists do not deny that evaluative terms make descriptive presuppositions, but claim that once we agree that something meets the descriptive criteria and get down to the evaluation, no additional fact makes the applicable of the evaluative term correct or incorrect. *At that point* it is simply a matter of opinion.

This point applies to the plausibility of metacompatibilism. As a free will subjectivist, I admit that it is linguistically incorrect for me to blame you for intentionally stepping on my toe if you did not step on my toe. My point is that we can agree that all the toe-stepping episodes of the world are determined and *still* argue just as plausibly that most intentional toe-steppers are blameworthy *and* that all such persons should be exonerated. Indeed, we may assert either claim passionately (as strident subjectivists would) or modestly (as sheepish subjectivists would).

4. THE FREE WILL PROBLEM PSYCHOLOGIZED

Given my metaphilosophy of Philosophy as Worldview Construction, metaethical subjectivism, and free will subjectivism, I view philosophers' debates over free will as more a psychological topic than do most philosophers. According to my view, the free will debate ceases to be a conceptual puzzle over the correct analysis of "free will" followed by a metaphysical inquiry over whether persons in fact have free will. The debate between the compatibilists and incompatibilists over *the objectively correct view* of free will becomes fruitless. The free will problem becomes psychologized, much as metaethical subjectivism turns the search for moral truth into moral psychology and the phenomenology of moral thinking.

One of the topics I find most interesting is the motivation of philosophers to adopt the positions they do. I claim no particular expertise at answering this question, nor do I know of any psychological research concerning it. Here I can only surmise, but because I think about the topic every time I read a book or article on free will, I cannot resist the temptation to indulge.

4.1. What Motivates Philosophers to Accept Libertarianism?

Dennett (1984) wonders whether the desire of some libertarians for a real state of responsibility is "a purely metaphysical hankering." Putting the most favorable gloss on this, most libertarians believe moral responsibility needs a grounding in the nature of things. For them, as for Kant and James, compatibilism is a "wretched subterfuge." The hankering may also evince a desire for linguistic tidiness. Plato thought there must be a Form of justice to underpin our talk of just acts. Libertarians might suppose there is a real state of responsibility to underpin our just-deserts talk. Somewhat less flatteringly, one's metaphysical hankering may be aimed at overcoming a visceral reaction to subjectivism. Simon Blackburn criticizes the analogous view regarding metaethical subjectivism with biting sarcasm:

> It might be that there are people who cannot "put up with" the idea that values have a subjective source. . . . But this will be because such people have a defect . . . in their sensibilities—one that has taught them that things do not matter unless they matter to God, or throughout infinity, or to a world conceived apart from any particular set of concerns or desires, or whatever. One should not adjust one's metaphysics to pander to such defects (Blackburn 1993: 157)

A less favorable gloss would be that libertarians wish to defend moral responsibility to reduce the cognitive dissonance at the thought that we are giving unjust deserts to those we punish retributively. An even less favorable gloss is provided by Nietzsche, who sees the belief in moral responsibility as an excuse for our natural barbarism and lust for revenge.

Additional libertarian motivation may lie in metaphilosophy. Some may seek to ground our practices and emotional reactions. Part of this desire may be a familiar Praxis fear: Without free will and moral responsibility, humanity will revert to savagery. Some libertarians who see the aim of philosophy as underpinning religion give libertarianism extra points if their religions are libertarian.

4.2. What Motivates Philosophers to Accept Compatibilism?

Compatibilists may avail themselves of the libertarian desire to underpin moral responsibility, while being convinced that indeterminism cannot do the job. I would like to find out how many compatibilists endorse what I call "CP" ("Under certain conditions, determined choices can be free") on its own merits, and how many accept it grudgingly only because they want *some* account of moral responsibility and believe that indeterministic free will does not exist or that it is worse than deterministic free will. As support for the latter possibility, note that most compatibilists champion a less blood-chilling kind of moral responsibility than do most libertarians, perhaps revealing of a lack of compatibilist confidence in

CP. As a meta-compatibilist, I see no reason why compatibilists *have* to adopt a weaker notion of responsibility than the libertarians do, but most do, which in turn encourages the libertarians to think that theirs is the only way to vindicate moral responsibility.

4.3. What Motivates Philosophers to Accept Hard Determinism?

I suspect that many hard determinists lament determinism and others wish they could accept compatibilism's way of accommodating determinism. For such thinkers, being a hard determinist is the price one pays for being a good epistemic agent who follows the argument even when it leads to an unhappy conclusion. We should not forget, however, the compassionate hard determinists such as Skinner and his kindred thinker, Waller, who find retributive moral responsibility a pernicious misconception in need of eradication. These latter thinkers have Praxis motivations for rejecting moral responsibility as well as philosophical arguments. Here again, I find interesting the question of how much Praxis motivation and how much Worldview Construction motivation contribute to hard determinism. (See the essays in this volume by Honderich, Pereboom and Smilansky for further insight into these issues, chs. 20, 21, and 22 respectively.)

4.4. What Motivates Philosophers to Accept Subjectivism?

A Praxis motivation for accepting subjectivism could be the desire to undermine the ontological ground of moral responsibility. One could charge subjectivists with fostering a totalitarian rejection of responsibility, as is sometimes charged against hard determinists, but that criticism holds less force against subjectivism. Strident subjectivists can acknowledge their own subjectivism and continue to blame, and even sheepish subjectivists can blame in their self-conscious, embarrassed way. So, if one had a burning Praxis motivation to attack moral responsibility, one could serve one's Praxis cause better by adopting hard determinism or no-free-will-either-way theory. Believing that there can be no such thing as objective moral responsibility will tend to take the edge off even the most strident, antiretributive subjectivist. By definition, strident subjectivists believe that there is nothing ontological that could make adopting sheepish subjectivism false. Thus, all varieties of subjectivism have the recognition of its limitations built into them, and, psychologically, recognizing one's limitations tends to modulate one's passions. This makes free will subjectivism a modulating position in a debate between passionate foes.

Given my commitment to subjectivism, I find that free will subjectivism coheres with what I think are the most plausible answers to several areas of philosophy: from aesthetics, to metaethics, to epistemology, to the nature of the physical world. This makes free will subjectivism attractive to me as a Worldview thinker. Moreover, free will subjectivism is an application of the only normative view I have ever been able to understand.

NOTES

I am grateful to Mark Bernstein and Bruce Waller for helpful comments on earlier drafts of this essay. I owe a special debt to Robert Kane.

1. Suppose the only options an individual had were (1) adoption of false, self-flattering beliefs (such as thinking one is better liked or more competent than one really is) or poor epistemic strategies (such as never entertaining criticisms of you-the-person as opposed to your behavior) and (2) leading a deeply depressed, suicide-prone life. In this case, I think there is a compelling moral case for adopting (1). See Double (1988a).

2. What I call *Philosophy as Conversation* after Richard Rorty (1979, 1989) sees philosophy as a kind of literature that contributes to our intellectual lives without pronouncing on the character of ultimate reality. This contribution may be viewed aesthetically and evaluated as one does literary works, or viewed as a technical genre, full of modal operators and analyses of subjunctive conditionals, the sort of philosophy Rorty sees promulgated in the elite philosophy graduate schools of our day.

Philosophy as Underpinnings sees philosophy's role as supporting some other area or areas of intellectual interest. Historically, philosophy has served religion, science, and common sense. Unsympathetically portrayed, the Underpinning metaphilosophy can be characterized as *Philosophy for Defending What I Already Believe* or *Philosophy Supporting Conventional Wisdom*. Other metaphilosophies could be included such as *Philosophy as Flaunting Common Sense, Philosophy as Stirring Up Controversy, Philosophy as Furthering My Dissertation Advisor's Research Program*, and *Philosophy as Ego Aggrandizement*. Also, there is a blurred line between a metaphilosophy and a favorite strategy one uses in a pinch. For example, we could consider the following as metaphilosophies or argumentative strategies. *Philosophical Snootiness*: Here philosophers give extra points to views simply because philosophers-in-the-right-circles endorse them. *Studied Myopia to Avoid Critical Challenges*: Here philosophers treat minutiae with great precision, while ignoring broader challenges to their technical concerns. Because philosophers have various motivations, they might instance more than one metaphilosophy.

3. I owe this point to Robert Kane.

4. Kane (1996a: 144) acknowledges this degree of looseness, which he calls "lack of antecedent determining control" over our choices but replies, controversially, that the type of control that free will requires is instead "plural voluntary control." For Kane, free persons manifest the latter when they control their choices *at the time* they make them, not before they make them.

CHAPTER 24

AUTONOMY, SELF-CONTROL, AND WEAKNESS OF WILL

ALFRED R. MELE

IT is commonly held that personal autonomy encompasses self-control.[1] The root notion of autonomy (from *autos* + *nomos*) is "self-rule" or "self-government," and there is at least a superficial link between this root notion and self-control. The terms *self-control* and *autonomy* are used in a variety of senses. To avoid confusion, some guidance should be offered at the outset about my use of these terms in this essay. I understand *self-control* as, roughly, the contrary of *akrasia* (want of self-control, incontinence, weakness of will). (*Akrasia* is discussed in section 2.) By *autonomy*, taking etymology seriously, I mean, again roughly, "self-rule" or "self-government." Joel Feinberg usefully distinguishes among four "meanings" of the term *autonomy* as applied to individuals: "It can refer either to the *capacity* to govern oneself . . . ; or to the *actual condition* of self-government . . . ; or to an *ideal of character* derived from that conception; or . . . to the *sovereign authority* to govern oneself" (1986: 28). My concern with autonomy in this essay is as an actual condition of individual agents.

I should add that *autonomy*, as I understand it, is associated with a family of *freedom*-concepts: free will, free choice, free action, and the like. In some of the philosophical literature that I will discuss, issues are framed in terms of freedom rather than autonomy, but we are talking about (aspects of) the same thing.

1. Autonomy and Moral Agency

Autonomy is sometimes used to name a property that, by stipulative definition, only agents who engage in *moral* conduct can have. I make no such stipulation. In his *Nicomachean Ethics* (1915b) Aristotle mentions hypothetical gods who have no need for the moral virtues (bk. 10.7). Perhaps we can imagine, in the same vein, a universe whose only sentient inhabitants are self-sufficient, divine beings who devote their lives to various solitary intellectual activities, as they judge best, and want nothing from one another. Having no need or desire that calls for interaction with other beings, they act in total isolation from one another. A being of this kind may be self-ruled or self-governed. Even so, the being may also be utterly *amoral*, on some conceptions of morality. Now, it might turn out that according to some acceptable conception of morality, even beings of the imagined kind engage in moral conduct. Perhaps any such being has moral duties to itself, for example; and it may discharge those duties or fail to do so. I leave this issue open. Whether all possible self-ruled or self-governed beings engage in moral conduct is a substantive issue that hinges on the outcome of substantive disputes about the nature of morality.

On the assumption that the hypothetical deities at issue are autonomous, the following claims from Kant's *Foundations of the Metaphysic of Morals* (1959) jointly place them, or their "wills," "under moral laws": "a free will and a will under moral laws are one and the same"; "freedom and the will's enactment of its own laws are indeed both autonomy" (ibid.: 98, 104). As Onora O'Neill observes, Kant's conception of autonomy is by no means standard in twentieth-century literature on autonomy (1989: 53–54, 66, 75–76). Readers are forewarned that it is no part of my aim to explore a specifically Kantian notion of autonomy here.

2. Self-Control, Akrasia, and the Self-Controlled Person

Common acceptance of the idea that individual autonomy encompasses self-control may be more nominal than substantive, depending upon the extent to which its proponents share a conception of self-control. The view of self-control that I will sketch has its roots in the ancient project of explaining intentional behavior. Aristotle asks, in chapter 7 of *De Motu Animalium* (1915a: 701a7–8),

"How does it happen that thinking is sometimes followed by action and sometimes not, sometimes by motion, sometimes not?" A proper answer requires understanding of how it happens that we sometimes act in accordance with our judgments about what it would be best to do and sometimes fail even to *attempt* so to act, pursuing instead a course of action at odds with what we judge best.

What Aristotle called *akrasia* is, very roughly, a trait of character exhibited in uncompelled, intentional behavior that goes against the agent's best or better judgment. This is a judgment—made from the perspective of the agent's own values, desires, beliefs, and the like—to the effect that it would be best to do A, or (instead) better to do A than to do B. *Enkrateia* (self-control, continence, strength of will) is, again roughly, a trait of character exhibited in behavior that conforms with one's best or better judgment in the face of temptation to act to the contrary. (For stylistic reasons, I will sometimes use "better judgment" in a broad sense that includes best judgments as well.) The akratic person, Aristotle writes, "is in such a state as to be defeated even by those [pleasures] which most people master," while the self-controlled person is in such a state as "to master even those by which most people are defeated" (*Nicomachean Ethics* 1150a11–13).

I will follow Aristotle in understanding *self-control* and *akrasia* as two sides of the same coin. According to a view that I have defended elsewhere, self-controlled individuals are agents who have significant motivation to conduct themselves as they judge best and a robust capacity to do what it takes so to conduct themselves in the face of (actual or anticipated) competing motivation (Mele 1995). Akratic individuals, conversely, suffer from a deficiency in one or both of these connections. Human beings *wholly* lacking self-control are at the mercy of whatever desires happen to be strongest—even when the desires clash with their better judgments.

It may be appropriate to distance oneself from Aristotle on a number of counts. Aristotle limits the sphere of *enkrateia* and *akrasia*, like that of temperance and self-indulgence (*Nicomachean Ethics* 3.10, 7.7), to "pleasures and pains and appetites and aversions arising through touch and taste" (ibid.: 1150a9–10).[2] On the conception of self-control being sketched, its sphere extends well beyond the bodily appetites. People exhibit self-control not only in (overt) actions that accord with their evaluative judgments—including judgments unrelated to bodily appetites—but also in their acquisition or retention of *beliefs*. Just as people can *act* akratically, they can *believe* akratically (Davidson 1985; Heil 1984; Mele 1987: ch. 8; Pears 1984; A. Rorty 1983), as in some cases of self-deception. By the same token, in successfully resisting actual or anticipated motivation to the contrary, agents may believe *continently* and manifest self-control (Mele 1995: ch. 5). The sphere of self-control—and of *akrasia*—extends, as well, to which emotions we have or lack at a particular time: not only do we sometimes have control over how or whether our emotions manifest themselves in our behavior, we sometimes have control over which emotions we have or lack (ibid.: ch. 6). It extends even further—to our assessment, revision, and acceptance of values and principles (ibid.: ch. 7).

One may reasonably depart from Aristotle on a metaphysical matter as well. He views the self-controlled agent as a person whose "desiring element" is "obedient" to his "reason" or "rational principle," though less obedient than the virtuous person's (*Nicomachean Ethics* 1102b26–28). A human being "is said to have or not to have self-control," Aristotle writes, "according as his reason has or has not the control (*kratein*), on the assumption that this is the man himself" (ibid.: 1168b34–35). Given his contention that "reason more than anything else is man" (1178a7; compare 1166a17, 22–23; 1168b27ff.; compare also Plato, *Republic* 588b–592b), Aristotle's identification of self-control with control by one's "reason" is predictable.

On an alternative, holistic view of human beings, the "self" of self-control is identified with the whole person rather than with reason. Even when one's passions and emotions run counter to one's better judgment, they often are not plausibly seen as alien forces. A conception of self-controlled individuals as, roughly, people who characteristically are guided by their better judgments even in the face of strong competing motivation does not commit one to viewing emotion, passion, and the like as having no place in the "self" of self-control. Self-control can be exercised in support of better judgments partially based on a person's appetites or emotional commitments. In some cases, our better judgments may indicate our evaluative ranking of competing *emotions* or *appetites*.

Self-control may be either regional or global, and it comes in degrees (Rorty 1980a). A scholar who exhibits remarkable self-control in adhering to the demanding work schedule that he decisively judges best for himself may be "weak-willed" about eating. He is self-controlled in one "region" of his life and weak-willed in another. Further, some self-controlled individuals apparently are more self-controlled than others. Agents possessed of global self-control—self-control in all regions of their lives—would be particularly remarkable, if, in every region, their self-control considerably exceeded that of most people.[3]

In Mele (1995), I developed an account of an ideally self-controlled person and I argued that the possession and successful exercise of such self-control is insufficient for autonomy. The ideally self-controlled person *perfectly* manifests what I called "perfect self-control." The relevant perfection has four dimensions: range, object, frequency, and effectiveness.

1. *Range.* Perfect self-control is perfectly global. It is manifested in overt actions, mental actions, intentions, beliefs, and emotions, in practical reasoning and practical evaluative judgments, in the assessment, acceptance, and revision of values and principles, and so on. It has, we may say, *maximal categorial range.*[4]

2. *Object.* Exercises of self-control combat something in support of something else. Ideally self-controlled agents never exercise self-control *errantly* (see Mele 1995: ch. 4), but only in support of "pure" items—*non-akratically held* better judgments, values, principles, and the like. The objects of exercises of self-control in ideally self-controlled agents are, in this sense, *perfect.*

3. *Frequency.* Ideally self-controlled agents exercise self-control whenever they reflectively deem it appropriate to do so.

4. *Effectiveness.* Ideally self-controlled agents' exercises of self-control always succeed in supporting what they are aimed at supporting. They are perfectly effective. This is not a matter of luck or causal deviance. Rather, ideally self-controlled agents consistently *intentionally* bring about the success of their exercises of self-control.

Obviously, ideally self-controlled agents are imaginary beings. Do super-agents of this kind—even assuming that they exercise self-control regularly in all areas of their lives and enjoy mental health—have everything that personal autonomy requires.[5] Such super-agents, in being self-conscious, self-reflective, self-assessing beings, are at a great remove from cats and dogs, animals that can act intentionally but are too "simpleminded" for autonomous action (on standard views). These super-agents also have qualities that we normal human beings only approximate. But are these agents' capacities and numerous flawless executions thereof sufficient for autonomous agency?

Incompatibilists on the subject of autonomy will note that my ideally self-controlled agents can inhabit a deterministic world. Since they take determinism to preclude autonomy, my super-agents fall short of their requirements for autonomy. Incompatibilism is discussed at length in other chapters of this volume. Here, I take up another worry.

Gerald Dworkin contends that "autonomy is a second-order capacity to reflect critically upon one's first-order preferences and desires, and the ability either to identify with these or to change them in light of higher-order preferences and values" (1988: 108). An ideally self-controlled person has this capacity and ability. However, even ideal self-control—no matter how frequently and successfully exercised—might not suffice for autonomy. If, as it seems, every process of critical reflection is regulated or guided by principles or values already in place, some principle or value will be presupposed or taken for granted in each process. If the principles or values taken for granted are products of brainwashing or other forms of "mind control," the process is tainted. To be sure, one can advert to a capacity for third-order reflection on second-order preferences, but the problem can be repeated at that level too. Nor is the problem solved by evoking the image of Neurath's boat and observing that agents can criticize each of their values from the perspective of some other value(s) without ascending a level; for an agent's collection of values may be engineered in such a way as to dictate the results of such criticism.

Apparently, an agent who is ideally self-controlled in my sense might ultimately be controlled by his brainwasher. Although the agent rigorously and effectively exercises an impressive capacity to master motivation that runs counter to his decisive better judgments about action, belief-formation, value-revision, and the like, the foundation on which these judgments rest might be wholly due to a malicious "mind-controller." Arguably, then, an autonomous agent must have some feature that even an ideally self-controlled person can lack. If so, how may self-control be supplemented to arrive at autonomy? I return to this question in section 5.

3. Personal Autonomy and Control

Articulating just what autonomy amounts to has proved difficult. Part of the problem is that theorists have had quite different theoretical uses for a notion of individual autonomy.[6] When an account of a concept is developed for a particular theoretical purpose, it can easily fail to suit other purposes. A possible tack is to construct a characterization of autonomy with the goal of accommodating *all* plausible theoretical demands that have been placed on something so named. However, the theoretical workload would then be enormous, and one may take comfort in the suggestion that no *one* specific concept is at work in all of these connections (Dworkin 1988: 6).

It is a platitude that autonomous agents (if there are any) have and exercise some degree of control over their lives. This platitude lies near the heart of familiar debate between compatibilists and incompatibilists about freedom of action and freedom of the will. One way to see the debate is in terms of *control*: incompatibilists contend that determinism is incompatible with our having the control over ourselves required for free will and free action, and for *autonomy*, in my sense; and compatibilists deny this.

Sometimes it is claimed that agents have no control at all if determinism is true. That claim is false. When I drive my car (under normal conditions), I am in control of the turns it makes, even if our world happens to be deterministic. I certainly am in control of my car's movements in a way in which my passengers and others are not. A distinction can be drawn between compatibilist or "non-ultimate" control and a species of control that might be available to agents in some indeterministic worlds—"ultimate" control.[7] I have the former kind of control over my car, and I might have the latter kind as well. Ultimate control might turn out to be remarkably similar to the control that many compatibilists have in mind; the key to its being *ultimate* control might be its indeterministic setting (Mele 1995: 213).

A familiar argument against incompatibilists who hold that (some) human beings are autonomous can be crudely stated as follows: autonomously willing and acting requires that agents exercise control over their "willings" and their actions; but control is a causal phenomenon and causation is essentially deterministic, so autonomy depends on determinism.[8] Unfortunately, it often is not made clear exactly what deterministic thesis is supposed to be required for causation. Determinism has been understood in a variety of ways, and distinct deterministic theses have prompted philosophical debate. Consider Peter van Inwagen's (orthodox) definition of *determinism* as "the thesis that there is at any instant exactly one physically possible future" (van Ihwagen 1983: 3). It is determinism in this sense that van Inwagen argues is incompatible with free will, but causation seems not to depend on the absence of alternative physically possible futures. For dramatic effect, imagine that "a tiny bit of radioactive substance" has been rigged to a bomb in Al's house—a bit "so small, that *perhaps* in the course of one hour one of the atoms decays, but also, with equal probability, perhaps not."[9] If, within one hour, any of the atoms decays, the causally undetermined decay-event will cause the bomb to detonate, which in turn will cause Al's house to blow up. If, alternatively, no such decay occurs in the specified period, the bomb will not explode. So there is more than one physically possible future. As it happens, an atom decays and the bomb is *caused* to explode.

A related objection to incompatibilist belief in autonomy is more worrisome. Agents' *control* is the yardstick by which the bearing of chance or luck on their autonomy and moral responsibility is measured.[10] Luck (good or bad) becomes problematic when it seems significantly to impede agents' control over themselves (for recent versions of this worry, see Haji 1999a; Mele 1995: 195–204, 1999a; Strawson 1994a; and Waller 1988). To the extent that it is causally undetermined whether, for example, an agent intends or decides in accordance with a better judgment that she made, the agent may seem to lack some control over what she intends or decides; perhaps a positive deterministic connection here would be more conducive to autonomy. Weakness of will is bad enough; an indeterministic connection between better judgments and intentions that allows, in addition, for "random" failures to intend as one judges best seems problematic. I return to this issue in section 6.

At any rate, that control is a causal phenomenon is difficult to deny. Try to imagine one being controlling another in the absence of any causal connection between them—Connie controlling Al, say. If there is no causal connection between them, Connie has no *effect* on Al. And if she has no effect on Al, Connie is not controlling Al: one does not control a being on whom one has no effect. Of course, one may *have the power* to control a being on whom one in fact has no effect; one may consistently refrain from exercising that power, perhaps because the being's conduct happens to accord with one's desires. But that is another matter. Given that causation is not essentially deterministic, it is open not only to compatibilists but also to incompatibilists to provide a causal account of the control required for autonomy. In sections 5 and 6, I address compatibilist and incompatibilist accounts of autonomy.[11]

4. AUTONOMY AND PRO-ATTITUDES

The capacities involved in personal autonomy are of at least two kinds, broadly conceived. Some are directed specifically at one's environment. Assuming some autonomy for Prometheus, he was considerably less autonomous bound than unbound; chained to the rock, he possessed only a severely limited capacity to affect his environment. Others have a pronounced inner-directedness, their outward manifestations notwithstanding. Capacities for decision-making and for critical reflection on one's values, principles, preferences, and beliefs fall into the second group. Capacities of both kinds have at least a partly psychological basis. Although beings lacking a mental life may affect their environment, they cannot do so autonomously; and, of course, such beings are incapable of decision and reflection. Reserving the expression "psychological autonomy" for the kind of autonomy open even to a shackled Prometheus, one can ask what it requires.

Three species of psychological autonomy that agents may, in principle, have regarding their pro-attitudes (for example, their values and desires) are distinguishable. There are differences among (1) an agent's autonomously *developing* a pro-attitude over a stretch of time; (2) an agent's autonomously *possessing* a pro-attitude during a stretch of time; and (3) an agent's being autonomous regarding the *influence* of a pro-attitude on his intentional behavior.[12]

I made this tripartite distinction elsewhere (Mele 1993) in criticizing a thesis advanced by John Christman (1991). Brief discussion of that thesis will prove useful. Christman maintains that "an agent is autonomous vis-à-vis some desire if the influences and conditions that gave rise to the desire were factors that the agent approved of or did not resist, or would not have resisted had she attended to them, and that this judgment was or would have been made in a minimally rational, non-self-deceived manner" (ibid.: 22). This claim is undermined by the following case.[13]

Alice, a specialist on drug addiction, once decided after careful reflection to make herself a heroin addict so that she could directly experience certain phenomena (see Frankfurt 1988: 14). She strove, accordingly, to develop irresistible desires for heroin and she fully accepted the developmental process on the basis of self-reflection that was at least minimally rational and involved no self-deception. Alice was careful to reflect on the process only when clearheaded. In due time, Alice developed irresistible desires for heroin; by hypothesis, she *autonomously* developed these desires. At present, while in the grip of an irresistible desire to use the drug, Alice rationally judges that it would be best to refrain from using it now; she explicitly and rationally judges, as well, that it would be best to eradicate her standing desire for heroin, beginning immediately. She is convinced that the experiment is more dangerous than she had realized and that it is time to start setting things right. However, Alice is incapable of resisting her present desire for heroin. Moreover, she is incapable of immediately eradicating her standing desire for heroin, and she is presently incapable of strategically eradicating it anytime soon (during *t*, say).

Although, by hypothesis, Alice autonomously developed irresistible desires for heroin, she is not autonomous with respect to the influence of her present desire for heroin on her present behavior. A clear sign of her nonautonomy in that connection is her *inability*, even in a compatibilist sense of *ability*, to refrain from acting on that desire even though she judges it best not to use the drug now. (Notice that part of Alice's aim in cultivating her irresistible desires might have been to enable herself to experience what it is like to be *nonautonomous* regarding the influence of a desire on one's behavior.) Furthermore, Alice is not autonomous (or self-governing) vis-à-vis her current possession of her standing desire for heroin, nor her continued possession of it during *t*—even though she satisfies Christman's conditions for being "autonomous vis-à-vis [that] desire."[14] If she were self-governing with respect to her possession of that desire, she would rid herself of it, as she judges best. Instead, she is stuck with the standing desire and victimized by it, while rationally preferring its eradication. Despite these problems, Christman may be on to something in his search for a developmental or historical aspect of autonomy.

5. AUTONOMY AND HISTORY

Do agents' histories have a special bearing on psychological autonomy? An *internalist* view of autonomy maintains that agents' histories are relevant to their psychological autonomy only insofar as their histories yield rationality, an ability to acquaint oneself with relevant facts, reliable capacities for decision-making and action, current psychic integration, and the like. Given that the traits and capacities are in place and are exercised with appropriate care and suitable frequency, all else is irrelevant to psychological autonomy, including how the agents came to be as they are. On an *externalist* view, there is more to being psychologically autonomous over a stretch of time than what goes on inside a person during that time. The autonomy of (some) individuals also depends, for example, upon how they came to possess values and desires that guide self-reflection, decision-making, and the like: it depends on agents' *causal histories*.[15] It has been suggested that compatibilists are committed to internalism. Later, I will sketch some grounds for rejecting this claim.

Bernard Berofsky writes: "[A]utonomy is not the freedom to express our origins; it is the freedom from those origins" (Berofsky 1995: 225). What he terms "liberation from self" might also have been termed "liberation from one's history." Berofsky contends that autonomy is "a feature of the agent grounded in his current relation to himself and his world" and that "differences in autonomy are to be identified "in terms of differences in rationality, independence, objectivity, or personal integrity" (ibid.: 211). With a possible exception that I am not sure how to interpret (ibid.: 214–18), he advocates an internalist conception of autonomy.

Gerald Dworkin apparently endorses internalism:

> Autonomy is a second-order capacity to reflect critically upon one's first-order preferences and desires, and the ability either to identify with these or to change them in light of higher-order preferences and values. By exercising such a capacity we define our nature, give meaning and coherence to our lives, and take responsibility for the kind of person we are. (Dworkin 1988: 108)

On this account, psychological autonomy seemingly is a wholly internal matter; it is possessed independently of facts about how the capacities and abilities came to be present in agents. Thus, beings who are, as it were, psychological twins over an interval *t* are equal with respect to psychological autonomy during *t* (see Schoeman 1978). Harry Frankfurt's bold endorsement of an internalist conception of free, or autonomous, action also sheds light on the general shape of an internalist conception of psychological autonomy:

> [T]o the extent that a person identifies himself with the springs of his actions, he takes responsibility for those actions and acquires moral responsibility for them; moreover, the questions of how the actions and his identifications with their springs are caused are irrelevant to the questions of whether he performs the actions *freely* or is morally responsible for performing them. (Frankfort 1988: 54; my italics)

Internalism is problematic. A pair of agents who now share, in the same measure, the nonhistorical properties that Berofsky, Dworkin, and Frankfurt identify as ingredients of autonomy may nevertheless have come to be the way they are in such radically different ways that we would be strongly inclined to regard one as significantly less autonomous than the other. Imagine, for example, that both Alan and Bob just now happily made enormous sacrifices for their children's sake, but that whereas Alan developed into an extraordinarily loving parent on his own, Bob's present disposition toward his children and his identification with his new parental values are products of covert brainwashing conducted last night. Prior to brainwashing, Bob had taken only a modest interest in his children's welfare; a futuristic social services department thought that it would be best for all concerned if he were like Alan. Other things being equal, one is naturally inclined to see Bob's pertinent action as less autonomous than Alan's—even if Bob does not fall short of Alan with respect to the nonhistorical properties these three philosophers have identified.

Keith Lehrer contends that what he dubs "the *power preference*" (*PP*) empowers agents and makes them autonomous: A(PP) I have the preference structure concerning my preference that *p* because I prefer to have that preference structure concerning my preference that *p*" (Lehrer 1997: 100). He argues that *PP* solves the problems posed by external manipulation and chance: "If I have the preference structure that I do because I prefer to have it, then it cannot be the case that the preferences of it are imposed by another, nor, for that matter, can they be fortuitous" (ibid.: 101).

This is doubtful. If I have the preference structure I prefer to have, including my preference to have that preference structure, *only* because I prefer to have it, then, as Lehrer says, external manipulation has no part in explaining my having the preferences I do. But it is likely that my preferring to have the preference structure I have does not fully explain my having that structure: presumably, some of my preferences, including my preference to have the preference structure I have, are influenced by past experiences of mine. It might be claimed that my preferring to have the preference structure I have, including that very preference, is the *proximate explanation* of my having that preference structure. But this is consistent with the fact that this preference resulted from external manipulation. Suppose expert manipulators cause me to prefer a certain preference structure, a structure that includes my preference to have it. My having this higher order preference might be the proximate explanation of my having the preference structure I do, even though a fuller explanation includes external manipulation. If I had not been manipulated, I would not have the preference structure that I now have. What Lehrer calls "the external manipulation problem" remains a problem for internalists about psychological autonomy.

A familiar reaction is that autonomy requires what Dworkin has termed "procedural independence" (1988: 18; compare Benn 1988; Haworth 1986; and Lindley 1986). The requirement, as Dworkin sometimes represents it, is externalist. He writes: "Second-order reflection cannot be the whole story of autonomy. For those reflections, the choice of the kind of person one wants to become, may be influenced by other persons or circumstances in such a fashion that we do not view those evaluations as being the person's own" (Dworkin 1988: 18). Thus, oddly, a human being can have and exercise precisely the capacities and abilities that Dworkin identifies with autonomy, and yet not be autonomous, on his view. (This indicates that Dworkin's identification should be construed as a conditional one—that is, conditional upon the person's having "procedural independence.")

Although Dworkin offers no analysis of procedural independence, he does sketch a program:

> Spelling out the conditions of procedural independence involves distinguishing those ways of influencing people's reflective and critical faculties which subvert them from those which promote and improve them. It involves distinguishing those influences such as hypnotic suggestion, manipulation, coercive persuasion, subliminal influence, and so forth, and doing so in a non ad hoc fashion. (ibid.: 18)

For some readers, this passage will have an internalist ring. If the proscribed influence amounts to the destruction or severe impairment—subversion in *that* sense—of agents' capacities for second-order reflection and the like, internalists can happily endorse the proscription. There is, however, a way of understanding the subversion of a person's reflective and critical faculties as at least sometimes an externalistic matter. By manipulating the perspective or orientation from which such faculties operate in another agent, one can subvert the faculties without dulling their edge. By controlling which principles or values an agent takes for granted, one can make another person's critical and reflective capacities serve one's own purposes—purposes perhaps violently opposed by the individual prior to manipulation. Perhaps Dworkin means to count subversion of this kind, too, as precluded by procedural independence. If so, his position is externalist.

An externalist may suggest that the autonomous possession of a pro-attitude requires *authenticity* regarding that pro-attitude. Brief commentary on two conceptions of authenticity will prove useful. Dworkin, in an influential article, understands authenticity as *identification* with one's motivations (Dworkin 1976: 25). Since brainwashed Bob identifies with his new motivations, authenticity in Dworkin's sense does not suit an externalist's needs. Joel Feinberg writes, in a similar vein:

> A person is authentic to the extent that . . . he can and does subject his opinions and tastes to rational scrutiny. He is authentic to the extent that he can and does alter his convictions for reasons of his own, and does this without guilt or anxiety. . . . He will select his life style to match his temperament, and his political attitudes to fit his ideals and interests. (Feinberg 1986: 33)

But brainwashed Bob can scrutinize his opinions and tastes, alter his convictions in accordance with his values (some of which are products of brainwashing), and select (or at least embrace) a lifestyle that fits his current temperament. Feinberg's expression, "reasons of his own," might leave open what we need, if reasons of one's own are not simply identical with one's reasons.[16] A theorist might hold that one's reasons count as "reasons of [one's] own" only under certain history-sensitive conditions. On such a reading, Feinberg's conception of authenticity is closer to what the externalist needs than is the more streamlined notion of authenticity as identification.

As most contributors to the literature on autonomy observe, including Dworkin and Feinberg, autonomy does not entail being a wholly self-made person. Any conception of authenticity that requires individuals who possess that property to be the sole source of their values, preferences, and the like would be poorly suited to our needs. External influences on our values are considerable; a view of autonomy that placed autonomous individuals above all that would exclude all of us. Still, apparently, some instances of effective external influence greatly reduce psychological autonomy, and attention to authenticity might help us see why.

Compare an authentic dollar bill with a perfect counterfeit. Both will get you a Coke from a vending machine. But only one of them can function in a *legal* purchase. Whether the two bills have the same causal powers is open to dispute. Some might claim that only one of them has the power to function—causally, of course—in your legally acquiring a Coke. Others might urge that because the distinction between the acquisition of a Coke and the *legal* acquisition of a Coke is a wholly conceptual matter, it has nothing whatever to do with causal powers: the bills have the same causal powers; but because only one of them is authentic, "purchasing" a Coke with the other does not *count as* a legal acquisition. This dispute may be set aside for present purposes. It suffices to note that, given certain conventions (in this case, laws), the bills cannot function in precisely the same ways: both get you the Coke, but only one gets it for you legally.

What are the conventions or principles with respect to which the sort of authenticity that an externalist needs would make a difference? One obvious answer is conventions or principles governing the attribution of *responsibility* to agents for their values, preferences, principles, and the like—or, more generally, for their *character*. To the extent that we view psychologically autonomous agents, in virtue of their autonomy, as responsible (in some measure, at least) for their character, we are likely to consider an authenticity that bears on responsibility for one's character as bearing on personal autonomy, as well.[17] Now, even if we see Alan as responsible for his character, do we see brainwashed Bob as responsible for the pertinent aspects of his new character, given what we know about the way that he came to be like Alan?

Assume that determinism is true and assume as well that its truth is compatible with personal autonomy and responsibility.[18] It might be argued that, with these assumptions in place, (1) the notion of responsibility for one's *character* must be jettisoned and (2) the best account we can give of autonomy regarding one's way of life is that such autonomy is precisely a matter of living in accordance with preferences and desires that one identifies with "in light of higher order preferences and values." In the former connection, it may be claimed that character is *ultimately* a product of external causes present prior even to our own existence, and that, having no control over such causes (events), we have no control over—hence no responsibility for—our character.[19] In the latter, it may be argued that if autonomy in a given practical domain suffices for an agent's responsiblity for his intentional actions in that domain, brainwashed Bob is responsible for his Alan-like behavior. He, like Alan, conducts himself in accordance with higher order preferences and values with which he identifies, is capable of critical reflection, and so on.

So much the worse for determinism and compatibilism, some will respond. But a philosopher may leave both theses open and take another approach. If a history-sensitive externalism about psychological autonomy is acceptable to a compatibilist about psychological autonomy, that is worth knowing. Richard Double has claimed—wrongly, I have argued (Mele 1995: ch. 9)—that "the internalistic view is implicit in compatibilism" and that "compatibilism has not a chance of plausibility without [internalism], since otherwise the incompatibilist abhorrence of determinism will destroy it" (Double 1991: 56–57). The apparent problem is that once agents' histories are allowed to have a relevance of the sort discussed here to their autonomy, their having *deterministic* histories also is relevant, and in a way that undermines compatibilism. It may be thought that if instances of manipulation of the sort that I have mentioned block psychological autonomy, they do so only if they *causally determine* crucial psychological events or states, and that determinism consequently is in danger of being identified as the real culprit.[20]

Assuming the truth of determinism, is it true that the internalist account of autonomy just sketched is the best possible? Well, determinists are in a position to distinguish among different causal routes to the collections of values (and "characters") agents have at a time. They are also in a position to provide principled grounds for holding that distinct routes to two type-identical collections of values may be such that one and only one of those routes blocks autonomy regarding a life lived in accordance with those values. An analogue of the familiar compatibilist distinction between *caused* and *compelled* (or constrained) *behavior* may be used here.[21] Perhaps in engineering Bob's parental values, the civic-minded brainwashers *compelled* him to have Alan-like pro-attitudes. Even so, a true and complete causal story about Alan's having the values that he has, might involve no compulsion. If Bob was compelled to possess his Alan-like values while Alan was not, we have some apparent grounds, at least, for taking the latter alone to be responsible for the pertinent aspects of his character and for value-guided deeds of the pertinent sort. And if these grounds are deemed irrelevant to responsibility, compatibilism is threatened. If the causal production and sustaining of values and other pro-attitudes are indistinguishable from the compulsive production and sustaining of such things, then determinists would have to hold that all of our pro-attitudes are effects of compulsion, and none "merely" of causation—in which case, arguably, the causally determined behavioral consequences of our pro-attitudes are themselves (indirectly) compelled, and no one is responsible for any behavior at all that is driven by pro-attitudes.[22]

6. Autonomism: Libertarian, Compatibilist, and Agnostic

Libertarians argue that determinism precludes autonomy by, for example, precluding an agent's ultimate responsibility for anything (see Kane 1996a). Some compatibilist believers in autonomy argue that libertarians rely on indeterminism in a way that deprives us of autonomous control over our decisions (for example, Berofsky 1995). Theorists who contend that no human being is autonomous ("nonautonomists") can benefit from arguments on both sides, alleging that libertarians decisively reveal the ordinary person's notion of autonomy, an incompatibilist notion, and that compatibilist critics of libertarianism show that the notion is incoherent or unsatisfiable. Is there a way to use the resources both of libertarianism and of compatibilism in an argument for the following thesis: the claim that there are autonomous human beings is more credible than the claim that there are none?

Suppose that Ann, on the basis of careful, rational deliberation, judges it best to A. And suppose that, on the basis of that judgment, she decides to A and then acts accordingly, intentionally A-ing. Suppose further that Ann has not been subjected to autonomy-thwarting mind control or relevant deception, that she is perfectly sane, and so on. To make a long story short, suppose that she satisfies an attractive set of sufficient conditions for *compatibilist* autonomy regarding her A-ing (see Mele 1995: ch. 10.5). Now add one more supposition to the set: while Ann was deliberating, it was not causally determined that she would come to the conclusion she did.

In principle, an agent-internal indeterminism may provide for indeterministic agency while blocking or limiting our ("nonultimate") control over what happens only at junctures at which we have no greater control on the hypothesis that our world is deterministic (Mele 1995: ch. 12; compare Dennett 1978: 294–99; Ekstrom 103–29; and Kane 1985: 101–10). Ordinary human beings have a wealth of beliefs, desires, hypotheses, and the like, the great majority of which are not salient in consciousness during any given process of deliberation. Plainly, in those cases in which we act on the basis of careful deliberation, what we do is influenced by at least some of the considerations that "come to mind"—that is, become salient in consciousness—during deliberation and by our assessments of considerations. Now, even if determinism is true, it is false that, with respect to *every* consideration—every belief, desire, hypothesis, and so on—that comes to mind during our deliberation, we are in control of its coming to mind; and some considerations that come to mind without our being in control of their so doing may influence the outcome of our deliberation. Furthermore, a kind of internal indeterminism is imaginable that limits our control only in a way that gives us no less nonultimate control than we would have on the assumption that determinism is true, while opening up alternative deliberative outcomes. (Although, in a deterministic world, it would never be a matter of genuine chance that a certain consideration came to mind during deliberation, it may still be a matter of luck relative to the agent's sphere of control.) As I put it elsewhere, "Where compatibilists have no good reason to insist on determinism in the deliberative process as a requirement for autonomy, where internal indeterminism is, for all we know, a reality, and where such indeterminism would not diminish the nonultimate control that real agents exert over their deliberation even on the assumption that real agents are internally deterministic—that is, at the *intersection* of these three locations—libertarians may plump for ultimacy-promoting indeterminism."[23]

Space constraints preclude much elaboration here, but I will point out that the modest indeterminism at issue allows agents ample control over their deliberation. Suppose a belief, hypothesis, or desire that is relevant to a deliberator's present practical question comes to mind during deliberation but was not causally determined to do so (perhaps unlike the great majority of considerations that come to mind during this process of deliberation).[24] Presumably, a normal agent would be able to *assess* this consideration. And upon reflection, he might rationally reject the belief as unwarranted, rationally judge that the hypothesis does not merit investigation, or rationally decide that the desire should be given little or no weight in his deliberation. Alternatively, reflection might rationally lead him to retain the belief, to pursue the hypothesis, or to give the desire significant weight. That a consideration comes to mind indeterministically does not entail that the agent has no control over how he responds to it.

Considerations that indeterministically come to mind (like considerations that deterministically come to mind) are nothing more than input to deliberation. Their coming to mind has at most an indirect effect on what the agent decides, an effect that is mediated by the agent's own assessment of them. They do not settle matters. Moreover, not only do agents have the opportunity to assess these considerations, they also have the opportunity to search for additional relevant considerations before they decide, thereby increasing the probability that other relevant considerations will indeterministically come to mind. They have the opportunity to cancel or attenuate the effects of bad luck (for example, the unde-termined coming to mind of a misleading consideration or an undetermined failure to notice a relevant consideration). And given a suitable indeterminism regarding what comes to mind in an assessment process, it is not causally deter-mined what assessment the agent will reach.

Compatibilists who hold that we act autonomously even when we are not in control of what happens at certain specific junctures in the process leading to action are in no position to hold that an indeterministic agent's lacking control at the same junctures precludes autonomous action. And, again, real human be-ings are not in control of the coming to mind of everything that comes to mind during typical processes of deliberation. If this lack of perfect nonultimate control does not preclude its being the case that autonomous actions sometimes issue from typical deliberation on the assumption that we are deterministic agents, it also does not preclude this on the assumption that we are *indeterministic* agents.

Is a modest indeterminism of the kind I have sketched useful to libertarians? Elsewhere, I have suggested that at least some libertarians might prize something that compatibilist autonomy does not offer them, a species of agency that gives them a kind of independence and an associated kind of explanatory bearing on their conduct that they would lack in any deterministic world (Mele 1996, 1999a). The combination of the satisfaction of an attractive set of sufficient conditions for *compatibilist* autonomy, including all the nonultimate control that involves, and a modest agent-internal indeterminism of the sort I have described would give them that. Agents of the imagined sort would make choices and perform actions that lack deterministic causes in the distant past. They would have no less control over these choices and actions than we do over ours, on the assumption that we are deterministic agents. And given that they have at least robust *compatibilist* responsibility for certain of these choices and actions, they would also have *ulti-mate* responsibility for them. These choices and actions have, in Robert Kane's words, "their ultimate sources" in the agents, in the sense that the collection of agent-internal states and events that explains these choices and actions does not itself admit of a deterministic explanation that stretches back beyond the agent (1996a: 98).

Now, even if garden-variety compatibilists can be led to see that the problem of luck is surmountable by a libertarian, how are theorists of other kinds likely to respond to the libertarian position that I have been sketching? There are, of course, philosophers who contend that moral responsibility and autonomy are illusions and that we lack these properties whether our world is deterministic or indeter-ministic (see, for example, Double 1991 and G. Strawson 1986). Elsewhere, I have argued that the impossible demands this position places on moral responsibility and autonomy are *unwarranted* demands (Mele 1995: chs. 12 and 13).

Modest libertarians can also anticipate trouble from traditional libertarians, who want more than the modest indeterminism that I have described can offer.

It is incumbent upon traditional libertarians to show that what they want is coherent. That requires showing that this does not entail or presuppose a kind of luck that would itself undermine moral responsibility.[25] The traditional libertarian wants both indeterminism and significant control at the moment of choice or decision. This is the desire that prompts a serious version of the worry about luck sketched in section 3.[26]

Must one choose between compatibilism and incompatibilism regarding the issue of autonomy? No. One can be agnostic. Moreover, consistently with agnosticism, one can make a case for the existence of autonomy. In Mele (1995), I defended what I dubbed "agnostic autonomism," the conjunction of the agnosticism just identified with the belief that there are autonomous human beings. This position can draw upon the resources both of compatibilism and of libertarianism. It can offer both a robust, satisfiable set of sufficient conditions for compatibilist autonomy and a coherent set of conditions for incompatibilist autonomy that, for all we know, is satisfied by real human beings. It has the resources to resolve alleged, determinism-neutral problems for compatibilist accounts of autonomy, to conquer (along lines sketched earlier in this section) the problem about "luck" or control that libertarianism traditionally faces, and to show that *if* compatibilism is true, belief in the existence of human autonomy is warranted. Further, agnostics have the advantage of not having certain disadvantages. Agnostics do not insist that autonomy is compatible with determinism; nor need they insist that we are internally indeterministic in a way useful to libertarians. But if it were discovered that we are not suitably indeterministic, they would have compatibilism to fall back on.

I claimed then, and still believe, that agnostic autonomism is more credible than the view that no human being is autonomous (nonautonomism). Consider the following propositions:

a. Some human beings are autonomous and determinism is compatible with autonomy (compatibilist belief in autonomy).
b. Some human beings are autonomous and determinism is incompatible with autonomy (libertarianism).
c. Either *a* or *b* (agnostic autonomism).
d. No human beings are autonomous (nonautonomism).

Imagine that each proposition has a probability between 0 and 1. Then (c) has a higher probability than (a) and a higher probability than (b), since (c) is the *disjunction* of (a) and (b). So what about (d)? I argued that nonautonomism, at best, fares no better than (a) and no better than (b) (1995: ch. 13). If that is right, then since (c) has a higher probability than each of (a) and (b), (c) has a higher probability than (d): agnostic autonomism beats nonautonomism! The nature of the claimed victory is such as to call for further work on all sides.

NOTES

Much of this essay derives from Mele (1995: chs. 1, 7, 8, 9, 12, and 13); part derives from Mele (1999).

1. See Audi (1991a), Benn (1988: ch. 10), Feinberg (1986: ch. 18), Haworth (1986), Lindley (1986: ch. 5), and Young 1986.

2. For other restrictive features of Aristotle's notion of *enkrateia*, see Charlton 1988: 35–41.

3. An issue that has received significant attention in the philosophical literature on self-control revolves around an interesting puzzle about how an exercise of self-control against one's strongest desires at the time is possible. I lack the space to review it here. See Alston (1977), Kennett and Smith (1996, 1997), McCann (1995a), Mele (1987: ch. 5, 1995: ch. 3, 1997a, 1998a), Pugmire (1994), and Velleman (1992).

4. More strictly, ideal self-control has maximal range relative to the psychological and physical life of a being. Immaterial beings incapable of overt action may be perfectly self-controlled; the same may be true of some hypothetical emotionless beings. But such beings are not my primary concern. By "maximal categorial range" in 1, I mean, roughly, the full range of self-control open to a being whose life is at least as robust and complex, physically and psychologically, as that of the average reader of this chapter.

5. The assumption is motivated partly by the possibility that some ideally self-controlled person rarely, if ever, needs to exercise his powers of self-control. On the relevance of mental health, see Mele (1995: 122–26).

6. Indeed, some theorists have used autonomy as a theoretical *foil* (for example, Wolf 1990).

7. Refer to Fischer's distinction between "guidance" and "regulative" control, Fischer (1994: 132–35).

8. For more sophisticated versions of this argument, see Ayer (1954), Bergmann (1977: 234–35), Hobart (1934), Nowell-Smith (1948), and Smart (1961); compare 1960 Hume: bk. II, pt. III, sec. 2 and item 1955. sec. 8.

9. The quoted words are from Schrödinger (1983: 157). On triggering cases of this general kind, also see Anscombe (1981: 144–47), Lewis (1986a, vol. 20 176), Sorabji (1980: 28), and van Inwagen (1983: 191–92).

10. The connection between control and "moral luck" is a major theme in Nagel's "Moral Luck" (1979: 24–38).

11. Since agent-causation is a central topic of other essays in this volume, I will not discuss it here.

12. This tripartite distinction is not intended to be exhaustive.

13. For further discussion of Christman (1991), see Mele (1993), where essentially this case appears.

14. This is not to deny that Alice is *responsible* (causally or morally) for her continued possession of the desire.

15. In Mele (1995), I compared the distinction between internalist and externalist conceptions of psychological autonomy with the distinction between internalism and externalism about the individuation of psychological states (a major issue in the philosophy of mind), and I suggested some ways in which the distinctions are independent of

one another (ibid.:146–47). D. Zimmerman (1999) is a fascinating exploration of the comparative issue.

16. For an attempted distinction along these lines, see Dworkin (1976: 25). See Mele (1995: ch. 7.5) on a putative distinction between "his own" and "his."

17. The kinds of responsibility associated with autonomy may vary with the kind of agent at issue. If even the various actions and omissions of the morality-transcending Aristotelian gods I mentioned have no moral significance, *moral* responsibility does not apply to these beings. (Imagine that these gods are the sole sentient inhabitants of their universe.)

18. The determinism at work here need not be a perfectly universal one. It may, instead, be a deterministic theory specifically of human development and behavior. For a detailed deterministic theory of the latter kind, see Honderich (1988, vols. 1 and 2).

19. See, for example, Waller (1990), who argues that determinism is compatible with freedom but not with moral responsibility. If there is a sense of *freedom* in which this is true, most compatibilist believers in freedom are seeking something more robust.

20. Roughly this idea is a theme in various "mind-control" arguments against compatibilism, as Blumenfeld (1988) observes. For a view of *moral responsibility* that is explicitly externalist *and* compatibilist, see Fischer (1987). (Fischer does not there endorse the compatibility of determinism with freedom to do *otherwise*, but compatibilists about determinism and free action need not be compatibilists about determinism and freedom to do otherwise.) Fischer's externalism about moral responsibility is developed further in Fischer and Ravizza (1994 and 1998).

21. See, for example, Audi (1993: chs. 7 and 10), Ayer (1954), Grünbaum (1971), Mill (1979: ch. 26, esp. 464–67), and Schlick 1962: ch. 7. Also see Hume's remarks on the liberty of spontaneity versus the liberty of indifference (1960 bk. II, pt. III, sec. 2).

22. An internalist might claim that agents are autonomous with respect to their possession of a pro-attitude if and only if they are able (at least in a compatibilist sense of *able*) to shed the attitude. In Mele (1995), I argue that agents can autonomously possess attitudes that they are "practically unable" to shed, and that "psychological twins," owing to different histories, may be such that although one of them is autonomous regarding a practically unsheddable attitude, the other is not (ibid. 149–73). The issue is complicated; owing to space constraints, I cannot explore it here.

23. Mele (1995: 235). On the relative theoretical utility of internal versus external indeterminism, see ibid. (195–96).

24. Regarding the parenthetical clause, bear in mind that not all causally determined events need be part of a deterministic chain that stretches back even for several moments, much less close to the Big Bang.

25. Just as I distinguished between ultimate and nonultimate control, one may distinguish between ultimate and nonultimate *luck*. Perhaps millions of years ago, in a deterministic universe, conditions were such that today Karl would be an exceptionally kind person whereas Carl would be a ruthless killer. Here we have ultimate luck—good and bad. Libertarians have been much more impressed by it than by nonultimate luck.

26. In section 3, I mentioned recent worries about luck articulated by Haji, Mele, Strawson, and Waller (1988). See Kane (1996a) for a libertarian reply to Waller and Strawson, and Kane (1999 and b) for replies to Haji and Mele. Also see Kane's essay in this volume, chapter 18.

PART VIII

NEUROSCIENCE AND FREE WILL

....

CHAPTER 25

DO WE HAVE FREE WILL?

....

BENJAMIN LIBET

I have taken an experimental approach to the question of whether we have free will. Freely voluntary acts are preceded by a specific electrical change in the brain (the "readiness potential", RP) that begins 550 msec. before the act. Human subjects became aware of intention to act 350–400 msec. *after RP* starts, but 200 msec. before the motor act. The volitional process is therefore *initiated* unconsciously. But the conscious function could still control the outcome; it can veto the act. Free will is therefore not excluded. These findings put constraints on views of how free will may operate; it would not initiate a voluntary act but it could *control* performance of the act. The findings also affect views of guilt and responsibility.

But the deeper question still remains: Are freely voluntary acts subject to macro-deterministic laws or can they appear without such constraints, nondetermined by natural laws and "truly free"? I shall present an experimentalist view about these fundamental philosophical opposites.

The question of free will goes to the root of our views about human nature and how we relate to the universe and to natural laws. Are we completely defined by the deterministic nature of physical laws? Theologically imposed fateful destiny ironically produces a similar end-effect. In either case, we would be essentially sophisticated automatons, with our conscious feelings and intentions tacked on as epiphenomena with no causal power. Or do we have some independence in making choices and actions, not completely determined by the known physical laws?

I have taken an experimental approach to at least some aspects of the question. The operational definition of free will in these experiments was in accord with common views. First, there should be no external control or cues to affect the occurrence or emergence of the voluntary act under study; that is, it should be endogenous. Second, the subject should feel that he or she wanted to do it, on her or his own initiative, and feel he or she could control what is being done, when to do it or not to do it. Many actions lack this second attribute. For example, when the primary motor area of the cerebral cortex is stimulated, muscle contractions can be produced in certain sites in the body. However, the subject (a neurosurgical patient) reports that these actions were imposed by the stimulator, that is, that he did not will these acts. And there are numerous clinical disorders in which a similar discrepancy between actions and will occurs. These include the involuntary actions in cerebral palsy, Parkinsonism, Huntington's chorea, Tourette's syndrome, and even obsessive compulsions to act. A striking example is the "alien hand syndrome." Patients with a lesion in a fronto-medial portion of premotor area may find that the hand and arm on the affected side performs curious purposeful actions, such as undoing a buttoned shirt when the subject is trying to button it up; all this occurs without or even against the subject's intention and will. (See Spence and Frith 1999: 23.)

1. Timing of Brain Processes and Conscious Will

Performance of "self-paced" voluntary acts had, surprisingly, been found to be preceded by a slow electrical change recordable on the scalp at the vertex (Kornhuber and Deecke 1965). The onset of this electrical indication of certain brain activities preceded the actual movement by up to 1 sec or more. It was termed the "Bereitschaftpotential" or "readiness potential" (RP). To obtain the RP required averaging the recordings in many self-paced acts. Subjects were therefore asked to perform their acts within time intervals of 30 sec. to make the total study manageable. In our experiments, however, we removed this constraint on freedom of action; subjects performed a simple flick or flexion of the wrist at any time they felt the urge or wish to do so. These voluntary acts were to be performed capriciously, free of any external limitations or restrictions (Libet et al. 1982). RPs in these acts began with onsets averaging 550 msec. before activation of the involved muscle (Figure 25.1).

The brain was evidently beginning the volitional process in this voluntary act well before the activation of the muscle that produced the movement. My question then became, *When* does the *conscious* wish or intention (to perform the act) appear? In the traditional view of conscious will and free will, one would expect conscious will to appear before, or at the onset, of the RP, and thus command the brain to perform the intended act. But an appearance of conscious will 550 msec. or more before the act seemed intuitively unlikely. It was clearly important to establish the time of the conscious will relative to the onset of the brain process (RP); if conscious will were to *follow* the onset of RP, that would have a fundamental impact on how we could view free will.

To establish this temporal relation required a method for measuring the time of appearance of the conscious will in each such act. Initially, that seemed to me an impossible goal. But after some time it occurred to me to try having the subject report a "clock-time" at which he or she was *first aware* of the wish or urge to act (Figure 25.2) (Libet et al., 1983a). The clock had to be much faster than the usual clock, in order to accommodate time differences in the hundreds of msec. For our clock, the spot of light of a cathode ray oscilloscope was made to revolve around the face of the scope like the sweep-second hand of an ordinary clock, but at a speed approximately 25 times as fast. Each of the marked off "seconds" around the periphery was thus equivalent to about 40 msec. When we tried out this method, we were actually surprised to find that each subject reported times for *first awareness of wish to act* (W) with a reliability of 20 msec., for each group of 40 such trials. A test for the accuracy of such reports was also encouraging. In this, the subject remained relaxed and did *not* perform any voluntary act. Instead, a weak electrical stimulus was delivered to the skin of the same hand. The stimulus was applied at random times in the different trials. The experimental observers knew the actual time for each stimulus. The subject did not know this actual time but was asked to report the clock-time at which he felt each such stimulus. Subjects accomplished this with an error of only −50 msec.

1.1. The Experiment

In the actual experiment, then, each RP was obtained from an averaged electrical recording in 40 trials. In each of these trials, the subject performed the sudden flick of the wrist whenever he or she freely wanted to do so. After each of these trials, the subject reported W, the clock-time associated with the first awareness of the wish to move (Libet et al. 1983a).

1.2. Brain Initiates Voluntary Act Unconsciously

The results of many such groups of trials are diagrammed in Figure 25.3. For groups in which all the voluntary acts were freely spontaneous, with no reports

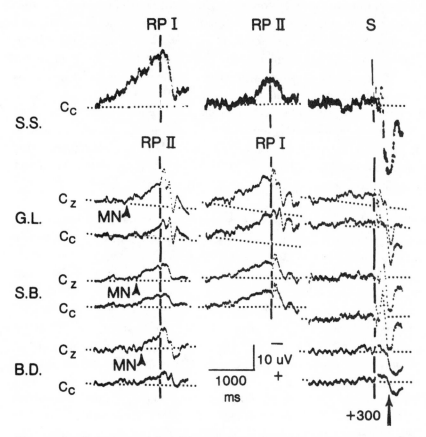

Fig. 25.1 Readiness potentials (RP) preceding self-initiated voluntary acts. Each horizontal row is the computer-averaged potential for 40 trials, recorded by a DC system with an active electrode on the scalp, either at the midline-vertex (Cz) or on the left side (contralateral to the performing right hand (Cc).

When every self-initiated quick flexion of the right hand (fingers or wrist) in the series of 40 trials was (reported as having been) subjectively experienced to originate spontaneously and with no planning by the subject, RPs labeled type II were found in association. (Arrowheads labeled MN indicate onset of the "main negative" phase of the vertex recorded type II RPs in this figure; see Libet et al 1982. Onsets were also measured for 90% of the total area of RP). When an awareness of a general intention or planning to act sometime within the next second or so was reported to have occurred before some of the 40 acts in the series, type I RPs were recorded (ibid). In the last column, labeled S, a near-threshold skin stimulus was applied in each of the 40 trials at a randomized time unknown to the subject, with no motor act performed; the subject was asked to recall and report the time when he became aware of each stimulus in the same way he reported the time of awareness of wanting to move in the case of self-initiated motor acts.

The solid vertical line through each column represents 0 time, at which the electromyogram (EMG) of the activated muscle begins in the case of RP series, or at of rough planning of when to act, the onset of RP averaged −550 msec. (before the muscle was activated). The W times for first awareness of wish to act averaged about −200 msec., for all groups. This value was the same even when subjects reported having pre-planned roughly when to act! If we correct W for the −50 msec. error in the subjects' reports of timings of the skin stimuli, we have an average corrected W of about −150 msec. Clearly, the brain process (RP) to prepare for this voluntary act began about 400 msec. before the appearance of the conscious will to act (W). This relationship was true for every group of 40 trials and in every one of the nine subjects studied. It should also be noted that the actual difference in times is probably greater than the 400 msec; the actual initiating process in the brain probably starts before our recorded RP, in an unknown area that then activates the supplementary motor area in the cerebral cortex. The supplementary motor area is located in the midline near the vertex and is thought to be the source of our recorded RP.

2. ANY ROLE FOR CONSCIOUS WILL?

The initiation of the freely voluntary act appears to begin in the brain unconsciously, well before the person consciously knows he wants to act!. Is there, then, any role for conscious will in the performance of a voluntary act? (see Libet, 1985) To answer this it must be recognized that conscious will (W) does appear about 150 msec. before the muscle is activated, even though it follows onset of the RP.

---

which the stimulus was actually delivered in the case of S series. The dashed horizontal line represents the DC baseline drift.

For subject S.S., the first RP (type I) was recorded before the instruction "to let the urge come on its own, spontaneously" was introduced; the second RP (type II) was obtained after giving this instruction in the same session as the first. For subjects G.L., S.B., and B.D., this instruction was given at the start of all sessions. Nevertheless, each of these subjects reported some experiences of loose planning in one of the 40-trial series, those series exhibited type I RPs rather than type II. Note that the slow negative shift in scalp potential that precedes EMGs of self-initiated acts (RP) does not precede the skin stimulus in S series. However, evoked potentials following the stimulus are seen regularly to exhibit a large positive component with a peak close to +300 ms. (arrow indicates this time), this P300 event-related potential had been shown by others to be associated with decisions about uncertain events (in this case, the time of the randomly delivered stimulus), and it also indicates that the subject is attending well to the experimental conditions.

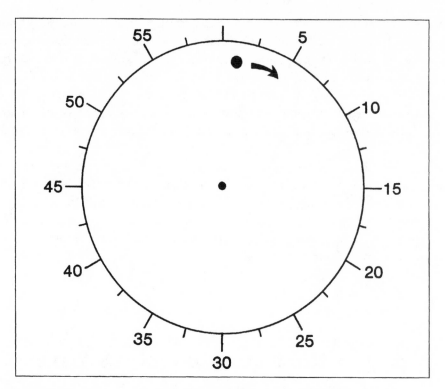

Fig. 25.2 Oscilloscope "clock." Spot of light revolves around periphery of screen, once in 2.56 sec. (instead of 60 sec. for a sweep-second hand of a regular clock). Each marked off "second" (in the total of 60 markings) represents 43 msec. of actual time here. The subject holds his gaze to the center of the screen. For each performed quick flexion of the wrist, at any freely chosen time, the subject was asked to note the position of the clock spot when he or she first became aware of the wish or intention to act. This associated clock time is reported by the subject later, after the trial is completed.

An interval of 150 msec. would allow enough time in which the conscious function might affect the final outcome of the volitional process. (Actually, only 100 msec. is available for any such effect. The final 50 msec. before the muscle is activated is the time for the primary motor cortex to activate the spinal motor nerve cells. During this time the act goes to completion with no possibility of stopping it by the rest of the cerebral cortex.)

Potentially available to the conscious function is the possibility of stopping or vetoing the final progress of the volitional process, so that no actual muscle action ensues. *Conscious will could thus affect the outcome* of the volitional process even though the latter was initiated by unconscious cerebral processes. Conscious will might block or veto the process, so that no act occurs.

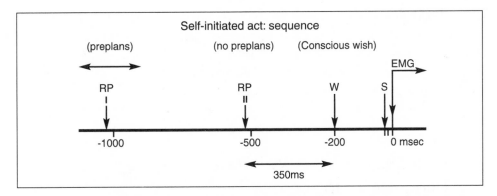

Fig. 25.3 Diagram of sequence of events, cerebral and subjective, that precede a fully self-initiated voluntary act. Relative to 0 time, detected in the electromyogram (EMG) of the suddenly activated muscle, the readiness potential (RP an indicator of related cerebral neuronal activities) begins first, at about −1050 ms. when some planning is reported (RP I) or about −550 ms. with spontaneous acts lacking immediate planning (RP II). Subjective awareness of the wish to move (W) appears at about −200 ms., some 350 ms. after onset even of RP II; however, W does appear well before the act (EMG). Subjective timings reported for awareness of the randomly delivered S (skin) stimulus average about −50 ms. Relative to actual delivery time (from Libet 1989).

The existence of a veto possibility is not in doubt. The subjects in our experiments at times reported that a conscious wish or urge to act appeared but that they suppressed or vetoed that. In the absence of the muscle's electrical signal when being activated, there was no trigger to initiate the computer's recording of any RP that may have preceded the veto; thus, there were no *recorded* RPs with a vetoed intention to act. We were, however, able to show that subjects could veto an act planned for performance at a prearranged time. They were able to exert the veto within the interval of 100 to 200 msec. before the preset time to act (Libet et al., 1983b). A large RP preceded the veto, signifying that the subject was indeed *preparing* to act, even though the action was aborted by the subject. All of us, not just experimental subjects, have the experience of vetoing a spontaneous urge to perform some act. This often occurs when the urge to act involves some socially unacceptable consequence, like an urge to shout some obscenity at the professor. (Incidentally, in the disorder called Tourette's syndrome, subjects do spontaneously shout obscenities. These acts should not be regarded as freely voluntary. No RP appears before such an act. A quick reaction to an unwarned stimulus also lacks a preceding RP, and it is not a freely voluntary act.)

Another hypothetical function for conscious will could be to serve as a "trigger" that is required to enable the volitional process to proceed to final action. However, there is no evidence for this, such as there is for a veto function, and the "trigger" possibility also seems unlikely on other grounds. For example, voluntary acts that become somewhat "automatic" can be performed with no reportable conscious wish to do so; the RP is rather minimal in amplitude and duration before such automatic acts. Automatic acts clearly go to completion without any conscious trigger available.

2.1. Does The Conscious Veto Have a Preceding Unconscious Origin?

One should, at this point, consider the possibility that the conscious veto itself may have its origin in preceding unconscious processes, just as is the case for the development and appearance of the conscious will. If the veto itself were to be initiated and developed unconsciously, the choice to veto would then become an unconscious choice of which we *become* conscious, rather than a consciously causal event. Our own previous evidence had shown that the brain "produces" an awareness of something only after about a 0.5 sec. period of appropriate neuronal activations (see reviews by Libet 1993, 1996).

Some have proposed that even an unconscious initiation of a veto choice would nevertheless be a genuine choice made by the individual and could still be viewed as a free will process (for example. Velmans 1991). I find such a proposed view of free will to be unacceptable. In such a view, the individual would not consciously control his actions; he would only become aware of an unconsciously initiated choice. He would have no direct conscious control over the nature of any preceding unconscious processes. But a free will process implies one could be held consciously responsible for one's choice to act or not to act. We do not hold people responsible for actions performed unconsciously, without the possibility of conscious control. For example, actions by a person during a psychomotor epileptic seizure, or by one with Tourette's syndrome, and so on, are not regarded as actions of free will. Why, then, should an act unconsciously developed by a normal individual, a process over which he also has no conscious control, be regarded as an act of free will?

I propose, instead, that the conscious veto may *not* require or be the direct result of preceding unconscious processes. The conscious veto is a *control* function, different from simply becoming aware of the wish to act. There is no logical imperative in any mind-brain theory, even identity theory, that requires specific neural activity to precede and determine the nature of a conscious control function. And there is no experimental evidence against the possibility that the control process may appear without development by prior unconscious processes.

Admittedly, to be conscious of the decision to veto does mean one is aware of the event. How may one reconcile this with my proposal? Perhaps we should revisit the concept of awareness, its relation to the content of awareness, and the cerebral processes that develop both awareness and its contents. Our own previous studies have indicated that *awareness* is a unique phenomenon in itself, distinguished from the contents of which one may become aware. For example, awareness of a sensory stimulus can require similar durations of stimulus trains for somatosensory cortex and for medial lemniscus. But the *content* of those awarenesses in these two cases is different, in the subjective timings of sensations (Libet et al. 1979). The content of an unconscious mental process (for example correct detection of a signal in the brain *without any awareness* of the signal) may be the same as the content *with awareness* of the signal. But to become aware of that same content required that stimulus duration be increased by about 400 msec (see Libet et al. 1991).

In an endogenous, freely voluntary act, awareness of the intention to act is delayed for about 400 msec after brain processes initiate the process unconsciously (Libet et al. 1983; Libet 1985). Awareness developed here may be thought of as applying to the whole volitional process; that would include the content of the conscious urge to act and the content of factors that may affect a conscious veto. One need not think of awareness of an event as restricted to one detailed item of content in the whole event.

The possibility is not excluded that factors, on which the decision to veto (control) is *based*, do develop by unconscious processes that precede the veto. However, the *conscious decision to veto* could still be made without direct specification for that decision by the preceding unconscious processes. That is, one could consciously accept or reject the program offered up by the whole array of preceding brain processes. The *awareness* of the decision to veto could be thought to require preceding unconscious processes, but the *content* of that awareness (the actual decision to veto) is a separate feature that need not have the same requirement.

3. WHAT SIGNIFICANCE DO OUR FINDINGS HAVE FOR VOLUNTARY ACTS IN GENERAL?

Can we assume that voluntary acts other than the simple one studied by us also have the same temporal relations between unconscious brain processes and the appearance of the conscious wish/will to act? It is common in scientific researches to be limited technically to studying a process in a simple system; and then to find that the fundamental behavior discovered with the simple system does indeed represent a phenomenon that appears or governs in other related and more complicated systems. For example, the charge on a single electron was measured by Milliken in one isolated system, but it is valid for electrons in all systems. It should also be noted that RPs have been found by other investigators to precede other more complex volitional acts, such as beginning to speak or to write; they did not, however, study the time of appearance of the conscious wish to begin such acts. We may, therefore, allow ourselves to consider what general implications may follow from our experimental findings, while recognizing that an extrapolation to encompass voluntary acts in general has been adopted.

We should also distinguish between *deliberations* about what choice of action to adopt (including planning of when to act on such a choice) and the final intention actually "to act now." One may, after all, deliberate all day about a choice but never act; there is *no voluntary act* in that case. In our experimental studies we found that in some trials subjects engaged in some conscious planning of roughly when to act (in the next second or so). But even in those cases, the subjects reported times of the conscious wish to actually act to be about −200 msec.; this value was very close to the values reported for fully spontaneous voluntary acts with no planning. The onset of the unconscious brain process (RP) for preparing to act was well before the final conscious intention "to act now" in all cases. These findings indicated that the sequence of the volitional processes "to act now" may apply to all volitional acts, regardless of their spontaneity or prior history of conscious deliberations.

4. ETHICAL IMPLICATIONS OF HOW FREE WILL OPERATES

The role of conscious free will would be, then, not to initiate a voluntary act, but rather to *control* occurrences of the act. We may view the unconscious initiatives for voluntary actions as "bubbling up" in the brain. The conscious-will then selects which of these initiatives may go forward to an action or which ones to veto and abort, with no act appearing.

This kind of role for free will is actually in accord with religious and ethical strictures, which commonly advocate that you "control yourself" Most of the Ten Commandments are "do not" orders.

How do our findings relate to the questions of when one may be regarded as guilty or sinful, in various religious and philosophical systems? If one experiences a conscious wish or urge to perform a socially unacceptable act, should that be regarded as a sinful event even if the urge has been vetoed and no act has occurred? Some religious systems answer yes. President Jimmy Carter admitted to having had urges to perform a lustful act. Although he did not act, he apparently still felt sinful for having experienced a lustful urge.[1] But any such urges would be initiated and developed in the brain unconsciously, according to our findings. The mere appearance of an intention to act could not be controlled consciously; only its final consummation in a motor act could be consciously controlled. Therefore, a religious system that castigates an individual for simply having a mental intention or impulse to do something unacceptable, even when this is not acted out, would create a physiologically insurmountable moral and psychological difficulty.

Indeed, insistence on regarding an unacceptable urge to act as sinful, even when no act ensues, would make virtually all individuals sinners. In that sense such a view could provide a physiological basis for "original sin"! Of course, the concept of "original sin" can be based on other views of what is regarded as sinful.

Ethical systems deal with moral codes or conventions that govern how one behaves toward or interacts with other individuals; they are presumably dealing with actions, not simply with urges or intentions. Only a motor act by one person can directly impinge on the welfare of another. Since it is the performance of an act that can be consciously controlled, it should be legitimate to hold individuals guilty of and responsible for their acts.

5. Determinism and Free Will

There remains a deeper question about free will that the foregoing considerations have not addressed. What we have achieved experimentally is some knowledge of the way free will may operate. But we have not answered the question of whether our consciously willed acts are fully determined by natural laws that govern the activities of nerve cells in the brain, or whether acts and the conscious decisions to perform them can proceed to some degree independently of natural determinism. The first of these options would make free will illusory. The conscious feeling of exerting one's will would then be regarded as an epiphenomenon, simply a by-product of the brain's activities but with no causal powers of its own.

First, it may be pointed out that free choices or acts are *unpredictable*, even if they should be completely determined. The "uncertainty principle" of Heisenberg precludes our having a complete knowledge of the underlying molecular activities. Quantum mechanics forces us to deal with probabilities rather than with certainties of events. And, in chaos theory, a random event may shift the behavior of a whole system, in a way that was not predictable. However, even if events are not predictable in practice, they might nevertheless accord with natural laws and therefore be determined.

Let us rephrase our basic question as follows: *Must* we accept determinism? Is non-determinism a viable option? We should recognize that both of these alternative views (natural law determinism versus nondeterminism) are unproven theories, that is, unproven in relation to the existence of free will. Determinism has, on the whole, worked well for the physical observable world. That has led many scientists and philosophers to regard any deviation from determinism as absurd and witless, and unworthy of consideration. But no evidence, nor even a proposed experimental test design, definitively or convincingly demonstrates the validity of natural law determinism as the mediator or instrument of free will.

There is an unexplained gap between the category of physical phenomena and the category of subjective phenomena. As far back as Leibniz, it was pointed out that if one looked into the brain with a full knowledge of its physical makeup and nerve cell activities, one would see nothing that describes subjective experience. The whole foundation of our own experimental studies of the physiology of conscious experience (beginning in the late 1950s) was that externally observable and manipulable brain processes and the related reportable subjective introspective experiences must be studied simultaneously, as independent categories, to understand their relationship. The assumption that a deterministic nature of the physically observable world (to the extent that may be true) can account for subjective conscious functions and event, is a speculative *belief*, not a scientifically proven proposition.

Nondeterminism, the view that conscious will may, at times, exert effects not in accord with known physical laws, is of course an unproven speculative belief. The view that conscious will can affect brain function in violation of known physical laws takes two forms. In one it is held that the violations are not detectable, because the actions of the mind may be at a level below that of the uncertainty allowed by quantum mechanics. (Whether this last proviso can in fact be tenable is a matter yet to be resolved). This view would thus allow for a nondeterministic free will without a perceptible violation of physical laws. In a second view it may be held that violations of known physical laws are large enough to be detectable, at least in principle. But, it can be argued, detectability in actual practice may be impossible. That difficulty for detection would be especially true if the conscious will is able to exert its influence by minimal actions at relatively few nerve elements; these actions could serve as triggers for amplified nerve cell patterns of activity in the brain. In any case, we do not have a scientific answer to the question of which theory (determinism or nondeterminism) may describe the nature of free will.

However, we must recognize that the almost universal experience that we can act with a free, independent choice provides a kind of prima facie evidence that conscious mental processes can causatively control some brain processes (Libet, 1992, 1994). This creates, for an experimental scientist, more difficulty for a determinist than for a non-determinist option. The phenomenal fact is that most of us feel that we do have free will, at least for some of our actions and within certain limits that may be imposed by our brain's status and by our environment. The intuitive feelings about the phenomenon of free will form a fundamental basis for views of our human nature, and great care should be taken not to believe allegedly scientific conclusions about them that actually depend upon hidden ad hoc assumptions. A theory that simply interprets the phenomenon of free will as illusory and denies the validity of this phenomenal fact is less attractive than a theory that accepts or accommodates the phenomenal fact.

In an issue so fundamentally important to our view of who we are, a claim for illusory nature should be based on fairly direct evidence. Such evidence is not available; nor do determinists propose even a potential experimental design to test the theory. Actually, I myself proposed an experimental design that could test whether conscious will could influence nerve cell activities in the brain, doing so via a putative "conscious mental field" that could act without any neuronal connections as the mediators (Libet 1994). This difficult though feasible experiment has, unfortunately, still to be carried out. If it should turn out to confirm the prediction of that field theory, there would be a radical transformation in our views of mind-brain interaction.

My conclusion about free will, one genuinely free in the nondetermined sense, is then that its existence is at least as good, if not a better, scientific option than is its denial by determinist theory. Given the speculative nature of both determinist and nondeterminist theories, why not adopt the view that we do have free will (until some real contradictory evidence may appear, if it ever does)? Such a view would at least allow us to proceed in a way that accepts and accommodates our own deep feeling that we do have free will. We would not need to view ourselves as machines that act in a manner completely controlled by the known physical laws. Such a permissive option has also been advocated by the neurobiologist Roger Sperry (see Doty 1998).[2]

I close, then, with a quotation from the great novelist Isaac Bashevis Singer that relates to the foregoing views. Singer stated his strong belief in our having free will. In an interview (Singer 1968) he volunteered that "The greatest gift which humanity has received is free choice. It is true that we are limited in our use of free choice. But the little free choice we have is such a great gift and is potentially worth so much that for this itself life is worthwhile living."

NOTES

1. President Carter was drawing on a Christian tradition deriving from the following two verses in the Sermon on the Mount: "[Jesus said], 'Ye have heard that it was said by them of old time, Thou shalt not commit adultery: But I say unto you, That whosoever looketh on a woman to lust after her hath committed adultery with her already in his heart' " (Matthew 5.27–28).

2. The belief by many people that one's fate is determined by some mystical reality or by divine intervention produces a difficult paradox for those who also believe we have free will and are to be held responsible for our actions. Such a paradox can arise in the Judeo-Christian view that (a) God is omnipotent, knows in advance what you are going to do, and controls your fate, while (b) also strongly advocating that we can freely determine our actions and are accountable and responsible for our behavior. This difficulty has led to some theological attempts to resolve the paradox. For example, the Kabbalists proposed that God voluntarily gave up his power to know what man was going to do, in order to allow man to choose freely and responsibly and to possess free will.

CHAPTER 26

NEUROPHILOSOPHY OF FREE WILL

HENRIK WALTER

1. FRONTAL CORTEX AND INTELLIGIBILITY

Imagine that you have invited friends to dinner at the last minute. Since the refrigerator is empty, you must shop on your way home from the office. You quickly make up a shopping list. Time is lacking and you must still drive home and also prepare the meal. You must visit various shops, so you decide upon a sequence. And you must take care not to get distracted by other interesting wares, conversation with the salesperson, or sudden ideas. Normally, performing this task is not a big deal. But it is for patients with lesions of the frontal lobes; they are hopelessly overtaxed. They cannot comply with the demands of this scenario. We plan our actions in advance (anticipation) and choose from various options (selection). When time is limited, it is important that we ignore distractions (suppress response), do not follow up on sudden ideas (control impulses), and stick to our task (concentrate). Finally, we must also remember which shops we have been to and what we have already purchased (working memory). We don't want to serve crackers without cheese!

According to neuropsychological findings, all these functions are attributed to the frontal cortex (Kolb and Wishaw 1996: 305–33). We now need some neuro-anatomical information: The frontal cortex comprises three parts—the primary motor cortex, the premotor cortex, and the so-called prefrontal (association) cortex. The primary motor cortex is a thin strip, which on both sides of the head stretches from the middle toward the front up to the temples. It relays motor commands to the muscles via the spinal cord. The premotor region is in front of this strip, six times as large and also concerned with motor functions (Freund 1990). In its medial section sits the supplementary motor area, the SMA, which is presumably the source of the readiness potential.[1] Both areas are closely linked to the biggest part of the frontal cortex, namely the prefrontal cortex. In terms of evolution, it is the youngest part of the human brain. While in cats it makes up only about 3.5% of the cortex surface, in chimpanzees it is about 17% and in humans it is 29%, that is, almost a third of the entire brain surface.[2] It is no wonder, then, that the prefrontal cortex is involved in typically human cognitive functions. We roughly distinguish two different sections of the prefrontal cortex: one part lies on the side and top (dorso-lateral section) and the other lies below and toward the center (ventral medial section). The ventral medial sections becomes important in section 2, on agency, so I need not discuss it here. The dorso-lateral section contains the motor speech center.

Very generally, we can say that the function of the frontal cortex is to organize behavior through time. While the motor area is concerned with organizing and executing movements, it is the job of the prefrontal cortex to "control" cognitive processes that ensure that suitable movements are selected at the right time for the right place. Regarding intelligible action, it is interesting to know why a movement occurs. It is the agent's having a reason that makes a movement understandable and turns it into an action. Most of our actions are embedded in a larger framework. They are often not spontaneous, but planned. That makes them directly relevant to our topic. Joaquin Fuster, author of a major work on the frontal cortex (Fuster 1989), writes:

> What leads to the decision to act, and to act in a certain way? The question is almost inextricable from the argument about free will. . . . [T]he decision to act, like the formulation of the plan, is the result of the competition between diverse, sometimes conflicting, neural influences converging on prefrontal cortex. (idem 1996: 51)

Patients with larger lesions (damage) of the cortex show a typical clinical syndrome. Their strategic thinking skills are strongly impaired, once they have made plans they cannot be persuaded to alter them, and they have difficulty adapting their behavior to altered circumstances (Kolb and Wishaw 1996: 305–33). It is as if some ordering mechanism that controls the coordination and harmonizing of diverse activities were missing. Neuropsychologist T. Shallice (1988) therefore assigns the frontal cortex the function of attentive supervision. Within the hierarchy of cortical systems, this occupies the highest level, above all automatic routine systems. It particularly becomes active when a person is confronted with new situations that cannot be dealt by means of habitual behavior routines. It is involved in making plans and selects subroutines appropriate for the situations, while it simultaneously registers and acts on mistakes in executing plans of action.

Now that sounds promising. Are these not the functions involved in decision-making? Not only lesion studies provide evidence for this. By means of functional imaging it has been proven for normal persons that during willed action a specific activation of the dorsolateral prefrontal cortex occurs (Frith et al. 1991; Hyder et al. 1997; Phelps et al. 1997). In experiments the activation of the brain was measured during movements and while the subjects were thinking about words. Comparisons were made between passive conditions (moving a touched finger, silently repeating a word) and active, willed, self-generated action (the test persons chose one of two movements, or made up a word).

In addition, these studies also showed a slight specific activation of the anterior cingulate. That is the foremost part of a cerebral convolution that is shaped like a sickle, situated on the inner surface of the cortex, bordering on both the SMA and the frontal lobes. Many researchers believe that it belongs to the frontal cortex. The authors of the works mentioned earlier discuss it only in passing. But new findings indicate that the anterior cingulate plays an important part in "volition." It is involved in many mental functions.[3] In addition to its role in selecting actions, it is an interface between emotion and cognition (see section 3) and can be viewed as a kind of energy center or driving force: Where there is selective damage, the syndrome of akinetic mutism occurs. Damasio and van Hoesen (1983) describe the case of a woman who had this disorder. Directly after damage, the patient rested in bed with a wide-awake facial expression and apparently reacted not at all to her environment. Closer inspection revealed that she was observing the people in the room. She did not speak voluntarily nor verbally answer any inquiries. But she did seem to understand the questions, because sometimes she nodded her head. She was able to repeat words and sentences, albeit very slowly. In a nutshell, her reactions to the environment were very limited and rather stereotypical. A month later she had largely recovered. She reported that she had been unbothered by not being able to communicate. Although she was able to follow conversations, she did not say anything because she "had nothing to say." Her "mind" was "empty." When Francis Crick, discoverer of the DNA double helix and for decades a renowned brain research specialist, read that description, he immediately thought; "This woman has lost her will!" And so he writes, with naiveté meant to provoke:

> I went over for tea one day and announced to Patricia Churchland and Terry Sejnowski that the seat of the Will had been discovered! It is at or near the anterior cingulate. (Crick 1994: 268)

What did Crick mean? What this woman lacked was obviously any kind of drive, any motivation, to become active. As she herself reported, the reason was not that she did not understand what was happening around her nor that she could not produce any language. It was more that she did not want to do or say anything. She did not make an effort to do or say anything. A neuroanatomical solution suggests itself: The anterior cingulate lies at the interface between the frontal cortex and motor centers and is part of the limbic system connected with emotions and motivation. Therefore, it is likely that the anterior cingulate plays a part in the behavior of striving, which Kane (1996a) says is a form of the will (and O'Shaughnessy 1980 calls the striving will).

In view of these findings, it is no wonder that some authors try to locate "the will" in the prefrontal cortex or in the anterior cingulate. But let me issue a general warning: When trying to locate things, we must be careful not to fall into the homunculi trap and attribute all mental capacities to a little guy (or region) in the brain. While it is true that attributing those functions to the frontal cortex rests on hard neuropsychological facts, the sum of those facts is so great that there is almost nothing that the frontal cortex is not supposed to be able to do. Some critics therefore chaff and speak of "frontal lobology as a new pseudoscience" (David 1992). We should therefore take pains not to think of the prefrontal cortex as the knowledgeable initiator and top commander of mental planning and decision-making. That would ultimately return us to the problem of an infinite regress:

> Thus, to assign will to any frontal region obviously begs the question of prior command on that region from another structure; the same question can be asked about that other structure, whatever it may be, and then about its precursor, and so on. (Fuster 1996: 296).

As Fuster emphasizes, it is important to see that the frontal cortex is embedded in a network of actions that he calls the "perception–action–cycle." Sensory information is processed neuronally which leads to movements, which in turn lead to changes in the environment (internal and external), which again lead to new sensory input, and so on. At the lowest level, this cycle is realized as a reflex. Around it and enclosing it there are further cycles—from sensory to motor—with involvement of "control instances" such as the prefrontal cortex. The perception–action–cycle thus consists of several, partially overlapping, bidirectional cycles, with the environment at the bottom. Given this idea of a perception-action cycle, an idea that alludes to Viktor von Weizäcker's "Gestaltkreis" (1950), the question of an initiator, an absolute source of actions (first initiation), becomes secondary. We should not conceive of human action as being too linear nor think in terms of stimuli and commands, but rather in terms of intersecting cycles, for which the determination of an absolute point of departure for any act is purely arbitrary. This is similar to Rheinwald's argumentation (see 1990: 197–210). She insisted that the matter of ascribing preceding factors becomes less important the farther we move along in a hierarchy of unreal conditional propositions. It would make more sense to speak of modulations of neuronal activity by certain cerebral systems at various levels of organization.

But how, then, does the prefrontal cortex fulfill its selecting function? We get a clue by looking at another deficiency that is evident after damage to the frontal cortex. It concerns the so-called working memory. And, in fact, one of the main functions of the dorsolateral prefrontal cortex is that of a working memory. The prefrontal cortex contains a great quantity of information about objects and can make the representations of those available for planning actions for a while. People with defective working memories depend on hints from the environment to control their behavior. Their behavior is not guided by internalized and active knowledge, but by circumstance. This is exemplified by patients with frontal cortex lesions who have difficulty suppressing reactions to external stimuli. In the example given earlier (shopping for dinner), such patients might suddenly start shopping for shoes or be distracted from their purposes by a conversation.

The prefrontal cortex plays an important role in Changeux and Dehaene's (1989, 1995) theory of mental Darwinism. In an approach similar to that of neurosemantics, these authors have suggested that we seek the variation-selection process in the brain's cognitive activity in a psychological time screen. They distinguish three kinds of neuronal representations (idem 1989: 87): (1) percepts; (2) images, concepts, and intentions; and (3) prerepresentations. Percepts consist of a correlated activity of neurons that is determined by the outer world and disintegrates as soon as external stimulation terminates. Images, concepts, and intentions are actualized objects of memory, which result from activating a stable memory trace. (Recall Edelman's thesis of "remembered present.") Prerepresentations are multiple, spontaneously arising unstable and transient activity patterns that can be selected or eliminated.[4] Prerepresentations that come and go without having meaning could nonetheless acquire it when the organism is confronted with new situations. In a new situation, the organism might not readily have appropriate representations in store. Selection would occur from an abundance of spontaneously occurring prerepresentations, namely those that are adequate to the new circumstances and fit existing percepts and concepts. Changeux calls this adaptation process resonance. Such an adaptation process also occurs at higher cognitive levels:

> A basic function of the frontal cortex is to capture errors in the unfolding of a motor program. Similarly, intentions might be subjected to internal tests. The validation of a proposition, for example, would then result from a context-dependent compatibility of a chain of mental objects within a given semantic frame with already-stored mental objects. Such tests for compatibility or adequateness might be viewed, from a neural point of view, as analogues of the matching by resonance (or unmatching by dissonance) of percepts with prerepresentations. (Changeux and Dehaene 1989: 97f)

Changeux and Deheane have also implemented their theory in a model by designing network models of frontal functions (Changeux and Dehaene 1996).[5] They show that in their model there are rule-coding neurons, whose activity varies randomly and which are then selected in a process in which the matching with memories and external stimuli is central. In their model newly generated rules can be tested in an auto-evaluation process. The authors consider this to be a simple form of thinking.

To summarize—planning and decision making result from a selective adaptation process. Representations, or prerepresentations, generated by chance, are selected in an adaptive process (matching, resonance). As in evolution, this could be a random recombination of representations. The meaning of the representations involved is not given by their neuronal form, but by their proper functions. Plans generated in this way are intelligible because they are appropriate for the situation, which is accomplished by matching plans for action with neuronal representations of the situation at hand. The prefrontal cortex fulfills this matching function by providing various representations (working memory). Naturally, linguistically coded representations could therein also be of central importance. Movement does not—as the Libet theory implied—come from nothing; it results from adapting an already available movement pattern in a larger framework. No Cartesian consciousness is necessary for that, no consciousness that performs the whole work of understanding and reason. It is sufficient to have a series of ultra-fast adaptation processes that adhere to physiological laws.

Even though all these theories are still fairly hypothetical, it should be obvious by now that the idea of ultra-fast adaptation has already been introduced into neurobiological ruminations. Referring to adaptive neurosemantics, we can begin to understand how our brains allow us to generate new semantic content in short periods of time. Yet we still do not have an explanation for what agency can mean from a neurophilosophical perspective.

2. AGENCY AND AUTHENTICITY

Every theory of the self or the person needs a satisfactory theory of agency. In this section we shall look for a neurophilosophical foundation on which we can build such a theory. The question we want to answer is how a person makes a decision her own. In neurophilosophy, attitudes and beliefs can be understood as sophisticated adaptive brain states, which can be modeled as relaxation states of a neuronal net or as attractors of a multidimensional phase space.

In a situation that demands a decision the following happens: While weighing diverse alternatives for action, we not only make plans and think up arguments, we also imagine the possible outcomes of possible decisions, that is, we imagine future scenarios. To express it somewhat more technically, we mentally simulate counterfactual situations. The prefrontal cortex generates these scenarios of future events (see the discussion that follows). Simultaneously the amygdala and hypothalamus (hormone control center) also affect one's body, particularly the visceral functions (heart, intestines, blood pressure, and so on.). The body reacts as it has in similar past situations and, via feedback loops, it reports its state back to the brain. An instinct for similar future situations that arises in this way is usually a fairly reliable sign for decisions—similar to the way in which a pain, without requiring much thought or rationalization tells us whether our present situation is acceptable or whether we must change something. VM patients are unable to make evaluations using their feelings because the relevant region in their brains is damaged, namely the region that coordinates the integration of body state representations and imagined scenarios, that is, the ventromedial section of the frontal cortex. Loss of that function severs the physiological link between the prefrontal cortex, the limbic system, and body state representations. That their bodies no longer react as do those of healthy persons is evidenced by a lack of electric skin response. This is a neurobiological explanation for a disorder in cognitive procedure brought about by interrupting emotional mechanisms. Since a decision cannot be supported by the feeling that it is right, many of the decisions these patients make are useless and not in their own interests. So not only is insight crucial, but also whether a decision is consistent with one's emotional values!. . . .

There is direct empirical evidence that interruption in the circuits as described here in turn causes a disturbance in the feeling of agency. One pathological symptom discussed in this regard is the *alien hand syndrome* (Goldberg and Bloom 1990; Gasquoine 1993). It occurs after damage in the anterior cingulate and neighboring areas. A person with this disorder makes movements with his left hand, for example, but does not feel responsible for that action. Usually this involves rather simple and stereotype motions. It can happen that the hand grasps for a nearby object "by itself," as it were. In some cases the patients cannot let go of the object with the sick hand and must pry it out using the healthy hand. In one case a patient could not willingly open his hand, but he was able to do so by giving his hand a command. He said out loud, "Let go!" At the level of conscious experience, we would say that the movement did not happen willingly. But what we are essentially saying is that the owner of the hand is no longer the agent of the movement. One patient described by Spence (1996) reported that his hand "has a will of its own." In agreement with Damasio's theory, these phenomena can be explained by noting that the connection has been severed that normally exists between the regions controlling the movement of the hand and the other parts of the neural body-self.

Psychiatry provides a wealth of disturbances in volition and agency that certainly will be a major source for future empirically supported theories of autonomy. The development of neuroimaging opens a new era of explanation for some well-known but previously mysterious phenomena. An appropriate portrayal of these sources would require a book by itself. But I would like to mention a few findings relevant to our topic. In states of depression as well as a subclass of schizophrenia, it has been shown that there is reduced activity in the left dorsolateral frontal lobes (Andreasen 1997). This finding is not considered specific for the illness, but specific for the symptom, because both disorders exhibit a "hypovolitional" syndrome, which means reduced drive and impeded initiative, combined with flat affects in some schizophrenics (the syndrome of psychomotor poverty, Liddle 1987). This is what one would expect, given the dorsolateral prefrontal cortex function for "willed action." Another important subclass of schizophrenic patients, who clinically are said to have the disorganization syndrome, exhibited reduced activity in the right ventromedial frontal cortex and hyperactivity in the anterior cingulati on the right (Liddle et al. 1992; Liddle 1994). The authors propose that these patients exhibit an abnormality in the ventromedial cortex, which causes the tendency toward inappropriate behavior.

Another important illness, obsessive compulsive disorder (OCD), exhibits just the opposite symptoms. In this case functional neuroimaging has shown that the ventromedial cortex (and the subcortical motor regions connected to it) exhibit increased activity (Baxter et al. 1992; Breiter et al. 1996). Patients suffering from OCD must do certain things or must think certain thoughts, although they claim that they do not want to and often desperately try to fight it. Baxter's hypothesis (Baxter et al. 1990; see also Kischka et al. 1997) is that this occurs because a "worry input" entered through the frontal lobes is fed into the subcortical basal ganglia via the ventromedial cortex. The (probably primarily) reduced filter function of the caudate nucleus (part of the basal ganglin) reduces the impeding effect of another structure (the thalamus) on the ventromedial cortex, so that a positive feedback loop occurs, whose activity then spreads to other brain regions. In my view, the reason patients with compulsory disorders do not feel that they themselves produce their thoughts and actions is that the circuit has become autonomous and uncoupled from the representation of the body-self.

One of the most interesting phenomena for the feeling of agency is, perhaps, the so-called I-disorder (Ich-Störung).[6] Typically, it is exhibited by schizophrenics. The patient feels that his own psychic procedures no longer belong to himself; he experiences them as produced outside of himself. Patients are under the impression that their thoughts can spread to other people, that their thoughts are taken away from them, or that foreign ideas are put into their minds. It is also sometimes thought of as a disorder of "belonging to oneself" (or "me-ness," as Met-zinger (1993: 78) puts it). It includes more experiences of alien control. Patients have the feeling that they can control things they cannot really control ("I control the movements of the sun!"), or that they are influenced by things that do not really influence them ("An electronic remote control is controlling me!"). What could cause these types of phenomena? Obviously, they are phenomenologically connected to the concept of agency. Philosophically interested psychiatrists discuss these phenomena in connection with Frankfurt's compatibilistic theory of agency (Stephens and Graham 1996). We can speculate that self-disorders have something to do with irregularity in those brain sections dealing with agency, that is, in the ventromedial cortex, including the anterior cingulate or the body represen-tations in the right hemisphere. Some empirical findings, in fact, indicate this. In a recent, and—for this field of work—methodically very tidy study, Spence et al. (1997) used positron emission tomography to investigate the brain activity of schizophrenic patients suffering from passivity phenomena (one form of Ich-Störungen) during a willed motor task. Symptom-specific activity was discovered when the data was compared with brain activity of normal persons and with that of schizophrenic patients not suffering from passivity phenomena. Which brain regions were involved? As expected, activity was in the motor, premotor, and parietal regions. The seven patients with self-disorders, five of whom experienced passivity phenomena *during* the experiment (exclaiming: "I feel like a machine" or "I feel guided by a female spirit who has entered me"), in addition also exhib-ited symptom-specific activity. This activity was found in exactly those areas pre-viously discussed, namely, in the right inferior parietal cortex and the anterior cingulate. Both regions are central to the representation of a body-self during willed actions. However, the activity in those regions was increased and not re-duced, an event not necessarily inconsistent with the hypothesis of the neural base of a self-body image. Instead of thinking along the lines of reduced or increased brain activity in particular brain regions, we should perhaps think in terms of regulation disorders in cerebral circuits. Hyperactivity, for example, could be an attempt to compensate for a functional disconnection to another station in the circuit.

In summary, the traditional notion that feelings obstruct reflective and re-sponsible decision making is not true. Emotions actually constitute a foundation for our subjective values. We cannot do without them when making authentic and prudent decisions with implications for our own futures. Central body-representation joins the emotional basis of decisions with the physical basis of the self, by implicitly containing the past history of the individual. This neurophilo-sophical thesis about the components of the agency of willed actions is based on empirical findings, thereby transforming the phenomenon of agency from a phil-osophically obscure thesis to an empirically researchable topic.

3. NATURAL AUTONOMY

Freedom of will is an illusion, if by it we mean that under *identical* conditions we would be able to do or decide otherwise, while simultaneously acting only for reasons and considering ourselves the true *originators* of our actions. We can do justice to many libertarian intuitions, however, with a neurophilosophical concept of autonomy that includes mild forms of all three components (being able to do otherwise, acting intelligibly for reasons, and being originators of our actions). What remains is a kind of autonomy, that, loyal to the naturalistic approach, I call *natural autonomy*.

Since natural autonomy is not the same as the free will in the strong (libertarian) sense, part of that interpretation *is* lost. Natural autonomy can sustain neither our traditional concept of guilt, for example, nor certain attitudes and hopes about our lives. But we are also not mere marionettes nor puppets without thoughts and ideas that influence events in our lives. The lack of a strong form of free will does not imply that all moral order collapses or that we need abandon every concept of responsibility.

If deterministic chaos should in fact turn out to be a ubiquitous phenomenon within the nervous system, that would explain why we can make different choices in similar situations. It would explain why even in comparable situations we do not always take the same path, how we keep natural alternatives open, and why our thinking is so flexible. It would also explain why the subjective impression of being able to do otherwise seems so irrefutable. Often enough, we do experience a feeling that in comparable situations we would act differently, although we cannot always explain it rationally. Not only can chaotic processes help explain quasi-indeterministic capacities to act otherwise and flexibility; under certain conditions, they also produce stable and predictable behavior. Part of our predictable behavior is presumably within the realm of intermittence—in a realm of order in the midst of chaos.

Intelligibility (the term I chose to mean "understandable actions due to reasons") is the most difficult, and traditionally the least discussed, component of free will. It is closely connected to the problem of intentional causation, that is, the question of how reasons can be causally effective. For the dualist, humankind belongs to a second, intelligible world. This creates the problem of how that world can be causally effective within the first and natural world. In connection with the concept of consciousness, the second component is often taken as evidence that free decisions are not predetermined by past events but made with the assistance of reason. On the other hand, indeterminism is hardly compatible with a notion of intelligible behavior. So, without introducing rationality dualism, it is difficult to theoretically comprehend intelligibility. The only alternative is to design a naturalistic theory of intelligibility (such as I have done in this work).

For the component called *agency*, I discussed the most important theories of incompatibilism and compatibilism. I rejected the incompatibilistic theory of agent causation that views agency as origination through the agent alone. Hierarchical compatibilism centers around the concept of identification, the process through which a person makes her volitions her own. This, according to neurophilosophical arguments, does not in fact—as the theory assumes—happen purely rationally but is rather the result of essentially emotional mechanisms. An emotional break-off mechanism solves the regress problem of traditional identification theories. There are concrete neurobiological hypotheses about this mechanism. The dorsolateral section of the frontal cortex is important in simulating future counterfactual situations. The ventromedial section admits mental sample actions into the evaluation circuit. This circuit joins emotional centers, the body, and its neuronal representation. Changes in the body's state and the secondary feelings associated with it contain a subjective, experience-dependent evaluation aspect. Emotionally fixed points thus prevent purely rational reflection from ending in a regress. We can describe the process of emotional identification as a cognitively nontransparent, but economical and efficient test for whether actions are consistent with one's own past. It thus fulfills the function of a self-compatibility test. I suggest that we call this kind of agency *authenticity*. Presumably, the neuronal body-self is a necessary basis of a self-model, in which, during the course of a lifetime, other, more sophisticated cognitive models of the self become integrated.

I want to summarize the idea of natural autonomy in one sentence. We possess natural autonomy when under very similar circumstances we could also do other than we actually do (because of the chaotic nature of our brain), and this choice is understandable (intelligible; it is determined by past events, by immediate adaptation processes in the brain, and partially by our linguistically formed environment), and it is authentic (when through reflection loops with emotional adjustments we can identify with that action). This kind of autonomy suits a compatibilistic concept of responsibility and supplements it in some areas.

NOTES

1. The lateral sections of the premotor cortex are particularly relevant for movements triggered by external stimuli, while the medial sections (including SMA) are concerned with internally generated (not directly initiated by external stimuli) movements (Passingham 1993).

2. Newest research questions the exceptional status of humans. The differences in size of the frontal cortex are not noteworthy within the family of primates (H. Damasio 1996: 12).

3. The best survey is in Devinsky et al. (1995). See also Joseph (1996).

4. Changeux and Dehaene (1995: 135) sometimes call the prefrontal cortex the generator of diversity (which incidentally forms the acronym god). But it is unclear whether it performs that task, or whether diversity occurs spontaneously.

5. These are models of two widely used neuropsychological tests that are held to be specifically for frontal functions; the delayed response test and the Wisconsin card sorting test.

6. Philosophers may find it interesting that the classification as "I-disorder" is only common in German psychiatric discourse, where it is called *Ich-Störung*; Anglo-American literature calls this phenomenon "delusion of alien control" or "passivity phenomenon." This may be due to Kant's influence and the associated idea of a transcendental self.

References

Abelson, Raziel. 1988. *Lawless Mind*. Philadelphia: Temple University Press.

Adams, Marilyn. 1987. *William Ockham*. Notre Dame: Notre Dame University Press.

———. 1967. "Is the Existence of God a 'Hard' Fact?" *The Philosophical Review* 76: 492–503.

Adams, Robert Merrihew. 1994. *Leibniz: Determinist, Theist, Idealist*. New York: Oxford University Press.

———. 1991. "An Anti-Molinist Argument." *Philosophical Perspectives* 5: 343–54.

———. 1985. "Involuntary Sins." *Philosophical Review* 94: 3–31.

———. 1982. "Leibniz's Theories of Contingency." In M. Hooker, ed., *Leibniz: Critical and Interpretive Essays*. Minneapolis: University of Minnesota Press, 243–83.

———. 1977. "Middle Knowledge and the Problem of Evil." *American Philosophical Quarterly* 14: 1–12.

Adler, Mortimer, ed. 1958. *The Idea of Freedom*. 2 vols. New York: Doubleday.

Albert, David. 1994. "Bohm's Alternative to Quantum Mechanics." *Scientific American* (May): 32–39.

———. 1992. *Quantum Mechanics and Experience*. Cambridge, MA: Harvard University Press.

Albritton, Rogers. 1985. "Freedom of the Will and the Freedom of Action." Presidential Address. *Proceedings of the Americal Philosophical Association* 59: 239–51.

Allen, Colin. 1995. "It Isn't What You Think: A New Idea about Intentional Causation." *Nous* 29: 115–26.

Allen, Robert. 1997. "Re-examining Frankfurt Cases." *Southern Journal of Philosophy* 37: 363–76.

———. 1995. "Responsibility and Motivation." *Southern Journal of Philosophy* 35: 289–99.

Allison, Henry. 1990. *Kant's Theory of Freedom*. Cambridge: Cambridge University Press.

Alston, William. 1989. *Divine and Human Language*. Ithaca: Cornell University Press.

———. 1986. "Does God Have Beliefs?"*Religious Studies* 22: 287–306.

———. 1985. "Divine Foreknowledge and Alternative Conceptions of Human Freedom." *International Journal for Philosophy of Religion* 18: 19–32.

———. 1977. "Self-Intervention and the Structure of Motivation." In T. Mischel, ed., *The Self: Philosophical and Psychological Issues*. Oxford: Oxford University Press, pp. 65–102.

Andreasen, N. C. 1997. "Linking Mind and Brain in the Study of Mental Illnesses." *Science* 275: 1586–93.

Anglin, W. S. 1990. *Free Will and the Christian Faith*. Oxford: Oxford University Press.

Anscombe, G. E. M. 1981. "Causality and Determination." In *The Collected Philosophical Papers of G. E. M. Anscombe*. Vol. 2. Minneapolis: University of Minnesota Press: 139–163. Reprinted in Ekstrom 2000c: 57–73.

———. 1971. *Causality and Determinism*. Cambridge: Cambridge University Press.

———. 1958. *Intention*. Oxford: Blackwell.

Antoniou, I., and I. Prigogine. 1993. "Intrinsic Irreversibility and Integrability of Dynamics." *Physica A* 192: 443–64.

Aquinas, Saint Thomas. 1945. *Basic Writings of St. Thomas Aquinas*. Vol. I. Ed. A. Pegis. New York: Random House.

Aristotle. 1915a. *De Motu Animalium*. In *The Works of Aristotle*. Vol. 5. Ed. W. D. Ross. London: Oxford University Press.

———. 1915b. *Nichomachean Ethics*. In *The Works of Aristotle*. Vol. 9 Ed. W. D. Ross. London: Oxford University Press.

Armstrong, D. M. 1997. *A World of States of Affairs*. Cambridge: Cambridge University Press.

———. 1983. *What Is a Law of Nature?* Cambridge: Cambridge University Press.

Aspect, A., J., Dalibard, and G. Roger. 1982a. "Experimental Realization of Einstein-Podolsky-Rosen-Bohm Gedankenexperiment: A New Violation of Bell's Inequalities." *Physical Review Letters* 49: 91–94.

———. 1982b. "Experimental Test of Bell's Inequalities Using Time-Varying Analyzers." *Physical Review Letters* 49: 1804–7.

Audi, Robert. 1993. *Action, Intention and Reason*. Ithaca: Cornell University Press.

———. 1991a. "Autonomy, Reason and Desire." *Pacific Philosophical Quarterly* 11: 1–14.

———. 1991b. "Responsible Action and Virtuous Character." *Ethics* 101: 304–21.

———. 1989. *Practical Reasoning*. London: Routledge & Kegan Paul.

———. 1986. "Acting for Reasons." *Philosophical Review* 95: 511–46.

———. 1981. "Inductive Nomological Generalizations and Psychological Laws." *Theory and Decision* 13: 229–49.

———. 1979. "Weakness of Will and Practical Judgment." *Nous* 13: 73–96.

———. 1974. "Moral Responsibility, Freedom and Compulsion." *American Philosophical Quarterly* 19: 25–39.

———. 1973. "Intending." *Journal of Philosophy* 70: 387–403.

Augustine. 1964. *On the Free Choice of the Will*. Indianapolis: Bobbs-Merrill.

Aune, Bruce. 1977. *Reason and Action*. Dordrecht: Reidel.

———. 1970. "Free Will, 'Can,' and Ethics: A Reply to Lehrer." *Analysis* 30: 77–83.

———. 1967. "Hypotheticals and 'Can': Another Look." *Analysis* 27: 191–95.

Austin, J. L. 1961. "Ifs and Cans." In *Philosophical Papers*, ed. J. O. Urmson and G. Warnock. Oxford: Clarendon Press: 153–80. Reprinted in Berofsky, 1966: 295–321.

Ayer, A. J. 1963. "Fatalism." In his *Concept of a Person and Other Essays*. New York: St. Martin's Press: 235–68.

———. 1954. "Freedom and Necessity." In his *Philosophical Essays*. New York: St. Martin's Press, 3–20.

———. 1952. *Language, Truth and Logic*. 2nd ed: New York: Dover.

Ayers, M. R. 1968. *The Refutation of Determinism*. London: Methuen.

Babcock, William. 1988. "Augustine on Sin and Moral Agency." *Journal of Religious Ethics* 16: 40–56.

Babloyantz, A., and A. Destexhe. 1985. "Strange Attractors in the Human Cortex." In *Temporal Disorder in Human Oscillatory Systems.* Ed. L. Rensing et al., New York: Springer: 132–43.

Baier, Kurt. 1958. *The Moral Point of View.* Ithaca: Cornell University Press.

Baker, G. L., and J. P. Gollub. 1990. *Chaotic Dynamics: An Introduction.* Cambridge: Cambridge University Press.

Baker, Lynne Rudder. 1993. "Metaphysics and Mental Causation." In Heil and Mele, 1993: 75–96.

Baker, S. 1999. "Counterfactuals, Probabilistic Counterfactuals and Causation." *Mind* 108: 427–69.

Balaguer, Mark. 1999. "Libertarianism as a Scientifically Reputable View." *Philosophical Studies* 93: 189–211.

Barrett, William. 1958. "Determinism and Novelty." In Hook, 1958: 46–54.

Barrow, J. D., and F. J. Tipler. 1988. *The Anthropic Cosmological Principle.* Oxford: Oxford University Press.

Basinger, David. 1993. "Simple Foreknowledge and Providential Control." *Faith and Philosophy* 10: 421–27.

———. 1986. "Middle Knowledge and Classical Christian Thought." *Religious Studies* 22: 407–22.

Batterman, Robert. 1993. "Defining Chaos." *Philosophy of Science* 60: 43–66.

Baxter, L. E., J. Schwartz, K. Bergman, et al. 1992. "Caudate Glucose Metabolic Rate Changes with Both Drug and Behavior Therapy for Obsessive Compulsive Disorder." *Archives of General Psychiatry* 49: 681–89.

Baxter, L. E., J. Schwartz, B. Guze, K. Bergman, and M. Szuba. 1990. "Neuroimaging in Obsessive-Compulsive Disorder." In *Obsessive Compulsive Disorders.* Ed. M. Jenike et al., St. Louis MO: Mosby Yearbook, 167–88.

Beaty, Michael D. ed. 1990. *Christian Theism and the Problems of Philosophy.* Notre Dame: University of Notre Dame Press.

Beck, F., and J. Eccles. 1992. "Quantum Aspects of Brain Activity and the Role of Consciousness." *Proceedings of the National Academy of Science US* 89: 11357–61.

Beckermann, Ansgar, Hans Flohr, and Jaegwon Kim, eds. 1992. *Emergence or Reduction? Essays on the Prospects of Nonreductive Physicalism.* Berlin: Walter de Gruyter.

Bell, J. S. 1987. *Speakable and Unspeakable in Quantum Mechanics.* Cambridge: Cambridge University Press.

Benn, Stanley. 1988. *A Theory of Freedom.* Cambridge: Cambridge University Press.

Bennett, Jonathan. 1995. *The Act Itself.* Oxford: Oxford University Press.

———. 1980. "Accountability." In *Philosophical Subjects.* Ed. Z. van Straaten, Oxford: Clarendon Press: 86–103.

Benson, Paul. 1987. "Freedom and Value." *Journal of Philosophy* 84: 465–87.

———. 1994. "Free Agency and Self-Worth." *Journal of Philosophy* 91: 650–68.

Bergmann, Fritjoh. 1977. *On Being Free.* Notre Dame: Notre Dame University Press.

Bergson, Henri. 1960. *Time and Free Will.* New York: Harper & Row. Originally published in 1890.

Berkeley, 1998a. *Three Dialogues Between Hylas and Philonous.*

———. 1998b. A Treatise Concerning the *Principles of Human Knowedge.* Ed. J. Dancy. Oxford: Oxford University Press. Originally published in 1710.

Berlin, Isaiah. 1980. "From Hope and Fear Set Free." In *Concepts and Categories* Oxford: Oxford University Press: 108–127.

———. 1969. *Four Essays on Liberty*. Oxford: Oxford University Press.

Bernstein, Mark. 1995. "Kanean Libertarianism." *Southwest Philosophy Review* 11: 151–57.

———. 1992. *Fatalism*. Lincoln: University of Nebraska Press.

———. 1989. "Fatalism and Time." *Dialogue* 28: 461–71.

———. 1983. "Socialization and Autonomy." *Mind* 93: 120–23.

Berofsky, Bernard. 2000. "Ultimate Responsibility in a Determined World." *Philosophy and Phenomenological Research* 60: 135–40.

———. 1995. *Liberation from Self*. Cambridge: Cambridge University Press.

———. 1992. "On the Absolute Freedom of the Will." *American Philosophical Quarterly* 29: 279–89.

———. 1987. *Freedom from Necessity*. London: Routledge & Kegan Paul.

———. 1971. *Determinism*. Princeton: Princeton University Press.

———. ed. 1966. *Free Will and Determinism*. New York: Harper & Row.

Betzler, Monika, and Barbara Guckes, eds. 2000a. *Freiheit und Autonomie: Ausgewalte Texte zur Philosophie Harry G. Frankfurts*. Berlin: Academie.

———. 2000b. *Autonomes Handeln: Beitrage zur Philosophie Harry G. Frankfurts*. Berlin: Academie.

Bigelow, John, S. Dodds, and R. Pargetter. 1990. "Temptation and the Will." *American Philosophical Quarterly* 27: 39–49.

Bishop, John. 1989. *Natural Agency*. Cambridge: Cambridge University Press.

———. 1986. "Is Agent-Causality a Conceptual Primitive?" *Synthèse* 67: 225–47.

———. 1983. "Agent-Causation." *Mind* 92: 61–79.

Bishop, Robert C. 1999. "Chaotic Dynamics, Indeterminacy and Free Will." Ph.D. Dissertation. University of Texas at Austin.

———. n.d.(a) "On Separating Predictability and Determinism." Unpublished Ms.

———. n.d.(b). "Brussels-Austin Nonequilibrium Statistical Mechanics in the Early Years: Similarity Transformations Between Deterministic and Probabilistic Description:" Submitted to *Studies in History and Philosophy of Modern Physics*.

———. n.d.(c). "Brussels-Austin Nonequilibrium Statistical Mechanics in the Later Years: Large Poincaré Systems." Submitted to *Studies in History and Philosophy of Modern Physics*.

Bishop, Robert C., and Frederick K. Kronz. 1999. "Is Chaos Indeterministic?" In *Language, Quantum, Music: Selected Contributed Papers of the Tenth International Congress of Logic, Methodology & Philosophy of Science*. Ed. Maria Luisa Dalla Chiara, Roberto Guintini, and Federico Laudisa. Florence, August 1995. London: Kluwer Academic Publishers: 129–41.

Bishop, Robert C., and Frank Richardson. Forthcoming. "Physique, Sciences humaines et fin des Certitudes." In *L'homme devant l'incertain*. Ed. D. Driebe and I. Prigogine. Paris: Editions Odile Jacob

Blackburn, Simon. 1999. *Thinking*. Oxford: Oxford University Press.

———. 1993. *Essays in Quasi-Realism*. New York: Oxford University Press.

Blauvelt, Whit. 1999. "Y's Domain." In Libet, Freeman and Sutherland, 1999.: 269–74.

Blum, Alex. 2000. " 'N'." *Analysis* 60: 284–86.

———. 1990. "On a Mainstay of Incompatibilism." *Iyyum* 39: 267–79.

Blumenfeld, David. 1988a. "Freedom and Mind Control." *American Philosophical Quarterly* 25: 215–27.

———. 1988b. "Freedom, Contingency and Things Possible in Themselves." *Philosophy and Phenomenological Research* 49: 178–199.

———. 1971. "The Principle of Alternative Possibilities." *Journal of Philosophy* 68: 339–45.

Bohm, David. 1986. "The Implicate Order." In *Beyond Mechanism* Ed. D. Schindler. New York: The University Press of America: 67–95.

———. 1984. *Causality and Chance in Modern Physics*. London: Routledge.

———. 1952a. "A Suggested Interpretation of the Quantum Theory in Terms of 'Hidden Variables' I." *Physical Review* 85: 166–79.

———. 1952b. "A Suggested Interpretation of the Quantum Theory in Terms of 'Hidden Variables' II." *Physical Review* 85: 180–93. (Reprinted in Wheeler and Zurek 1983: 369–96.)

Bohm, David, and B. J. Hiley. 1993. *The Undivided Universe: An Ontological Interpretation of Quantum Mechanics*. London: Routledge.

Bok, Hilary. 1998. *Freedom and Responsibility*. Princeton: Princeton University Press.

Bonjour, Laurence. 1976. "Determinism, Libertarianism and Agent Causation." *Southern Journal of Philosophy* 14: 145–56.

Bourke, Vernon. 1964. *Will in Western Thought*. New York: Sheed and Ward.

Boyle, J., G. Grisez, and D. Tollefson. 1976. *Free Choice: A Self-Referential Argument*. Notre Dame: Notre Dame University Press.

Bradley, F. H. 1927. "The Vulgar Notion of Responsibility in Connexion with the Theories of Free Will and Necessity." In *Ethical Studies*. Oxford: Clarendon Press, 3–57.

Bramhall, John. 1844. *The Works of John Bramhall*. Oxford: John Henry Parker.

Brand, Myles. 1984. *Intending and Acting*. Cambridge, MA: MIT Press.

Brand, Myles, and D. Walton, eds. 1976. *Action Theory*. Dordrecht: D. Reidel.

Brandt, Richard. 1958. "Blameworthiness and Obligation." In *Essays in Moral Philosophy*. Ed. A. I. Melden. Seattle: University of Washington Press: 3–39

Bransen, Jan. 2000. "Alternatives *of* Oneself." *Philosophy and Phenomenological Research* 60: 1–21.

———. 1998. "Making X Happen: Prolepsis and the Problem of Mental Determination." In *Human Action, Deliberation and Causation*. Ed. J. Bransen and S. E. Cuypers. Dordrecht: Kluwer Academic Publishers, 131–53.

Brant, Dale Eric. 1997. "On Plantinga's Way Out" *Faith and Philosophy* 14: 378–87.

Bratman, Michael. 1999. *Faces of Intention*. Cambridge: Cambridge University Press.

———. 1996. "Identification, Decision and Treating as a Reason." *Philosophical Topics* 24: 1–18. Reprinted in Bratman 1999: 67–85

———. 1987. *Intentions, Plans and Practical Reason*. Cambridge: Harvard University Press.

———. 1984. "Two Faces of Intention." *The Philosophical Review* 93: 178–203.

Breiter, H., S. Rauch, K. Kwong, et al. 1996. "Functional Magnetic Resonance Imaging of Symptomatic Provocation in Obsessive-Compulsive Disorder." *Archives of General Psychiatry* 53: 595–606.

Bricklin, Jonathan. 1999. "A Variety of Religious Experience: William James and the Non-Reality of Free Will." In Libet, Freeman and Sutherland, 1999: 77–98.

Brink, David O. 1989. *Moral Realism and the Foundations of Ethics*. Cambridge: Cambridge University Press.

Broad, C. D. 1952. "Determinism, Indeterminism and Libertarianism." In C. D. Broad, *Ethics and the History of Philosophy*. London: Routledge & Kegan Paul, 195–217. Reprinted in Berofsky 1966: 135–59.

Broadie, Sarah. 1991. *Ethics with Aristotle*. Oxford: Oxford University Press.

Brown, Mark. 1990. "Action and Ability." *Journal of Philosophical Logic* 19: 95–114.

———. 1988. "On the Logic of Ability." *Journal of Philosophical Logic* 17: 1–26.

Brown, Robert F. 1991. "Divine Omniscience, Immutability, Aseity and Human Free Will" *Religious Studies* 27: 285–95.

Brueckner, Anthony. 2000. "On an Attempt to Demonstrate the Compatibility of Divine Foreknowledge and Human Freedom." *Faith and Philosophy* 17: 132–34.

Bruner, Jerome. 1986. *Actual Minds, Possible Worlds*. Cambridge: Harvard University Press.

Bub, Jeffrey. 1997. *Interpreting the Quantum World*. Cambridge: Cambridge University Press.

Bunge, Mario. 1998. *Philosophy of Science* Vol 1: *From Problem to Theory*. New Bruswick, NJ: Transaction Publishers.

Burms, A. and H. DeDijn. 1979. "Freedom and Logical Contingency in Leibniz." *Studia Leibnitiana* 11: 124–33.

Burrington, Dale. 1999. "Blameworthiness." *Journal of Philosophical Research* 24: 505–27.

Buser, P. A., and A. Rougel-Buser eds. 1978. *Cerebral Correlates of Conscious Experience*. Amsterdam: North-Holland.

Buss, Sarah. 1994 "Autonomy Reconsidered." *Midwest Studies in Philosophy* 19: 95–121.

Buss, Sarah, and Lee Overton, eds. Forthcoming *The Contours of Agency: Essays in Honor of Harry Frankfurt*. Cambridge, MA: MIT Press.

Cahn, Steven M. 1977. "Random Choices." *Philosophy and Phenomenological Research* 37: 549–51.

———. 1967. *Fate, Time and Logic*. New Haven: Yale University Press.

Calvin, William H. 1990. *The Cerebral Symphony: Seashore Reflections on the Structure of Consciousness*. New York: Bantam.

Campbell, C. 1967. *In Defense of Free Will*. London: Allen & Unwin.

———. 1957. "Has the Self Free Will?" In *On Selfhood and Godhood*. London: Allen and Unwin, *Lecture 9*: 128–42.

———. 1951. "Is Free Will a Pseudo-Problem?" *Mind* 60: 446–65. Reprinted in Berofsky 1966: 112–35.

Campbell, Donald. 1960. "Blind Variation and Selective Retention in Creative Thought." *Psychological Review* 67: 380–400.

Campbell, Joseph Kiem. 1997. "A Compatibilist Theory of Alternative Possibilities." *Philosophical Studies* 67: 339–44.

Carpenter, R. H. S. 1999. "A Neural Mechanism that Randomises Behavior." *Journal of Consciousness Studies* 6: 13–22.

Carr, Craig. 1985. "Coercion and Freedom." *American Philosophical Quarterly* 25: 59–67.

Carr, E. H. 1961. *What Is History?* London: Macmillan.

Carter, W. R. 1979. "On Transworld Event Identity." *The Philosophical Review* 88: 443–52.

———. 1989. *Nature's Capacities and their Measurements*. Oxford: Oxford University Press.

Cartwright, Nancy. 1983. *How the Laws of Physics Lie*. Oxford: Oxford University Press.

Castañeda, H.-N. 1975. *Thinking and Doing*. Dordrecht: Reidel.

Caston, Victor. 1997. "Epiphenomenalism: Ancient and Modern." *The Philosophical Review* 106: 309–63.

Changeux, J.-P., and S. Dehaene. 1995. "Neuronal Models of Cognitive Functions Associated with the Prefrontal Cortex." In Damasio et al. 1996: 125–44.

———. 1989. "Neuronal Models of Cognitive Functions." *Cognition* 33: 63–109.

Charlton, William. 1988. *Weakness of Will*. Oxford: Blackwell.

Chisholm, R. M. 1995. "Agents, Causes and Events." In O'Connor 1995a: 95–100.

———. 1982a. "Self-Profile" and "Replies." In *Roderick M. Chisholm*. Ed. R. J. Bogdan. Dordrecht: Reidel: 1–16; 141–65.

———. 1982b. "Human Freedom and the Self." In Watson, 1982: 24–35.

———. 1979. "Objects and Persons: Revisions and Replies." In *Essays on the Philosophy of Roderick Chisholm*. Ed. E. Sosa. Amsterdam: Rodopi.

———. 1976a. *Person and Object*. Lasalle, IL.: Open Court.

———. 1976b. "The Agent as Cause." In Brand and Walton 1976, 199–211.

———. 1971. "Reflections on Human Agency." *Idealistic Studies* 1: 33–46.

———. 1967. "He Could Have Done Otherwise." *Journal of Philosophy* 64: 409–18.

———. 1966. "Freedom and Action." In Lehrer 1966a: 11–44.

———. 1964. "J. L. Austin's Philosophical Papers." In Berofsky, 1966: 339–45.

Christman, John. 1991a. "Autonomy and Personal History." *Canadian Journal of Philosophy* 21: 1–24.

———. 1991b. "Liberalism and Individual Positive Freedom." *Ethics* 101: 343–59.

———. ed., 1989. *The Inner Citadel: Essays on Individual Autonomy*. Oxford: Oxford University Press.

———. 1988. "Constructing the Inner Citadel: Recent Work on Autonomy." *Ethics* 99: 109–24.

Churchland, Patricia S. 1994. "Can Neurobiology Teach Us Anything about Consciousness?" Presidential Address. *Proceedings of the American Philosophical Association* 67: 23–40.

———. 1986. *Neurophilosophy*. Cambridge, MA.: MIT Press.

Churchland, Paul M. 1996. *The Engine of Reason, The Seat of the Soul*. Cambridge, MA: MIT Press.

———. 1988. *Matter and Consciousness*. Cambridge, MA: MIT Press.

Cicero, Marcus Tullius. 1960. *De Oratore, De Fato*. Trans. H. Rackham. London: Heinemann.

Clark, Thomas W. 1999. "Fear of Mechanism: A Compatibilist Critique of 'The Volitional Brain.'" In Libet, Freeman and Sutherland, 1999: 279–93.

Clarke, Randolph. Forthcoming. "Freedom of the Will." In Stephen Stich and Ted Warfield, eds., *The Blackwell Guide to Philosophy of Mind*.

———. 2000. "Modest Libertarianism." *Philosophical Perspectives* 14. 21–45.

———. 1999. "Free Choice, Effort and Wanting More." *Philosophical Explorations* 2: 20–41.

———. 1997. "On the Possibility of Rational Free Action." *Philosophical Studies* 88: 37–57.

———. 1996a. "Agent Causation and Event Causation in the Production of Free Action." *Philosophical Topics* 24: 19–48.

———. 1996b. "Contrastive Rational Explanation of Free Choice." *The Philosophical Quarterly* 46: 185–201.

———. 1995a. "Freedom and Determinism: Recent Work." *Philosophical Books* 36: 9–18.

———. 1995b. "Indeterminism and Control." *American Philosophical Quarterly* 32: 125–38.

———. 1994. "Ability and Responsibility for Omissions." *Philosophical Studies* 73: 195–208.

———. 1993. "Towards a Credible Agent-Causal Account of Free Will." *Nous* 27: 191–203. Reprinted in O'Connor, 2000: 201–15.

———. 1992a. "A Principle of Rational Explanation." *The Southern Journal of Philosophy* 30: 1–12.

———. 1992b. "Deliberation and Beliefs about One's Abilities." *Pacific Philosophical Quarterly* 73: 101–13.

Claxton, Guy. 1999. "Whodunnit? Unpicking the 'Seems' of Free Will." In Libet, Freeman and Sutherland, 1999: 99–114.

Collins, John. 2000. "Premptive Prevention." *Journal of Philosophy* 97: 223–34.

Compton, A. H. 1935. *The Freedom of Man.* New Haven: Yale University Press.

Copp, David. 1997. "Defending the Principle of Alternative Possibilities: Blameworthiness and Moral Responsibility." *Nous* 31: 441–56.

Cover, Jan, and John O'Leary-Hawthorne. 1996. "Free Agency and Materialism." In D. Howard-Snyder and J. Jordan, 1996: 47–71.

Craig, William Lane. 1998. "On Hasker's Defense of Anti-Molinism." *Faith and Philosophy* 15: 236–40.

———. 1994. "Robert Adams's New Anti-Molinist Argument" *Philosophy and Phenomenological Research* 54: 857–61.

———. 1990. *Divine Foreknowledge and Human Freedom.* Brill's Studies in Intellectual History 19. Leiden: E. J. Brill.

Crick, Francis. 1994. *The Astonishing Hypothesis.* New York: Scribner's and Sons.

Crick, Francis, and Christof Koch. 1990. "Towards a Neurobiological Theory of Consciousness." *Seminars in the Neurosciences* 4: 263–76.

Crisp, Thomas, and Ted Warfield. 2000. "The Irrelevance of Indeterministic Counterexamples to Principle Beta." *Philosophy and Phenomenological Research* 61: 173–84.

Cullity, Garrett, and Berys Gaut. 1997. *Ethics and Practical Reason.* Oxford: Oxford University Press.

Cuypers, Stefaan. Forthcoming. "Autonomy beyond Voluntarism: In Defense of Hierarchy." *Canadian Journal of Philosophy.*

Damasio, A. R. 1994. *Descartes' Error: Emotion, Reason, and the Human Brain.* New York: Avon Books.

Damasio, A. R., H. Damasio, and Y. Christen, eds. 1996. *Neurobiology of Decision Making.* New York: Springer.

Damasio, A. R., and G. W. van Hoesen. 1983 "Emotional Disturbances Associated with Focal Lesions of the Limbic Frontal Lobe." In Heilman, K. M. and P. Satz (eds.) *Neuropsychologie of Human Emotions.* New York: Guilford Press: 87–103.

Damasio, H. 1996. "Human Neuroanatomy Relevant to Decision Making." In A. Damasio, et al. 1996: 2–12.

Danieri, A., A. Loinger, and G. Prosperi. 1983. "Quantum theory of Measurement and Ergodicity Conditions." In Wheeler and Zurek 1983: 657–79.

Darwall, Stephen. 1996. "Ethical Theory." *The Encyclopedia of Philosophy* (Supplement).

Davenport, John. 2000 Review of Fischer and Ravizza 1998. *Faith and Philosophy* 17: 382–92.

David, A. S. 1992. "Frontal Lobology—Psychiatry's New Pseudoscience." *British Journal of Psychiatry* 161: 244–48.

Davidson, Donald. 1985. "Deception and Division." In *Actions and Events*. Ed. E. LePore and B. McLaughlin. Oxford: Basil Blackwell 138–48.

———. 1980. *Essays on Actions and Events*. Oxford: Clarendon Press.

———. 1973. "Freedom to Act." In Honderich, 1973: 67–86. Reprinted in Davidson 1980.

———. 1970. "How Is Weakness of Will Possible?" In *Moral Concepts*. Ed. J. Feinberg. Oxford: Clarendon Press. Reprinted in Davidson 1980.

———. 1963. "Actions, Reasons and Causes." In Davidson 1980: 5–20.

Davies, Martin. 1983. "Boethius and Others on Divine Foreknowledge." *Pacific Philosophical Quarterly* 8: 313–29.

Davies, P., and J. R. Brown. 1986. *The Ghost in the Atom*. Cambridge: Cambridge University Press.

Davis, Lawrence. 1979. *Theory of Action*. Englewood Cliffs, NJ: Prentice-Hall.

Davison, Scott. 1999. "Moral Luck and the Flicker of Freedom." *American Philosophical Quarterly* 36: 241–51.

Deeke, L., B. Grotzinger, and H. H. Kornhuber. 1976. "Voluntary Finger Movement in Man: Cerebral Potentials and Theory." *Biological Cybernetics* 23: 99.

Dekker, Eef. 2000. *Middle Knowledge*. Leuven: Peeters.

Della Rocca, Michael. 1998. "Frankfurt, Fischer and Flickers." *Nous* 32: 99–105.

Dennett, Daniel. 1995. *Darwin's Dangerous Idea*. New York: Touchstone.

———. 1991. "Real Patterns." *Journal of Philosophy* 88: 27–51.

———. 1988. "Coming to Terms with the Determined" (Review of Honderich 1988) *The Times Literary Supplement* (November 4–10): 1219–20.

———. 1984. *Elbow Room*. Cambridge, MA: MIT Press.

———. 1978. "On Giving Libertarians What They Say They Want." In Dennett, *Brainstorms*. Cambridge, MA: MIT Press: 286–99.

———. 1973. "Mechanism and Responsibility." In Honderich, 1973: 159–84.

Denyer, Nicholas. 1981. *Time, Action and Necessity*. London: Duckworth.

Descartes, René. 1955. *Philosophical Works*. Vol. I. Ed. and trans. J. Haldane and W. Ross. New York: Dover.

d'Espagnat, Bernard. 1989. *Reality and the Physicist*. Cambridge: Cambridge University Press.

Deutsch, David. 1998. *The Fabric of Reality*. London: Penguin.

Deutsch, David, and Michael Lockwood. 1994. "The Quantum Physics of Time Travel." *Scientific American*. (March): 50–57.

Devinsky, O. F. Putnam, J. Grafman, E. Bromfield, and W. Theodore. 1995. "Contributions of Anterior Cingulate Cortex to Behavior." *Brain* 118: 279–306.

DeVito, Scott. 1996. "Completeness and Indeterministic Causation." *Philosophy of Science* 63 (Proceedings): S177–S184.

DeWitt, R., and N. Graham, (eds). 1973. *The Many-Worlds Interpretation of Quantum Mechanics*. Princeton: Princeton University Press.

Diesmann M., M-O. Gewaltig, and A. Aertsen 1999. "Stable Propagation of Synchronous Spiking in Cortical Neural Networks." *Nature* 402: 529, 533.

Dilman, Ilham. 1999. *Free Will: An Historical and Philosophical Introduction*. London: Routledge.

Diósi, L. 1989. "Models for Universal Reduction of Macroscopic Quantum Fluctuations." *Physical Review* A 40: 1165–74.

———. 1988. "Quantum Stochastic Processes as Models for State Vector Reduction." *Journal of Physics* A 21: 2885–98.

Diósi, L., N. Gisin, and W. T. Strunz. 1998. "Non-Markovian Quantum State Diffusion." *Physical Review* A 58: 1699–1712.

Dirac, P.A.M. 1958. *The Principles of Quantum Mechanics*. 4th ed. Oxford: Oxford University Press.

Donagan, Alan. 1987. *Choice*. London: Routledge & Kegan Paul.

Doty, R. W. 1998. "Five Mysteries of the Mind and their Consequences." In *Views of the Brain*. Ed. A. Puente. Washington DC: American Psychological Association: 127–45.

Double, Richard. 1999. "In Defense of the Smart Aleck: A Reply to Ted Honderich." *Journal of Philosophical Research* 24: 305–9.

———. 1997. "Misdirection on the Free Will Problem." *American Philosophical Quarterly* 34: 359–68.

———. 1996a. *Metaphilosophy and Free Will*. Oxford: Oxford University Press.

———. 1996b. "Honderich on the Consequences of Determinism." *Philosophy and Phenomenological Research* 56: 847–54.

———. 1993. "The Principle of Rational Explanation Defended." *The Southern Journal of Philosophy* 31: 133–42.

———. 1991. *The Non-Reality of Free Will*. Oxford: Oxford University Press.

———. 1988a. "What's Wrong with Self-Serving Epistemic Strategies?" *Philosophical Psychology* 2: 341–48.

———. 1988b. "Libertarianism and Rationality." *The Southern Journal of Philosophy* 26: 431–39.

———. 1988c. Review of Kane *1985*. *Philosophical Books* 29: 96–97.

———. n.d. "The Moral Hardness of Libertarianism."

Dray, William. 1957. *Laws and Explanations in History*. Oxford: Oxford University Press.

Dretske, Fred. 1988. *Explaining Behavior: Reasons in a World of Causes*. Cambridge, MA.: MIT Press.

———. 1977. "Laws of Nature." *Philosophy of Science* 44: 248–68.

Duggan, Timothy, and Bernard Gert. 1979. "Free Will and the Ability to Will." *Nous* 13: 197–217.

Dummett, Michael. 1964. "Bringing about the Past." *Philosophical Review* 73: 338–59.

Dunn, Robert. 1987. *The Possibility of Weakness of Will*. Indianapolis: Hackett.

Dupré, John. 1996. "The Solution to the Problem of the Freedom of the Will." *Philosophical Perspectives* 10: 385–402.

———. 1993. *The Disorder of Things*. Cambridge, MA: Harvard University Press.

Dworkin, Gerald. 1988. *The Theory and Practice of Autonomy*. Cambridge: Cambridge University Press.

———. 1986. Review of Dennett's *Elbow Room*. *Ethics* 96: 423–25.

———. 1976. "Autonomy and Behavior Control." *Hastings Center Report* 6: 23–28.

————. 1970a. "Acting Freely." *Nous* 4: 367–83.

————. ed., 1970b. *Determinism, Free Will and Moral Responsibility*. Englewood Cliffs: Prentice-Hall.

Earman, John.1986. *A Primer on Determinism*. Dordrecht: Reidel.

Eccles, John. 1994. *How the Self Controls Its Brain*. Berlin: Springer.

————. 1970. *Facing Reality*. New York: Springer-Verlag.

Eccles, John, and Karl Popper. 1977. *The Self and Its Brain*. New York: Springer-Verlag.

Eckhorn, J., R. Bauer, W. Jordan, M. Brosch, W. Kruse, M. Monk, and H. Reitbueck. 1988. "Coherent Oscillations: A Mechanism of Feature Linking in the Neural Cortex?" *Biological Cybernetics* 60: 121–30.

Edelman, G. M. 1993. *Bright Air, Brilliant Fire*. New York: Basic Books.

————. 1987. *Neural Darwinism*. New York: Basic Books.

Eddington, Arthur. 1929. *The Nature of the Physical World*. London: Dent.

Edwards, Jonathan. 1969. *The Freedom of the Will*. Indianapolis: Bobbs-Merrill. Originally published in 1754.

Edwards, Paul. 1958. "Hard and Soft Determinism." In Hook, 1958: 117–25.

Eells, Ellery. 1991. *Probabilistic Causality*. Cambridge: Cambridge University Press.

Ehring, Douglas. 1997. *Causation and Persistence: A Theory of Causation*. New York: Oxford University Press.

Einstein, A. 1931. "About Free Will." In *The Golden Book of Tagore*. Ed. Ramananda Chatterjee. Calcutta: Golden Book Committee: 77–84.

Einstein, A., B. Podolsky, and N. Rosen. 1935. "Can Quantum-Mechanical Description of Physical Reality Be Considered Complete?" *Physical Review* 47: 777–80.

Ekstrom, Laura Waddell. 2001a. *Agency and Responsibility: Essays on the Metaphysics of Freedom*. Boulder, CO: Westview Press.

————. 2001b. "Indeterminist Free Action." In Ekstrom 2000: 138–57.

————. 2000. *Free Will: A Philosophical Study*. Boulder, CO: Westview Press.

————. 1998a. "Freedom, Causation and the Consequence Argument." *Synthese* 115: 333–54.

————. 1998b. "Protecting Incompatibilist Freedom." *American Philosophical Quarterly* 35: 281–91.

————. 1995. "Causes and Nested Conditionals." *Australasian Journal of Philosophy* 73: 574–8.

Engel, Andreas K., Pieter R., Roelfsema, Peter König, and Wolf Singer. 1997. "Neurophysiological Relevance of Time." In *Time, Temporality, Now: Experiencing Time and Concepts of Time in an Interdisciplinary Perspective*. Ed. Harald Atmanspacher and Eva Ruhnau. Berlin: Springer-Verlag: 133–57.

Erasmus, Desiderius and Martin Luther. 1961. *Discourse on Free Will*. New York: Frederick Unger. Originally published in 1524–1525.

Falk, Arthur. 1981. "Some Modal Confusions in Compatibilism." *American Philosophical Quarterly* 18: 141–48.

Farrell, Daniel. 1985. "The Justification of General Deterrence." *The Philosophical Review* 104: 176–210.

Farrer, Austin. 1967. *The Freedom of the Will*. New York: Scribner's.

Feldman, Fred. 1986. *Doing the Best We Can*. Dordrecht: D. Reidel.

Feinberg, Joel. 1986. *Harm to Self*. New York: Oxford University Press.

Felt, James, S. J. 1994. *Making Sense of Your Freedom*. Ithaca: Cornell University Press.

Feuer, Lewis, ed. 1959. *Marx and Engels: Basic Writings*. New York: Doubleday.

Finch, Alicia, and Ted Warfield. 1999. "Fatalism: Logical and Theological." *Faith and Philosophy* 16: 233–38.

———. 1998. "The *Mind* Argument and Libertarianism." *Mind* 107: 515–28.

Fine, Arthur. 1993. "Indeterminism and the Freedom of the Will." In *Philosophical Problems of the Internal and External World*. Ed. J. Earman et al. Pittsburgh: University of Pittsburgh Press, 551–570.

———. 1971. "Probability in Quantum Mechanics and Other Statistical Theories." In *Problems in the Foundations of Physics*. Ed. M. Bunge. New York: Springer, 79–92.

Fine, Gail. 1981. "Aristotle on Determinism." *The Philosophical Review* 90: 561–79.

Fischer, John Martin. Forthcoming "Frankfurt-type Compatibilism." In Buss and Overton Forthcoming.

———. 2000. "The Significance of Free Will." *Philosophy and Phenomenological Research* 60: 141–48

———. 1999a. "Responsibility and Self-Expression." *Journal of Ethics* 3: 277–97.

———. 1999b. "Recent Work on Moral Responsibility." *Ethics* 110: 91–139.

———. 1996. "A New Compatibilism." *Philosophical Topics* 24: 49–66.

———. 1995. "Libertarianism and Avoidability: A Reply to Widerker." *Faith and Philosophy* 12: 119–25.

———. 1994. *The Metaphysics of Free Will: A Study of Control*. Oxford: Blackwell.

———. 1991. "Snapshot Ockhamism." *Philosophical Perspectives* 5: 355–72.

———. ed., 1989. *God, Freedom and Foreknowledge*. Stanford: Stanford University Press.

———. 1988. "Freedom and Miracles." *Nous* 22: 235–52.

———. 1987. "Responsiveness and Moral Responsibility." In Schoeman, 1987: 81–106.

———. ed. 1986a. *Moral Responsibility*. Ithaca: Cornell University Press.

———. 1986b. "Power Necessity." *Philosophical Topics* 14: 77–91.

———. 1985/86. "Responsibility and Failure." *Proceedings of the Aristotelian Society* 86: 251–70.

———. 1985a. "Scotism." *Mind* 94: 231–43.

———. 1985b. "Ockhamism." *Philosophical Review* 94: 81–100.

———. 1983a. "Incompatibilism." *Philosophical Studies* 43: 127–37.

———. 1983b. "Freedom and Foreknowledge." *Philosophical Review* 92: 67–79.

———. 1982. "Responsibility and Control." *Journal of Philosophy* 79: 24–40.

Fischer, John Martin, and Paul Hoffman. 1994. "Alternative Possibilities: A Reply to Lamb." *Journal of Philosophy* 91: 321–26.

Fischer, John Martin, and Mark Ravizza. 1998. *Responsibility and Control: A Theory of Moral Responsibility*. Cambridge: Cambridge University Press.

———. 1996. "Free Will and the Modal Principle." *Philosophical Studies* 83: 213–30.

———. 1994. "Responsibility and History." *Midwest Studies in Philosophy* 19: 430–51.

———. eds., 1993. *Perspectives on Moral Responsibility*. Ithaca: Cornell University Press.

———. 1992a. "Responsibility, Freedom and Reason." *Ethics* 102: 368–89.

———. 1992b. "When the Will Is Free." In *Philosophical Perspectives*. Ed. J. Tomberlin. Vol. 6. Atascadero, CA.: Ridgview Publishing, 423–51. Reprinted in O'Connor 1995a: 239–69.

Flanagan, Owen. 1992. *Consciousness Reconsidered*. Cambridge, MA: MIT Press.

Flew, Antony, and Godfrey Vesey. 1987. *Agency and Necessity*. Oxford: Blackwell.

Flint, Thomas. 1998. *Divine Providence: The Molinist Account*. Ithaca: Cornell University Press.

———. 1997a. "Praying for Things to Have Happened." *Midwest Studies in Philosophy* 21: (ed. Peter French et al) 61–82.

———. 1997b. "Providence and Predestination." In Quinn and Taliaferro, eds.: 569–76.

———. 1991. "In Defense of Theological Compatibilism." *Faith and Philosophy* 8: 237–43.

———. 1990. "Hasker's *God, Time, and Knowledge.*"*Philosophical Studies* 60: 103–15.

———. 1987. "Compatibilism and the Argument from Unavoidability." *Journal of Philosophy* 84: 423–40.

Foley, Richard. 1979. "Compatibilism and Control over the Past." *Analysis* 39: 70–74.

———. 1978. "Compatibilism." *Mind* 87: 421–28.

Foot, Philippa. 1957. "Free Will as Involving Determinism." *The Philosophical Review* 66: 439–50. Reprinted in Berofsky, 1966, 95–108.

Ford, Joseph. 1989. "What Is Chaos?" In *The New Physics*. Ed. P. Davies. Cambridge: Cambridge University Press, 348–71.

Forrest, Peter. 1985. "Backwards Causation in Defense of Free Will." *Mind* 94: 210–17.

Foster, John. 1991. *The Immaterial Self*. London: Routledge.

Frankfurt, Harry. 1999a. "Responses." *Journal of Ethics* 3: 367–72.

———. 1999b. *Necessity, Volition and Love*. Cambridge: Cambridge University Press.

———. 1994a. "An Alleged Asymmetry between Actions and Omissions." *Ethics* 104: 620–23.

———. 1994b. "Autonomy, Necessity and Love." In *Vernunftbegriffe in der Moderne*. Ed. H. Friedrich and R-P. Horstmann. Stuttgart: Klett-Cotta, 433–47.

———. 1993. "On the Necessity of Ideals." In *The Moral Self*. Ed. G. G. Noam and Thomas Wren, Cambridge, MA.: MIT Press, 16–27.

———. 1992a. "The Faintest Passion." Presidential Address. *Proceedings of the American Philosophical Association* 66: 5–16.

———. 1992b. "On the Usefulness of Final Ends." *Iyyun* 41: 3–19.

———. 1988. *The Importance of What We Care about*. New York: Cambridge University Press.

———. 1987. "Identification and Wholeheartedness." In Schoeman, 1987: 27–45.

———. 1971. "Freedom of the Will and the Concept of a Person." *Journal of Philosophy* 68: 5–20.

———. 1969. "Alternate Possibilities and Moral Responsibility." *Journal of Philosophy* 66: 829–39.

Freddoso, Alfred. 1988. Trans and intr. to Luis de Molina On Divine Foreknowledge. Part IV of *Concordia, Liberi Arbitrii cum Gratio Donis*. Originally published in 1588. Ithaca: Cornell University Press.

———. 1983. "Accidental Necessity and Logical Determinism." *Journal of Philosophy* 80: 257–78.

———. 1982. "Accidental Necessity and Power over the Past." *Pacific Philosophical Quarterly* 63, 54–68.

Freeman, Anthony. 1999. "Decisive Action: Personal Responsibility All the Way Down." In Libet, Freeman, and Sutherland, 1999.: 275–78.

French, Peter. 1992. *Responsibility Matters*. Lawrence: University of Kansas Press.

———. ed. 1972. *Individual and Collective Responsibility*. Cambridge, MA: Shenkman.

Freund, H.-J. 1990. "Premotor Area and Preparation of Movement." *Review of Neurology* 146: 543–47.

Friedman, Marilyn. 1986. "Autonomy and the Split-Level Self." *Southern Journal of Philosophy* 24: 19–35.

Frith, C., K. Friston, P. Liddle, and R. Frackowiack. 1991. "Willed Action and the Prefrontal Cortex in Man." *Proceedings of the Royal Society* B 244: 241–46.

Frohlich, H. 1986. "Coherent Activation in Active Biological Systems." In *Modern Bioelectrochemistry*. Ed. F. Gutman and H. Keyzer. New York: Plenum, 241–61.

Fuster, J. M. 1996. "Frontal Lobe and the Cognitive Foundation of Behavioral Action." In Damasio et al. 1996.: 47–62.

———. 1989. *The Prefrontal Cortex: Anatomy, Physiologie and Neuropsychology of the Frontal Lobe*. New York: Raven Press.

Gadamer, Hans-Georg. 1989. *Truth and Method*. New York: Continuum.

Gallagher, David. 1994. "Free Choice and Free Judgment in Thomas Aquinas." *Archiv für Geshichte der Philosophie* 76: 247–77.

Gallois, Andre. 1977. "Van Inwagen on Free Will and Determinism." *Philosophical Studies* 32: 99–105.

Garson, James. 1993. "Chaos and Free Will." Paper delivered to the American Philosophical Association, Pacific Division Meeting, March.

———. 1994. "Molina on Divine Foreknowledge and the Principle of Bivalence." *Journal of the History of Philosophy* 32: 551–71.

Gaskin, R. 1993. "Conditionals of Freedom and Middle Knowledge." *The Philosophical Quarterly* 43: 412–30.

Gasking, Douglas. 1955. "Causation and Recipes." *Mind* 64: 479–87.

Gasquoine, P. G. 1993. "Alien Hand Sign." *Journal of Clinical and Experimental Neuropsychology* 15: 653–67.

Gauthier, David. 1986. *Morals by Agreement*. Oxford: Clarendon Press.

Gazzaniga, M. S. 1993. *Nature's Mind*. New York: Basic Books.

Gell-Mann, Murray. 1994. *The Quark and the Jaguar*. London: Little, Brown.

Gensler, Harry. 1989. Review of Kane 1985. *The Modern Schoolman* 66: 160–62.

Gert, Bernard, and T. Duggan. 1979. "Free Will as the Ability to Will." *Nous* 13: 197–217.

Ghirardi, G. C., A. Rimini, and T. Weber. 1986. "Unified Dynamics for Microscopic and Macroscopic Systems." *Physical Review* D 34: 470–91.

Giere, Ronald. 1999. *Science without Laws*. University of Chicago Press.

Gilbert, Scott F., and Sahotra Sarkar. 2000. "Embracing Complexity: Organicism for the Twenty-first Century." Forthcoming in *Developmental Dynamics* 219: 1–9.

Ginet, Carl. 1996. "In Defense of the Principle of Alternative Possibilities: Why I Don't find Frankfurt's Argument Convincing." *Philosophical Perspectives* 10: 403–17.

———. 1990. *On Action*. Cambridge: Cambridge University Press.

———. 1983. "In Defense of Incompatibilism." *Philosophical Studies* 44: 391–400.

———. 1980. "The Conditional Analysis of Freedom." In van Inwagen, 1980: 171–86.

———. 1966. "Might We Have No Choice?" In Lehrer 1966a: 87–104.

Gisin, Nicolas. 1989. "Stochastic Quantum Dynamics and Relativity." *Helvetica Physica Acta* 62: 363–71.

———. 1984. "Quantum Measurements and Stochastic Processes." *Physical Review Letters* 52: 1657–60.

Gisin, Nicolas, and Ian C. Percival. 1992. "The Quantum-State Diffusion Model Applied to Open Systems." *Journal of Physics A: Mathematical and General* 25: 5677–91.

Giulini, D., E. Joos, C. Kiefer, J. Kupsch, I.-O, Stamatescu, and H. D. Zeh, 1996. *Decoherence and the Appearance of a Classical World in Quantum Theory.* Berlin: Springer.

Glannon, Walter. 1997. "Sensitivity and Responsibility for Consequences." *Philosophical Studies* 75: 5–24.

———. 1995. "Responsibility and the Principle of Possible Action." *Journal of Philosophy* 92: 261–74.

Glass, Leon, and Michael Mackey. 1988. *From Clocks to Chaos: The Rhythms of Life.* Princeton: Princeton University Press.

Globus, Gordon. 1995. "Kane on Incompatibilism: an Exercise in Neurophilosophy" (unpublished paper).

Glover, Jonathan. 1970. *Responsibility.* London: Routledge & Kegan Paul.

Glymour, Clark. 1971. "Determinism, Ignorance and Quantum Mechanics." *Journal of Philosophy* 68: 744–51.

Goetz, Stewart C. Forthcoming. "Stump on Libertarianism and Alternative Possibilities." Forthcoming in *Faith and Philosophy.*

———. 1999. "Stumping for Widerker." *Faith and Philosophy* 16: 83–89.

———. 1997. "Libertarian Choice." *Faith and Philosophy* 14: 195–211.

———. 1988. "A Non-Causal Theory of Agency." *Philosophy and Phenomenological Research* 49: 303–16.

Goldberg, G., and K. Bloom. 1990. "The Alien Hand Sign." *American Journal of Physical Medical Rehabilitation* 69: 228–38.

Goldman, Alvin. 1970. *A Theory of Human Action.* Englewood Cliffs: Prentice-Hall.

Gomberg, Paul. 1975. "Free Will as Ultimate Responsibility." *American Philosophical Quarterly* 15: 205–12.

Gomes, Gilberto. 1999. "Volition and the Readiness Potential." In Libet, Freeman, and Sutherland, 1999: 59–76.

Good, I. J. 1962. "A Causal Calculus II." *The British Journal for the Philosophy of Science* 12: 43–51.

———. 1961. "A Causal Calculus I." *The British Journal for the Philosophy of Science* 11: 305–18.

Goris, Harm J. M. J. 1996. *Free Creatures of an Eternal God: Thomas Aquinas on God's Foreknowledge and Irresistible Will.* Utrecht/Louvain: Thomas Instituut/Peeters.

Gosling, J. 1990. *Weakness of Will.* London: Routledge.

Gosselin, Phillip. 1987. "The Principle of Alternative Possibilities." *Canadian Journal of Philosophy* 17: 91–104.

Goswami, Amit. 1990. "Consciousness in Quantum Physics and the Mind-Body Problem." *Journal of Mind and Behavior* 11: 75–96.

Graham, George. 1993. *The Philosophy of Mind.* Oxford: Blackwell.

Graham, N. 1973. "The Measurement of Relative Frequency." In DeWitt and Graham 1973: 229–52.

Gray, C., and W. Singer. 1989. "Stimulus Specific Neuronal Oscillations in Orientation Columns of the Lateral Visual Cortex." *Proceedings of the National Academy of Sciences*, USA 86: 1689–1702.

Greenspan, P. S. 1993. "Free Will and the Genome Project." *Philosophy and Public Affairs* 22: 31–43.

———. 1978. "Behavior Control and Freedom of Action." *Philosophical Review* 87: 225–40.

———. 1976. "Wiggins on Historical Inevitability and Incompatibilism." *Philosophical Studies* 29: 235–47.

Gribbin, John. 1985. *In Search of Schrodinger's Cat*. London: Corgi.

Griffin, David, and John B. Cobb. 1976. *Process Theology: An Introductory Exposition*. Philadelphia: Westminster Press.

Grünbaum, Adolph. 1971. "Free Will and the Laws of Human Behavior." *American Philosophical Quarterly* 8: 299–317.

———. 1953. "Causality and the Science of Human Behavior." In *Readings in the Philosophy of Science*. Ed. H. Feigl and M. Brodbeck. New York: Appleton-Century Crofts, 752–80.

Gunter, Pete A. Y. 1991. "Bergson and Non-linear, Non-equilibrium Thermodynamics." *Revue Internationale de Philosophie* 177: 108–21.

Haji, Ishtiyaque. 1999a. "Indeterminism and Frankfurt-style Examples." *Philosophical Explorations* 2: 42–58.

———. 1999b. "Moral Anchors and Control." *Canadian Journal of Philosophy* 175–203.

———. 1998. *Moral Appraisability*. New York: Oxford University Press.

———. 1993. "Alternative Possibilities, Moral Obligation and Moral Responsibility." *Philosophical Papers* 22: 41–50.

———. 1992. "A Riddle Regarding Omissions." *Canadian Journal of Philosophy* 22: 485–502.

Hall, Ned. 2000. "Causation and the Price of Transitivity." *Journal of Philosophy* 97: 198–222.

Hameroff, Stuart, and Scott Hagen. 2000. "Quantum Computation in the Brain? Decoherence and Biological Feasibility." Paper presented at Tucson *Toward a Science of Consciousness* conference, April (see www.u.arizona.edu/~hameroff).

Hameroff, Stuart, Alwyn Scott, and Al Kaszniak, eds. 1998. *Toward a Science of Consciousness II*. Cambridge MA: MIT Press.

Hardie, W. F. R. 1968. "Aristotle and the Freewill Problem." *Philosophy* 43: 274–78.

Harman, Gilbert. 1986. "Willing and Intending." In *Philosophical Grounds of Rationality* Ed. Richard Grandy and R. Warner. Oxford: Clarendon Press, 92–116.

———. 1977. *The Nature of Morality*. New York: Oxford University Press.

Harper, William L., and Brian Skyrms, eds. 1988. *Causation in Decision, Belief Change, and Statistics: Proceedings of the Irvine Conference on Probability and Causation*. Vol. 2. Dordrecht: Kluwer Academic.

Hart, H. L. A. 1970. *Punishment and Responsibility*. Oxford: Clarendon Press.

Hart, H. L. A. and A. M. Honoré. 1959. *Causation in the Law*. Oxford: Clarendon Press.

Hartshorne, Charles. 1967. *A Natural Theology for Our Time*. Lasalle: Open Court.

———. 1941. *Man's Vision of God*. NY: Harper and Bros.

Hasker, William. 2000. "Anti-Molinism Is Undefeated!" *Faith and Philosophy* 17: 126–31.

———. 1999. *The Emergent Self*. Ithaca: Cornell University Press.

———. 1998. "No Easy Way Out—A Response to Warfield." *Nous* 32: 361–63.

———. 1997. "Explanatory Priority: Transitive and Unequivocal, a Reply to William Craig." *Philosophy and Phenomological Research* 57: 389–93.

———. 1995. "Middle Knowledge: A Refutation Revisited." *Faith and Philosophy* 12: 223–36.

———. 1993. "Zagzebski on Power Entailment." *Faith and Philosophy* 10: 250–55.

———. 1989a. *God, Time and Knowledge*. Ithaca: Cornell University Press.

———. 1989b. "Hard Facts and Theological Fatalism." In Fischer: 159–77.

———. 1989c. "Foreknowledge and Necessity." In Fischer 1989: 216–57.

———. 1985. "Foreknowledge and Necessity." *Faith and Philosophy* 2: 121–57.

Hawking, Stephen. 1988. *A Brief History of Time*. NY: Bantam.

Hawkins, David. 1967. *The Language of Nature*. Garden City: Doubleday.

Haworth, Laurence. 1986. *Autonomy*. New Haven: Yale University Press.

Heil, John. 1992. *The Nature of True Minds*. Cambridge: Cambridge University Press.

———. 1984. "Doxastic Incontinence." *Mind* 93: 56–70.

Heil, John, and Alfred Mele, eds, 1993. *Mental Causation*. Oxford: Oxford University Press.

Heinaman, Robert. 1986. "Incompatibilism without the Principle of Alternative Possibilities." *Australasian Journal of Philosophy* 64: 266–76.

Heller, Mark. 1990. *The Ontology of Physical Objects*. Cambridge: Cambridge University Press.

Herbert, Nick. 1993. *Elemental Mind*. NY: Dutton.

Hilborn, Robert C. 1994. *Chaos and Nonlinear Dynamics: An Introduction for Scientists and Engineers*. Oxford: Oxford University Press.

Hill, Christopher. 1992. "Van Inwagen on the Consequence Argument." *Analysis* 52: 49–55.

———. 1984. "Watsonian Freedom and Freedom of the Will." *Australasian Journal of Philosophy* 62: 294–98

Hill, Thomas. 1991. *Autonomy and Self-Respect*. Cambridge: Cambridge University Press.

———. 1987. "The Importance of Autonomy." In *Women and Moral Theory*. Ed. E. Feder Kittay and D. Meyers. Totowa, NJ: Rowman and Littlefield: 129–318.

Hitchcock, Christopher. 1993. "A Generalized Probabilistie Theory of Causal Relevance." *Synthese* 97: 335–64.

Hobart, R. E. 1934. "Free Will as Involving Determinism and Inconceivable without It." *Mind* 43 (1934): 1–27. Reprinted in Berofsky, 1966: 63–95.

Hobbes, Thomas. 1962. *The English Works of Thomas Hobbes*. Vol 5. Ed. W. Molesworth. London: Scientia Aalen. Original publication 1654.

———. 1958. *Leviathan*. Indianapolis: Bobbs-Merrill. Originally published in 1651.

Hobbs, Jesse. 1991. "Chaos and Indeterminism." *Canadian Journal of Philosophy* 21: 141–64.

Hocutt, Max. 1992. "A Review of Bruce Waller's *Freedom Without Responsibility*." *Behavior and Philosophy* 20: 71–76.

Hodgson, David. 1999. "Hume's Mistake." In Libet, Freeman, and Sutherland, 1999: 201–24.

———. 1996. "Nonlocality, Local Indeterminism, and Consciousness." *Ratio* 9: 1–22.

———. 1995. "Probability: The Logic of the Law—a Response." *Oxford Journal of Legal Studies* 14: 51–68.

———. 1991. *The Mind Matters*. Oxford: Clarendon Press.

Hoffman, Joshua, and Gary Rosenkrantz. 1984. "Hard and Soft Facts." *Philosophical Review* 93: 419–34.

Holland, Peter R. 1993. *The Quantum Theory of Motion: An Account of the de Broglie-Bohm Causal Interpretation of Quantum Mechanics.* Cambridge: Cambridge University Press.

Holmstrom-Hintikka, Ghita and Raimo Tuomela. 1997. *Contemporary Action Theory* Vol. 1. Dordrecht: Kluwer.

Honderich, Ted. 2001. "Mind the Guff: A Response to John Searle." *Journal of Consciousness Studies* 8 (4): 62–78.

———. 2000. *Philosopher: A Kind of Life.* London: Routledge.

———. 1996. "Compatibilism, Incompatibilism and the Smart Aleck." *Philosophy and Phenomenological Research* 56: 855–62.

———. 1993. *How Free Are You?* Oxford: Oxford University Press.

———. 1988. *A Theory of Determinism.* 2 vols. Oxford: Clarendon Press.

———. ed. 1973. *Essays on Freedom of Action.* London: Routledge & Kegan Paul.

Hook, Sidney, ed., 1958. *Determinism and Freedom in the Age of Modern Science.* New York: Collier-Macmillan.

Horgan, Terence. 1985. "Compatibilism and the Consequence Argument." *Philosophical Studies* 47: 339–56.

Horgan, Terence, and George Graham. 1991. "In Defense of Southern Fundamentalism." *Philosophical Studies* 62: 107–34.

Horgan, Terence, and James Woodward. 1985. "Folk Psychology Is Here to Stay." *The Philosophical Review* 94: 197–226.

Hornsby, Jennifer. 1993. "Agency and Causal Explanation." In Heil and Mele, 1993: 161–88.

———. 1980. *Actions.* London: Routledge & Kegan Paul.

Hospers, John. 1958. "What Means This Freedom?" In Hook, 1958.: 126–42.

Howard-Snyder, Daniel, and Jeff Jordan, eds. 1996. *Faith, Freedom and Rationality.* Lanham, MD: Rowman and Littlefield.

Huberman, P., and G. Hogg. 1987. "Phase Transitions in Artificial Intelligence Systems." *Artificial Intelligence* 33: 155–72.

Huby, Pamela. 1967. "The First Discovery of the Free Will Issue." *Philosophy* 42: 333–62.

Hume, David. 1960. *A Treatise on Human Nature.* Ed. L. A. Selby-Bigge. Oxford: Clarendon Press. Originally published in 1739.

———. 1955. *An Enquiry concerning Human Understanding.* Ed. L. A. Selby-Bigge. Oxford: Clarendon Press. Originally published in 1743.

Humphreys, Paul. 1989. *The Chances of Explanation: Causal Explanation in the Social, Medical and Physical Sciences.* Princeton: Princeton University Press.

———. 1980. "Probabilistic Causality and Multiple Causation." Ed. P. D. Asquith and R. N. Giere. In *PSA*, Vol. 2. East Lansing, MI: Philosophy of Science Association 25–37.

Hunt, David. 2000. "Moral Responsibility and Avoidable Action." *Philosophical Studies* 97: 195–227.

———. 1999. "On Augustine's Way Out." *Faith and Philosophy* 16: 3–26.

———. 1997. "Two Problems with Knowing the Future." *American Philosophical Quarterly* 34 (April): 273–85. Reprinted in *Essays on Time and Related Topics: Selected Papers of the Philosophy of Time Society Proceedings, 1995–1999.* Ed. L. Nathan Oaklander. Dordrecht: Kluwer, forthcoming.

———. 1996a. "Frankfurt Counterexamples : Some Comments on the Widerker-Fischer Debate." *Faith and Philosophy* 13: 395–401.

———. 1996b. "Augustine on Theological Fatalism: The Argument of *De Libero Arbitrio* III.1–4." *Medieval Philosophy and Theology* 6: 1–30.

———. 1995a. "Does Theological Fatalism Rest on an Equivocation?" *American Philosophical Quarterly* 32: 153–65.

———. 1995b. "Dispositional Omniscience." *Philosophical Studies* 80: 243–78.

———. 1993a. "Simple Foreknowledge and Divine Providence." *Faith and Philosophy* 10: 394–414.

———. 1993b. "Prescience and Providence: A Reply to My Critics." *Faith and Philosophy* 10: 428–38.

———. 1992. "Omnisprescient Agency." *Religious Studies* 28: 351–69.

———. n.d. "Freedom, Foreknowledge and Frankfurt."

Hunt, G. M. K. 1981. "Determinism, Prediction and Chaos." *Analysis* 49: 129–32.

Hurley, Susan. Forthcoming. "Luck, Responsibility, and the 'Natural Lottery.'" In Hurley, *Justice Luck and Knowledge*. Cambridge Ma: Harvard University Press.

Hurley, Paul. 1993. "How Weakness of Will Is Possible." *Mind* 102: 329–34.

Huxley, Aldous. 1989. *Brave New World*. San Francisco: Harper-Collins.

Hyder, R., E. Phelps, C. Wiggens, K. Labar, A. Blamire, and R. Shulman. 1997. "Willed Action." *Proceedings of the National Academy of Science, USA.* 94: 6989–94.

Ingvar, David H. 1999. "On Volition: A Neurophysiologically-Oriented Essay." In Libet, Freeman, and Sutherland, 1999: 1–10.

Irwin, Terence. 1992. "Who Discovered the Will?" In *Philosophical Perspectives*. Vol. 6. Ed. J. Tomberlin. Atascadero, CA.: Ridgview, 405–22.

———. 1988. *Aristotle's First Principles*. Oxford: Oxford University Press.

———. 1980. "Reason and Responsibility in Aristotle." In A. Rorty, 1980a: 72–91.

Jackson, Frank. 1985. "Internal Conflicts in Desires and Morals." *American Philosophical Quarterly* 22: 105–14.

———. 1984. "Weakness of Will." *Mind* 93: 1–18.

James, William. 1956. *The Will to Believe and Other Essays*. New York: Dover.

———. 1907. *The Principles of Psychology*. Vol. 1. New York: Henry Holt.

Jeffrey, Richard. 1974. "Preferences among Preferences." *Journal of Philosophy* 71: 377–91.

———. 1971. "Statistical Explanation and Statistical Relevance." In Salmon et al. 1971: 19–28.

Jibu, M., and K. Yasue. 1995. *Quantum Brain Dynamics and Consciousness: An Introduction*. Amsterdam: Benjamin.

Joseph, R. 1996. *Neuropsychiatry, Neuropsychology and Clinical Neuroscience*. Baltimore: Williams and Wilkens.

Kane, Robert, ed. 2001. *Free Will*. Oxford: Blackwell.

———. 2000a. "Precis of *The Significance of Free Will*" and "Responses to Bernard Berofsky, John Martin Fischer and Galen Strawson." *Philosophy and Phenomenological Research* 60: 129–34, 157–67.

———. 2000b. "The Dual Regress of Free Will and the Role of Alternative Possibilities." *Philosophical Perspectives* 14. Oxford: Blackwell Publishers, 57–80.

———. 1999a. "Responsibility, Luck and Chance: Reflections on Free Will and Indeterminism." *Journal of Philosophy* 96: 217–40.

———. 1999b. "On Free Will, Responsibility and Indeterminism: Responses to Clarke, Haji and Mele." *Philosophical Explorations: An International Journal for the Philosophy of Mind and Action* 2: 105–21.

———. 1999c. "New Directions on Free Will." *Proceedings of the 20th World Congress of Philosophy*. Boston.: Boston University Press: 135–42.

———. 1999d. Review of Bok 1998 and Fischer and Ravizza 1998. *The Times Literary Supplement* (August 13).

———. 1996a. *The Significance of Free Will*. Oxford: Oxford University Press.

———. 1996b. "Free Will, Responsibility and Will-Setting." *Philosophical Topics* 24:2: 67–90.

———. 1995. "Acts, Patterns, and Self-Control." *Behavioral and Brain Sciences* 18: 131–32.

———. 1994. "Free Will: The Elusive Ideal." *Philosophical Studies* 75: 25–60.

———. 1991. Review of Anglin 1991, Double 1991, S. Wolf, 1990 and Zagzebski 1991. *The Times Literary Supplement* (September): 25.

———. 1989. "Two Kinds of Incompatibilism." *Philosophy and Phenomenological Research* 50: 219–54. Reprinted in O'Connor, 1995a: 115–50.

———. 1988. "Libertarianism and Rationality Revisited." *The Southern Journal of Philosophy* 26: 441–60.

———. 1986. "Principles of Reason." *Erkenntnis* 24: 115–36.

———. 1985. *Free Will and Values*. Albany, NY: State University of New York Press.

———. n.d. "Responsibility, Incompatibilism and Frankfurt-style Examples."

Kaneko, Kunihiko, I. Tsuda, and T. Ikegami, eds. 1994. "Constructive Complexity and Artificial Reality: Proceedings of the Oji International Seminar on Complex Systems." *Physica D* 75. 103–89.

Kant, Immanuel. 1993. *Opus Posthumum*. Trans. B. Förster and M. Rosen. Cambridge; Cambridge University Press.

———. 1960. *Religion within the Bounds of Reason Alone*. Trans. T. Greene and H. Hudson. New York: Harper & Row. Originally published in 1804.

———. 1959. *Foundations of the Metaphysics of Morals*. Trans. L. W. Beck. Indianapolis: Bobbs-Merrill. Originally published in 1785.

———. 1958. *Critique of Pure Reason*. Trans. N. K. Smith. London: Macmillan. Originally published in 1881 (2nd Ed. 1787).

———. 1956. *Critique of Practical Reason*. Trans. L. W. Beck. Indianapolis: Bobbs-Merrill. Originally published in 1788.

———. 1793. *Die Religion innerhalb der Grenzen der blossen Vernunft*. Königsberg: Nicolovius.

———. 1788. *Kritik der praktischen Vernunft [Critique of Practical Reason]*. Riga: Hartknoch.

———. 1785. *Grundlegung zur Metaphysik der Sitten*. Riga: Hartknoch; revised 1786. Trans. H. J. Paton as *The Moral Law* (London: Hutchinson, 1948); republished as *Groundwork of the Metaphysic of Morals* (New York: Harper, 1948).

Kapitan, Tomis. 2000. "Autonomy and Manipulated Freedom." *Philosophical Perspectives* 14 (forthcoming).

———. 1996. "Modal Principles in the Metaphysics of Free Will." *Philosophical Perspectives* 10: 419–45.

———. 1994. "Critical Study of R. Double's *The Non-Reality of Free Will*." *Nous* 28: 90–95.

———. 1993. "Providence, Foreknowledge, and Decision Procedure." *Faith and Philosophy* 10: 415–20.

———. 1991a. "Ability and Cognition: A Defense of Compatibilism." *Philosophical Studies* 63: 231–43.

———. 1991b. "How Powerful Are We?" *American Philosophical Quarterly* 28: 331–38.

———. 1990. Review of G. Strawson 1986. *Nous* 24: 807–10.

———. 1989. "Doxastic Freedom: A Compatibilist Alternative." *American Philosophical Quarterly* 26: 31–41.

———. 1986a. "Freedom and Moral Choice." *Nous* 20: 241–60.

———. 1986b. "Deliberation and the Presumption of Open Alternatives." *The Philosophical Quarterly* 36: 230–51.

Kauffman, Stuart. 1995. *At Home in the Universe*. New York: Oxford University Press.

Kellert, Stephen. 1993. *In the Wake of Chaos*. Chicago: University of Chicago Press.

Kennett, J., and M. Smith. 1997. "Synchronic Self-Control Is Always Non-Actional." *Analysis* 57: 123–31.

———. 1996. "Frog and Toad Lose Control." *Analysis*. 56: 63–73.

Kenny, Anthony. 1993. *Aquinas on Mind*. London: Routledge.

———. 1978. *Free Will and Responsibility*. London: Routledge & Kegan Paul.

———. 1975. *Will, Freedom, and Power*. Oxford: Basil Blackwell.

———. 1969a. "Divine Foreknowledge and Human Freedom." In *Aquinas: A Collection of Critical Essays*. Ed. A. Kenny. University of Notre Dame Press: 63–81.

———. 1969b. *Aristotle's Theory of the Will*. London: Blackwell's.

———. 1963. *Action, Emotion, and Will*. London: Routledge & Kegan Paul.

Kent, Bonnie. 1995. *Virtues of the Will: The Transformations of Ethics in the Late Thirteenth Century*. Washington: Catholic University Press.

Kim, Jaegwon. 1999. "Making Sense of Emergence." *Philosophical Studies* 95: 3–36.

———. 1998. *Mind in the Physical World*. Cambridge, MA: MIT Press.

———. 1993. *Supervenience and Mind*. Cambridge: Cambridge University Press.

———. 1984. "Epiphenomenal and Supervenient Causation." *Midwest Studies in Philosophy*. 257–70 Ed. P. French et al.

———. 1974. "Noncausal Connections." *Nous* 8: 41–52.

Kischka, U., M. Spitzer, and T. Kammer. 1997. "Frontal-subkortikale Schaltkreise." *Fortschrifte Neurologie Psychiatrie* 65: 221–31

Klein, Martha. 1990. *Determinism, Blameworthiness and Deprivation*. Oxford: Oxford University Press.

Knuuttila, Simo. 1993. *Modalities in Medieval Philosophy*. London: Routledge.

Kolb, B., and I. Wishaw. 1996. *Neuropsychologie*. 4th ed. Weinheim: Spektrum.

Kolb, Edward W., and Michael S. Turner. 1990. *The Early Universe*. Reading, MA: Addison-Wesley.

Kolb, Edward W., Michael S. Turner, David Lindley, Keith Olive, and David Seckel, eds. 1986. *Inner Space Outer Space: The Interface between Cosmology and Particle Physics*. Chicago: University of Chicago Press.

Koons, Robert. 2000. *Realism Regained: An Exact Theory of Causation, Teleology and Mind*. Oxford: Oxford University Press.

———. 1992. *Paradoxes of Belief and Strategic Rationality*. Cambridge: Cambridge University Press.

Kornhuber, H., and L. Deecke. 1965. "Hirnpotentialanderungen bei Willkurbewegungen und passiven Bewegungen des Menschen." *Pfluegers Arch Gesamte Physiologie Menschen Tiere* 284: 1–17.

Körner, Stephen. 1973. "Rational Choice." *Proceedings of the Aristotelian Society* 47: 1–17.

Kristjansson, Kristjan. 1996. *Social Freedom: The Responsibility View*. Cambridge: Cambridge University Press.

Kuppers, Bernd-Olaf. 1992. "Understanding Complexity." In Beckermann, Flohr, and Kim 1992: 241–56.

———. 1990. *Information and the Origin of Life*. Cambridge, MA: MIT Press.

Kvanvig, Jonathan. 1986. *The Possibility of an All-Knowing God*. New York: St. Martin's Press.

Lahav, Ran. 1991. "Between Pre-Determination and Arbitrariness: A Bergsonian Approach to Free Will." *The Southern Journal of Philosophy*. 29: 487–500.

Lamb, James. 1993. "Evaluative Compatibilism and the Principle of Alternative Possibilities." *Journal of Philosophy* 90: 517–27.

———. 1977. "On a Proof of Incompatibilism." *The Philosophical Review* 86: 20–35.

Landé, Alfred. 1958. "The Case for Indeterminism." In Hook, 1958: 83–89.

Lanier, Jaron. 1999. "And Now a Brief Word from Now: Logical Dependencies between Vernacular Concepts of Free Will, Time and Consciousness." In Libet, Freeman and Sutherland, 1999.: 261–68.

Laplace, P. S. 1951. *A Philosophical Essay on Probabilities*. New York: Dover. Originally published in 1812.

LaRochfoucauld, François. 1678. *Maxims*. Trans. L. Tancock. Hammondsworth: Penguin, 1959.

Leftow, Brian. 1991a. "Timelessness and Foreknowledge." *Philosophical Studies* 63: 309–25.

———. 1991b. *Time and Eternity*. Ithaca: Cornell University Press.

Lehnertz, K., C. E. Elger, J. Arnhold, and P. Grassberger, eds. Forthcoming "Chaos in the Brain?" Singapore: *Proceedings of the World Scientific Workshop*.

Lehrer, Keith. 1997. *Self-Trust: A Study of Reason, Knowledge and Autonomy*. Oxford: Clarendon Press.

———. 1980. "Preferences, Conditionals and Freedom." In van Inwagen, 1980: 76–96.

———. 1976. " 'Can' in Theory and Practice: A Possible Worlds Analysis." In *Action Theory*. Ed. M. Brand and D. Walton. Dordrecht: Reidel, 67–97.

———. 1968. " 'Can's Without 'If's." *Analysis* 29:29–32.

———. ed. 1966a. *Freedom and Determinism*. New York: Random House.

———. ed. 1966b. "An Empircial Disproof of Determinism." In Lehrer, 1966a: 175–202.

———. 1964. " 'Could' and Determinism." *Analysis* 24: 159–60.

Leibniz, G. W. F. 1988. *Discourse on Metaphysics*. Trans. R. Martin, D. Niall, and S. Brown. Manchester: Manchester University Press. Originally published in 1716.

———. 1951. *Selections*. Ed. P. Wiener. New York: Scribner's.

Leiter, Brian. 1998. "The Paradox of Fatalism and Self-Creation in Nietzsche." In *Willing and Nothingness: Schopenhauer as Nietzsche's Educator*. Ed. C. Janaway. Oxford: Oxford University Press.

Lennon, Kathleen. 1990. *Explaining Human Action*. Peru, IL: Open Court.

LeShan, L., and H. Margenau. 1982. *Einstein's Space and van Gogh's Sky*. New York: Macmillan.

Levin, Michael. 1979. *Metaphysics and the Mind-Body Problem*. Oxford: Oxford University Press.

Lewis, David. 2000. "Causation as Influence." *Journal of Philosophy* 97: 182–97.

————. 1986a. *Philosophical Papers.* 2 Vols. Oxford: Oxford University Press.

————. 1986b. *On the Plurality of Worlds.* Oxford: Blackwell

————. 1981. "Are We Free to Break the Laws?" *Theoria* 47: 113–21. Reprinted in Lewis 1986a, vol. 2: 291–98.

————. 1979. "Counterfactual Dependence and Time's Arrow." *Nous* 13: 455–76.

————. 1973a. *Counterfactuals.* Cambridge, MA: Harvard University Press.

————. 1973b. "Causation." *Journal of Philosophy* 70: 556–67.

Libet, B. 1996. "Neural Time Factors in Conscious and Unconscious Mental Function." In *Toward a Science of Consciousness.* Ed. S. Hameroff et al. Cambridge, MA: MIT Press. 156–171.

————. 1994. "A Testable Field Theory of Mind-Brain Interaction." *Journal of Consciousness Studies* 1: 119–26.

————. 1993. "The Neural Time Factor in Conscious and Unconscious Mental Events." In Ciba Foundation Symposium #174. *Experimental and Theoretical Studies of Consciousness.* Chichester: Wiley. 210–23.

————. 1989. "Conscious Subjective Experience vs. Unconscious Mental Functions." In *Models of Brain Function.* Ed. R. M. J. Cotterill. New York: Cambridge University Press. 68–79.

————. 1987. "Are the Mental Experiences of Will and Self-Control Significant for the Performance of a Voluntary Act?" *Behavioral and Brain Sciences.* 10: 783–91.

————. 1985. "Unconscious Cerebral Initiative and the Role of Conscious Will in Voluntary Action." *Behavioral and Brain Sciences* 8: 529–66.

Libet, B., Anthony Freeman, and Keith Sutherland, eds. 1999. *The Volitional Brain: Towards a Neuroscience of Free Will.* Thorverten, UK: Imprint Academic.

Libet B., C. Gleason, E. Wright, and D. Pearl. 1983a. "Time of Conscious Intention to Act in Relation to Cerebral Potential." *Brain* 106: 623–42.

————. 1983b. "Preparation—or Intention to Act in Relation to Pre-Event Potentials." *Electroencephalograph and Clinical Neurophysiology* 56: 367–72.

Libet, B., D. Pearl, D. Morledge, C. Gleason, Y. Hosoguchi, and N. Barbaro. 1991. "Control of the Transition from Sensory Detection to Sensory Awareness in Man by the Duration of a Thalamic Stimulus." *Brain* 114: 1731–57.

Libet, B., E. Wright, B. Feinstein, and D. Pearl. 1979. "Subjective Referral for a Timing for a Conscious Sensory Experience." *Brain* 102: 191–222.

Libet, B., E. Wright, and C. Gleason. 1982. "Readiness Potentials Preceding Unrestricted Spontaneous Pre-Planned Voluntary Acts." *Electroencephalograph and Clinical Neurophysiology* 54: 322–25.

Liddle, P. F. 1994. "Volition and Schizophrenia." In *The Neuropsychology of Schizophrenia.* Ed. A. David et al. Hillsdale NJ: Erlbaum: 39–49.

————. 1987. "The Symptoms of Chronic Schizophrenia." *British Journal of Psychiatry* 151: 145–51.

Liddle, P. F. K. Friston, C. Frith, T. Jones, S. Hirsch, and R. Frackowiack. 1992. "Patterns of Cerebral Blood Flow in Schizophrenia." *British Journal of Psychiatry* 160: 179–89.

Lindley, Richard. 1986. *Autonomy.* London: Macmillan.

Linville, Mark D. 1993. "Divine Foreknowledge and the Libertarian Conception of Freedom." *International Journal for Philosophy of Religion* 33: 165–86.

Llinas, Rudolfo, and D. Pare. 1991. "Of Dreaming and Wakefulness." *Neuroscience* 44: 521–35.

Llinas, Rudolfo, and U. Ribary. 1993. "Coherent 40 Hz. Oscillation Characterizes Dream State in Humans." *Proceedings of the National Academy of Sciences* 90: 2078–81.

Locke, Don. 1974. "Reasons, Wants and Causes." *American Philosophical Quarterly* 11: 169–79.

Locke, John. 1959. *An Essay Concerning Human Understanding*. Ed. A. C. Fraser. New York: Dover. (Originally published in 1689.)

Lockwood, Michael. n.d. "Taking Space-Time Seriously."

———. 1989. *Mind, Brain and Quantum*. Oxford: Oxford University Press.

Loewer, Barry. 1996. "Freedom from Physics: Quantum Mechanics and Free Will." *Philosophical Topics* 24: 91–112.

London, F., and E. Bauer. 1983. "The Theory of Observation in Quantum Mechanics." In Wheeler and Zurek 1983: 217–59.

Loughran, Thomas. 1994. "Freedom and Good in the Thomistic Tradition." *Faith and Philosophy* 11: 414–35.

Lowe, E. J. 1999. "Self, Agency and Mental Causation." In Libet, Freeman and Sutherland 1999: 225–40.

———. 1990. "Conditionals, Context and Transitivity." *Analysis* 50: 80–87.

Lucas, J. R. 1993. *Responsibility*. Oxford: Oxford University Press.

———. 1989. *The Future: An Essay on God, Temporality, and Truth*. London: Blackwell.

———. 1970. *The Freedom of the Will*. Oxford: Oxford University Press.

Lutyens, M. 1983. *Krishnamurti: The Years of Fulfilment*. London: John Murray.

Lycan, William. 1987. *Consciousness*. Cambridge, MA: MIT Press.

———. 1984. "A Syntactically Motivated Theory of Conditionals." *Midwest Studies in Philosophy* 9. Minneapolis: University of Minnesota Press. 439–55.

MacDonald, Scott. 1999. "Primal Sin." In *The Augustinian Tradition*. Ed. G. Matthews. Berkeley, CA: University of California Press, 110–39.

———. 1998. "Aquinas's Libertarian Account of Free Choice." *Revue Internationale de Philosophie* 52: 309–28.

MacDonald, Scott, and Eleonore Stump. 1998. *Aquinas's Moral Theory*. Ithaca: Cornell University Press.

Machina, Kenton. 1994. "Challenges for Compatibilism." *American Philosophical Quarterly* 31: 213–22.

MacKay, D. M. 1967. *Freedom of Action in a Mechanistic Universe*. Cambridge: Cambridge University Press.

———. 1960. "On the Logical Indeterminacy of a Free Choice." *Mind* 69: 31–40.

Mackie, J. L. 1985. "Morality and the Retributive Emotions." In Mackie, *Persons and Values:*. Vol. 2. Oxford: Clarendon Press, 117–134.

———. 1977. *Ethics: Inventing Right and Wrong*. New York: Penguin.

Magill, Kevin. 2000. "Blaming, Understanding and Justification." In T. van den Beld 2000: 183–197.

———. 1997. *Experience and Freedom: Self-Determination without Illusions*. London: MacMillan.

Malcolm, Norman. 1968. "The Conceivability of Mechanism." *Philosophical Review* 77: 45–72. Reprinted in Watson 1982: 127–49.

Manekin, C. H., and M. Kellner, eds. 1997. *Freedom and Moral Responsibility: General and Jewish Perspectives*. College Park, MD: University of Maryland Press.

Mansel, Henry. 1851. *Prolegomena Logica*. Oxford: William Graham.

Margenau, Henry. 1984. *The Miracle of Existence* Woodbridge, CT: OxBow.

Marshall, I. N. 1989. "Consciousness and Bose-Einstein Condensates." *New Ideas in Psychology.* 7: 81–87.

Martin, Jack, and Jeff Sugarman. 1999. "Psychology's Reality Debate: A 'Levels of Reality' Approach." *Journal of Theoretical and Philosophical Psychology.* 19: 177–94.

Mates, Benson. 1961. *Stoic Logic.* Berkeley: University of California Press.

Matson, Wallace. 1987. *A New History of Philosophy.* Vol. 1. New York: Harcourt, Brace, Jovanovich.

Mavrodes, George. 1984. "Is the Past Preventable?" *Faith and Philosophy* 1: 131–46.

Maxwell, Nicholas. 1988. "Quantum Propensiton Theory: A Testable Resolution of the Wave/Particle Dilemma." *British Journal of Philosophy of Science* 39: 1–50.

———. n.d. "Can There Be Free Will in a Physically Comprehensible Universe?" (Unpublished manuscript).

May, Larry. 1992. *Sharing Responsibility.* Chicago: University of Chicago Press.

McCall, Storrs. 1999. "Deliberation Reasons and Explanation Reasons." In *Language, Logic and Concepts.* Ed. R. Jackendoff et al. Cambridge, MA: MIT Press, 97–108.

———. 1994. *A Model of the Universe.* Oxford: Clarendon Press.

———. 1987. "Decision." *Canadian Journal of Philosophy* 17: 261–88.

———. 1984. "Freedom Defined as the Power to Decide." *American Philosophical Quarterly* 21: 329–38.

McCann, Hugh. 1998. *The Works of Agency: On Human Action, Will and Freedom.* Ithaca: Cornell University Press.

———. 1997. "On When the Will Is Free." In Holmstrom-Hintikka and Tuomela, 1997: 219–32.

———. 1995a. "Intention and Motivational Strength." *Journal of Philosophical Research* 20: 283–96.

———. 1995b. "Divine Sovereignty and the Freedom of the Will." *Faith and Philosophy* 12: 582–98.

———. 1986. "Intrinsic Intentionality." *Theory and Decision* 20: 247–73.

———. 1974. "Volition and Basic Action." *Philosophical Review* 83: 451–73.

McCrone, John. 1999. "A Bifold Model of Free Will." In Libet, Freeman, and Sutherland 1999: 241–59.

———. 1994. "Quantum States of Mind." *New Scientist* 20 August: 35–38.

McGinn, Colin. 1991. *The Problem of Consciousness.* Oxford: Blackwell.

McIntyre, Alison. 1994. "Compatibilists Could Have Done Otherwise: Responsibility and Negative Agency." *Philosophical Review* 103: 453–88.

McKay, Thomas, and David Johnson. 1996. "A Reconsideration of an Argument against Compatibilism." *Philosophical Topics* 24: 113–22.

McKenna, Michael. 1998a. "Does Strong Compatibilism Survive Frankfurt-style Examples?" *Philosophical Studies* 91: 259–64.

———. 1998b. "The Limits of Evil and the Role of Address." *Journal of Ethics* 2: 123–42.

———. 1997. "Alternative Possibilities and the Failure of the Counterexample Strategy." *Journal of Social Philosophy* 28: 71–85.

McKenna, Michael, and David Widerker, eds. Forthcoming. *Freedom, Responsibility and Agency: Essays on the Importance of Alternative Possibilities.* Burlington, VT: Ashgate Press.

McLaughlin, J. A. 1925. "Proximate Cause." *Harvard Law Review* 39: 149–55.

Melden, A. I. 1961. *Free Action*. London: Routledge & Kegan Paul.

Mele, Alfred. 2000. "Deciding to Act." *Philosophical Studies* 100: 81–108.

———. 1999a. "Ultimate Responsibility and Dumb Luck." *Social Philosophy and Policy* 16: 274–93.

———. 1999b. "Kane, Luck and the Significance of Free Will." *Philosophical Explorations* 2: 96–104.

———. 1998a. "Synchronic Self-Control Revisited: Frog and Toad Shape Up." *Analysis* 58: 305–10.

———. 1998b. Review of Kane, 1996a. *Journal of Philosophy* 95: 581–84.

———. 1997a. "Strength of Motivation and Being in Control: Learning from Libet." *American Philosophical Quarterly* 34: 319–33.

———. ed. 1997b. *The Philosophy of Action*. Oxford: Oxford University Press

———. 1997c. "Agency and Mental Action." *Philosophical Perspectives* 11: 231–49.

———. 1996. "Soft Libertarianism and Frankfurt-style Scenarios." *Philosophical Topics* 24: 123–41.

———. 1995. *Autonomous Agents: From Self-Control to Autonomy*. New York: Oxford University Press.

———. 1993. "History and Personal Autonomy." *Canadian Journal of Philosophy* 23: 271–80.

———. 1992a *Springs of Action: Understanding Intentional Behavior*. Oxford: Oxford University Press.

———. 1992b. "Akrasia, Self-control and Second-Order Desire." *Nous* 26: 281–302.

———. 1987. *Irrationality*. New York: Oxford University Press.

Mele, Alfred, and David Robb. 1998. "Rescuing Frankfurt-style Cases." *The Philosophical Review* 107: 97–112.

Mellema, Gregory. 1984. "On Being Fully Responsible." *American Philosophical Quarterly* 21: 189–93.

Mellor, D. H. 1999. *The Facts of Causation*. London: Routledge.

———. 1986. "Fixed Past, Unfixed Future." *Contributions to Philosophy*: Michael Dummett, B. Taylor The Hague: Dordrecht. 166–86.

———. 1971. *The Matter of Chance*. Cambridge: Cambridge University Press.

Menzies, P. 1996. "Probabilistic Causation and the Pre-Emption Problem." *Mind* 105: 85–118.

Mermin, D. 1985. "Is the Moon There When Nobody Looks?" *Physics Today* (April): 38–47.

Metzinger, T. 1993. *Subjekt und Selbstmodell*. Paderborn: Mentis.

Meyer, Susan. 1993. *Aristotle on Moral Responsibility*. Oxford: Blackwell.

Mill, J. S. 1979. *An Examination of Sir William Hamilton's Philosphy*. Ed. J. Robson. Toronto: Routledge and Kegan Paul. Orginally published in 1865.

———. 1947. *On Liberty*. Oxford: Blackwell. Originally published in 1860.

———. 1874. "From an Examination of Sir William Hamilton's Philosophy." In Morgenbesser and Walsh, 1962: 57–69.

Milo, Ronald D. 1984. *Immorality*. Princeton: Princeton University Press.

Mohrhoff, Ulrich. 1999. "The Physics of Interactionism." In Libet, Freeman and Sutherland 1999: 165–84.

Mongkin, Charles, and Menachem Kellner, eds. 1998. *Free Will and Moral Responsibility: General and Jewish Perspectives*. College Park, MD: University of Maryland Press.

Montague, Richard. 1974. *Formal Philosophy: Selected Papers of Richard Montague*. Ed. Richard H. Thomason. New Haven: Yale University Press.

Moore, G. E. 1912. "Free Will." In Moore *Ethics*. Oxford: Oxford University Press: 84–95.

Moreland, J. P., and Scott B. Rae. 2000. *Body and Soul*. Downer's Grove, IL: Intervarsity Press.

Morgenbesser, Sidney, and J. H. Walsh, eds. 1962. *Free Will*. Englewood Cliffs: Prentice-Hall.

Mortimore, G. W., ed. 1971. *Weakness of Will*. London: Macmillan.

Moser, Paul, and Alfred Mele. 1994. "Intentional Action." *Nous* 28: 39–68.

Moya, Carlos. 1991. *The Philosphy of Action*. Oxford: Blackwell.

Murray, Michael. 1995. "Leibniz on Divine Foreknowledge, Future Contingents and Human Freedom." *Philosophy and Phenomenological Research* 55: 75–108.

Murray, Michael, and David Dudrick. 1995. "Are Coerced Actions Free?" *American Philosophical Quarterly* 32: 109–23.

Nagel, Thomas. 1987. "Is That You, James?" *London Review of Books* 9 (Oct. 1): 35–6.

———. 1986. *The View from Nowhere*. New York: Oxford University Press.

———. 1979. "Moral Luck." In Nagel, *Mortal Questions*. Cambridge: Cambridge University Press. 24–38.

———. 1970. *The Possibility of Altruism*. New York: Oxford University Press.

Narveson, Jan. 1977. "Compatibilism Defended." *Philosophical Studies* 32: 83–88.

Nathan, Nicholas. 1997. "Self and Will." *International Journal of Philosophical Studies* 5: 81–94.

———. 1992. *Will and World*. Oxford: Oxford University Press.

Naylor, Margery Bedford. 1984. "Frankfurt on the Principle of Alternative Possibilities." *Philosophical Studies* 46: 249–58.

Neely, Wright. 1974. "Freedom and Desire." *The Philosophical Review* 83: 32–54.

Nietzche, F. 1889. *Götterdämmerung, oder Wie man mit dem Hammer philosophirt [Twilight of the Idols, or: How to Philosophize with a Hammer]* Leipzig: Naumann.

———. 1886. *Jenseits von Gut und Böse [Beyond Good and Evil]*. Leipzig: Naumann.

Noordorf, Paul. 1999. "Probabilistic Causation, Preemption and Counterfactuals." *Mind* 108: 95–125.

———. 1998. "Critical Notice: Causation, Probability, and Chance." *Mind* 107: 855–876.

Norretranders, T. 1991/1998. *The User Illusion: Cutting Consciousness Down to Size*. London Penguin.

Nowell-Smith, P. 1960. "Ifs and Cans." *Theoria* 26 Part 2: 85–101. Reprinted in Berofsky, 1966: 322–39.

———. 1954. "Freedom and Responsibility." In *Ethics*. Hammondsworth: Penguin, 285–90.

———. 1948. "Free Will and Moral Responsibility." *Mind* 57: 45–61.

Nozick, Robert. 1995. "Choice and Indeterminism." In O'Connor, 1995a: 101–14.

———. 1981. *Philosophical Explanations*. Cambridge, MA.: Harvard University Press.

Ockham, William. 1983. *Predestination, Foreknowledge, and Future Contingents*. 2nd ed. Trans. Marilyn McCord Adams and Norman Kretzmann. Indianapolis: Hackett. Written approx. 1335.

O'Connor, Timothy, 2000. *Persons and Causes: The Metaphysics of Free Will*. New York: Oxford University Press.

———. 1996. "Why Agent Causation?" *Philosophical Topics* 24: 143–58.

———. ed. 1995a. *Agents, Causes and Events: Essays on Free Will and Indeterminism.* Oxford: Oxford University Press.

———. 1995b. "Agent Causation." In O'Connor, 1995a: 173–200.

———. 1994. "Thomas Reid on Free Agency." *Journal of the History of Philosophy* 32: 605–22.

———. 1993a. "Indeterminism and Free Agency: Three Recent Views." *Philosophy and Phenomenological Research* 53: 499–526.

———. 1993b. "On the Transfer of Necessity." *Nous* 27: 204–18.

Odegard, Douglas. 1985. "Moral Responsibility and Alternatives." *Theoria* 51: 125–36.

Oldenquist, Andrew. 1967. "Choosing, Deciding and Doing." *Encyclopedia of Philosophy.*

Olson, Eric T. 1997. *The Human Animal: Personal Identity without Psychology.* New York: Oxford University Press.

Omnès, Roland. 1994. *The Interpretation of Quantum Mechanics.* Princeton: Princeton University Press.

O'Neill, Onora. 1989. *Constructing Reason.* Cambridge: Cambridge University Press.

Oshana, Marina. 1997. "Ascriptions of Responsibilty." *American Philsophical Quarterly* 34: 71–83.

O'Shaughnessy, Brian. 1980. *The Will.* 2 vols. Cambridge: Cambridge University Press.

Otsuka, Michael. 1998. "Incompatibilism and the Avoidability of Blame." *Ethics* 108: 685–701.

Padgett, Alan. 1992. *Eternity and the Nature of Time.* New York: St. Martin's Press.

———. n.d. "Divine Foreknowledge and the Arrow of Time: On the Impossibility of Retrocausation." In *God and Time.* Ed. Paul Helm, Alan Padgett, William Lane Craig, and Nicholas Wolterstorff. Downer's Grove, IL: Intervarsity Press.

Pascal, Blaise. 1966. *Pensées.* Trans. A. Krailsheimer. Hammondsworth: Penguin Books. Originally published in 1670.

Passingham, R. E. 1993. *The Frontal Lobes and Voluntary Action.* Oxford: Oxford University Press.

Paul, L. A. 2000. "Aspect Causation." *Journal of Philosophy* 97: 235–56.

Paull, R. Cranston. 1992. "Leibniz and the Miracle of Freedom." *Nous* 26: 218–35.

Peacocke, Christopher. 1999. *Being Known.* Oxford: Clarendon Press.

———. 1979. *Holistic Explanation.* Oxford: Clarendon Press.

Pearl, J. 2000. *Causality: Models, Reasoning, and Inference.* Cambridge: Cambridge University Press.

———. 1997. *Probabilistic Reasoning in Intelligent Systems: Networks of Plausible Inference.* San Francisco: Morgan Kaufmann.

Pears, David. 1985. *Motivated Irrationality.* Oxford: Oxford University Press.

Penrose, Roger. 1997. *The Large, the Small and the Human Mind.* Cambridge: Cambridge University Press.

———. 1994. *Shadows of the Mind.* Oxford: Oxford University Press.

———. 1989. *The Emperor's New Mind.* Oxford: Oxford University Press.

Pereboom, Derk. 2001. *Living without Free Will.* Cambridge: Cambridge University Press.

———. 2000. "Alternate Possibilities and Causal Histories." *Philosophical Perspectives* 14: 119–38

———. 1995. "Determinism Al Dente." *Nous* 29: 21–45.

Peters, R. S. 1960. *The Concept of Motivation.* London: Routledge & Kegan Paul.

Petrosky, T., and I. Prigogine, 1997. "The Extension of Classical Dynamics for Unstable Hamiltonian Systems." *Computers & Mathematics with Applications* 34: 1–44.

———. 1996. "Poincaré Resonances and the Extension of Classical Dynamics." *Chaos, Solitons & Fractals* 7: 441–97.

Pettit, Phillip, and Michael Smith. 1996. "Freedom in Belief and Desire." *Journal of Philosophy* 9: 429–49.

Phelps, E., F. Hyder, A. Blamire, and R. Schulman. 1997. "FMRI of the Prefrontal Cortex during Overt Verbal Fluency." *Neuroreport* 8: 561–65.

Pike, Nelson. 1993. "A Latter-Day Look at the Foreknowledge Problem." *International Journal for Philosophy of Religion* 33: 129–64.

———. 1965. "Divine Omniscience and Voluntary Action." *Philosophical Review* 74: 27–46.

Pink, T. L. 1997. "Reason and Agency." *Proceedings of the Aristotelian Society*: 263–80.

———. 1996. *The Psychology of Freedom*. Cambridge: Cambridge University Press.

———. 1991. "Purposive Intending." *Mind* 103: 343–60.

Pinnock, Clark, Richard Rice, John Sanders, William Hasker, and David Basinger. 1994. *The Openness of God: A Biblical Challenge to the Traditional Understanding of God*. Downers Grove, IL: Intervarsity Press.

Plantinga, Alvin. 1986. "On Ockham's Way Out." *Faith and Philosophy* 3: 235–69.

———. 1977. *God, Freedom, and Evil*. Grand Rapids, MI: Eerdmans.

———. 1974. *The Nature of Necessity*. Oxford: Oxford University Press.

———. 1973. "Which Worlds Could God Have Created?" *Journal of Philosophy* 70: 539–55.

Plato. 1937. *The Dialogues of Plato*. Trans. B. Jowett. Vol. 2. New York: Random House.

Plenio, M. B. and P. L. Knight. 1998. "The Quantum-Jump Approach to Dissipative Dynamics in Quantum Optics." *Reviews of Modern Physics* 70: 101–44.

Polkinghorne, John. 1996. *Beyond Science*. Cambridge: Cambridge University Press.

———. 1991. *Reason and Reality: The Relationship between Science and Theology*. Valley Forge, PA: Trinity Press.

———. 1989. *Science and Providence: God's Interaction with the World*. Boston: Shambhala.

———. 1988. *Science & Creation: The Search for Understanding*. London: Society for Promoting Christian Knowledge.

Popper, Karl. 1982. *The Open Universe—An Argument for Indeterminism*. London: Hutchinson.

———. 1972. "Of Clouds and Clocks." In his *Objective Knowledge*. Oxford: Oxford University Press, 206–55.

———. 1965. *Conjectures and Refutations*. New York: Harper Torchbooks.

Popper, Karl, and John Eccles. 1977. *The Self and Its Brain*. New York: Springer.

Posth, Matthew. 1990. "Freedom and Realism." Ph. D. Dissertation, Northwestern University.

Price, Huw. 1994. "A Neglected Route to Realism about Quantum Mechanics." *Mind* 103: 303–36.

———. 1992. "Agency and Causal Asymmetry." *Mind* 101: 501–20.

———. 1991. "Saving Free Will." *New Scientist* 12: 55–56.

Priestley, Joseph, and Richard Price. 1778. *A Free Discussion of the Doctrine of Materialism and Philosophical Necessity*. London.

Prigogine, Ilya. 1997. *The End of Certainty: Time, Chaos, and the New Laws of Nature*. New York: Free Press.

Prigogine, I., and I. Stengers. 1984. *Order out of Chaos*. New York: Bantam.

Primas, Hans. 1998. "Emergence in Exact Natural Sciences." *Acta Polytechnica Scandinavica* 91: 83–98.

Pugmire, D. 1994. "Perverse Preference: Self-Beguilement or Self-Deception." *Canadian Journal of Philosophy* 24: 73–94.

Purtill, Richard. 1988. "Fatalism and the Omnitemporality of Truth." *Faith and Philosophy* 5: 185–92.

Putnam, Hilary. 1975. *Mind, Language and Reality*. London: Cambridge University Press.

———. 1967. "Time and Physical Geometry." *Journal of Philosophy* 64: 167–89.

Quante, Michael. 1998. "Freiheit, Autonomie Und Verantwortung in der Neueren Analytischen Philosophie." *Philosophischer Literaturanzeiger* 51. Part 1: 281–310; Part II: 387–414.

———. 1997. "Personal Autonomy and the Structure of the Will." In *Right, Morality, Ethical Life*. Ed. J. Kotkavirta. Jyvaskyla: University of Jyvaskyla Press. 45–74.

Quine, W. V. O. 1980. "Reference and Modality." In *From a Logical Point of View*. 2nd ed., revised. Cambridge, MA: Harvard University Press. 139–59.

———. 1969. "Propositional Objects." In Quine, *Ontological Relativity*. New York: Columbia University Press, 68–82.

Quinn, Philip, and Charles Taliaferro, eds. 1997. *A Companion to Philosophy of Religion*, Oxford: Blackwell.

Rachlin, Howard. 1995. "Self-Control: Beyond Commitment." *Behavioral and Brain Sciences* 18: 109–21.

———. 1994. *Behavior and Mind*. Oxford: Oxford University Press.

Rae, Alastair 1986. *Quantum Physics: Illusion or Reality?* Cambridge: Cambridge University Press.

Railton, Peter. 1978. "A Deductive-Nomological Model of Probabilistic Explanation." *Philosophy of Science* 45: 206–26.

Rauf, M. A. 1970. "The Qur'an and Free Will." *The Muslim World* 60: 289–99.

Ravizza, Mark. 1994. "Semi-Compatibilism and the Transfer of Non-Responsibility." *Philosophical Studies* 75: 61–94.

Rawls, John. 1971. *A Theory of Justice*. Cambridge, MA: Harvard University Press.

Raz, J. 1986. *The Morality of Freedom*. Oxford: Clarendon Press.

Reichenbach, Bruce. 1988. "Fatalism and Freedom." *International Philosophical Quarterly* 28: 271–85.

———. 1987. "Hasker on Omniscience." *Faith and Philosophy* 4: 86–92.

Reichenbach, Hans. 1956. *The Direction of Time*. Berkeley: University of California Press.

Reid, Thomas. 1983. *The Works of Thomas Reid*. Ed. W. Hamilton: Hildeshein: George Ulm Verlag.

———. 1969. *Essay on the Active Powers of the Human Mind*. Cambridge, MA: MIT Press, originally published in 1788.

Rheinwald, R. 1990. "Zur Frageder Vereinbarkeit von Freiheit und Determinismus." *Zeitschrift für Philosophiseke Forshung* 44: 194–219.

Richardson, Frank C., and Robert C. Bishop. n.d. "Physics, the Human Sciences, and the End of Certainty." In *Facing the Uncertain*, Ed. D. Driebe and I. Prigogine. Dordrecht: Kluwer.

Robinson, Kirk. 1991. "Reason, Desire and Weakness of Will." *American Philosophical Quarterly* 28: 287–98.

Robinson, Michael D. 1995. *Eternity and Freedom: A Critical Analysis of Divine Timelessness as a Solution to the Foreknowledge/Free Will Debate*. Lanham, MD: University Press of America.

Rockwell, W. Teed. 1994. "Beyond Determinism and Indignity: A Reinterpretation of Operant Conditioning." *Behavior and Philosophy* 22: 53–66.

Rorty, Amelie O. 1983. "Akratic Believers." *American Philosophical Quarterly* 20: 175–83.

———. 1980a. "Akrasia and Conflict." *Inquiry* 22: 193–212.

———. 1980b. "Self-deception, Akrasia and Irrationality." *Social Science Information* 19: 905–22.

———, ed., 1980c. *Essays on Aristotle's Ethics*. Berkeley: University of California Press.

Rorty, Richard. 1989. *Contingency, Irony and Solidarity*. Cambridge: Cambridge University Press.

———. 1979. *Philosophy and the Mirror of Nature*. Princeton: Princeton University Press.

Ross, W. D. 1939. *Foundations of Ethics*. Oxford: Clarendon Press.

Rowe, William. 1999. "Problem of Divine Sovereignty and Human Freedom." *Faith and Philosophy* 16: 98–101.

———. 1991. *Thomas Reid on Freedom and Morality*. Ithaca: Cornell University Press.

———. 1989. "Causing and Being Responsible for What Is Inevitable." *American Philosophical Quarterly* 26: 153–59.

———. 1987. "Two Concepts of Freedom." Presidential Address. *Proceedings of the American Philosophical Association* 62: 43–64. Reprinted in O'Connor, 1995: 151–72.

Ruben, David-Hillel, ed. 1993. *Explanation*. Oxford: Oxford University Press.

Rumi, Jalalu'ddin. 1956. *Rumi, Poet and Mystic*. Trans and ed. R. A Nicholson. London: George Allen & Unwin.

Runzo, Joseph. 1981. "Omniscience and Freedom for Evil." *International Journal for Philosophy of Religion* 12: 131–47.

Russell, Bertrand. 1953. "On the Notion of Cause, with Applications to the Free-Will Problem." *Readings in the Philosophy of Science*, Ed. Herbert F. and M. Brodbeck. New York: Appleton-Century-Crofts.

Russell, Paul. 2000. "Compatibilist-Fatalism." In van den Beld 2000: 199–218.

———. 1995. *Freedom and Moral Sentiment*. New York: Oxford University Press.

———. 1992. "Strawson's Way of Naturalizing Responsibility." *Ethics* 102: 287–302.

———. 1988. "Causation, Compulsion and Compatibilism." *American Philosophical Quarterly* 25: 313–21.

———. 1984. "Sorabji and the Dilemma of Determinism." *Analysis* 44: 166–72.

———. n.d. "Responsibility, Moral Sense and Symmetry."

Ryle, Gilbert. 1949. *The Concept of Mind*. New York: Barnes and Noble.

Salmon, Wesley. 1998. *Causality and Explanation*. Oxford: Oxford University Press.

———. 1993. "Probabilistic Causation." In Causation. Ed. E. Sosa and M. Tooley. Oxford: Oxford University Press. 137–53.

———. 1984. *Scientific Explanation and the Causal Structure of the World*. Princeton: Princeton University Press.

Salmon, Wesley, R. Jeffrey, and T. Greeno, eds. 1971. *Statistical Explanation and Statistical Relevance*. Pittsburgh: University of Pittsburgh Press.

Sanders, John. 1997. "Why Simple Foreknowledge Offers No More Providential Control than the Openness of God." *Faith and Philosophy* 14: 26–40.

Sanford, David. 1991. " 'Could's,' 'Might's,' 'If's' and 'Can's'." *Nous* 25: 208–11.

Sankowski, Edward. 1977. "Some Problems about Determinism and Freedom." *American Philosophical Quarterly* 17: 291–99.

Sartre, Jean-Paul. 1962. "From *Being and Nothingness*." In Morgenbesser and Walsh, 1962: 95–113.

Sartre, Jean-Paul. 1948. *Existentialism is a Humanism*. London: Methuen.

Saunders, John Turk. 1968. "The Temptations of Powerlessness." *American Philosophical Quarterly* 5: 100–108.

Scanlon, Thomas M. 1988. "The Significance of Choice." In *The Tanner Lectures on Human Values*. Ed. S. McMurrin. Cambridge: Cambridge University Press, 151–216.

Schick, F. 1991. *Understanding Action*. Cambridge: Cambridge University Press.

Schlick, Moritz. 1966. "When Is a Man Responsible?" In Berofsky, 1966: 54–62.

———. 1962. *Problems of Ethics*. Trans D. Rynin. New York: Dover.

Schlossberger, Eugene. 1986. *Moral Responsibility and Persons*. Philadelphia: Temple University Press.

Schoeman, F. ed., 1987. *Responsibility, Character and Emotions*. Cambridge: Cambridge University Press.

———. 1979. "On Incapacitating the Dangerous." *American Philosophical Quarterly* 16: 56–67.

———. 1978. "Responsibility and the Problem of Induced Desires." *Philosophical Studies* 34: 293–301.

Schopenhauer, Arthur. 1999. *Prize Essay on the Freedom of the Will*. Trans. E. J. F. Payne. Ed. with an introduction by Gunter Zoller. Cambridge: Cambridge University Press. Originally published in 1841.

———. 1889. "The Fourfold Root of the Principle of Sufficient Reason." In *Two Essays by A. Schopenhauer*. Trans. K. Hillebrand. London: George Bell and Sons. 1–82. Originally published in 1813.

Schrodinger, Erwin. 1983. "The Present Situation in Quantum Mechanics." In Wheeler and Zurek, 1983: 152–67.

———. 1967. *What Is Life?* Cambridge: Cambridge University Press.

Schultz, Wolfram. 1999. "The Primal Basal Ganglia and the Voluntary Control of Behavior." In Libet, Freeman and Sutherland, 1999: 31–46.

Schwartz, Jeffrey M. 1999. "A Role for Volition and Attention in the Generation of New Brain Circuitry." In Libet, Freeman and Sutherland, 1999: 115–42.

Scott, George P. 1991. "Dissipative Structures and the Mind-Body Problem." In Scott, 1991b: 259–72.

———. ed., 1991b. *Time, Rhythms and Chaos in the New Dialogue With Nature*. Ames: Iowa State University Press.

Scott, George P., and Michael McMillen, eds. 1980. *Dissipative Structures and Spatiotemporal Organization Studies in Biomedical Research*. Ames: Iowa State University Press.

Scotus, John Duns. 1962. "From the *Oxford Commentary*." In Morgenbesser and Walsh, eds.: 35–39. Originally written circa 1300.

Searle, John. 2000. "Consciousness, Free Action and the Brain," *Journal of Consciousness Studies* 7(10):3–22.

———. 1992. *The Rediscovery of the Mind*. Cambridge, MA: MIT Press.

————. 1983. *Intentionality*. Cambridge: Cambridge University Press.

Sehon, Scott. 1994. "Teleology and the Nature of Mental States." *American Philosophical Quarterly* 31: 63–72.

Seife, C. 2000. "Cold Numbers Unmake the Quantum Mind." *Science* 287 #5454, (Feb. 4).

Sellars, Wilfrid. 1980. "Volitions Reaffirmed." In *Action Theory*. Ed. M. Brand and D. Walton. Dordrecht: Reidel, 72–96.

Senchuk, Dennis M. 1991. "Consciousness Naturalized: Supervenience Without Physical Determinism." *American Philosophical Quarterly* 28: 37–47.

Sennett, James. 1999. "Is There Freedom in Heaven?" *Faith and Philosophy* 16: 69–82.

Shaffer, Jonathan. 2000. "Trumping Preemption." *Journal of Philosophy* 97: 165–81.

Shallice, T. 1988. *From Neuropsychology to Mental Structure*. Cambridge: Cambridge University Press.

Shanley, B. 1998. "Divine Causation and Human Freedom in Aquinas." *American Catholic Philosophical Quarterly* 72: 99–122.

————. 1997. "Eternal Knowledge of the Temporal in Aquinas." *American Catholic Philosophical Quarterly* 71: 197–224.

Shatz, David. 1997. "Irresistible Goodness and Alternative Possibilities." In Manekin and Kellner, 1997: 13–51.

————. 1988. "Compatibilism, Values and 'Could Have Done Otherwise.'" *Philosophical Topics* 16: 151–200.

————. 1985. "Free Will and the Structure of Motivation." *Midwest Studies in Philosophy*. Vol. 10. Ed. P. French, Minneapolis: University of Minnesota Press, 451–82.

Sher, George. 1979. *Desert*. Princeton: Princeton University Press.

Shiffer, Stephen. 1976. "A Paradox of Desire." *American Philosophical Quarterly* 13: 195–203.

Showalter, K., R. Noyes, and H. Turner. 1979. "Detailed Studies of Trigger Wave Initiation and Detection." *Journal of the American Chemical Society* 101: 746–49.

Siderits, Mark. 1987. "Beyond Compatibilism: A Buddhist Approach to Freedom and Determinism." *American Philosophical Quarterly* 24: 149–59.

Simonton, Dean K. 1988. *Scientific Genius*. Cambridge: Cambridge University Press.

Singer, I. B. 1968. Interview of I. B. Singer by H. Flender. In *Writers at Work*. Ed. G. Plimpton. New York: Penguin, 1981, 104–18

Sinnott-Armstrong, Walter. 1988. *Moral Dilemmas*. Oxford: Blackwell.

Skarda, C., and W. Freeman. 1987. "How Do Brains Make Chaos in Order to Make Sense of the World?" *Behavioral and Brain Sciences* 10: 161–95.

Skinner, B. F. 1971. *Beyond Freedom and Dignity*. New York: Vintage.

————. 1948. *Walden Two*. New York: Macmillan. Reprinted in 1962.

Skyrms, Brian, ed. 1999. Synthèse: Special Issue on Statistics and Causation. Dordrecht: Kluwer.

Skyrms, Brian, and William L. Harper. 1988. *Causation, Chance and Credence: Proceedings of the Irvine Conference on Probability and Causation*, Vol. 2. Dordrecht: Kluwer.

Sleigh, Robert. 1994. "Leibniz on Divine Foreknowledge." *Faith and Philosophy* 11: 547–71.

————. 1990. *Leibniz and Arnauld: A Commentary on Their Correspondence*. New Haven: Yale University Press.

Slote, Michael. 1985. Review of van Inwagen 1983. *Journal of Philosophy* 82: 327–30.

————. 1982. "Selective Necessity and the Free Will Problem." *Journal of Philosophy* 79: 5–24.

————. 1980. "Understanding Free Will." *Journal of Philosophy* 77: 136–51.

Smart, J.J.C. 1963. "Free Will, Praise and Blame." *Mind* 70: 291–306.

————. 1961. *Philosophy and Scientific Realism.* New York: Humanities Press.

Smilansky, Saul. 2001. "Free Will: From Nature to Illusion." *Proceedings of the Aristotelian Society* (forthcoming).

————. 2000. *Free Will and Illusion.* Oxford: Clarendon Press.

————. 1997. "Can a Determinist Help Herself?" In Manekin and Kellner 1997: 85–98.

————. 1994. "The Ethical Advantages of Hard Determinism." *Philosophy and Phenomenological Research* 54: 355–63.

————. 1993. "Does the Free Will Debate Rest on a Mistake?" *Philosophical Papers* 22: 173–88.

————. 1990a. "Van Inwagen on the 'Obviousness' of Libertarian Moral Responsibility." *Analysis* 50: 29–33.

————. 1990b. "Is Libertarian Free Will Worth Wanting?" *Philosophical Investigations* 13: 273–76.

Smith, Michael. 1997. "A Theory of Freedom and Responsibility." In Cullity and Gaut 1997: 293–319.

Sobel, Jordan Howard. 1998. *Puzzles for the Will.* Toronto: University of Toronto Press.

Sober, Elliott. 1987. "Explanation and Causation" (review of Salmon 1984). *British Journal for the Philosophy of Science* 38: 243–57.

Sorabji, Richard. 1980. *Necessity, Cause and Blame: Perspectives on Aristotle's Philosophy.* Ithaca: Cornell University Press.

Speak, Daniel. 1999. "Fischer and Avoidability: A Reply to Widerker and Katzoff." *Faith and Philosophy* 16: 239–47.

Spence, S. A., and Commentaries. 1996. "Free Will in the Light of Neuropsychiatry." *Philosophy, Psychiatry and Psychology* 3: 75–100.

Spence, S. A., D. Brooks, S. Hirsch, P. Liddle, J. Meehan, and P. Grasby. 1997. "A PET Study of Voluntary Movement in Schizophrenic Patients Experiencing Passivity Phenomena." *Brain* 120: 1997–2011.

Spence, S. A., and C. Frith. 1999. "Towards a Functional Anatomy of Volition." *Journal of Consciousness Studies* 6, 8–9: 11–29.

Sperry, R. W. 1980. "Mind-Brain Interaction: Mentalism, Yes, Dualism, No." *Neuroscience* 5: 195–206.

Spinoza, B. 1985. *Ethics.* Trans. E. Curley. Princeton: Princeton University Press. Originally published posthumously in 1677.

Spitzer, Manfred. 1999. *The Mind within the Net.* Cambridge, MA: MIT Press.

Squires, Euan. 1994. "Quantum Theory and the Need for Consciousness." *Journal of Consciousness Studies* 1: 201–4.

————. 1991. "One Mind or Many—A Note on the Everett Interpretation of Quantum Theory." *Synthèse* 89: 283–86.

————. 1990. *Conscious Mind in the Physical World.* Bristol: Adam Hilger.

Stalnaker, Robert. 1968. "A Theory of Conditionals." In *Studies in Logical Theory.* Ed. N. Rescher. Oxford: Blackwell, 86–116.

Stampe, Dennis, and Martha Gibson. 1992. "Of One's Own Free Will." *Philosophy and Phenomenological Research* 52: 529–56.

Stapp, Henry P. 2000. "Decoherence and Quantum Theory of Mind: Closing the Gap between Being and Knowing." http://www-physics.lbl.gov; sh~stapp/stappfiles

———. 1999. "Attention, Intention and Will In Quantum Physics." In Libet, Freeman, and Sutherland, 1999: 143–64.

———. 1998. "Pragmatic Approach to Consciousness." In *Brain and Values*. Ed. K. H. Pribram Thieme: Erlbaum: 237–48.

———. 1997. "Science of Consciousness and the Hard Problem." *Journal of Mind and Behavior* 18: 171–93.

———. 1993. *Mind, Matter and Quantum Mechanics*. New York: Springer.

———. 1990. "A Quantum Theory of the Mind-Body Interface." Unpublished Presentation. Conference on Consciousness within Science, University of California at San Francisco.

Stebbing, L. S. 1937. *Philosophy and the Physicists*. London: Penguin.

Stephens, G. Lynn, and George Graham. 1996. "Psychopathology, Freedom and the Experience of Externality." *Philosophical Topics* 24: 159–82.

Stone, Mark A. 1989. "Chaos, Prediction and LaPlacean Determinism." *American Philosophical Quarterly* 26: 123–31.

Strasser, Mark. 1988. "Frankfurt, Aristotle and PAP." *Southern Journal of Philosophy* 26: 235–46.

Strawson, Galen. 2000. "The Unhelpfulness of Indeterminism." *Philosophy and Phenomenological Research* 60: 149–56.

———. 1998. "Free Will." *Routledge Encyclopedia of Philosophy*.

———. 1994a. "The Impossibility of Moral Responsibility." *Philosophical Studies* 75: 5–24.

———. 1994b. *Mental Reality*. Cambridge, MA: MIT Press.

———. 1989. "Consciousness, Free Will and the Unimportance of Determinism." *Inquiry* 32: 3–27.

———. 1986. *Freedom and Belief*. Oxford: Oxford University Press.

Strawson, Peter F. 1962. "Freedom and Resentment." *Proceedings of the British Academy* 48: 1–25. Reprinted in Watson ed., 1982: 59–80.

———. 1959. *Individuals: An Essay in Descriptive Metaphysics*. London: Methuen.

Stump, Eleonore. 1999a. "Dust, Determinism and Frankfurt: A Reply to Goetz." *Faith and Philosophy* 16: 413–22.

———. 1999b. "Alternative Possibilities and Moral Responsibility: The Flicker of Freedom." *The Journal of Ethics* 3: 299–324.

———. 1996a. "Libertarian Freedom and the Principle of Alternative Possibilities." In Howard-Snyder and Jordan, 1996: 73–88.

———. 1996b. "Persons, Identification and Freedom." *Philosophical Topics* 24: 183–214.

———. 1995. "Cartesian Dualism and Materialism Without Reductionism." *Faith and Philosophy* 12: 505–31.

———. 1993. "Sanctification, Hardening of the Heart, and Frankfurt's Concept of the Will." In Fischer and Ravizza, eds.: 211–34.

———. 1990. "Intellect, Will, and the Principle of Alternative Possibilities." In Beaty, 1990: 254–85.

Stump, Eleonore, and Norman Kretzmann. 1992. "Eternity, Awareness, and Action." *Faith and Philosophy* 9: 463–82.

———. 1991. "Prophecy, Past Truth, and Eternity." *Philosophical Perspectives* 5: 395–424.

———. 1981. "Eternity." *Journal of Philosophy* 78: 429–58.

Sudbery, A. 1986. *Quantum Mechanics and the Particles of Nature*. Cambridge: Cambridge University Press.

Suppe, Frederick. 1989. *The Semantic Conception of Theories and Scientific Realism*. Urbana: University of Illinois Press.

Suppes, Patrick. 1984. *Probabilistic Metaphysics*. Oxford: Blackwell.

———. 1979. "Quantum Mechanics and the Nature of Continuous Physical Magnitudes." *Journal of Philosophy* 76: 345–61.

———. 1970. *A Probabilistic Theory of Causality*. Amsterdam: North Holland.

Swanton, Christine. 1992. *Freedom: A Coherence Theory*. Indianapolis: Hackett.

Swinburne, Richard. 1989. *Responsibility and Atonement*. Oxford: Clarendon Press,

———. 1986. *The Evolution of the Soul*. Oxford: Clarendon Press.

Szabo, Laszlo E. 1994. "Quantum Mechanics in a Deterministic Universe." *International Journal of Quantum Physics* 56: 540–55.

Talbott, Thomas. 1993. "Theological Fatalism and Modal Confusion." *International Journal for Philosophy of Religion* 33: 65–88.

———. 1988. "On Free Agency and the Concept of Power." *Pacific Philosophical Quarterly* 69: 241–54.

———. 1986a. "On Divine Foreknowledge and Bringing About the Past." *Philosophy and Phenomenological Research* 46: 455–68.

———. 1986b. Review of Kane 1985. *International Philosophical Quarterly* 20: 300–302.

———. 1979. "Indeterminism and Chance Occurrences." *The Personalist* 61: 253–61.

Taurek, John. 1972. "Determinism and Moral Responsibility." Ph. D. dissertation. University of California at Los Angeles.

Taylor, Charles. 1982. "Responsibility for Self." In Watson, 1982: 111–26.

———. 1964. *The Explanation of Behavior*. London: Routledge & Kegan Paul.

Taylor, Gabriele. 1985. *Pride, Shame and Guilt*. Oxford: Clarendon Press.

Taylor, Richard. 1982. "Agent and Patient." *Erkenntnis* 18: 223–32.

———. 1974. *Metaphysics*. Englewood Cliffs, NJ: Prentice-Hall.

———. 1966. *Action and Purpose*. Englewood Cliffs, NJ: Prentice-Hall.

———. 1964. "Deliberation and Foreknowledge." *American Philosophical Quarterly* 1: 73–80.

Teller, Paul. 1979. "Quantum Mechanics and the Nature of Continuous Physical Magnitudes." *Journal of Philosophy* 76: 435–61.

Thalberg, Irving. 1989. "Hierarchical Analyses of Unfree Action." In Christman, 1989: 123–36.

———. 1977. *Perception, Emotion and Action*. Oxford: Blackwell.

Thomson, Judith. 1977. *Acts and Other Events*. Ithaca: Cornell University Press.

Thornton, Mark. 1990. *Do We Have Free Will?* New York: St. Martin's Press.

Thorp, John. 1980. *Free Will: A Defense against Neurophysiological Determinism*. London: Routledge & Kegan Paul.

Tooley, Michael. 2000. "Freedom and Foreknowledge." *Faith and Philosophy* 17: 212–24.

———. 1987. *Causation: A Realist Approach*. Oxford: Oxford University Press.

———. 1977. The Nature of Law." *Canadian Journal of Philosophy* 7: 667–98.

Trusted, Jennifer. 1984. *Free Will and Responsibility*. Oxford: Oxford University Press.

Tuomela, Raimo. 1977. *Human Action and Its Explanation*. Dordrecht: Reidel.

Ullmann-Margolit, Edna, and Sidney Morgenbesser. 1977. "Picking and Choosing." *Social Research* 77: 757–85.

Unger, Peter. Forthcoming. "Free Will and Scientiphicalism." *Philosophy and Phenomenological Research*.

———. 1996. *Living High and Letting Die*. New York: Oxford University Press.

———. 1986. "The Cone Model of Knowledge." *Philosophical Topics* 14: 125–78.

———. 1984. *Philosophical Relativity*. Minneapolis: University of Minnesota Press.

———. 1975. *Ignorance: A Case for Scepticism*. Oxford: Clarendon Press.

Uus, Undo. 1986. "The Cone Model of Knowledge." *Philosophical Topics* 14: 125–78.

———. n. d. "The Libertarian Imperative and Its Implications for Consciousness Studies" (unpublished manuscript).

van den Beld, Ton, ed. 2000. *Moral Responsibility and Ontology*. Dordrecht: Kluwer.

Vandervert, Larry. 1997. "Understanding Tomorrow's Mind: Advances in Chaos Theory, Quantum Theory, and Consciousness in Psychology." *Journal of Mind and Behavior* 30: 25–35.

van Fraassen, Bas. 1991. *Quantum Mechanics: An Empiricist View*. Oxford: Oxford University Press.

———. 1988. *Laws and Symmetry*. Oxford: Clarendon Press.

van Gulick, R. 1990. "What Difference Does Consciousness Make?" *Philosophical Topics* 17: 211–30.

van Inwagen, Peter. 1997a. *The Possibility of Resurrection and Other Essays in Christian Apologetics*. Boulder, CO: Westview Press.

———. 1997b. "Against Middle Knowledge." *Midwest Studies in Philosophy* 21: 50–69.

———. 1994. "When Is the Will Not Free." *Philosophical Studies* 75: 95–114.

———. 1990a. "Logic and the Free Will Problem" and "Response to Slote." *Social Theory and Practice* 16: 277–90, 385–95.

———. 1990b. "Four-Dimensional Objects." *Nous* 24: 245–56.

———. 1989. "When Is the Will Free?" *Philosophical Perspectives*. Vol. 3. Ed. J. Tomberlin. Atascadero, CA.: Ridgeview., 399–422. Reprinted in O'Connor 1995: 219–38.

———. 1983. *An Essay on Free Will*. Oxford: Clarendon Press.

———. ed., 1980a. *Time and Cause*. Dordrecht: Reidel.

———. 1980b. "Compatibilism and the Burden of Proof." *Analysis* 40: 98–100.

———. 1978. "Ability and Responsibility." *The Philosophical Review* 87: 201–24.

———. 1977a. "Reply to Gallois." *Philosophical Studies* 32: 107–11.

———. 1977b. "Reply to Narveson." *Philosophical Studies* 32: 89–98.

———. 1975. "The Incompatibility of Free Will and Determinism." *Philosophical Studies* 27:185–99.

———. 1974. "A Formal Approach to the Problem of Free Will and Determinism." *Theoria* 24 (Part I): 9–22.

van Rensselaer Wilson, H. 1955. "Causal Discontinuity in Fatalism and Indeterminism." *Journal of Philosophy* 52: 134–58.

van Straaten, Zak, ed. 1980. *Philosophical Subjects: Essays Presented to P. F. Strawson*. Oxford: Oxford University Press.

Velleman, David. 2000. *The Possibility of Practical Reason*. Oxford: Oxford University Press.

———. 1992. "What Happens When Someone Acts?" *Mind* 101: 461–81.

———. 1989. *Practical Reflection*. Princeton, NJ: Princeton University Press.

Velmans, M. 1991. "Is Human Information Processing Conscious?" *Behavioral and Brain Sciences* 3: 651–69.

Vihvelin, Kadri. 1995a. "Causes, Effects and Counterfactual Dependence." *Australasian Journal of Philosophy* 73: 560–73.

———. 1995b. "Reply to 'Causes and Nested Conditionals.' " *Australasian Journal of Philosophy* 73: 579–81

———. 1994. "Are Drug Addicts Unfree?" In *Drugs, Morality and the Law*. ed. S. Luper-Foy and C. Brown. New York: Garland: 51–78.

———. 1991. "Freedom, Causation and Counterfactuals." *Philosophical Studies* 64: 161–84.

———. 1990. "Freedom, Necessity and Laws of Nature as Relations Between Universals." *Australasian Journal of Philosophy* 68: 371–81.

———. 1988. "The Modal Argument for Incompatibililism." *Philosophical Studies* 53: 227–44.

———. n.d. "Libertarian Compatibilism."

Viney, Donald Wayne. 1986. "William James on Free Will and Determinism." *Journal of Mind and Behavior* 7: 555–66.

Viney, Wayne, D. Waldman, and J. Barchilon. 1982. "Attitudes Toward Punishment in Relation to Free Will and Determinism." *Human Relations* 35: 939–50.

Vitiello, G., and E. del Giudice. 1984. "Boson Condensation in Biological Systems." In *Nonlinear Electrodynamics of Biological Systems*. Ed. W. Aden and A. Laurence. New York: Plenum Books.

von Neumann, John. 1955. *Mathematical Foundations of Quantum Mechanics*. Princeton: Princeton University Press.

von Weizacker, V. 1950. *Der Gestaltkreis* (The Gestalt Circle). Stuttgart: Thieme.

von Wright, G. H. 1971. *Explanation and Understanding*. Ithaca: Cornell University Press.

Vuoso, George. 1987. "Background, Responsibility and Excuse." *Yale Law Journal*. 96: 1661–86.

Walker, Arthur F. 1989. "The Problem of Weakness of Will." *Nous* 23: 653–76.

Wallace, R. Jay. 1994. *Responsibility and the Moral Sentiments*. Cambridge, MA: Harvard University Press.

Waller, Bruce. 1992. "A Response to Kane and Hocutt." *Behavior and Philosophy* 20: 83–88.

———. 1990. *Freedom without Responsibility*. Philadelphia: Temple University Press.

———. 1988. "Free Will Gone Out of Control: A Critical Study of R. Kane's *Free Will and Values*." *Behaviorism* 16: 149–67.

Walls, Jerry. 1990. "Is Molinism as Bad as Calvinism?" *Faith and Philosophy* 7: 85–98.

Walter, Henrik. 2001. *Neurophilosophy of Free Will*. Cambridge, MA: MIT Press.

———. 1998. *Neurophilosophie der Willensfreiheit: Von Libertarischen Illusionem zum Konzept natürlicher Autonomie*. Paderborn: Schoningh. 2nd ed. 1999. Paderborn: Mentis. (Walter 2001 is the Englich translation of this work.)

Warfield, Ted. 2000. "On Freedom and Foreknowledge: A Reply to Two Critics." *Faith and Philosophy* 17: 255–59.

———. 1997. "Divine Foreknowledge and Human Freedom Are Compatible." *Nous* 31: 80–6.

———. 1996. "Determinism and Moral Responsibility Are Incompatible." *Philosophical Topics* 24: 215–26.

Warner, Richard. 1987. *Freedom, Enjoyment and Happiness*. Ithaca: Cornell University Press.

Watson, Gary. 1996. "Two Faces of Responsibility." *Philosophical Topics* 24: 227–48.

———. 1987a. "Free Action and Free Will." *Mind* 96: 145–72.

———. 1987b. "Responsibility and the Limits of Evil: Variations on a Strawsonian Theme." In Schoeman, 1987: 256–86.

———. 1986. Review of Dennett's 1984. *Journal of Philosophy* 83: 517–22.

———. ed. 1982. *Free Will*. Oxford: Oxford University Press.

———. 1977. "Scepticism about Weakness of Will." *Philosophical Review* 86: 316–39.

———. 1975. "Free Agency" *Journal of Philosophy* 72: 205–20. Reprinted in and cited from Watson 1982: 96–110.

Weatherford, Roy. 1991. *The Implications of Determinism*. London: Routledge.

Weinberg, S. 1993. *Dreams of a Final Theory*. London: Vintage.

Wheeler, J. A., and W. H. Zurek, eds. 1983. *Quantum Theory and Measurement*. Princeton: Princeton University Press.

Whitaker, A. 1996. *Einstein, Bohr and the Quantum Dilemma*. Cambridge: Cambridge University Press.

White, Michael. 1985. *Agency and Integrality*. Dordrecht: Reidel.

White, Morton. 1993. *The Question of Free Will: A Holistic View*. Princeton: Princeton University Press.

Whitehead, A. N. 1978. *Process and Reality*. Ed. D. R. Griffin and D. Sherburne. New York: Macmillan Press. Originally published in 1929.

Widerker, David. 2000a. "Frankfurt's Attack on the Principle of Alternative Possibilities." *Philosophical Perspectives* 14 (forthcoming)

———. 2000b. "Theological Fatalism and Frankfurt Counterexamples to the Principle of Alternate Possibilities." *Faith and Philosophy* 17: 249–54.

———. 1996. "Contra Snapshot Ockhamism." *International Journal for Philosophy of Religion* 39: 95–102.

———. 1995a. "Libertarianism and Frankfurt's Attack on the Principle of Alternative Possibilities." *Philosophical Review* 104: 247–61.

———. 1995b. "Libertarian Freedom and the Avoidability of Decisions." *Faith and Philosophy* 12: 113–18.

———. 1991a. "Frankfurt on 'Ought' implies 'Can' and Alternative Possibilities." *Analysis* 49: 222–24.

———. 1991b. "A Problem for the Eternity Solution." *International Journal for Philosophy of Religion* 29: 87–95.

———. 1990. "Troubles with Ockhamism." *Journal of Philosophy* 87: 462–80.

———. 1989. "Two Forms of Fatalism." In Fischer, 1986: 97–110.

———. 1987. "On an Argument for Incompatibilism." *Analysis* 47: 37–41.

Widerker, David, and Charlotte Katzoff. 1996. "Avoidability and Libertarianism: A Response to Fischer." *Faith and Philosophy* 13: 415–21.

Wierenga, Edward. 1991. "Prophecy, Freedom, and the Necessity of the Past." *Philosophical Perspectives* 5: 425–46.

———. 1989. *The Nature of God*. Ithaca: Cornell University Press.

Wiggins, David. 1973. "Towards a Reasonable Libertarianism." In Honderich 1973: 31–61.

Wigner, E. P. 1983. "Remarks on the Mind-Body Question." In Wheeler and Zurek 1983.

Wilbur, J. A. 1979. *The Worlds of the Early Greek Philosophers*. Buffalo, NY: Prometheus Books.

Williams, Bernard. 1986. *How Free Does the Will Have to Be?* Lindley Lecture (1985). Lawrence: University of Kansas Press.

Williams, Clifford.1980. *Free Will and Determinism*. Indianapolis: Hackett.

Wilson, David. 1999. "Mind-Brain Interaction and Violation of Physical Laws." In Libet, Freeman, and Sutherland 1999.: 185–99.

Wilson, George. 1997. "Reasons as Causes *for* Actions." In Holmstrom-Hintikka and Tuomela, 1997: 65–82.

————. 1989. *The Intentionality of Human Action*. Stanford, CA.: Stanford University Press.

Winch, Peter. 1958. *The Idea of a Social Science*. London: Routledge & Kegan Paul.

Winfield, Richard Dien. 1991. *Freedom and Modernity*. Albany: State University of New York Press.

Wolf, F. A. 1986. *The Body Quantum*. New York: Macmillan.

————. 1984. *Mind and the New Physics*. London: Heinemann.

Wolf, Susan. 1990. *Freedom within Reason*. Oxford: Oxford University Press.

————. 1987. "Sanity and the Metaphysics of Responsibility." In Schoeman, 1987.: 45–64.

————. 1981. "The Importance of Free Will." *Mind* 90: 386–405.

————. 1980. "Asymmetrical Freedom." *Journal of Philosophy* 77: 151–66.

Wood, Allen. 1984. "Kant's Compatibilism." In *Self and Nature in Kant's Philosophy*. Ed. Allen Wood. Ithaca: Cornell University Press, 136–59.

Woody, J. Melvin. 1998. *Freedom's Embrace*. Philadelphia, PA: University of Pennsylvania Press.

Wyma, Keith. 1997. "Moral Responsibility and the Leeway for Action." *American Philosophical Quarterly* 34: 57–70.

Yaffe, Gideon. Forthcoming. *Liberty Worth the Name: Locke on Free Agency*. Princeton: Princeton University Press.

————. "Free Will and Agency at its Best." In *Philosophical Perspectives* 14 (2000): 203–29.

Young, Robert. 1986. *Personal Autonomy*. New York: St. Martin's Press.

————. 1982. "The Value of Autonomy." *Philosophical Quarterly* 32: 35–44.

————. 1979. "Compatibilism and Conditioning." *Nous* 13: 361–78.

————. 1975. *Freedom, Responsibility and God*. London: MacMillan.

Zagzebski, Linda T. 2000. "Does Libertarian Freedom Require Alternate Possibilities?" *Philosophical Perspectives* 14 (forthcoming).

————. 1997. "Foreknowledge and Freedom." In Quinn and Taliaferro, eds. Oxford: Blackwell. 291–99.

————. 1994. "Religious Luck." *Faith and Philosophy* 11: 397–413.

————. 1993. "Rejoinder to Hasker." *Faith and Philosophy* 10: 256–60.

————. 1991. *The Dilemma of Freedom and Foreknowledge*. Oxford: Oxford University Press.

————. 1990. "A New Foreknowledge Dilemma." *Proceedings of the American Catholic Philosophical Association* 63: 139–45.

Zemach, Eddy M., and David Widerker. 1987. "Facts, Freedom, and Foreknowledge." *Religious Studies* 23: 19–28.

Zimmerman, David. 2000. "Making Do: Troubling Stoic Tendencies in an Otherwise Compelling Theory of Autonomy."*Canadian Journal of Philosophy* 30: 25–54.

———. 1999. "Born Yesterday: Personal Autonomy for Agents without a Past." *Midwest Studies in Philosophy* 23: 236–66.

———. 1994. "Acts, Omissions, and Semi-Compatibilism." *Philosophical Studies* 73: 209–23.

———. 1981. "Hierarchical Motivation and the Freedom of the Will." *Pacific Philosophical Quarterly* 62: 354–68.

Zimmerman, Michael. 1996. *The Concept of Moral Obligation.* Cambridge: Cambridge University Press.

———. 1992. Review of John Bishop's *Natural Agency. The Philosophical Review* 101: 687–90.

———. 1988. *An Essay on Moral Responsibility.* Totowa, NJ: Rowman and Littlefield.

———. 1984. *An Essay on Human Action.* New York: Peter Lang.

Zohar, Danah. 1990. *The Quantum Self.* London: Bloomsbury.

Zohar, D., and I. Marshall. 1994. *The Quantum Society.* London: Bloomsbury.

Zurek, Wojciech H. 1991. "Decoherence and the Transition from Quantum to Classical." *Physics Today* 44, 10:36–44.

———. 1982. "Environment-Induced Superselection Rules." *Physical Review* D 26: 1862–80.

———. 1981. "Pointer Basis of Quantum Apparatus: Into What Mixture Does the Wave Packet Collapse?" *Physical Review* D 24: 1516–25.

Index